CHINA'S NEW SOURCES OF ECONOMIC GROWTH

vol. 2

Human Capital, Innovation and Technological Change

Other titles in the China Update Book Series include:

1999 China: Twenty Years of Economic Reform
2002 China: WTO Entry and World Recession
2003 China: New Engine of World Growth
2004 China: Is Rapid Growth Sustainable?
2005 The China Boom and its Discontents
2006 China: The Turning Point in China's Economic Development
2007 China: Linking Markets for Growth
2008 China's Dilemma: Economic Growth, the Environment and Climate Change
2009 China's New Place in a World of Crisis
2010 China: The Next Twenty Years of Reform and Development
2011 Rising China: Global Challenges and Opportunities
2012 Rebalancing and Sustaining Growth in China
2013 China: A New Model for Growth and Development
2014 Deepening Reform for China's Long-Term Growth and Development
2015 China's Domestic Transformation in a Global Context
2016 China's New Sources of Economic Growth: Vol. 1

The titles are available online at press.anu.edu.au/publications/series/china-update-series

CHINA'S NEW SOURCES OF ECONOMIC GROWTH

vol. 2

Human Capital, Innovation and Technological Change

Edited by Ligang Song, Ross Garnaut, Cai Fang and Lauren Johnston

Australian National University
PRESS

社会科学文献出版社
SOCIAL SCIENCES ACADEMIC PRESS (CHINA)

Published by ANU Press
The Australian National University
Acton ACT 2601, Australia
Email: anupress@anu.edu.au
This title is also available online at press.anu.edu.au

National Library of Australia Cataloguing-in-Publication entry

Title: China's new sources of economic growth : human capital, innovation and technological change. Volume 2 / Ligang Song, Ross Garnaut, Cai Fang, Lauren Johnston, editors

ISBN: 9781760461294 (paperback : Volume 2.) 9781760461300 (ebook)

Series: China update series ; 2017.

Subjects: Economic development--China.
Sustainable development--China.
Climatic changes--Government policy--China.
China--Economic policy--2000-

Other Creators/Contributors:
Song, Ligang, editor.
Garnaut, Ross, editor.
Cai, Fang, editor.
Johnston, Lauren, editor.

Cover design and layout by ANU Press

Contents

Figures

Tables

Contributors

Ross Garnaut
Professorial Research Fellow in Economics, University of Melbourne, Melbourne

Cai Fang
Vice President, Chinese Academy of Social Sciences, Beijing

Ligang Song
Crawford School of Public Policy, The Australian National University, Canberra

Lauren Johnston
Research Fellow, Melbourne Institute of Applied Economic and Social Research, Faculty of Business and Economics, University of Melbourne, Melbourne

Yiping Huang
National School of Development, Peking University, Beijing

Wing Thye Woo
Economics Department, University of California, Davis; Institute of Population and Labor Economics, Chinese Academy of Social Sciences, Beijing; Jeffrey Cheah Institute on Southeast Asia, Sunway University, Kuala Lumpur

Yixiao Zhou
Curtin Business School, Curtin University, Perth

Yanrui Wu
Economics, Business School, University of Western Australia, Perth

Xiumei Guo
Curtin University Sustainability Policy Institute, Faculty of Humanities, Curtin University, Perth

Prema-chandra Athukorala
Professor of Economics, Arndt-Corden Department of Economics, Crawford School of Public Policy, The Australian National University, Canberra

Ross Kendall
International and Economic Research Departments, Reserve Bank of Australia, Sydney

Jonathan Lees
International and Economic Research Departments, Reserve Bank of Australia, Sydney

Chunlai Chen
Crawford School of Public Policy, The Australian National University, Canberra

Biliang Hu
Professor of Economics, Dean of Emerging Markets Institute, Beijing Normal University, Beijing

Shang-Jin Wei
N.T. Wang Professor at Columbia University, New York, and Research Associate at the National Bureau of Economic Research

Zhuan Xie
Research Fellow in the State Administration of Foreign Exchange (SAFE) of China, Beijing

Xiaobo Zhang
Distinguished Professor at Peking University, Beijing, and Senior Research Fellow at the International Food Policy Research Institute, Washington

Marina Rudyak
Institute of Chinese Studies, Heidelberg University, Heidelberg

Zhifeng Yin
School of Economics, Central University of Finance and Economics, Beijing

Hao Mao
Development & Research Center, State Intellectual Property Office, Beijing

Alanna Krolikowski
China Institute, University of Alberta, Alberta

Yu Sheng
Associate Professor, School of Advanced Agricultural Sciences; Deputy Director, China Center for Agricultural Policy, Peking University, Beijing

Qing Yi
PhD Candidate, School of Advanced Agricultural Sciences; Deputy Director, China Center for Agricultural Policy, Peking University, Beijing

Jiang Kejun
Senior Researcher, Energy Research Institute, China

Yan Shen
National School of Development, Peking University, and Senior Research Fellow at the Institute of Digital Finance, Peking University, Beijing

Qiuzi Fu
National School of Development, Peking University, Beijing

Yang Yao
Dean and Professor, National School of Development, Peking University, Beijing

Mengqi Wang
National School of Development, Peking University, Beijing

Jane Golley
Associate Professor and Deputy Director, Australian Centre on China in the World, The Australian National University, Canberra

Sherry Tao Kong
Associate Professor at the Institute of Social Science Survey, Peking University, Beijing

Xiaojing Zhang
Deputy Director-General of National Institution for Finance & Development, Chinese Academy of Social Sciences, Beijing

Shenglang Yang
Crawford School of Public Policy, The Australian National University, Canberra

Dora Marinova
Curtin University Sustainability Policy Institute, Faculty of Humanities, Curtin University, Perth

Chaofeng Yang
Institute of Scientific & Technical Information of China, Beijing

Zhiyun Zhao
Institute of Scientific & Technical Information of China, Beijing

Zhijuan Zhang
Institute of Scientific & Technical Information of China, Beijing

Qingjie Liu
Postdoctoral Researcher, Emerging Markets Institute, Beijing Normal University, Beijing

Jiao Yan
Doctoral Candidate, School of Economics and Resource Management, Beijing Normal University, Beijing

Acknowledgements

The China Economy Program gratefully acknowledges the financial support for the *China Update 2017* provided by Rio Tinto through the Rio Tinto–ANU China Partnership, as well as coordination and editorial assistance provided by Program Manager Elizabeth Buchanan and our colleagues at the East Asia Forum at The Australian National University. This is the 17th edition in the *China Update Series* and we sincerely thank our contributors from around the world for their valuable contributions to the book series and the *Update* events throughout these years. Thanks also go to the ANU Press team, notably Emily Hazlewood and Jan Borrie, for the expeditious publication of the book series, and to Social Sciences Academic Press (China) in Beijing for translating and publishing the Chinese versions of the *Update* book series to make the research work available to the readers in China.

Abbreviations

AfDB	African Development Bank
AIIB	Asian Infrastructure Investment Bank
ASEAN	Association of Southeast Asian Nations
ASEAN-5	Association of Southeast Asian Nations Five
ASIEC	Annual Survey of Industrial Enterprises in China
AVIC	Aviation Industry Corporation of China
BEC	Broad Economic Classification (United Nations)
BIS	Bank for International Settlements
BRI	Belt and Road Initiative
BRICS	Brazil, Russia, India, China and South Africa
CAICCF	China–Africa Industrial Capacity Cooperation Fund
CAS	Chinese Academy of Sciences
CASC	Chinese Aerospace Science and Technology Corporation
CASIC	Chinese Aerospace Science and Industry Corporation
CCAP	Center for Chinese Agricultural Policy
CCDC	China Central Depository & Clearing
CDB	China Development Bank
CEC	China Electricity Council
CEO	chief executive officer
CEPII	Centre d'Etudes Prospectives et d'Informations Internationales (Centre for Prospective Studies and International Information)
CFPS	China Family Panel Studies
Comac	Commercial Aircraft Corporation of China
Complant	China National Complete Plant Import Export Corporation
CPC	Communist Party of China
CPI	consumer price index
CPPCC	Chinese People's Political Consultative Conference
CSFAGC	China State Farms Agribusiness Group Corporation
CSP	concentrating solar power
CUI	catch-up index
DID	difference-in-difference
EC	efficiency change

EEU	Eurasian Economic Union
EIB	European Investment Bank
EU	European Union
Exim Bank	Export–Import Bank of China
FDI	foreign direct investment
FE	fixed-effects model
FIE	foreign-invested enterprise
FIT	feed-in tariff
FOCAC	Forum On China–Africa Cooperation
FTA	free-trade agreement
GDP	gross domestic product
GFC	Global Financial Crisis
GMM	generalised method of moments
GPN	global production network
GW	gigawatt
GWh	gigawatt-hour
HH	Herfindahl–Hirschman
HRS	household responsibility system
HS	Harmonised System
HSR	high-speed rail
ICOR	incremental capital–output ratio
IEE	Institute of Electrical Engineering
IFDI	inward foreign direct investment
IID	independent and identically distributed
IMF	International Monetary Fund
IPAC	Integrated Policy Assessment Model for China
IPO	initial public offering
ISSS	Institute of Social Science Survey
IT	information technology
kW	kilowatt
kWh	kilowatt-hour
LCOE	levelised cost of electricity
LMERR	Lagrange Multiplier Error
LMLAG	Lagrange Multiplier Lag
LP	Levinsohn and Petrin

m/s	metres per second
M&A	merger and acquisition
M1	narrow money supply
M2	broad money supply
MITH	middle-income trap hypothesis
ML	maximum likelihood method
MNE	multinational enterprise
MOFCOM	Ministry of Commerce of China
MOFTEC	Ministry of Foreign Trade and Economic Cooperation
MW	megawatt
NAFTA	North American Free Trade Agreement
NASA	National Aeronautics and Space Administration
NBS	National Bureau of Statistics of China
NDRC	National Development and Reform Commission
NEA	National Energy Administration
NEI	new-economy index
NFS	National Fixed-point Survey
NPC	National People's Congress
NPL	non-performing loan
ODA	official development assistance
OECD	Organisation for Economic Co-operation and Development
OFDI	outward foreign direct investment
OLS	ordinary least squares
OOF	other official flow
PBC	People's Bank of China
PBS	Provincial Bureau of Statistics
PMI	purchasing manager index
PPI	producer price index
PPP	purchasing power parity
PRC	People's Republic of China
PV	photovoltaic
R&D	research and development
RBA	Reserve Bank of Australia
RCEP	Regional Comprehensive Economic Partnership
RE	random-effects model

repo	repurchase agreement
RLCL	Rural Land Contracting Law
RMB	renminbi
S&GA	selling, general and administrative expenses
S&T	science and technology
SCO	Shanghai Cooperation Organisation
SDR	special drawing right
SEM	spatial error model
SEZ	special economic zone
SIC	Standard Industrial Classification
SIPO	State Intellectual Property Office of China
SITC	Standard International Trade Classification
SLM	spatial lag model
SME	small and medium enterprise
SOE	state-owned enterprise
TCE	tonnes of coal equivalent
TFP	total factor productivity
toe	tonnes of oil equivalent
TP	technological progress
TPP	Trans-Pacific Partnership
TVE	township and village-owned enterprise
TWh	terawatt-hour
UK	United Kingdom
UNCTAD	United Nations Conference on Trade and Development
UNDP	United Nations Development Programme
US	United States
USPTO	United States Patent and Trademark Office
VAI	value added in the manufacturing industry
VAT	value-added tax
WEO	World Economic Outlook
WIPO	World Intellectual Property Organization
WTO	World Trade Organization

1. China's Path Towards New Growth: Drivers of Human Capital, Innovation and Technological Change

Ligang Song, Cai Fang and Lauren Johnston[1]

Introduction

Since the last China Update volume, sluggish world growth, of a touch above 3 per cent in 2016, has added to concerns about China's financial sector and sustainable growth prospects at least in the near term. Geopolitical shocks in the United States and United Kingdom have exaggerated the uncertainty around whether China will be able to navigate away from an export, capital and resource-intensive growth model towards a new model of economic growth.

In the 2016 book, we covered China's economy from the perspectives of reform, energy and resources and climate change as volume one. This year's book explores topics in China's progress in advancing the new growth frontiers of human capital, innovation and technological change.

The new growth path that China seeks to tread is broadly that followed by today's advanced economies in earlier times. It involves substitution of intangibles such as innovation and technology for tangible components of factors of production such as land, labour and physical capital (Maddison 1982). Many countries, however, get stuck in that transition and fail over decades in their attempt to enter the high-income group—a circumstance known as the 'middle-income trap' (Eichengreen et al. 2013).

For China, the transition towards new, advanced-economy growth drivers offers a route to continued economic development. It means relying less on industries that are resource- and pollution-intensive, such as steel and construction, and on labour-intensive and low-quality manufacturing. It means instead shifting the growth model towards consumption, services, higher value-added manufacturing and innovation. China has already made significant progress towards the development of new high-tech industries in high-speed rail (HSR) transportation,[2] high value-added

1 We thank Shenglang Yang for his help with assembling the data used in this chapter.

2 The total length of China's high-speed rail reached 12,000 km in 2016.

manufacturing including super-fast quantum computing, aviation[3] and space technologies.[4] It has similarly made progress in reducing the adverse environmental spillovers of the economy and fostering high-tech manufacturing—not least by becoming a world leader in new-energy technology including solar panels, wind turbines, hybrid cars and new materials.

This year's book takes a closer look at the role of human capital, innovation and technological change in affecting the pattern of growth and general development of the Chinese economy. First, we explore recent macroeconomic developments, alongside trends in education and innovation. We also look at how structural change is preparing the economy for a more advanced set of economic growth drivers.

Macroeconomic development

China's economy is now growing at a consistently slower 'new normal' rate than the double-digit growth of the first decade or so of this century. Nonetheless, it continues to grow faster than all other major economies. Figure 1.1 shows that the Chinese economy grew at 6.7 per cent in 2016, and illustrates the persistent growth deceleration. The slowdown is causing immense overcapacity problems in some industries. Overcapacity has to be managed alongside major challenges of uncertainty about the nature of contemporary change and the risks and problems of inequality of access in the financial sector.

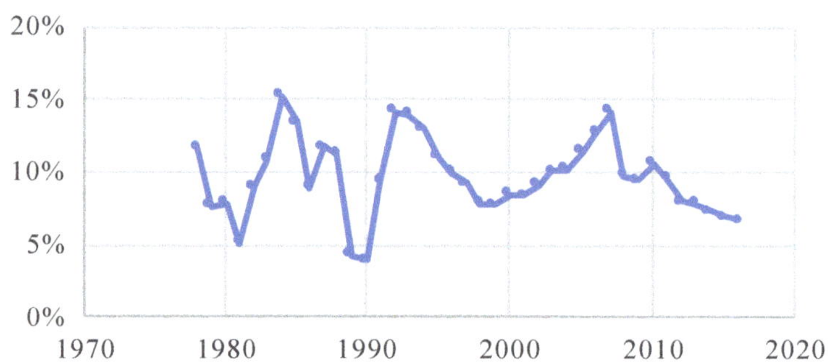

Figure 1.1 GDP growth rates, 1975–2016

Source: NBS (various years).

3 China's first commercial jet aircraft (C919) conducted its first test flight on 5 May 2017.

4 This includes the prospect that China will own and operate the world's only space station from 2022.

China has made progress in recent years in rebalancing the economy towards household consumption and away from fixed capital investment (Figure 1.2).

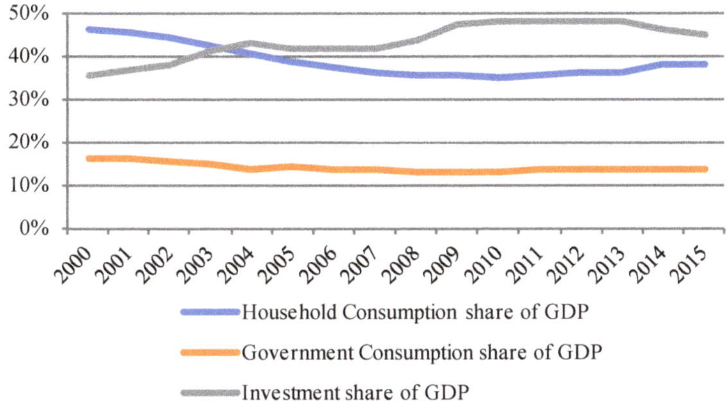

Figure 1.2 Consumption and investment, 2000–15

Source: NBS (various years).

As required by China's new model of growth, the tertiary sector has continued to increase its relative size, accounting for 52 per cent of gross domestic product (GDP) in 2016, while secondary (40 per cent share in 2016) and primary (8 per cent) industries have continued their relative decline (Figure 1.3).

China's new growth model allocates a lesser place for exports as a driver of growth. Over the first 30 years of reform, China benefited from a more favourable trading environment. The share of exports in China's GDP rose from about 5 per cent in 1980 to a peak of 37 per cent in 2006 (Figure 1.4), but has fallen since.

China became the largest trading nation in the world, surpassing the United States, in 2013 and has retained that status since.

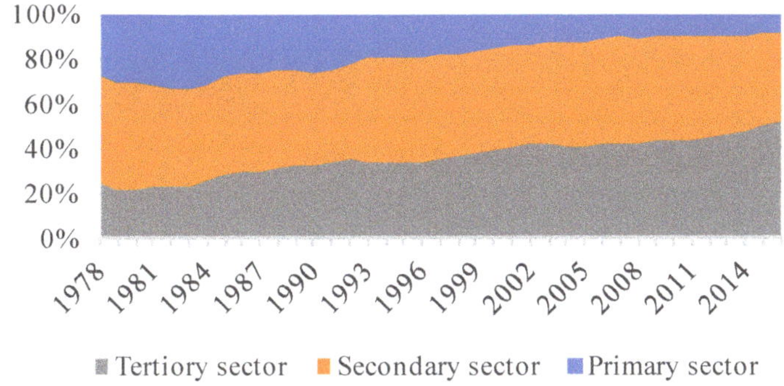

Figure 1.3 Sector shares in total GDP, 1978–2016

Source: NBS (various years).

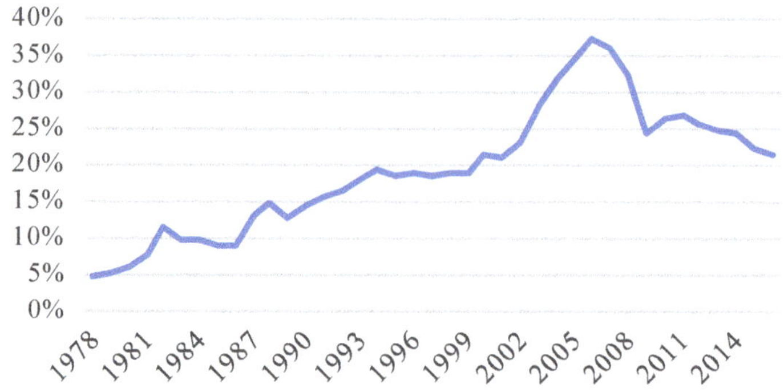

Figure 1.4 China's export share in GDP, 1978–2016
Source: NBS (various years).

Consistent with the new model of growth, China's trade surpluses have fallen as shares of GDP (Figure 1.5). China's total foreign reserves have also fallen considerably, to about US$3 trillion in 2016. After a long period of currency appreciation and pressure for more, in recent years, the pressure has now been for renminbi (RMB) depreciation against the US dollar.

The decline in Chinese trade surpluses has eased global imbalances; however, reduced export orientation of the Chinese economy has contributed to the deceleration of global trade growth. Developments in China have been a major factor in the decline of trade in global economic activity since 2012.

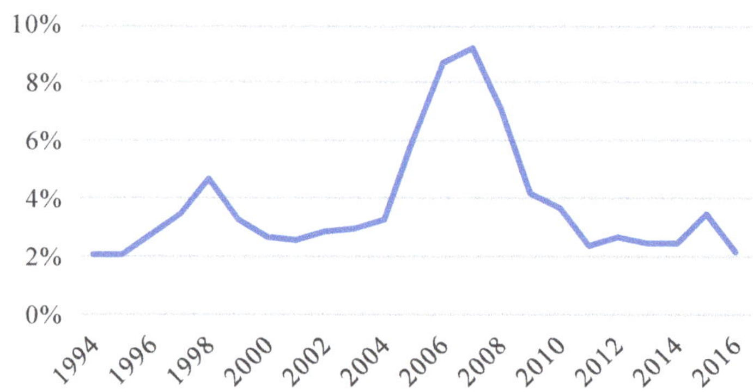

Figure 1.5 Share of China's trade surpluses in GDP, 1994–2016
Source: NBS (various years).

China's share of global trade grew more rapidly than its share of output until the Global Financial Crisis (GFC), but more slowly since (Figure 1.6).

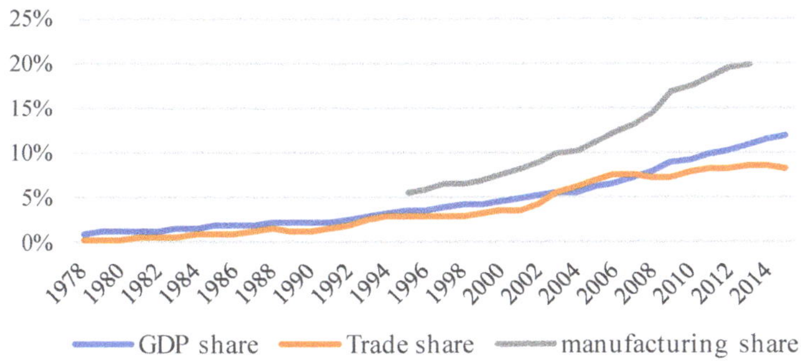

Figure 1.6 Shares of China's GDP and trade in global totals, 1978–2014 (2010 constant US$)

Sources: World Bank (databank.worldbank.org/data/home.aspx) and NBS (various years).

Data from The Conference Board (2015) show a modest increase in total factor productivity (TFP) growth in 2015 after several years of stagnation. According to some estimates, the contribution of TFP to China's economic growth has fallen consistently since 2008 (Figure 1.7). This may be explained by the massive increase in investment through the fiscal stimulus package that was a response to the GFC and which was associated with a large decline in returns to capital. The decline in the labour force in recent years and the lower rate of urbanisation have also contributed to higher capital/labour ratios and lower capital productivity growth. The share of people of working age in the population has been falling since 2012.

These factors are behind the rising imperative for China to find new ways to boost productivity.

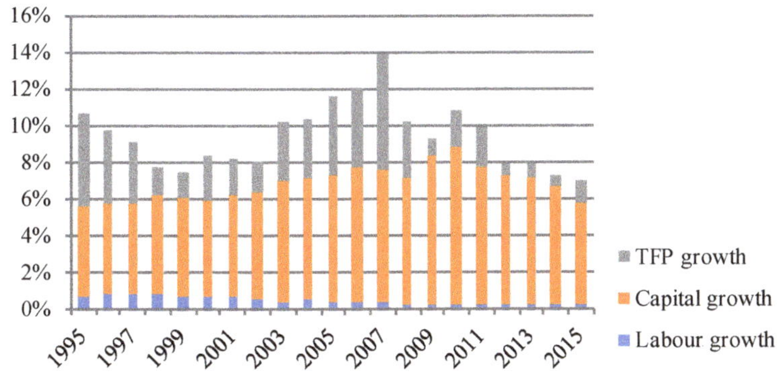

Figure 1.7 Decomposition of China's GDP growth, 1995–2015

Note: Growth is calculated as a log-difference.

Source: The Conference Board (2015).

China has made strides over recent decades in developing its human capital, its innovative capacities and technological potential. Transforming these into growth drivers that allow China to climb through the middle-income trap into the high-income group of countries depends on how resources of all kinds are allocated to the most productive uses. This requires structural reform.

Structural reform within China's new model of growth has been highlighted in most recent China Update books. This year's book concentrates on human capital, innovation and technology.

Human capital

Improvements in education and skills can considerably increase the productivity and earnings of labour. But the capacity to absorb and use physical capital may be limited by, among other things, investment in human capital. There may thus be a close association between education and the mainsprings of technological progress (Thirlwall and Pacheco-Lopez 2017: 210).

> Rising levels of human capital per capita could make the average individual better at discovering and sharing ideas. As was the case in OECD [Organisation for Economic Co-operation and Development] countries in the second half of the twentieth century, if new institutions change incentives, the fraction of the available human capital that is devoted to producing and sharing ideas could continue to rise. To that end, there is enormous potential for similar economic and innovation-driven transformation in countries like China and India. It is possible even that growth at the technological frontier could continue for the foreseeable future, and who knows, it might even increase again in this century compared to the last (Jones and Romer 2010: 235).

For China, in particular, capital per worker must rise in the new phase of its development. An effective way of preventing diminishing returns to capital is to increase China's human capital per worker, which could sustain a continual improvement in productivity. Towards that goal, China may benefit from its unusual workforce structure, in which human capital is highly skewed in favour of younger workers. This offers an implicit new productivity potential that structurally is not open to economies where the human capital of older workers is closer to that of younger workforce entrants.

In its review of educational priorities for China in the coming century, the World Bank (1999: 9; see also 2013) reinforces both the positive correlation between education and economic growth and the increasing relevance of education:

> That link is strengthening with increasing globalization, competition for markets and dependence of economies on knowledge and information. Skill is replacing other factors as a basis for competitive advantage in the global economy; the economic strength of a nation will become more dependent upon its ability to develop, utilize and manage its human resources.

Continuous improvement in productivity is expected to become the primary mechanism by which Chinese authorities can promote economic growth in the next century. Education has played an important role in China's economic growth through the reform period. Changes in government education policy have brought rapid change in tertiary education (Figure 1.8), and the share of education expenditure in GDP has been rising in recent years, even approaching the level of developed countries (Figure 1.9). According to Jones and Romer (2010: 241), '[t]he rising supply of highly educated labour tilts technical change in its own direction'.

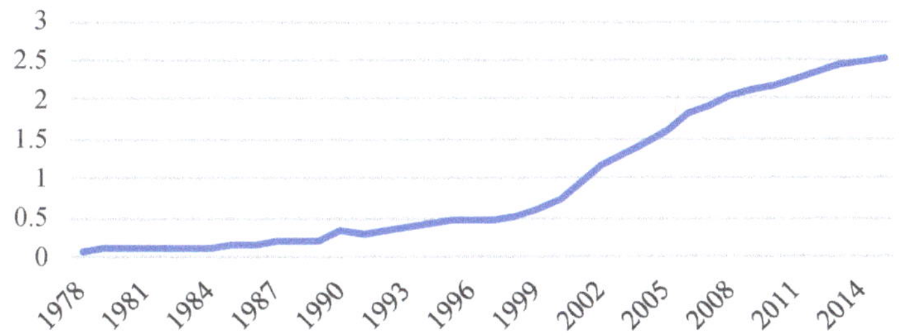

Figure 1.8 University students per 100 population, 1978–2014
Source: NBS (various years).

Nonetheless, China must do more to improve the quality of education at all levels and also to create an environment in which human capital investment is duly recognised and respected. In the university sector, through projects such as Project 985 and 211, China has, for two decades, invested heavily in ensuring that the country is home to some world-class universities. Peking University and Tsinghua University are now ranked in the top 100 universities worldwide, at 29 and 35, respectively, according to the 2017 Times Higher Education World University rankings. Continued investments in this direction are crucial if China is to become a more innovative and productive economy and society.

Harnessing the benefits of rising human capital through improved institutions (and, thereby, incentives) is another key to sustaining China's future economic growth, including its contribution to future global growth and wellbeing (Glazebrook and Song 2013).

Innovation and technology

The economic growth literature of the past half-century has identified the importance of technological change. Invention and innovation are the sources of technological change and can create knowledge that might spill over to entities that were not responsible for the original creation (Hall and Rosenberg 2010: 6). This suggests a need for policy to encourage the appropriate level of investment in these activities (Arrow 1962).

To encourage innovation, the Chinese Government and Chinese industrial enterprises have invested more and more in research and development (R&D) (Figure 1.9).

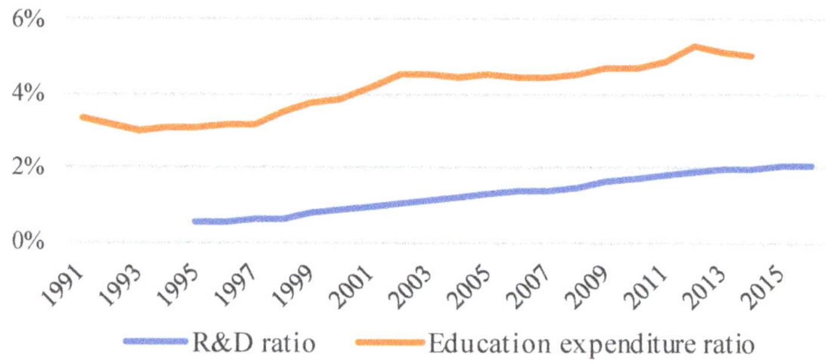

Figure 1.9 China's shares of R&D and total education expenditure in GDP, 1991–2015

Source: NBS (various years).

Technological change has been accelerating in several key sectors, including transport, space technologies and telecommunications. Increased competition, government subsidises and the chance to learn from frontier markets abroad through opening up and reform have supported that process. Contributing factors include collaboration between firms and scientific and research institutions, including universities, and the strengthening of incentives (Figure 1.10).

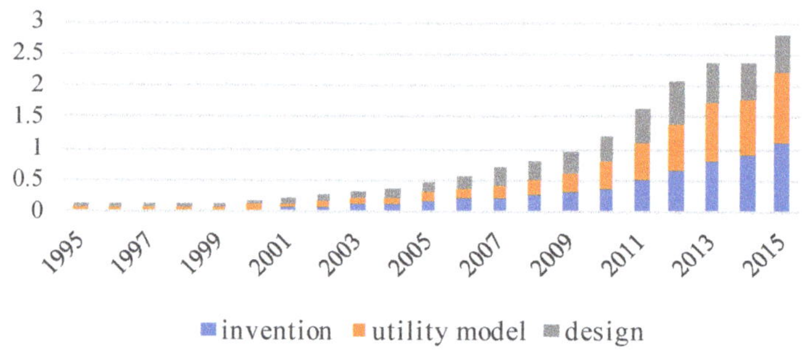

Figure 1.10 Number of patent applications, 1995–2015 (million)

Source: NBS (various years).

Such efforts are intended to support technological development in China while also enabling continuous learning from other countries. The goal is for China to contribute increasingly to extending the global technological frontiers.

Nurturing private entrepreneurship is important in that context. Enhancing competition and improving the productive use of resources can be supported by lowering and removing entry barriers to private enterprises in industries providing essential services to growing industries—particularly financial and banking services.

The increased participation of private firms in service industries will also improve private sector access to resources, especially capital and credit, which are critical for private sector innovation and development.

Government policy and regulation seeking to advance the role of the private sector in the allocation of key resources can drive increasing productivity in China (Son and Song 2015).

Finding ways to increase the efficiency and effectiveness of R&D expenditure is an important concern, for governments and entrepreneurs alike.

We are living in a new era when modern technologies are increasingly affecting all aspects of our life. China is making great efforts to embrace these new developments across the entire country, but faces tremendous challenges. This 2017 volume is an attempt to contribute deeper analysis of the role of human capital, innovation and technological change in a transitional economy and to discuss ways in which China's experience has offered some important lessons for China itself and for other countries, too.

Structure of the book

Part I: Reform and macroeconomic development

Four chapters provide perspectives on recent macroeconomic developments in China. First, Cai and Zhang (Chapter 2) explain the additional reform challenges of China's 'new normal' growth era. Thereafter, Huang et al. (Chapter 3) explain the official goal of 'making progress while maintaining stability'. The authors outline a new economy index that helps to measure 'progress' and draw attention to issues of stability, especially in the financial sector. Yao and Wang (Chapter 4) estimate the potential for a successful process of internal convergence to sustain China's long-run growth. Woo (Chapter 5) rounds out the first section by bridging the domestic 'new normal' and the more recent 'international new normal' arising from the election of US President Donald Trump and the Brexit transition.

Cai and Zhang (Chapter 2) elaborate China's new and ongoing policy changes in the 'new normal' era of slower growth. They note that reform is now more difficult, especially since many necessary reforms have shifted from being characterised by 'Pareto improvement'—in which the majority of people benefit and no one suffers—to 'Kaldor improvement', which requires a balance to be struck between the winners and losers from reform. Key areas of reform within that challenging context therefore include legal and property rights protection reforms, a shift from industrial to competition policy and optimising the roles of the market and government in deciding the allocation of resources. The authors note that defining boundaries for the market and government is a practical matter and that, during a catch-up phase, distortions in that balance may be more pronounced. Compared with the states of other major economies, the Chinese Government owns a relatively high share of the national wealth. Towards reforming the incentive mechanism, policymakers must now much better understand the benefits or costs associated with reform and work to reach consensus on the direction of the roadmap across government and society. This will not only better support greater competition and entrepreneurship, but also ensure collective support for an ongoing and deeper reform process.

Huang et al. (Chapter 3) explain how the combination of slowing growth and financial risk led the December 2016 Central Economic Work Conference and the more recent National People's Congress (NPC) meetings to decide on an economic policy goal of 'making progress while maintaining stability'. This means a proactive fiscal policy with prudent monetary policy, increasing exchange rate flexibility while retaining basic exchange stability and resolving systemic risk as macroeconomic policy priorities. In this chapter, the recent rise in economic momentum is attributed to cyclical factors, including public infrastructure spending, implying uncertainty for the medium term. The cause of that broader slowdown and transition uncertainty relates to the fact that earlier growth-driving industries have lost competitiveness, but new ones have not replaced them. An index of the new economy composed and elaborated on in Chapter 3 finds that the new economy accounts for about 30 per cent of the total economy at the moment. As a greater share of resources shift into the new-economy sector, the identified crowding-out effect of the relatively high share of investment currently going to old-economy sectors will diminish and will, in turn, help to ensure a sustainable growth path. Over time, this may also serve to directly and indirectly facilitate a smoother regional progression towards the new economy. At present, southeastern China is ahead of the rest of the country in that transition. Overall, such progress will also reduce systemic financial risk, which probably relates to slow growth, high leveraging, low productivity and limited policy flexibility.

Yao and Wang (Chapter 4) examine how internal convergence—regional, efficiency and technological—can sustain China's long-run growth. The authors estimate growth equations for China's three geographic regions and for the whole country, finding different speeds of regional convergence, different levels of investment efficiency and different speeds of technological progress in the three regions. The authors calculate that regional convergence in China could offer a growth dividend of almost 12 per cent, technological convergence could increase China's growth potential by one-third and convergence of investment efficiency in the two inland regions towards that of the eastern region would not have a large effect on the level or rate of growth.

There are, however, a number of obstacles to realising these potential growth gains: it is difficult to attract talent to China's lesser-developed inland regions and the persistence of structural challenges such as the issue of zombie firms. Removing these obstacles would add momentum for economic convergence.

In a year of conflicting signals for China's economy, Woo (Chapter 5) completes part one with a study of three important economic issues for China: the current trajectory of the economy, the policy options to influence that trajectory and some possible additional elements to be incorporated into international economic relations. He specifically takes on conflicting interpretations of China's economic challenges, especially the difference between optimists and pessimists. Adopting a new framework classifying China's policy challenges—into 'hardware' and 'software' categories—the author proposes a reform agenda that will also help China to avoid underlying 'power failure'. This includes structural reforms to rationalise the state-owned enterprise (SOE) sector, deregulation of markets for capital, labour and land and structural reform of governance institutions such as the *hukou* household registration system and rural landownership. In addition, in the context of the 'new international normal'—the absence of hegemonic stability—the author argues China should now more actively shape globalisation in such ways as to expand on former Chinese president Hu Jintao's notion of a 'harmonious' society and transform it into a concept of a 'harmonious world'.

Part II: Education and human capital

Education provides the building blocks for the accumulation of human capital. China's progress in accumulating human capital and trends in capturing the benefits of such productive capacity over time have been mixed. Part two looks at two elements of that story. First, Golley and Kong (Chapter 6) compare the educational outcomes of Chinese citizens born over five decades after 1940 and identify a number of factors that have served to undermine equal opportunity in China's education system over time. Second, Yang and Zhou (Chapter 7) use China's input–output table to study the role of intangible capital in the country by industrial sector.

Golley and Kong (Chapter 6) show that China's workforce is, on average, poorly educated compared with an OECD average benchmark. Against that backdrop and China's aspiration to close the gap between the domestic and frontier economies, the authors study the educational outcomes of Chinese citizens born over the half-century from 1940 with a focus on whether gaps were driven by 'inequality of opportunity'. Data from the China Family Panel Studies (CFPS) provide years of schooling for rural and urban population samples. After identifying the key determinants of educational outcomes—among which are China's *hukou* system, paternal education levels and birth cohort—the authors calculate the share of 'inequality of opportunity' in overall educational inequality. They conclude with a call for policies to reduce the impact of factors exaggerating educational inequality in China, especially in light of China's attempt to transition towards a higher value-added and innovative economy.

Yang and Zhou (Chapter 7) utilise data from China's input–output tables to study the role of intangible capital by industrial sector. In the process, the authors also offer a new methodology for measuring the role of intangible capital for economies with poor data. The authors find that growth in intangible capital can explain almost 20 per cent of the TFP growth over the period 1997–2012. This result is robust under various forms of sensitivity analysis. At the sector level, R&D is found to play a more important role in agriculture than economic competency and computerised information; but the role of economic competency is more important in the services and light industry sectors than that of R&D and computerised information.

Part III: Innovation and productivity

Part III explores in greater detail China's transition towards a more innovative economy. First, Wei et al. (Chapter 8) uses firm-level data to find that, despite being at a disadvantage in competing for funds with the state sector, private firms embracing international markets and finding creative ways to adapt to rising labour costs are pushing the frontier of China's transition up the productivity and manufacturing value chains. Wu et al. (Chapter 9) present new estimates of China's productivity growth rates by province. They find productivity gains are now consistently higher in inland areas than coastal areas, and that services sector growth in coastal areas is promisingly robust and thus may be able to sustain growth in these areas in future.

Yang et al. (Chapter 10) find that regional innovation capacity is playing a role in determining the rate of regional convergence in China and argue that this must be accounted for in China's policies to reduce regional economic inequalities.

Yin and Mao (Chapter 11) study firm-level patent-seeking and its impact on R&D expenditure. They find that both market-driven patent-seeking and the number of patents held are among factors associated with higher levels of R&D activity among firms.

Finally, Krolikowski (Chapter 12) explores the cultural habits and industrial progress of China's frontier aeronautical and space research communities.

Wei et al. (Chapter 8) open with a reminder of the scale of China's demographic challenge. After more than three decades of high growth based on exploitation of demographic and wage cost advantages, interacting with international and market-oriented reforms, China now confronts higher wages and a shrinking workforce. Future growth now must depend more on innovation and increased productivity. Chapter 8 assesses the likelihood of China making the transition. It uses matched firm-level data on patent applications, receipts and citations and a survey of manufacturing firms. It finds that embracing new international opportunities and adapting to rising labour costs are two factors leading China's increasingly innovative economy. A result is that the quality of Chinese exports is increasing, but there is also evidence of resource misallocation affecting innovation: state-owned firms receive a greater share of innovation subsidies, but private firms are more successful innovators. The authors argue that the transition to an innovation-led economy will progress more quickly if this resource misallocation can be tackled.

In Chapter 9, Wu et al. note that the greater importance of innovation and entrepreneurship as new drivers of China's economy has led to an intense debate about the role and dynamics of productivity growth in China. The authors present an update on this area of the literature. Most studies agree that while TFP made a significant and positive contribution to China's economic growth in recent decades, both TFP and economic growth rates in China have slowed in recent years. Whether this downward trend continues has important implications for China's economic development. Somewhat optimistically, new estimates presented here find that China's inland regions have maintained high growth and have outperformed coastal regions across all sectors: primary, manufacturing and services. Whereas manufacturing TFP in coastal areas has suffered in recent times, services sector TFP growth in coastal China is robust and could thus help to sustain growth in these regions into the future.

Yang et al. (Chapter 10) offer an empirical analysis of the convergence of real GDP per capita of 31 Chinese provinces and municipalities over the period 2001–15. They explore the impact of innovation capability on economic convergence and identify three key results: 1) after considering the spatial effect, China's regional economic development has both conditional convergence and absolute convergence; 2) the trend towards regional economic development convergence is increasing; and 3) after regional innovation capacity is taken into account, the convergence speed of China's regional economy will deteriorate. In other words, innovation ability has a significant effect on the speed of economic convergence. In turn, if the excessive concentration of innovation resources along China's coastal region is not better spread across the country, China's economic development will experience innovation-led regional divergence. In formulating innovation policy, the government should thus pay attention to spatial interaction.

In Chapter 11, Yin and Mao use data from the 2013 National Patent Survey to study the causal relationship between Chinese patent protection and enterprise R&D expenditure, and the more specific effects on promoting R&D of patent motivation (e.g. protection of inventions and strategic blocking behaviour), accumulation and choice of protection model. The findings include patent filing is market-driven and closely associated with R&D expenditure, firms that hold a higher number of patents on average spend more on R&D and the type of patents held (patent quality) is not significantly associated with R&D expenditure. Since patent motivation has an important impact on consequential innovation, the chapter concludes that Chinese policymakers should pay attention to patent motivation when incentivising innovators and, similarly, that both firms and the state, if relevant, should encourage patent quality over quantity. Finally, China's unique 'double-track' judicial and administrative patent rights enforcement and protection mechanism should be strengthened.

Krolikowski (Chapter 12) offers a fascinating introduction to what is possibly the world's most rapidly advancing space program. Moreover, China is also poised to enter the technologically demanding large-carrier segment of the global aircraft industry. Within that dynamic system, Chapter 12 informs us how these particular scientific expert clusters share specialised knowledge and culture. They are also concentrated in two large state-owned defence-industry groups—the Chinese Aerospace Science and Technology Corporation (CASC) and the Chinese Aerospace Science and Industry Corporation (CASIC)—several government agencies, military organs and technical universities and research institutes. Their culture over time has become more meritocratic, but these agencies and areas of expertise in general remain relatively insular. They do, however, have a unique role to play in shaping China's innovation policy, especially the long-term ideal of national control over satellite and launch vehicle manufacture. Understanding the cultures and hierarchies of these scientific communities and their interrelationships with policymakers and national goals can shed light on China's progress towards the high-tech frontiers of the aerospace sector.

Part IV: Technological change by sectors

Technological change within key economic sectors lies at the heart of a bigger story of transformation. Part IV comprises three chapters that study one topic from each of the primary, secondary and tertiary sectors.

Sheng et al. (Chapter 13) present an interesting idea for deepening the mechanisation of China's agricultural sector and raising productivity levels without increasing average farm size. Jiang (Chapter 14) looks at renewable energy technologies and presents a thorough review of industrial structure and progress for hydropower, wind, solar and biomass energy. Kendell and Lees (Chapter 15) round out Part IV with an exploration of frontier financing in China. They demonstrate the dexterity of China's financial policymakers in recently advancing China's 'repo' markets as an additional and increasingly important source of shorter-term financing in the country.

Sheng et al. (Chapter 13) tackle a longstanding constraint to the productivity growth of agricultural production in developing countries: small farm size. The authors argue that, in place of agglomerating small farms into larger ones, contract mechanisation services (in particular, capital outsourcing) could offer an alternative route to increasing farm productivity. This, in turn, can raise the capital–labour ratio of medium-sized and small farms, complementing earlier Chinese land consolidation reform towards continued improvement in industry-level agricultural productivity. Such institutional creativity could offer China's small farming households the opportunity to continue to increase productivity via 'increasing returns to scale' and frontier technologies—without having to make prohibitively large investments. However, they point out that market-based outsourced mechanisation services are constrained by market friction, high transaction costs and various institutional barriers. Institutional innovation is therefore required to reduce market transaction costs to facilitate the use of outsourced mechanisation services to deal with the issue of small farm size in agricultural production along with land consolidation reform.

In Chapter 14, Jiang sheds light on China as a leading player in renewable energy development. Renewable energy capacity in China accounts for some one-third of the global total, and growth in the industry has been especially strong since 2011. Growth has been especially rapid in solar, which has grown by 110 per cent per annum over this period. Strong policy support has led to technological progress and large falls in prices. Chapter 14 describes these trends, especially with respect to developments in hydro, wind, solar and biomass power capacity and industrial development in China. Chinese authorities are committed to reaching the climate change–related targets of the Paris agreement. The author highlights that China reaching its energy transition and clean air targets are central to the realisation of international climate change goals.

Kendell and Lees (Chapter 15) explore the market for repurchase agreements ('repo'), which are an important source of short-term funding for financial institutions operating in China. Used by the People's Bank of China to manage domestic liquidity conditions through open market operations, repos are likely to become increasingly important as a channel for the transmission of monetary policy. The authors describe the characteristics of China's repo market. They initially focus on the interbank market and then look at recent developments and their impact on the bond market. They show that lower and less volatile repo rates over the past couple of years have contributed to greater risk-taking in financial markets and policy settings in China have been dynamic in shaping and responding to these developments.

Part V: Technologies with trade and investment

Part V explores China's progress in innovation in trade, investment and development finance globally. First, Athukorala (Chapter 16) studies China's trade balances in terms of the evolution of East Asian production networks and, despite views being trumpeted internationally, the chapter suggests that punitive tariffs against China may, paradoxically, hurt competing international business interests more than those in China. Chen (Chapter 17) studies empirically the impact of China's outward foreign direct investment (OFDI) on its economic growth by using a province-level panel dataset covering 30 provinces and the period 2004–14.

The final two chapters of the 2017 volume elaborate issues that are important to China's prominent 'One Belt, One Road' initiative and its new globalisation push. Hu et al. (Chapter 18) study existing economic patterns and make suggestions for policies that will deepen ties between China and a section of the 'Road': the five countries of the Eurasian Economic Union (EEU). Johnston and Rudyak (Chapter 19) make an important contribution in the context of China's new globalisation. They identify political and economic points of inflection and influences that shaped China's own globalisation as a means to understanding how China may shape globalisation itself.

In Chapter 16, Athukorala explores the implications of China's evolving role in East Asian global production networks. The context of the chapter is increasing recent international trade friction and the role of regional and international production networks. He argues that China's widening trade imbalances with many economies are a structural phenomenon driven by a process of global production sharing and the decades-deep pivotal role played by China within East Asian–centred global production networks. Global production sharing is an integral part of economic globalisation, so the underlying story of the US–Sino trade gap is more complicated than can be revealed by standard trade-flow analysis. China's final assembly export networks are not only extensive across East Asia and the Organisation for Economic Co-operation and Development (OECD), but also extend increasingly to Africa, Latin America and the Middle East. As a result, punitive tariffs on China are bound to face opposition from American business interests and the impact on global production network flows may be less damaging than is commonly thought.

Chen (Chapter 17) finds that both OFDI from provincial firms and OFDI from central government–controlled state-owned enterprises (SOEs) have a statistically significant positive impact on China's provincial economic growth. The positive impact of OFDI on provincial economic growth may be the result of reverse knowledge spillovers from OFDI to the home province's economy through demonstration and imitation, labour movement, backward and forward industrial linkages, information flows, promoting the exports of local firms and facilitating industrial restructuring and technological upgrading of home economies, thus increasing the productivity and efficiency of local firms and promoting growth of the home economy. Overall, the study offers strong empirical evidence that OFDI contributes to China's economic growth. Policies should aim to develop a more open and market-oriented OFDI regime, encourage R&D and technological development to increase the ownership advantages of home-economy domestic firms and encourage interaction between home-economy multinational enterprises (MNEs) and home-economy domestic firms to enhance and accelerate the diffusion of positive reverse knowledge spillovers from OFDI to China's economy.

Hu et al. in Chapter 18 explore '5 + 1' cooperation between China and the five countries of the EEU: Russia, Belarus, Kazakhstan, Kyrgyzstan and Armenia. These countries are central to the 'Belt' in China's 'One Belt, One Road' initiative. The authors compare resource endowments in China and EEU countries and examine the potential for greater mutual and global connectivity around infrastructure investment, as well as deeper trade and investment ties. The authors make a series of policy suggestions to foster greater collaboration between China and the five EEU countries. These include encouraging greater financial integration—directly through the establishment of Chinese financial institutions in the five EEU countries and indirectly through expanding funding levels and mechanisms for development projects. Similarly, greater use of the renminbi within the region may reduce currency instability, which recently has been an issue. Away from finance, the authors suggest more visa-free mobility and enhanced trade and industrial policy coordination as mechanisms for facilitating greater economic activity among member countries.

Johnston and Rudyak (Chapter 19) bring the 2017 volume to a close with their chapter on one of the most important features of China's new globalisation agenda: foreign aid and development finance. In his plenary speech to the World Economic Forum in Davos in early 2017, the Chinese President Xi Jinping noted that China should 'adapt to and guide economic globalization, cushion its negative impact, and deliver its benefits to all countries and all nations'. With the stated goal of China playing a greater leadership role in globalisation, including through delivering benefits to other developing countries, Xi drew attention to the role of China's foreign aid in contributing to global growth. Since understanding China's own experience with foreign aid could shed light on the potential directions of its new globalisation agenda, the authors present a chronology that helps explain how and why China may now develop its own economic interests and those of other developing countries by being more active in shaping globalisation. Africa has been an especially important focus of China's aid policy, since half of China's foreign aid to Africa is also a focus of the 'One Belt, One Road' initiative.

References

Arrow, K. (1962), Economic welfare and the allocation of resources for invention, in R. R. Nelson (ed.), *The Rate and Direction of Inventive Activity*, pp. 609–26, Princeton, NJ: Princeton University Press. doi.org/10.1515/9781400879762-024.

The Conference Board (2015), *The Conference Board Total Economy Database*, New York: The Conference Board. Available from: www.conference-board.org/data/economydatabase/.

Dosi, G. and Nelson, R. R. (2010), Technical change and industrial dynamics as evolutionary processes, in B. H. Hall and N. Rosenberg (eds), *Handbook of the Economics of Innovation: Volume 1*, Amsterdam: Elsevier. doi.org/10.1016/S0169-7218(10)01003-8.

Eichengreen, B., Park, D. and Shin, K. (2013), *Growth slowdowns redux: New evidence on the middle-income trap*, NBER Working Paper No. w18673, National Bureau of Economic Research, Cambridge, Mass.

Glazebrook, K. and Song, L. (2013), Is China up to the test? A review of theories and priorities for education investment for a modern China, *China & World Economy* 21(4): 56–78. doi.org/10.1111/j.1749-124x.2013.12028.x.

Hall, B. H. and Rosenberg, N. (2010), Introduction to the handbook, in B. H. Hall and N. Rosenberg (eds), *Handbook of the Economics of Innovation: Volume 1*, pp. 3–9, Amsterdam: Elsevier. doi.org/10.1016/S0169-7218(10)01001-4.

Jones, C. I. and Romer, P. M. (2010), The new Kaldor facts: Ideas, institutions, population, and human capital, *American Economic Journal: Macroeconomics* 2(1): 224–45. doi.org/10.1257/mac.2.1.224.

Maddison, A. (1982), *Phases of Capitalist Development*, Oxford: Oxford University Press.

National Bureau of Statistics of China (NBS) (various years), *China Statistical Yearbook*, Beijing: China Statistics Press.

Son, N. C. and Song, L. (2015), Promoting private entrepreneurship for deepening market reform in China: A resource allocation perspective, *China & World Economy* 23(1): 747–77.

Thirlwall, A. P. and Pacheco-Lopez, P. (2017), *Economics of Development: Theory and evidence*, London: Palgrave Macmillan. doi.org/10.1057/978-1-137-57795-5.

World Bank (1999), *Strategic goals for Chinese education in the 21st century*, Report No. 18969-CHA, The World Bank, Washington, DC. Available from: documents.worldbank.org/curated/en/203951468768863829/Strategic-goals-for-Chinese-education-in-the-21st-century.

World Bank (2013), *China 2030: Building a modern, harmonious, and creative society*, Report No. 76299, The World Bank, Washington, DC. Available from: documents.worldbank.org/curated/en/781101468239669951/China-2030-building-a-modern-harmonious-and-creative-society.

Part I: Reform and Macroeconomic Development

2. Reform Dividends to Sustain China's Economic Growth

Cai Fang and Xiaojing Zhang

Introduction

After three decades of double-digit growth, China's economy has now moved into a period of slower potential growth rates known as the 'new normal'. To realise sustainable growth in this period, China must capture dividends from reform. This chapter studies the features of current reforms, including the adjustment of interest structure, non-Pareto improvement reform, the interplay between top-level reform design and grassroots innovation, achieving unity between a problem-oriented and a goal-oriented approach to reform and the necessity of having a legal basis for reforms. Second, it analyses the progress of reforms, including efforts to increase market competition and promote a level playing field, reform of the government's role in resource allocation and improving the property rights protection system. Such reforms seek to deepen market-oriented reforms that began in the late 1970s. To that end, this chapter concludes that the best way for China to capture reform dividends is to further clarify the direction of reform, to promote pragmatic reforms and to restructure incentive mechanisms to mobilise the enthusiasm of the whole society.

The keys to China's economic miracle over the past few decades were reform and opening-up—the continuation of which is an important choice for the future. After the 18th National People's Congress of the Communist Party of China (CPC) held in 2012, and especially following the third plenary session of the 18th CPC Central Committee held in November 2013, a new agenda for reform was set, including the following:

1. China should continue to promote improvement and development of the socialist system with Chinese characteristics, and further develop social productivity, thereby releasing the creativity of the whole society.
2. To promote sustainable and healthy development, and to continue to improve people's wellbeing, China needs to solve major problems.
3. China should maintain the vitality of the socialist system in a context of global interdependence and institutional competition.

Reform itself is continuous in transitional economies such as China's as well as in developed market economies, such as the United States, Japan and European countries. From a global perspective, institutional competition and reform will become more entrenched. In institutional economics, it is recognised that the forces driving the evolution of internal and external systems include not only the indirect effects on international trade and mobility of production factors, but also direct institutional adjustment to competition. Globalisation has led to 'institutional (or system) competition' (Kasper and Streit 1999). Since the 2008 Global Financial Crisis (GFC), rebalancing and structural reforms have become more prominent themes in global development. China has implemented a comprehensive reform agenda, as deployed via the third through sixth plenary sessions of the 18th CPC Central Committee. The United States, Japan and Europe have also launched structural reform programs and strategies for long-term growth. This suggests intense competition for reform has already begun in the wake of the tighter growth conditions after the GFC.

The ability and determination of one country to promote reforms depend mainly on its state capacity. The Irish thinker Edmond Burke argued in his book *Reflections on the Revolution in France*: 'A state without the means of some change, is without the means of its own conservation' (Burke 1986). A state without such means for change will inevitably have to take a risk, which is to say it will lose the part of its system that it wants to preserve the most. This is the force driving the comprehensively deepening reforms in China that are aimed at 'preserving' the fundamental nature of the socialist system.

In a sense, for China, the pursuit of internal reform in a context of intensified global competition provides the underlying logic of its reform and opening-up. Indeed, in the 1980s, paramount leader Deng Xiaoping pointed out that the purpose of the reform (of that time) was to establish a solid foundation for sustainable development in the next decade and the first half of the twenty-first century. Without reform, there would be no sustainable development in the future. As with all aspects of reform, we should focus not just on short-term measures and results, but also on those impacting over the longer term. Reform, therefore, must continue (Deng 1993).

New features of reform

China's economy has entered a period in which growth of around 6–7 per cent is normal, compared with annual growth of 10 per cent in the previous three decades. Only through reform can China sufficiently adapt to the new normal and enter a new era of growth. Without reform, China's continued economic development will suffer reduced vitality, could fail to achieve sustainable growth and may even fall into the 'middle-income trap'. The challenges in China's current economic landscape, however, highlight the fact that deepening structural reform is an urgent task. We now elaborate distinctive new features of China's reform requirements, compared with the experiences of the past 30 years.

The deep-water reform zone

After 'the reform without losers' in the early years of economic transition (Lau et al. 2000), China has now entered a deep-water reform zone with more challenges and difficulties. This means that this era of reform necessitates confronting multiple fundamental and sensitive problems, such as deep-rooted social conflicts, vested interests and lack of social mobility. Little progress has been made on such issues over many years of reform. This can be attributed, to a large extent, to China's gradualist approach to reform, in which some relatively easy tasks have been pushed forward first and the difficult ones have been put aside. This gradual approach has, however, also supported the persistence of the so-called protective umbrella of vested interests, which refers to the capacity of actors to access individual benefits through abuse of public power and to impede the general public's access to the benefits of reform. The 'umbrella' thus restrains economic vitality and social creativity, harms the efficiency of resource allocation, reduces social mobility and, more importantly, has become a major obstacle to further deepening of reform.

No longer a 'Pareto improvement'

Adjustment of the role played by vested interests is vital to the process of reform, and is now unavoidable. Earlier reforms were typically characterised as offering a 'Pareto improvement', in which the majority of people benefit and no one suffers. Current reforms, however, are likely to have the nature of a 'Kaldor improvement', in which there is a necessary coexistence of improvement (namely, benefiting from a bigger pie) and adjustment (benefiting from dividing up the pie). Thus, policymakers need to more dynamically and comprehensively consider the likely beneficiaries before, during and after implementation of reform, and give top priority to the interests of ordinary people. Policymakers also need to coordinate the interests of various groups and should focus on the overall long-term benefits, thereby enabling the greatest share of people to enjoy the fruits of any reform. This, in turn, will enable 'the building of a moderately prosperous (*xiaokang*) society in all respects with no region, no ethnic group and no individual left behind'.[1] It means that policymakers need to not only alleviate and prevent poverty, but also help people achieve all-round economic, political, cultural, social and ecological improvement. It means also that policymakers should increase the size of the social wealth 'pie' and distribute it fairly to create a more equitable and wealthy society full of hope for all.

1 See cpc.people.com.cn/xuexi/n/2015/0303/c385476-26629388.html.

Interplay between top-level design and grassroots innovation

Four major problems need to be addressed via top-level design. First, it is important to look at the overall picture. Reform is a systemic project, in which opportunities and challenges are entangled, and piecemeal adjustment and repair are often unfeasible. There must be comprehensive systemic reform and improvement in all fields, which in turn means that top-level design and overall planning of reform process are sorely needed. Second, innovations at the grassroots level should be consistent with the general direction of reform. Third, there is a need to define what can and cannot be done. Fourth, there is a need to break the deadlock due to vested interests. Precisely because China's reform has entered a deep-water zone, top-level leadership may be needed to break vested interests' resistance to reform and to add new momentum to the project. At the same time, innovation at the grassroots level should be encouraged. Many top-down reform designs provide only broad guidance, whereas extensive experimentation is needed to promote reforms. Problems that are difficult to solve in theory can often be better addressed in practice. Therefore, innovation at the grassroots level is of great importance for the development of theory and would not only help achieve practical results, but also contribute to institutional innovation.

Problem-oriented and goal-oriented unity

China's reform process has been driven by the need to solve practical problems; therefore, problem-oriented research is of great significance. In particular, to open new prospects for reform, China's policymakers and scholars should aim to solve the structural challenges hindering the country's development. At the same time, focusing on problems can lead to the 'fragmentation' of reform efforts—that is, restricting focus and causing an incoherent approach. It is therefore essential to have clear goals for reform and a clear blueprint for achieving it.

Legal basis of reform

In this new era, policymakers seek the best combination of reform and rule of law: reform should be promoted under the rule of law and the rule of law needs improving in the process of reform. Problems incurred during the passage of reform should be solved only within the framework of the rule of law and there must be a legal basis for those reforms. The comprehensive deepening of reforms should be advanced with courage to 'break' institutional barriers and change the status quo.

On the other hand, the ultimate goal of breaking such barriers is to thereafter establish a set of new, stable and efficient laws and regulations; therefore, reforms should not supersede the law. Unlike three decades ago, China has integrated itself much more deeply into the global system, where regard for the rule of law is necessary for the common achievement of human civilisation. China must now promote reform through lawful means to create a favourable external environment.

New progress of reform

Since the third plenary session of the 18th CPC Central Committee in 2013, great progress has been made in the comprehensive deepening of reform in China. The main framework for reform, with multiple key 'pillars', has been established and a new, albeit preliminary, pattern of reform has emerged. Achievements include the creation of healthy and fair market competition, innovation in the government's role in resource allocation, promotion of the compilation of the Civil Code and emphasis on the property rights system as a cornerstone of the socialist market economy. All these efforts have helped to clarify the direction of reform and stabilise public expectations. On the whole, these reforms—focusing on how to allow market forces to play a decisive role in the economy and to improve the government's role—constitute the continuation of the market-oriented reforms that began in the late 1970s, and on which we elaborate further below.

Ensuring a level playing field

In the new normal era, developing a level playing field is of even greater importance than before to the vitality and efficiency of the economy, and to achieving innovation-driven development and maintaining sustainable economic growth. There are three keys to facilitating fair competition.

The first is tackling local protectionism—that is, policymakers need to break regional blockades and local protection measures, remove market barriers and promote the mobility of goods and production factors across regions within the country. This will aid the formation of a truly unified domestic market, which is vital to ensuring healthy local competition.

Second is the need to tackle industrial monopolies—in particular, the imposing challenge of the administrative monopoly of state-owned enterprises (SOEs). A study by Li et al. (2014) found that after the large-scale reform of SOEs in the late 1990s, Chinese industry formed a vertical industrial structure, in which SOEs continued to dominate and monopolise some of the key upstream industries (such as energy, finance and telecommunications), while the majority of downstream industries (such as the manufacture of consumer goods, hospitality, entertainment and other consumer-oriented services) have, to some extent, been liberalised and are now dominated by private enterprises. In the process of structural transformation (i.e. industrialisation) and trade globalisation, private enterprises in downstream industries have experienced continuous growth by making full use of China's abundant and cheap labour and by taking advantage of China's accession to the World Trade Organization (WTO) in 2001, which led to rapid economic growth in the country. With the expanding scale of production, downstream private enterprises have also experienced a growing demand for critical inputs and intermediate services, such as energy, telecommunications, finance and so on. SOEs, with their monopoly on these key upstream products and services, gain proportionately from the higher productivity, output and exports of private enterprises. Currently, the nature of the SOEs' monopoly is mainly administrative—meaning the government helps some enterprises gain market resources and access, government procurement opportunities and so on, to ensure they remain in an absolute monopoly position. Only by breaking the administrative monopoly of SOEs—in particular, withdrawing SOEs from some competitive areas—can a level playing field gradually emerge.

The third factor is enabling a shift from traditional industrial policy with a focus on infant industry protection to new development policy with focuses on competition and improving market institution. Traditional industrial policy can play an active role during a period of economic catch-up, because the government can support the market to make use of the advantages of backwardness by imitating and introducing new technology. This allows the absorption of all kinds of information relating to frontier technologies and emerging industries at low cost, and thereafter determines the technical route for industry to follow, actively mobilises necessary resources and promotes indigenous research, industrialisation and technological innovation (developing countries rely on 'importation' for more than 80 per cent of their new technology; Manyika et al. 2015). As the advantage of backwardness progressively shrinks, however, the uncertainty of frontier technological innovation increases and the government's ability to collect information and make appropriate decisions is significantly reduced. The industrial policy strategy of 'the government picking the winner' therefore fails. Due to these challenges, in a more developed economy, there is a need for a better institutional environment to nurture original innovation. The more seeds of innovation that are sown, the more novel ideas will sprout. This highlights the need for China to now shift from a selective to an inclusive industrial policy, to pay more attention to competition policy and to let market forces play a greater role in innovation and related incentives.

Reforming the government's role in resource allocation

Thanks to the deepening of market-oriented reform and opening-up in China, the role of the market in resource allocation has been increasingly enhanced—as has the role of government.

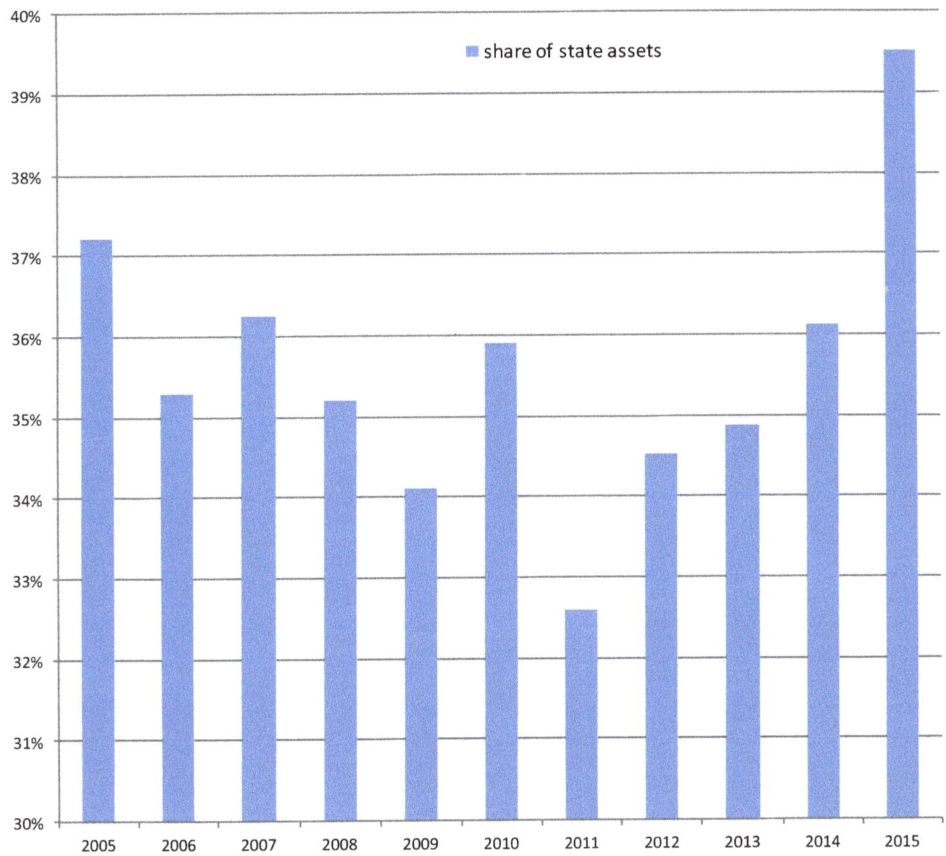

Figure 2.1 Trends in the relative size of state-owned assets (as percentage of total assets in the corporate sector)

Sources: NBS (various issues); authors' estimates.

An important aspect of government resource allocation is how to accumulate and manage public assets. We can explore the issue from different perspectives. Our estimates indicate that: 1) as of 2015, state-owned assets (including non-financial and net financial assets) accounted for nearly 40 per cent of total assets in the corporate sector (Figure 2.1); 2) in 2015, the government's sovereign net worth reached about RMB100 trillion (Figure 2.2); and 3) the proportion of general government net wealth in national net wealth is close to one-quarter, in comparison with Germany and Japan, where this ratio is less than 1 per cent, and the United Kingdom and the United States, where this ratio is in fact negative (Figure 2.3). The result is closely related to China's ownership structure (with the domination of public ownership) and its development stage (government-driven catch-up growth).

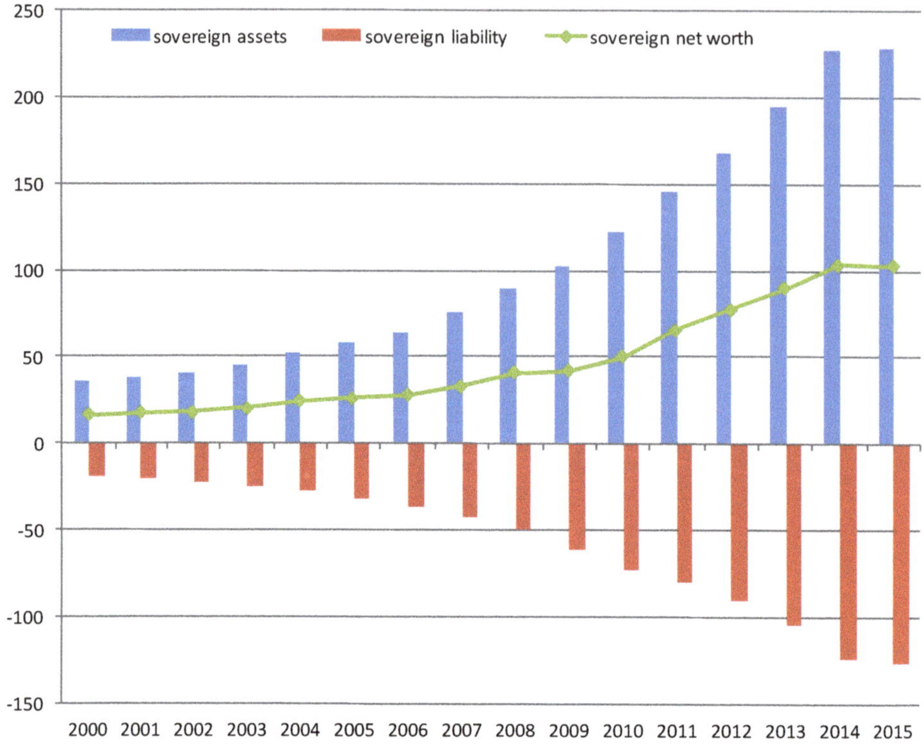

Figure 2.2 China's sovereign assets, liabilities and net worth (RMB trillion)
Sources: NBS (various issues); authors' estimates.

From a comparative perspective, the wealth held by the Chinese Government is strikingly large, even by conservative estimates. According to Detter and Folster (2015), a 1 per cent increase in the rate of return on those assets would generate US$750 billion (estimated at US$75 trillion in global public commercial assets) of public revenue. Obviously, this figure does not include large amounts of non-commercial (or non-operating) assets, such as natural resources and assets held by administrative institutions (such as China's science, education, culture and health institutions). Given the tremendous holdings of economic resources, reforming the government's role in resources allocation, as well as greater efficiency of resource use, will be an increasingly important aspect of future reforms.

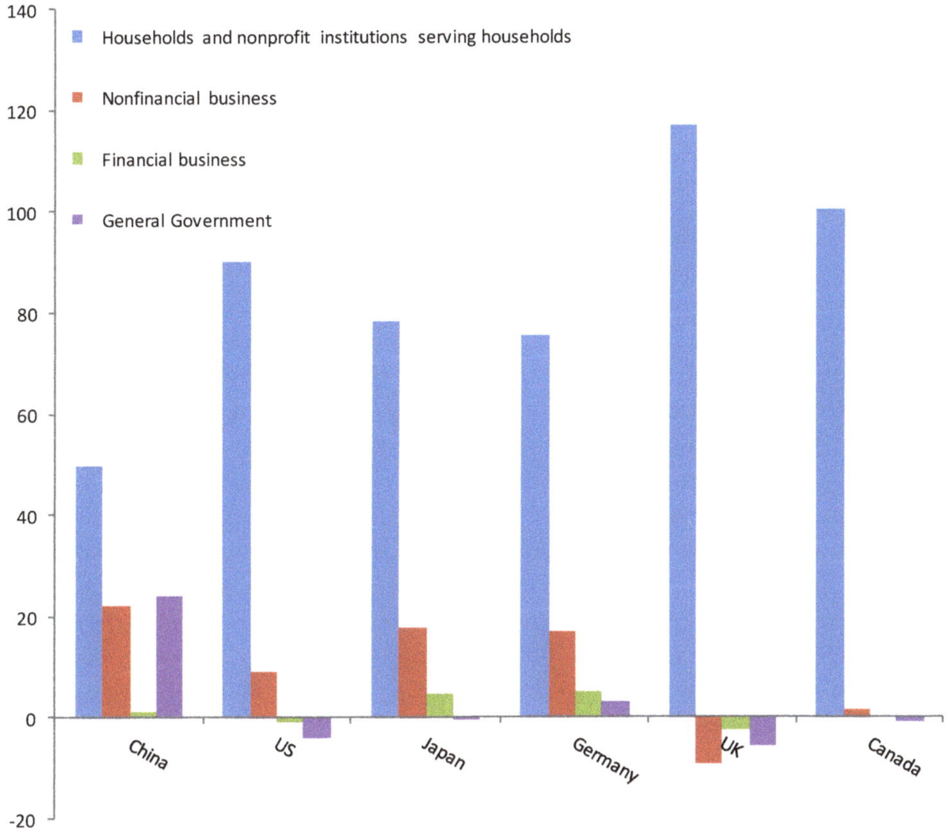

Figure 2.3 International comparison of China's net worth structure, 2015 (per cent)

Notes: Data for China are from 2013 and from 2014 for other countries. For Canada, non-financial and financial sectors have been consolidated. General government assets in China include state-owned business assets, non-business assets, natural resource assets, foreign assets, social security funds and government deposits at the central bank.

Sources: NBS (various issues); authors' estimates.

Resources allocated by the Chinese Government include natural resources and resources held by SOEs and public institutions, which are owned on behalf of the state and the people. To address outstanding problems—including market price distortion and the inefficient allocation and insufficient supply of public services—it is necessary to shift allocative decisions away from the state and towards market mechanisms to improve the efficiency and effectiveness of resource allocation.

First, access to and use of natural resources should be based on the establishment of a property rights system. In China, the law clearly stipulates that all natural resources—such as land, minerals, water, forests, mountains, grasslands, wasteland, sea areas, uninhabited islands, beaches and so on—are owned collectively. For this type of public resource, a clear property rights system should be established and the related usage administration improved. In particular, the role of spatial planning in guiding the allocation of natural resources needs more attention. 'Radio spectrum' should also be allocated and managed on the basis of market competition and a user-pays system.

Second, the allocation and management of state-owned assets should be reformed. For state-owned financial and non-financial operating assets, it is necessary to establish a sound management system with an emphasis on capital allocation and efficiency, sectoral distribution and investment and withdrawal. To optimise the distribution of state-owned capital, the government should concentrate its efforts in key industries and infrastructure projects that relate to national security, the foundation of the national economy and the people's livelihood, as well as forward-looking strategic industries and advancing enterprises with core competitiveness. Policymakers should similarly improve the exit mechanism for state-owned capital, explore what is a reasonable proportion for state-owned shareholding in financial institutions and maintain control of financial institutions of systemic importance. The ownership structure of other institutions should be optimised in accordance with the principle of market competition and provide incentives to non-state investment. There is also an increasing need to improve the system of authorisation and franchising of the operations of state-owned capital. Further policy efforts are needed to establish a state-owned asset supervision system with a focus on capital management, to restructure or set up state-owned capital investment and operation companies and to carry out pilot projects in which the government authorises state-owned capital investment and encourages operating companies to fulfil their responsibilities as capital contributors. Policymakers should also keep a focus on capital management, aiming to enhance the liquidity of state-owned capital and actively change the form of public capital, such as securitisation of operating state-owned assets, and also emphasise the role of public capital in the country's macroeconomic regulation and control, long-term development strategy and the protection of people's basic livelihoods.

Third, regarding non-operating state-owned assets for the purpose of public administration and public service provision, policymakers should adhere to a principle of fair distribution and actively introduce competition mechanisms to increase allocation efficiency and thus improve the accessibility and fairness of basic public services. Government departments and public institutions should be distinguished by their different functions, as should government administration and business operation. That is, policymakers should clearly define the different functions of the government as a capital owner and as an industry regulator, improve mechanisms for direct resource allocation and strengthen the regulatory functions of departments/institutions in the education, health, social security, culture, sports and other sectors. The government must also be innovative with respect to the supply mode for public services. Policymakers should establish a diversified public service supply system with a focus on government leadership, social engagement, independent operation and public oversight. All localities and departments can expand and improve the supply of public goods and services through franchising and government procurement of services, according to their needs and financial conditions. The government should promote the integration and sharing of non-operating state-owned assets. With clearly defined property rights and accurate assessments of assets and capital, the government needs to abolish the administrative segmentation of departments and build a shared platform for the dissemination of public knowledge, education, health care, culture and other non-material resources.

Improving the property rights protection system

In November 2016, China issued 'The Opinions of the CPC Central Committee and the State Council on Improving the Protection System of Property Rights and the Protection of Property Rights in Accordance with Law'. The document stresses that the property rights system is the cornerstone of the socialist market economy and that the protection of property rights is an inevitable requirement to adhere to the fundamental socialist economic system. As an old Chinese saying goes, 'one shall have his (or her) peace of mind when he (or she) possesses a piece of land', so the effective protection and recognition of the property rights of economic agents serve as the basis of sustainable and healthy socioeconomic development.

A large number of studies from outside China suggest that reform of the property rights system has, to some extent, been ignored in China's reform process (see, among others, Murphy et al. 1992; Young 2000; Brandt and Rawski 2008). Other studies recognise that China's property rights system in fact has many distinctive features and that these are open to change as China experiments to find the best property rights structure. First, in an economy dominated by public ownership, the contracting out of property use rights (exemplified especially by the rural household responsibility system (HRS)) has been solidified from the abstract and often ill-defined ownership of 'whole people' or 'collectivity'. Second, making further effort to respecting private ownership of various factors of production, including capital, labour, technology and entrepreneurship. Third, private property rights have been redefined or new forms recognised. The need for further transfers of property to preserve and increase property values has seen the emergence of market transactions. In particular, transfer rights, pricing power, the right to bid and bargaining power have been recognised, and have resulted in the market playing an increasingly important role in resource allocation; the system of central economic planning is gradually being dismantled as well. Fourth, in the framework of the shareholding system, contracts can be concluded for various types of property rights that could be recognised and protected, and corporate enterprises with clear property rights can be established (Zhou 2010).

As China's reform process continues, challenges with the definition and protection of property rights should not be underestimated. First, regarding the protection of state-owned property rights, the relationship between owners and agents is not clear and there are some problems—such as insider control and related party transactions—that could lead to the loss of state-owned assets. Second, the protection of private property rights also remains weak, and is often encroached on by public power. Third, the protection of intellectual property rights is still weak and infringements are pervasive with low penalties.[2] Therefore, the government should focus on the following three factors to improve the property rights protection system.

First, public property rights need to be defined and protected. China's economic system is dominated by public ownership, with allowances for the development of other types of ownership. Therefore, the protection of public property rights—which involves the protection of land, natural resources and state-owned assets—can be viewed as a fundamental feature of China's political-economic institutions.

Second, private property rights need to be defined and protected. China's planned economy has long discriminated against private ownership. Policymakers therefore need to break the ideological constraint of 'public versus private' and strengthen the equal protection of property rights for all kinds of economic organisations and agents. The most urgent is to get rid of the 'original sin', and to strictly follow the principles of non-retroactivity, *nullum crimen sine lege* (no crime without law), *in dubio pro reo* '(when) in doubt, for the accused' and 'to rectify whatever is wrong', as well as application of the existing law unless a lesser punishment is stipulated in the new law. In taking the perspectives of history and development, the irregularities of the enterprises, especially private enterprises, should be properly handled in full consideration of their contexts, where the legal system and market institutions were immature. This will strengthen confidence in development and property security and help to stimulate entrepreneurs' spirit of innovation.

Third, intellectual property rights must be protected. Further work is needed to refine the laws and regulations relevant to intellectual property rights protection, to gradually establish a punitive damages mechanism for intellectual property infringements to prevent infringement behaviour and to improve compulsory remedial measures after infringement. Enforcement of intellectual property rights protection is essential, as is eliminating any arbitrariness and selectivity in such enforcement. The government's simplistic interventions on patents, specific industrial policies and talent policies must be reduced to promote technological

2 As an example, we refer to a recent report released by the Global Intellectual Property Center (2016), which measures efforts in the legal enforcement of intellectual property rights in the 38 economies including China, United States, the United Kingdom, and India. On a scale in which the highest score is 6, China's law enforcement efforts were given 1.51 points, ranking it the 31st of 38 countries. In the context of weak intellectual property rights protection, imitation becomes the norm for enterprises' 'innovation', and even piracy and counterfeiting can become common—cultivating a cultural atmosphere in which intellectual property rights are not respected.

innovation. Policymakers should also gradually improve market incentives, allowing market forces to become the main drivers of growth in patent quantity and quality. The definition and protection of the human capital property rights of scientific and engineering personnel in the public sector must be examined to release the innovative capabilities of scientific researchers.

Policy recommendations and perspectives on reform

The third plenary session of the 18th CPC Central Committee in 2013 outlined a blueprint for China's reform. Given the success of reforms and the attainment of the 'two centenary goals',[3] China now needs to focus on the following four factors: 1) further clarifying the direction of reform; 2) promoting the implementation and practical achievement of reform; 3) reconstructing incentive mechanisms to mobilise the enthusiasm of private and public economic agents; and 4) capitalising on the benefits of the reform dividend to achieve sustainable growth.

Further clarifying the direction of reform

China's process of economic catch-up over more than three decades has been accompanied by a variety of distortions,[4] including price distortions in favour of industrial products, financial repression, trade protection and industrial policy with the intention of infant industry protection. Broadly speaking, distortions can be viewed as different forms of government intervention. There is an extensive literature on the role of government in economic development. A prime example is the study of the 'developmental state', which refers to government playing an extremely proactive role in promoting economic growth through strong and direct intervention, including extensive regulation and planning (see Johnson 1982; Woo-Cummings 1999). Governments in East Asia, including China, are typical of those in the developmental state. Interestingly, we can also find a parallel but much earlier strong push from the hand of government in most developed countries in their early stages of development, such as mercantilist Holland and the United Kingdom in the sixteenth to eighteenth centuries and emerging Germany and the United States in the late nineteenth century.

3 See Hu Jintao's *Report at 18th CPC National Congress*, held in November 2012. For an English translation of the report, see: news.xinhuanet.com/english/special/18cpcnc/2012-11/17/c_131981259.htm.

4 In economics, the standard definition of distortion is deviation from the optimal equilibrium state of the market.

The role of distortion, either positive or negative, is closely related to the economy's development stage. When an economy is in an early stage of development—characterised by an immature industrial system, imperfect market mechanisms and unfavourable international competition—intensive policy distortions are often required to mobilise economic resources, foster domestic industries and assist the formation of comparative advantages. As the economy enters a higher income stage of development—characterised by a more mature industrial system and sound market mechanisms—too much policy distortion is no longer conducive to the efficient allocation of economic resources and often results in changes in incentives and behaviour through 'rent-seeking' for public power. This then serves to inhibit innovation and the sustainability of growth. Zhang et al. (forthcoming) support the above argument with evidence from international and Chinese experiences. The recent study of Bardhan (2016) also confirms this view.

Although many agree about the reduction or elimination of policy distortions and interventions, there are still some controversies and ambiguities on the topic. For example, when it comes to allowing the market to play a decisive role in resource allocation and improving the government's role, some thinking remains unclear on how to deal with the relationship between the market and government.

With the Central Committee having clearly outlined the general direction of China's reform, the challenge now is how to achieve practical results. First, however, some basic theoretical questions remain unanswered. For example, the aforementioned twofold emphasis on allowing the market to play a decisive role in resource allocation and improving the government's role may not only lead to a more balanced relationship between the market and government, but also throw up substantial obstacles to the promotion of reform in practice. Different departments, interest groups and social classes will have their own interpretation of this argument, with some emphasising the market and others the government. As an example, the recent fierce debate on industrial policy in China shows that consensus has not yet been reached on the issue of the market–government relationship.[5]

Defining the respective boundaries of the market and government is a practical matter (which is the case in both developed and developing economies); however, if, in theory, some 'moderate distortions', albeit ill defined, are believed necessary during the catch-up stage, such distortions will appear pervasively. Indeed, 'improving the government's role' mainly implies that the government cannot be absent from its essential functions—for example, providing public goods, fairness, justice and good governance. China's economy on a per capita level is currently moving from middle income towards the high-income level. Only by eliminating all remaining distortions during the catch-up period can China better promote sustainable development.

5 See a news report on the debate between Yifu Lin and Weiying Zhang, two economists of influence in China. Available from: finance.sina.com.cn/roll/2016-09-26/doc-ifxwevmf2320320.shtml [in Chinese].

In this sense, China needs 'limited' government that follows the logic of the market and serves the market. Therefore, policymakers need to further clarify and highlight the decisive role of the market in the next stages of reform.

Promoting reform plans

In his book *An Economist in the Real World: The art of policymaking in India*, Basu (2015) argued that although former prime minister Jawaharlal Nehru and other leaders in India participated in the development of economic planning, they were concerned more with the quality of the wording than with the content of the plan. It is not surprising, then, that South Korea worked out the most effective method of planning, while India's planning is written with the most literary grace.

And yet, it is also possible that the wording of China's reform plans is also a literary effort (even better than India's). The issue is how to promote these texts so they can be implemented in practice. The phenomenon of the 'implementation of documents by documents' is not uncommon, and worries about incompetence in implementing reforms are also pervasive. Among many factors leading to difficulties in the implementation of reform plans, the following should receive more attention from policymakers.

First, the dividends of reform are not fully understood. Structural reform—through which China could achieve real dividends—is not a substitute for economic growth, but is a catalyst or even prerequisite for growth. However, this argument has not yet been widely recognised and the incentives for reform are often weak and incompatible. For a long time, there has been a view both in China and abroad that there is a waxing and waning relationship between reform and growth—such that economic growth should be sacrificed to achieve breakthroughs in reform. In view of this, for government departments or local governments concerned about the pace of growth, the stimulus strategies on the demand side are usually visible in terms of the means of implementation, and the results or outcomes are often rapid. The policy tools also correspond to their effects quite well. On the contrary, for structural reform of the supply side, policy instruments seem to be invisible and there is no clear correspondence between the policy tools and their effects.

Second, the various incentives for reform are often incompatible. Due to the lack of appropriate standards with which to define the responsibilities of government at different levels, many reforms involving costs and benefits that need to be shared appropriately across all levels have not yet begun. Even if the economic agents understand that they can benefit from reform in principle, there is inconsistency as to which bodies will bear the reform-related costs and which will enjoy the benefits; therefore, some departments and localities have a wait-and-see attitude towards reform due to the asymmetry between cost and benefit. To some extent, this is also the case in countries other than China; thus, when promoting structural reforms, there is a need for persuasion and specific institutional arrangements to achieve incentive compatibility (Rajan 2004). In some areas of reform in China, such as that of the household registration system (*hukou*), a proper mechanism for sharing the expected costs and benefits is the key to promoting timely reform.

The third area for attention is deviation from the reform roadmap. In the presence of the above obstacles, reform initiatives in some areas are likely to be avoided, delayed, deformed or distorted in disregard of the original intention of the reform, so reform in practice deviates from the timetable set out by the CPC Central Committee. Related problems include: 1) when deciding on the balance between a supply-side structural reform program and a demand-side stimulus plan, some promoters prefer the latter, which is relatively easy to implement, thus creating a dependence on stimulus policies that results in the delay of structural reform. 2) Some reform officials focus only on statistics and indicators—which are crucial for government performance assessment and thus officials' prospects for promotion (meeting related political goals)—rather than on deep reform of institutions and mechanisms. As a result, even if some old problems can be temporarily resolved, the institutional flaws left untouched will create new problems. 3) Some reform promoters tend to avoid the important problems and focus on the trivial ones, and even count quotidian and routine management activities as reform initiatives. As a result, they have failed to fundamentally reform the existing institutional system and mechanisms, which, in particular, protect vested interests.

In short, to promote reform plans and achieve practical results, Chinese policymakers need to improve the public's understanding of the benefits or dividends of and costs associated with reform, and reach a consensus on the direction of reform across all levels of government and society. Policymakers should appeal to a sense of responsibility, political courage and perseverance to ensure further reform efforts. They should welcome experimentation and innovation at the grassroots level and promote positive interaction with top-level reform designs. They should encourage differentiated pilot programs and reform experiments in different regions and respond to people's concerns, especially the difficulties in their lives, by promoting targeted reform measures. They should also ensure the compatibility of incentives, so that government departments, localities and ordinary people can benefit from reform.

Restructuring the incentive mechanism

Thanks to strict governance by the CPC, its tough stance on corruption and the establishment of rules and regulations, solid regulatory mechanisms have gradually been established since the 18th CPC National Congress and, particularly, the third plenary session of the 18th CPC Central Committee. This is an important achievement; however, an appropriate incentive mechanism, which is also necessary for the success of reform, is still in the making.

First, in principle, competition among localities can continue to play a positive role in boosting market dynamics and economic development. In the past four decades, interregional competition and local vitality have underpinned China's economic success, which is also recognised internationally as an important component of the 'Chinese characteristics' defining its system. But the same institutional competition has produced a series of adverse impacts, such as vicious competition, local protectionism and market segmentation, structural distortion, homogenisation of development, overcapacity and so on. In view of this, China should redirect local competition—shifting from competition for gross domestic product (GDP) to competition for public goods and services. It is widely argued that until now local competition in China has centred on GDP growth performance. In the process of rapid urbanisation in recent years, the provision of public goods and services—including public security, education, health care, community services, social security and social housing—has become a 'short board' for socioeconomic development. Therefore, policymakers should focus on the type, quantity and quality of public goods and services to assess the performance of local governance and, in so doing, foster a new type of local competition for this new phase of development. In addition, evaluation of local government performance should be gradually shifted from a 'top-down' to a 'bottom-up' approach. If the past competition for GDP was mainly evaluated through a top-down approach, competition for public services needs to be evaluated through a bottom-up approach—because ordinary people should have a say about these public services. A bottom-up approach would also rely on the supervision of local people's congresses, the Chinese People's Political Consultative Conference (CPPCC), the media and independent third parties. The central–local government relationship must also be restructured in terms of establishing rights and responsibilities and setting up mechanisms for compatible incentives. At present, local government expenditure makes up about 80 per cent of total public expenditure, while local revenue is only about 40 per cent of the total. This mismatch leads to problems, such as land-based public finance, local debt risks and so on. Local government should therefore be provided with a greater range of sources of tax revenue, such as taxes on real estate and household consumption, and an increased proportion of the revenue from value-added tax (VAT). Local issuance of bonds should also be allowed. Local government power over legislation should be enhanced to facilitate the exercise of discretion over local matters.

Second, entrepreneurship should be stimulated and protected. 'Original sin' must be tackled and private property rights protected. A new type of government–business relations must be established so that entrepreneurs can more clearly follow the rules of the game. From a government perspective, it should improve its role in creating an environment conducive to enterprise development. On the one hand, the Chinese Government needs to treat enterprises with different ownership structures equally, create a legal environment to protect the legitimate rights and interests of entrepreneurs and accelerate the formation of a market environment conducive to fair competition and business integrity. Information exchange and communication with entrepreneurs, especially those in the private sector, should also be strengthened, and the streamlining of administration and institutional decentralisation should continue, to provide efficient and pragmatic quality services and practical solutions for businesses and entrepreneurs. On the other hand, it is necessary to make a clear distinction between public and private interests in the interaction between entrepreneurs and government officials. In particular, the latter should not abuse their power for personal gain or engage in collusion between power and money. Nor should they shift responsibility on to others. The income distribution system must be improved to enable entrepreneurs to take risks equivalent to their potential gains. Indeed, by taking a greater risk in the innovation process, entrepreneurs can be viewed as a kind of scarce resource. Therefore, China should also further improve mechanisms for long-term incentives so that the gains of entrepreneurs are matched with their contribution to innovation and management, as well as with their responsibilities and risks. There should be greater tolerance for and encouragement of innovation by entrepreneurs. Although the entrepreneurial spirit—especially the spirit of innovation—often manifests as unusual thoughts and behaviour, as long as these are within legal boundaries, they should be respected. In particular, the government needs to create an atmosphere of respect for and encouragement of private innovation and entrepreneurship. Fundamentally, the Chinese Government needs to establish a legal system that protects the rights of entrepreneurs and recognises their contribution.

Third, policymakers should ensure that people benefit sufficiently from any reform dividends. Ordinary people should be allowed to participate in and share more of the gains of reform (a recent field study in Jiangxi province by the authors found that, in some regions, poverty levels and poverty-reduction efforts are basically determined by the government and local people have little say). The reason past reforms were promptly promoted lies in the fact that they brought substantial benefits to most people as well as opportunities for equal participation and development. This is the fundamental driving force for reform that is supported by the majority of people. For the comprehensive deepening of reforms, the government needs to make its starting point the promotion of social equity and justice and the enhancement of the wellbeing of the general public. Therefore, it is necessary to establish fair and effective institutional mechanisms so the dividends of reform and the fruits of development can be shared equitably among all people. To achieve this, first, the government should protect the interests of the poor and low-income individuals and families, so they have greater access to opportunities for development through and as a result of reform; and second, it must allow the gradual expansion of the middle class and give it greater space for development. The government should also protect the legitimate interests of the high-income group and create a better development environment to give them incentives to invest and innovate. It is important to actualise the full potential of different social groups and allow labour, knowledge, technology, managerial expertise, capital and other sources of wealth to play their full part in invigorating the market, thereby ensuring that all social groups can benefit from, and thus support, the reform process.

Achieving sustainable growth through reform dividends

In the new normal era of China's economic development, the country confronts a decline in its potential growth rate. How to benefit from continued reform and improve the potential growth rate are key issues for achieving sustainable economic growth in China.

In theory, there are two ways to increase the potential growth rate. The first is to maintain the traditional growth momentum. This does not mean maintaining the traditional model of growth, which was driven by factor accumulation, but rather means focusing on the exploration of potential production factors, especially the potential supply of labour (namely, to extend the demographic dividend). The second is to develop new drivers of economic growth. This is mainly about increasing human capital accumulation and total factor productivity (TFP) growth. Both these sources of economic growth are related to reform dividends and embody the following aspects.

First, the participation rate of workers in sectors of high productivity needs to be increased. Indeed, almost all the factors causing China's economic slowdown can be attributed to the fading of China's demographic dividend, meaning there is no longer an unlimited supply of new (and low-cost) labour. Thus, increasing the supply of labour in productive sectors can help alleviate the decline in the potential growth rate. As a result of changes in the population age structure, not only is the working-age population (those aged 15–59 years) now decreasing, but also current labour force participation rates suggest the growth rate of the economically active population will be negative after 2018. That is, after that point, it will be difficult to increase the size of the total labour force. The only way to increase the potential supply of labour will be to improve the labour participation rate. Due to the size of China's working-age population, an increase of 1 per cent in the labour force participation rate in 2015 would have corresponded to more than nine million active workers. Simulation shows that across the period 2011–22, if the labour participation rate of the non-agricultural sector increases by 1 per cent per year, China will increase its potential growth rate by 0.88 per cent (Cai and Lu 2013). With this prospect in mind, we think the most important measures to improve the labour force participation rate include reform of the household registration system and improvements in urbanisation, both of which would help to stabilise and improve the employment of migrant workers in the urban economy and non-agricultural industries.

Second, population policies could increase the total fertility rate and establish a balanced population age structure in the future. Chinese President Xi Jinping has asked the country to 'stand on the strategic height of the long-term development of the Chinese nation and promote the balanced development of the population'.[6] According to international and Chinese experience, a decline in fertility is a typical result of economic and social development, and fertility policy itself plays a role only at the margins in most cases. For 35 years from the early 1980s, China implemented its 'one-child' family planning policy. Recent reforms to this policy now allow two children per family and are expected to significantly raise the fertility rate over time. It is hoped this adjustment to fertility policy is able to increase, or at least slow the decrease of, the fertility rate, which is currently believed to be about 1.5, and move it towards a balanced replacement level—namely 2.1. Policy simulations show that, if the fertility rate increases to 1.8 from the benchmark rate of 1.6, the potential growth rate in the period 2036–40 could be increased by 0.2 per cent (Cai and Lu 2016). It is worth noting that reform aiming to balance population development should not be limited to fertility policy adjustments. It also requires improving the supply of public services and reducing the financial burden of raising children to allow people to decide the number of children they have in accordance with policy requirements.

Third, there is a need to maintain a reasonable pace of human capital accumulation. As shown in the experiences of East Asian economies, economic development characterised by structural transformation is often followed by a stage of development driven by human capital accumulation. One of our research simulations (Cai and Lu 2016) shows that, under some scenarios with improved human capital due to development of education and training, China's future potential growth rate could increase by about 0.1 per cent. This number cannot be ignored for China, which is seeking to maintain medium–high growth in the new normal era. Moreover, our simulations consider only the quantity of human capital. If the quality of education is taken into account, the effect of human capital on economic growth will become more significant, and could even surpass the contribution to economic growth of productivity progress (Manuelli and Seshadri 2005).

Fourth, further policy efforts should be made in favour of the rate of TFP growth, thereby obtaining a more sustainable source of growth. The theoretical literature and empirical analysis (e.g. Cai and Lu 2016) show that although an increase in the labour participation rate will help boost the potential growth rate, that impact gradually diminishes over time. By contrast, the contribution of TFP growth to potential growth is not only immediately effective, but also endures over the long term. Growth in China is approaching that of the neoclassical model. On the one hand, China's economy is increasingly dependent on scientific and technological

6 See health.people.com.cn/n1/2016/0819/c398004-28648312.html.

innovation to maintain its sustainability; on the other, there is still plenty of room to improve the efficiency of resource allocation by eliminating institutional barriers. Our simulation shows that if the average annual growth rate of TFP increases by 1 per cent over 2011–22, the rate of potential growth will increase by 0.99 per cent over the same period (Cai and Lu 2013).

Based on the hypothetical contribution of reform of the household registration system, the education and training system, SOEs and population policies, as well as changes to the labour participation rate, human capital accumulation and TFP, we considered different scenarios that could generate reform dividends. We find that different intensities of reform will produce significantly different growth trajectories in both the short and the long term (Figure 2.4).

As for long-term growth prospects, Figure 2.4 illustrates that, on the one hand, we should not expect a V-shaped recovery that is attributed to cyclical (short-term) factors. On the other hand, under the different assumptions about supply-side structural reform, the growth prospects also differ. Looking at Figure 2.4 from left to right, and comparing the benchmark scenario without effective reform initiatives, we can conclude that there is a positive correlation between in-depth reform and growth performance and, moreover, that the deeper the reform, the more likely it is that growth follows an L-shaped trajectory.

In sum, as China's economy transitioned into the 'new normal'—characterised by economic slowdown and other socioeconomic structural changes—its market-oriented reform program encountered new challenges and opportunities. In this new context, how to achieve sustainable growth via the promotion of reform becomes an issue of primary importance. With these considerations in mind, this chapter has examined some emerging features of China's economy in the new era, with an emphasis on adjustment of interest structure and reforms of non-Pareto improvement. The current study also discusses some policy issues regarding reforms and sustainable growth, which include top-level design and grassroots innovation, legal reforms, government restructuring, local competition and property rights protection. Finally, this chapter concludes that the best way for China to capture reform dividends is to further clarify the direction of its reform program, promote pragmatic reforms and restructure incentive mechanisms to mobilise the enthusiasm of the whole society.

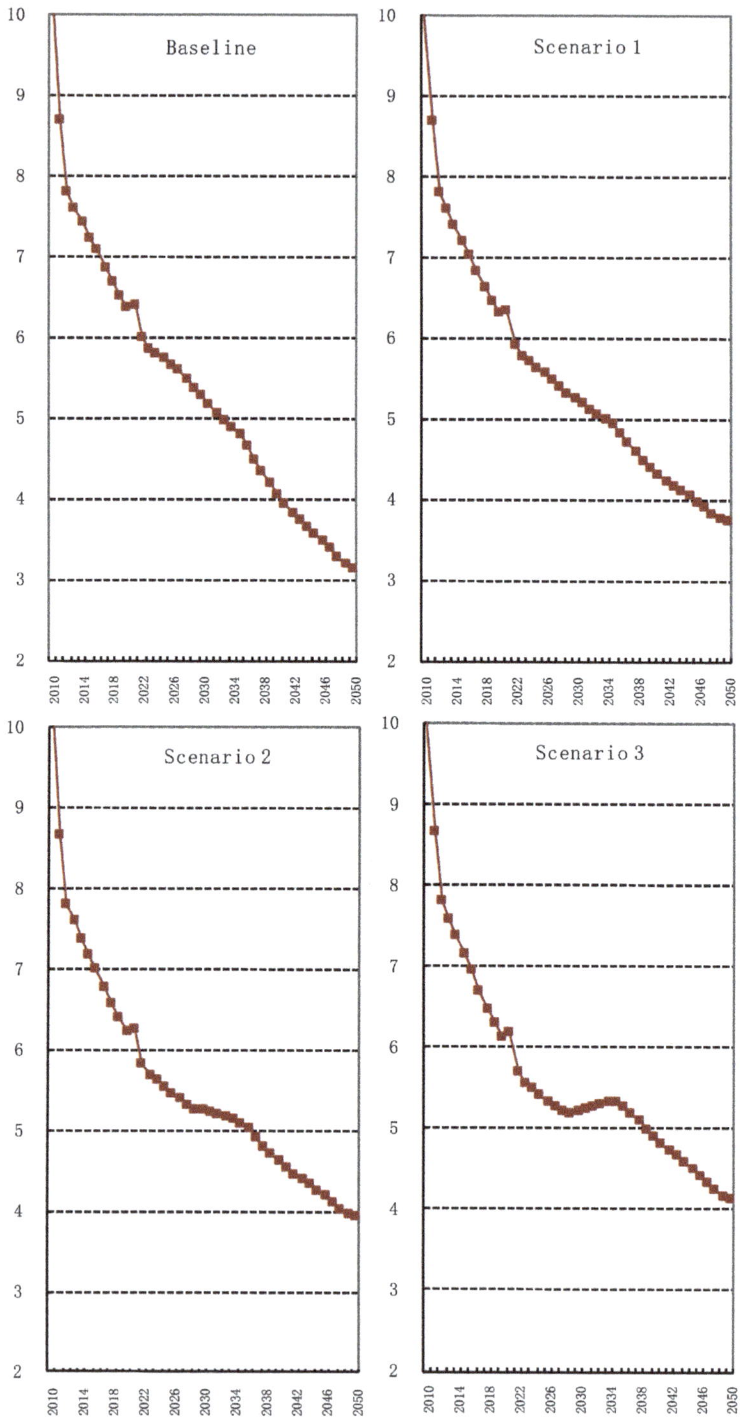

Figure 2.4 Supply-side structural reform and growth scenarios
Source: Cai and Lu (2016).

References

Bardhan, P. (2016), State and development: The need for a reappraisal of the current literature, *Journal of Economic Literature* 54(3): 862–92. doi.org/10.1257/jel.20151239.

Basu, K. (2015), *An Economist in the Real World: The art of policymaking in India*, Cambridge, Mass.: MIT Press. doi.org/10.7551/mitpress/9780262029629.001.0001.

Brandt, L. and Rawski, T. G. (eds) (2008), *China's Great Economic Transformation*, Cambridge: Cambridge University Press.

Burke, E. (1986 [1790]), *Reflections on the Revolution in France*, Reprint, London: Penguin Classics.

Cai, F. and Lu, Y. (2013), The end of China's demographic dividend: The perspective of potential GDP growth, in R. Garnaut, F. Cai and L. Song (eds), *China: A New Model for Growth and Development*, pp. 55–74, Canberra: ANU E Press.

Cai, F. and Lu, Y. (2016), Take-off, persistence, and sustainability: The demographic factor in Chinese growth, *Asia & the Pacific Policy Studies* 3(2): 203–25. doi.org/10.1002/app5.139.

Deng, X. (1993), *Deng Xiaoping Wenxuan. Volume 3*, Beijing: Renmin Publishing House.

Detter, D., and Folster, S. (2015), *The Public Wealth of Nations*, London: Palgrave Macmillan.

Global Intellectual Property Center (2016), *Infinite Possibilities: US Chamber International IP Index*, 4th edition, Washington: US Chamber of Commerce.

Johnson, C. (1982), *MITI and the Japanese Miracle*, Stanford, CA: Stanford University Press.

Kasper, W. and Streit, M. E. (1999), *Institutional Economics: Social order and public policy*, Cheltenham, UK: Edward Elgar.

Lau, L., Qian, Y., and Roland, G. (2000), Reform without losers: An interpretation of China's dual-track approach to transition, *Journal of Political Economy*, 108 (1): 120-143.

Li, X., Liu, X. and Wang, Y. (2014), A model of China's economic growth, *China Journal of Economics* 1(4): 1–48.

Manuelli, R. E. and Seshadri, A. (2005), Human capital and the wealth of nations, manuscript, Department of Economics, University of Wisconsin, Madison, May.

Manyika, J., Woetzel, J., Dobbs, R., Remes, J., Labaye, E. and Jordan, A. (2015), *Global growth: Can productivity save the day in an aging world?* Report, January, McKinsey Global Institute, New York.

Murphy, K. M., Shleifer, A. and Vishny, R. W. (1992), The transition to a market economy: Pitfalls of partial reform, *Quarterly Journal of Economics* 107(3): 889–906. doi.org/10.2307/2118367.

National Bureau of Statistics of China (NBS) (various issues), *China Statistical Yearbook*, China Statistics Press.

Rajan, R. (2004), Why are structural reforms so difficult? *Finance & Development*, June: 56–7.

Woo-Cummings, M. (ed.) (1999), *The Developmental State*, Ithaca, NY: Cornell University Press.

Young, A. (2000), The razor's edge: Distortions and incremental reform in the People's Republic of China, *Quarterly Journal of Economics* 115(4): 1091–135. doi.org/10.1162/003355300555024.

Zhang, X., Li, C. and Li, Y. (forthcoming), *Distortions, catching-up growth and middle income trap*, ADBI Working Paper, Asian Development Bank Institute, Tokyo.

Zhou, Q. (2010), Zhonguo Jingji Zengzhang de Jichu (The foundation of the economic growth in China, *Journal of Beijing University (Philosophy and Social Sciences)*, vol. 1.

3. China's Macroeconomic Balancing Act: Shifting to New Drivers of Growth and Sustaining Financial Stability

Yiping Huang, Yan Shen and Qiuzi Fu

Introduction

At the National People's Congress (NPC) meeting in early March 2017, the Chinese Government set its annual growth target at 6.5 per cent, a notch down from the actual performance of 6.7 per cent in the previous year. It vowed, however, to achieve better results, if possible (see Figure 3.1). In the first quarter of 2017, better than expected results were recorded, with growth in gross domestic product (GDP) reaching 6.9 per cent. High-frequency economic data, such as those on industrial production, trade and fixed-asset investment, also confirm that, since mid-2016, economic momentum has continued to improve. Analysts' views on the economic outlook through 2017, however, remain divided. Some believe the economy will do better than in the previous year while others predict a sharp moderation of growth across the year.

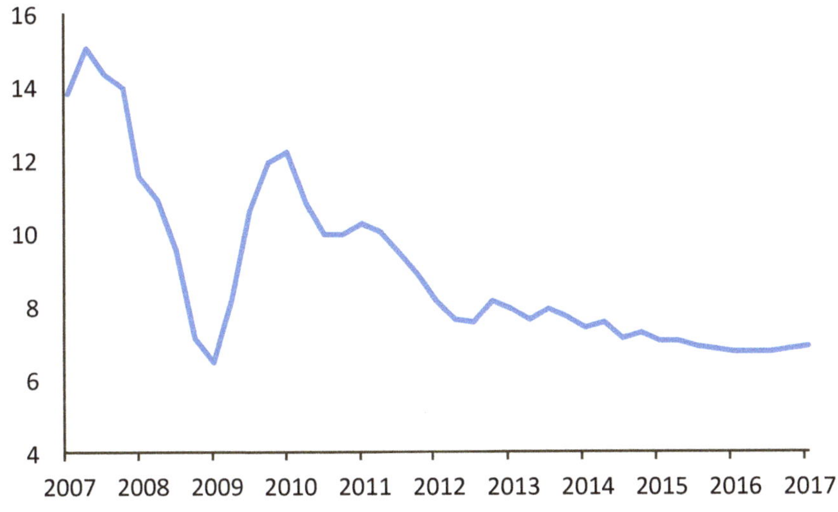

Figure 3.1 Quarterly GDP growth in China, 2007–16 (percentage year-on-year)
Source: CEIC Database: www.ceicdata.com.

We are cautiously confident of the continuation of the current upswing, partly because some of the key drivers of the improvement in economic activity over the past several quarters might not be sustainable. This does not necessarily imply, however, that the Chinese economy will be unable to achieve its growth target. Across various levels, the government is especially committed to supporting growth in the lead-up to the 19th NPC in the third quarter of 2017.

At both the Central Economic Work Conference in December 2016 and the recent NPC, policymakers set the basic tone for economic policy as 'making progress while maintaining stability'. They specifically outlined three key features of macroeconomic policies for 2017: 1) adopting proactive fiscal policy but prudent/neutral monetary policy; 2) increasing exchange rate flexibility while maintaining basic exchange rate stability; and 3) prioritising the control and resolution of systemic financial risks.

Any bottoming out of economic growth in the near term will likely be short-lived. Since 2010, economists have been debating the nature of the growth slowdown. Some argue that it is a cyclical phenomenon, while others believe it is mainly a change in trend. While these assessments are certainly correct, they probably do not pay sufficient attention to the structural shifts that the current growth slowdown is making necessary, and thus could lead to inappropriate policy suggestions.

The most important cause of the current growth slowdown is a structural one: most of the industries that supported strong economic growth during the past several decades have lost competitiveness, but new industries and the forces driving them, such as consumption, have not developed sufficiently to carry the Chinese economy forward with the previous levels of momentum. In the past, two engines—export and investment—were the main drivers of Chinese growth, while consumption was relatively weak. These two engines were facilitated, respectively, by the labour-intensive manufacturing industries along the southeast coast and the resource-based heavy industries in the northeast and northwest of the country. Both have since lost competitiveness.

In a way, China is confronting challenges today that are typical of the 'middle-income trap' hypothesis. That is, prior to an economy reaching the industrial competitiveness frontier—or at least before momentum in that direction is sufficiently large—downward pressure on growth continues. During the past six years, economists have repeatedly forecast the bottoming out of growth in every quarter. But every bottoming out was followed by even slower growth—a trend that evidently continues.

In this chapter, we: 1) briefly forecast the performance of the Chinese economy in the near term; 2) estimate the scale of China's transition towards those identified 'new' drivers of growth; 3) elaborate on the risks and potential of useful policies for maintaining growth in the future; and 4) suggest some appropriate policy strategies.

The remainder of this chapter is organised as follows. The next section discusses some of the key drivers of the short-term growth outlook and concludes that, while some important uncertainties remain, the economy should be able to achieve its growth target of 6.5 per cent. The third section outlines the new-economy index (NEI), developed by one of the authors of this chapter, to draw some implications from the recent literature. In particular, the share of the new economy in the overall economy remains relatively small and there is a clear trade-off between the new and the old economies. Section four analyses the key risks facing the Chinese economy, especially zombie firms and systemic financial risks, followed by some policy recommendations in the final section.

Cyclical versus structural factors

High-frequency official data, grassroots surveys and independent big data analyses agree that Chinese economic momentum picked up after mid-2016. This improved economic outlook was led by three factors: infrastructure investment, property investment and manufacturing investment (see Figure 3.2). Between March and August 2016, growth in infrastructure investment slowed steadily but quickly stabilised thereafter. Property investment also increased marginally after July 2016, while manufacturing investment picked up even more visibly after June 2016.

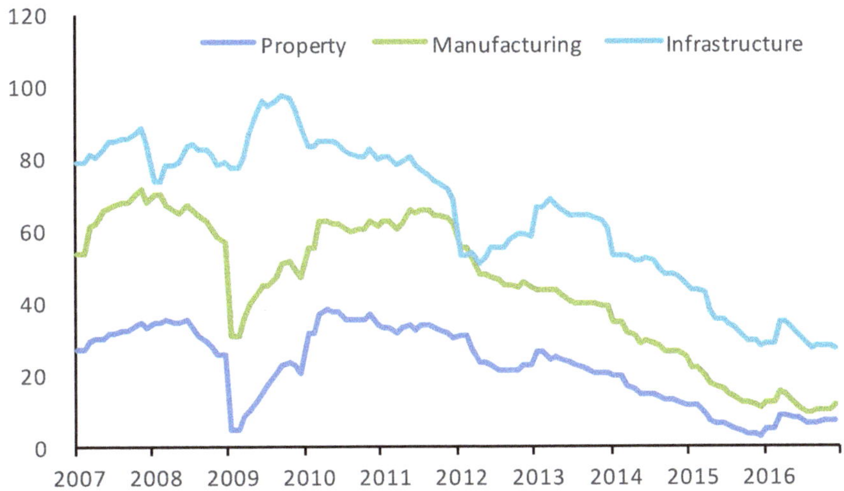

Figure 3.2 Monthly growth of fixed-asset investment in property, infrastructure and manufacturing, 2007–16 (percentage year-on-year)

Source: Wind Database: www.wind.com.cn.

It is important to ask whether these trends are likely to continue throughout the year ahead. Property sales, for example, have already softened in several major cities, after widespread tightening policies introduced during the National Day holiday in 2016. Interestingly, growth in property sales started to moderate from early 2016. Property prices, however, are far more resilient, even after the tightening policies were introduced (see Figure 3.3). Levels of property investment continue to do well in early 2017; however, if sales do not recover, it will be a matter when, not if, property investment weakens.

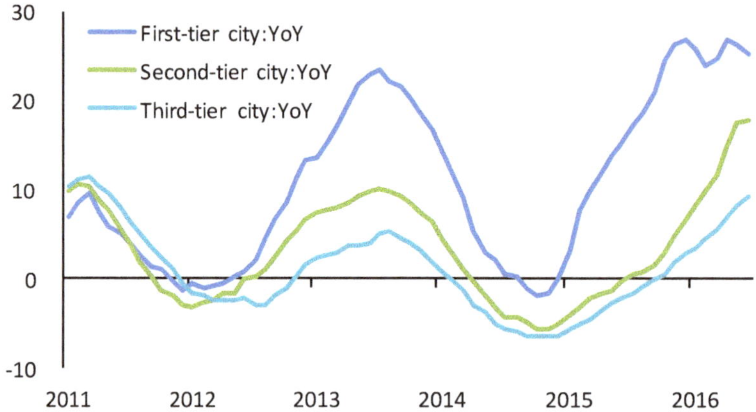

Figure 3.3 Monthly growth of property prices for groups of cities, 2007–16 (per cent)

Source: Wind Database: www.wind.com.cn.

Improvements in manufacturing investment, especially in the private sector, come as something of a surprise, explained in part by the sharp turnaround of the producer price index (PPI). After experiencing more than 50 continuous months of negative growth, the PPI turned positive in September 2016 and rose to 7.8 per cent in February 2017. This change—heavily associated with changes in commodities markets—was likely driven by the Chinese Government's efforts to reduce excess capacity, especially in steel and coal, and also by an improved global economic outlook. The end of deflation in particular has provided important support for investor confidence.

Whether or not this improvement can be sustained depends partly on transmission from the PPI to the consumer price index (CPI). For instance, in February 2017, while the PPI hit a cyclical high, the CPI stayed at 0.5 per cent (Figure 3.4). This led to concern that any rise in upstream industry prices could squeeze the profit margins of downstream industries, leading to an abrupt end to the improvement in manufacturing investment. Some analysts, however, believe that what happened in February was temporary because: 1) the CPI excluding food was in fact in the more healthy 2–3 per cent range; 2) transmission from the PPI to the CPI could be experiencing a time lag; and 3) broad-based improvements in manufacturing profitability started to emerge.

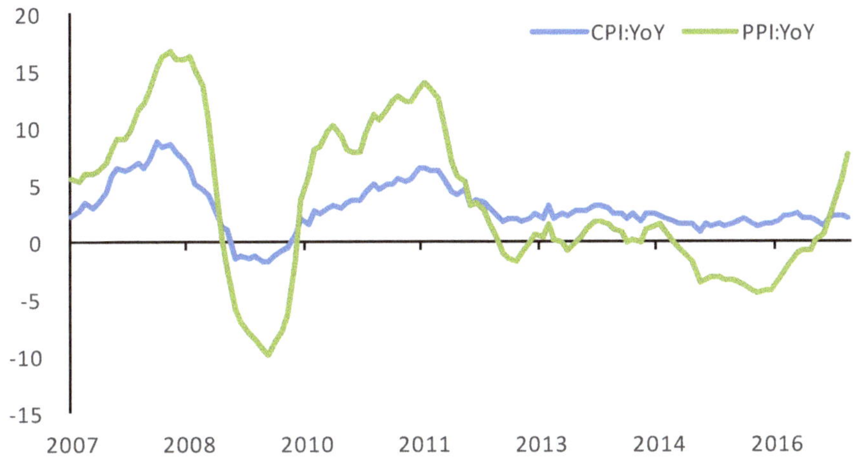

Figure 3.4 Monthly PPI and CPI, 2007–16 (per cent)
Source: Wind Database: www.wind.com.cn.

Despite uncertainty about the sustainability of the recovery in property and manufacturing investment growth, there are two important factors underpinning China's growth performance in the near term. First, the growth outlook has brightened somewhat for most developed economies, especially the United States, Japan and the European Union (EU), which could induce increased demand for China's exports. Second, as Chinese leaders emphasise the importance of stability ahead of the party congress, local governments are strongly motivated to support growth. Therefore, the Chinese economy will likely be able to achieve the 6.5 per cent growth target in 2017, even if some of the downside risks do materialise.

This otherwise benign scenario, however, may not continue for long because current improvements in economic momentum are being driven mainly by cyclical and not structural factors. During the past several years, there has been heated debate about the nature of the current growth slowdown, with some commentators believing it to be cyclical while others claim it is a long-term trend. Among the important challenges is the need for industrial upgrading in response to the fact that industries that previously supported rapid economic growth are no longer sufficiently competitive or generating enough demand to achieve the previous levels of growth. During the first three decades of its economic reform, China's surging economic growth was driven by exports and capital investment. More recently, consumption levels have been rising relative to GDP (Figure 3.5). Before any industrial upgrading is complete, any bottoming out and upturn in economic activity could be short-lived. To some extent, this is typically reflective of the middle-income trap phenomenon.

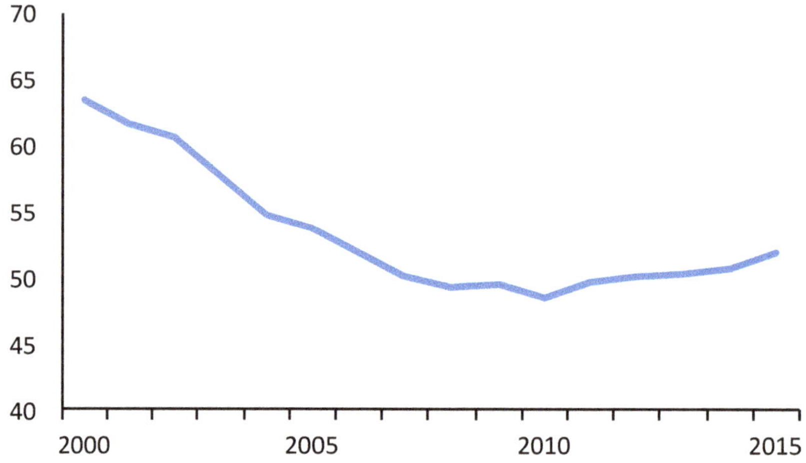

Figure 3.5 Consumption share of GDP, 2000–15 (per cent)
Source: CEIC Database: www.ceicdata.com.

Assessing the emergence of the 'new' economy

After more than three decades of rapid economic growth, China has entered the 'new normal' stage in which economic growth is slowing and the earlier export-oriented, investment-pulling growth pattern is no longer sustainable. Moreover, space for further export growth appears to be limited given that China's share in global exports grew from 0.8 per cent in 1978 to 14 per cent in 2015, surpassing Germany (12.1 per cent in 1987) and Japan (9.52 per cent in 1988) at their peak levels. The after-tax return to capital dropped from 12 per cent before 2005 to 4.17 per cent in 2013 (Bai et al. 2006; Bai and Zhang 2014). In parallel, labour costs have been increasing as the demographic dividend began to disappear from around 2013. From 1982 to 2000, the demographic dividend was an important source of growth, contributing 26.8 per cent of the growth in per capita GDP (Cai and Wang 2005). In terms of population structure, China is 'ageing before affluence', and the share of those aged 60 and above is projected to increase from 10 per cent of the population in 2000 to about 30 per cent in 2050 (Cai 2010)—increasing the burden of providing support to the elderly.

As China's previous sources of rapid growth become less effective, the capacity of the 'new economy' to offset this slowdown will determine whether China can enjoy sustainable growth from now on. China's ongoing economic transition will be considered successful only if these new sectors can drive productivity increases and technological advancement. To better gauge the extent of China's economic transition, it may be useful to measure the size of the new-economy sector and understand how it interacts with the traditional-economy sector. However, partly because of the lack of a clear definition of what constitutes the 'new-economy' sector, official statistics cannot help us answer these questions. To fill the void, we have constructed an index that tracks the size and change of the new-economy sector in China using big data collected from the internet.

The new-economy index

To construct the NEI, we first need to specify the scope of the new-economy sector, which includes both newly developed industries and upgraded existing industries. Based on international experience and observations about China, we define an industry as belonging to the new-economy sector if: 1) it is human-capital intensive, technology intensive and/or has a low share of fixed capital investment in its cost structure; and 2) its development follows the country's industrial policies. We use the Industry Input–Output Table for 2010 and the Sixth Economics Census[1] data to identify industries satisfying these standards.

Specifically, we consider an industry to be human-capital intensive if the sum of income from labour and the operating surplus is more than 70 per cent of the value added, the average level of workers' education is more than 12 years and its share of research and development (R&D) is among the top 10 per cent for that industry. The industrial policies we refer to include documents such as the *Guidance for Accelerating the Development of High-Tech Service Industries*, issued by the State Council in 2011; the *Decision to Accelerate the Cultivation and Development of Strategic Emerging Industries*, released in 2012; and *Made in China 2025*, released in 2015. Ten industries are identified as belonging to the new-economy sector: energy conservation and environmental protection, new energy, new energy vehicles, new materials, new information technology (IT) and information services, recreation, high-tech services and R&D, biological medicine, financial and legal services and high-tech equipment manufacturing.[2]

It is not feasible to directly measure the size of the new-economy sector, as the official statistics do not yet measure its contribution to GDP. We instead focus on the share of the new-economy sector in the whole economy, and particularly its share of inputs. If a Cobb–Douglas production function is employed, the share of the new economy in total output can be calculated from the relative shares of capital, labour and technology, with appropriate weights. The focus of the construction then becomes how to measure capital, labour and technology for both the new-economy and the traditional-economy sectors.

1 National Bureau of Statistics of China: www.stats.gov.cn.

2 The four-digit industry code for the new-economy sector can be found in our technical report. Available from: mt.sohu.com/20160504/n447633738.shtml.

As official statistics do not measure the above input factors for the two sectors separately, we rely on the big data obtained from the internet to accomplish this task. The data include information on registration for each new enterprise, patents and commercialisation of patents (measuring technology), millions of posts on the websites of major internet recruitment companies, population mobility via rail and air (labour), information on venture capital investment, bidding and companies listed on the New Third Board market (capital). After using machine-learning techniques to separate these inputs into the new-economy and the traditional-economy sectors, we construct the NEI and its capital, labour and technology subindices (for details, see Shen et al. 2016).[3]

Figure 3.6 presents the average share of new-economy industries in terms of the percentage of inputs that has been distributed to this sector between December 2015 and March 2017. The three largest industries are new IT and information services (12 per cent), financial and legal services (6 per cent) and bio-medicine (3 per cent). IT and financial services have grown relatively rapidly over the years, so it is not surprising this is the largest industry in the new-economy sector. The industry with the lowest share in the new-economy sector is new energy vehicles, which is consistent with the observation that this industry is heavily supported by industrial policies but may not have enough innovation to increase its market share.

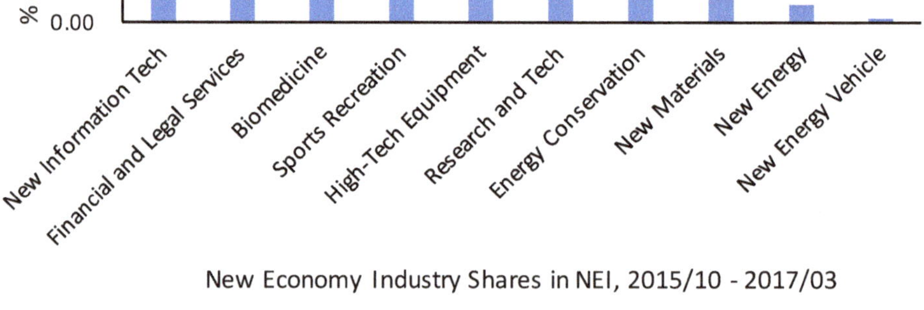

Figure 3.6 NEI industries and their shares

Source: Authors' calculations.

3 Appendix 3.1 provides the main websites from which we collected the data.

Can the new-economy sector outpace the traditional-economy sector?

We document the size of our NEI and track its relative change over time. Figure 3.7 delivers two messages about the NEI. First, the new-economy sector accounts for about one-third of China's GDP; this share increased from 31.4 per cent in October 2015 to 35 per cent in February and March 2016, and then fluctuated around 33 per cent in March 2017. Second, and worryingly, there appears to have been a declining trend in recent months, even though the series is too short for reliable seasonal adjustment. In particular, the March 2017 NEI share is 2 percentage points, or 6 per cent, lower than that of March 2016, indicating that the relative share of the new-economy sector in 2017 is lower than it was in 2016.

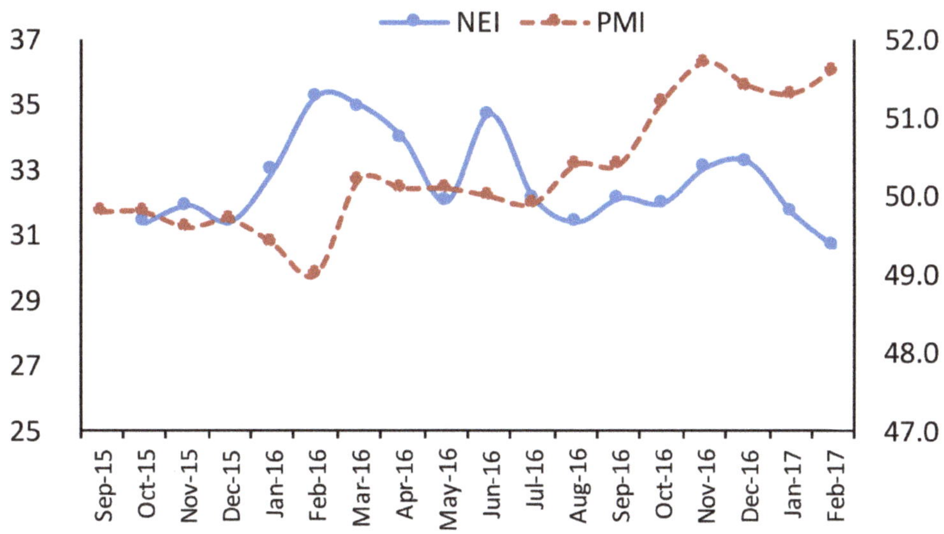

Figure 3.7 NEI (left-hand side) (per cent) and PMI in China

Source: Authors' calculations.

As the NEI documents the relative share, the shrinkage of the new-economy sector may be due to recovery in the traditional-economy sector, the slower pace of growth in the new-economy sector or both. To find out whether the recovery of the traditional-economy sector is the main driver, we also compare the NEI with the official purchasing manager index (PMI) for manufacturing industries (Figure 3.7). The PMI is constructed based on surveys of representative firms to obtain information on their expectations about the economy. A PMI score lower than 50 indicates a pessimistic attitude towards economic prospects, and a score higher than 50 shows an optimistic attitude. As the firms surveyed in the PMI come predominantly from the traditional-economy sector, growth momentum in this sector is likely driving the PMI. Figure 3.7 clearly shows that there is a negative relationship between the NEI and the PMI—that is, when the PMI increases, the NEI tends to decrease and vice versa. This is true for 14 of the 17 months for which we have records of the NEI.

Figure 3.7 suggests there is a trade-off between the development of the new-economy and the traditional-economy sectors. In particular, starting from July 2016, the PMI passed 50, entering the zone of optimistic attitudes towards the traditional-economy sector. Even in the new-economy sector, there is evidence that industries more closely related to the traditional economy appear to attract more resources. Figure 3.8 plots the shares of the capital, labour and technology subindices in the NEI. It shows that between July 2016 and March 2017, the share of capital inputs has increased, but labour and technology decreased. We therefore need to carefully investigate whether the new-economy sector is being sacrificed to meet the short-term goal of stabilising the wider economy.

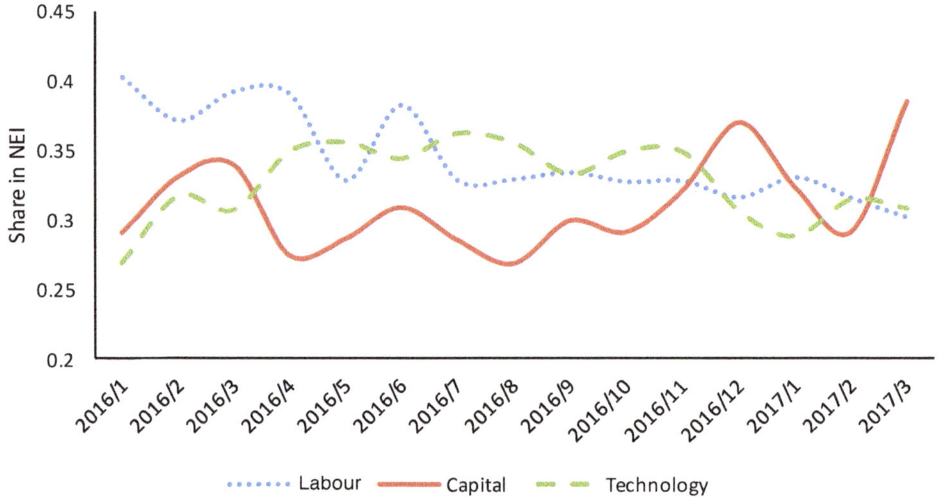

Figure 3.8 Capital, labour and technology subindices

Source: Authors' calculations.

In Figure 3.9, we compare the NEI with the month-on-month growth rate of value added in the manufacturing industry (VAI). An interesting pattern emerges if the series is split into two periods: before and after July 2016. Before July 2016, the NEI and VAI appear to have a positive relationship; however, after July 2016, this relationship switches to negative. To be more specific, the correlation coefficient for the NEI and VAI is 0.15 before July 2016 but changes to –0.71 after that time.

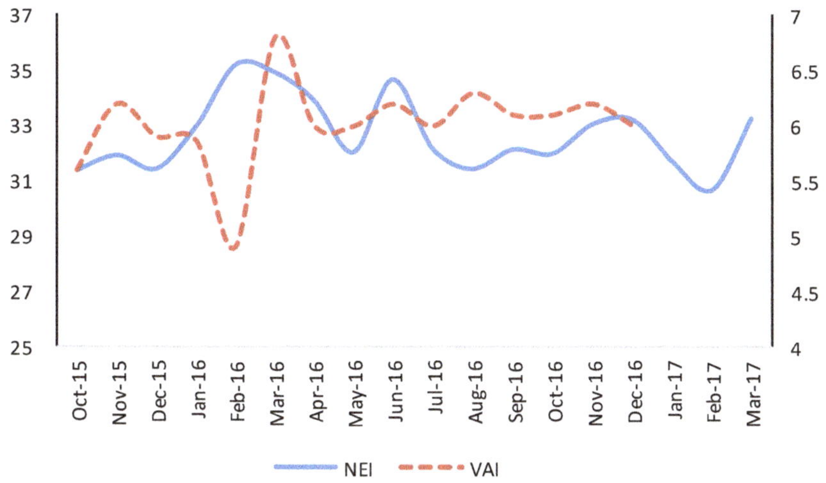

Figure 3.9 NEI (left-hand side) and month-on-month value-added growth rate (per cent)

Source: Authors' calculations.

The trends presented here suggest that recovery of the traditional economy may hurt the development of the new economy—something also reflected in Figure 3.10, in which we compare the NEI with the month-on-month growth rate of investment in infrastructure. Again, we observe very different patterns before and after July 2016. After July 2016, an increase in the infrastructure growth rate is accompanied by a drop in the NEI, and vice versa. Figure 3.10 indicates that when more investment is directed to infrastructure, fewer resources will be accessed by the new-economy sector, limiting its growth space.

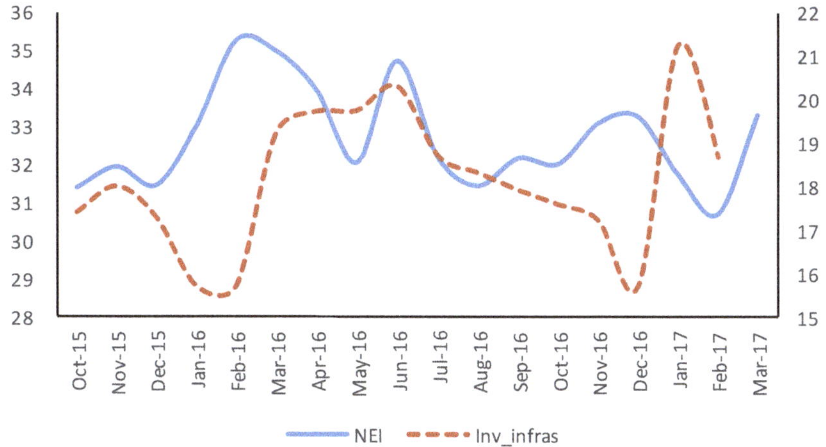

Figure 3.10 NEI (left-hand side) and month-on-month growth rate of infrastructure investment (per cent)

Source: Authors' calculations.

Here we have described the emergence of China's new-economy sector and established an index via which to measure it. We find that the new-economy sector comprises about one-third of the whole economy, so it will take some time to replace the traditional-economy sector as the main engine for growth. From the comparisons of the NEI with the PMI, with VAI and with the growth rate of infrastructure investment, we find a disturbing phenomenon that suggests that, in recent months, more resources have been redirected to the traditional-economy sector, limiting the growth of the new-economy sector. Policymakers may need to carefully balance the trade-off between relying on the traditional-economy sector to 'stabilise growth' in the short run and developing the new-economy sector to create space for sustainable, long-run and high-quality growth. Rebalancing capital structure by reducing capacity in the traditional-economy sector, eliminating 'zombie firms' and increasing investment in the new-economy sector could increase the efficiency of capital utilisation. As development in the new-economy sector often means exploring new business models, the market needs to be the determining factor in fostering the environment for that sector's prosperity.

Rising systemic financial risks

At the Central Economic Work Conference in December 2016, the NPC in March 2017 and the Politburo meeting in April 2017, China's leaders—for the first time in recent years—made repeated warnings about rising systemic financial risks.

Indeed, during the past couple of years, many financial areas—from equity and bond markets to shadow banking, property markets, digital finance and foreign exchange markets—have experienced various financial risks. For example, the Shanghai A-share Index rose from about 2,000 in May 2014 to 4,500 in May 2015, before dropping below 3,000 in May 2016. The average ratio of commercial banks' non-performing loans (NPLs) jumped by 75 per cent during the past two years (Figure 3.11). Although the absolute ratio is still relatively low, many analysts believe that number could be significantly underestimated. The property market has also gone through three cycles since 2009, with each becoming increasingly violent (see Figure 3.3). The most recent example of financial risk is the pressure for capital flight and currency depreciation. The fact that financial risks rotate around different markets could be an important warning sign that such risks have become systemic.

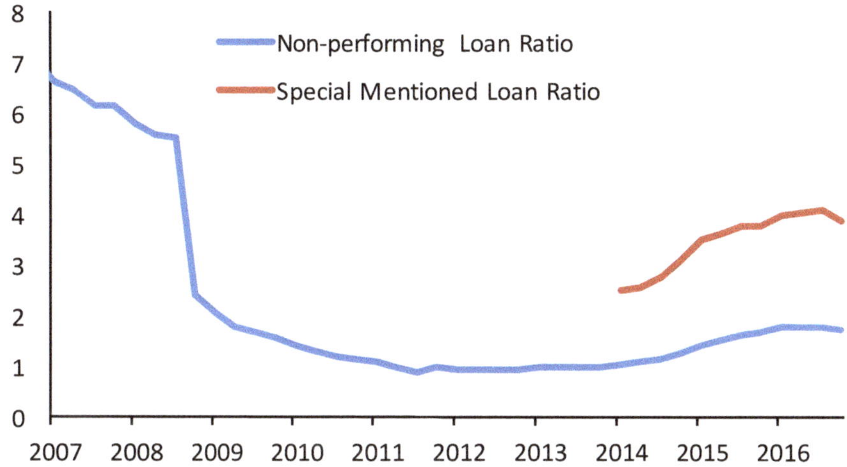

Figure 3.11 Commercial banks' average NPL ratio (per cent)
Sources: Wind Information Company; CEIC Data Company.

To date, China remains the only major emerging market economy that has not experienced a serious financial crisis—probably for two reasons. First, continued rapid economic growth helped to subdue or hide financial risk. Second, government guarantees have supported investor confidence. A good example of this was that although the Chinese banks' average NPL ratio probably reached 30–40 per cent at the height of the Asian Financial Crisis, China did not experience a banking crisis. With an implicit, blanket guarantee for bank deposits, depositors were not worried about the safety of their money even though the banks were technically insolvent. Therefore, the government had the time to write-off NPLs, inject capital, introduce strategic investors and list banks' initial public offerings (IPOs) on domestic and international capital markets. Several years later, the banks were among the strongest in the world, in terms of both size of assets and profits.

Now, however, it will be increasingly difficult for China to maintain that no-crisis record. China's current macroeconomic conditions are falling within those for a phenomenon the Bank for International Settlements (BIS) calls the 'risky trinity': rising leverage ratios, declining productivity and shrinking policy flexibility. On the first, between 2007 and 2014, China's total non-financial borrowing as a proportion of GDP increased by more than 65 percentage points (Figure 3.12). Data also confirm China's slowing total factor productivity (TFP) gains since 2008, with the incremental capital–output ratio (ICOR) rising from 3.5 in 2007 to 5.9 in 2015—implying declines in the efficiency of capital use, the effectiveness of stimulus policy and returns to investment. Finally, compared with 2007, the government's ability to adopt expansionary fiscal and monetary policies is now more limited. Such trends suggest that the government might be less able to contain financial risks than in the past.

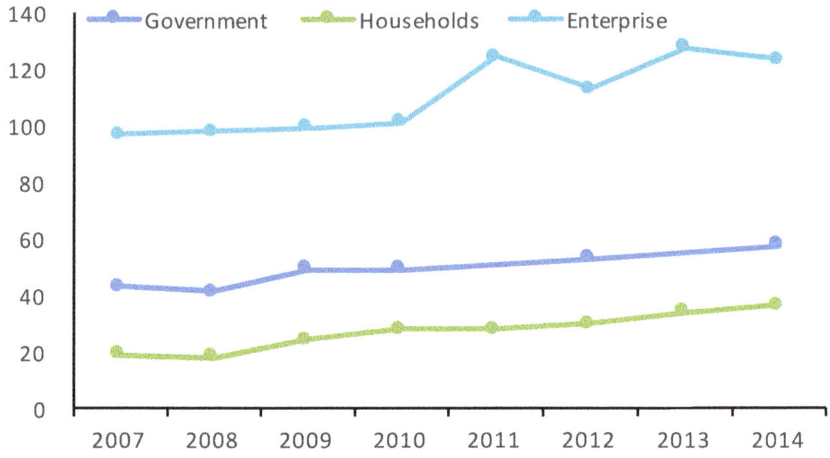

Figure 3.12 China's leverage ratios (percentage of GDP)
Source: Wind Information Company.

In the meantime, financial risks have grown rapidly. Alongside a rising leverage ratio and falling productivity, the persistent growth slowdown and structural shifts have led to a significant deterioration of corporate balance sheets and produced large numbers of zombie firms. In a way, zombie firms have become a key source of China's current economic problems: they hinder industrial upgrading, lower financial efficiency and increase financial risks. If we look around the country, industrial upgrading is progressing unevenly between regions. In the south of the country, where the market functions relatively effectively and entrepreneurs are empowered to play active roles in the economy, industrial upgrading is proceeding smoothly. In the north, however, where zombie firms are concentrated, industries are stuck in a state of excess capacity and innovation is proving extremely difficult. These factors are clearly reflected in the differing growth performance of individual provinces (Figure 3.13).

In addition, broad money supply (M2) reached 210 per cent of GDP at the end of 2016, which is among the highest in the world. China's relatively high M2–GDP ratio is partly attributable to the banks' domination of its financial system. Any financial transactions are reflected in forms of money supply and borrowing. More important, as a result of the government's guarantee against financial risks, there is a built-in acceleration mechanism for money supply: when the economy does well, M2 must accelerate to facilitate expansion of economic activities; and when the economy does not do well, M2 must also accelerate to stabilise growth and financial markets.

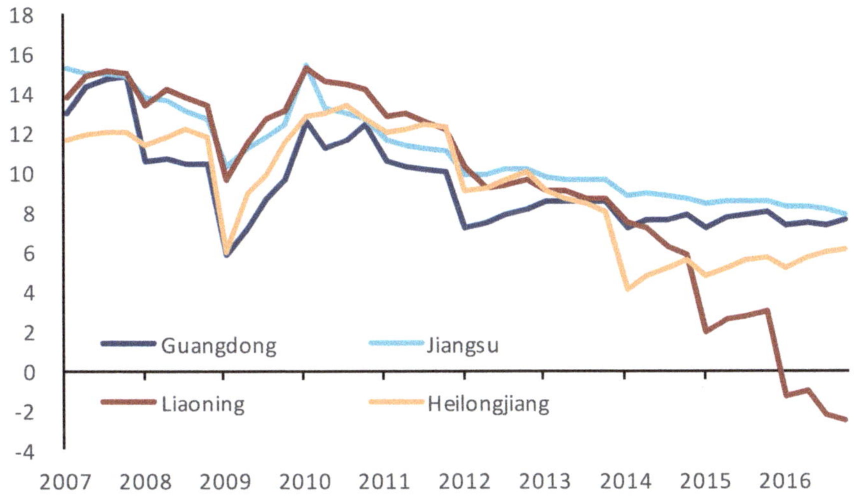

Figure 3.13 Provincial GDP growth of Guangdong, Jiangsu, Liaoning and Heilongjiang, 2007–16 (per cent)

Source: Wind Information Company.

The combination of large volumes of liquidity and limited investment channels (the other side of the coin of a bank-dominated financial system) could easily be equated with financial instability; when large amounts of liquidity flow to a single market, asset prices could quickly skyrocket, followed by a bursting bubble. This is exactly what happened during the past few years in the equity, bond, property, wealth management, digital finance and foreign exchange markets. There was one important reason financial risks were suddenly exacerbated. In the past in China, as in many other countries, M2 growth always exceeded growth in narrow money supply (M1). However, in China from October 2015, M1 growth suddenly accelerated, far exceeding the pace of M2. This essentially implies a massive transfer of funds from term to saving deposits. Depositors, however, were no longer happy with low interest rates on their term deposits and wanted to make better use of their funds; but, because of limited investment opportunities in the domestic market, wherever the funds flew, there was always first a boom and then a bust.

Concluding remarks and policy implications

China's two fundamental macroeconomic challenges today are achieving growth sustainability and maintaining financial stability. After more than three decades of remarkable economic performance, China's GDP has moderated steadily since 2010. Although there was an upturn in growth from late 2016, there are doubts about whether and for how long it will be sustainable. China is also the only major emerging market economy that has not yet experienced a serious financial crisis—but how much longer can it retain this record?

Analyses in this chapter led us to three important conclusions. First, recent increased economic momentum was driven mainly by cyclical factors, especially public infrastructure spending and investment in property and manufacturing. The outlook for property investment depends on future property sales, while prospects for manufacturing investment hinge on manufacturing profitability. There is little doubt, however, that China's economy should realise its growth target in the near term given the combination of an improved global economic outlook and the fact that governments at all levels in China are strongly motivated to support growth ahead of the 19th party congress.

Second, the medium-term picture for China's economy is less rosy, or at least less certain. The underlying cause of the slowdown in China's economy is an incomplete transition to new drivers of growth; old industries that had previously supported China's growth have lost competitiveness, but new industries and new drivers of growth are not yet sufficiently developed to carry China forward with equivalent momentum. The NEI discussed in this chapter suggests that the new economy accounts for only 30 per cent of the total economy so far, and, to some extent, there are clear trade-offs between the new and old economies. Recent strengthening of property and infrastructure investment, while supporting the near-term growth outlook, could actually dim the outlook in the medium term. Before the process of industrial upgrading is complete, any bottoming out and pick up in growth may be short-lived.

Third, there has been an escalation of systemic financial risks in China recently. This is probably related to slow growth, high leveraging, low productivity and limited policy flexibility. Abundant liquidity and limited investment channels have exaggerated the challenge. In recent years, financial risks have rotated between and within different markets, including the equity, property, bonds, wealth management product, digital financial and foreign exchange markets. This suggests that China's first financial crisis might be closer than we think.

So what should the government do? Since July 2016, Chinese President Xi Jinping has advocated pushing for 'supply-side reform'. Although interpretations of this are often diverse and sometimes confusing, in essence, supply-side reform means improving productivity instead of concentrating on cyclical demand. In 2016, the government identified five policy objectives that could be regarded as detailed tasks of supply-side reform: reducing excess capacity and housing inventory, deleveraging, lowering costs and overcoming bottlenecks.

The overall objectives of supply-side reform should be to help achieve growth sustainability and maintain financial stability. For the former, the key is to facilitate industrial upgrading—clearing out old industries and developing new ones. And, for the latter, the key is to control overall financial risks—eliminating old risks and containing new ones.

To achieve these two goals, there are lots of policy steps the government could take. Of these, the most important measures should include enforcing market discipline and improving financial regulation.

Letting market forces play a more decisive role in resource allocation was a reform principle decided by the third plenum of the 18th party congress. This is especially important today because government controls present selective challenges to growth sustainability and financial stability. One of the most sticky such issues is how to deal with zombie firms. In past years, governments at various levels have made significant efforts to develop new industries. The continued presence of old industries, especially where these have become zombie industries, reduces the urgency and space for developing new industries. Moreover, zombie firms themselves generate many financial challenges and risks. Therefore, dealing with zombie firms should be a top policy priority.

Compared with those in the 1990s, today's zombie firms are fewer in number but much greater in size. Although the economy-wide effects of the exit of zombie firms should be much more limited now, the more localised effects on economies and societies could be much more damaging. For some zombie firms, which still enjoy competitiveness in certain areas but suffer from temporary market setbacks, measures such as granting shares to management, mixed ownership, mergers and acquisitions (M&A) and debt–equity swaps may be used to re-energise them. For others, which continuously lose money and are in old-economy industries, bankruptcy might be the only option. The central government should set up a special fund to help ease the pain of any bankruptcies in local society.

In addition, the financial regulation framework should be revamped to preserve financial stability, as the current system suffers from a number of problems. For example, regulators are not independent, so their policies are often compromised by other policy considerations, such as pressure for economic growth and achieving industrial development goals. Regulators also lack an effective coordination mechanism because of the segregated setup, which often leads to either repetition or a regulatory vacuum. Macro prudential regulation, meanwhile, remains immature and needs to be improved significantly to contain systemic financial risks.

References

Bai, C. and Zhang, Q. (2014), The return to capital in China, *World Economy* (10): 3–30.

Bai, C., Hsieh, C. and Qian, Y. (2006), The return to capital in China, *Brookings Papers on Economic Activity* (2): 61–101.

Cai, F. (2010), Demographic transition, demographic dividend, and Lewis turning point in China, *China Economic Journal* 3(2): 107–19.

Cai, F. and Wang, D. (2005), China's demographic transition: Implications for growth, in R. Garnaut and L. Song (eds), *The China Boom and Its Discontents*, pp. 34–52, Canberra: Asia Pacific Press.

Shen, Y., Shen, M. G. and Chen, Q. (2016), Measurement of the new economy in China: Big data approach, *China Economic Journal* 9(3): 304–16.

Appendix 3.1

Main websites of data sources for the NEI

On labour demand

www.51job.com/ [in Chinese]

www.zhaopin.com/ [in Chinese]

www.58.com [in Chinese]

www.liepin.com/ [in Chinese]

On newly registered businesses

www.gsxt.gov.cn/index.html [in Chinese]

On capital

www.pedata.cn/ [in Chinese]

www.qianlima.com/ [in Chinese]

www.bidchance.com/ [in Chinese]

On transportation

www.ly.com/huochepiao/train [in Chinese]

www.umetrip.com (airlines) [in Chinese]

On patents

www.sipo.gov.cn/zhfwpt/zljs/ [in Chinese]

4. Internal Convergence and China's Growth Potential

Yang Yao and Mengqi Wang

Introduction

Amid declining growth rates, the debate about China's growth potential has re-emerged. Something overlooked in this debate, however, is the role played by internal convergence. China's unprecedented growth over the past 30 years or so, and particularly in the years before the Global Financial Crisis (GFC), has been concentrated in its coastal provinces, while the vast inland areas have largely lagged behind. By 2015, per capita gross domestic product (GDP) in the eastern provinces was 1.8 times that in the central and western regions. Shanghai, the richest province in China, enjoyed a per capita GDP of $15,265 in 2015, 3.5 times that of Guizhou, one of the poorest provinces in China. Since the GFC, growth in the eastern provinces has slowed, while growth in the inland provinces has picked up. Internal convergence could serve as a driver for the growth of China's inland provinces.

This chapter studies how internal convergence can contribute to China's long-run growth. In particular, we study three kinds of convergence: regional, efficiency and technological. Regional convergence is the convergence of provinces within China's eastern (coastal), central (inland) and western (inland) regions, and allows China's inland provinces to enjoy the advantage of backwardness to sustain a longer period of high-speed growth. Efficiency convergence is the convergence of the two inland regions towards the efficiency level maintained by the eastern region, and pulls inland provinces to the production frontier, so the growth rates in their transition paths become higher. Technological convergence is the convergence of the two inland regions towards the speed of technological progress achieved by the eastern region, and raises the inland regions' steady-state growth rates. Technological convergence also increases inland regions' growth rates in their transition paths because the steady-state growth rate is part of the growth rate in the transition path. The three kinds of convergence thus have the potential to greatly enhance China's overall long-term growth.

Our analysis is organised as follows. In the next section, we introduce the theoretical framework of our analysis, which is based on the neoclassical growth model and China's regional growth disparities. In section three, we introduce the data and correction methods to the growth figures reported for various provinces.

In section four, we estimate the growth equations for each region and nationally and, in section five, we present our forecast for the growth potential of each region and for the country as a whole. Using that forecast, we then conduct several policy experiments as well as a counterfactual analysis to study the effects of the three kinds of convergence. Section six concludes the chapter.

The theoretical framework

The theoretical basis for the three types of convergence studied in this chapter is neoclassical growth theory. It is well known that the theory predicts conditional convergence among countries or regions (Barro and Sala-i-Martin 1992). Specifically, since countries/regions have a steady state (where growth in per capita GDP is the rate of technological progress), countries/regions with lower levels of per capita GDP (or lower levels of capital stock) should grow faster than those with higher levels of per capita GDP (or higher levels of capital stock). Ultimately, therefore, per capita GDP converges (σ-convergence).

In reality, countries/regions may not have the same steady state, in terms of having the same rates of saving and technological progress in particular. Thus, income convergence is not realised. However, given its own steady-state growth rate, a country/region nonetheless grows faster when its per capita GDP is low than when its per capita GDP becomes higher (so-called β-convergence). This provides the basis for the advantage of backwardness, which, in turn, forms the basis of the first kind of convergence to be examined in this chapter: regional convergence.

In the past 20 years, China's growth has been concentrated in its coastal provinces (the eastern region), while the two inland areas lagged behind. The reasons for this include the fact that the eastern region: 1) maintains a higher level of resource efficiency; and 2) has faster rates of technological progress. Eastern provinces are now close to their steady states, so their growth rates have declined. Inland provinces, however, remain at a distance from their steady states, so their growth rates, at least theoretically, can be high relative to those of the eastern region. If the inland regions can realise higher growth rates, the country as a whole can maintain a higher growth rate.

The second type of convergence sees inland regions obtaining the investment efficiency of the eastern region, and the third type sees them reaching the technological progress levels of the east. To provide a more structured view of the three types of convergence, let us consider the following variant of the Solow model with technological progress.

Let a region's production function be expressed by Equation 4.1.

Equation 4.1

$Y = (K^{\delta})^{a}(AL)^{1-a},\ 0 < a < 1$

In Equation 4.1, K captures the stock of capital, L is the stock of labour (population), Y is output and a is the output elasticity of capital (so $1-a$ is the output elasticity of labour). In addition, δ is an index of the efficiency of capital utilisation and A is an index of a labour-augmenting technology. The efficiency of capital utilisation is constant and A grows at a constant rate, η. The population grows at a constant rate of n. $L^{*} = AL$ is the stock of effective labour, which has a growth rate of $\hat{L}^{*} = \eta + n$. Output per effective labour is shown as Equation 4.2.

Equation 4.2

$$y^{*} = Y / L^{*} = \left(K^{\delta} / AL\right)^{a}$$

Output per labour unit is therefore $y = Ay^{*}$, and we can now show that in the transition path the growth rate of output per effective labour is shown as Equation 4.3.

Equation 4.3

$$\hat{y}^{*} = a\left(\delta\hat{K} - \hat{L}^{*}\right) = a\left[\delta\hat{k} - (1-\delta)n - \eta\right]$$

In Equation 4.3, $k = K/L$ is capital stock per unit of labour, so the growth rate of output per labour unit (or GDP per capita) in the transition path is shown as Equation 4.4.

Equation 4.4

$$\hat{y} = a\left[\delta\hat{k} - (1-\delta)n\right] + (1-a)\eta$$

In other words, the growth of GDP per capita in the transition path is derived from two sources. First—represented by the terms in the right-hand bracket—is growth of capital stock per capita adjusted by the efficiency of capital utilisation. Second, is the growth of the labour-augmenting technology, the rate of which is η. The two sources are weighted by the output elasticities of capital and labour, respectively.

In the steady state, output per effective labour becomes constant. By Equation 4.3, we get Equation 4.5.

Equation 4.5

$$\delta\hat{k} = (1-\delta)n + \eta$$

From Equation 4.5, we in turn obtain the growth rate of GDP per capita in the steady state (Equation 4.6).

Equation 4.6

$$\hat{y} = \eta$$

That is, the growth rate of GDP per capita at the steady state is equal to the rate of technological progress. This is the standard result of the Solow model for technological progress.

The above model informs our understanding of the three kinds of convergence we have defined. First, Equation 4.5 implies β-convergence: when per capita GDP is low, the rate of growth of per capita capital stock, $\hat{k}$, is large,[1] as is the rate of growth of per capita GDP. This is what we refer to as regional convergence. The two inland regions still have low per capita GDP, meaning their growth rates should be higher when they follow their own rates of convergence than when they follow the national rate of convergence. In other words, regional (club) convergence could help China maintain a higher growth period for longer.

Second, Equation 4.5 also explains the second kind of convergence. The equation informs us that a higher efficiency index, *d*, increases the growth rate of GDP per capita. To the extent that the eastern region has the highest level of investment efficiency, convergence of the two inland regions towards that level will increase their growth rates. The national growth rate will, in turn, also rise. Last, Equations 4.5 and 4.6 tell us that a higher rate of technological progress boosts the growth rate of per capita GDP in the steady state as well as in the transition path. Again, because the eastern region has the highest rate of technological progress, convergence of the two inland regions towards the rate of the eastern region will increase not only their own growth rates, but also the national growth rate.

Data

Data used in this study include real GDP per capita and its growth rate, alongside the growth rate of real investment per capita across 28 provinces[2] in China and over the period 1984–2015. We collect the data from *China Statistics Yearbooks* (NBS 1985–2016) and *The Gross Domestic Product of China: 1952–1995* (NBS 1997).

One issue when using provincial GDP data is a tendency by local governments to overstate growth rates. It is widely acknowledged that the published growth rates of almost all provinces in China have been consistently higher than the published national growth rate. To account for this, we adopt a method of deflation to correct provincial growth rates as follows.

1 This result comes from one of the standard assumptions made by the Solow model—namely, the national saving rate is exogenous and constant.

2 We leave out Tibet, Chongqing and Hainan due to missing data.

First, we calculate the national average growth rate of real GDP among all provinces for each year, weighted by their shares of real GDP in the national total. Second, to obtain the deflator for each year, we divide this average growth rate by the national growth rate as published by the National Bureau of Statistics of China (NBS). Third, we deflate each province's growth rate in any particular year by the common deflator for that year. Fourth, assuming that the GDP figures of the base year (1984) were not inflated, we then apply the deflated growth rates to capture the 'true' GDP figures for each year thereafter. Finally, by dividing the deflated GDP by each province's population, we get each province's per capita GDP for each year.

Our study involves estimation of the growth equation, during which we will study only one input: the real growth rate of investment per capita. Since the NBS publishes only nominal figures of investment, we obtain the real growth rates of investment by deflating the value of investment by the price indices of fixed investment. Depreciation rates for investment after 1995 are from the *China Statistics Yearbooks* (NBS 1985–2016) and those before 1995 are constructed according to Zhang et al. (2004) and using investment data from *The Gross Domestic Product of China: 1952–1995* (NBS 1997).

The 28 provinces are divided into three regions: eastern, central and western.[3] Summary statistics of the main variables by region are presented in Table 4.1. The national data are simple averages of the 28 provinces.

Table 4.1 Summary statistics

	Real GDP per capita (RMB100)	Growth rate of real GDP per capita	Growth rate of real investment per capita
Panel A: Eastern			
Observations	288	288	288
Mean	49.497	0.085	0.127
Std deviation	45.758	0.049	0.141
Maximum	243.329	0.227	1.384
Minimum	4.700	–0.110	–0.244
Panel B: Central			
Observations	320	320	320
Mean	23.523	0.086	0.127
Std deviation	20.367	0.038	0.138
Maximum	114.853	0.198	0.973
Minimum	2.985	–0.043	–0.370

3 The eastern region provinces are: Beijing, Tianjin, Hebei, Shanghai, Jiangsu, Zhejiang, Fujian, Shandong and Guangdong; central region: Shanxi, Liaoning, Jilin, Heilongjiang, Anhui, Jiangxi, Henan, Hubei, Hunan and Guangxi; western region: Inner Mongolia, Sichuan, Guizhou, Yunnan, Shaanxi, Gansu, Qinghai, Ningxia and Xinjiang.

	Real GDP per capita (RMB100)	Growth rate of real GDP per capita	Growth rate of real investment per capita
Panel C: Western			
Observations	288	288	288
Mean	18.848	0.084	0.135
Std deviation	15.989	0.062	0.147
Maximum	87.995	0.555	0.729
Minimum	2.683	–0.347	–0.288
Panel D: National			
Observations	896	896	896
Mean	30.369	0.085	0.130
Std deviation	32.840	0.050	0.142
Maximum	243.329	0.555	1.384
Minimum	2.683	–0.347	–0.370

Notes: The period covered is 1984–2015. Tibet, Hainan and Chongqing are not included due to missing data. GDP and its growth rates are modified under the assumption that the national figures reported by the NBS are correct.

Source: Original data are from NBS (1985–2016).

Figure 4.1 shows the growth of GDP per capita in each region using the modified GDP data. On average, the eastern region has grown faster than the two other regions. As a result, the economies of the country's coastal provinces and those of its inland provinces have diverged. The gap between the central region and the western region has also grown over the years. By 2015, the per capita GDP of the eastern region was two times that of the central region, while per capita GDP in the western region was 23 per cent lower than in the central region. These contrasts provide the basis for this study. Since the gap is greatest between the eastern region and the other two regions, we will study the catch-up process of the two inland regions.

Figure 4.2 presents each region's average growth rate of real GDP per capita and Figure 4.3 shows the average growth rate of real investment per capita for each region over the period 1984–2015. The eastern region led the growth of real GDP until 2007, after which it was overtaken by the two inland regions. The eastern region had higher rates of investment growth than the two inland regions until the middle of the 1990s, but much lower rates since 2000. Clearly, investment efficiency has been lower in the two inland regions, particularly across China's high-growth period of 2001–08. This provides the basis for the potential internal convergence of efficiency.

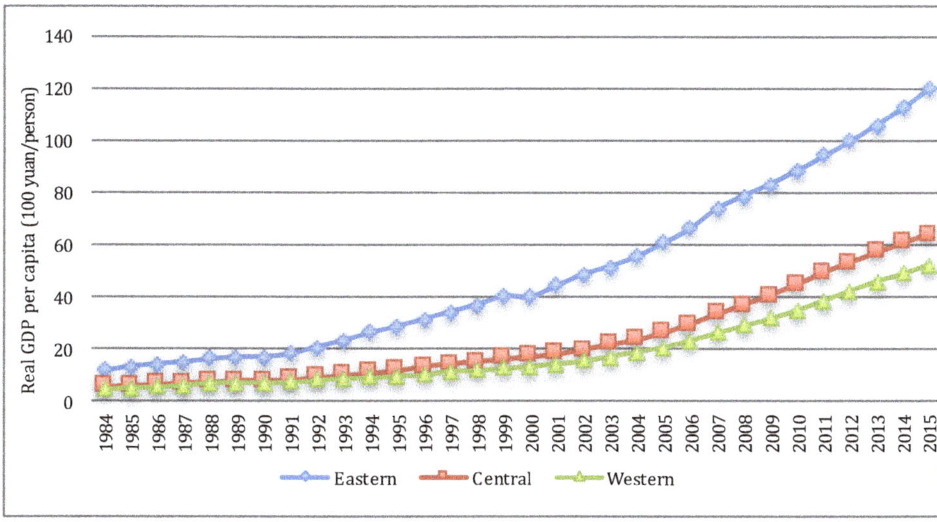

Figure 4.1 Real GDP per capita (RMB100 per capita)

Note: GDP per capita is measured in 1984 renminbi and is adjusted under the assumption that the national growth rates published by the NBS are correct.

Source: Original data from NBS (1985–2016).

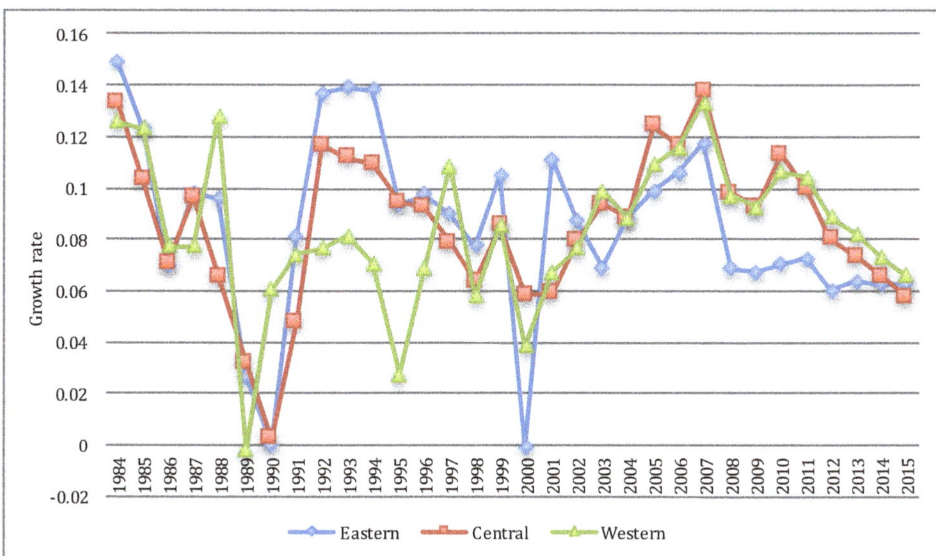

Figure 4.2 Growth rates of real GDP per capita

Note: The growth rates presented are adjusted under the assumption that the national growth rates published by the NBS are correct.

Source: Original data from NBS (1985–2016).

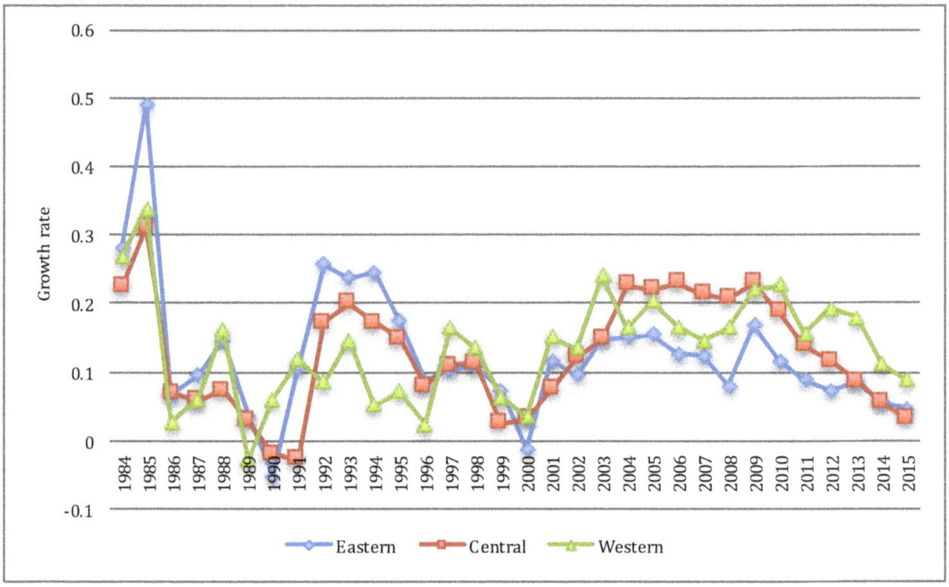

Figure 4.3 Growth rates of real investment per capita

Source: The growth rates of real investment are obtained by applying the price indices of fixed investment to the nominal investment data published by NBS (1996–2016). The price indices before 1995 are constructed according to Zhang et al. (2004) using investment data from NBS (1997).

Estimation of the growth equations

Econometric setups

We estimate two growth equations: one to determine the conditional convergence of each region and the other to determine the conditional convergence of the whole country. Both are consistent with the theoretical model introduced in the previous section. The first equation assumes heterogeneous parameters for individual regions and takes the following specification (Equation 4.7).

Equation 4.7

$$g_{it} = \alpha + \beta_E \ln(y_{i,t-1}) + \beta_C \ln(y_{i,t-1}) * D_C + \beta_W \ln(y_{i,t-1}) * D_W + \delta_E G_{it} + \delta_C G_{it} * D_C + \delta_W G_{it} * D_W + \eta_E (t - 1983) + \eta_C (t - 1983) * D_C + \eta_W (t - 1983) * D_W + \phi_i + \varepsilon_{it}$$

In Equation 4.7, the dependent variable g_{it} is the modified annual growth rate of real GDP per capita for province i in year t. On the right-hand side, $\ln(y_{i,t-1})$ is log-lagged real GDP per capita, which aims to capture the convergence effect. We allow for different speeds of convergence in different regions. D_C and D_W are two dummy variables representing the central and western regions, respectively. As a result, β_E measures the speed of convergence in the eastern region and $\beta_E + \beta_C$ and $\beta_E + \beta_W$ measure, respectively, the speeds of convergence in the central and western regions. Next, G_{it} is the growth rate of real investment per capita in province i in year t. To capture the different levels of efficiency in individual regions, we estimate a different coefficient for G_{it} for each region. We expect that δ_E, the efficiency coefficient for the eastern region, is larger than that for the other two regions—that is, δ_C and δ_W should be negative. To measure the rate of technological progress in each region, we estimate a linear time trend for each. The parameters η_E, $\eta_E + \eta_C$ and $\eta_E + \eta_W$ are, respectively, the speeds of technological progress in the eastern, central and western regions. We expect that η_E is positive and the other two parameters, η_C and η_W, are negative. We also add province fixed effects to control the influences of unobserved province-specific and time-invariant factors. Last, ε_{it} is an independent and identically distributed (IID) error term.

By Equation 4.7, we can calculate the steady-state growth rate for each region. In the steady state, the growth rate of investment per capita is constant, as is the growth rate of GDP per capita. So, for any two consecutive periods, t and $t - 1$, we have the following (Equation 4.8).

Equation 4.8

$$\hat{\beta}_j^*[\ln(y_{j,t}) - \ln(y_{j,t-1})] = \hat{\eta}_j^*,\ j=E,\ C,\ and\ W$$

In Equation 4.8, $\hat{\beta}_j^*$ represents the estimates for β_E, $\beta_E + \beta_C$ and $\beta_E + \beta_W$ and $\hat{\eta}_j^*$ represents the estimates for η_E, $\eta_E + \eta_C$ and $\eta_E + \eta_W$. As a result, the steady-state growth rate, which equals $\ln(y_{j,t}) - \ln(y_{j,t-1})$, is shown as Equation 4.9.

Equation 4.9

$$\hat{g}_j^* = \frac{\hat{\eta}_j^*}{\hat{\beta}_j^*},\ j = E,\ C,\ and\ W$$

This, of course, is a restatement of a result derived by the neoclassical growth model: the growth rate of GDP per capita in the steady state is equal to the long-term speed of technological progress.

To study convergence nationally, we estimate the following common-parameter equation (Equation 4.10).

Equation 4.10

$$g_{it} = \alpha + \beta\ln(y_{i,t-1}) + \delta G_{it} + \eta(t - 1983) + \varphi_i + \varepsilon_{it}$$

In this specification, we assume common speeds of convergence, efficiency of investment and technological progress in all provinces.

Estimation results

We report the results of Equations 4.7 and 4.10 in Table 4.2. The first three columns show the estimated parameters for each of the three regions in the heterogeneous-parameter specification. The speeds of convergence in the eastern, central and western regions are, respectively, 8 per cent, 7.1 per cent and 7.7 per cent. The eastern region converges the fastest because it has the highest per capita GDP and is therefore closer to its steady state than the other two regions. It is interesting, however, to find that the western region has a higher speed of convergence than the central region. The western region has a lower per capita GDP than the central region at the moment, so it must also have a lower per capita GDP than the central region in the steady state. This is one piece of evidence that the western region has impediments to its long-term technological progress.

Table 4.2 Regression results

	Eastern	Central	Western	National
Ln(lagged real GDP per capita)	–0.080***	–0.071***	–0.077*	–0.076***
	(0.015)	(0.021)	(0.044)	(0.016)
Investment growth	0.160***	0.141***	0.157***	0.154***
	(0.047)	(0.020)	(0.032)	(0.019)
Time trend	0.00613***	0.00606***	0.00601*	0.00606***
	(0.00127)	(0.00181)	(0.00327)	(0.00129)
Steady-state growth rate	7.66%	8.54%	7.81%	7.97%
Average province fixed effect	–0.020	–0.089	–0.092	–0.056
Constant	0.270***	0.270***	0.270***	0.239***
	(0.043)	(0.043)	(0.043)	(0.041)
Province FEs	Yes	Yes	Yes	Yes
R-squared	0.300	0.300	0.300	0.297
Observations	896	896	896	896

* significant at 10 per cent

** significant at 5 per cent

*** significant at 1 per cent

Notes: This table shows the regression results of Equations 4.1 and 4.3. Columns 1–3 are results from Equation 4.1. Parameters are consolidated for the regions. Column 4 presents the results from Equation 4.4.

A 1 percentage point increase in the rate of investment growth can bring increases in the GDP growth rate of 0.16 percentage point for the eastern region, 0.141 for the central region and 0.157 for the west. As expected, the eastern region has the highest level of investment efficiency, while the level of investment efficiency in the western region is higher than in the central region. Technological progress in the eastern region is the fastest, growing at 0.613 per cent each year, followed by the central region on 0.606 per cent and the western region on 0.601 per cent.

Based on Equation 4.3, we calculate the growth rate for each region in their respective steady states and present them in Table 4.2. We find that in their steady states, the eastern region would grow at 7.66 per cent, the central region at 8.54 per cent and the west at 7.81 per cent. These rates are high, for which we can see two reasons: the first is that the period studied was one of very high growth; and second is Chinese provinces are, on average, likely still far from reaching their steady states. Both of these factors can inflate the estimates of technological progress. As it is not the purpose of this chapter to make a forecast of China's growth prospects, but rather to study how internal convergence raises China's growth potential, attention should be paid to comparisons between different scenarios of convergence and not the growth rate levels.

The last column of Table 4.2 presents the regression results of Equation 4.4 for the national average. The speed of convergence is 7.6 per cent per annum, which is within the range obtained for the three regions. The rate of investment contribution is 0.154, which is also within the range obtained for the three regions. Finally, the speed of technological progress is 0.606 per cent, which is the same as that for the central region. Because the rate of convergence is higher nationally than in the central region, national growth in the steady state ends lower, at 7.97 per cent.

Forecast and analysis

With the estimation results in Table 4.2, we proceed to offer a forecast for China's growth potential in the period 2016–30. Our focus is not the forecast itself, but analysis of the effects of internal convergence. Specifically, we study three kinds of convergence: 1) the two inland regions converge to their own steady-state growth rate with the speed of convergence of the eastern region; 2) the two inland regions reach the investment efficiency of the eastern region; and 3) the two inland regions reach the speed of technological progress of the eastern region. Because the eastern region has faster convergence than the other two regions, regional convergence would lower the GDP growth rates of the other two regions. This counterfactual analysis thus shows that the backwardness of the two inland regions actually offers the potential for China to sustain higher rates of growth into the future. The second kind of convergence helps the inland regions reach the efficiency frontier maintained by the eastern region. As a result, it increases the inland regions' growth rates in their transition paths towards steady states. Last, the third kind of convergence raises the rates of the inland regions' long-term technological progress to the level of the eastern region so they would have higher GDP growth rates in their steady states.

The steady-state growth rates of the three regions and the whole country were presented in Table 4.2. Our forecasting task is to estimate the GDP growth rates in the transition pathways. For region *j*, we use the following equation to iterate our forecast, starting in 2016 (Equation 4.11).

Equation 4.11

$$\bar{g}_{jt} = \hat{\alpha} + \hat{\beta}_j \ln(\bar{y}_{j,t-1}) + \hat{\delta}_j \bar{G}_{jt} + \hat{\eta}_j (t - 1983) + \hat{\bar{\phi}}_j, j = E, M, W, \quad t = 2016, 2018, \dots, 2030$$

In Equation 4.11, the variables with the bars are the averages for the given region, and the key is to forecast the average growth rate of investment.

Forecasting investment growth

China has broadly followed a unique path of high savings and high investment since the People's Republic was established in 1949. But in the decade leading up to 2012, the saving and investment rates were particularly high, reaching above 50 per cent of GDP. Although in the past several years the economy has embarked on a path of rebalancing, China's saving and investment rates are still high by international standards. This makes it difficult to use an international benchmark to forecast China's future investment growth. In this chapter, we adopt the time-series analysis model ARIMA (2, 2) to forecast China's investment growth rates for the period 2016–30. Once again, our focus is not on the levels forecast; rather, the forecast offers a basis for us to study the effects of the three convergence types.

Our forecast adopts 2015 as the base year. Based on the observed investment growth rates in the period 1984–2015, we apply the ARIMA (2, 2) model to predict the investment growth rates of each region across the period 2016–30. The national forecast for each year is the weighted average of the three regions. Forecast per capita investment growth rates are presented in Figures 4.4a–d, alongside greater details listed in Appendix Table 4.A1. In all three regions, investment growth is predicted to pick up from 2016, but this is not what is observed that year.

Investment growth continued to decline in 2016. Again, however, our primary purpose is not to obtain exact estimates for the levels of investment growth; rather, we are more concerned with how improvements in investment efficiency would sustain higher growth rates in China. The future growth rates of investment in the eastern region are predicted to converge to 11.7 per cent from 2022. In the central region, investment growth will converge to 10.9 per cent from 2027. In the western region, investment has grown by very high rates in recent years, but it is expected to quickly converge to 12.8 per cent from 2021.

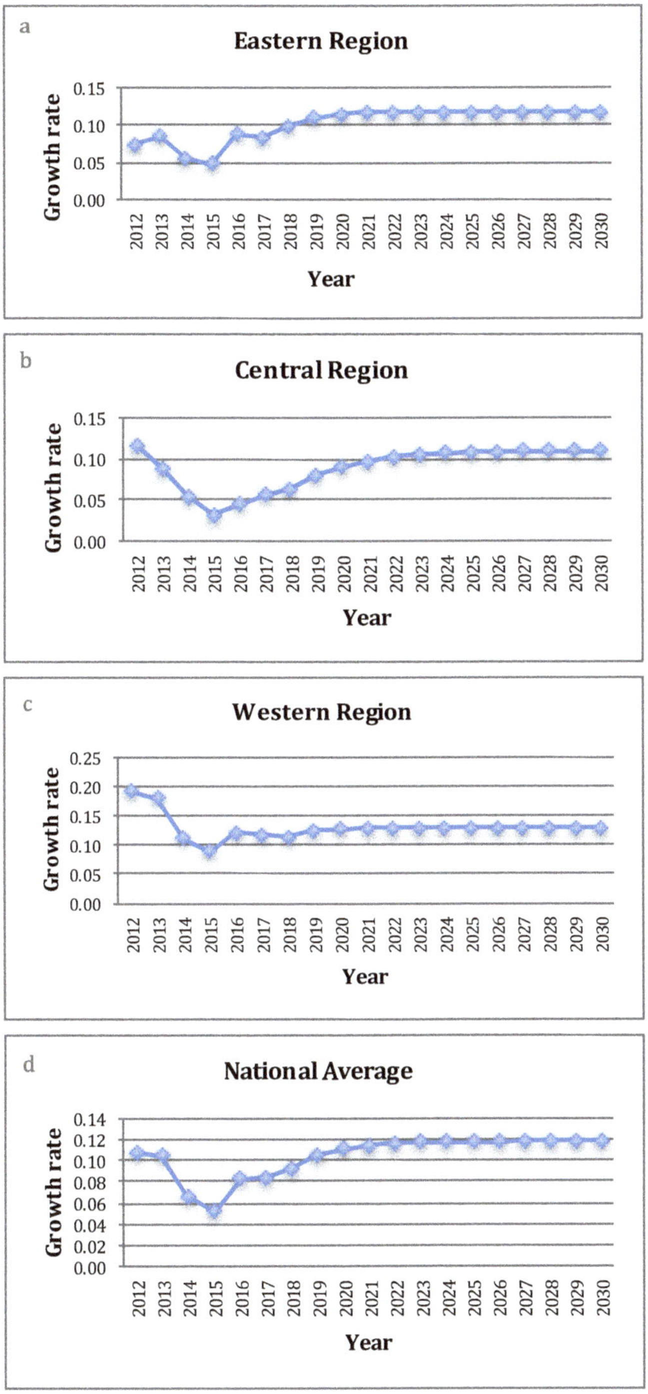

Figures 4.4a–d Forecast investment growth rates

Note: The forecast for each region is done using ARIMA (2, 2) based on the data for the period 1984–2015. The national average is the weighted average of the three regions' growth rates.

Source: Authors' calculation.

Forecasting GDP growth

Based on the forecast investment growth rates and applying Equation 4.11, we can forecast future growth rates of GDP per capita for each region. We can then compute the national weighted average growth rates.[4] These forecasts are presented in Figures 4.5a–d together with their corresponding historical records. Detailed numbers are presented in Appendix Table 4.A2. In sum, all three regions see rising GDP growth rates over the coming decade—mostly brought about by the predicted higher investment growth rates in the ensuing few years and the positive speed of technological progress, as reported in Table 4.2. By 2025, however, growth rates for the three regions will have stabilised,[5] although they will still be higher than in their respective steady states. That is, convergence towards the steady state will not begin in the 2016–30 period.

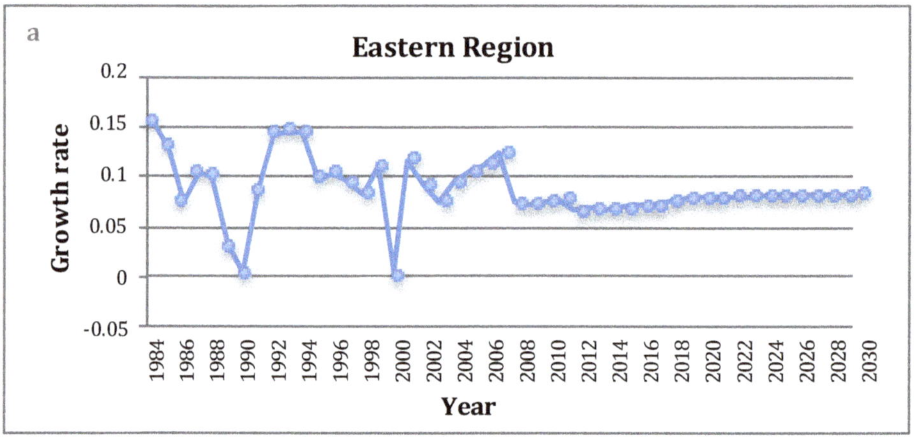

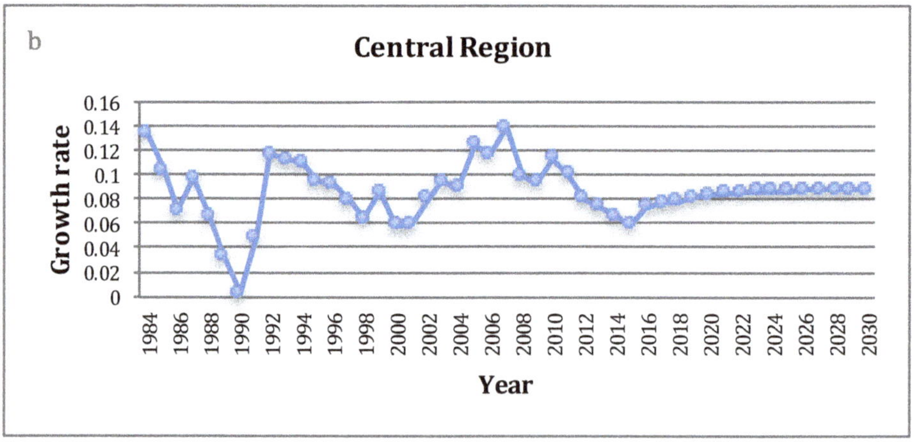

4 The population in each region is assumed to be constant from 2015 onwards.

5 The average half-life of convergence in the three regions is nine years, which is consistent with this finding.

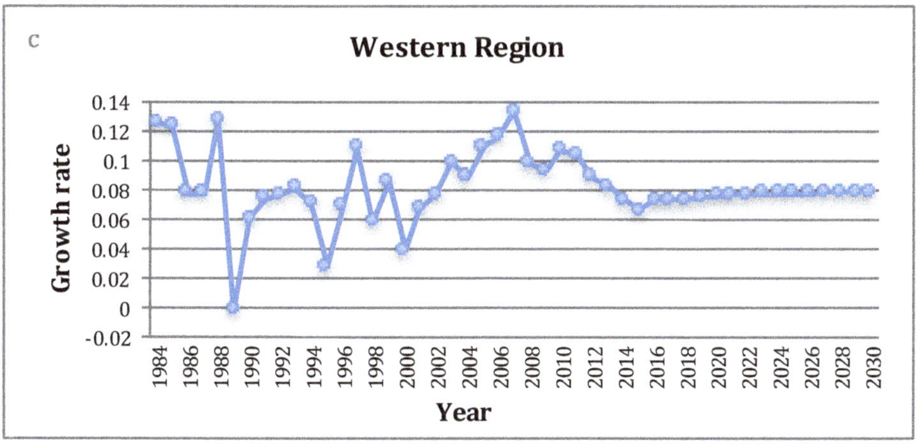

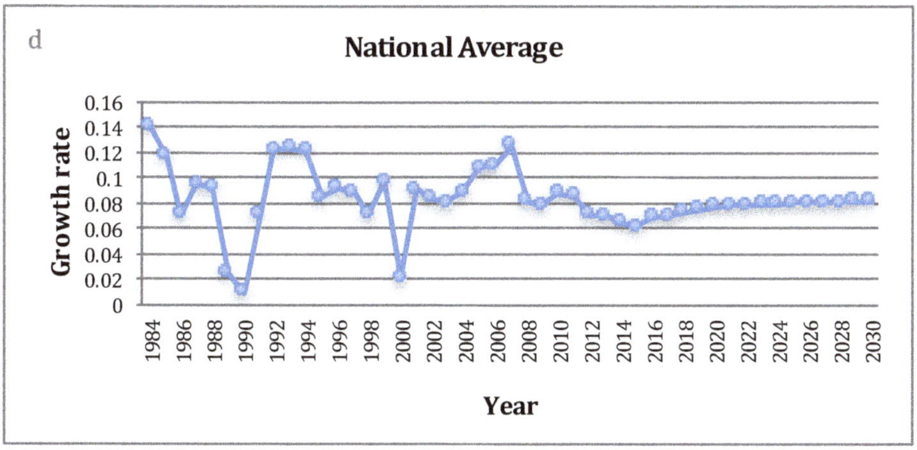

Figures 4.5a–d Forecast growth rates of GDP per capita

Note: The forecasts are done following Equation 4.11 and the forecast investment growth rates reported in Figure 4.4.

Source: Authors' calculation.

Comparative analyses

As we have emphasised, our main purpose is to study the effects of the three kinds of convergence, which we will do in this subsection. Before this, however, we show that ignoring regional convergence could lead to underestimation of national growth potential. It amounts to making a comparison between the national growth rates calculated as the weighted averages of the forecast regional growth rates introduced above and the counterfactual in which the national growth rates are forecast by the estimated results of the national growth equation (Equation 4.10), the results of which are presented in the last column of Table 4.2.

Equation 4.10 assumes that all provinces share the same speed of convergence, have the same level of investment efficiency and converge to the same steady state. Subsequently, we will call estimates derived using Equation 4.10 'common-parameter estimates'. These form the counterfactual because, in reality, provinces in the three regions converge to different steady states at different speeds and have different levels of efficiency. Depending on the composition of those factors, the national growth rates calculated by the weighted averages of the three regions' growth rates can be higher than the national growth rates forecast by the common-parameter estimates. Figure 4.6 shows that this is indeed the case here. The weighted-average forecast is 1.51 percentage points higher than the common-parameter forecast. In other words, this illustrates that ignoring regional convergence can lead to underestimation of the national growth potential. There are probably two explanations for this. First, the eastern region is more efficient and has a higher steady-state growth rate than the other two regions. In the meantime, its share of national GDP is also large (about 60 per cent). Second, the two inland provinces have slower convergence than the eastern region, meaning their high growth can be sustained for a longer period.

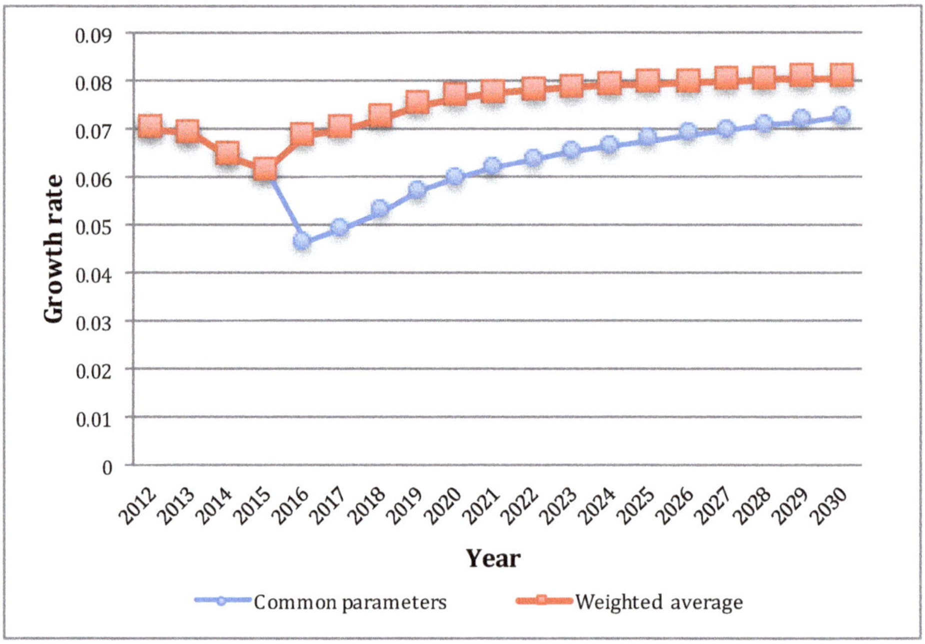

Figure 4.6 Common-parameter estimation versus heterogeneous-parameter estimation

Note: The common-parameter forecast uses the results of the national regression reported in Table 4.2 and the national investment growth rates forecast by the weighted averages of the three regions.

Source: Authors' calculation.

We now study the effects of the first kind of convergence: regional convergence. We compare the central and western regions' growth rates forecast by their respective growth equations with their growth rates in the counterfactual in which their speed of convergence catches up with the speed of convergence in the eastern region. The results are presented in Figures 4.7a–c, which also present a comparison with the national average. As expected, reaching the eastern region's speed of convergence would lower the growth rates in the central and western regions. This is more the case in the central region than in the west because the central region has the lowest speed of convergence (Table 4.2). On average, the central region's growth would slow by 2.7 per cent, while the western region's growth would slow by only 0.8 per cent. Together, this would lead to an average reduction of 0.9 per cent in the national growth rate, which is equal to 11.7 per cent of the average national growth rate of 7.7 per cent that was originally forecast for the period 2016–30. In other words, the lower speeds of convergence in the two inland regions that result from the advantage of backwardness can indeed sustain higher national growth rates in China.

Coming to the effects of convergence on investment efficiency, we find these are very small—mostly because the coefficients of investment growth for the three regions (Table 4.2) do not differ much. On average, the growth rate in the central region would be increased by only 0.1 percentage points if the region's investment efficiency caught up with that of the eastern region. In addition, the investment growth rate in the western region would stabilise at a higher rate than that of the eastern region, which would cancel the efficiency gains of the latter. As a result, the growth rates of the western region would be almost unchanged if it obtained the investment efficiency of the east.

Last, we study the effects of the convergence of technological progress. Technological progress has cumulative effects on the growth rate in the transition path, so convergence towards the level of technological progress in the eastern region would allow the other two regions to have substantially higher rates of growth in their transition path (although Table 4.2 shows that the eastern region does not lead the other two regions by large margins). Figures 4.8a–c illustrate these results, including that the improvements in technological progress are substantial. On average, the central region would grow 4.7 percentage points faster and the west 4.8 percentage points. As a result, the national economy would grow an average of 2.6 percentage points faster. This is more than one-third of the average national growth rate originally forecast for the period 2016–30. Therefore, convergence of technological progress has by far the largest effect of the three kinds of convergence on regional and national growth.

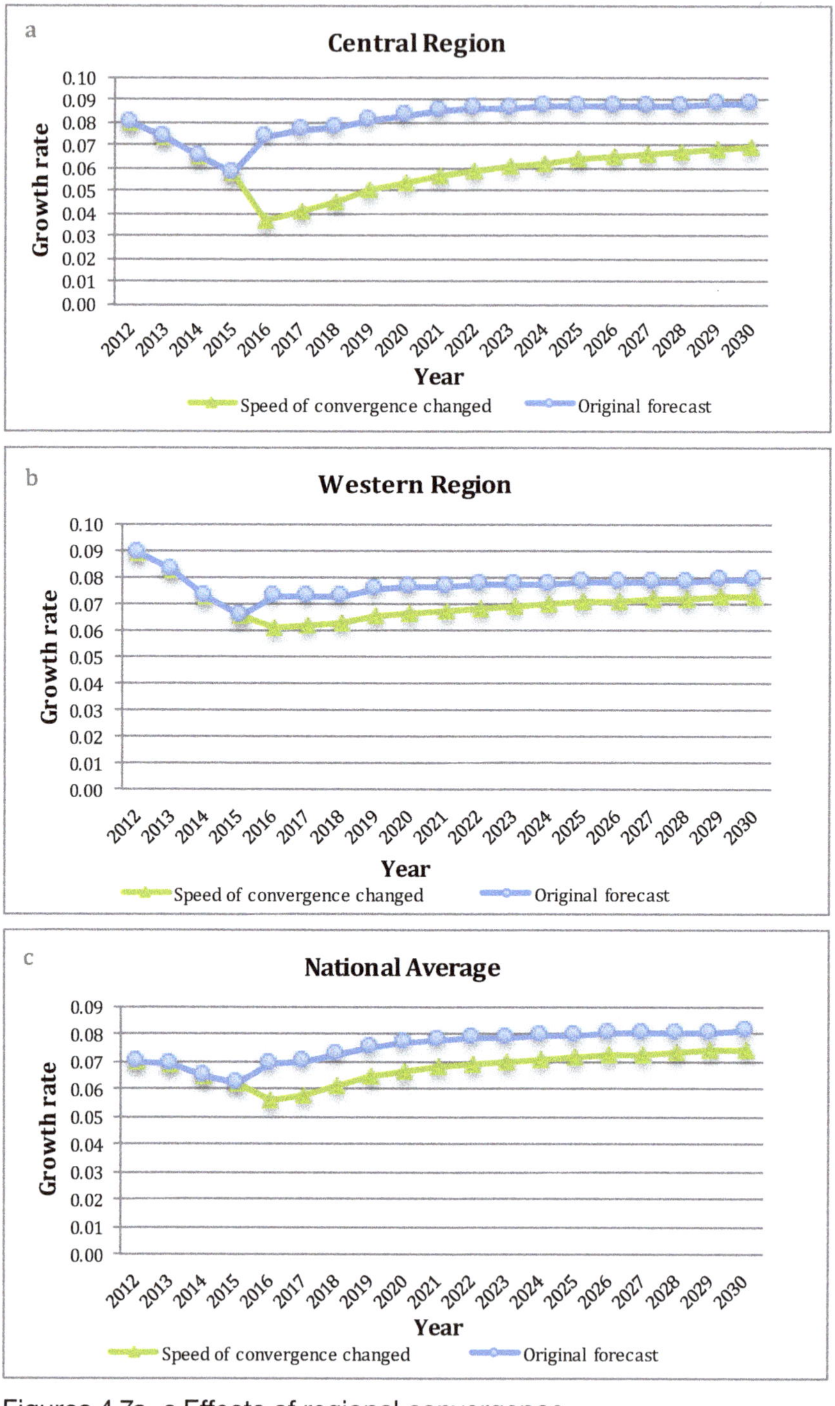

Figures 4.7a–c Effects of regional convergence

Notes: Original forecasts are the same as those presented in Figures 4.5a–d. The counterfactual forecasts assume that the central and western regions adopt the speed of convergence of the eastern region.

Source: Authors' calculation.

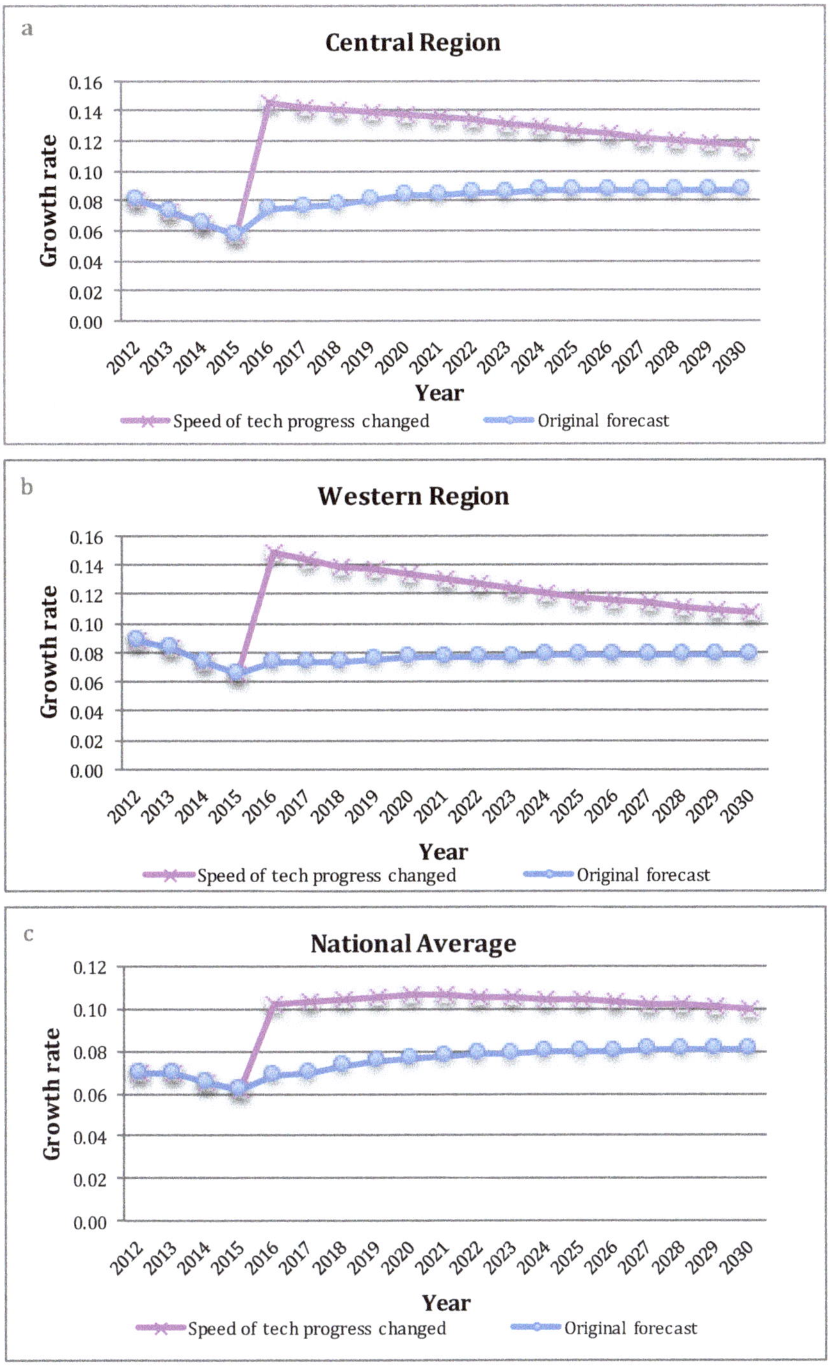

Figures 4.8a–c Effects of the convergence of technological progress

Note: Original forecasts are the same as those presented in Figure 4.5; the counterfactual forecasts assume that the central and western regions adopt the speed of technological progress of the eastern region.

Source: Authors' calculation.

Conclusion

In this chapter, we have estimated growth equations for China's three geographic regions and for the whole country. We have found different speeds of regional convergence, different levels of investment efficiency and different speeds of technological progress in the three regions, which provide the basis for regional convergence, efficiency convergence and technological convergence, respectively. Second, our counterfactual analysis found that: 1) the advantage of backwardness in the two inland regions produces their lower speeds of convergence relative to the eastern region, which increases China's future growth potential by 11.7 per cent; 2) convergence of technological progress in the two inland regions towards the speed of the eastern region would increase China's growth potential by more than one-third; and 3) convergence of investment efficiency in the two inland regions towards that of the eastern region does not have a large effect on either the growth rate or the level of income, mainly because the eastern region's advantages over the other two regions are not large.

To realise the identified gains from convergence of technological progress, the two inland regions should improve their policy environments and their stocks and quality of human capital. One challenge in achieving that goal, however, is the fact that China's inland provinces are in a disadvantageous position when it comes to attracting talent. To that end, efforts to improve the policy environment may be particularly important. In addition, the provision of affordable housing, good education for the next generation, an amiable work environment and preferential taxation arrangements is probably the most important and effective measure to attract and retain talent.

In addition, there is potential to improve investment efficiency in all three regions. As measured by the incremental capital–output ratio (ICOR), however, the efficiency of investment in China seems to have declined since a new investment drive was started after the GFC. Specifically, the ICOR increased from four in the period 2000–07 to 14 in 2015.[6] Growth in infrastructure-related investment, which has low rates of return, could explain part of this increase, but the ICOR data suggest that falling investment efficiency is also likely to be a major cause. In general, China has been on the downside of a business cycle since 2013, and overcapacity has become a serious issue in several key sectors. This may also account for part of the efficiency decline. As China's economy has already started to recover from that downturn, it is expected that the level of investment efficiency will increase in the next few years. Ongoing supply-side structural reforms that help reduce excess capacity and address the issue of zombie firms should also help improve efficiency in the economy.

6 Authors' calculations based on data released by NBS (various years).

References

Barro, R. and Sala-i-Martin, X. (1992), Convergence, *Journal of Political Economy* 100(2)(April): 223–51. doi.org/10.1086/261816.

National Bureau of Statistics of China (1985–2016), *China Statistics Yearbook*, Beijing: China Statistics Press.

National Bureau of Statistics of China (NBS) (1997), *The Gross Domestic Product of China: 1952–1995*, Dalian: Dongbei University of Finance and Economics Press.

Zhang, J., Wu, G. and Zhang, J. (2004), The estimation of China's provincial capital stock: 1952–2000, [in Chinese], *Economic Research Journal* 10(October): 35–44.

Appendix 4.1

Table 4.A1 Forecast investment growth rates

Year	Eastern	Central	Western	National
2012	0.073	0.116	0.192	0.107
2013	0.085	0.087	0.179	0.104
2014	0.055	0.055	0.112	0.066
2015	0.048	0.032	0.089	0.052
2016	0.087	0.044	0.121	0.083
2017	0.083	0.056	0.118	0.084
2018	0.098	0.062	0.113	0.092
2019	0.109	0.079	0.124	0.105
2020	0.114	0.090	0.127	0.111
2021	0.116	0.097	0.128	0.114
2022	0.117	0.102	0.128	0.116
2023	0.117	0.105	0.128	0.117
2024	0.117	0.106	0.128	0.117
2025	0.117	0.108	0.128	0.118
2026	0.117	0.108	0.128	0.118
2027	0.117	0.109	0.128	0.118
2028	0.117	0.109	0.128	0.118
2029	0.117	0.109	0.128	0.118
2030	0.117	0.109	0.128	0.118

Notes: The forecast for each region is made using ARIMA (2, 2) based on data for the period 1984–2015. The national average is the weighted average of the three regions' growth rates.

Table 4.A2 Forecast GDP growth rates

	Original forecast				Common speed of convergence			Common investment efficiency			Common rate of technological progress		
Year	Eastern	Central	Western	National	Central	Western	National	Central	Western	National	Central	Western	National
2012	0.060	0.080	0.089	0.070	0.080	0.089	0.070	0.080	0.089	0.070	0.080	0.089	0.070
2013	0.064	0.074	0.082	0.069	0.074	0.082	0.069	0.074	0.082	0.069	0.074	0.082	0.069
2014	0.062	0.065	0.073	0.065	0.065	0.073	0.065	0.065	0.073	0.065	0.065	0.073	0.065
2015	0.063	0.058	0.066	0.062	0.058	0.066	0.062	0.058	0.066	0.062	0.058	0.066	0.062
2016	0.065	0.074	0.073	0.069	0.036	0.061	0.056	0.074	0.073	0.069	0.145	0.149	0.102
2017	0.066	0.076	0.073	0.070	0.041	0.062	0.058	0.077	0.073	0.070	0.143	0.144	0.103
2018	0.069	0.078	0.073	0.072	0.045	0.062	0.061	0.079	0.073	0.073	0.141	0.139	0.104
2019	0.072	0.081	0.075	0.075	0.050	0.065	0.065	0.083	0.075	0.076	0.140	0.136	0.106
2020	0.073	0.083	0.076	0.077	0.054	0.067	0.067	0.085	0.076	0.077	0.138	0.133	0.106
2021	0.074	0.085	0.077	0.078	0.056	0.068	0.068	0.086	0.077	0.078	0.136	0.130	0.106
2022	0.074	0.086	0.077	0.078	0.059	0.068	0.069	0.087	0.077	0.079	0.134	0.127	0.106
2023	0.075	0.086	0.077	0.079	0.061	0.069	0.070	0.088	0.078	0.079	0.131	0.124	0.105
2024	0.075	0.087	0.078	0.079	0.062	0.070	0.071	0.088	0.078	0.080	0.129	0.121	0.105
2025	0.076	0.087	0.078	0.080	0.064	0.070	0.072	0.088	0.078	0.080	0.127	0.118	0.104
2026	0.076	0.087	0.078	0.080	0.065	0.071	0.072	0.088	0.078	0.080	0.124	0.116	0.103
2027	0.076	0.087	0.078	0.080	0.066	0.072	0.073	0.089	0.078	0.081	0.122	0.113	0.102
2028	0.076	0.088	0.078	0.080	0.067	0.072	0.073	0.089	0.079	0.081	0.120	0.111	0.102
2029	0.077	0.088	0.079	0.081	0.068	0.072	0.074	0.089	0.079	0.081	0.118	0.109	0.101
2030	0.077	0.088	0.079	0.081	0.069	0.073	0.074	0.089	0.079	0.081	0.117	0.107	0.100

Notes: Forecasts under 'Common speed of convergence', 'Common investment efficiency' and 'Common rate of technological progress' assume that the central and western regions adopt the speed of convergence, level of investment efficiency and rate of technological progress, respectively, of the eastern region. They are made following Equation 4.11 and the forecast investment growth rates reported in Appendix Table 4.A1.

5. Adjusting to the New Domestic Normal and the New International Normal: Supply-side Structural Reform 2.0

Wing Thye Woo[1]

On the eve of the 19th party congress

The past year has been one of conflicting signals for China's economy. Real estate prices in the largest cities (e.g. Beijing and Shenzhen) and in most second-tier cities (e.g. Xiamen and Qingdao) have continued to soar, but the phenomenon of 'ghost cities' continues to haunt many inland and smaller cities. Excess capacity still plagues heavy industry (e.g. iron and cement). Together with the large inventory of unsold houses in ghost cities, this has, however, not caused the proportion of non-performing bank loans to rise much.

How should one interpret the fact that the number of bank loans in the 'special-mention' category (i.e. loans that have potential weakness) has increased significantly in the past two years? Is this caused by temporary difficulties in debt servicing that will disappear after cost-cutting measures by firms? Or is this development the outcome of the special-mention category being the hiding place for non-performing loans (NPLs) and a prelude to a jump in the NPL rate?

China's trade surplus remains large and has fallen little in the past three years. The stock of foreign exchange reserves of the People's Bank of China has, however, continued to decline. This implies that the deficit of the non–central bank component of the Financial Account[2] is larger than the trade surplus. These symptoms suggest that the renminbi (RMB) has been overvalued for at least the past three years—a suspicion that is reinforced by the steady tightening of capital controls on outflows.

Is this massive capital outflow the result of a similarly massive loss of confidence in China's future economic prospects? Or is this the result of massive flight of ill-gotten wealth induced by the widening of investigations in the campaign

1 I am most grateful to Lauren Johnston for excellent editing and insightful critical review that improved this chapter tremendously.

2 The Financial Account is known as the Capital Account in the old terminology in balance of payments accounts.

against corruption? Or is this a speculative bet against the current value of the renminbi? The first interpretation signals a dim economic future for China, while the second means a brighter economic future. The third interpretation signals a temporary state of affairs that could be reversed at any time by the government, but the economic implications (good or bad) would depend on how the government reduced capital outflow.

At the same time, conflicting signals are also seen at the international level, and China's geopolitical positioning is changing amid broader global shifts. The unexpected election of Donald Trump has resulted in the United States withdrawing from the Trans-Pacific Partnership (TPP) and demanding renegotiations of the North American Free Trade Agreement (NAFTA). In parallel, the United Kingdom (UK) has voted to leave the European Union (EU), threatening the process of further European integration and, potentially, existing European unity. Partly in response to these developments, China is moving more decisively than ever into the role of a responsible global stakeholder. At the January 2017 meeting of the World Economic Forum in Davos, Chinese President Xi Jinping pledged his country's leadership in the fight to prevent deglobalisation:

> We should commit ourselves to growing an open global economy to share opportunities and interests through opening-up and achieve win-win outcomes. One should not just retreat to the harbor when encountering a storm, for this will never get us to the other shore of the ocean. We must redouble efforts to develop global connectivity to enable all countries to achieve inter-connected growth and share prosperity. (Xi 2017)

The Wall Street Journal reported that at the 'One Belt, One Road' summit in Beijing on 14–15 May 2017:

> Mr Xi portrayed China as a committed free trader and pledged more than $100 billion in new financing and assistance for projects and countries involved in an updated revival of ancient Silk Road trading … Mr Xi said over the last three years China has invested more than $50 billion in Silk Road countries, and Chinese officials have branded the venture as a new form of globalization, one that is more inclusive and fairer than previous tides of world commerce. (Wong 2017)

It is therefore jarring that *The Wall Street Journal* also carried on its website at the same time a video recording of Charlene Barshefsky, the former US trade negotiator for China's World Trade Organization (WTO) accession, claiming that President Xi had 'stopped the process of economic reform and opening' in China (Barshefsky 2017). In her opinion, China has been retreating from economic liberalisation since 2007 and President Xi has accelerated the introduction of mercantilist policies with programs such as those relating to 'pillar industries', 'strategic emerging industries' and 'Made in China 2025'. Barshefsky described President Xi's economic strategy as a 'techno-nationalist push across-the-board'—that is, 'an import-substitution strategy' à la Brazil of many years ago—to 'Sinicize the Chinese economy' with homemade replacements (e.g. cloud computing, integrated circuits, new materials) unleashed by 'indigenous innovations'.[3] Barshefsky also described China's globalisation strategy as 'a zero-sum game' because it is focused on making sure that 'everyone else's market is open'.

How could Barshefsky have described the 'One Belt, One Road' initiative—the key mechanism of China's globalisation strategy—as a zero-sum game? While the construction of bridges, dams and railroads in Pakistan and South-East Asia would certainly help alleviate the excess capacity problems in China's heavy industries, it cannot be denied that the additional infrastructure will also enrich these neighbouring countries. Similarly, the greatly improved rail link between the Central Asian republics and Europe will enrich the economies of both Central Asia and Europe—not just China.

The above conflicting interpretations of various Chinese economic features show clearly that there are some deep misunderstandings about China's economy and the government's policy choices, and deep suspicions about the motives of China's economic policymakers. It must be recognised that at the heart of the Xi–Barshefsky disagreement is the fact that the US-dominated post–World War II world order is no longer viable, and there is now a tussle to shape the architecture of the new framework within which countries conduct their affairs internally and internationally.

This chapter is an effort to clarify understanding on three issues relating to the Chinese economy: the current trajectory of the economy, the policy options to influence that trajectory and possible additional elements to be incorporated into international economic relations. Our view is that for China to embark on dynamic sustainable development that will put the country in the ranks of the most advanced countries in the medium term, China must comprehensively scale up its program of supply-side structural reform by broadening it to include not only policy realignments in other domestic spheres (e.g. the socioeconomic rights of the rural population), but also an ambitious revamping of the institutional arrangements of international governance (e.g. the nature of collective global leadership). Bold implementation of the revised reform program, which we call 'supply-side structural reform 2.0', will hopefully begin on conclusion of the 19th Communist Party Congress in late 2017.

3 A low-key summary of Charlene Barshefsky's speech is reported in Cheng (2017).

The current trajectory of China's economy

The average annual growth rate of China's gross domestic product (GDP) in the period 1979–2010 was 10 per cent. After economic growth came in at 7.9 per cent in 2012 and 7.8 per cent in 2013, the government announced, in 2014, that the Chinese economy had reached a different development stage, called the 'new normal'. Many analysts at that time took this to mean an implicit growth target of 7 per cent. Growth shrank to 7.3 per cent in 2014 and remained sluggish in mid-2015, so the government announced in late 2015 that the target growth rate for the next Five-Year Plan (2016–20) would be in the range of 6.5–7 per cent. Growth was 6.9 per cent in 2015 and 6.7 per cent in 2016.

The diagnoses by leading China experts of the cause of the steady decline in the growth rate since 2010 are all over the map. Naturally, their advice to China's policymakers is also all over the map. Broadly speaking, the identified causes for the post-2010 slowdown range from temporarily insufficient aggregate demand created by cyclical factors to inescapable productivity collapses created by deep-seated structural flaws. In other words, the first key differentiating factor in competing diagnoses of China's economy is the degree of optimism about the sustainability of the three-decade-long high growth rates up to 2010.

Justin Lin (2016) typifies the optimistic faction of analysts when he identifies 'external and cyclical factors, not some natural limit' as the primary causes of the growth slowdown. He therefore urges boosting domestic demand—through 'improvements in infrastructure, urbanization efforts, environmental management, and high-tech industries' (Lin 2016)—to reach the official growth targets. The underlying basis for Lin's optimism is his observation that the Sino–US ratio of GDP per capita (in purchasing power parity (PPP) dollars) was 20 per cent in 2008, which was the level of the Japanese–US ratio in 1951 and the South Korean–US ratio in 1977. Japan and South Korea went on to grow 9.2 per cent and 7.6 per cent annually, respectively, for the next 20 years. Lin (2015) concludes that 'in the 20 years after 2008, China should have a potential growth rate of roughly 8%'.

Other notable members of the optimistic faction are Michael Spence and Fred Hu (2016). They feel that, despite challenges such as significant industrial overcapacity and excessive credit expansion, 'the reality is that China's transition to a more innovative, consumer-driven economy is well underway. This suggests that the economy is experiencing a bumpy deceleration, not a meltdown.' Importantly, 'bumpy' refers to a temporary deviation from the norm. Because Spence and Hu choose to focus on how to moderate the bump rather than how to raise the level of the norm, they advise the Chinese Government to increase the transparency of its decision-making and to communicate its policy decisions more effectively. The defining characteristic of these optimists is that they do not mention (or emphasise) in their articles any specific structural or institutional reform.

Keyu Jin (2016a), on the other hand, is pessimistic about sustaining the high growth of the past because she sees the state-owned enterprise (SOE) sector 'as choking the private sector' through unfair competition resulting from the preferential treatment given to SOEs (such as cheap land and cheap capital). Jin calls for root-and-branch reform of the entire social system: 'The economic reforms China needs now presuppose political reform … it will have to overhaul its governance system—and the philosophy that underpins it' (Jin 2016a).

Like Jin, Zhang Jun (2016b) identifies 'a far-reaching restructuring of large SOEs [involving the] sale or transfer of state-owned assets' as the most effective remedy for the biggest threats to China's economy. Private firms must be allowed to enter the 'SOE-dominated, capital-intensive, and high-end service industries', zombie SOEs should be shut down and the rollback of the SOE reforms undertaken earlier by Zhu Rongji should be reversed. Optimally, 'the role of SOEs needs to be once again limited to a few relevant sectors' (Zhang 2016b).

Unlike Jin, however, Zhang makes no mention of sociopolitical changes as the required complement to economic reform. This omission highlights the fact that the second key differentiating factor among China analysts (besides the optimist–pessimist divide) is the degree to which they see complementary linkages between political reform and economic reform.

To some segments of the Western media, the recent political developments in China re-concentrating power from the periphery to the centre (specifically from other members of the Standing Committee to President Xi), strengthening censorship of the domestic media and beefing up the 'Great Firewall' to reduce access to foreign websites are usually regarded as setbacks to sociopolitical progress (possibly also resulting in setbacks for economic progress later on). Keyu Jin (2016b), however, disagrees with this interpretation.

According to Jin (2016a), the reason the Chinese Government has not implemented necessary economic reform is because of its concern about 'the potential for mass protest and civil unrest'. Jin (2016b) hails the ongoing process of amassing power in the hands of Xi Jinping on the grounds that the President needs greatly enhanced political power to be able 'to strengthen China'. According to Jin, the situation is that 'over three decades of lax governance, some local authorities have formed political cliques that work together to protect their illicit gains and economic interests', thereby producing the present sociopolitical and economic malaise.

It must therefore be emphasised that optimism about China's future economic performance is not a minority opinion. As noted, even Keyu Jin, who calls for sweeping sociopolitical reforms to remove deeply embedded barriers to socioeconomic progress, is pessimistic only about the economy at present and in the short run. She is very optimistic about the inevitability of radical reforms that will be enacted to entrench dynamism into China's economy (perhaps after the 19th party congress in late 2017?).

Another analyst embodying Lin's optimism about the present and Jin's optimism about the future is Stephan Roach (2016), who is convinced that 'China has the strategy, wherewithal, and commitment to achieve a dramatic structural transformation into a services-based consumer society while successfully dodging daunting cyclical headwinds'.

On the question of whether the post-2010 growth slowdown was caused by cyclical factors or by a decline in the potential growth rate, one could hedge by stating that the slowdown was caused by both factors. While this cautious answer is likely true, it is not useful unless it also specifies the relative contribution of each set of causes to the decline in the growth rate.

Yu Yongding (2016b) states that 'China faces two separate challenges: the long-term issue of a declining potential growth rate and the immediate problem of below-potential actual growth'. Yu (2016a) therefore points out that 'another stimulus package that increases aggregate demand through infrastructure investment is needed'. Yu adds that the 'key will be to finance projects mainly with government bonds, instead of bank credit'. While this suggestion would help to prevent a future banking crisis created by NPLs, this additional debt servicing could contribute to a future fiscal crisis.[4]

Moreover, financial soundness is not sufficient to justify Lin's and Yu's enthusiastic endorsements for another round of macro-stimulus because policymakers should also consider whether there is a trade-off between short-term macroeconomic stability and long-term economic dynamism. Experience shows that the usual types of macro-stimulus (e.g. generalised monetary loosening and more investments chosen at the discretion of local governments) generally keep zombie firms alive, support disproportionate growth of the SOE sector and result in the eventual appearance of large excess production capacity in heavy industry (see Tan et al. 2016).

In other words, the usual macro-stimulus in China enables more of the wasteful behaviour associated with the soft-budget constraint hypothesis. But, as China's surplus labour diminishes and the demographic dividend fades, this type of macro-stimulus reduces the potential growth rate of the economy, and hence accelerates the decline in the actual growth rate. The more frequent is the use of the usual

4 An infrastructure project that does not generate a private rate of return high enough to cover the loan rate will create an NPL for the bank. An infrastructure project that does create enough (direct and indirect) revenue to the government to cover the servicing of the infrastructure bonds will create a fiscal crisis if it increases the government budget deficit substantially, necessitating large cuts in important government programs.

type of Chinese stimulus to keep zombie firms alive, the higher is the probability that China will fall into the middle-income trap, where its growth rate is not high enough to close the development gap between it and the advanced economies.[5]

The exit of most zombie firms is a necessary condition for the long-term dynamism of the Chinese economy, and the key is to reduce the pain of shutting them down through targeted assistance to displaced workers. The right kinds of fiscal stimulus to accompany the tightening of the soft-budget constraint would have as their key components the enlargement of unemployment insurance and the expansion of job retraining programs.

To avoid unemployment, China must stop using the usual types of macro-stimulus that maintain the status quo of output composition—for example, choosing infrastructure investment to reduce excess capacity in specific heavy industries and dispensing subsidies and loans to firms that cannot sell all the goods they produce. These traditional types of stimulus actually encourage such heavy industries to expand their production capacity. The existence of this trade-off between short-term macroeconomic stability and long-term economic dynamism is the reason official commentary on economic policies since November 2015 has overwhelmingly emphasised supply-side structural reform.

It is reasonable to assume that Xi Jinping has concluded that the primary cause of the growth slowdown is the decline in the potential growth rate. This reading of Xi's assessment is consistent with the comment of the mysterious 'authoritative official' featured on the front page of the *People's Daily* on 9 May 2016, that 'boosting growth by increasing leverage was like "growing a tree in the air" and that a high leverage ratio could lead to a financial crisis' (Zhou 2016). The Sino–US ratio of GDP per capita (in PPP dollars) is about 30 per cent today, showing that there are still significant possibilities for large increases in China's productivity through technological catch-up. So why are China's policymakers pessimistic about the sustainability of high growth?

There are two good reasons to be wary of the sustainability of the pre-2010 growth rate. First, there is no reason to believe that technological catch-up is an automatic process or even the dominant outcome. Taking the five largest Latin American countries as a group, their GDP per capita (in PPP dollars) was about 30 per cent of the US level in 1955, and it is still roughly that level today. The absolute standard of living has improved in Latin America, but the size of the development gap between it and the United States has not changed for more than 60 years. This failure to catch-up is what is meant by the term 'middle-income trap'.

5 Woo (2012) defines a catch-up index (CUI) as the ratio of the Chinese living standard to the US living standard (both measured in PPP dollars). The size of the development gap is 100 minus the country's CUI value. A middle-income trap is the phenomenon where CUI is stuck in the 25–50 per cent range.

The economic stagnation of Latin America is not unique. Malaysia reached 30 per cent of the US standard of living in 1994 and about 35 per cent in 2016, reducing the development gap by only 5 percentage points after 22 years. Thailand reached 27 per cent of the US standard living in 1994 and has been stuck there since. The significant growth slowdown in these two South-East Asian countries has resulted in people dressed in different-coloured clothes (Red Shirts versus Yellow Shirts) fighting each other in the streets. Such confrontations hark back to the political disruptions of the Brown Shirts, Black Shirts and Blue Shirts in Europe in the 1930s.

Japan, Taiwan and South Korea are the only Asian economies of significant size to have rapidly narrowed their development gaps with the United States. China cannot simply count on the economic exceptionalism of these economies to relieve it of worry about losing its shirt in the middle-income trap, especially as many of its problems are much larger in scale and more varied and complex in nature.

The second reason for China to be cautious about the sustainability of past growth rates is that it is rapidly becoming an ageing society. An ageing population will have fewer savings (and hence will undertake less investment) and will accumulate human capital more slowly. An ageing society will also become one with a declining population, and this reduces the efficiency gains from economies of scale in production and from synergy-induced innovation.

It must be pointed out that some economists anticipated the post-2010 growth slowdown. Cai Fang (2011) pointed out that China—unlike Japan and South Korea—was ageing before becoming affluent, and warned that this demographic factor could cause China to fall into the middle-income trap.[6] The abrupt drop in Japanese growth rates occurred in the early 1990s when the Japanese dependency ratio (the proportion of the population younger than 15 and older than 60 years) started rising sharply, after increasing very slowly in the period 1970–90. Similarly, South Korea's growth rates slowed significantly after its dependency ratio bottomed out in 2010 and started climbing rapidly.

China's dependency ratio bottomed out in 2010, and its subsequent rise has been quite rapid although still a little slower than in Japan after 1995 and in South Korea after 2010. Cai Fang called for the relaxation of the one-child policy and the household registration (*hukou*) system to retard the rise of the dependency ratio via a higher fertility rate and to increase the labour participation rate via more rapid urbanisation.

6 See Johnston et al. (2016) for a sceptical assessment of Cai's hypothesis.

In 2013, before the present slowdown in China's trend growth rate was recognised by most analysts, Cai Fang and Lu Yang (2013) used demographically adjusted growth accounting to determine that the average annual potential growth rate would be 7.19 per cent in the period 2011–15 and 6.08 per cent in 2016–20. This prediction might have become reality earlier but for two reasons—the first of which was the frequent monetary and fiscal stimulus to keep zombie SOEs alive, enlarge the inventory of unoccupied housing in some regions and increase the demand for goods made by firms with excess capacity. The second reason is the implementation of some fundamental reforms such as cancellation of the one-child policy and further relaxation of *hukou* restrictions.

Cai Fang's work alerts us to a general methodological issue. Justin Lin had looked at the Japanese–US and South Korean–US ratios of GDP per capita and predicted continued high growth (8 per cent) for China in the next 20 years. Cai Fang studied the relationship between the dependency ratio and the GDP growth rate in Japan and South Korea and predicted a drop in China's annual growth rate. Which is the right variable to pick for comparison across countries to project the trajectory of another variable?

The answer is that cross-country comparison is useful only when the analyst is well informed about the specific conditions in each country and the relative importance of these specific conditions to the trajectory of the variable of interest in that country. In short, cross-country institutional knowledge is needed to supplement standard economic theory to assess the relative importance of the economic mechanisms listed in textbooks.

Country-specific knowledge is absolutely essential because the same observed outcome could be produced by different factors. China might be caught in the middle-income trap because of the accelerated ageing of its population and the unusually slow process of rural–urban migration. Malaysia is in the middle-income trap for an entirely different set of reasons: a comprehensive ethnic preferential system that has spawned rampant rent-seeking, promoted massive capital flight and created a continuing and large brain drain; and an overly centralised administrative structure that suppresses local development initiatives. Thailand has also been forced into the middle-income trap because of the intense political conflict caused by the refusal of the traditional elite to accommodate new social forces.

Andrew Sheng and Xiao Geng (2016) warn that 'the success of the structural rebalancing that China needs to ensure sustainable long-term growth is far from certain'. They believe the origin of China's economic problems lies in the interaction between imperfect markets and an imperfect bureaucracy. While they do not identify whether the greater severity of such problems is due to increased imperfections in the markets or increased imperfections in the bureaucracy, they are confident that the solution to today's more difficult problems requires the government to go beyond structural reform to 'institutional reform'.

The one institutional reform that Sheng and Xiao chose to mention is:

> the central and local authorities must clearly delineate property rights with regard to land, capital, and natural resources, and establish industrial standards and best practices. Such clarity is critical to curtail a surge in disputes over rights, which block productivity-enhancing market-oriented adjustments. (Sheng and Xiao 2016)

It would have been helpful if Sheng and Xiao had indicated how to operationalise their advice.

The most common way to clearly delineate property rights is to privatise state-controlled assets; and the most common way to establish industrial standards and best practice in a country is to adopt standards and practices from abroad and carefully adapt them to ensure their effectiveness under local conditions. China's approach to economic reform should continue to be based on the adage that there is no need to reinvent the wheel for most issues (Woo 2001). There is only the need to have adequate knowledge of how local conditions differ from the conditions in the country from which standards are borrowed so that appropriate modifications can be made.

What is to be done?

Framework for classifying policy challenges

At the China Update 2010 conference, Woo (2010) compared the performance of China's economy during the past three decades to a speeding car. He classified what could cause the car to crash (or stop) under three headings: hardware failure, software failure and power supply failure.

Using the Marxist distinction between base structure and superstructure, Woo (2010) called the breakdown of an *economic mechanism* a crisis in the base structure, which he termed a *hardware failure*. Probable hardware failures include a banking crisis, a budget crisis and a productivity crisis. He called a crisis in the superstructure a *software failure* because it refers to a flaw in *governance* that creates frequent, widespread social disorder that disrupts economy-wide production and discourages private investment. Software failures usually result from not having the right institutional incentives to guarantee good governance—for example, technocratic competence in economic management and effective administrative responses to social concerns over severe inequality, serious corruption and political repression.

Woo (2010) inserted cyber-terminology into the Marxist dichotomy to create a comprehensive framework to capture the phenomenon of a *power supply failure*, where the economy stalls after reaching either *a natural limit* or *an externally imposed limit*. Examples of power supply failures are an environmental collapse, a nuclear war (not necessarily involving China) and a trade war.

We will make the case that there is now a 'new international normal' (of which the election of Donald Trump is a manifestation) in which enlightened self-interest requires China to become a responsible stakeholder and help supply global public goods to meet existential global threats—that is, threats of power supply failures at the global level. China must help to build effective collective global leadership to mobilise the global community to achieve the 17 Sustainable Development Goals adopted by the United Nations General Assembly in 2015. Global progress under the new international normal necessitates collective action to prevent power supply failures such as climate change, nuclear proliferation, technological stagnation and military confrontation.

The hardware reform agenda

At the China Update 2016 conference, Woo (2016) identified the two most likely types of hardware failure under the present policy regime as: 1) fiscal stress from having to bail out the state banks by taking over the NPLs generated by the soft-budget constraint of SOEs; and 2) low productivity growth from the disproportionate expansion of the SOE sector. These two hardware failures have been mainly unintentional outcomes of China's use of SOEs as instruments of macro-stimulus. The stimulus-through-SOEs mechanism creates a trade-off between maintenance of full capacity utilisation in the short run and sustaining a high rate of capacity expansion in the long run.

Chinese policymakers should now replace the stimulus-through-SOEs mechanism with three new interrelated market-friendly macro-stabilisation tools and growth drivers. First, they should foster new private entrepreneurs; second, they should promote urbanisation according to the principles of future homeownership and consumer location choice; and third, they should develop a modern financial system in which the private sector has a greatly enhanced role.

Foster new private entrepreneurs

In section two, we identified the taming of SOEs as the most common element in the policy advice that is offered to China to raise its potential growth rate. This common element does not reflect ideological bias but rather the reality that SOEs constitute a growing burden on the economy. There should be rationalisation of the sector by privatising some, but not all, SOEs. There is no need to privatise most of the largest SOEs provided the government allows free entry into their industries (with exceptions such as armaments), imposes the hard-budget constraint on both SOEs and private firms (no SOE bias and no crony capitalism) and practices free trade (with exceptions such as opium).

The state can partly offset the contractionary effects of the shrinking state sector by mobilising the laid-off workers to form an entrepreneurial force. Many of these workers could start their own factory workshops to take advantage of the increased cost competitiveness in China's inland provinces created by the explosive extension of the national transportation network since the 2008 Global Financial Crisis (GFC). Because the primary barrier to the emergence of this group of owner-operators is the availability of credit, the government should legalise small and medium-sized private banks as they have comparative advantage over the four large state banks in catering to the needs of these new entrepreneurs.

Promote urbanisation

The second new growth-oriented macro-stabilisation instrument is urbanisation based on the principles of affordable future homeownership and consumer location choice. The prolonged rapid growth of the real estate sector and the large increases in housing prices reflect not just speculative demand but also genuine pent-up demand for housing and genuine accommodation of the rapid rate of the joint industrialisation–urbanisation process. The bulk of new arrivals from the countryside, however, do not qualify for bank mortgages, so many investors have been buying multiple housing units to rent to new arrivals with the intention of raising the rents over time in line with the income growth of the renters. In this sense, much of the recent housing demand has been speculative.

As financial sector development is a protracted process, efficient markets for mortgage loans are a long time coming. Meanwhile, China should significantly scale up its low-cost housing program by allowing new arrivals to the cities to rent for seven years and then have the first right to buy these units at a price based on the cost of construction. This 'future ownership' form of urbanisation would prevent the problem of empty housing being held for speculative reasons and escalating into NPLs. China can afford a massive public housing program because the expensive part of such programs in other countries is the cost of land and not the cost of the structures, and land in China is mostly owned by the state.

To prevent the very real possibility of any massive low-cost housing scheme turning into a ghost town, the government must abandon its present practice of forcing real estate development to follow a preconceived (bureaucratically determined) distribution of city size (that is, the preconceived notion of what the proportions of large, medium and small cities ought to be) and a preconceived notion about what the absolute size of a large city should be.

The interaction of these two preconceived notions of urbanisation and the *hukou* system[7] has produced an urbanisation strategy that favours the growth of small cities at the expense of the growth of large cities. Lu and Wan (2014: 674) point out that this anti–big cities strategy has created many abnormalities such as:

> urbanization lagging behind development and industrialization status; urban land expanding much faster than urban population growth; open discrimination against migrants; a significant proportion of urban residents being excluded from urban society; and serious distortions in the urban system with too many small cities and too few big cities.

Since 2003, the central government has increased the share of land-use quotas allocated to the country's central and western regions to support their development. Liang et al. (2016: 70) found that this 'relative decline in land supply in the eastern regions' caused rapid growth of housing prices that were then accommodated by higher wages. The result of China's pro–small cities land policy is a reduction in the economic competitiveness of the eastern regions. Since the eastern regions are advantageously located for international trade, the land policy has decreased China's overall economic efficiency.

Furthermore, because 'the large cities are not large enough' (Lu and Wan 2014: 671), China's economic growth has insufficiently benefited from agglomeration effects. The primary agglomeration effect is human capital externality, the primary manifestation of which is multidimensional creativity, which, when appropriately harnessed, translates into efficiency gains across the board.

Gao and Lu (2015: 126) use probit models of employment determination to investigate the influence of city scale on employment levels. They find:

> A 1 percent increase in city scale increases one's employment probability by between 0.044 and 0.050 percentage points. Moreover, the scale advantage of big cities is heterogeneous among individuals with different levels of human capital, with the least-skilled workers benefiting the most.

The first reform that is necessary to support urbanisation as a driver of growth is to let the locational preferences of Chinese residents determine both the size distribution and the absolute size of cities. The state should limit its role to linking cities with adequate infrastructure and to treating all cities on an equitable basis. For example, one way to make housing more affordable in the most desired cities is to allow these cities to expand in land area according to demand.

7 The *hukou* system prevents mobility across locations and not just between urban and rural areas.

The second reform to maximise the growth effects of urbanisation is to phase out the *hukou* system to allow the size and composition of the urban population to reach their optimum values. We will have more to say about this correction in our discussion of the superstructure (software) reforms below.

Develop a modern financial system

Our third, interrelated new growth-oriented macro-tool is the true legalisation of privately owned financial institutions. First, the legalisation of private banks is fundamental to allowing the smooth working of the first two new growth drivers: the emergence of new dynamic entrepreneurs, and the emergence of an efficient mortgage market and thus a more rational pattern of urbanisation. Second, the legalisation of private banks is also an independent driver of growth in its own right.

The healthy development of new private banks would of course require that the system of prudential supervision be strengthened and that interest rates be deregulated.

The emergence of a strong small–medium banking sector will reduce the dominance of the state-controlled banks and hence make the economy less vulnerable to their collapse from potential NPLs. The entry of private banks (domestic and foreign) will reduce the probability of any one of the big four state banks remaining too big to fail, and hence reduce the soft-budget protection enjoyed by the monopoly state banking system. The development of a modern banking system with a major role for the private sector will therefore increase the quality and the quantity of bank loans. The replacement of the usual macro-stimulus of SOE-led investments with market-directed investments will reduce the generation of NPLs.

The software reform agenda

Former president Hu Jintao made the establishment of a 'harmonious society' the overarching objective of his administration. This emphasis reveals his judgement that the probability of a software failure is higher than the probability of a hardware failure because fixing the former is much more difficult.[8] There are two reasons for the greater difficulty. First, popular expectations of administrative performance have risen dramatically with income growth and, more importantly, with increasing knowledge of the outside world. Second, successful reconfiguration of the administrative software requires not just highly developed political skills, but also favourable circumstances in the domestic political arena and a benign international environment—both of which are beyond the reach of most politicians.

8 Judging from China's passive stance at the WTO negotiations in Potsdam in 2007 and its uncooperative position at the climate change conference in Copenhagen in 2009, power supply failure was not something that was on the radar screens of Hu Jintao or Wen Jiabao.

The satisfactory functioning of a market economy requires a wide array of regulatory institutions, ranging from straightforward administration of law and order to complicated legal adjudication. The lack of accountability (because of the absence of a mechanism for popular political competition) and the lack of transparency (the absence of a free press) have resulted in inefficient governance on many fronts. The ongoing anticorruption campaign that China has enforced since 2012 represents a serious attempt to improve governance.

Other important institutional reforms that should be started to enhance economic dynamism are reform of the *hukou* system and reform of rural landownership. These two reforms are really complementary and mutually reinforcing. The *hukou* system has created great disparities in access to public services (such as education, health care, public housing and social security) between cities and between urban and rural residents. For example, until recently, admission into almost all universities required lower academic scores for students who were legal residents in the towns in which the universities were located. This is particularly unfair to students who attend rural schools that are less well funded and less well staffed.

Many rural people are working in cities as residents with no *hukou* in these cities, leaving their rural residences mostly unoccupied and their rural farms untended. 'Permanent nonlocal labor without local *Hukou* has already exceeded a third of the total urban population in the big cities of the eastern region, and is over 50% in Guangdong', according to Lu and Wan (2014: 678). Because these migrant workers are usually not entitled to any public services, their children normally stay in the rural area with aged relatives, resulting in widespread underinvestment in the human capital of rural children.

The *hukou* system is grossly unfair as well as economically inefficient. We agree with the suggestion of Lu Ming and Wan Guanghua (2014: 678) that:

> Hukou reforms should be simultaneously advanced on two fronts. First, the thresholds for nonlocal residents to obtain local urban Hukou should be gradually lowered. Second, steady, moderate equalization in urban–rural and interregional basic public services should be promoted through central fiscal transfers.
>
> … Who should be granted local urban Hukou? The key is to give priority to those pursuing employment over those pursuing public services. Therefore, the criteria should mainly be employment and social security contribution records. One could use years of work and unbroken residence in one area as conditions for conferring Hukou. At the same time, educational level and professional qualifications should be removed from the list of requirements. For university graduates, their actual employment status, not their educational qualifications, should be used as conditions for entry.

> … [There should be] a series of parallel reforms in social security and public services. Portability of social security benefits is urgently needed, and the link between local Hukou and social security benefits needs to be weakened. The gap in social services between permanent residents with and without local Hukou should be narrowed through central fiscal transfers.

Presently, rural land is collectively owned, but the right to use the land is assigned to individuals, usually for 30 years. When the legal status of a rural resident changes to 'urban resident', this person loses their claim to the use of the piece of rural land assigned to them. Because of the large-scale privatisation of collectively owned assets in urban areas in the 1990s, many rural residents have the expectation that rural land will also one day be privatised. This expectation has therefore rendered many rural residents reluctant to accept legal urban resident status when offered.

Land in rural areas is divided between that for residential use and that for farming use, and the state decides the amount of land set aside for each. The administrative land area of a Chinese city contains land for urban construction and rural land (divided into residential use and farming use), and the amount of each type of land is set by the state.

There are many good reasons rural land should be privatised to existing leaseholders. One common objection to rural land privatisation is that it will increase inequality because rural land in poor provinces is worth a fraction of the rural land within the limits of big cities in the rich provinces. This objection is facetious because privatisation would mean formal recognition of existing inequalities in access to high-value land rather than the creation of more inequality. Privatisation of urban housing to the existing occupants and privatisation of small state enterprises to their staff occurred more than 20 years ago; it is hard to find economic or moral reasons to continue discriminating against rural residents.

If rural land cannot be privatised, China should adopt the 'mechanism to enable the trading of land usage rights' suggested by Lu and Wan (2014: 680):

> The core of our proposal is to enable long-term migrants to convert their rural residential land into construction-use land quotas which are then transferred to the city of their employment for urban expansion. The residential land at the origin is then restored into farmland. The migrants win as they obtain urban Hukou and associated benefits. The native urbanites also win because some of the gains from the appreciation of suburban land (as it becomes construction-use land) can be used to fund public services and social security for themselves as well as for new migrants. In fact, all parties involved will win …
>
> The population-inflow region's government represents local residents in obtaining a portion of the land appreciation gains while the population-outflow region's government also shares part of the gains as they restore abandoned residential land to farmland for productive use, which in turn provides revenues for funding

local public services to be enjoyed by those staying behind. To make this win-win proposal a reality, a nation-wide construction-use land quota trading system could be established, to maximize the gains from construction-use land usage rights while preserving sufficient land for farming or food security.

The policy agenda to avert power supply failures

At the China Update 2010 conference, Woo (2010) emphasised the importance of environmental protection in China and of harmonious international relations in enabling the rate of China's economic catch-up to remain high. China's severe air pollution shortens lifespans at home and in neighbouring countries, and China's management of water from the Tibetan Plateau affects the economic development in northern versus southern China and in its southern neighbours such as India, Thailand and Vietnam. The win-win solutions for most types of power supply failures will involve both technological breakthroughs and creative international diplomacy. In both cases, the probability of success is greatly increased when there is cooperation with foreign partners.

The global situation in 2017 requires that China doubles down on its cooperation with foreign actors because globalisation is now under threat and China is (arguably) the biggest beneficiary of globalisation. Popular dissatisfaction with different aspects of globalisation played an important part in the unexpected victories of the Brexit movement in the United Kingdom and the election of Donald Trump in the United States.

The British public could accept the free movement of goods and capital but could not countenance the free movement of people because of its threat to ethnic identity. The American white working class and white middle class in the rust belt had a lot to be resentful about: the loss of their manufacturing jobs to foreign imports and to relocation of production plants abroad, the potential dilution of their cultural identity by the inflow of immigrants, the venality of the US financial industry that caused many workers to lose their homes and savings, the unresponsiveness of the conservative political class to their need for assistance, the contemptuousness of the liberal political class towards their values relating to guns and religion and the blow to their national pride from the decline in the international standing of the United States.

Globalisation was seen as the process that brought many of these ills to American shores and also as the process that strengthened many of America's enemies. The deepening and widening of US interaction with China were perceived to be responsible for a significant part of the United States' problems. After all, even the ever-reasonable Ben Bernanke, former chairman of the US Federal Reserve, had identified surplus savings from China as one of the key factors in the meltdown of US financial markets in 2008.

Furthermore, China was also seen as the quiet ally of the seemingly mad North Korean regime and of the highly antagonistic Iranian theocracy, both of which constantly threaten the destruction of US allies. Seeking advantage from the growing Sino-phobia, candidate Trump promised to impose a 40 per cent tariff on Chinese imports and embraced the 'America first' economic agenda of US economist Peter Navarro (2015), who penned the conspiratorial tract *Crouching Tiger: What China's militarism means for the world.*

US President Donald Trump has stayed true to many of his key campaign promises so far—albeit in sometimes inscrutable ways. He confronted China at the beginning of his term by speaking with the Taiwanese President, but he then also ended former president Barack Obama's pivot to Asia by pulling the United States out of the TPP. Trump's gutting of the TPP is unfortunate because it denies the Association of Southeast Asian Nations (ASEAN) and Australia the option of adopting the formally neutral position of being in both the US-led TPP and the China-led Regional Comprehensive Economic Partnership (RCEP), effectively pushing them into de facto alliance with China.

For good measure, Trump also declared the withdrawal of the United States from the Paris Climate Treaty, expressed strong approval for Brexit, proposed rollbacks of prudential supervision of financial institutions and removed regulations on fossil fuel industries. Trump's eagerness to play the 'Ugly American'—for example, slamming down the phone on Australian Prime Minister Malcolm Turnbull and building the 'Great Wall' that Mexico would somehow be made to pay for—has left the world lacking adult leadership on the provision of global public goods. This vacuum in global leadership is threatening to unravel globalisation.

Even though it is true that the governance of globalisation by the major powers and international agencies has often been incompetent and unfair in many ways, we urge that the rollback of globalisation be resisted because we know that globalisation-induced socioeconomic problems can be solved without deglobalisation. Deepening globalisation does not require the less developed countries to fall even further under the thumb of the International Monetary Fund (IMF) (which acted as the collector of Latin American debt on behalf of the US banks in the 1980s and mishandled the Asian Financial Crisis in the 1990s)[9] nor does it require the strengthening of the two-decade trend in international trade agreements that favours multinational corporations at the expense of less developed countries (e.g. the removal of the adjudication of commercial disputes involving foreign investors from domestic courts to external private arbitration bodies).[10]

9 To be fair, the IMF has learned from its mistakes and improved its performance.

10 The Investor–State Dispute Settlement Mechanism reduces the regulatory space of the host country.

In the face of the US withdrawal from global roles, major countries in the G20, including China, should step up to the plate and change the governance of the international economy for the better, to prevent deglobalisation. We must keep in mind the conclusion of Charles Kindleberger in his magisterial book *The World in Depression, 1929–1939* that the mechanism responsible for the depth and length of the 1929 Great Depression was deglobalisation: 'When every country turned to protect its national private interest, the world public interest went down the drain, and with it the private interests of all' (Kindleberger 1973: 291).

The fundamental insight in Kindleberger's book is the hegemonic stability thesis. The ultimate reason the world experienced the Great Depression rather than a great recession, according to Kindleberger, was the absence of a benevolent hegemon during the period 1929–39—the absence of:

> a dominant economic power able and willing to take the interests of smaller powers and the operation of the larger international system into account by stabilising the flow of spending through the global or at least the North Atlantic economy, and doing so by acting as a lender and consumer of last resort. (DeLong and Eichengreen 2012)

The essence of the hegemonic stability thesis is that whenever the global economy is hit by sizeable shocks, it becomes unstable unless some country intervenes to stabilise it. The United Kingdom played that stabilising role in the nineteenth century and up to 1913, but, by 1929, it had declined to middle-power status and no longer had the overwhelming economic power to hold back collapsing global demand and to mobilise others to join countervailing actions. The United States in 1929 was not yet big enough to be the global hegemon, but, even if it had been, it was not mentally willing to take on that role. It was only after World War II that the United States became the unchallenged global hegemon and developed the mindset to play that role.

A global hegemon no longer exists in 2017 because the size of the Chinese economy measured in PPP dollars is now as large as the US economy. Will China emerge as the global hegemon in 2060 if it succeeds in catching up to the US standard of living by that time? The answer is no. If India maintains its present pace of economic catch-up, its economy in 2060 will be at least as big as China's. In 2060, the standard of living in India might still be lower than in China, but the Indian population will be significantly larger, making India's GDP as large as China's.

In brief, the world from this point would no longer have a monopoly economic power that could act as the global hegemon. An oligopolistic distribution of economic power would henceforth be the norm: China–United States–European Union in 2017 and India–China–United States–European Union in 2060.[11]

11 The bold prediction here is that the European Union will have achieved total political integration by 2060.

The new international normal is a multipolar world. From the lens of the hegemonic stability thesis, this is a terrible development because a leaderless world is prone to adopting self-defeating protectionism. The world is now facing the challenge of Karl Marx's (1852) observation that 'History repeats itself, first as tragedy and then as farce'.

The most common outcome in a situation of oligopolistic distribution of power is the division of the world into spheres of influence because of the security concerns of each major power. The present squabbles in Ukraine and the South China Sea could be the beginning of this process. However, it could be a mistake to see the future as a replay of the past; it would certainly signal a lack of imagination if we were to do so.

With the right regional arrangements and interregional agreements in place to address the security concerns of each major power, a new form of benign globalisation could emerge. The sphere of influence of each major power could become a geographical cluster for economic development and not a geographical cluster for economic exploitation (as between Africa and Europe in the first half of the twentieth century) or a geographical cluster for political domination (as between Eastern Europe and the Soviet Union in the second half of the twentieth century). Given the existence of economies of scale in production, every geographical cluster must practise open regionalism to maximise economic prosperity. Existing global institutions such as the United Nations and its agencies, the World Bank, the IMF and the G20 will have the additional task of regional coordination to ensure global economic integration.

Each major power would be the chief funder of economic institutions in its own cluster—for example, the European Stabilisation Fund, the Asian Infrastructure Investment Bank (AIIB) and the Inter-American Development Bank. The existence of competing/complementary regional institutions means there are multiple independent analytical centres in the world instead of a monopoly international financial institution and a monopoly international development bank. This outcome would minimise the possibility of wrong diagnoses and/or the wrong prescriptions, avoiding a repeat of the mistakes made by the IMF and the World Bank in the past.

As China will continue to grow in relative size, it can play an important role in making collective leadership for global governance successful and in fostering the creation of these clusters for economic development. China's engagement with its neighbours through the 'One Belt, One Road' initiative, the AIIB and the RCEP is very much in line with a multipolar world in which each development-oriented cluster practises open regionalism.[12] However, for globalisation to deepen and widen, China must take greater leadership in the supply of global public goods such as fighting climate change and species extinction, stopping nuclear proliferation

12 For a good recent discussion of the foreign aid practices of China, see Johnston and Rudyak (2016).

and international terrorism, stabilising the international monetary system by internationalising the RMB to broaden the choice of reserve currencies to reduce currency risks from globalisation, and getting the world to agree to a worldwide minimum tax rate on capital to prevent a race to the bottom in financing social safety nets.

The new international normal of a multipolar world would necessarily mean the political and economic fragmentation of the post–World War II global order. There is, however, good fragmentation as well as bad fragmentation. Good fragmentation protects globalisation in a setting of effective collective leadership and bad fragmentation is the situation in which Kindleberger's hegemonic stability thesis applies and Marx's dictum on repetitive history rules.

Final remarks

China has now achieved middle-income status through the marketisation and internationalisation of its economy. The internal economic conditions in China have also changed: the supply of surplus labour is exhausted, the demographic dividend is ending, and the natural environment is under severe stress. This outcome creates a new domestic normal that requires the creation of reform dividends to drive growth. Specifically, China must undertake: 1) structural reform of economic mechanisms such as rationalising the SOE sector and deregulating the markets for capital, labour and land; 2) structural reform of governance institutions such as administrative accountability, the *hukou* system and rural landownership; and 3) structural reform of institutional incentives to protect the environment. These three sets of reform measures in response to the new domestic normal comprise what we call 'supply-side structural reform 1.0'.

At the same time, the global picture that China faces has changed, and this change is part of China's making. The architecture of global governance that rested on the hegemonic stability provided by the United States is crumbling because China's rise has ended the days when the US had such overwhelming economic power that it could impose order on economic dwarfs. The inevitable emergence of India as a global superpower guarantees that hegemonic stability will stay in the garbage bin of history. A multipolar world is now the new international normal.

Having helped bury hegemonic stability, China must now help make collective global leadership work by expanding Hu Jintao's concept of a harmonious society to the concept of a harmonious world. Out of enlightened self-interest, China must help mobilise the world to work together to protect the global environmental commons, the global trading system and global security; and to promote continued globalisation to maximise the synergy for global progress created by interaction.

Finally, the 1992 *nanxun*-inspired[13] economic strategy that has so impressively transformed China for the better is no longer adequate because China today faces a new set of domestic conditions (the new domestic normal) and a new set of international challenges (the new international normal). For China to avoid the middle-income trap, it must now take a path of dynamic sustainable development to continue the process of economic catch-up. In this chapter, we have provided a sketch of such a strategy under the new domestic normal and the new international normal, which we call supply-side structural reform 2.0.

Chinese and world socioeconomic progress, as well as the necessity for environmental protection, require decisive reforms in both the structure of domestic incentives[14] that determines domestic production, and in the structure of international governance[15] that determines the provision of global public goods.[16]

In a multipolar world, the business-as-usual outcome is the partition of the world into competing spheres of influence where deglobalisation is the by-product. However, if enlightened self-interests prevail in the major countries, the outcome will instead be geographical clusters for sustainable economic development based on the principle of open regionalism. The world is likely to be now at the critical point where each of the major powers is choosing either to be enlightened enough to act according to its long-term interests or to be cynical and continue to play the usual zero-sum *realpolitik* game. The outcome of benign globalisation in a multipolar world need not be a dream.

References

Barshefsky, C. (2017), Barshefsky: China stepped up reform push reversals, [video], *The Wall Street Journal Video*, 15 May. Available from: www.wsj.com/video/barshefsky-china-stepped-up-reform-push-reversals/E64003AE-5D47-4569-BF3E-6683A8D546B2.html.

Cai, F. (2011), Aging before affluence in China, *Project Syndicate*, 19 October.

13 *Nanxun* refers to the tour of Southern China by Deng Xiaoping in 1992, in which he re-ignited the process of economic reform and opening by rejecting absolutely the applicability of Soviet-style central planning to the Chinese economy.

14 For example, rural land and urbanisation policies.

15 For example, regional financial institutions, international maritime resources oversight bodies, and global climate agencies.

16 We hope over the coming year to make progress on research that will flesh out more of the Supply-Side Structural Reform 2.0 program, and that will, hopefully, be worthy of inclusion in the China Update 2018 meeting of the China Economy Program of the Crawford School at The Australian National University in Canberra.

Cai, F. and Yang, L. (2013), The end of China's demographic dividend: The perspective of potential GDP growth, in R. Garnaut, F. Cai and L. Song (eds), *China: A new model for growth and development*, pp. 55–74, Canberra: ANU E Press.

Cheng, J. (2017), Former US trade representative urges renegotiation with China, *The Wall Street Journal*, 15 May. Available from: www.wsj.com/articles/former-u-s-trade-representative-urges-renegotiation-with-china-1494898590.

DeLong, B. and Eichengreen, B. (2012), New preface to Charles Kindleberger, 'The World in Depression, 1929–1939', 12 June, *VOX: CEPR's Policy Portal*, Centre for Economic Policy Research, London. Available from: voxeu.org/article/new-preface-charles-kindleberger-world-depression-1929-1939.

Gao, H. and Lu, M. (2015), Inclusive urban employment: How does city scale affect job opportunities for different people? *Asian Economic Papers* 14(2): 98–128. doi.org/10.1162/ASEP_a_00352.

Jin, K. (2016a), Overhauling China, *Project Syndicate*, 2 November.

Jin, K. (2016b), Xi Jinping is no Mao Zedong, *Project Syndicate*, 4 August.

Johnston, L. and Rudyak, M. (2016), China's 'innovative and pragmatic' foreign aid: Shaped by and now shaping globalization, Paper presented at China: Wealth and Power conference, College of Asia and the Pacific, The Australian National University, Canberra, 7–8 April.

Johnston, L., Liu, X., Yang, M. and Zhang, X. (2016), Getting rich after getting old: China's demographic and economic transition in dynamic international context, in R. Garnaut, L. Song, F. Cai and L. Johnston (eds), *China's New Sources of Economic Growth. Volume 1: Reform, resources and climate change*, pp. 215–46, Canberra: ANU Press.

Kindleberger, C. (1973), *The World in Depression, 1929–39*, Berkeley: University of California Press.

Liang, W., Lu, M. and Zhang, H. (2016), Housing prices raise wages: Estimating the unexpected effects of land supply regulation in China, *Journal of Housing Economics* 33: 70–81. doi.org/10.1016/j.jhe.2016.07.002.

Lin, J. Y. (2015), How fast will China grow? *Project Syndicate*, 29 January.

Lin, J. Y. (2016), Why China can grow according to plan, *Project Syndicate*, 25 March.

Lu, M. (2015), *Myths and realities of China's urbanization*, Paulson Policy Memorandum, 18 August, Paulson Institute, Chicago.

Lu, M. and Wan, G. (2014), Urbanization and urban systems in the People's Republic of China: Research findings and policy recommendations, *Journal of Economic Surveys* 28(4): 671–85. doi.org/10.1111/joes.12078.

Marx, K. (1852), The eighteenth brumaire of Louis Napoleon, *Die Revolution*. Available from: www.marxists.org/archive/marx/works/1852/18th-brumaire/ch01.htm.

Navarro, P. (2015), *Crouching Tiger: What China's militarism means for the world*, Amherst, NY: Prometheus Books.

Roach, S. (2016), The world economy without China, *Project Syndicate*, 24 October.

Sheng, A. and Xiao, G. (2016), Beyond structural reform in China, *Project Syndicate*, 29 July.

Spence, M. and Hu, F. (2016), China's volatile growth, *Project Syndicate*, 28 February.

Tan, Y., Huang, Y. and Woo, W. T. (2016), Zombie firms and the crowding-out of private investment in China, *Asian Economic Papers* 15(3): 32–55. doi.org/10.1162/ASEP_a_00474.

Wong, C. H. (2017), China's President Xi casts country as guardian of globalization, *The Wall Street Journal*, 14 May.

Woo, W. T. (2001), Recent claims of China's economic exceptionalism: Reflections inspired by WTO accession, *China Economic Review* 12(2–3): 107–36. doi.org/10.1016/S1043-951X(01)00047-5.

Woo, W. T. (2010), Avoiding economic crashes on China's road to prosperity, in R. Garnaut, J. Golley and L. Song (eds), *China: The next twenty years of reform and development*, pp. 269–92, Canberra: ANU E Press.

Woo, W. T. (2012), China meets the middle-income trap: The large potholes in the road to catching-up, *Journal of Chinese Economic and Business Studies* 10(4): 313–36. doi.org/10.1080/14765284.2012.724980.

Woo, W. T. (2016), The demand-side supplement to supply-side structural reform: Termination of the soft-budget constraint, in R. Garnaut, L. Song, F. Cai and L. Johnston (eds), *China's New Sources of Economic Growth: Reform, resources and climate change*, pp. 139–58, Canberra: ANU Press. doi.org/10.2139/ssrn.2798763.

Xi, J. (2017), President Xi's speech to Davos in full, World Economic Forum, Davos, Switzerland, 17 January. Available from: www.weforum.org/agenda/2017/01/full-text-of-xi-jinping-keynote-at-the-world-economic-forum.

Yu, Y. (2016a), China's next stimulus, *Project Syndicate*, 24 March.

Yu, Y. (2016b), China's incomplete growth strategy, *Project Syndicate*, 25 May.

Zhang, J. (2016a), China's painful structural transformation, *Project Syndicate*, 19 August.

Zhang, J. (2016b), Three threats to China's economy, *Project Syndicate*, 28 October.

Zhou, X. (2016), China heading for big economic policy shift, says mystery 'authoritative' source in People's Daily, *South China Morning Post*, 9 May.

Part II: Education and Human Capital

6. Educating 'the Masses' in China: Unequal Opportunities and Unequal Outcomes

Jane Golley and Sherry Tao Kong

Introduction

Following a staggering growth rate of 10 per cent per annum between 1979 and 2010, China's growth has steadily decelerated over the past five years, from 7.9 per cent in 2012 to 6.7 per cent in 2016. Yet it remains by far the fastest-growing major economy in the world. In the decades ahead, China aims to sustain its progress of development and to advance from middle-income to high-income status by mid-century. The road towards this ambitious goal is mapped out by a comprehensive reform plan, geared towards switching from a reliance on an abundance of cheap labour to a more innovative, skilled workforce. The success of this transition will require concerted effort on various fronts, among which significant improvements in human capital will be critical.

Compared with the high-income-country group that China aspires to join, the education level of China's current labour force is shockingly poor. As of 2010, the share of China's labour force that had ever attended senior high school (24 per cent) is less than one-third of the average upper secondary attainment rate in Organisation for Economic Co-operation and Development (OECD) countries (Khor et al. 2016). Moreover, as this chapter will demonstrate, there is a substantial degree of inequality of educational opportunity across China's cities and countryside, as well as across a number of other dimensions. While successive generations of Chinese children are better educated than their parents, these unequal opportunities will constrain the country's human capital potential in the decades ahead.

Inequality of opportunity in education (or in any other measure of economic 'advantage') is quite distinct from inequality in educational outcomes. In particular, while there is no clear consensus as to what constitutes the 'optimal' or 'ideal' level of inequality in outcomes, there is broad consensus that inequality resulting from unequal 'effort' is ethically acceptable, while inequality resulting from unequal 'circumstances' or opportunities—which lie beyond the control of an individual—is not.

A rapidly growing literature has used this idea as the basis for measuring the extent of inequality of opportunity for a range of economic outcomes—including per capita income, earnings, wealth, consumption and health—in a wide range of countries, confirming that the ideal of equality of opportunity is by far the exception, not the rule. Ferreira and Gignoux (2011), for example, in their analysis of six Latin American countries, find that the share of inequality of opportunity in outcome inequality is substantial, ranging from 23 per cent in Colombia to 34 per cent in Guatemala for household per capita income. Zhang and Eriksson (2010) likewise find a very high share of inequality of opportunity in individual income inequality in China—increasing steadily from 46 per cent in 1989 to 63 per cent in 2006. These papers identify a range of 'circumstances' that contribute to inequality of opportunity, with one's place of birth, gender and parental education levels almost always playing significant roles.

In this chapter, we take it as given that equality of opportunity—as opposed to equality of outcomes—has indisputable merit, and set out to examine the extent to which the educational outcomes of Chinese citizens born between 1940 and 1989 diverge from this ideal. For a country intent on raising the level of human capital to support productivity, growth and a higher value-added economy in the future, equality of opportunity seems like a very good place to start.

The next section introduces the methodology used to calculate inequality of opportunity and identifies the set of 'circumstance' variables that we use to measure this in the case of China's educational attainment (measured in years of schooling), using the China Family Panel Studies (CFPS) surveys for 2010 and 2012. The following section confirms the importance of these variables using regressions for the nationwide sample, and separately for the urban and rural samples, as a way of assessing the unequal opportunities not only between urban and rural populations, but also within them. We then present the key empirical results regarding inequality of opportunity in education in China, before concluding with some policy implications.

Measuring 'inequality of opportunity'

Method

Attempts to measure 'inequality of opportunity' begin with the premise that the observed inequality in any particular economic outcome can be attributed to two components. The first component derives from the different circumstances in which individuals find themselves and over which they have no control—for example, their gender, place of birth or the socioeconomic status of their parents. The second derives from the different levels of effort that individuals may exert to influence a given outcome—for example, how hard they study. This distinction has long been recognised as critical for assessing the extent to which equal opportunity does or does not prevail.

In his seminal paper, Roemer (1998) defines equality of opportunity as a situation in which the distribution of a given outcome is independent of circumstances or, in other words, that all individuals who exert the same effort would achieve the same outcome, regardless of their circumstances. Partitioning the population into groups or 'types' of people with identical circumstances and measuring the extent to which this condition is *not* satisfied provide one measure of inequality of opportunity. An alternative, weaker criterion for equality of opportunity is that the mean outcome levels—rather than the entire distributions—are identical across types, as proposed by Van de Gaer (1993). This criterion involves suppressing 'intra-type' inequality and calculating the extent of 'between-type' inequality based on the mean levels for each type as a measure of inequality of opportunity.

These ideas have been developed and applied in a burgeoning empirical literature that adopts a range of methods to measure the degree of inequality of opportunity in a range of countries and for a range of different outcomes.[1] Here, we follow the methodology of Ferreira and Gignoux (2011), which has emerged as the most common approach,[2] adapting it to suit our economic advantage of interest: years of education.

In particular, we begin with a stylised model of advantage (here, years of schooling) of the form $y = f(C, E, u)$, where C is a vector of circumstance variables, E is a vector of effort variables and u represents random unobserved variables. While circumstances are exogenous by definition (that is, they cannot be influenced by any actions of the individual), it is likely that effort will be influenced by a range of factors, including circumstances.[3] This implies that the model is more accurately expressed as $y = f(C, E(C, v), u)$. For a number of reasons, touched on further below (and expanded on at length in Ferreira and Gignoux 2011), we choose to treat effort as unobserved and estimate the reduced-form regression (Equation 6.1).

Equation 6.1

$$y_i = \beta \boldsymbol{C}_i + \varepsilon$$

1 For alternative approaches, see Checchi and Peragine (2010); Lefranc et al. (2008); Bourguignon et al. (2007).

2 For some key examples, see the survey by Brunori et al. (2013); also Bourguignon et al. (2007); Marrero and Rodríguez (2012); Singh (2012). For a more detailed discussion, see Golley and Kong (in press).

3 For example, it could be the case that less-educated rural parents place less pressure on their children to study hard, encouraging them instead to leave school early because of the financial burden and opportunity cost of keeping them in school. Yi et al. (2012) provide some evidence of this in their analysis of why students in poor rural areas in China are failing to complete junior high (using a survey of 7,800 students in 2009 and 2010).

In Equation 6.1, y_i is the years of schooling attained by individual i, and $\boldsymbol{C}_i$ is a vector of discrete circumstance variables pertaining to that individual, which allows a partition into types as described above. For example, if there were just two circumstance variables—gender and *hukou* (household registration) status—there would be a total of four 'types': rural boys, rural girls, urban boys and urban girls. Using the estimated coefficients, $\hat{\beta}$, and the actual values of circumstances, we construct a distribution, $\{\hat{y}\}$, in which $\hat{y}_i = \hat{\beta}\boldsymbol{C}_i$. That is, y is replaced with its prediction, *given the vector of circumstances*, which is identical for all individuals in any given type, thus eliminating all intra-group inequality. This gives us an *absolute* scalar measure of inequality of opportunity, $IOA = I(\{\hat{y}\})$. The corresponding *relative* measure, $IOR = I\{\hat{y}\}/I\{y\}$, determines inequality of opportunity as a share of total inequality, for an appropriate inequality measure, I.

Only certain indexes of inequality satisfy the critical property of additive decomposability that enables total inequality to be decomposed into its between-type and intra-type components—including the generalised entropy class, but not the Gini coefficient. Neither GE(0) (mean log deviation) nor GE(1) (the Theil entropy index) is an option for measuring inequality in educational outcomes as they both involve log values and there are many individuals with no years of schooling (which is not the case in the more standard analyses focused on earnings or consumption). This leaves GE(2), half the coefficient of variation, as the best scalar measure of inequality, which we use below.

We are also interested in the partial contributions of each of the circumstance variables. To assess these, we produce a counterfactual distribution, $\hat{y}^J$, where $\hat{y}_i^J = \hat{\beta}\boldsymbol{C}_i^{j\neq J} + \beta\overline{\boldsymbol{C}}_i^{\,j=J}$, which assigns the mean level of circumstance J to all individuals, one circumstance at a time. Note that the corresponding partial measures of both the absolute and the relative inequality of opportunity—the latter being $IOR_P = I\{(\hat{y}^J\}/I(\{y\}$—will be *lower* for a variable that has a *larger* impact on inequality of opportunity. That is, by eliminating the variation in that variable, inequality of opportunity will fall by a greater amount.

Whatever the number of circumstance variables included in the regression above, an important property of the estimates for *IOA* and *IOR* is that they are lower-bound estimates of inequality of opportunity.[4] This is because the vector of observed circumstances will necessarily be a subset of all relevant circumstances that impact on individual outcomes, with the implication that the estimates for *IOA* and *IOR* would be higher if unobserved circumstances were added to the vector *C*. This lower-bound result, however, applies only to the overall measures of *IOA* and *IOR*. In particular, excessive weighting will be attributed to an observable circumstance if

4 For a formal proof, see Ferreira and Gignoux (2011).

it is correlated with an unobservable or omitted one. In this case, $\hat{\beta}$ will still provide a reasonable measure of all the factors that are linked to the observable circumstances, but it means that the partial estimates, IOR_p, should be treated with caution.

Our decision to treat effort as unobserved is for both practical and logical reasons. We can think of only one variable—hours of study—that could possibly be classified as effort when educational attainment is the outcome of interest, and which is necessarily omitted, as it is not recorded in the survey data utilised below. Whether this is treated as an omitted 'effort' variable or an omitted 'circumstance' variable, however, the implications are the same. In particular, either it has no correlation with the observed circumstance variables, in which case its omission will not impact on the inequality of opportunity estimates, or it is itself impacted by observed circumstances, in which case this impact will be *indirectly* incorporated into the estimated coefficients. While this again points to the need for caution in interpreting the regression coefficients as *causal* links between a given circumstance and the outcome, it is not critical to the measurement of inequality of opportunity, which is the primary concern of this chapter. For a more in-depth discussion on this point, see Golley and Kong (in press).

Which circumstances matter?

Throughout the era of the People's Republic, China has achieved remarkable advances in expanding its education system and raising the average level of education achieved by its vast population. However, these advances have also resulted in significant educational inequalities along a number of dimensions.

The most prominent dimension of these inequalities is the rural–urban divide, which was solidified by the introduction of the *hukou* system of household registration in the late 1950s, and which effectively divided—and continues to divide—Chinese citizens into two distinct groups, with starkly different access to China's expanding education system. An extensive literature has documented the persistent gap in educational attainments between urban and rural China since this time, with weaknesses in the rural education system reflected in higher dropout rates and lower participation at every level of the system, from preschool through to college (see Qiao 2008; Wang et al. 2009; Golley and Kong 2012, 2013; Knight et al. 2012; Yi et al. 2012; Wu 2013; Li et al. 2015).

Another critical dimension of educational inequality in China—and in a large number of other countries as well—stems from intergenerational persistence in educational attainment.[5] An ongoing debate centres on the extent to which this

5 See, in particular, Hertz et al.'s (2007) study of 50-year time trends in 42 countries, and also Checchi et al. (2008) and Black and Devereux (2010).

observed persistence is directly causal (for example, the likelihood that better-educated parents may have greater intellectual capacity *because* of their own education, rather than because of their innate ability, to invest in educating their children) as opposed to *indirectly* causal (for example, due to higher genetic intelligence or the greater financial capacity of parents with higher incomes to invest in higher-quality schools) (Black and Devereux 2010). The reason for persistence is not central to the analysis here. Suffice to say that, in its presence, children with better-educated parents find themselves in a relatively enviable circumstance with regard to their prospects, or opportunities, for educational advancement. There is ample evidence to suggest that this is the case in China (see Golley and Kong 2012, 2013; Knight et al. 2012).

The observed persistence in educational attainment across generations feeds into the importance of family origin or socioeconomic status more generally, which has been shown to be of particular significance in China during both the Maoist era (see, for example, Deng and Treiman 1997; Meng and Gregory 2002; Sato and Li 2008) and beyond. A wealth of evidence concurs that during the reform era, the educational advantages of the 'dominant' or higher socioeconomic classes—whether measured in terms of parents' class origins, Communist Party membership, educational levels, occupations or incomes—have been restored and strengthened, with educational inequalities increasing as a result.[6]

The literature reveals a number of other dimensions that have contributed to a widening gap between the most and the least advantaged members of society: across regions, provinces and counties (with children in richer areas achieving higher education levels on average) (Hannum and Wang 2006; Heckmann 2005; Zhang and Kanbur 2005), between different ethnic groups (Hannum 2002) (with Han Chinese maintaining their traditional lead), between genders (Zhang et al. 2007; Zhang and Chen 2014) (with girls being out-educated by boys across all educational levels at nearly all points in time) and between children from families of varying size—invoking Becker and Lewis's (1973) 'quantity–quality trade-off' (see Li et al. 2008; Rosenzweig and Zhang 2009).

Crucially, all the dimensions identified above are essentially 'circumstances' into which each individual is born, rather than facing by choice: their *hukou* status (in childhood), father's education, parents' socioeconomic status, province of birth, ethnicity, gender and the number of siblings they have all fall into this category.

We use the CFPS survey, which is a nationally representative biannual longitudinal survey of Chinese communities, families and individuals produced by the Institute of Social Science Survey (ISSS) of Peking University. The CFPS collects individual, family and community-level longitudinal data covering a wide range of economic

6 For a few of the countless examples, see: Zhou et al. (1998); Liu (2006); Sato and Li (2008); Wu (2009); Emran and Sun (2015); Zhang and Chen (2014).

activities, education outcomes, family dynamics and relationships, migration and health. In the 2010 baseline survey, the CFPS successfully interviewed 14,960 households and 42,590 individuals, with an approximate response rate of 79 per cent. Respondents are tracked through annual follow-up surveys, and we draw on the 2012 survey to take advantage of the supplementary parental information that is missing from the 2010 baseline dataset.

Given the available data, we select the following set of circumstance variables: father's education level, for which we use three dummy variables—primary school, junior high and senior high and above (with illiteracy as the fourth, excluded category); *hukou* status at age 12 (urban = 1); gender (male = 1); parents' Communist Party membership (= 1 if either parent is a member); number of siblings (dummy variables for one or two siblings and three or more siblings, with only children as the third, excluded category); ethnic minority status (= 1 if Han Chinese, 0 for others); and province (with Beijing as the excluded category). To account for the significant variation in educational policies and outcomes over time, we also include dummy variables for each of 10 five-year birth cohorts, from 1940–44 through to 1985–89, before running separate regressions for each of these cohorts. We further investigate the determinants of educational outcomes—and the sources of inequality of opportunity—within the rural and urban subsamples.

Due to data limitations, we do not include parental income or occupation, which, along with education levels, are indicators of socioeconomic status. We also exclude mother's education level because of the high degree of 'marriage matching' observed in China, and hence the high correlation between parents' education levels (Knight et al. 2012). These variables are hence treated as omitted circumstance variables, which, if correlated with the included variables, will bias their estimated coefficients. This seems most likely for father's education. While this means we need to be careful interpreting the coefficients on the fathers' education dummies, it is not problematic for our estimate of inequality of opportunity; it just means that it is a lower-bound result, as discussed above.

Some preliminary statistics for these variables are shown in Table 6.1. This confirms the educational gaps between each of the circumstance variables across the entire national sample, and within the urban and rural samples as well. Not surprisingly, average years of schooling are higher for urban children, boys, Han Chinese, only children and children with parents who are Communist Party members.

One final point worth noting is that our classification of rural or urban based on *hukou* status 'at the age of 12' means that virtually all migrants remain 'rural' in the analysis here, with the rural sample accounting for 84 per cent of the total. This is indicative of just how rapid urbanisation has been in recent decades, given a 2013 split of 36–64 per cent for urban and rural *hukou* holders, respectively, and an even greater share of the population actually living in urban areas, at 54 per cent.

Table 6.1 Preliminary statistics

Education (%)	Nationwide	Urban	Rural
Illiterate	22.7	3.7	26.6
Primary school	20.8	6.0	23.8
Junior high school	32.0	29.4	32.5
Senior high school	13.8	28.5	10.8
College and above	10.8	32.4	6.4
Average schooling (years)	7.4	11.5	6.6
Male (YES = 1, %)	51.3	51.4	51.2
Male average schooling (years)	8.1	11.6	7.4
Female average schooling (years)	6.7	11.4	5.8
Father's education (%)			
Illiterate (no schooling)	44.9	22.3	49.4
Primary school	27.4	26.0	27.7
Junior high school	16.8	23.9	15.4
Senior high school	8.6	18.3	6.6
College and above	2.4	9.6	0.9
Father's average schooling (years)	4.5	7.3	3.9
Parents party member (YES = 1, %)	12.9	22.2	11.1
Party member average schooling (years)	9.0	12.4	7.7
Non-party member average schooling (years)	7.2	11.2	6.5
Family size (%)			
Only child	8.9	23.0	6.0
One or two siblings	40.5	43.2	40.0
Three or more siblings	50.6	33.9	54.0
Only child average schooling (years)	10.0	13.3	7.4
One or two siblings average schooling (years)	8.4	11.7	7.8
Three or more siblings average schooling (years)	6.2	10.1	5.7
Han Chinese (YES = 1, %)	89.3	94.4	88.4
Han average schooling (years)	7.7	11.4	6.9
Minority average schooling (years)	5.4	12.1	4.7
No. of observations	25,937	4,364	21,573

Note: All figures are weighted by CFPS sample weights to be nationally representative.

Sources: CFPS (2010, 2012).

Unequal educational outcomes and their determinants

Before presenting the inequality of opportunity results, this section presents a general picture of trends in educational outcomes across birth cohorts, and their determinants. Figure 6.1 illustrates the rise in average years of schooling attained by successive generations in China, from just 3.9 years for the oldest cohort to 10.1 years for the youngest one nationwide, with children in each cohort being 'out-educated' compared with their parents by a large margin. While these average gains are impressive, the figure also shows the persistent gap between the rural and urban populations, peaking at 5.6 years for the 1950–54 cohort and with still a substantial gap of 4.1 years for the youngest cohort.

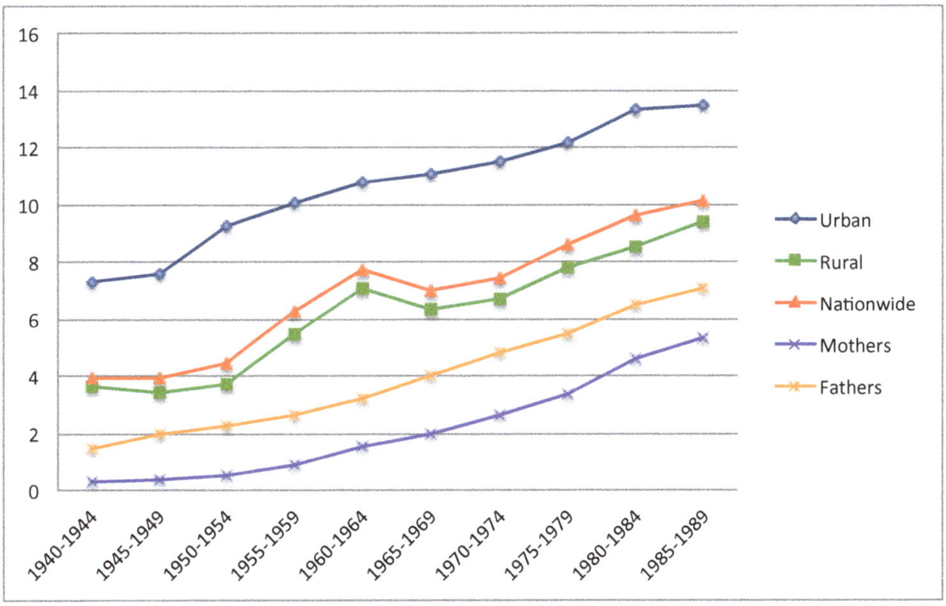

Figure 6.1 Years of schooling across two generations, 1940–89

Sources: CFPS (2010, 2012) and authors' calculations.

The distributions of educational outcomes for the urban and rural populations are illustrated in Figures 6.2a and 6.2b, respectively. For the urban population, the most striking increase has been at the college level, accounting for just 11 per cent of the 1940–44 cohort compared with 61 per cent of the 1985–89 cohort. The reduction in the urban shares of people either receiving no education (i.e. illiterate) or completing only primary school also stands out, falling from 25 per cent and 24 per cent to 1.7 per cent and 2.1 per cent, respectively, from the oldest to the youngest cohort.

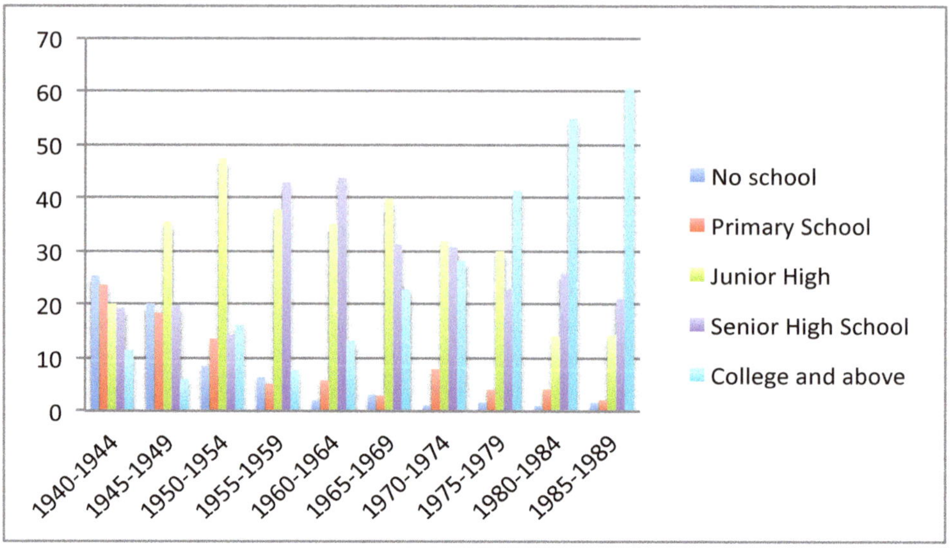

Figure 6.2a Educational attainment, urban China (per cent)

Sources: CFPS (2010, 2012) and authors' calculations.

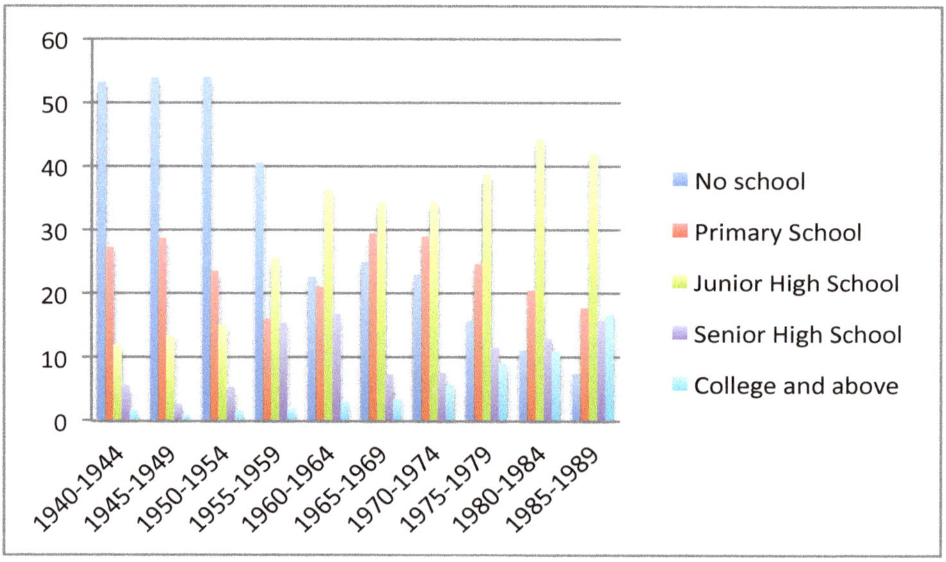

Figure 6.2b Educational attainment, rural China (per cent)

Sources: CFPS (2010, 2012) and authors' calculations.

For the rural population, the most dramatic change is the reduction in illiteracy, declining from a peak of 54 per cent of the 1945–49 cohort to 7.5 per cent of the youngest cohort. Until the 1960s cohorts, the share of those completing college remained below 4 per cent, increasing substantially since then but still remarkably lower than the equivalent urban share, at just 16.8 per cent for the 1985–89 cohort. As discussed at length in an earlier China Update book (Golley and Kong 2012), the dominant educational attainment in rural China is junior high, remaining at 42 per cent for the youngest cohort.

Table 6.2 presents our chosen measure of inequality in educational outcomes, GE(2), for the national, urban and rural samples (in Column 1) and for each of the 10 five-year cohorts (also illustrated in Figure 6.3). Panel A reveals the overall downward trend in nationwide outcome inequality beginning with the 1945–49 cohort, with the only increase coming between the 1960–64 and 1965–69 cohorts. These trends broadly mirror the rural ones in Panel C—which is to be expected given the dominance of people classified as rural in the sample—and are notably higher than the urban measures for all cohorts. The urban measures in Panel B reveal a steady decline through to the 1960–64 cohort, fluctuating at low levels thereafter.

For comparative purposes, Table 6.2 also presents the Gini coefficients as an alternative measure of outcome inequality,[7] and one that is more easily interpreted. Importantly, the trends across birth cohorts are the same as those for GE(2) in all three panels, and the values for the rural sample are consistently and substantially higher than those for the urban sample, with values lying between 0.09 for the youngest urban cohort and 0.59 for the 1945–49 rural cohort. The key point here is that the distributions of rural and urban educational outcomes—whether described in terms of the population shares in each education level or summarised as a scalar inequality measure—are significantly different from each other and vary substantially across birth cohorts.

A further point worth noting is that while lower inequality in the urban sample is coupled with higher educational outcomes, this need not necessarily be the case. For example, a Gini of zero would be recorded if all individuals had identical educational outcomes, whether that was illiteracy or college-level education, while if one individual held a PhD, or indeed any positive level of schooling, and the rest of the population was illiterate, the Gini would be one. In this sense, it is impossible to say categorically that any particular level of outcome inequality is better or worse than another. This is what makes measures of inequality of opportunity so valuable, as they reflect the part of inequality that is, quite simply, unjust.

7 The Gini coefficient's lack of additive decomposability is not problematic for examining total inequality of *outcome*; it just means that it cannot be used for the decomposition exercise below.

Table 6.2 Inequality in educational outcomes

Cohort	1940–49	1940–44	1945–49	1950–54	1955–59	1960–64	1965–69	1970–74	1975–79	1980–84	1985–89
Panel A: Nationwide											
GE(E)	0.21	0.62	0.59	0.54	0.31	0.16	0.20	0.18	0.13	0.10	1.09
Gini	0.35	0.59	0.57	0.56	0.44	0.30	0.34	0.33	0.28	0.25	0.22
Panel B: Urban											
GE(2)	0.05	0.25	0.17	0.08	0.06	0.03	0.04	0.04	0.04	0.03	0.03
Gini	0.17	0.40	0.32	0.21	0.16	0.13	0.15	0.16	0.15	0.13	0.12
Panel C: Rural											
GE(2)	0.24	0.66	0.66	0.67	0.39	0.19	0.22	0.21	0.15	0.11	0.09
Gini	0.38	0.60	0.60	0.61	0.49	0.33	0.36	0.35	0.29	0.25	0.23

Sources: CFPS (2010, 2012) and authors' calculations.

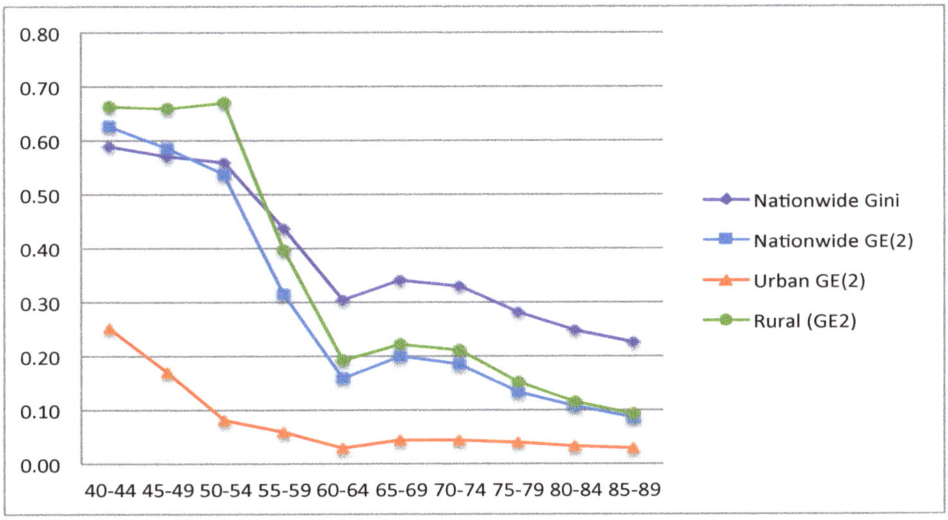

Figure 6.3 Inequality of educational outcomes by cohort

Sources: CFPS (2010, 2012) and authors' calculations.

Table 6.3 presents the results of the regressions based on Equation 6.1, conducted for the national sample, and separately for the urban and rural samples. Column 1 presents the nationwide results, with all coefficients taking on their expected signs and being highly significant at the 1 per cent level, with the exception of the 1950–54 birth cohort dummy. Most notably, urban *hukou* status is still associated with an additional three years of schooling (compared with five years in the raw data). It is also clear that better-educated fathers have better-educated children, with primary school, junior high and senior high and above associated with (if not directly causing) an additional 1.6, 2.2 and 3.2 years of schooling, respectively, compared with their illiterate counterparts. Provincial dummies (not reported here for space reasons) are all highly significant and negative, with the exception of Shanghai's (which is insignificant), with the years of education attained in Beijing exceeding those in Jiangxi, Sichuan and Guizhou by more than three years. The coefficients for the birth cohorts reflect the nationwide trends in educational attainment illustrated in Figure 6.1—generally rising across birth cohorts, with the exception of the 1945–49 and 1965–69 cohorts.

Columns 2 and 3 use the same set of variables (excluding *hukou* status) for the urban and rural samples, respectively. Most notably, father's education appears to matter more for rural individuals than for urban ones at every level, peaking at an additional 3.1 years compared with 2.6 years for senior high school and above.

Table 6.3 Determinants of years of schooling: Nationwide, urban and rural

Sample	National	Urban	Rural
Independent variables			
Father: Primary school (YES = 1)	1.61***	0.58***	1.70***
Father: Junior high (YES = 1)	2.18***	1.28***	2.29***
Father: Senior high and above (YES = 1)	3.20***	2.71***	3.11***
Hukou at age 12 (Urban = 1)	3.10***		
Male (YES = 1)	1.37***	–0.03	1.66***
Parents party member (YES = 1)	0.80***	0.81***	0.78***
One or two siblings (YES = 1)	0.04	–0.56***	0.19
Three or more siblings (YES = 1)	–0.42***	–0.73***	–0.32*
Han Chinese (YES = 1)	0.86***	–0.05	0.94***
Birth cohort:			
1945–49	–0.34*	0.23	–0.39*
1950–54	0.03	1.56**	–0.17
1955–59	1.53***	2.33***	1.45***
1960–64	2.89***	3.07***	2.93***
1965–69	2.01***	2.89***	1.90***
1970–74	2.22***	3.25***	2.09***
1975–79	3.03***	3.45***	3.05***
1980–84	3.50***	4.13***	3.42***
1985–89	4.09***	4.31***	4.06***
Provinces	Yes	Yes	Yes
Constant	4.21***	8.85***	5.34***
Observations	23,601	3,775	19,826
R-squared	0.39	0.32	0.31

*** $p < 0.01$

** $p < 0.05$

* $p < 0.1$

Sources: CFPS (2010, 2012) and authors' own regressions.

Table 6.4 presents the regression results for each birth cohort separately. What is most striking in the nationwide regressions in Panel A is that *hukou* status is a highly significant determinant of educational outcomes for all cohorts, peaking at 4.5 additional years for urban residents for the 1950–54 cohort and falling to a low of 2.3 years for the youngest cohort. Other interesting points include the declining advantages of being male, to the point of being insignificant for the two youngest cohorts; the consistently positive benefits of having a parent with Communist Party membership; and the significantly negative association of educational attainment with family size for the 1980s cohorts.

Panels B and C reveal some key differences between the urban and rural samples. First, gender clearly matters more in rural areas than urban ones, with the male coefficient insignificant in the latter from the 1960–64 cohort onwards, and even negative for the two youngest cohorts. Second, the schooling advantages associated with parents' Communist Party membership also differ. For example, for the urban sample, it is insignificant for the 1950s cohorts (the two main Cultural Revolution cohorts), as well as the 1975–79 and 1980–84 cohorts (who would have benefited from the introduction of the compulsory education law in 1986), while it is significant for most rural cohorts apart from the youngest one (possibly reflecting the delayed implementation of the compulsory education law in rural areas). Third, ethnic minority status is significant for the rural sample from the 1970–74 cohort onwards, while for the urban sample it is insignificant throughout.

Finally, the coefficients on the dummies for fathers' education levels vary substantially across birth cohorts and between the rural and urban samples. For the urban sample, only the senior high school dummy is consistently significant, although notably less so for the oldest cohorts, and reaching a low in magnitude for the 1960–64 cohort—the last of the three cohorts directly impacted by the Cultural Revolution. The coefficient then rises through to the 1975–79 cohort, declining only slightly thereafter but remaining well above those from the pre-reform era, confirming the increasing importance of family socioeconomic status during the reform period. In contrast, for the rural sample, the coefficients on *all* levels of father's education tend to be highly significant, with only a few exceptions. Notably, father's education brings a premium that is greater than for their urban counterparts in all cohorts, suggesting a higher degree of intergenerational persistence.[8]

8 Note that this finding differs from that in Golley and Kong (2012), where we found greater persistence in the urban sample. This difference stems from our definition of 'rural' here, which includes those people who migrated after the age of 12, while in our earlier work these people were classified as 'urban'. Given that these migrants generally have better-educated fathers and higher levels of education themselves (with 27 per cent attaining senior high and above, compared with 17 per cent for the rural sample overall), including them in the rural sample here results in higher intergenerational persistence.

Table 6.4 Determinants of years of schooling by cohort

Cohort	1940–44	1945–49	1950–54	1955–59	1960–64	1965–69	1970–74	1975–79	1980–84	1985–89
Independent variables										
Panel A: Nationwide										
Father: Primary school (YES = 1)	2.0***	1.6***	1.4***	1.5***	1.2***	1.8***	1.9***	2.0***	1.5***	1.6***
Father: Junior high (YES = 1)	–0.2	1.2*	0.6	1.6***	1.4***	2.1***	2.5***	2.9***	2.6***	2.3***
Father: Senior high and above (YES = 1)	0.34	2.4***	1.8***	1.2**	3.0***	2.7***	3.8***	4.1***	3.2***	3.7***
Hukou at age 12 (Urban = 1)	2.8***	3.3***	4.5***	3.9***	3.1***	3.5***	3.0***	2.4***	2.6***	2.3***
Male (YES = 1)	3.2***	2.2***	2.8***	3.0***	1.9***	1.5***	1.3***	0.6***	0.1	0
Parents party member (YES = 1)	–0.02	0.5	0.9***	0.6*	0.7***	1.1***	0.6***	0.5***	1.1***	0.9***
One or two siblings (YES = 1)	0.4	–0.1	–0.1	0.7	1.5***	0.7	0.9**	–0.2	–0.8***	–0.7**
Three or more siblings (YES = 1)	0.6	0.1	–0.4	0.6	1.5***	0.4	0.1	–0.8**	–2.3	–2.1***
Han Chinese (YES = 1)	0.1	–0.1	0.3	–0.1	0.9*	–0.1	1.3***	1.2***	1.5***	1.0***
Provinces	Yes	Yes	Yes	Yes	Yes	Yes	Yes	Yes	Yes	Yes
Constant	6.91**	5.0***	4.2***	2.9**	5.5***	5.4***	6.0***	6.7***	8.6***	9.0***
Observations	1,108	1,757	2,451	2,389	2,753	3,268	3,158	2,328	2,079	2,310
R-squared	0.31	0.2	0.3	0.3	0.3	0.3	0.3	0.4	0.4	0.3
Panel B: Urban										
Father: Primary school (YES = 1)	1.4	2.3**	0.8	0.6	0.3	–0.2	1.1**	–0.3	0.2	1.6
Father: Junior high (YES = 1)	0.6	1.8	1.9**	1.3	0.3	0.4	1.0*	1.3*	2.4**	2.4
Father: Senior high and above (YES = 1)	0.6	2.0	2.0**	1.8**	1.4***	1.6***	3.6***	3.3***	3.2***	3.9***
Male (YES = 1)	–0.3	1.0	1.0**	0.7	0.2	0.2	0	0	–0.8**	–1.2***
Parents party member (YES = 1)	11.3***	1.1	0.5	0.1	0.3	1.2***	0.9***	0	1.0**	0.7
One or two siblings (YES = 1)	1.4	–0.3	–0.9	–0.5	1.6***	–0.7	–1.0	–0.2	–1.3***	–0.7*
Three or more siblings (YES = 1)	–0.3	0.4	0.3	–1.2	1.0*	–0.9	–1.5**	–0.6	–3.7***	–0.8

Cohort	1940–44	1945–49	1950–54	1955–59	1960–64	1965–69	1970–74	1975–79	1980–84	1985–89
Independent variables										
Han Chinese (YES = 1)	–2.9	–2.2	–0.4	3.6	–0.6	0.9	–0.5	1.0	0.1	–0.8
Provinces	Yes	Yes	Yes	Yes	Yes	Yes	Yes	Yes	Yes	Yes
Constant	11.3***	9.0***	9.6***	6.2*	11.3***	10.6***	12.8***	11.7***	12.9***	13.4***
Observations	103	242	393	432	466	400	452	403	453	431
R-squared	0.7	0.4	0.2	0.2	0.2	0.2	0.3	0.3	0.3	0.3
Panel C: Rural										
Father: Primary school (YES = 1)	2.0***	1.6***	1.5***	1.7***	1.4***	1.9***	1.9***	2.1***	1.5***	1.4***
Father: Junior high (YES = 1)	–0.7	0.9	0.5	1.5***	1.6***	2.3***	2.8***	3.0***	2.7***	2.0***
Father: Senior high and above (YES = 1)	0	2.5***	1.2	0.3	3.3***	2.7***	3.4***	3.8***	2.9***	3.4***
Male (YES = 1)	3.3***	2.3***	3.1***	3.4***	2.4***	1.6***	1.5***	0.7***	0.5**	0.2
Parents party member (YES = 1)	–0.3	0.4	1.1***	0.6*	0.9***	1.1***	0.5*	0.6*	1.0***	1.1**
One or two siblings (YES = 1)	0.3	0.2	0	1.2**	1.8***	1.0*	1.7***	–0.3	–0.5	–0.7**
Three or more siblings (YES = 1)	0.5	0.2	–0.5	1.1**	1.9***	0.8	0.9	–0.8*	–1.8***	–2.2***
Han Chinese (YES = 1)	0	0.1	0.3	–0.2	0.9*	–0.2	1.5***	1.1***	1.8***	1.3***
Provinces	Yes	Yes	Yes	Yes	Yes	Yes	Yes	Yes	Yes	Yes
Constant	14.5***	7.8***	6.0***	8.3***	4.8***	6.0***	6.0***	6.1***	9.5***	9.7***
Observations	1,005	1,515	2,058	1,957	2,287	2,868	2,706	1,925	1,626	1,879
R-squared	0.3	0.2	0.2	0.2	0.2	0.2	0.2	0.3	0.3	0.2

*** $p < 0.01$

** $p < 0.05$

* $p < 0.1$

Note: Standard errors supressed for space reasons.

Sources: CFPS (2010, 2012) and authors' own regressions.

Inequality of opportunity

Using the regressions reported in Tables 6.3 and 6.4, and the method described above, Table 6.5 presents measures of both the absolute and the relative indexes of inequality of opportunity, *IOA* and *IOR*, respectively, along with the inequality of outcome index, GE(2). National trends for these three indexes are illustrated in Figure 6.4, while Figure 6.5 illustrates *IOR* for the nationwide, urban and rural samples. There are a number of key points.

First, as seen in Figure 6.4, trends in the absolute measure of inequality of opportunity, *IOA*, are quite distinct from those for inequality of outcomes, GE(2); for some cohorts they move in the same direction, but, for others, the opposite is true. Thus, there is no evidence to suggest that the observed reductions in inequality of outcome have occurred because of an equalising of educational opportunities. More to the point, reductions in inequality of outcome have coincided with increases in inequality of opportunity.

Second, the share of inequality of opportunity in total inequality (*IOR*) for the nationwide sample fluctuates only slightly for the oldest cohorts, ranging from 24.5 to 32.7 per cent through to the 1965–69 cohort. It is higher than this for every subsequent cohort, peaking at 43.1 per cent of total inequality for the 1980–84 cohort. This confirms that inequality of opportunity has become an increasingly important determinant of unequal educational outcomes during the reform period—and that is not a good sign.

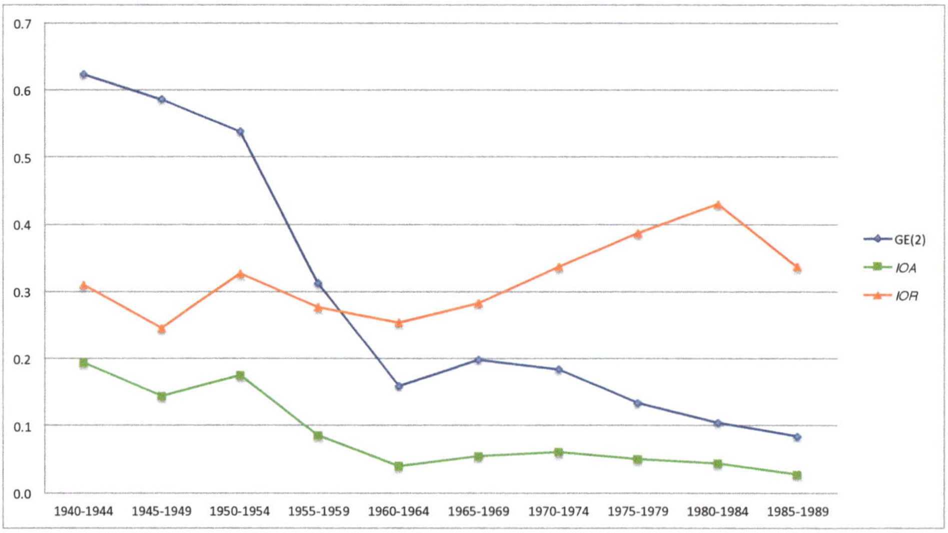

Figure 6.4 Nationwide trends in inequality of outcome and inequality of opportunity

Sources: CFPS (2010, 2012) and authors' calculations.

Third, as seen in Figure 6.5, trends in the share of inequality of opportunity are quite different in the urban and rural samples—most strikingly, for the three oldest cohorts, but also for the youngest two. The downturn for the youngest rural cohort is a positive sign that opportunities may be improving for the least disadvantaged Chinese children in rural areas. The upturn for the youngest urban cohort is a cause of concern.

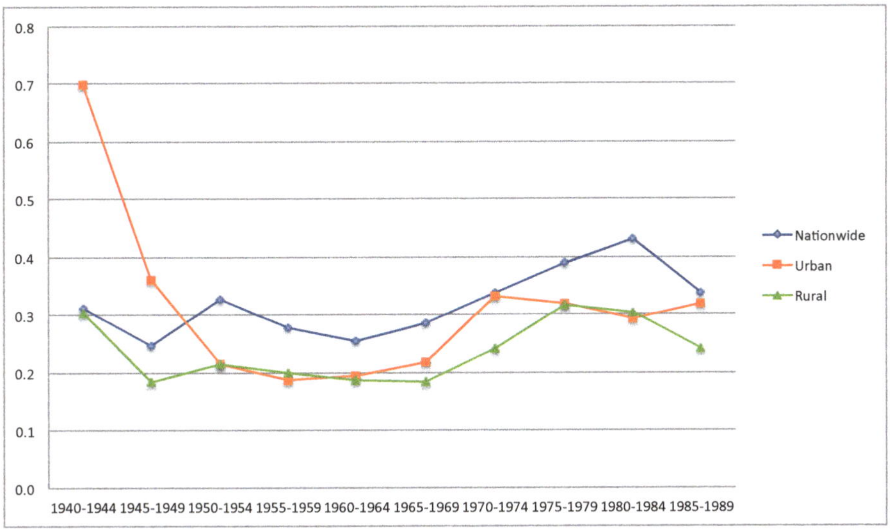

Figure 6.5 Share of inequality of opportunity in inequality of outcome (*IOR*)

Sources: CFPS (2010, 2012) and authors' calculations.

And fourth, the nationwide measures of both the absolute and the relative measures of inequality of opportunity in Panel A in Table 6.5 are higher than both the urban and the rural ones from the 1950s onwards (Panels B and C). The reason for this is quite simple: the *hukou* system, which extends the set of circumstances in the national sample beyond those in the urban and rural samples, clearly creates greater inequality of opportunity in the process.

To push this crucial point further, Table 6.6 presents the partial contributions of each of the circumstance variables. For example, to calculate the partial contribution from *hukou* status, we assign every individual the 'average' value for the dummy variable—that is, equal to the proportion of people with urban *hukou*, rerun the regressions to generate new predicted values for years of schooling and then calculate the IOR_p associated with these predictions.

The results are ranked in order of importance, revealing that the largest single contributor to inequality of opportunity is *hukou* status. Both this and father's education play a stronger role than either one's province or one's year of birth, which is quite astounding. Having parents with Communist Party membership ranks above being male, coming from a single-child family or being Han Chinese. Clearly, however, each of these factors plays a role in preventing equality of opportunity from being achieved in China's educational outcomes.

Table 6.5 Inequality of opportunity: Nationwide, urban and rural

		By birth cohort									
	All	1940–44	1945–49	1950–54	1955–59	1960–64	1965–69	1970–74	1975–79	1980–84	1985–89
Panel A: Nationwide											
Total (outcome) inequality											
GE(2)	0.207	0.624	0.585	0.538	0.313	0.158	0.198	0.185	0.134	0.105	0.085
Inequality of opportunity											
Absolute: *IOA*	0.082	0.194	0.143	0.176	0.086	0.040	0.056	0.062	0.052	0.045	0.029
Relative: *IOR*	0.393	0.311	0.245	0.327	0.276	0.253	0.284	0.338	0.388	0.431	0.338
Panel B: Urban											
Total (outcome) inequality											
GE(2)	0.052	0.250	0.170	0.079	0.057	0.030	0.044	0.042	0.041	0.033	0.028
Inequality of opportunity											
Absolute: *IOA*	0.016	0.175	0.061	0.017	0.011	0.006	0.010	0.014	0.013	0.010	0.009
Relative: *IOR*	0.316	0.700	0.361	0.214	0.187	0.194	0.218	0.331	0.319	0.292	0.319
Panel C: Rural											
Total (outcome) inequality											
GE(2)	0.238	0.662	0.658	0.671	0.395	0.190	0.221	0.211	0.149	0.113	0.091
Inequality of opportunity											
Absolute: *IOA*	0.073	0.200	0.121	0.144	0.079	0.036	0.040	0.051	0.047	0.034	0.022
Relative: *IOR*	0.306	0.303	0.184	0.214	0.200	0.187	0.183	0.241	0.317	0.304	0.240

Sources: CFPS (2010, 2012) and authors' calculations based on regression results in Tables 6.3 and 6.4.

Table 6.6 Partial contributions to relative inequality of opportunity (IOR_P)

			By birth cohort																			
Circumstance	All		1940–44		1945–49		1950–54		1955–59		1960–64		1965–69		1970–74		1975–79		1980–84		1985–89	
Hukou at age 12	0.22	1	0.12	2	0.08	1	0.10	1	0.12	1	0.14	1	0.14	1	0.19	2	0.26	2	0.29	1	0.24	1
Father's education	0.24	2	0.31	4	0.11	3	0.19	3	0.23	3	0.15	2	0.19	1	0.19	3	0.24	1	0.33	3	0.25	2
Birth year cohort	0.24	3																				
Province	0.25	4	0.06	1	0.08	2	0.15	2	0.29	6	0.15	3	0.20	3	0.18	1	0.29	3	0.30	2	0.26	3
Parents party member	0.33	5	0.31	5	0.20	5	0.24	5	0.24	4	0.22	5	0.22	4	0.29	5	0.35	4	0.36	4	0.29	4
Male	0.33	6	0.17	3	0.15	4	0.19	4	0.18	2	0.20	4	0.23	5	0.28	4	0.36	6	0.43	6	0.34	6
Number of siblings	0.37	7	0.40	7	0.25	7	0.29	6	0.34	7	0.38	7	0.33	7	0.38	6	0.36	5	0.36	5	0.03	5
Han Chinese	0.49	8	0.33	6	0.24	6	0.37	7	0.27	5	0.32	6	0.28	6	0.47	7	0.51	7	0.58	7	0.41	7

Sources: CFPS (2010, 2012) and authors' calculations based on regression results in Table 6.4: Panel A.

Conclusions

This chapter investigated trends in educational inequality in China, focusing on the contribution of 'inequality of opportunity' to these trends. Utilising the CFPS survey results for 2010 and 2012, we measured the inequality in individual educational outcomes (years of schooling) for the nationwide sample and for separate rural and urban subsamples, in aggregate and for each of 10 birth cohorts. Our regressions identified the key determinants of these outcomes, all of which, we argued, could be classified as 'circumstances' that lie beyond the control of each individual, revealing important variations in the magnitude and significance of key determinants across birth cohorts and between the rural and urban subsamples. These results were used to calculate the share of inequality of opportunity in overall educational inequality. The lack of equal opportunity for Chinese citizens with regard to their educational outcomes was shown to stem primarily from the divisive *hukou* system, with further significant contributions from father's education level, birth cohort, province, parents' Communist Party membership, gender, family size and ethnicity, in that order.

Unequal educational attainments across a diverse population—with diverse aptitudes, aspirations and motivations—are to be expected, and there is no sense in which our results suggest this should be otherwise. Rather, what matters is the extent to which these unequal outcomes are determined by factors for which an individual is not responsible and which they cannot change; and there is a very clear case to be made for policies that minimise the impact of these factors and promote equal opportunity for all. The ethical imperative for the ruling Communist Party to address this issue is compounded by the economic importance of finding new sources of growth, particularly in the context of an ageing population and diminishing workforce.

It certainly does not follow that the coefficients on *all* of the selected circumstance variables should have been insignificantly different from zero. The omission of unobserved variables meant that the estimated coefficients were likely to exhibit some bias and could not be treated as causal. The most obvious of these was the coefficient on father's education, which likely incorporated not only the omitted impacts of his (and the mother's) income and occupation, but also reflected some degree of genetic inheritability, which would and should generate inequality in educational outcomes; beyond all others, this coefficient clearly should not be zero.

This point about causality notwithstanding, the results presented in this chapter provide a basis for identifying some reasonable 'equal opportunity policies' in China's education sphere. On the rural–urban gap, *hukou* system reforms that grant the children of rural migrant workers access to the urban schooling systems where they live are clearly a step in the right direction. Other equalising measures could target a reduction in the private educational costs borne by rural residents who are least able to afford them, such as the *liangmian yibu* ('the two waivers, one subsidy') program that became national law in 2006, and the forbidding of charges and other miscellaneous fees for primary and junior high school. More generally, in a country where intergenerational persistence and educational costs are both on the rise, policies to facilitate the poorest rural children—and, for that matter, the poorest urban children, too—remaining in school for as long as they have the capacity and desire to do so, seem eminently reasonable. Making education accessible and affordable for all should be the number one priority in this regard.

Another set of policy actions relates to the possibility of using affirmative action to address unequal opportunities, by applying different test score standards or admission requirements depending on an individual's circumstances. This has been a longstanding practice for China's ethnic minorities (as discussed in Sautman 1999; Yang and Wu 2009), and one that continues to make sense based on our results here, particularly given the concentration of ethnic minorities in the country's most remote poor rural areas. One practice that makes less sense would be any kind of affirmative action *in favour of boys*, despite the fact that girls have begun to outperform them in recent years—as evidenced by revelations in 2012 that girls were required to have higher admission scores than boys for entry into the same university courses, a practice that has since been banned. As found in a detailed study by Zhang et al. (2012) on this point, this likely reflects the fact that girls study harder—and they certainly should not be discriminated against because of that.

China has made remarkable progress in advancing the average level of educational attainment during the past seven decades, with considerable expansion of rural education programs in recent times. However, the education gaps between children living in cities and those in villages, in first-tier metropolitan cities such as Beijing and Shanghai and the rest of the country, and from different socioeconomic backgrounds more broadly remain substantial.

To successfully transform into a more technology-based economy capable of long-term sustainable growth, China will require an increasingly skilled labour force. Efforts to ensure that all those children who are most capable, rather than just those who are most fortunate, can access the quality and quantity of education they deserve will raise the likelihood of achieving this development goal. Our results lend quantitative support to the necessity of such an effort.

References

Becker, G. and Lewis, H. (1973), On the interaction between the quantity and quality of children, *Journal of Political Economy* 81(2): 773–824. doi.org/10.1086/260166.

Black, S. E. and Devereux, P. J. (2010), Recent developments in intergenerational mobility, *Handbook of Labor Economics* 4(B): 1487–541.

Bourguignon, F., Ferreira, F. and Menendez, M. (2007), Inequality of opportunity in Brazil, *Review of Income and Wealth* 53(4): 585–618. doi.org/10.1111/j.1475-4991.2007.00247.x.

Brunori, P., Ferreira, F. and Peragine, V. (2013), *Inequality of opportunity, income inequality and economic mobility: Some international comparisons*, IZA Discussion Paper No. 7155, Institute of Labor Economics, Bonn. Available from: ftp.iza.org/dp7155.pdf. doi.org/10.1596/1813-9450-6304.

Checchi, D. and Peragine, V. (2010), Inequality of opportunity in Italy, *Journal of Economic Inequality* 8(4): 429–50. doi.org/10.1007/s10888-009-9118-3.

Checchi, D., Fiorio, C. V. and Leonardi, M. (2008), Intergenerational persistence in educational attainment in Italy, Paper presented at 30th General Conference of The International Association for Research in Income and Wealth, Dresden, Germany, August.

Deng, Z. and Treiman, D. J. (1997), The impact of the Cultural Revolution on trends in educational attainment in the People's Republic of China, *The American Journal of Sociology* 103(2): 391–428. doi.org/10.1086/231212.

Emran, M. S. and Sun, Y. (2015), *Magical transition? Intergenerational educational and occupational mobility in rural China: 1988–2002*, Policy Research Working Paper 7316, June, Office of the Chief Economist for East Asia and the Pacific Region, The World Bank, Washington, DC. Available from: documents.worldbank.org/curated/en/229911468000896844/pdf/WPS7316.pdf.

Ferreira, F. and Gignoux, J. (2011), The measurement of inequality of opportunity: Theory and an application to Latin America, *Review of Income and Wealth* 57(4): 622–57. doi.org/10.1111/j.1475-4991.2011.00467.x.

Golley, J. and Kong, S. T. (2012), Climbing the intergenerational ladder of education in urban, rural and migrant China, in H. Mackay and L. Song (eds), *Rebalancing and Sustaining Growth in China*, Canberra: ANU E Press.

Golley, J. and Kong, S. T. (2013), Inequality in the intergenerational mobility of education in China, *China and the World Economy* 21(2): 15–37.

Golley, J. and Kong, S. T. (in press), Inequality of opportunity in China's educational outcomes, *China Economic Review*. doi.org/10.1016/j.chieco.2016.07.002.

Hannum, E. (2002), Educational stratification by ethnicity in China: Enrolment and attainment in the early reform years, *Demography* 39(1): 95–117. doi.org/10.1353/dem.2002.0005.

Hannum, E. and Wang, M. (2006), Geography and educational inequality in China, *China Economic Review* 17: 253–65. doi.org/10.1016/j.chieco.2006.04.003.

Heckman, J. (2005), China's human capital investment, *China Economic Review* 16(1): 50–70. doi.org/10.1016/j.chieco.2004.06.012.

Hertz, T., Jayasundera, T., Piraino, P., Selcuk, S., Smith, N. and Verashchagina, A. (2007), The inheritance of educational inequality: International comparisons and fifty-year trends, *The B. E. Journal of Economic Analysis and Policy* 7(2): 1–46.

Khor, N., Pang, L., Liu, C., Chang, F., Mo, D., Loyalka, P. and Rozelle, S. (2016), China's looming human capital crisis: Upper secondary educational attainment rates and the middle-income trap, *The China Quarterly* 228: 905–26. doi.org/10.1017/S0305741016001119.

Knight, J., Sicular, T. and Yue, X. (2012), *Educational inequality in China: The intergenerational dimension*, CIBC Working Paper Series No. 2011-13, Centre for Human Capital and Productivity, University of Western Ontario, London.

Lefranc, A., Pistolesi, N. and Trannoy, A. (2008), Inequality of opportunities vs. inequality of outcomes: Are Western societies alike? *The Review of Income and Wealth* 54(4): 513–46. doi.org/10.1111/j.1475-4991.2008.00289.x.

Li, H., Loyalka, P., Rozelle, S., Wu, B. and Xie, J. (2015), *Unequal access to college in China: How far have poor, rural students been left behind?* SFI Working Paper Series No. SFIWP0046, Shanghai Finance Institute, Shanghai.

Li, H. J., Zhang J. and Zhu, Y. (2008), The quality–quantity trade-off of children in a developing country: Identification using Chinese twins, *Demography* 45(1): 223–43. doi.org/10.1353/dem.2008.0006.

Liu, J. (2006), Expansion of higher education in China and inequality in entrance opportunities, [in Chinese], *Chinese Journal of Sociology* 26(3): 158–79.

Marrero, G. and Rodríguez, J. G. (2012), Inequality of opportunity in Europe, *Review of Income and Wealth* 58(4): 597–620. doi.org/10.1111/j.1475-4991.2012.00496.x.

Meng, X. and Gregory, R. G. (2002), The impact of interrupted education on subsequent educational attainment: A cost of the Chinese Cultural Revolution, *Economic Development and Cultural Change* 50(4): 935–59. doi.org/10.1086/342761.

Qiao, J. (2008), Differentiation of entrance opportunity for higher education in urban and rural areas, [in Chinese], *Journal of Education Studies* 4(5): 92–6.

Roemer, J. (1998), *Equality of Opportunity*, Cambridge, Mass.: Harvard University Press.

Rosenzweig, M. and Zhang, J. (2009), Do population control policies induce more capital investment? Twins, birth weight and China's 'one-child' policy, *Review of Economic Studies* 76(3): 1149–74. doi.org/10.1111/j.1467-937X.2009.00563.x.

Sato, H. and Li, S. (2008), *Class origin, family culture, and intergenerational correlation of education in rural China*, Global COE Hi-Stat Discussion Paper Series 007, Institute of Economic Research, Hitotsubashi University, Tokyo.

Sautman, B. (1999), Expanding access to higher education for China's national minorities: Policies of preferential admissions, in G. A. Postiglione (ed.), *China's National Minority Education: Culture, schooling and development*, pp. 173–210, New York: Falmer Press.

Singh, A. (2012), Inequality of opportunity in earnings and consumption expenditure: The case of Indian men, *Review of Income and Wealth* 58(1): 79–106. doi.org/10.1111/j.1475-4991.2011.00485.x.

Van de Gaer, D. (1993), Equality of opportunity and investment in human capital, PhD dissertation, Catholic University of Louvain, Louvain-la-Neuve, Belgium.

Wang, X., Liu, C., Zhang, L., Luo, R., Glauben, T., Shi, Y., Rozelle, S. and Sharbono, B. (2009), *What is keeping the poor out of college? Enrolment rates, educational barriers and college matriculation in China*, REAP Working Paper 210, September, Rural Education Action Program, Stanford University, California.

Wu, X. (2009), Economic transition, school expansion and educational inequality in China, 1990–2000, [in Chinese], *Chinese Journal of Sociology* 29(5): 88–113.

Wu, Y. (2013), The inequality and evolution of China's urban–rural educational opportunities, 1978–2008, [in Chinese], *China Social Science* (3): 4–21.

Yang, R. and Wu, M. (2009), Education for ethnic minorities in China: A policy critique, *SA-eDUC Journal* 6(2): 117–31.

Yi, H., Zhang, L., Luo, R., Shi, Y., Mo, D., Chen, X., Brinton, C. and Rozelle, S. (2012), Dropping out: Why are students leaving junior high in China's poor rural areas? *International Journal of Educational Development* 32: 555–63. doi.org/10.1016/j.ijedudev.2011.09.002.

Zhang, J., Pang, X., Zhang, L., Medina, A. and Rozelle, S. (2012), *Gender inequality of education in China: A meta-regression analysis*, REAP Working Paper 239, May, Rural Education Action Program, Stanford University, California.

Zhang, X. and Kanbur, R. (2005), Spatial inequality in education and healthcare in China, *China Economic Review* 16: 189–204.

Zhang, Y. and Eriksson, T. (2010), Inequality of opportunity and income inequality in nine Chinese provinces, 1986–2006, *China Economic Review* 21(4): 607–16. doi.org/10.1016/j.chieco.2010.06.008.

Zhang, Y., Kao, G. and Hannum, E. (2007), Do mothers in rural China practice gender equality in educational aspirations for their children? *Comparative Education Review* 51(2): 131–57. doi.org/10.1086/512023.

Zhang, Z. and Chen, Q. (2014), The expansion of higher education admissions and the gender equalization of higher education opportunity: An empirical study based on Chinese General Social Survey (CGSS2008) data, *The Journal ofChinese Sociology* 1: 1–19. doi.org/10.1186/s40711-014-0001-7.

Zhou, X., Moen, P. and Brandon Tuma, N. (1998), Educational stratification in urban China: 1949–94, *Sociology of Education* 71(3): 199–222. doi.org/10.2307/2673202.

7. Intangible Capital and China's Economic Growth: Evidence from Input–Output Tables

Shenglang Yang and Yixiao Zhou[1]

Introduction

This study uses data from input–output tables and a methodology adopted from Corrado et al. (2009) to provide empirical evidence of the role of intangible capital in China according to industrial sector. In so doing, it offers a new methodology for measuring the role of intangible capital in a country where data on intangible capital are inadequate. It finds that growth in intangible capital explains almost 20 per cent of total factor productivity (TFP) growth in China over the period 1997–2012. Moreover, these effects of intangible capital remain robust under various forms of sensitivity analysis including bootstrap regressions, the Levinsohn and Petrin (LP) (2003) approach and changes in the depreciation rate. At the sectoral level, we find that research and development (R&D), which embodies innovation, plays a more important role in agriculture than do economic competency or computerised information, but the role of economic competency is more important in the services and light-industry sectors than are R&D and computerised information.

China has enjoyed rapid growth since its reform and opening-up policies were implemented in 1978. China's real gross domestic product (GDP) per capita in 1978 was only one-fortieth of the US level and one-tenth of the Brazilian level (Zhu 2012). By 2015, however, China had real GDP per capita that was equal to almost one-quarter of the US level and at the same level as Brazil.[2] Growth in total factor productivity (TFP) has played a critical role in China's growth miracle. According to Zhu (2012), positive change in TFP accounts for 78 per cent of the growth in China's GDP per capita between 1978 and 2007. The transition from

1 We much appreciate the helpful comments on earlier versions of this chapter from Ligang Song and the conference participants at the Crawford School of Public Policy, The Australian National University. All remaining errors are our own.

2 GDP per capita is calculated using the purchasing power parity (PPP) approach (constant 2011 international currency); data are from the World Bank International Comparison Program (www.worldbank.org/en/programs/icp).

a planned to a market economy is a major source of TFP growth and has significantly improved China's TFP, but this source of TFP growth cannot last forever as returns from earlier reforms are diminishing.

From 2012, Chinese economic growth has been slowing and has entered a stage called the 'new normal', the official definition of which is that China will maintain stable and relatively lower growth compared with earlier growth rates. What could be China's new source of growth in the new normal? Text on the back of any iPhone may provide a hint. It reads: 'Designed by Apple in California. Assembled in China.' Payments to Chinese workers and the profits of non-Apple companies account for only 1.8 per cent and 9.2 per cent, respectively, of the value added of an iPhone, while Apple's profits are 58.5 per cent of the total value added in 2010, according to Kraemer et al. (2011). This striking fact has an important implication: the distribution of value added in the global value chain favours those who own the product design and hold the market power, rather than those who manufacture the products.

Product design and market power embody a broader concept called intangibles (Corrado et al. 2009). Intangible capital consists of the stock of non-material resources that enter the production process and is important for the creation or improvement of products as well as production processes (Arrighetti et al. 2014). Intangible capital has been playing an increasingly important role in boosting productivity and economic growth since the 'information technology revolution'. In developed economies, the relative use of tangible capital is decreasing while the relative use of intangible capital—such as production technologies, product design, market power and intangibles embodied in employees and firm structure—has been increasing (Fukao et al. 2009; van Ark et al. 2009; Marrano et al. 2009; Corrado and Hulten 2010; Miyagawa and Hisa 2013; Chun and Nadiri 2016).

The literature on intangible capital is significant and includes the discussion of intangible capital as a source of growth in various countries at national and industry levels (Fukao et al. 2009; van Ark et al. 2009; Marrano et al. 2009; Corrado and Hulten 2010; Borgo et al. 2013; Corrado et al. 2013; Haskel and Wallis 2013; Miyagawa and Hisa 2013; Chun and Nadiri 2016), the discussion of intangible capital in the valuation and productivity of firms (Atkeson and Kehoe 2005; Tronconi and Marzetti 2011; Arato and Yamada 2012; Eisfeldt and Papanikolaou 2013, 2014; Gourio and Rudanko 2014b; Clausen and Hirth 2016) and the discussion of incorporating intangible capital to solve macroeconomic puzzles (McGrattan and Prescott 2010, 2014; Goodridge et al. 2013; Gourio and Rudanko 2014a). However, studies on intangible capital in China are scarce, due both to the lack of data and to the recent importance of intangible capital to the economy. Hulten and Hao (2012) calculate the intangible capital of China between 2000 and 2008 and conduct growth accounting of national data using the income-share method. The authors gather only nine observations, which is not sufficient for a comprehensive analysis. Given China's shifting growth model and the possibility of utilising alternative data sources, it is timely to further investigate the role of intangible capital in China's growth.

To the best of our knowledge, this study is the first empirical test of how intangibles enhance economic growth at the sectoral level in China. In contrast to national-level studies, an industry-level study has the advantage of generating more observations and thus allows more statistical freedom to analyse how different categories of intangible capital impact on economic growth. This will provide a better way to assess the role of intangibles in an economy.

We divided 100 sectors from China's input–output tables for 1997, 2002, 2007 and 2012[3] into four subgroups—agriculture, light industry, heavy industry and services—to alleviate the problem of parameter heterogeneity between sectors. The selected input–output tables are constructed using data from China's National Bureau of Statistics (NBS), based on input–output surveys, and are relatively reliable. The measurement of intangible investment in this study follows the literature in capitalising either the intangible intermediates or intangible expenditure. Use of intermediates from input–output tables to estimate intangibles is common in the literature,[4] including in Miyagawa and Hisa (2013), Haskel et al. (2014) and Chun and Nadiri (2016).

Unlike Corrado et al. (2009), Fukao et al. (2009) and Hulten and Hao (2012), however, this study uses a proxy approach—that is, we use the entries relevant to intangible investment as proxies and make the assumption that the ratios of intangible investments to the proxies remain constant over time. Using the proxy approach and assuming the ratio of true value to proxies is constant over time are also common in the literature on intangible capital. For example, Gourio and Rudanko (2014b) proxy selling, general and administrative expenses (S&GA) for investment in customer capital, while Tronconi and Marzetti (2011) and Eisfeldt and Papanikolaou (2014) proxy S&GA for investment in organisational capital. Although this assumption is often found to be invalid, it is the best this study could adopt based on the available data; and, if this assumption is true, the study will avoid the inaccurate measurement problems found in Corrado et al. (2009) and Fukao et al. (2009).

When conducting growth accounting, we adopt the Cobb–Douglas parameter estimation based on econometrics instead of income/cost shares, along the lines of Niebel et al. (2017). The advantage of this approach is to allow for the existence

3 The reason we exclude the input–output tables for 1987 and 1992 is that these two tables are inaccurate and include few of the intangible intermediates.

4 Intangible investment produced within firms is not reflected in input–output tables; however, as long as the ratio of actual intangible expenditure to the intangible expenditure manifest in the input–output tables remains constant over time, the coefficients in the empirical analysis will not be biased.

of error terms. In contrast, the income-share method used by Corrado et al. (2009), Fukao et al. (2009) and Hulten and Hao (2012) may underestimate the contribution of resource reallocation to economic growth when the economy is in disequilibrium, according to Nadiri (1970). A transitional economy such as China's is likely to remain in disequilibrium over time; therefore, the income-share method is not suitable here. Our choice of econometric approach allows for an error term, which alleviates the problems arising from disequilibrium.

Our study also conducts bootstrap regressions to confirm the robustness of the results, which is new to the existing literature. Limited by the time span (T = 4), the standard generalised method of moments (GMM) approach is not suitable for this study. Bootstrap regressions are the only feasible method given data limitations. Studies on intangible capital often suffer from small sample size. Bootstrap regressions alleviate this problem to some extent. Moreover, the depreciation rate of intangible capital is debatable. To confirm the significance of the impacts of intangible capital, we will conduct a sensitivity analysis by experimenting with various depreciation rates.

This study consists of five sections. In the next section, the methodology of growth accounting at the industry level is discussed and a traditional growth accounting approach excluding intangible capital is conducted. Section three provides empirical evidence of the relationship between intangible capital and TFP. In section four, a growth accounting approach incorporating intangible capital is conducted, while section five concludes.

How do we conduct growth accounting with sectoral data?

Growth accounting often utilises the Cobb–Douglas production function (Equation 7.1).

Equation 7.1

$$Y = AK^{ak}L^{al}$$

In Equation 7.1, Y is GDP, A is TFP and K is capital. If the object is a nation, we take the logarithm of both sides and run a regression. The parameters ak and al can be estimated in this way. However, with sectoral data, there is a problem: the parameters of each industry may vary from one another. If a pooled regression is conducted, the heterogeneity of parameters will cause bias of the estimates. Moreover, each industry may have its own initial TFP value, which implies different intercepts of various industries. To overcome the problem of parameter heterogeneity, we categorise the industries according to the similarities of parameters, following previous literature such as Harris and Robinson (2002). In this study, the subgroups are defined as follows: light industry, heavy industry, agriculture and services.[5] We then assume a Cobb–Douglas production function (Equation 7.2).

Equation 7.2

$$Y_{it} = A_{it}K_{it}^{ak}L_{it}^{al}$$

Y_{it} is the value added of sector i at time t; A_{it} is the TFP of sector i at time t; K_{it} is capital according to the traditional definition (excluding most intangibles); L_{it} is the level of labour inputs; and *ak* and *al* are the capital and labour elasticities of output, respectively. Due to sectoral heterogeneity, the initial values of TFP may be different across sectors. We therefore assume Equation 7.3.

Equation 7.3

$$A_{it} = A_{i0eyt}$$

Taking the logarithm of both sides, we get Equation 7.4.

Equation 7.4

$$\ln Y_{it} = \ln A_{it} + ak\ln k_{it} = al\ln L_{it}$$

Equation 7.4 can be estimated by either the fixed-effects (FE) model or the random-effects (RE) model, depending on whether A_{i0} varies from sector to sector within a subgroup.

A key issue in production function estimation is, however, correlation between the unobservable productivity shocks and input levels. An industry responds to positive productivity shocks by expanding output and input. Negative shocks lead an industry to reduce output and input usage. When true, ordinary least squares (OLS) estimations of production functions are likely to be biased, which leads to biased estimates of productivity. Olley and Pakes (1996) develop an estimation approach using investment as a proxy for these unobservable shocks. More recently, Levinsohn and Petrin (2003) point out that investment is lumpy. If this is true, the investment proxy may not respond smoothly to productivity shocks. Levinsohn and Petrin (2003) suggest that using intermediate inputs can solve this problem.

5 The list of subgroups is demonstrated in Appendix 7.1.

Therefore, here we also adopt growth accounting without intangibles[6] using the Levinsohn and Petrin (LP) approach. The proxy used in this study is the usage of electricity, heating, fuel and water intermediates at 1997 constant prices.[7]

The growth rate of TFP is backed out as Equation 7.5.

Equation 7.5

$$g\_tfp = g_y - akg_k - alg_l$$

Capital and labour inputs at the sectoral level as detailed as those in China's input–output tables are not available. Luckily, China's input–output tables have two variables: total wages for labour and capital depreciation. We adjust the nominated depreciation of capital to the real depreciation using the Price Index of Investment in Fixed Assets from the NBS.

We assume a constant depreciation rate, θ, as is the convention in the existing literature (Equation 7.6).

Equation 7.6

$$\theta K_{it} = \text{real depreciation}_{it}$$

It is clear that real depreciation$_{it}$ has a strictly linear relationship with K_{it} and therefore is a perfect proxy for capital. As for the quantity of labour, we have Equation 7.7.

Equation 7.7

$$L_{it} = \frac{\text{total wage}_{it}}{\text{average wage}_{it}}$$

Total wage$_{it}$ is from China's input–output table and average wage$_{it}$ is from the China Labour Statistical Yearbook (NBS various years); however, the sectoral classifications in these yearbooks are not as detailed as those in China's input–output tables. Therefore, the average wage in the upper level of classification is used as a proxy for the average wage in individual sectors.[8]

We substitute K_{it} in Equation 7.4 with Equation 7.6 (Equation 7.8).

6 This approach allows only one capital variable; however, when incorporating intangible capital, there are at least two capital variables. Therefore, we do not conduct growth accounting with intangible capital using the LP approach.

7 Deflators are obtained from the National Bureau of Statistics of China and the World Input Output Database (www.wiod.org/).

8 The proxy is based on an assumption that the ratio of the average wage in a lower sector to that in the upper-level sector remains constant over time. If this assumption holds, the constant ratio becomes a part of the intercept, similar to Equation 7.8. The coefficient of the proxy is then the same as the true coefficient.

Equation 7.8

$$\ln Y_{it} = \ln A_{it} - ak\ln(\theta) + ak\ln \text{Capital\_proxy}_{it} + al\ln L_{it}$$

It is clear that substituting the capital proxy (real depreciation$_{it}$) for K_{it} is appropriate because the coefficient of real depreciation$_{it}$ is the same as that of K_{it}. The depreciation rate, θ, becomes part of the intercept. The growth rate of K_{it} that is used for the calculation of TFP is exactly the same as the growth rate of real depreciation$_{it}$.

Table 7.1 reports the descriptive statistics of the variables used in regressions for the period 1998–2012. It is clear that the ranges of value added, capital proxy, labour and different categories of intangible capital are large. This sample consists of 100 sectors in China across 14 years and therefore has nearly 400 observations.

Table 7.1 Descriptive statistics

Variable		Mean	Std dev.	Min.	Max.	Observations
ln(Value added)	Overall	15.83	1.21	12.29	19.21	N = 400
	Between		1.07	13.10	18.55	n = 100
	Within		0.59	12.31	17.94	T-bar = 4
ln(Capital proxy)	Overall	13.99	1.30	9.71	18.86	N = 398
	Between		1.08	11.35	17.57	n = 100
	Within		0.75	9.92	16.87	T-bar = 3.98
ln(labour)	Overall	5.39	1.27	1.06	9.72	N = 398
	Between		1.22	1.33	9.63	n = 100
	Within		0.38	1.71	6.88	T-bar = 3.98
ln(Intangible capital)	Overall	13.22	1.85	8.58	17.79	N = 398
	Between		1.20	10.57	15.84	n = 100
	Within		1.41	10.20	16.97	T-bar = 3.98
ln(R&D capital)	Overall	10.22	2.38	2.67	15.65	N = 394
	Between		1.68	3.76	13.37	n = 99
	Within		1.70	6.57	13.48	T-bar = 3.98
ln(EC capital)	Overall	12.93	1.82	8.46	17.65	N = 398
	Between		1.18	10.24	15.56	n = 100
	Within		1.38	9.82	16.74	T-bar = 3.98
ln(CI capital)	Overall	9.94	2.26	1.07	15.55	N = 397
	Between		1.86	3.59	14.25	n = 100
	Within		1.29	5.86	13.24	T-bar = 3.97

EC = economic competency

CI = computerised information

Source: Authors' calculations.

Table 7.2 Regression results for growth accounting without intangibles

	(1)	(2)	(3)	(4)	(5)	(6)	(7)	(8)	(9)	(10)	(11)	(12)
	Agriculture			Heavy industry			Light industry			Service		
Variables	RE	RE bootstrap	LP	RE	RE bootstrap	LP	FE	FE bootstrap	LP	FE	FE bootstrap	LP
ln(Capital)	0.42***	0.42***	0.62***	0.67***	0.67***	0.39**	0.70***	0.70***	0.60***	0.64***	0.64***	0.42**
	(0.14)	(0.14)	(0.18)	(0.08)	(0.07)	(0.17)	(0.03)	(0.03)	(0.06)	(0.05)	(0.05)	(0.19)
ln(Labour)	0.57***	0.57***	0.34**	0.26**	0.26*	0.30***	0.13**	0.13**	0.29***	0.22**	0.22**	0.44***
	(0.0979)	(0.133)	(0.133)	(0.123)	(0.147)	(0.116)	(0.0577)	(0.0577)	(0.0505)	(0.0796)	(0.0989)	(0.0585)
Constant	6.48***	6.48***		4.99***	4.99***		5.37***	5.37***		5.60***	5.60***	
	(1.27)	(1.11)		(0.87)	(0.65)		(0.50)	(0.50)		(0.48)	(0.62)	
Observations	20	20	20	138	138	138	144	144	144	96	96	96
R-squared	0.79	0.79		0.81	0.81		0.88	0.88		0.86	0.86	
Number of id	5	5		35	35		36	36		24	24	

*** $p < 0.01$

** $p < 0.05$

* $p < 0.1$

RE = random effects

FE = fixed effects

LP = Levinsohn and Petrin

Notes: Cluster robust standard errors are in parentheses. Number of bootstrap replications: 400 for normal bootstrap, 250 for LP. Number of id refers to the number of individuals within the sample.

Source: Authors' calculations.

The results for growth accounting are displayed in Table 7.2. According to Hausman tests, random-effects models are appropriate to study the agricultural and light-industry sectors, but fixed-effects models are used for the heavy industry and services sectors. Both labour and depreciation are highly significant economically and statistically, and remain robust when using bootstrap regressions. A 1 per cent change in capital stock is associated with a 0.42 per cent, 0.67 per cent, 0.70 per cent and 0.64 per cent change in value added in agriculture, heavy industry, light industry and services, respectively. A 1 per cent change in labour is associated with a 0.57 per cent, 0.26 per cent, 0.13 per cent and 0.22 per cent change in value added in agriculture, heavy industry, light industry and services, respectively. The growth rate of TFP is calculated according to Equation 7.5.

Intangible capital and TFP growth

According to Corrado et al. (2009), intangible investment includes investment in computerised information, innovative property and economic competency. Traditionally, intangible investment is classified as intermediate or expenditure and therefore is not manifest in national accounts. However, investment is the action of sacrificing today's consumption for increasing consumption in the future, according to Hulten (1979) and Corrado et al. (2009). Moreover, the effects of the intangible expenditure mentioned above last more than one year and those expenses should therefore be capitalised.

We follow the literature to measure intangibles by capitalising the intangible intermediates or intangible expenditure. Specifically, this study obtains relevant intermediate data from China's input–output tables and assumes that the ratio of the intermediate to the true intangible investment remains constant over time. The proxy approach is commonly adopted in measuring intangible investment and is well founded—for example, Gourio and Rudanko (2014b) proxy the S&GA for customer capital investment, and Tronconi and Marzetti (2011) and Eisfeldt and Papanikolaou (2014) proxy S&GA for organisational capital investment. Table 7.3 presents our proxies for intangible investment.

Table 7.3 Categories of intangible investment

	Proxy	Comments
1. Computerised information (mainly software)	Computer services and software intermediates	Includes software
2. Innovative property (a) Scientific R&D (b) Non-scientific R&D	Research industry intermediates	Includes R&D expenditure
3. Economic competencies (a) Brand equity (mainly advertising) (b) Firm-specific resources (organisational capital and staff training)	Culture, arts, radio, film and television industry intermediates	Includes parts of advertising expenditure
	Business service industry intermediates	Includes advertising expenditure and organisational investment
	Education industry intermediates	Includes staff training

Note: The intangible investment classification follows Corrado et al. (2009).
Source: Authors' construction.

Following Corrado et al. (2009), intangible investment is deflated to 1997 constant prices using the GDP deflator.[9] Since the interval of the input–output table is five years, we interpolate the missing data within the interval by assuming that the growth rate is constant within the five-year interval. The depreciation rate of intangible capital is set according to Corrado et al. (2009): 20 per cent for R&D, 33 per cent for computerised information, 60 per cent for brand equity and 40 per cent for firm-specific resources. Based on these, we assume 40 per cent for overall intangibles and 50 per cent for economic competency intangibles. Intangible capital in 1997 was set to zero and therefore 1998 is the first year for which this study calculates intangible capital. According to Corrado et al. (2009), the year in which initial capital stocks are zero has little effect on growth accounting analysis because the depreciation rates are high and much previous capital has been depreciated away by the date we start analysis—that is, 1998. Moreover, the amount of intangible capital in China was considerably smaller in the 1990s, as manifest by low R&D spending (0.57 per cent of GDP in 1996[10] and unavailable before that) and software use. Therefore, setting intangible capital in 1997 to zero will not cause significant problems.

9 The GDP deflator is obtained from the World Bank.
10 Data obtained from the World Bank.

Table 7.4 shows the trend of the sectoral average ratio of intangibles to tangibles. The amount of tangible capital is derived based on an assumed depreciation rate of 5 per cent.[11] The amount of intangible capital is calculated using the method explained above. Accompanying China's rapid economic growth over the past two decades has been a significant rise in its intangible–tangible ratio. However, compared with advanced economies, China's intensity of intangible capital use in production is still low and, therefore, there is plenty of room for catch-up in the future. For example, the intangible–tangible ratios of Japan, the United States and the United Kingdom in 2007 were 17 per cent, 22 per cent and 24 per cent,[12] respectively. Note that the parts of proxies include expenditure that is not intangible investment and excludes those that are produced within firms. This suggests that the actual intangible–tangible ratio might be lower or higher than the figures in Table 7.4.

Table 7.4 Increasing trend of intangibles in China (RMB thousand)

	1998	2002	2007	2012
Sectoral average intangibles	1,573,790	8,880,930	24,017,800	59,924,580
Sectoral average tangibles	216,289,200	333,212,600	697,231,200	1280,413,600
Ratio	0.7%	2.7%	3.4%	4.7%

Source: Authors' calculations using raw data from China's input–output tables.

Since TFP is the portion of output for which input cannot account (Comin 2004), we should be careful when linking TFP to intangible capital. Change in TFP is possibly caused by changes in human capital and institutional quality. The changes in human capital and institutions are often not sector-specific, which can be controlled for at the national level. To capture human capital and institutional quality changes, this study uses two proxies. The first is GDP per capita and the second is the time dummy that captures time effects. The positive correlation between economic development, human capital and institutional quality has been well documented (Weede and Kämpf 2002; Gwartney et al. 2004). The time dummy provides a different overall TFP growth rate for each year so we can separate the TFP growth at the national level from that caused by the change in intangible capital within individual industries. To control for the scale of an industry, the indicator of intangible capital is the ratio of intangibles to tangibles instead of the absolute amount of intangibles. Table 7.5 demonstrates the relationship between the growth rate of TFP and the growth rate of the intangible–tangible ratio. Note two types of TFP are used to check the robustness of our results: one is derived from RE/FE models and the other is LP derived from the LP models.

11 The most commonly used depreciation rate for the Chinese economy is 5 per cent.

12 Tangible capital data are obtained from the Penn World Table 8.1 (www.rug.nl/ggdc/productivity/pwt/pwt-releases/pwt8.1) and intangible capital data are from the cross-country intangible investment data website (www.intan-invest.net/).

Table 7.5 Relationship between the intangible–tangible ratio and TFP growth

	ΔIn(TFP)					ΔIn(TFP, LP)						
Variables	(1) OLS	(2) RE	(3) FE	(4) OLS	(5) RE	(6) FE	(7) OLS	(8) RE	(9) FE	(10) OLS	(11) RE	(12) FE
ΔIn(Intangible/tangible)	0.20***	0.20***	0.25***	0.20***	0.20***	0.25***	0.14***	0.14***	0.16***	0.14***	0.14***	0.16***
	(0.05)	(0.07)	(0.08)	(0.05)	(0.07)	(0.08)	(0.03)	(0.04)	(0.05)	(0.03)	(0.04)	(0.05)
ΔIn(GDP per capita)	0.42***	0.42**	0.56***				0.30**	0.30**	0.39***			
	(0.16)	(0.17)	(0.20)				(0.13)	(0.13)	(0.14)			
Constant	–0.33***	–0.33**	–0.45***	–0.16**	–0.16*	–0.23**	–0.12	–0.12	–0.19*	0.02	0.02	–0.02
	(0.12)	(0.14)	(0.17)	(0.07)	(0.09)	(0.11)	(0.09)	(0.10)	(0.11)	(0.05)	(0.06)	(0.07)
Observations	298	298	298	298	298	298	298	298	298	298	298	298
R-squared	0.18	0.18	0.23	0.27	0.27	0.32	0.11	0.11	0.15	0.25	0.25	0.30
Year fixed effects	NO	NO	NO	YES	YES	YES	NO	NO	NO	YES	YES	YES
Number of id		100	100		100	100		100	100		100	100

*** $p < 0.01$

** $p < 0.05$

* $p < 0.1$

Δ = first differenced

OLS = ordinary least squares

RE = random effects

FE = fixed effects

LP = Levinsohn and Petrin

Notes: Cluster robust standard errors in parentheses, except OLS; OLS is with robust standard error. Number of bootstrap replications: 400 for normal bootstrap, 250 for LP. TFP denotes the TFP derived from RE/FE models while 'TFP, LP' denotes TFP derived from LP models. Number of id refers to the number of individuals within the sample.

Source: Authors' calculations.

Importantly, the growth rate of the intangible–tangible ratio is economically and statistically significant across all specifications. A 1 per cent increase in the intangible–tangible ratio is associated with 0.26 per cent, 0.26 per cent, 0.31 per cent, 0.26 per cent, 0.26 per cent and 0.31 per cent growth in TFP according to models (1)–(6), respectively. A 1 per cent increase in the intangible–tangible ratio is associated with 0.14 per cent, 0.14 per cent, 0.16 per cent, 0.14 per cent, 0.14 per cent and 0.16 per cent growth in 'TFP, LP' according to models (7)–(12), respectively. Growth of the intangible–tangible ratio also explains a significant amount of TFP change, at 17 per cent according to model (4) and 11 per cent according to model (10).[13] The significant impact of intangibles on TFP is consistent with the findings of Haskel et al. (2014), who regress TFP on intangibles, information and communication technology and other variables and find that intangible capital is the only one that is significant. With GDP per capita and time effects as the control variables and the fixed-effects estimator, the intangible–tangible ratio is still statistically and economically significant, which suggests the finding is robust. Based on the above evidence, we thus conclude that intangible capital does play a significant role in China's productivity increase.

Another interesting question to ask is how the contributions of different categories of intangible capital to TFP growth differ. Table 7.6 shows the results of the effects of different intangible capital on TFP growth. When using the TFP derived from RE/FE models, all categories of intangible capital play important roles in the growth of TFP, being robust across all models. Specifically, according to model (4), a 1 per cent increase in the ratio of computerised information capital to tangible capital is associated with 0.08 per cent growth in TFP, 1 per cent growth in the ratio of R&D capital to tangible capital is associated with 0.11 per cent growth in TFP and 1 per cent growth in the ratio of economic competency capital to tangible capital is associated with 0.13 per cent growth in TFP. This is consistent with Chun et al. (2012), who find that innovative property is the most significant among all sorts of intangible investments when they are used to explain the growth of TFP in the Japanese economy. However, when the method of deriving TFP changes from FE/RE models to LP models, the results differ. Although the scale of the coefficients has not changed dramatically, the statistical significance has. The computerised information capital is no longer significant and the economic competency capital is insignificant when year effects are not controlled. R&D capital remains generally significant. When it comes to the scale of the effects, according to model (8), a 1 per cent increase in the ratio of computerised information capital to tangible capital is associated with a 0.03 per cent increase in 'TFP, LP', a 1 per cent increase

13 The square of partial correlation coefficient between $\Delta\ln(TFP)/\Delta\ln(TFP, LP)$ and $\Delta\ln(Intangible/tangible)$ is the percentage of variance in $\Delta\ln(TFP)/\Delta\ln(TFP, LP)$ that can be explained by $\Delta\ln(Intangible/tangible)$ in a model specification. Therefore, the 17 per cent and 11 per cent here are the squares of partial correlation coefficients between the two variables of interest in model (4) and model (10).

in the ratio of R&D capital to tangible capital is associated with a 0.04 per cent increase in 'TFP, LP' and a 1 per cent increase in the ratio of economic competency capital to tangible capital is associated with a 0.11 per cent increase in 'TFP, LP'.

Table 7.6 Impact of growth of different categories of intangible–tangible ratio on growth of TFP

	Δln(TFP)				Δln(TFP, LP)			
Variables	(1) OLS	(2) RE	(3) OLS	(4) RE	(5) OLS	(6) RE	(7) OLS	(8) RE
Δln(CI/Tangible)	0.07**	0.07**	0.06*	0.06*	0.05	0.05	0.03	0.03
	(0.03)	(0.03)	(0.03)	(0.03)	(0.03)	(0.03)	(0.03)	(0.03)
Δln(R&D/Tangible)	0.11***	0.11***	0.07**	0.07***	0.09***	0.09***	0.04	0.04*
	(0.03)	(0.03)	(0.03)	(0.03)	(0.03)	(0.03)	(0.03)	(0.02)
Δln(EC/Tangible)	0.08*	0.08*	0.12***	0.12***	0.05	0.05	0.11***	0.11***
	(0.04)	(0.04)	(0.04)	(0.04)	(0.03)	(0.03)	(0.03)	(0.03)
Constant	–0.05	–0.05	–0.14***	–0.14***	0.07*	0.07**	–0.05	–0.05
	(0.04)	(0.04)	(0.05)	(0.04)	(0.04)	(0.04)	(0.04)	(0.04)
Observations	196	196	196	196	196	196	196	196
R-squared	0.30	0.30	0.35	0.35	0.21	0.21	0.31	0.31
Year fixed effects	NO	NO	YES	YES	NO	NO	YES	YES
Number of id		98		98		98		98

*** $p < 0.01$

** $p < 0.05$

* $p < 0.1$

OLS = ordinary least squares

RE = random effects

Notes: Cluster robust standard errors in parentheses except OLS; OLS is with robust standard error. Cluster robust standard error is unavailable when using FE models due to insufficient rank, so FE models are not used. CI is computerised information (mainly software); R&D is innovative property; EC is economic competency; TFP denotes TFP derived from RE/FE models; while 'TFP, LP' is TFP derived from LP models. Number of id refers to the number of individuals within the sample.

Source: Authors' calculations.

Growth accounting incorporating intangible capital

According to Corrado et al. (2009), the production function could be written as Equation 7.9 when intangible capital is incorporated.

Equation 7.9

$$Y = AK^{ak}I^{ai}L^{al}$$

In Equation 7.9, *I* is the intangible capital stock and *ai* is the output elasticity of intangible capital. When intangible expenditure is viewed as investment, it should be counted as value added according to its national accounts identity (Corrado et al. 2009). Therefore, when conducting growth accounting with intangible capital, an even more accurate measurement of intangible investment is required. In this study, however, we do not know the ratio of the true intangible investment to proxies. One feasible action is to assume 100 per cent as the base case.[14]

Table 7.7 demonstrates the results of growth accounting incorporating intangible capital. The impacts of intangibles on the economic growth of all subgroups are economically and statistically significant. A 1 per cent increase in intangible capital is associated with 0.16 per cent, 0.22 per cent, 0.14 per cent and 0.24 per cent output growth in agriculture, heavy industry, light industry and services, respectively. This indicates that intangible capital has become an important source of growth in the Chinese economy.

Table 7.7 Results of growth accounting with intangibles

	(1)	(2)	(3)	(4)	(5)	(6)	(7)	(8)
	Agriculture		Heavy industry		Light industry		Services	
Variables	RE	RE bootstrap	RE	RE bootstrap	FE	FE bootstrap	FE	FE bootstrap
ln(Tangibles)	0.36***	0.36***	0.29***	0.29**	0.40***	0.40***	0.32***	0.32***
	(0.09)	(0.13)	(0.11)	(0.12)	(0.04)	(0.04)	(0.08)	(0.09)
ln(Labour)	0.54***	0.54***	0.44***	0.44***	0.37***	0.37***	0.39***	0.39***
	(0.04)	(0.09)	(0.11)	(0.10)	(0.06)	(0.06)	(0.07)	(0.10)
ln(Intangibles)	0.16***	0.15**	0.22***	0.22***	0.14***	0.14***	0.24***	0.24***
	(0.05)	(0.08)	(0.05)	(0.05)	(0.02)	(0.02)	(0.05)	(0.06)
Constant	5.68***	5.65***	6.56***	6.56***	6.36***	6.36***	6.09***	6.09***
	(0.38)	(0.54)	(0.74)	(0.83)	(0.39)	(0.39)	(0.49)	(0.68)
Observations	20	20	138	138	144	144	96	96
R-squared	0.87	0.87	0.88	0.88	0.92	0.92	0.93	0.93
Number of id	5	5	35	35	36	36	24	24

*** $p < 0.01$

** $p < 0.05$

* $p < 0.1$

RE = random effects

FE = fixed effects

Notes: Cluster robust standard errors in parentheses, except OLS; OLS is with robust standard error. Number of id refers to the number of individuals within the sample.

Source: Authors' calculations.

14 The value of proportion does not matter for the results. When varying the proportion, the results remain similar. For the details of how the proportion is changed, please see Appendix 7.2.

As mentioned earlier, intangible capital can be divided into computerised information, innovative property and economic competency. A question to be investigated is whether their roles differ across industries. To answer this question, we first assume a production function in which the intangible capital is decomposed (Equation 7.10).

Equation 7.10

$$Y = AK^{ak}CI^{ai1}RD^{ai2}EC^{ai3}L^{al}$$

In Equation 7.10, CI is computerised information (mainly software); RD is innovative property (R&D); EC is economic competency; and *ai*1, *ai*2 and *ai*3 are the output elasticities of the three inputs, respectively.

Table 7.8 shows the results of growth accounting using the above production function. Not all categories of intangible capital are significant (e.g. economic competency within the agricultural sector and R&D within the services sector). One reason might be the strong positive correlation between different categories of intangible capital due to their co-movement. However, from the results in Table 7.8, we are able to obtain some information about the roles of different intangible capital in different industries. In agriculture, R&D is significant and positive. A 1 per cent increase in R&D capital is predicted to increase a sector's value added by 0.15 per cent. The coefficients of economic competency and computerised information are small, which may indicate that their effects are trivial. In heavy industry, all are economically and statistically significant. A 1 per cent increase in R&D, economic competency and computerised information is associated with 0.13 per cent, 0.11 per cent and 0.04 per cent growth in value added, respectively. In light industry, both R&D and economic competency capital are significant. A 1 per cent increase in R&D and economic competency is correlated with a 0.08 per cent and 0.14 per cent increase in value added, respectively. The coefficient of computerised information capital is insignificant and small. Therefore, economic competency capital is likely to play the most important role in China's light industry of the three categories of intangible capital. In services, only economic competency is significant. A 1 per cent increase in economic competency capital is associated with 0.25 per cent of value-added growth. The coefficients of both R&D and computerised information capital are insignificant and small in value, which may imply that economic competency is the most important category of intangible capital in the services sector.

Table 7.8 Results of growth accounting with detailed intangible capital

	(1)	(2)	(3)	(4)	(5)	(6)	(7)	(8)
	Agriculture		Heavy industry		Light industry		Services	
Variables	RE	RE bootstrap	RE	RE bootstrap	FE	FE bootstrap	FE	FE bootstrap
ln(Tangibles)	0.35***	0.35	0.22***	0.22**	0.30***	0.30***	0.29***	0.29***
	(0.08)	(0.27)	(0.09	(0.10)	(0.06)	(0.05)	(0.06)	(0.07)
ln(Labour)	0.52***	0.52**	0.49***	0.49***	0.44***	0.44***	0.39***	0.39***
	(0.06)	(0.21)	(0.07)	(0.07)	(0.08)	(0.08)	(0.07)	(0.11)
ln(RD)	0.15***	0.15	0.13***	0.13***	0.08**	0.08**	0.02	0.02
	(0.03)	(0.15)	(0.02)	(0.03)	(0.03)	(0.03)	(0.02)	(0.02)
ln(EC)	0.02	0.02	0.11***	0.11**	0.14***	0.14***	0.25***	0.25***
	(0.05)	(0.13)	(0.04)	(0.05)	(0.02)	(0.03)	(0.05)	(0.05)
Ln(CI)	–0.06***	–0.06	0.04**	0.04**	–0.01	–0.01	0.02	0.02
	(0.01)	(0.07)	(0.02)	(0.02)	(0.01)	(0.01)	(0.03)	(0.03)
Constant	6.57***	6.57***	7.02***	7.02***	6.78***	6.78***	6.05***	6.05***
	(0.81)	(1.70)	(0.60)	(0.79)	(0.39)	(0.43)	(0.41)	(0.67)
Observations	20	20	137	137	144	144	92	92
R-squared	0.99	0.99	0.93	0.93	0.94	0.94	0.94	0.94
Number of id	5	5	35	35	36	36	23	23

*** $p < 0.01$

** $p < 0.05$

* $p < 0.1$

RE = random effects

FE = fixed effects

Notes: Cluster robust standard errors in parentheses, except OLS; OLS is with robust standard error. CI is computerised information (mainly software); R&D is innovative property; and EC is economic competency. Number of id refers to the number of individuals within the sample.

Source: Authors' calculations.

Conclusion

Intangible capital and its various forms—technology, product design, marketing and organisational development—are the foundation of knowledge economies. According to our results, China, a transitional economy, has started to benefit from the rapid growth of intangible capital. Using China's input–output tables for various years, this study provides an important insight into the role of intangible capital in different industries in the context of an emerging knowledge economy. It is specifically found that the growth in intangible capital is significantly associated with TFP growth in China, and explains almost 20 per cent of TFP growth over the sample period. The results are generally robust across the different model specifications.

This study also reveals the relative importance of different categories of intangible capital in different industries. In agriculture, R&D is likely to play a critical role, but the role of other intangible capital is relatively trivial. In the heavy-industry sector, R&D, computerised information (mainly software) and economic competency are all important to growth, but R&D is the most important. While the effects of both economic competency and R&D are significant to the growth of light industry, R&D is more significant. Last but not least, in the services sector, the role of economic competency is critical while those of the other categories are relatively unimportant. In other words, the role of R&D is important across all non-service industries, while the role of economic competency is paramount across all non-agriculture industries.

The use of intangible capital in production in China, however, remains relatively small compared with that in advanced economies. In 2007, the intangible–tangible ratio in China was approximately 3.4 per cent, compared with 17 per cent in Japan, 22 per cent in the United States and 24 per cent in the United Kingdom. This is consistent with China's role at the assembly end of global value chains and the fact that investment in design, intellectual property and branding remains the preserve of more developed economies. Given that the productivity boost from China's reform and opening up is diminishing and the country has entered the new normal phase, it is clearly time for China to invest in new sources of growth—and intangible capital is one of them.

The transformation from 'made in China' to 'designed in China' has a long way to run, but the shifts in the intangible–tangible ratio identified here suggest that China is catching up with frontier economies. Given the gradually increasing intangible capital in China, there is every reason to believe that rapid growth in intangible capital will become an increasingly important driver of China's economic growth.

References

Arato, H. and Yamada, K. (2012), Japan's intangible capital and valuation of corporations in a neoclassical framework, *Review of Economic Dynamics* 15(4): 459–78. doi.org/10.1016/j.red.2012.01.001.

Arrighetti, A., Landini, F. and Lasagni, A. (2014), Intangible assets and firm heterogeneity: Evidence from Italy, *Research Policy* 43(1): 202–13. doi.org/10.1016/j.respol.2013.07.015.

Asker, J., Farre-Mensa, J. and Ljungqvist, A. (2015), Corporate investment and stock market listing: A puzzle? *Review of Financial Studies* 28(2)(February): 342–90. doi.org/10.1093/rfs/hhu077.

Atkeson, A. and Kehoe, P. J. (2005), Modeling and measuring organization capital, *Journal of Political Economy* 113(5): 1026–53. doi.org/10.1086/431289.

Awano, G., Franklin, M., Haskel, J. and Kastrinaki, Z. (2010), Measuring investment in intangible assets in the UK: Results from a new survey, *Economic & Labour Market Review* 4(7): 66–71. doi.org/10.1057/elmr.2010.98.

Borgo, M. D., Goodridge, P., Haskel, J. and Pesole, A. (2013), Productivity and growth in UK industries: An intangible investment approach, *Oxford Bulletin of Economics and Statistics* 75(6): 806–34. doi.org/10.1111/j.1468-0084.2012.00718.x.

Chun, H. and Nadiri, M. I. (2016), Intangible investment and changing sources of growth in Korea, *Japanese Economic Review* 67(1): 50–76. doi.org/10.1111/jere.12079.

Chun, H., Fukao, K., Hisa, S. and Miyagawa, T. (2012), *Measurement of intangible investments by industry and its role in productivity improvement utilizing comparative studies between Japan and Korea*, RIETI Discussion Paper Series 12-E-037, The Research Institute of Economy, Trade and Industry, Tokyo.

Clausen, S. and Hirth, S. (2016), Measuring the value of intangibles, *Journal of Corporate Finance* 40: 110–27. doi.org/10.1016/j.jcorpfin.2016.07.012.

Comin, D. (2004), Harrod–Domar model, in J. Segura and C. R. Braun (eds), *An Eponymous Dictionary of Economics: A guide to laws and theorems named after economists*, p. 105, Cheltenham, UK: Edward Elgar.

Corrado, C. A. and Hulten, C. R. (2010), How do you measure a 'technological revolution'? *The American Economic Review* 100(2): 99–104. doi.org/10.1257/aer.100.2.99.

Corrado, C., Haskel, J., Jona-Lasinio, C. and Iommi, M. (2013), Innovation and intangible investment in Europe, Japan, and the United States, *Oxford Review of Economic Policy* 29(2): 261–86.

Corrado, C., Hulten, C. and Sichel, D. (2009), Intangible capital and US economic growth, *Review of Income and Wealth* 55(3): 661–685. doi.org/10.1111/j.1475-4991.2009.00343.x.

Eisfeldt, A. L. and Papanikolaou, D. (2013), Organization capital and the cross-section of expected returns, *The Journal of Finance* 68(4): 1365–406. doi.org/10.1111/jofi.12034.

Eisfeldt, A. L. and Papanikolaou, D. (2014), The value and ownership of intangible capital, *The American Economic Review* 104(5): 189–94. doi.org/10.1257/aer.104.5.189.

Feenstra, R. C., Inklaar, R. and Timmer, M. P. (2015), The next generation of the Penn World Table, *The American Economic Review* 105(10): 3150–82. doi.org/10.1257/aer.20130954.

Fukao, K., Miyagawa, T., Mukai, K., Shinoda, Y. and Tonogi, K. (2009), Intangible investment in Japan: Measurement and contribution to economic growth, *Review of Income and Wealth* 55(3): 717–36. doi.org/10.1111/j.1475-4991.2009.00345.x.

Goodridge, P., Jonathan H., and Gavin W. (2013), Can intangible investment explain the UK productivity puzzle?, *National Institute Economic Review* 224(1): R48–R58. doi.org/10.1177/002795011322400104.

Gourio, F. and Rudanko, L. (2014a), Can intangible capital explain cyclical movements in the labor wedge? *The American Economic Review* 104(5): 183–8. doi.org/10.1257/aer.104.5.183.

Gourio, F. and Rudanko, L. (2014b), Customer capital, *The Review of Economic Studies* 81(3): 1102–36. doi.org/10.1093/restud/rdu007.

Gwartney, J. D., Holcombe, R. G. and Lawson, R. A. (2004), Economic freedom, institutional quality, and cross-country differences in income and growth, *Cato Journal* 24: 205.

Harris, R. and Robinson, C. (2002), The effect of foreign acquisitions on total factor productivity: Plant-level evidence from UK manufacturing, 1987–1992, *Review of Economics and Statistics* 84(3): 562–8. doi.org/10.1162/003465302320259556.

Haskel, J. and Wallis, G. (2013), Public support for innovation, intangible investment and productivity growth in the UK market sector, *Economics Letters* 119(2): 195–8. doi.org/10.1016/j.econlet.2013.02.011.

Haskel, J., Corrado, C. and Jona-Lasinio, C. (2014), *Knowledge spillovers, ICT and productivity growth*, Working Paper, Imperial College Business School, Imperial College, London.

Hayashi, F. and Prescott, E. C. (2002), The 1990s in Japan: A lost decade, *Review of Economic Dynamics* 5(1): 206–35. doi.org/10.1006/redy.2001.0149.

Hulten, C. R. (1979), On the 'Importance' of Productivity Change, *The American Economic Review* 69 (1): 126–36.

Hulten, C. R. and Hao, J. X. (2012), *The role of intangible capital in the transformation and growth of the Chinese economy*, NBER Working Paper No. 18405, National Bureau of Economic Research, Cambridge, Mass.

Hulten, C. R. and Hao, X. (2008), *What is a company really worth? Intangible capital and the 'market to book value' puzzle*, NBER Working Paper No. 14548, National Bureau of Economic Research, Cambridge, Mass.

Kraemer, K., Linden, G. and Dedrick, J. (2011), *Capturing value in global networks: Apple's iPad and iPhone*, Working Paper, Personal Computing Industry Center, University of California, Irvine. Available from: pcic.merage.uci.edu/papers/2011/value_ipad_iphone.pdf.

Levinsohn, J. and Petrin, A. (2003), Estimating production functions using inputs to control for unobservables, *The Review of Economic Studies* 70(2): 317–41. doi.org/10.1111/1467-937X.00246.

Marrano, M. G., Haskel, J., and Wallis, G. (2009), What happened to the knowledge economy? ICT, intangible investment, and Britain's productivity record revisited, *Review of Income and Wealth* 55(3): 686–716. doi.org/10.1111/j.1475-4991.2009.00344.x.

McGrattan, E. R. and Prescott, E. C. (2010), Unmeasured investment and the puzzling US boom in the 1990s, *American Economic Journal: Macroeconomics* 2(4): 88–123. doi.org/10.1257/mac.2.4.88.

McGrattan, E. R. and Prescott, E. C. (2014), A reassessment of real business cycle theory, *The American Economic Review* 104(5): 177–82. doi.org/10.1257/aer.104.5.177.

Miyagawa, T. and Hisa, S. (2013), Estimates of intangible investment by industry and productivity growth in Japan, *Japanese Economic Review* 64(1): 42–72. doi.org/10.1111/jere.12000.

Nadiri, M. I. (1970), Some approaches to the theory and measurement of total factor productivity: A survey, *Journal of Economic Literature* 8(4): 1137–77.

National Bureau of Statistics of China (NBS) (various years), *China Labour Statistical Yearbook*, Beijing: China Statistics Press.

Niebel, T., O'Mahony, M. and Saam, M. (2017), The contribution of intangible assets to sectoral productivity growth in the EU, *Review of Income and Wealth* 63(1). doi.org/10.1111/roiw.12248.

Olley, G. S. and Pakes, A. (1996), The dynamics of productivity in the telecommunications equipment industry, *Econometrica: Journal of the Econometric Society* 64(6): 1263–97. doi.org/10.2307/2171831.

Tronconi, C. and Marzetti, G. V. (2011), Organization capital and firm performance: Empirical evidence for European firms, *Economics Letters* 112(2): 141–3. doi.org/10.1016/j.econlet.2011.04.004.

van Ark, B., Hao, J. X., Corrado, C., and Hulten, C. (2009), Measuring intangible capital and its contribution to economic growth in Europe, *EIB papers* 14(1): 62–93. hdl.handle.net/10419/44905.

Weede, E. and Kämpf, S. (2002), The impact of intelligence and institutional improvements on economic growth, *Kyklos* 55(3): 361–80. doi.org/10.1111/1467-6435.00191.

Zhu, X. (2012), Understanding China's growth: Past, present, and future, *The Journal of Economic Perspectives* 26(4): 103–24. doi.org/10.1257/jep.26.4.103.

Appendix 7.1. Industry classification

	Name	Subgroup
1	Farming	Agriculture
2	Forestry	Agriculture
3	Livestock products	Agriculture
4	Fisheries	Agriculture
5	Agricultural services	Agriculture
6	Coalmining and processing	Heavy industry
7	Petroleum and natural gas extraction	Heavy industry
8	Ferrous metals mining and processing	Heavy industry
9	Non-ferrous metals mining and processing	Heavy industry
10	Non-metal minerals mining and processing	Heavy industry
11	Processing of petroleum and nuclear fuel	Heavy industry
12	Processing of coking coal	Heavy industry
13	Manufacture of chemical raw materials	Heavy industry
14	Manufacture of fertiliser	Heavy industry
15	Manufacture of pesticide	Heavy industry
16	Manufacture of organic chemical products	Heavy industry
17	Manufacture of rubber	Heavy industry
18	Manufacture of plastics	Heavy industry
19	Manufacture of cement and asbestos products	Heavy industry
20	Manufacture of non-metallic mineral products	Heavy industry
21	Iron and steel products	Heavy industry
22	Smelting of steel	Heavy industry

	Name	Subgroup
23	Smelting of iron alloys	Heavy industry
24	Smelting of nonferrous metals	Heavy industry
25	Processing of nonferrous metals	Heavy industry
26	Manufacture of boilers, engines and turbines	Heavy industry
27	Manufacturer of metal-working machines	Heavy industry
28	Manufacture of other general industrial machinery	Heavy industry
29	Manufacture of agricultural, forestry, animal husbandry and fishing machinery	Heavy industry
30	Manufacture of other special industrial equipment	Heavy industry
31	Manufacture of railway equipment	Heavy industry
32	Manufacture of automobiles	Heavy industry
33	Manufacture of ship equipment	Heavy industry
34	Manufacture of other transportation equipment	Heavy industry
35	Manufacture of generators	Heavy industry
36	Recycling and disposal of waste	Heavy industry
37	Production and distribution of electric power	Heavy industry
38	Production and distribution of gas	Heavy industry
39	Processing and distribution of tap water	Heavy industry
40	Construction	Heavy industry
41	Processing of crops, cooking oil and stock feed	Light industry
42	Manufacture of sugar	Light industry
43	Processing of meat	Light industry
44	Processing of aquatic products	Light industry
45	Processing of other food	Light industry
46	Manufacture of alcohol	Light industry
47	Manufacture of beverages and tea	Light industry
48	Manufacture of tobacco	Light industry
49	Manufacture of textiles from cotton	Light industry
50	Manufacture of textiles from wool	Light industry
51	Manufacture of textiles from fibre and silk	Light industry
52	Manufacture of knitted products	Light industry
53	Manufacture of textile products	Light industry
54	Manufacture of textile, apparel, footwear and caps	Light industry
55	Manufacture of leather, fur, feather and related products	Light industry
56	Processing of timber, manufacture of wood, bamboo, rattan, palm and straw products	Light industry
57	Manufacture of paper and paper products	Light industry
58	Printing and recorded media	Light industry
59	Manufacture of equipment for culture, education and sports activity	Light industry
60	Manufacture of chemical products for daily use	Light industry
61	Manufacture of other chemical products	Light industry

	Name	Subgroup
62	Manufacture of medicines	Light industry
63	Manufacture of chemical fibres	Light industry
64	Manufacture of glass and glass products	Light industry
65	Manufacture of pottery, china and earthenware	Light industry
66	Manufacture of fireproof products	Light industry
67	Manufacture of metal products	Light industry
68	Manufacture of household electrical appliances	Light industry
69	Manufacture of other electrical machinery and equipment	Light industry
70	Manufacture of computers	Light industry
71	Manufacture of communication and other electronic equipment	Light industry
72	Manufacture of other household electronic appliances	Light industry
73	Manufacture of electronic elements and devices	Light industry
74	Manufacture of measuring instruments	Light industry
75	Manufacture of articles for culture, education and sports activity	Light industry
76	Manufacture of artwork and other manufacturing	Light industry
77	Railway transport	Service
78	Road transport	Service
79	Pipeline transport	Service
80	Air transport	Service
81	Water transport	Service
82	Storage	Service
83	Postal services	Service
84	Telecommunications	Service
85	Catering	Service
86	Finance	Service
87	Insurance	Service
88	Real estate	Service
89	Accommodation	Service
90	Residential and other services	Service
91	Entertainment	Service
92	Polytechnic services	Service
93	Health care	Service
94	Education	Service
95	Sports	Service
96	Social welfare	Service
97	Culture, arts, radio and television	Service
98	Research and experimental development	Service
99	Geological prospecting	Service
100	Public administration and social organisation	Service

Source: Authors' construction.

Appendix 7.2. Sensitivity analysis

The depreciation rate of intangible capital is often not well grounded, in both this study and previous studies. To check the robustness of the results, a sensitivity analysis is conducted. The changes in parameters in this study are comprehensive and occur in two directions: either an increase or a decrease. If the changes in both directions make little difference, the contributions of intangible capital to economic growth are believed to be robust.

Table 7.A1 Changes of parameters in sensitivity analysis (per cent)

	Base case	Case									
		1	2	3	4	5	6	7	8	9	10
Proxy ratio	100	50	150								
δ(Intangible)	40			60	20						
δ(RD)	20					10	40				
δ(EC)	50							25	75		
δ(CI)	33									11	66

Notes: Proxy ratio refers to the ratio of the actual intangible investment to the proxy; δ is the depreciation rate; RD is R&D capital; EC is economic competency capital; and CI is computerised information capital (mainly software).

Source: Authors' construction.

All the sensitivity analysis results are available from the authors. The changes in parameters do not change the significance and signs of the intangibles and the changes in regression coefficient are small. Therefore, the impacts of intangible capital on productivity are considerably robust.

Part III: Innovation and Productivity

8. China's Transition to a More Innovative Economy: Progress and Challenges

Shang-Jin Wei, Zhuan Xie and Xiaobo Zhang[1]

Introduction

After more than three decades of high growth based on the exploitation of low-wage and demographic advantages interacted with incremental market-oriented reforms and international openness, China now confronts higher wages and a shrinking workforce. Future growth will therefore depend increasingly on innovation and increased productivity. We assess the likelihood of China making this transition, using matched firm-level data on patent applications, receipts and citations and a survey of manufacturing firms. We find that embracing new international opportunities and adaptation to rising labour costs are two leading factors in China's increasingly innovative economy. As a result, Chinese exports are increasing in quality; and the market share of Chinese exports relative to other countries has increased steadily, even after controlling the unit value. We also find, however, evidence of resource misallocation in the innovation area: state-owned firms receive a greater share of innovation subsidies, but private firms are the more successful innovators. The transition to an innovation-led economy would presumably progress even faster if this resource misallocation could be tackled.

Over the period 1980–2015, China's economy grew at an average annual rate of 8.7 per cent, increasing real per capita income by a cumulative rate of 1,759 per cent, or from $714 in 1980 (in 2011 international purchasing power

1 We thank *Journal of Economic Perspectives* editors Gordon Hanson, Enrico Moretti and especially Timothy Taylor for very helpful comments and suggestions. We are also grateful for comments received at seminars/conferences held at Hong Kong Baptist University, New York University, University of Michigan and University of Western Australia, and support from the Natural Science Foundation of China (approval number 71350002), the National Science Foundation (approval number 7675172) and the key research base of China's Ministry of Education (14JJD790027). We thank Lea Sumulong and Joy Glazener for excellent editorial assistance and Lintong Lin for outstanding research assistance. The chapter represents the personal views of the authors and not necessarily those of the institutions with which they are affiliated. A shorter version of the chapter has been published as 'From "made in China" to "innovated in China": Necessity, prospect, and challenges' in the *Journal of Economic Perspectives* (31(1): 49–70, 2017). The journal has granted permission to reprint the article here.

parity (PPP) dollars) to $13,277 in 2015 (based on the International Monetary Fund's World Economic Outlook (WEO) data). Only one other economy, Equatorial Guinea, grew by as much over the same period.

For 25 consecutive years from 1990, China's economy grew at more than 6 per cent a year. No other country has grown at that uninterrupted rate for even 20 years since 1980 (the starting year of the WEO database), let alone one-quarter of a century. Over the same period, a very short list of economies did grow at or better than that rate for some 10–20 years, but these were not consecutive. Those economies are Ethiopia (17 years); Equatorial Guinea and the Republic of Korea (16 years each); Albania and Turkmenistan (15 years); Armenia (14 years); Maldives and Myanmar (13 years); Georgia, Chinese Taipei and Thailand (all 12 years); Estonia, Latvia and Lithuania (11 years); and Argentina, Azerbaijan, Belarus, Bhutan, Botswana, Iraq, Moldova, Seychelles, Singapore, Sri Lanka, Uzbekistan and Vietnam (10 years). China's growth performance is spectacular and exceptional.

That exceptional growth was based fundamentally on a combination of low wages and a favourable demographic structure, the potential of which was converted into actual growth through a sequence of domestic market-oriented institutional reforms and greater openness to trade and foreign investment. That, in turn, supported a catch-up process in the direction of the high-income economic frontier (see, for example, Fan et al. 2014). When China began its process of reform and opening up in 1980, its per capita income of $714 ranked it 136 of the 138 economies with sufficient data to be included in the WEO database. Even in 2001, the year China acceded to the World Trade Organization (WTO), and after a long period of sustained growth, per capita income was still lower than in 77 other countries. Throughout the period 1980–2011, the Chinese working-age cohort as a share of the total population was unusually high, partly due to rapid fertility declines associated with strict family planning policies brought in around 1980. Relatively low wages, a large workforce and a favourable dependency ratio formed a powerful combination of fundamentals for economic development. Since 2000, accession to the WTO and an imbalanced gender ratio in the premarital-age cohort have inspired additional entrepreneurship and work effort, which have added perhaps 2 percentage points to the growth rate (Wei and Zhang 2011b).

Since 2011, however, the working-age cohort (aged 15–60) has started to shrink in absolute size (due in part to the family planning policies of the previous three decades). By 2015, China's income had reached $13,277 (in 2011 international PPP dollars), but the average wage rate in current US dollar terms was higher than that of most economies outside the Organisation for Economic Co-operation and Development (OECD). China's economy has now reached another crossroad. The importance of these structural shifts helps explain the slowdown in the growth rate of between 6 per cent and 7 per cent since 2014, which will likely moderate further even though the economy is otherwise also affected by a cyclical downturn (e.g. a relatively weak global economy).

A country's potential growth comes from the sum of the growth of its workforce and the growth of its labour productivity. The Chinese workforce has been shrinking since 2011 (Cai and Wang 2008). Policy changes to extend the official retirement age or to encourage more female labour force participation will at best moderate the decline in the workforce. The relaxation of the one-child policy in November 2015 will, over the next decade and a half, make the dependency ratio worse, without altering the size of the workforce (no couple can give birth to a 16-year-old) (Wei 2015).

Both the Chinese Government and scholars often refer to the challenges facing China in the context of a possible 'middle-income trap' (among many others, see OECD 2013; Ma 2016). The 'middle-income trap hypothesis' (MITH) claims that only in exceptional cases can a middle-income country ever manage to become a high-income economy thanks to the fact that these economies face a uniquely challenging growth environment. Contrary to the popular hypothesis, however, using a transition matrix analysis and a non-parametric analysis (by regression trees), Han and Wei (2015) are unable to support an unconditional MITH, but they do identify conditions under which growth may be more likely to stagnate or even regress.

Given such factors, growth in labour productivity must become an important driver of overall economic growth. In 2015, China's investment to gross domestic product (GDP) ratio, at 43.3 per cent, was already high by international standards, making it doubtful continued physical investment would deliver a higher rate of labour productivity growth. Moreover, Bai and Zhang (2014) estimated that returns to investment have in fact shown signs of decline since 2008. Increased productivity could, however, come from reducing resource misallocation (Hsieh and Klenow 2009), including via further reforms to factor and product markets such as reform of state-owned enterprises (SOEs). This area of potential productivity gains is, however, also limited. The pace of future reform is unlikely to be as aggressive as in the past, partly because many of the low-hanging fruits have already been picked and partly because society (read: interest groups) now has greater means to block reforms than in earlier decades. An additional potential source of productivity gains is the discovery of new products, new uses for existing products, new designs and production processes and the conversion of these innovations into new sales or cost reductions.

In this chapter, we study whether China can transition to a more innovation-driven growth model. Specifically, we study three questions. First, how much growth in innovation is actually occurring in Chinese firms? We approach this question from a comparative perspective and ask how China's rate of innovation compares with that in Brazil, Russia, India and South Africa (the BRICS economies) and also with South Korea. India has a lower per capita income than China but is comparable in population size, and, like China, it has a diaspora with a strong presence in science and technology, academic and elite chief executive officer (CEO) communities in the United States. Brazil, Russia and South Korea all have higher income per capita than China. South Korea, in particular, has experienced a growth miracle that leads China by about 25 years. Its industry includes a string of successful and innovative companies, such as Samsung and LG, and, in many ways, it presents a model that China wishes to emulate.

We draw comparison between China and the selected countries using data on patent applications by and patents granted to firms both at home and in the United States as a proxy for innovative activities. Patent data are sourced from the State Intellectual Property Office of China (SIPO), the US Patent and Trademark Office (USPTO) and the World Intellectual Property Organization (WIPO). We find evidence that China's performance on innovative activities—as measured by the pace of patent applications, patents granted and citations of patents—has been strong, particularly recently.

Second, we explore what accounts for the relatively rapid pace of innovation by Chinese firms as measured by patent applications. In particular, we explore whether this derives from China granting patents using a threshold lower than international standards, government subsidies for research and development (R&D) activities or disproportionate innovations by state-owned firms that have privileged access to resources. Or do Chinese firms embrace the challenge of rising wage costs and embark on innovation to adjust to the evolving comparative advantage?

China's accession to the WTO created greater market access for its exports, enabling export firms to better recover the cost of R&D investment, stimulating their innovative activities. We use export data to investigate whether Chinese firms have converted innovation into quality improvement and increased export market shares even in the face of progressively rising labour costs, including in comparison with competitor economies. We report evidence that the market share of Chinese exports does generally increase, even after controlling for the unit cost of its exports relative to those of its competitors. Facing rising labour costs, labour-intensive or routine-intensive firms have recently become increasingly innovative compared with capital-intensive firms. We find that, overall, rising wages and expanding markets are the two most important drivers of China's explosion in patents.

Third, since a feature of the Chinese economy is the significant presence of SOEs, we investigate possible resource misallocation in the innovation space. We find that although SOEs have received a relatively high share of government subsidies, their performance in innovation is lacklustre compared with that of private enterprises. Furthermore, the elasticity of patent filing or patents granted per renminbi (RMB) of subsidy is significantly higher for private sector firms than for SOEs. We interpret these patterns as reflecting the misallocation of public funds. Interestingly, we also find evidence that SOEs often face higher realised tax burdens than private firms (the sum of corporate income tax and value-added tax as a share of sales or profits). To improve the efficiency of resource allocation, policy reforms should perhaps put weight on simultaneous reductions in discretionary subsidies and taxes.

In the next section, we provide an overview of the sources of past economic growth. In section three, we examine the pace of innovation in Chinese firms, with particular attention to patent data. In section four, we examine the sources of innovation growth—in particular, the possible roles of the misreporting of and/or lax approval processes for patents, expanding market opportunities, subsidies and tax reductions and rising wages. In section five, we implement a robustness check, seeking evidence of quality improvement in Chinese exports in an era of rapidly rising local wages. In section six, we investigate resource allocation efficiency—especially government subsidies to firms of different ownership types—and its role in firms' innovation. We draw our conclusions in section seven.

Sources of historical growth

China's rapid growth in the past several decades has been driven by two sets of factors: 1) market-oriented policy reforms (which allowed market-determined output prices and factor prices to progressively replace administrative prices, and the introduction and strengthening of property rights) and the policy of opening up (reducing barriers to international trade and investment); and 2) economic fundamentals—a favourable demographic structure and low initial labour costs. Since we have discussed the wage and demographic factors, we will provide a brief review of the institutional reforms that allowed firms to use the economic fundamentals as a source of growth.

The Chinese growth miracle started with reform of the rural household responsibility system (HRS) in the early 1980s. Under the HRS, farmers were granted land cultivation rights so they could make their own production decisions. With better-aligned incentives, agricultural production and rural incomes increased dramatically in the ensuing years (Lin 1992). In just a few years, hundreds of millions of farmers were released from their land, providing the non-farm sector with a seemingly unlimited labour supply. In the 1980s, China's labour costs were among the lowest of the developing countries—lower than India and the Philippines. The availability of large numbers of low-wage workers ensured China's growth model in the subsequent three decades was based on low-cost production.

In the 1980s, township and village–owned enterprises (TVEs) grew rapidly thanks to abundant labour and rising market demand for daily goods after the successful rural reforms. TVEs were largely manufacturing firms in rural areas, and can be regarded as a second-best response to the institutional barriers to free relocation of labour across space; they provided a way for China to accelerate the movement of labour from low-productivity activities in rural areas to higher-productivity manufacturing activities before restrictions on internal migration were removed. Because they are second-best entities, TVEs also carry their own distortions, as their property rights have not always been clearly defined. In the 1990s, the government launched massive TVE and SOE reforms in an attempt to give entrepreneurs more incentives. Most TVEs were privatised. For SOEs, the government adopted a policy of 'grasping the big, letting go of the small' by privatising small SOEs and consolidating large ones (Hsieh and Song 2015). After the reforms, TVE employment plummeted from 129 million in 1995 to just 6 million in 2011, while SOE employment dropped from 113 million in 1995 to 67 million in 2011. The number of SOEs declined by 92 per cent, from 744,240 in 1995 to 61,204 in 2014 (Table 8.1).

Table 8.1 Number of Chinese firms

Year	No. of existing firms	No. of newly established firms	Private (%)	SOE (%)	Foreign (%)
1995	4,102,757	705,684	74.94	18.14	6.92
1996	4,628,316	676,993	76.71	17.98	5.31
1997	5,029,932	704,512	78.26	16.72	5.02
1998	5,328,497	803,088	80.13	15.67	4.19
1999	5,563,881	838,987	81.18	15.16	3.66
2000	5,752,414	849,768	83.81	12.00	4.20
2001	5,918,494	914,449	86.47	8.57	4.96
2002	6,079,731	1,043,979	88.04	6.82	5.14
2003	6,410,225	1,237,360	89.61	5.59	4.80
2004	6,896,890	1,356,846	91.11	3.96	4.93
2005	7,473,111	1,363,405	91.42	3.40	5.18
2006	8,061,934	1,361,640	92.50	2.83	4.67
2007	8,658,343	1,324,605	92.24	2.72	5.04
2008	9,050,977	1,311,798	92.50	2.74	4.75
2009	9,500,295	1,530,672	95.26	1.63	3.11
2010	10,230,384	1,802,531	96.09	1.24	2.66
2011	11,254,499	2,021,418	96.58	0.95	2.47
2012	12,463,854	2,002,236	96.82	0.9	2.28

Year	No. of existing firms	No. of newly established firms	Private (%)	SOE (%)	Foreign (%)
2013	13,544,658	2,611,083	97.69	0.63	1.68
2014	15,300,901	3,681,347	98.35	0.40	1.25
Annual growth rate (%)					
1995–2004	5.94	7.53	8.27	−10.54	2.02
2004–2014	8.29	10.50	9.13	−13.89	−5.59
1995–2014	7.17	9.08	8.72	−12.32	−2.06

Source: Tabulated by the authors based on the China Firm Registry Database.

In the short term, the reform was a painful process; large numbers of urban workers had to leave SOEs. Remarkably, the country avoided a big spike in the unemployment rate. The key was that the de facto privatisation was accompanied by aggressive reforms that lowered the entry barriers for private sector entrepreneurs. The inefficiency of the previous centrally planned, state-dominated economic system, together with high barriers to entry, meant there was a huge level of unexplored or underexplored opportunities for profit-making, and private sector entrepreneurs responded quickly. As a result, almost all of the jobs lost from TVEs and SOEs were offset by new job opportunities in the private sector. The number of private enterprises increased nearly fivefold, to more than 15 million, in the period 1995–2014 (see Table 8.1). By 2011, 193 million people worked in private enterprises (including those who were self-employed)—about three times the workforce in SOEs (NBS 2012). Therefore, in terms of employment share by ownership, the Chinese economy has clearly come to be dominated by the private sector. Indeed, Wei and Zhang (2011b), using firm-level census data for 1994 and 2005, document two 70 per cent rules: first, approximately 70 per cent of the growth in industrial value added came from private sector firms in this period; second, approximately 70 per cent of private sector growth in value added came from the increase in the number of new private sector firms (the extensive margin), while the remaining 30 per cent came from the growth of existing firms (the intensive margin).

China also reformed its financial system to provide local governments with better incentives to develop their economies. Under the arrangements introduced in the early 1980s, local governments and the central government follow a predetermined revenue formula (varying across regions as a result of local bargaining power), greatly stimulating local officials' incentive to create a more business-friendly environment. The system was reformed further in 1994, with the introduction of a value-added tax and a nationally uniform formula with which to divide revenue collection between the central and local governments. These reforms empowered entrepreneurs and local officials, providing them an impetus to pursue growth.

From the start of the Deng Xiaoping era in 1979, China adopted a development strategy of 'opening up' to the outside world. The government set up special zones in the coastal provinces to attract foreign direct investment (FDI) in the 1980s and 1990s, and integration with the global economy was accelerated after the country joined the WTO in December 2001. As China opened up, the external demand for its products increased, which in turn stimulated the growth of private enterprises. China's open-door policy and abundant cheaper labour attracted massive inflows of FDI. By 2003, China had become the largest recipient of inward FDI. The openness to trade and FDI has facilitated economic growth through many channels and has also had important impacts on the rest of the world (see Feenstra and Wei 2010).

As well as extensive growth in firms and augmented input use, knowledge growth and productivity improvement are key drivers of economic growth. The increase in productivity stems from sectoral innovation and the reallocation of resources (mainly labour) from low to highly productive sectors. Innovation and infrastructure investment are key pillars of intra-sector productivity improvement. The role of innovation in productivity growth has been widely discussed in the literature (Romer 1990). China's rapid build up in infrastructure gives it some advantage in improving productivity. Even though its first expressway was not built until 1988, China's total highway length reached 122,300 kilometres by 2015—more than any other country. The story of China's high-speed rail (HSR) is equally, if not more, remarkable. Starting from nothing in 2005, its constructed length had surpassed 19,300 km by 2015. In 2016, a Chinese HSR company went to the United States to negotiate building the first HSR in that country.[2]

As well as productivity growth within a firm or sector, structural change can also contribute to economic growth by shifting resources from less productive to more productive sectors, such as from the state sector to the private sector or from the agricultural sector to non-agricultural sectors (Zhu 2012). It is estimated that sectoral productivity increases and structural change accounted for 42 per cent and 17 per cent of economic growth, respectively, during 1978–95 (Fan et al. 2003).

Demographic factors were powerful drivers of China's growth in the past three-and-a-half decades (and are an important contributor to the recent growth slowdown). China's fertility rate should have dropped over the same period as its per capita income rose; however, the actual decline was more pronounced than that suggested by international experience because of the family planning policies implemented from 1979. The sharp decline in the fertility rate means there are fewer young dependants to support for a given working-age cohort. The share of prime-age population in the total population rose steadily for three decades, creating a demographic dividend, which in turn contributed to economic growth (Cai and Wang 2008).

2 www.wsj.com/articles/u-s-throws-china-off-high-speed-rail-project-1465465356.

The one-child policy yields an unintended consequence in distorting the sex ratio in favour of boys, meaning that as this generation reaches marriageable age, young men face a very competitive environment. To attract potential brides, families with sons choose to work harder, save more and take more risks, including exhibiting a higher propensity to become entrepreneurs (Wei and Zhang 2011a, 2011b; Chang and Zhang 2015; Wei et al. 2016). It is estimated that increasing competition in the marriage market due to sex ratio imbalances has contributed to about 2 percentage points of economic growth per annum (Wei and Zhang 2011b). It is important to note that this additional growth is of an immiserising type: social welfare is likely to decline even though GDP growth increases. The logic for this is explained in Wei and Zhang (2011b): the extra work effort and extra risk-taking that produce a higher GDP growth rate are motivated by a desire to improve one's chances (or one's children's chances) in the marriage market. Yet, the share of young men who will not get married in the aggregate is determined by the sex ratio, and not by the economy-wide work effort, risk-taking or GDP growth rate. In this sense, the extra work effort and risk-taking are futile; utility-maximising households would have happily given up this part of income growth if there were no sex ratio imbalance.

For three decades after the start of market-oriented reforms in the country, China appeared to have inexhaustible 'surplus labour' (low-productivity labour in rural areas). Signs of a labour shortage started to emerge, however, in the mid-2000s. According to Cai and Du (2011) and Zhang et al. (2011), wages for unskilled workers have shown double-digit growth since 2003–04, indicating the country might have crossed the so-called Lewis turning point, which means the era of surplus labour is over.

The exact timing of the sharp increase in the wage rate for unskilled workers is a subject of debate. Wang et al. (2011) report a turning point as early as 2000. On the other hand, Knight et al. (2011) and Golley and Meng (2011), for example, point out that barriers to internal migration—especially the rigid household registration system that prevents rural households from moving freely to urban areas—allow additional scope for rural–urban migration if and when the remaining barriers are dismantled. Either way, China is no longer a low-wage country.

Since the onset of the Global Financial Crisis (GFC) in 2008, external demand for Chinese products has weakened. The previous growth model based on exploiting cheap labour is no longer viable. As a result of the strict family planning policies implemented in the early 1980s, the number of entrants to the labour force fell below the number leaving from 2011. The usually favourable dependency ratio has become an unusually unfavourable ratio. Facing rising labour costs and weak external demand, firms have to make a tough choice: to move in, out, down or up. Moving 'in' means relocating factories from coastal to inland areas, where wages are lower. Given the pace of convergence within the country, this is at best a temporary strategy. Moving 'out' means engaging in outbound direct investment, combining Chinese knowhow with low wages in other countries. No doubt, some Chinese companies are pursuing this strategy. Moving 'down' means closing the business, which is an option for individual firms, but not for the country as a whole. Moving 'up' means engaging in innovation and upgrading so firms no longer need to depend on low-paid unskilled labour. While firms will employ a portfolio of such strategies, a decisive factor for China's economic future will be whether its firms can innovate and upgrade, and how fast they can do so. In the next section, we focus on innovation and quality upgrading and ask the question: can China transition to become a more innovative economy?

The pace of innovation as measured by growth in patents

Innovation can take the form of commercial secrets or patents, or it can be about improving business processes or models, in addition to inventing new products. Innovation can also take place outside the commercial space, such as in the cultural sphere. Due to data availability, we focus on patents lodged by firms as a measure of innovation.

Alongside rapid economic growth in China, the number of patents has exploded. The number of patent applications filed with SIPO leapt from less than 100,000 in 1995 to more than 2 million in 2014, with an annual growth rate of 19 per cent—doubling the per capita GDP growth rate in the same period. The annual growth rate of patent filings has accelerated from 17 per cent in the period 1995–2014 to 21 per cent between 2004 and 2014 (see Table 8.2). By 2011, China had overtaken the United States as the world's most prolific patent filer (WIPO 2012).

Among the three types of patents—invention, utility model and design—the share of applications for invention patents (arguably, the most technically intensive) rose from 26 per cent in 1995 to 39 per cent in 2014. In 1995, foreign patent filings accounted for more than 17 per cent of total applications, but the share of foreign filings dropped to a mere 6 per cent in 2014. The latter suggests that indigenous innovation has played an increasing role in the Chinese economy. Easy approvals, low-quality patent filings, government subsidies, expanded market opportunities and responses to rising labour costs have been offered as potential reasons for this explosion in Chinese patents. But how do these trends compare with the patent gains of the economies noted in the introduction?

Table 8.2 Number of Chinese patent applications, 1995–2014

Year	Total domestic applications	Of domestic patent applications				Total overseas applications
		Invention (%)	Utility model (%)	Design (%)	Foreign (%)	
1995	83,045	26	53	21	17	205
1996	102,735	28	48	24	20	201
1997	114,208	29	44	27	21	178
1998	121,989	29	42	28	21	259
1999	134,239	27	43	30	18	383
2000	170,682	30	40	29	18	652
2001	203,573	31	39	30	19	846
2002	252,631	32	37	31	19	1,138
2003	308,487	34	35	30	19	1,368
2004	353,807	37	32	31	21	2,365
2005	476,264	36	29	34	20	3,258
2006	573,178	37	28	35	18	5,293
2007	693,917	35	26	39	15	6,041
2008	828,328	35	27	38	13	7,099
2009	976,686	32	32	36	10	9,766
2010	1,222,286	32	34	34	9	11,703
2011	1,633,347	32	36	32	8	14,937
2012	2,050,649	32	36	32	7	19,627
2013	2,377,061	35	37	38	6	22,008
2014	2,361,243	39	37	24	6	26,356
Annual growth rate of total number of patents in different periods (%)						
1995–2004	17	22	11	23	20	31
2004–2014	21	22	23	18	7	27
1995–2014	19	22	17	20	13	29

Sources: Tabulated by the authors based on aggregate online data from SIPO (www.sipo.gov.cn/tjxx/) and WIPO (various years).

We start by drawing a comparison between the ease of patent approval in China and that in other countries. Figure 8.1 shows the patent approval rate in BRICS countries, South Korea and the United States. The Chinese ratio of 0.5 is not unusually high, *ceteris paribus*, indicating it is not especially easy to obtain patent approval. Approved patents have exhibited a pattern of rapid growth similar to that for patent applications. The annual growth rate of patents approved by SIPO between 1995 and 2014 is the same as that for patent applications—that is, 19 per cent (Table 8.3). The number of patents granted by developed countries grew by 28 per cent per annum during the same period. It is widely believed that Chinese firms, individuals and institutions tend to file high-quality patents in developed countries rather than with SIPO. The much more rapid growth in overseas patent applications signals an improvement in Chinese patent quality.

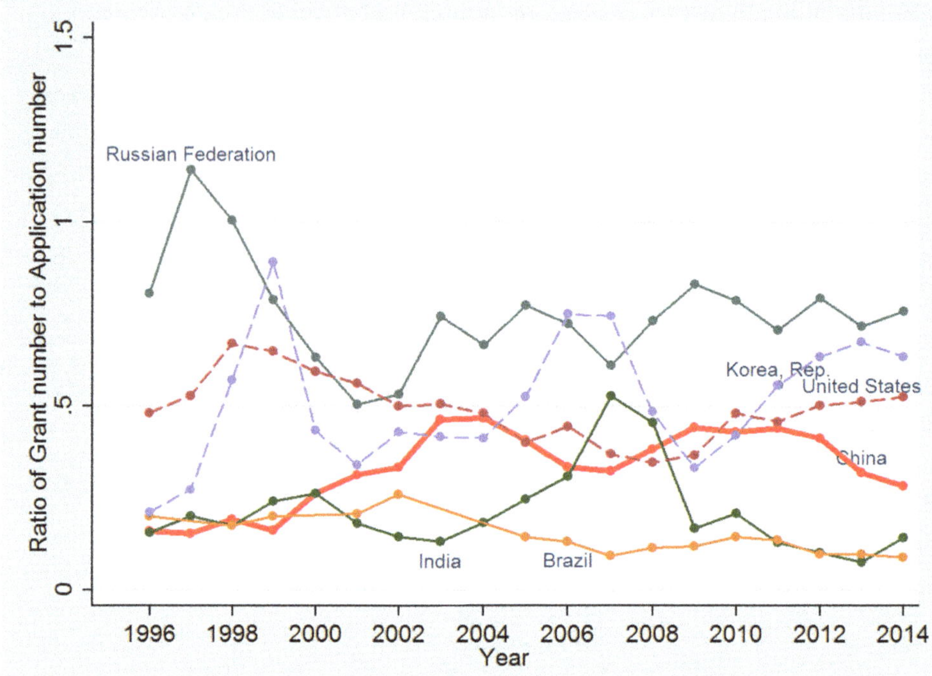

Figure 8.1 Patent approval rates in BRICS countries, South Korea and the United States

Note: The approval rate is defined as grant number in *T* divided by application number in *T*–1.

Source: WIPO (various years).

We investigate whether the rapid growth in patents reflects a low starting base. First, we divide the sample into two periods, 1995–2004 and 2004–14, and calculate the annual growth rate for each. If a low initial value is the major cause of the phenomenal growth in patents then we would expect to see a lower growth rate in the second period, when the initial base was much larger. In fact, we observe that the annual growth rate for both patent filings and patent approvals in the second period is 4 percentage points higher than in the initial period.

Table 8.3 Number of patents approved by SIPO and patents granted to Chinese applicants from overseas patent offices, 1995–2014

Year	Total domestically approved patents	Of domestically approved patents				Total approved patents overseas
		Invention (%)	Utility model (%)	Design (%)	Foreign (%)	
1995	45,064	8	68	25	8	99
1996	43,780	7	62	31	9	97
1997	50,996	7	54	40	9	91
1998	67,889	7	50	43	10	95
1999	100,156	8	56	36	8	126
2000	105,345	12	52	36	10	157
2001	114,251	14	48	38	13	225
2002	132,399	16	43	40	15	334
2003	182,226	20	38	42	18	362
2004	190,238	26	37	37	20	524
2005	214,003	25	37	38	20	539
2006	268,002	22	40	38	16	847
2007	351,782	19	43	38	14	1,013
2008	411,982	23	43	34	14	1,652
2009	581,992	22	35	43	14	2,234
2010	814,825	17	42	41	9	3,434
2011	960,513	18	42	40	8	4,255
2012	1,255,138	17	46	37	7	6,433
2013	1,313,000	16	53	31	6	8,337
2014	1,302,687	18	54	28	7	10,282
Annual growth rate in different periods (%)						
1995–2004	17	35	10	23	29	20
2004–2014	21	17	26	18	9	35
1995–2014	19	25	18	20	18	28

Sources: Tabulated by the authors based on aggregate online data from SIPO (www.sipo.gov.cn/tjxx/) and WIPO (various years).

Second, we look at the trend for foreign citations of patents approved by SIPO to gauge the quality of domestically approved patents in China. Although SIPO does not count the domestic citations of Chinese patents, patents granted in developed countries specify all the patents cited, including those approved by SIPO. Table 8.4 reports the number of citations of domestically approved invention and utility model patents in China from 1995 to 2014. During the period 1995–2004, the annual growth rate of foreign citations of Chinese invention patents was 34 per cent, and this accelerated to 49 per cent in the second period, 2004–14. The number of citations of utility model patents resembles that for invention patents, growing at

36 per cent per annum over the whole period. The growth in foreign citations of domestic patents even outpaces the growth of domestic patents, which suggests that at least a share of the Chinese patents filed are of citable quality internationally.

Table 8.4 Foreign patents citations on Chinese domestic patents approved by SIPO, 1995–2014

Year	Invention patents	Utility patents
1995	100	65
1996	114	62
1997	174	100
1998	201	98
1999	244	125
2000	303	198
2001	522	357
2002	667	440
2003	1,019	681
2004	1,358	851
2005	1,765	1,089
2006	2,984	1,830
2007	5,087	2,721
2008	9,183	4,084
2009	13,347	5,097
2010	20,781	7,752
2011	30,706	11,241
2012	45,364	16,132
2013	55,649	21,072
2014	71,383	23,544
Annual growth rate in different periods (%)		
1995–2004	34	33
2004–2014	49	39
1995–2014	41	36

Source: Tabulated by authors based on WIPO (various years).

Third, we compare patents by Chinese firms approved by the USPTO with patents by firms from other countries approved by USPTO to investigate whether China is an outlier. This could help us to control for differences in quality between patents approved by the USPTO and those granted by SIPO. Table 8.5 presents the number of patents granted by the USPTO to applicants from BRICS countries, as well as from Germany, Japan and South Korea. Of the sampled countries, between 1995 and 2014, China saw the fastest growth in the number of patents approved by the USPTO, with an annual growth rate of 28 per cent. Moreover, as the data in Table 8.5 reveal, the gap in the growth rate between China and the other countries has widened over time. The annual growth rate of Chinese patents approved by the USPTO in 2004–14 reached 33 per cent, 10 percentage points higher than the second-placed country, India. By comparison, patents granted to South Korea, Germany and Japan grew by 14 per cent, 4 per cent and 4 per cent per annum, respectively, during the period.

Table 8.5 Total number of patents granted by the USPTO to (corporate) applicants from BRICS countries, Germany, Japan and South Korea

Year	China	Brazil	India	Russia	South Africa	Germany	Japan	South Korea
1995	62	63	37	98	123	6,600	21,764	1,161
1996	46	63	35	116	111	6,818	23,053	1,493
1997	62	62	47	111	101	7,008	23,179	1,891
1998	72	74	85	189	115	9,095	30,841	3,259
1999	90	91	112	181	110	9,337	31,104	3,562
2000	119	98	131	183	111	10,234	31,296	3,314
2001	195	110	177	234	120	11,260	33,223	3,538
2002	289	33	249	200	114	11,278	34,859	3,786
2003	297	130	341	202	112	11,444	35,517	3,944
2004	404	106	363	169	100	10,779	35,348	4,428
2005	402	77	384	148	87	9,011	30,341	4,352
2006	661	121	481	172	109	10,005	36,807	5,908
2007	772	90	546	188	82	9,051	33,354	6,295
2008	1,225	101	634	176	91	8,915	33,682	7,549
2009	1,655	103	679	196	93	9,000	35,501	8,762
2010	2,657	175	1,098	272	116	12,363	44,814	11,671
2011	3,174	215	1,234	298	123	11,920	46,139	12,262
2012	4,637	196	1,691	331	142	13,835	50,677	13,233
2013	5,928	254	2,424	417	161	15,498	51,919	14,548
2014	7,236	334	2,987	445	152	16,550	53,849	16,469
Annual growth rate in different periods (%)								
1995–2004	23	6	29	6	–2	6	6	16
2004–2014	33	12	23	10	4	4	4	14
1995–2014	28	9	26	8	1	5	5	15

Note: The figures represent the total number of patents granted to applicants from these countries by the USPTO.

Source: Computed by authors based on data from WIPO (various years).

Assuming that talent is normally distributed evenly across countries, China, as the most populous country, enjoys a larger talent pool than other countries when it comes to generating innovative ideas. Its rapid growth in patents granted since the period of opening up and reform, both domestically and overseas, may have something to do with its large population size. To address this concern, we should control for population size when making the international comparisons. Similarly, the level of economic development also matters for the total number of patents: wealthier countries can afford to devote more resources to R&D and face a stronger necessity to innovate than poor countries. Thus, we should also control for per capita GDP in our comparisons.

For international comparison, we include OECD and BRICS countries in our sample. We regress the total number of invention patents granted by the USPTO on population size (log), per capita GDP (log), country fixed effects, year fixed effects and country × year fixed effects. Figure 8.2 plots the estimated coefficients for the country × year fixed effects for Japan, Germany, South Korea and BRICS countries versus their per capita GDP. The conditional plot reflects the time trend of patents approved by the USPTO from applicants in these countries after controlling for their population size and level of economic development. As revealed in the figure, along with economic growth, China has registered steady growth in invention patents, while other countries, with the exception of India, do not exhibit such a clear trend. In the sample period, India also displays a positive correlation between economic growth and patent growth, but China has come out ahead of India in terms of obtaining patent approvals from the USPTO.

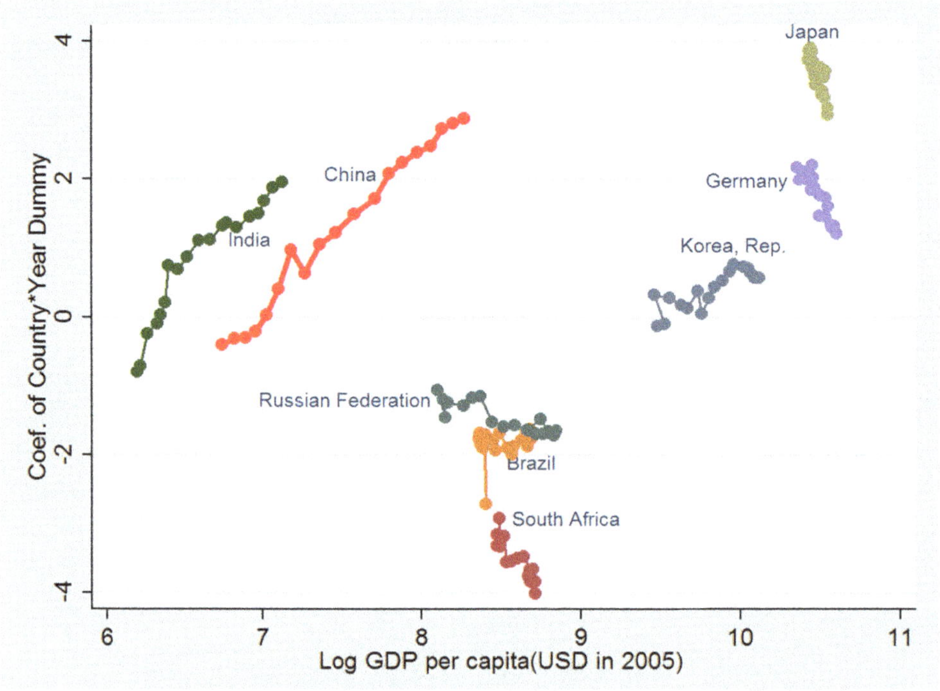

Figure 8.2 Invention patents granted by the USPTO for different countries

Note: Conditional plot by controlling for population, population squared and country and year fixed effects.

Sources: Based on data from OECD and, for BRICS countries, from WIPO (various years).

To understand the value of patents to innovators, it is useful to look at the frequency of citations of a patent by other patent applicants. In Figure 8.3, the total number of citations of patents by country in all patents granted by the USPTO in subsequent years (forward citations) replaces the total number of patents granted in Figure 8.2. Once again, China and India demonstrate a clear upward trend with GDP growth. Because China grew faster than India, the growth in citations of Chinese patents appears more remarkable in the figure. By comparison, the patterns are not apparent for other BRICS countries, Japan, Germany and South Korea. Importantly, if one fits a log linear line between patents cited and log income based on other countries' experiences, the graph appears to suggest that China is awarded more patents than other BRICS countries (except India) and more than the comparator advanced countries when their income level is comparable China's.

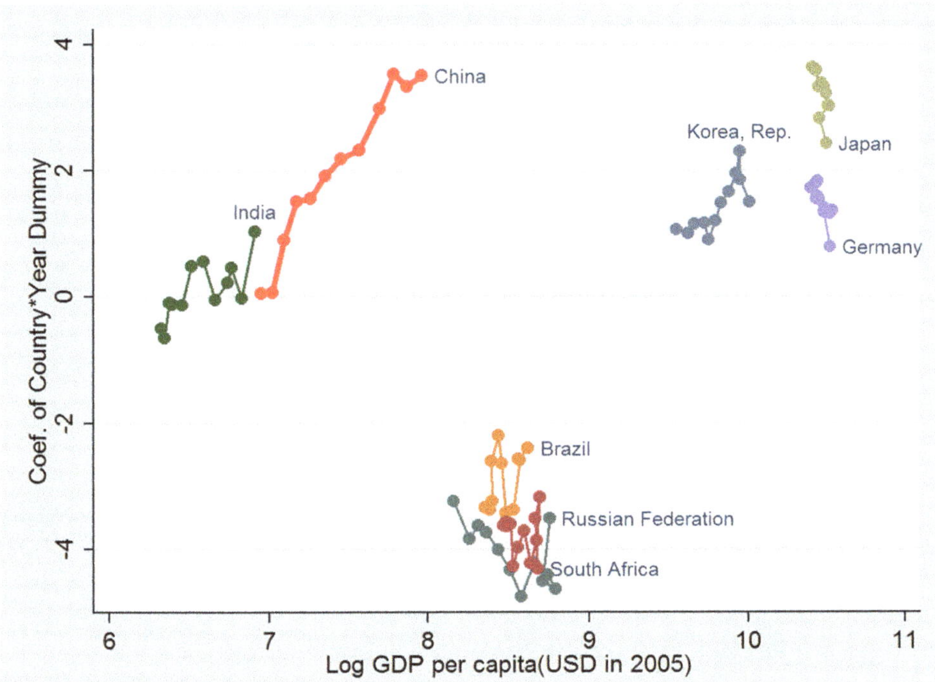

Figure 8.3 Citations of invention patents granted by the USPTO: Cross-country comparison

Note: Conditional plot by controlling for population, population squared and country and year fixed effects.

Sources: Based on data from OECD and, for BRICS countries, from WIPO (various years).

Overall, not only has the number of Chinese patents exploded, but so too has their quality, as measured by forward citation statistics. Chinese patent quality exhibits remarkable improvement over time, in absolute terms and when compared with other BRICS economies and leading patent-filing OECD countries. In short, the growth in innovation appears real and robust.

Sources of innovation growth

What are the sources of China's rapid growth in innovation as demonstrated by our analysis of China's patent filings? There are several potential factors. Government support for R&D, industrial competition, market size and changes in relative prices (such as rising wages) have been regarded as the major drivers of innovation. In this section, we study each of these factors individually and collectively to explore their role in driving China's recent patent success.

First, R&D investment is a key input for patents, and the Chinese Government has increasingly provided large subsidies to firms in support of their R&D activities. To gauge the degree of such subsidies, we merge the Chinese patent database with the Annual Survey of Industrial Enterprises in China (ASIEC). The ASIEC database covers all SOEs and above-scale private firms with annual sales exceeding RMB5 million from 1998 to 2009, including ownership information.[3] The patent database contains all patents granted by SIPO between 1985 and 2012. R&D data are taken from the ASIEC database, which provides firm-level annual R&D subsidy data.

Figure 8.4 plots the ratio of R&D subsidies to total sales for SOEs and for private firms, using data from the ASIEC firm database, and reflects a pattern that is similar to that when value added is used as the denominator. What is evident is that SOEs received a greater volume of subsidies than private firms across the period 1998–2007 (the period for which the ASIEC data are available). Even though small and medium SOEs were granted more subsidies than their private counterparts, they generally performed poorly when compared with private firms in generating patents. As shown in Table 8.6, during the period 1998–2009, the number of patents granted to private firms grew by an annual rate of 35 per cent, overtaking SOEs and foreign firms by 23 and 9 percentage points, respectively. The drop in the share of patents held by SOEs is due mainly to the shrinkage of the SOE sector. In 1998, SOEs accounted for 30 per cent of the total number of firms in the ASIEC database, while they dropped to just 2 per cent by 2009. Because of their massive numbers, private firms have become the engine of innovation.

3 While ASIEC data for 2010–14 float on the grey market, the quality appears suspect. To be conservative, we do not use these data in this chapter.

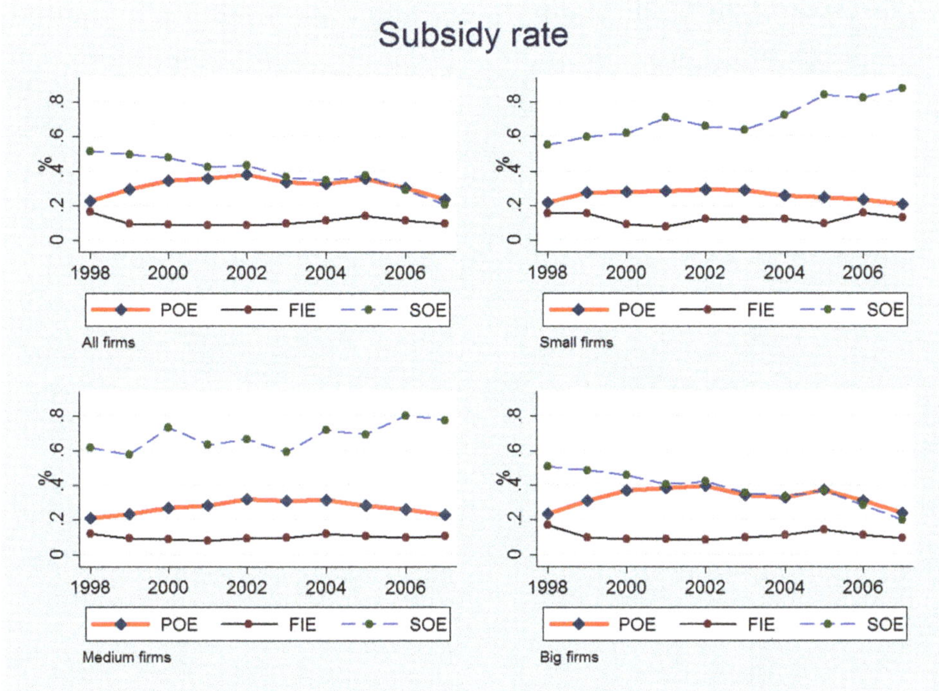

Figure 8.4 Ratio of subsidies to sales by firm ownership and size

Note: Firms are divided equally into three groups according to sales: small, medium and large.

Source: ASIEC database, 1998–2007.

Market size has been regarded as a key driver of innovation in the literature (Acemoglu and Linn 2004). In the past decades, the Chinese economy has become increasingly integrated with the global economy, particularly since China's 2001 accession to the WTO. When confronted by fierce international market competition, one way for export firms to maintain their competitiveness is to innovate. As revealed in Table 8.6 and Figure 8.5, China's exporting firms are indeed more innovative than its non-exporting firms.

Table 8.6 Distribution of domestically granted patents to firms, by firm type and year of application

	Share of patent numbers				Share of firm numbers			Patent per firm			Exporting firms (%)	Labour-intensive firms (%)
Year	Total	Private firm (%)	State-owned firms (%)	Foreign firm (%)	Private firm (%)	State-owned firms (%)	Foreign firm (%)	Private firm	State-owned firms	Foreign firm		
1998	8,776	37	23	40	53	30	17	0.043	0.049	0.148	59	55
1999	12,181	36	22	42	55	27	18	0.058	0.072	0.209	60	59
2000	14,613	39	19	42	59	22	19	0.069	0.094	0.229	59	56
2001	18,121	47	12	41	64	17	20	0.089	0.089	0.254	65	62
2002	26,028	49	11	39	67	13	20	0.121	0.140	0.320	64	63
2003	31,483	51	13	36	70	10	21	0.131	0.240	0.319	67	63
2004	41,739	52	8	40	72	6	21	0.119	0.211	0.311	73	66
2005	52,017	53	7	40	74	4	21	0.150	0.326	0.400	69	69
2006	68,960	54	6	40	76	3	21	0.180	0.450	0.483	69	69
2007	87,086	61	5	34	78	2	20	0.220	0.658	0.474	68	68
2008	122,558	61	5	34	80	2	18	0.248	0.877	0.602	73	67
2009	137,900	62	5	33	80	2	18	0.365	1.371	0.825	60	66
Annual growth rate (%)	28	35	12	26	11	−17	8	21	35	17	28	31

Notes: Private firms are either privately or collectively owned. If the state controls more than 50 per cent of a firm's share, it is defined as a state-owned enterprise. Foreign firms are companies with more than 10 per cent of shares controlled by foreigners or by individuals or companies from Hong Kong, Macau or Chinese Taipei. The definition of labour-intensive firms follows Qu et al. (2013).

Source: Calculated by the authors based on a firm patent database (1998–2009) from the merging of SIPO's national patent database and the ASIEC database.

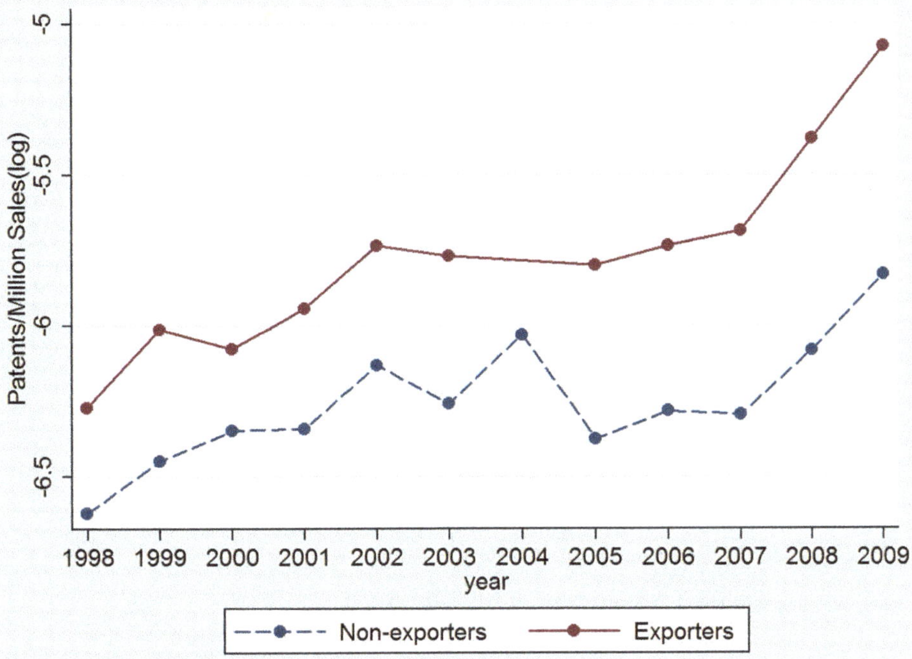

Figure 8.5 Patent intensity by firm's export status

Note: A firm is defined as an exporter if it exports in a particular year.

Source: Modified from Xie and Zhang (2015).

Since 2003, real wages in China have grown at a rate of more than 10 per cent a year. Some scholars argue that China has now passed the Lewis turning point, which means that the era of ultra-low wage production is over (see, for example, Zhang et al. 2011). Facing rising labour costs, firms exit the business, relocate to areas with cheaper labour and land costs or innovate. The last column of Table 8.6 reports the share of patents granted to labour-intensive firms in China over time. Specifically, such firms increased their share of total patents granted, from 55 per cent in 1998 to 66 per cent in 2009. As shown in Figure 8.6, patent intensity—measured as the ratio of the number of patents granted to sales—for labour-intensive firms has increased, while it declined among capital-intensive firms from 2003 to 2007, which is around the time real wages started to spike. Rising labour costs may have induced labour-intensive sectors to come up with more innovations to substitute for labour.

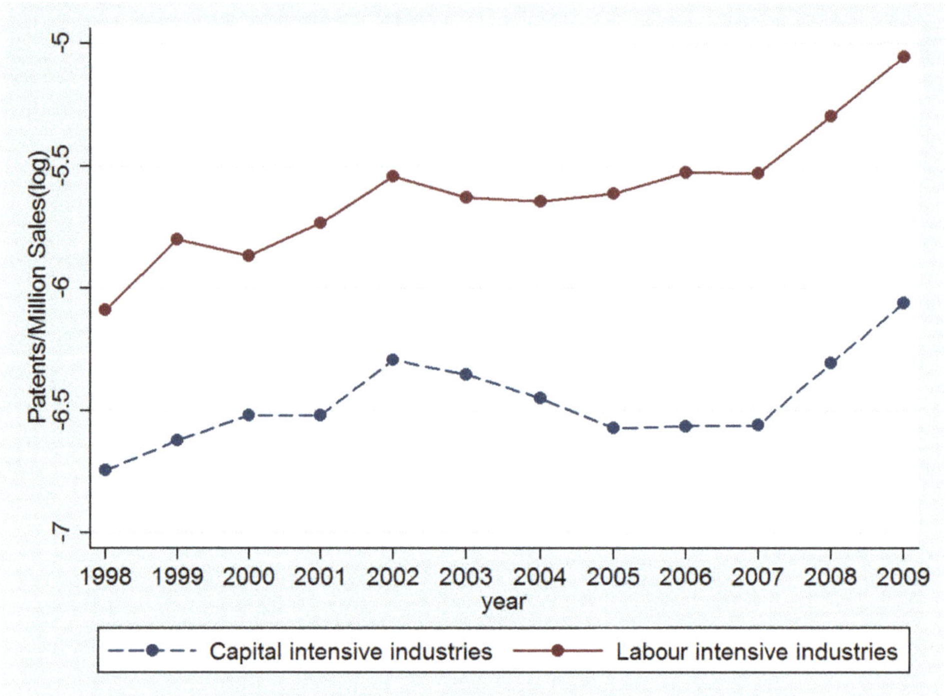

Figure 8.6 Patent intensity by firm's capital intensity

Note: For each year, we define a firm as capital intensive if the capital–labour ratio is greater than the median value.

Source: Modified from Xie and Zhang (2015).

Of course, the above descriptions are based on bivariate correlations and, as such, are only suggestive. To evaluate the relative importance of the contribution of these factors to firms' innovation, we now run multivariate regressions. Since many firms do not have patents and the patent count does not follow a log-normal distribution, we cannot use ordinary least squares (OLS) regressions by taking the log on patent count. A common approach in this situation is to use a negative binomial model; however, all the observations with zero patents will be dropped when including firm fixed effects. We therefore use the hybrid binomial estimation method proposed by Allison (2005) as follows: first, we compute the mean values of all the explanatory variables, X; second, we create a set of new variables by deducting the mean values from the original values of X—that is, X – mean of X; third, we run a random negative binomial model on the patent count using these newly created variables as independent variables. This method is a hybrid of the fixed effect and random effect models, and, importantly, it largely solves the shortcomings of the conditional estimated fixed effect negative binomial model, which automatically drops observations with zero values for the outcome variable for all years. The equation we estimate can be written as Equation 8.1.

Equation 8.1

$P_{ijt} = F(Sales_{it}, Wage_{jt}, Subsidy_{jt}, Tax\ rate_{jt}, Interest\ rate_{jt}, Tariff_{jt}, Export_{it}, HH_{jt},$ industry or firm fixed effects and year fixed effects)

In Equation 8.1, *P* is the number of approved patents for firm *i* in year *t*; *Sales* is firm *i*'s annual sales in year *t*; *Wage* is the average wage at the city–industry–year–firm ownership level (excluding the firm itself) in the cell where the firm is located; *Subsidy* is the ratio of subsidies received from the government to total sales at the firm level; *Tax rate* is the sum of income tax and value-added tax payments relative to total sales at the firm level in year *t*; *Interest rate* is the ratio of total interest paid to the average liability this year and last year at the firm level; *Tariff* is the weighted average of trading partners' tariff rates, based on matching product-level tariff data from the United Nations' Comtrade database with firm *i*'s Standard Industrial Classification two-digit (SIC-2) code (computed at the industry–year level);[4] *Export* is a dummy variable indicating whether a firm has positive exports in year *t*; and *HH* is the Herfindahl–Hirschman (HH) index at the industry–year level.[5]

Many of the regressors are undoubtedly endogenous. In the spirit of an instrumental variable approach, we replace the wage rate, subsidy rate, tax rate and interest rate from firm–year specific values with the average values of all other firms in the same cell of city–industry–ownership type–year. The idea (or assumption) is that the average values of all other firms in the same cell will more likely reflect local labour market conditions (in the case of wages) or local policy designs (in the case of the other three variables). To do this exercise, we also drop all cells with fewer than five observations. Note that we regard the tariff variable as exogenous since it is the average of trading partners' tariff rates, which are unlikely to be systematically manipulated by individual firms in China.

Table 8.7 reports the hybrid negative binomial regression estimates.[6] Several findings are apparent from the results. First, firm size, measured by sales, is positively associated with the number of patents approved. Unsurprisingly, larger firms tend to have more patents approved. Second, exporting firms are more innovative than non-exporting firms. We refrain from assigning a causal interpretation to these two coefficients; the positive correlations between firm size and level of innovation and between export status and level of innovation could reflect causal effects in either direction (and probably in both directions) and these are not empirically explored herein. We have simply treated these regressors as control variables.

4 We use Standard Industrial Classification two-digit (SIC-2) code mainly to improve the matching rate.

5 The HH index is calculated via the following steps: 1) for every four-digit industry and year *t*, compute each firm's market share; 2) for every four-digit industry and year *t*, sum the square of each firm's market share. The higher the HH index, the lower is the degree of competition.

6 As robustness checks, we have implemented other specifications as well, such as the fixed effect negative binomial model, the random effect negative binomial model and the fixed effect ordinal linear probability model. The coefficients for most variables are qualitatively similar and therefore robust.

Table 8.7 Hybrid negative binomial regressions on patent count: Baseline

Variables	(1) Total	(2) Invention	(3) Utility	(4) Design
Sales (log)	0.437***	0.491***	0.435***	0.424***
	(0.012)	(0.024)	(0.015)	(0.019)
Export	0.115***	0.181***	0.071**	0.157***
	(0.022)	(0.045)	(0.028)	(0.036)
Wage (log)	0.082***	0.224***	0.137***	0.072*
	(0.027)	(0.050)	(0.034)	(0.042)
Subsidy rate (log)	0.003	0.045***	0.003	0.010
	(0.006)	(0.011)	(0.007)	(0.009)
Tax rate (log)	–0.073***	–0.066**	–0.085***	–0.036
	(0.017)	(0.032)	(0.021)	(0.027)
Interest rate (log)	–0.025**	0.010	–0.042***	–0.036**
	(0.010)	(0.020)	(0.013)	(0.016)
Partner tariff	–1.048***	–0.843***	–1.123***	–0.482***
	(0.078)	(0.146)	(0.115)	(0.118)
HH index	0.143	–0.087	0.541**	0.358
	(0.224)	(0.425)	(0.267)	(0.328)
Observations	1,187,140	1,187,140	1,187,140	1,187,140
Firm fixed effects	YES	YES	YES	YES
Year fixed effects	YES	YES	YES	YES
Akaike Information Criterion (AIC)	438,522	114,137	270,400	213,959

*** represents 1% significant level.

Notes: *Wage* (log), *Subsidy rate* (log), *Tax rate* (log) and *Interest rate* (log) are averages at the city–industry–firm ownership type–year levels (except for the firm itself). Cells with fewer than six observations are dropped. *Sales* (log) and *Export* are still firm–year levels.

Third, lower import tariffs are positively associated with firms' innovation through the expansion of international markets for Chinese products. Because foreign tariffs are (largely) exogenous, we interpret this coefficient as reflecting a causal effect: the expansion of international markets or export opportunities induces firms to be more innovative. Results in Table 8.7 suggest that a reduction by 1 per cent in the weighted average of the partner firms' tariff rates in the relevant industry is associated, on average, with a 1 per cent increase in the number of patents granted.

Fourth, in terms of the effects of fiscal subsidies, there is some evidence that invention patents are positively associated with R&D subsidies, but the relationships therein for utility and design patents are not statistically significant. Since invention patents are often regarded as 'more innovative' than the other types, one cannot rule out the possibility that firms' innovative activities respond to fiscal incentives.

Meanwhile, a higher tax rate is negatively associated with innovation; the coefficients on the tax rate are negative in all four columns, but statistically significant for all patents combined, and individually for invention and utility patents.

Fifth, higher capital costs as measured by a higher implied interest rate are negatively associated with many types of innovative activities; the coefficients on log interest rates are negative and statistically significant for all patents, and for utility and design patents.

Finally, there is a robust positive relationship between the wage level and firms' innovation. If our strategy of using the average wages of all other firms in the same cell to replace individual firms' own wages succeeds in removing endogeneity, one might interpret the coefficient as saying that firms, on average, rise to the challenge of higher labour costs by engaging in more innovation. Of course, innovative industries tend to hire more skilled workers than less innovative industries. In general, skilled workers earn more than unskilled workers, and thereby could produce a positive correlation between average wages and firms' level of innovation at the industry level. Note that our regressions in Table 8.7 include separate firm and year fixed effects (therefore subsuming separate industry fixed effects). So the endogeneity has to come at the levels of industry–city–ownership–year. Nonetheless, to further remove endogeneity, we replace current average wages with those of others firms in the same cell by its lagged value, and find qualitatively the same results (see Appendix Table 8.A1). As a robustness check, we use the minimum wages at the city–year levels to replace the average wage of other firms in the same cell, and again find the same qualitative results (see Appendix Table 8.A2).

An absolute-level wage increase, however, presents a different relative cost shock to firms in labour-intensive and other industries. To explore this feature, we now add an interaction term between the average wage of other firms in the same cell and a dummy indicating that the industry in which the firm operates has a labour intensity (labour cost as a share of total cost) above the median at the beginning of the sample. Table 8.8 displays the estimation results. The coefficient for the interaction term is positive and statistically significant among three out of four regressions (for total patents, and for invention and design patents). These results are consistent with the induced innovation theory that suggests that rising labour costs induce labour-intensive firms to become more innovative to survive. The results in Table 8.8 are robust to the use of alternative wage variables (either lagged wages or legal minimum wages). To save space, the estimates using lagged wages and minimum wages are not reported here.

Table 8.8 Impacts of wages on the innovation levels of labour-intensive firms

Variables	(1) Total	(2) Invention	(3) Utility	(4) Design
Wage (log)*Labour-intensive dummy	0.163***	0.695***	–0.042	0.174***
	(0.038)	(0.073)	(0.052)	(0.059)
Sales (log)	0.436***	0.483***	0.433***	0.425***
	(0.012)	(0.024)	(0.015)	(0.019)
Export	0.108***	0.162***	0.064**	0.153***
	(0.022)	(0.045)	(0.028)	(0.036)
Wage (log)	0.010	–0.101*	0.184***	0.007
	(0.034)	(0.061)	(0.050)	(0.051)
Subsidy rate (log)	0.006	0.044***	0.008	0.012
	(0.006)	(0.011)	(0.007)	(0.009)
Tax rate (log)	–0.068***	–0.032	–0.082***	–0.031
	(0.017)	(0.033)	(0.021)	(0.027)
Interest rate (log)	–0.022**	0.021	–0.040***	–0.035**
	(0.011)	(0.020)	(0.013)	(0.017)
Partner tariff	–1.138***	–1.091***	–1.141***	–0.475***
	(0.082)	(0.148)	(0.120)	(0.122)
HH index	0.260	-0.090	0.597**	0.456
	(0.223)	(0.423)	(0.265)	(0.327)
Observations	1,187,140	1,187,140	1,187,140	1,187,140
Firm fixed effects	YES	YES	YES	YES
Year fixed effects	YES	YES	YES	YES
Akaike Information Criterion (AIC)	436,557	114,023	266,115	213,652

** represents 5% significant level

*** represents 1% significant level.

Notes: *Wage* (log), *Subsidy rate* (log), *Tax rate* (log) and *Interest rate* (log) are averages at the city–industry–firm ownership type–year levels (except for the firm itself). Cells with fewer than six observations are dropped. *Sales* (log) and *Export* are still firm–year levels. The dependent variable is the patent count. Hybrid negative binomial regression is used. See Qu et al. (2013) for the definition of labour-intensive industries.

Studies (Autor et al. 2003) have shown that computer technology has reduced the demand for jobs involving routine tasks. Following Autor et al. (2003), we create a dummy variable, 'routine', indicating whether an industry involves more routine tasks (1) or not (0). We expect to see firms facing rising labour costs and heavily involved in routine tasks, which are often done by low-skilled workers, to be more innovative for the purpose of substituting technology for labour. Similar to Table 8.7, we use a difference-in-difference (DID) approach to examine the impact of rising wages on routine task–intensive industries by including an interaction term between wages and a 'routine' dummy. As shown in Panel A of Table 8.9, the coefficient for the interaction term is statistically significant in all four regressions. In other words, in the presence of rising wages, the survival of firms (i.e. their ability to continue to produce) is linked to enhanced innovation, possibly by those firms taking advantage of computer technologies to replace labour in undertaking 'routine' tasks.

Table 8.9 Impact of wages on levels of innovation in routine-intensive industries and sunset industries

Variables	(1) Total	(2) Invention	(3) Utility	(4) Design
Panel A: Impact on routine-intensive industries				
Wage (log)*Routine	0.490***	0.992***	0.237***	0.759***
	(0.048)	(0.089)	(0.082)	(0.072)
Panel B: Impact on sunset industries				
Wage (log)*Sunset	0.040	–0.222***	–0.058	0.089
	(0.040)	(0.072)	(0.052)	(0.064)

*** represents 1% significant level.

Notes: Hybrid negative binomial regression estimates. Routine industries are defined according to Autor et al. (2003).

When facing rising labour costs, there are two possible routes for labour-intensive industries to take. In industries where innovation is possible, firms must innovate to survive. In industries in which international experience suggests that innovation is difficult (sunset industries), exit or closure is the likely outcome. In the sunset industries, with a dwindling market share, firms may be reluctant to make R&D investment for fear of failure to recoup the cost.

We define sunset industries in the case of China as follows: first, we select the top 40 economies according to GDP in 2000, excluding China. Next, we narrow the list by keeping countries with GDP per capita 1.5 times larger than that of China and lower than US$12,000 (constant in 2005). The remaining list includes Argentina, Brazil, Czech Republic, Mexico, Yemen, Poland, Russia, Turkey, Venezuela and Zambia. Third, using these economies as a reference point, we calculate the annual growth rate of each industry by country and obtain the aggregate growth rate for all countries in the list using GDP as a weight. An industry is defined as a sunset industry if its average growth rate during the period 1998–2007 is below the median growth rate among all industries.

Panel B of Table 8.9 shows the estimates for the interaction term between wages and the 'sunset' industry dummy. The coefficient is statistically negative only in the regression on invention patents. Invention patents normally involve more R&D input than utility model and design patents. The results are robust when using lagged values of minimum wages in the interaction term. When market prospects loom large, the surviving firms in the sunset industries are less likely to make large investments in R&D, thereby yielding fewer invention patents than other industries. Like the economies that are slightly richer than China, firms in the sunset industries in China will likely experience slower growth and will eventually be replaced with sunrise industries.

From quality improvement to export success

A rise in labour costs means a shift in comparative advantage, away from products that are intensive in unskilled labour. Chinese firms can maintain or increase their shares in the global market only through sufficient increases in productivity or product quality to offset rising labour costs. While this exercise does not use patent data, one might consider it an examination of quality improvement and innovation broadly defined. Here we examine whether the rapid growth in patents and in innovation in general has been transformed into export success.

Product quality is not directly observed in standard trade statistics. We measure export quality following the methodology originally proposed by Khandelwal (2010) and outlined in Amiti and Khandelwal (2013) (Equation 8.2).

Equation 8.2

$$\log Market\ share_{ijkt} = \beta_0 + \sum_{i\in A}\sum_{t=2}^{40}\beta_{1it} Interested\ country_i * Year_t + \beta_2 \log \text{GDP of } Exporter_{it} + \beta_3 \log \text{GDP of } Importer_{jt} + \beta_4 \log \text{GDP per capita of } Importer_{jt} + \sum_{k\in B} Product_k * Standardised \log \text{unit value}_{ijkt} + \alpha_t + \rho_k + \varepsilon_{ijkt}$$

In Equation 8.2, i is the exporting country, j is the importing (or destination) country, k is the six-digit Harmonised System (HS) product code and t denotes year, covering the period 1995–2014. Market shares and unit values are defined in Equation 8.3.

Equation 8.3

$$\log Market\ share_{ijkt} = \frac{Quantity_{ijkt}}{\sum_j Quantity_{ijkt}}$$

$$\log Unit\ value_{ijkt} = \frac{Export\ value_{ijkt}}{Quantity_{ijkt}}$$

Since the unit value is influenced by many factors, such as global resource prices, it may not purely reflect production quality. To remove the impact of sector-specific shocks on unit values, we standardise the unit value by subtracting the median unit value at the sector level—that is, Standardised log $Unit\ value_{ijkt}$ = log $Unit\ value_{ijkt}$ – Median log $Unit\ value_{ijkt}$.

We select the 40 largest economies in our sample as measured by absolute GDP. The findings are similar when using different samples, such as G20 economies or the top 70 economies measured in GDP. The group of importer countries is the same as the exporter countries, except for the BRICS countries, Germany, South Korea, Japan and the United States. The product group consists of China's top 500 export products in 2000, according to values. β_{1it} is the coefficient of interest to us.

We plot the estimated coefficient β_{1it} versus per capita GDP for nine countries of interest (Germany, Japan, South Korea, the United States and the BRICS economies) in Figure 8.7. Among the countries, China, India and Germany have gained export market share as their economies grow. The other three BRICS countries (Brazil, Russia and South Africa), Japan, South Korea and the United States saw a decline in export market share during the period. Based on the measure of conditional export market share, Chinese product quality has shown a steady improvement.

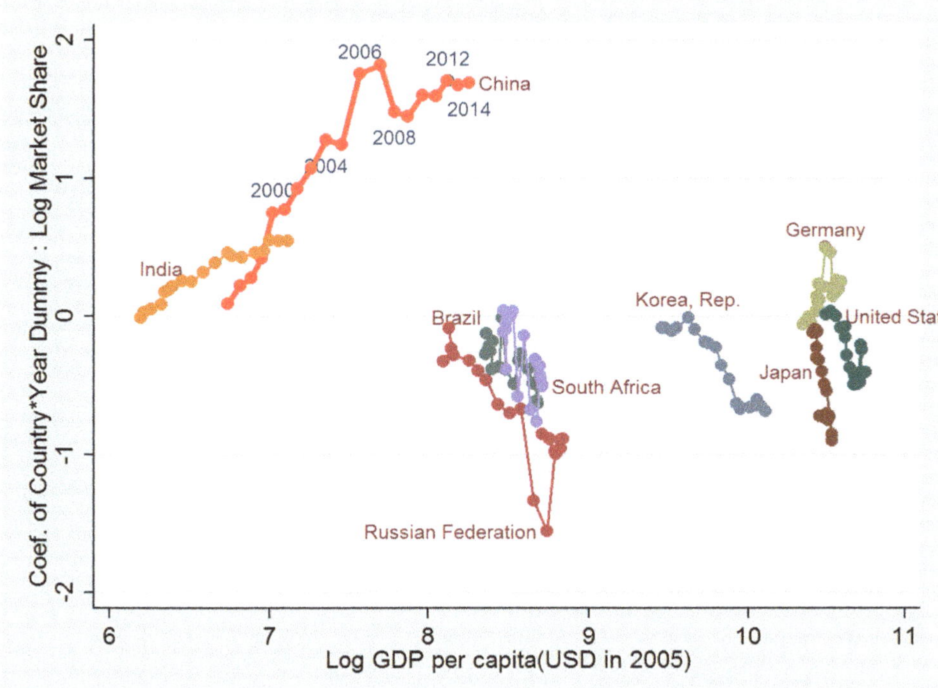

Figure 8.7 Export quality: Conditional plot of export market shares in selected countries

Note: The sample used in this figure covers G40 countries.

Source: Data from CEPII's BACI database (www.cepii.fr/CEPII/en/bdd_modele/presentation.asp?id=1).

Misallocation of R&D resources

Because state-owned firms still command non-trivial political weights and absorb non-trivial levels of resources, including government subsidies, in this section, we study the scope for China to improve the allocation efficiency of its R&D resources between SOEs and private firms.

Following the SOE reforms in the late 1990s, the share of SOEs in the overall number of firms dropped significantly, from 18.1 per cent (or 744,240 SOEs out of 4,102,757 firms) in 1995 to 0.4 per cent (or 61,204 out of 15,300,901 firms) in 2014 (Table 8.1). Almost all small SOEs were closed or privatised during the government's 'grasp the large, let go of the small' program. Most of the surviving SOEs are relatively large and are in upstream industries or strategically important sectors (Hsieh and Song 2015). They are subject to less competition than private enterprises, and, in addition, they receive more financial support from the government, such as bank loans and R&D subsidies.

Moreover, in the aftermath of both the 1997 Asian Financial Crisis and the 2008 GFC, the Chinese Government launched stimulus packages with massive liquidity injections into the economy, which were directed disproportionately to SOEs. The more favourable policies and massive stimulus funds have reduced the returns to capital of SOEs since 2008 (Bai and Zhang 2014), causing a decline in total factor productivity (TFP) in SOEs (Wu 2013) and providing a lifeline for inefficient zombie firms (Tan et al. 2016). Although the labour productivity of the remaining large SOEs converged to that of private enterprises, SOEs' returns to capital were still much lower than their private counterparts (Hsieh and Song 2015). Overall, SOEs lagged behind private firms in TFP (Brandt 2015).

As reviewed in Boeing (2016), most studies find that the government's R&D subsidies play a positive role in driving firms' levels of innovation. However, the finding does not imply that R&D subsidies have been allocated efficiently. Although, on average, SOEs received more R&D subsidies than private firms, private firms have experienced much faster growth in the number of approved patents than their SOE counterparts during the period 1998–2009, as shown in Table 8.6. This suggests that there are misallocations of R&D subsidies between SOEs and private enterprises.

As shown in Figure 8.4, SOEs, especially medium-sized and small SOEs, receive more subsidies per renminbi of sales than their private sector counterparts. This likely reflects subsidies from local governments to the SOEs they own. Large private firms and SOEs appear to be treated equally, reflecting both the fact that the central government offers less subsidies than do local governments and the fact that large private firms are perhaps more effective in obtaining a 'fair' share of subsidies. When looking at tax rates, we find that SOEs tend to also experience a higher effective tax rate [(income tax + value-added tax)/sales] than their private sector counterparts (see Figure 8.8). In fact, total taxes net of total subsidies tend to be higher for SOEs, and especially for large SOEs (Figure 8.9).

Table 8.10 Impact of R&D on patent output: Hybrid negative binomial regressions

Variables	(1) Total	(2) Invention	(3) Utility model	(4) Design
R&D (log)*FIE	–0.006	–0.006	0.002	–0.014**
	(0.004)	(0.006)	(0.004)	(0.006)
R&D (log)*SOE	–0.010**	–0.017**	–0.004	–0.014
	(0.005)	(0.007)	(0.005)	(0.010)
R&D (log)	0.016***	0.016***	0.013***	0.013***
	(0.002)	(0.004)	(0.003)	(0.004)
Sales (log)	0.278***	0.314***	0.259***	0.305***
	(0.022)	(0.040)	(0.027)	(0.037)
Constant	–5.558***	–7.135***	–4.979***	–6.414***
	(0.071)	(0.118)	(0.088)	(0.116)
Observations	783,229	783,229	783,229	783,229
Firm fixed effects	YES	YES	YES	YES
Year fixed effects	YES	YES	YES	YES
Akaike Information Criterion (AIC)	298,065	92,655	190,331	134,819

** represents 5% significant level

*** represents 1% significant level

Note: *Wage* (log), *Subsidy rate* (log), *Tax rate* (log) and *Interest rate* (log) are averages at the city–industry–firm ownership type–year levels (except for the firm itself). Cells with fewer than six observations are dropped. *Sales* (log) and *Export* are still firm–year levels. Since R&D data are available only for 2005–09, we include only these four years in the sample.

Table 8.10 presents the results of a regression of the patent count on firm R&D expenditure by controlling for firm sales, firm fixed effects and year fixed effects. To evaluate whether private firms and SOEs have different elasticity regarding R&D expenditure, we interact firm ownership with R&D expenditure in the regressions. The interaction term between the SOE dummy and the R&D variable is statistically negative, indicating that the elasticity of patents granted with respect to R&D expenditure is significantly higher for private firms than for SOEs. In other words, SOEs have not spent R&D resources as efficiently as have private firms. On the surface, there is prima facie evidence that the pattern of subsidies across firms represents resource misallocation. The economy-wide innovative outcomes would have been higher if the subsidies were more evenly spread across firm ownership.

Figure 8.8 Tax rate by firm ownership and size

Note: The tax rate is defined as [(income tax + value-added tax)/sales]. According to sales, firms are divided equally into three groups: small, medium and large.

Source: Calculated by the authors based on ASIEC database.

Since subsidies and taxes use different bases, distortions are introduced if one renminbi of tax is offset by one renminbi of subsidy. Considering a lower tax rate is associated with higher levels of firm innovation, the impact of subsidies is lukewarm and private firms use R&D expenditure more efficiently than SOEs, it makes economic sense to promote reforms to: 1) simultaneously reduce tax rates and subsidies (with zero impact on government net revenue); and 2) provide subsidies only in cases where the social returns exceed private returns (such as innovative activities), without regard to firm ownership type.

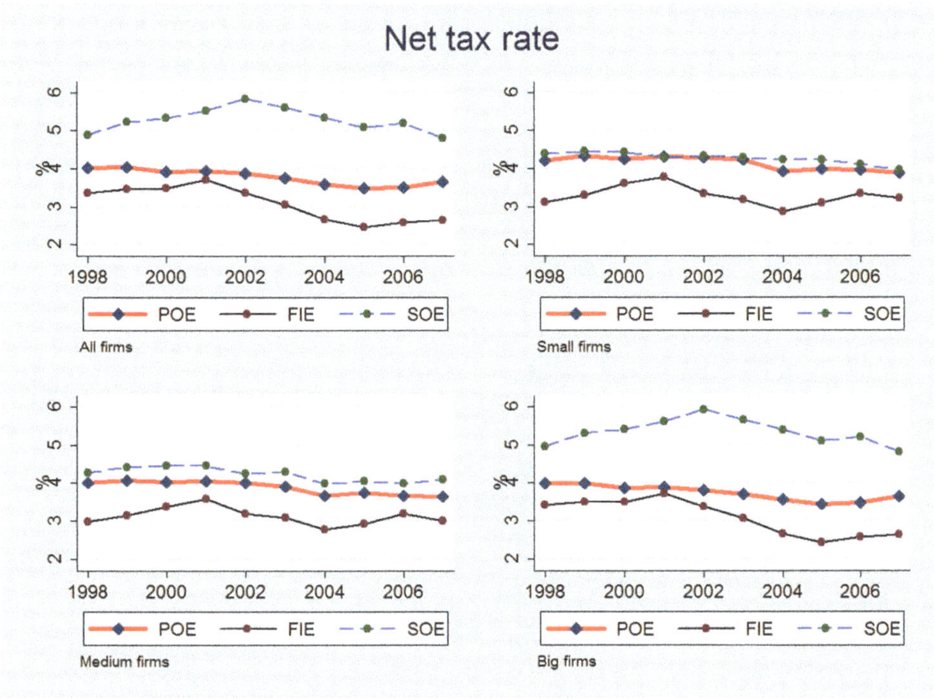

Figure 8.9 Net tax rate by firm ownership and size

Note: The net tax rate is defined as [(income tax + value-added tax – subsidy)/sales]. According to sales, firms are divided equally into three groups: small, medium and large.

Source: Calculated by the authors based on ASIEC database.

Conclusions

China's past success in economic growth means that the real manufacturing wage has increased by about 14-fold from 1980 to 2015. A shrinking workforce since 2011 has added to pressure on wages. By implication, China has to move to a growth model that is based more on innovation and productivity increases than in the past. Can China rise to the challenge?

By examining indicators on patents, our chapter shows that Chinese firms have become increasingly more innovative, in absolute terms and also relative to other major developing economies and major patent-filing economies. Specifically, the growth of patents granted to Chinese firms both at home and in the United States compares favourably with the experience of other BRICS countries and leading OECD countries, once one takes into account the country's size and income level. Taking advantage of the expanding global market and responding to rising labour costs are the two most important drivers of firms' levels of innovation.

Besides the correlation between firm size and level of innovation, and between export status and level of innovation, we find a number of patterns. First, expanding market opportunities in the form of lower tariffs from trading partners tend to promote innovation. Second, firms respond to higher wages by engaging in more innovation. This is especially true for firms in labour-intensive sectors and sectors with more routine tasks. This pattern suggests some reason for optimism in terms of the prospect of Chinese firms becoming more innovative as the country's income continues to rise. Third, Chinese products have taken an increasingly large market share after controlling for population size, economy size and the unit values of export products. The increasing competitiveness of Chinese products in the international market suggests that Chinese products have exhibited quality improvement over time.

There is some evidence that innovation responds positively to subsidies and negatively to taxes; however, subsidy allocation appears to be strongly biased in favour of SOEs, especially those owned by local governments. Yet, private sector firms exhibit a higher rate of innovation per renminbi invested in R&D than SOEs. If subsidies are meant to encourage innovation, the economy-wide innovation outcomes would have been greater if the bias towards SOEs in subsidy allocation was removed.

At the same time, the effective tax rate appears to vary not only across sectors, but also across firms. Interestingly, SOEs appear to face higher tax rates than private firms. Even after subtracting subsidies, SOEs—in particular, large ones—are still subject to higher tax burdens than private firms. This creates additional distortions. The desired direction of reforms is likely in the form of simultaneous reductions in subsidies and taxes and more uniform treatment of firms across ownership type. Levelling the playing field for firms of all ownership type, limiting the government's discretion in allocating subsidies for R&D and ensuring private sector firms have a fair chance at receiving those subsidies would reduce resource misallocation and improve efficiency. This will complement reforms strengthening protection of intellectual property rights and to the education system.

Patents are just one form of firm innovation. Some firms keep their business secrets and do not file patents for their product or production process innovations. In addition, business model innovations have been widely observed, but these types of innovation are not discussed in this chapter. More research is needed so that the comprehensive contributions of innovation to economic growth can be assessed.

References

Acemoglu, D. and Linn, J. (2004), Market size in innovation: Theory and evidence from the pharmaceutical industry, *Quarterly Journal of Economics* 119(3): 1049–90. doi.org/10.1162/0033553041502144.

Allison, P. D. (2005), *Fixed Effects Regression Methods for Longitudinal Data Using SAS*, Cary, NC: SAS Institute.

Amiti, M. and Khandelwal, A. K. (2013), Import competition and quality upgrading, *Review of Economics and Statistics* 95(2): 476–90. doi.org/10.1162/REST_a_00271.

Autor, D. H., Levy, F. and Murnane, R. J. (2003), The skill content of recent technological change: An empirical exploration, *Quarterly Journal of Economics* 118(4): 1279–333. doi.org/10.1162/003355303322552801.

Bai, C.-E. and Zhang, Q. (2014), Returns to capital and their determinants in China, [in Chinese], *World Economy* 10: 2–30.

Boeing, P. (2016), The allocation and effectiveness of China's R&D subsidies: Evidence from listed firms, *Research Policy* 45(9): 1774–89. doi.org/10.1016/j.respol.2016.05.007.

Brandt, L. (2015), Policy perspectives from the bottom up: What do firm level data tell China needs to do? Paper presented at the Asia Economic Policy Conference on Policy Challenges in a Diverging Global Economy, Federal Reserve Bank of San Francisco, San Francisco, 19–20 November.

Brandt, L., Tombe, T. and Zhu, X. (2013), Factor market distortions across time, space and sectors in China, *Review of Economic Dynamics* 16(1): 39–58. doi.org/10.1016/j.red.2012.10.002.

Cai, F. and Du, Y. (2011), Wage increases, wage convergence, and the Lewis turning point in China, *China Economic Review* 22(4): 601–10. doi.org/10.1016/j.chieco.2011.07.004.

Cai, F. and Wang, M. (2008), A counterfactual analysis on unlimited surplus labor in rural China, *China & World Economy* 16(1): 51–65. doi.org/10.1111/j.1749-124x.2008.00099.x.

Chang, S. and Zhang, X. (2015), Mating competition and entrepreneurship, *Journal of Economic Behavior & Organization* 116(C): 292–309. doi.org/10.1016/j.jebo.2015.05.004.

Dang, J. and Motohashi, K. (2015), Patent statistics: A good indicator for innovation in China? Patent subsidy program impacts on patent quality, *China Economic Review* 35(C): 137–55. doi.org/10.1016/j.chieco.2015.03.012.

Fan, S., Kanbur, R., Wei, S.-J. and Zhang, X. (eds) (2014), *The Oxford Companion to the Economics of China*, Oxford: Oxford University Press.

Fan, S., Zhang, X. and Robinson, S. (2003), Structural change and economic growth in China, *Review of Development Economics* 7(3): 360–77. doi.org/10.1111/1467-9361.00196.

Feenstra, R. and Wei, S.-J. (2010), *China's Growing Role in World Trade*, Chicago: University of Chicago Press. doi.org/10.7208/chicago/9780226239729.001.0001.

Golley, J. and Meng, X. (2011), Has China run out of surplus labour? *China Economic Review* 22(4): 555–72. doi.org/10.1016/j.chieco.2011.07.006.

Han, X. and Wei, S.-J. (2015), *Re-examining the middle income trap hypothesis (MITH): What to reject and what to revive?* CEPR Discussion Paper 10989, Centre for Economic Policy Research, London.

Hsieh, C.-T. and Klenow, P. J. (2009), Misallocation and manufacturing TFP in China and India, *Quarterly Journal of Economics* 124(4): 1403–48. doi.org/10.1162/qjec.2009.124.4.1403.

Hsieh, C.-T. and Song, Z. (2015), Grasp the large, let go of the small: The transformation of the state sector in China, *Brookings Papers on Economic Activity* 50(1): 295–366.

Khandelwal, A. (2010), The long and short (of) quality ladders, *Review of Economic Studies* 77(4): 1450–476. doi.org/10.1111/j.1467-937X.2010.00602.x.

Knight, J., Deng, Q. and Li, S. (2011), The puzzle of migrant labour shortage and rural labour surplus in China, *China Economic Review* 22(4): 585–600. doi.org/10.1016/j.chieco.2011.01.006.

Lin, J. (1992), Rural reforms and agricultural growth in China, *American Economic Review* 82(1): 34–51.

Ma, D. (2016), Can China avoid the middle income trap? *Foreign Policy*, 12 March.

National Bureau of Statistics of China (NBS) (2012), *China Statistical Yearbook*, Beijing: China Statistics Press.

Organisation for Economic Co-operation and Development (OECD) (2013), *The People's Republic of China: Avoiding the middle-income trap—Policies for sustained and inclusive growth*, September, Paris: OECD.

Qu, Y., Fang, C. and Zhang, X. (2013), Has the flying geese paradigm occurred in China? *China Economist* 8(6): 18–31.

Romer, P. M. (1990), Endogenous technological change, *Journal of Political Economy* 98(5): S71–S102. doi.org/10.1086/261725.

Tan, Y., Huang, Y. and Woo, W. T. (2016), Zombie firms and the crowding-out of private investment in China, *Asian Economic Papers* 15(3). doi.org/10.1162/ASEP_a_00474.

Wang, X., Huang, J., Zhang, L. and Rozelle, S. (2011), The rise of migration and the fall of self-employment in rural China's labor market, *China Economic Review* 22(4): 573–84. doi.org/10.1016/j.chieco.2011.07.005.

Wei, S.-J. (2015), The recent change in China's population policy and its implications for China and the world economy, Keynote address to the Asia Economic Policy Conference, Federal Reserve Bank of San Francisco, San Francisco, 19–20 November.

Wei, S.-J. and Zhang, X. (2011a), The competitive saving motive: Evidence from rising sex ratios and savings in China, *Journal of Political Economy* 119(3): 511–64. doi.org/10.1086/660887.

Wei, S.-J. and Zhang, X. (2011b), *Sex ratios, entrepreneurship and economic growth in the People's Republic of China*, NBER Working Paper No. 16800, National Bureau of Economic Research, Cambridge, Mass.

Wei, S.-J., Zhang, X. and Liu, Y. (2016), Home ownership as status competition: Some theory and evidence, *Journal of Development Economics*. First published online, 21 December. doi.org/10.1016/j.jdeveco.2016.12.001.

World Intellectual Property Organization (WIPO) (various years), *World Intellectual Property Indicators*, Geneva: WIPO.

Wu, H. X. (2013), Measuring and interpreting total factor productivity in Chinese industry, *Comparative Studies* 69. Available from: magazine.caixin.com/2013/cs_69/.

Xie, Z. and Zhang, X. (2015), The patterns of patents in China, *China Economic Journal* 8(2): 122–42.

Xu, C. and Zhang, X. (2009), *The evolution of Chinese entrepreneurial firms: Township–village enterprises revisited*, Discussion Paper No. 0854, International Food Policy Research Institute, Washington, DC.

Zhang, X., Yang, J. and Wang, S. (2011), China has reached the Lewis turning point, *China Economic Review* 22(4): 542–54. doi.org/10.1016/j.chieco.2011.07.002.

Zhu, X. (2012), Understanding China's growth: Past, present, and future, *Journal of Economic Perspectives* 26(4): 103–24. doi.org/10.1257/jep.26.4.103.

Appendix 8.1. Data

The export data come from the BACI database developed by the French Centre d'Etudes Prospectives et d'Informations Internationales (Centre for Prospective Studies and International Information, CEPII) at a high level of product disaggregation. Original data are provided by the United Nations Statistical Division's Comtrade database. BACI is constructed using an original procedure that reconciles the declarations of the exporter and the importer. This harmonisation procedure considerably extends the number of countries for which trade data are available, compared with the original dataset. BACI provides bilateral values and quantities of exports at the HS six-digit product disaggregation for more than 200 countries since 1995. It is updated every year. For more information, see: www.cepii.fr/CEPII/en/bdd_modele/presentation.asp?id=1.

The authors tabulated the total number of existing firms and new firms based on China's company registry database. The patent data used for international comparison come from WIPO and the USPTO.

The data used in regression tables are based on a merged firm patent database (1998–2009) of the national patent database from SIPO and the database of the ASIEC.

Appendix 8.2. Additional tables

Table 8.A1 Hybrid negative binomial regression on patent count: Using lagged wages

Variables	(1) Total	(2) Invention	(3) Utility	(4) Design
Sales (log)	0.419***	0.454***	0.418***	0.416***
	(0.013)	(0.026)	(0.016)	(0.021)
Export	0.119***	0.172***	0.065**	0.161***
	(0.025)	(0.049)	(0.031)	(0.041)
Lag wage (log)	0.510***	0.890***	0.790***	0.541***
	(0.058)	(0.113)	(0.074)	(0.090)
Subsidy rate (log)	–0.007	0.033***	–0.009	–0.003
	(0.006)	(0.012)	(0.008)	(0.010)
Tax rate (log)	–0.067***	–0.057	–0.080***	–0.036
	(0.020)	(0.036)	(0.025)	(0.032)
Interest rate (log)	–0.018	0.017	–0.034**	–0.031*
	(0.011)	(0.021)	(0.014)	(0.019)
Partner tariff	–0.850***	–0.314*	–0.666***	–0.454***
	(0.091)	(0.171)	(0.131)	(0.140)

Variables	(1) Total	(2) Invention	(3) Utility	(4) Design
HH index	0.238	–0.092	0.622**	0.337
	(0.240)	(0.429)	(0.279)	(0.361)
Observations	984,517	984,517	984,517	984,517
Firm fixed effects	YES	YES	YES	YES
Year fixed effects	YES	YES	YES	YES
Akaike Information Criterion (AIC)	368,333	99,218	229,716	173,836

* represents 10% significant level

** represents 5% significant level

*** represents 1% significant level

Notes: *Wage* (log), *Subsidy rate* (log), *Tax rate* (log) and *Interest rate* (log) are averages at the city–industry–firm ownership type–year levels (except for the firm itself). Cells with fewer than six observations are dropped. *Sales* (log) and *Export* are still firm–year levels. The value of the wage variable is lagged by one year.

Table 8.A2 Hybrid negative binomial regression on the patent count: Using minimum wages

Variables	(1) Total	(2) Invention	(3) Utility	(4) Design
Sales (log)	0.430***	0.441***	0.434***	0.435***
	(1.126)	(2.186)	(1.424)	(1.793)
Export	0.104***	0.172***	0.065**	0.148***
	(2.208)	(4.351)	(2.772)	(3.559)
Minimum wage (log)	0.318***	0.484***	0.607***	0.371***
	(4.890)	(9.569)	(6.354)	(7.597)
Subsidy rate (log)	–0.003	0.017*	–0.005	–0.013
	(0.526)	(0.978)	(0.664)	(0.859)
Tax rate (log)	0.050**	0.115***	0.026	0.053*
	(1.994)	(3.774)	(2.523)	(3.130)
Interest rate (log)	–0.012	–0.006	–0.040***	0.014
	(1.140)	(2.277)	(1.407)	(1.829)
Partner tariff	-9.156***	–6.279**	–8.354***	–4.772***
	(112.564)	(258.170)	(184.781)	(127.120)
HH index	0.358	0.085	0.486*	0.517
	(21.901)	(38.670)	(26.178)	(33.429)
Observations	1,305,376	1,305,376	1,305,376	1,305,376
Firm fixed effects	YES	YES	YES	YES
Year fixed effects	YES	YES	YES	YES
Akaike Information Criterion (AIC)	461,094	124,633	283,566	217,422

* represents 10% significant level

** represents 5% significant level

*** represents 1% significant level

Notes: *Wage* (log), *Subsidy rate* (log), *Tax rate* (log) and *Interest rate* (log) are averages at the city–industry–firm ownership type–year levels (except for the firm itself). Cells with fewer than six observations are dropped. *Sales* (log) and *Export* are still firm–year levels. Minimum wages are at the city and year levels.

9. Productivity, Innovation and China's Economic Growth

Yanrui Wu, Xiumei Guo and Dora Marinova

The role of productivity and innovation in China's economic growth is fiercely debated among economists.[1] With the economy currently progressing through the middle-income stages, China is forced to confront difficult areas of restructuring, and this has intensified that debate. Following the Global Financial Crisis (GFC), Chinese policymakers opted to make innovation and entrepreneurship new drivers of economic growth over coming decades.[2] This policy shift has merely intensified the debate about and research on productivity growth and innovation in China. This chapter presents an updated literature review and provides new estimates of productivity growth, innovation and efficiency changes in the Chinese economy. In addition, it explores what can be learnt from China's recent experience and how economic growth may be sustained through innovation and productivity improvement.

The chapter begins with a brief review of the literature on productivity growth analysis, before discussion of the literature on innovation and catch-up. Recent extensions in the field are investigated in the third section and new estimates of productivity growth at the sector level are reported in section four. Section five presents a comparison of productivity performance between coastal and non-coastal areas, while section six offers concluding remarks.

Productivity growth analysis

According to the traditional growth accounting framework, economic growth in a society arises as a result of changes in production inputs and technological progress (Solow 1957). The latter is also known as productivity or total factor productivity (TFP) growth. Consider the following Cobb–Douglas production function (Equation 9.1).

Equation 9.1

$$y = Ak^{\alpha}l^{\beta}$$

1 For comprehensive literature surveys, see Wu (2011); Tian and Yu (2012); and Zhang (2016).

2 For reviews of China's innovation capacity and development, refer to Wu (2012); and Fan (2014).

In Equation 9.1, it is assumed that capital (k) and labour (l) are employed to produce output (y) in the production process; α and β are the capital and labour income shares, respectively; and A provides a measure of productivity. Equation 9.1 can be converted into the following growth rate format (Equation 9.2).

Equation 9.2

$$\dot{y} = \dot{tfp} + (\alpha\dot{k} + \beta\dot{l})$$

In Equation 9.2, the superscript dot indicates the rate of growth and *tfp* is total factor productivity. Equation 9.2 implies that TFP growth is defined as the residual of output growth that is unexplained by input changes. Given this equation, conventionally, at least three terms—namely, TFP growth, technical change and technological progress—are used interchangeably by economists.

Many authors have followed this practice in their empirical analysis of the Chinese economy. For example, Wu (1993) presented a comprehensive survey of the relevant literature published up to and including 1992. A follow-up survey covering the period from 1993 reported 151 TFP growth estimates for the Chinese economy (Wu 2011). Wu (2011) observed substantial variation in the estimated TFP growth rates across the 74 studies reviewed, and derived a mean TFP growth rate of 3.62 per cent. That rate accounts for about one-third of China's average rate of economic growth during the period under study. Adopting a meta-analysis method, the study also demonstrated that the manufacturing sector in China outperforms agriculture in terms of TFP growth. An interesting additional observation by Wu (2011) was his claim that English-language journal articles tend to report relatively high TFP growth rates compared with those in Chinese.

Since the review by Wu (2011), more empirical studies have emerged in the literature. Zhu (2012) studied the period 1978–2007 and concluded that TFP growth was responsible for about 78 per cent of China's per capita gross domestic product (GDP) growth over those years. Morrison (2013) reported annual TFP growth rates rose from about 4 per cent in 2000 to a peak of around 9 per cent in 2007. From 2008 to 2012, however, Morrison (2013) found that TFP growth showed a sustained downward trend. International Monetary Fund (IMF) economists Anand et al. (2014) also observed this inverted-U shaped pattern of TFP growth in a comparative study of China, India and economies of the Association of Southeast Asian Nations Five (ASEAN-5). In particular, they considered capital utilisation. Their argument is that rapidly declining capital utilisation could lead to biased estimates of TFP growth. They identified that the observed inverted-U shape in the case without considering capital utilisation is much flatter than that with capital utilisation being adjusted.

Wang et al. (2013) estimated agricultural productivity growth using provincial data for the period 1985–2007 and found that TFP growth was responsible for more than 50 per cent of China's agricultural growth, with the coastal regions enjoying relatively faster productivity growth than non-coastal areas. They also found, however, that TFP growth showed a downward trend over time. Du et al. (2014) examined firm-level data for the period 1998–2007 and reported that TFP growth tended to decline over time, and approached zero at the end of their sample period. They argued that this situation was due to resource misallocation between the state and non-state sectors on the one hand, and reduction in technological progress in surviving firms on the other.

More recent studies include Yao (2015), H. Wu (2016) and Mallick (2017). Yao (2015) demonstrated that economic reform and the policy of opening up boosted China's productivity growth significantly, but this growth shows a declining trend over time and especially during the GFC. H. Wu (2016), on the other hand, found that TFP growth has played a minor role in China's economic growth, and TFP growth had even turned negative during the period 2007–12. Mallick (2017) compared China with India and showed that the contribution of TFP growth is substantial in China, but tends to decline over time.

Overall, research findings in the existing literature on the role of TFP in China's economic growth are mixed. But there is one consensus in the literature: most authors observed that China's TFP growth declined during the GFC. Maliszewski and Zhang (2015) drew comparison between this decline and that during the East Asian Financial Crisis in the 1990s. Lai (2015) claimed this productivity slowdown was responsible for China's slow economic growth in recent years.

Innovation and catch-up

The conventional concept of TFP growth has been extended to distinguish between innovation or technological progress and efficiency change or catch-up since the work of Aigner et al. (1977), Meeusen and van den Broeck (1977) and Battese and Corra (1977), to cite a few. In the extended framework, innovation refers to the shift of the production frontier while efficiency change captures movement towards best practice or the production frontier (Nishimizu and Page 1982; Lau and Brada 1990). The sum of the rates of technological progress and efficiency change gives the rate of TFP growth. In other words, TFP growth is decomposable into two components: technological progress and efficiency change. Since the 1980s, a large pool of literature has adopted this concept. Lovell (1996) and Greene (1997) provide reviews of that literature. The decomposition method has also been applied to analyse productivity growth in the Chinese economy. Wu (1995) was one of the earlier studies to use China's regional data, and showed technological progress to be the main driver of TFP growth in farming and rural and urban industries. He also observed variations across sectors as well as among China's three regions—namely, the coastal, central and western regions. Wu (2011) reviewed the earlier literature.

Recently, Li et al. (2011) investigated the source of TFP growth in Chinese agriculture and found significant productivity growth since the 1980s. They pointed out that since the 1980s this growth has been driven mainly by technological progress. Ma et al. (2013) derived a similar conclusion by analysing micro-level data. You and Sarantis (2013) observed that rural transformation or efficiency improvement has made an important contribution to TFP growth; however, its importance has declined over time and that of technological progress has increased. Gao (2015) adopted a data envelopment analysis approach and examined agricultural TFP by using regional data for the period 1992–2012, reaching a conclusion that confirms the findings by Li et al. (2011) and Ma et al. (2013).

Wang and Szirmai (2013) found that efficiency changes dominated industrial productivity growth in the 1980s while technological progress played the major role in the 1990s. This is consistent with the conclusion about China's rural sector by You and Sarantis (2013). Zhang et al. (2014) drew attention to the declining trend in the contribution of TFP to economic growth during the period 1978–2012, and raised the important related question of the sustainability of economic growth in China.

More recently, Han and Shen (2015) adopted the data envelopment method and showed an annual TFP growth rate of 5.9 per cent over the period 1990–2009. This growth is dominated by the rate of technological progress: 5.5 per cent. However, Yu et al. (2015) argued that China's catch-up process is characterised by 'creative restructuring' (or efficiency improvement) rather than 'creative destruction' (or innovation). Curtis (2016) argued that relocation of resources could account for 21.5 points of TFP growth during 1992–97. In sum, the views of the research community as to the role of technological progress and efficiency changes are varied overall. However, more evidence appears to support the idea that technological progress has dominated TFP growth in the Chinese economy in recent decades and that TFP growth tends to decline over time, particularly during the GFC.

Extensions

New growth theory recognises the role of non-traditional production factors such as human capital and research and development (R&D) spending in the growth process. A stream of literature has adopted new growth theory ideas in case studies on the Chinese economy. Wang and Yao (2003) were probably the first to provide human capital estimates for the period 1952–99 with incorporated human capital growth accounting. They found that rapid human capital accumulation and related productivity growth that arose during China's reform period (1978–99) made a positive contribution to economic growth. Ding and Knight (2011) found a positive impact of human capital formation on economic growth. Wei and Hao (2011) examined the role of human capital in China's TFP growth and found a significantly positive effect from human capital on provincial TFP growth during 1985–2004. The effect of human capital, however, is found to vary between the coastal, central and western regions. Luckstead et al. (2014) showed that human capital accounted for an average 24 per cent of TFP growth over the period 1952–78 and 42 per cent for the period 1979–2000. Chen and Funke (2013) explained how a sequencing of physical capital accumulation, human capital accumulation and innovation has driven China's growth since the 1980s.

A secondary body of research explores how additional variables have affected China's TFP growth. For example, Jiang (2011) found a negative relationship between regional openness and TFP growth. Later, however, Yu (2015) found tariff reduction was responsible for at least 14.5 per cent of China's economy-wide productivity growth. Lin et al. (2011) explored the relationship between foreign direct investment (FDI) and regional productivity, concluding that the overall effect of FDI on productivity is positive, especially in coastal regions. Hong and Sun (2011) support this finding. Choi et al. (2015) considered environmentally sensitive productivity growth, the rate of which is found to be low and relatively constant in China. They also observed that related productivity growth has been driven mainly by innovation.

Hu (2001) analysed firm-level data and found a strong link between private R&D and firm productivity. Ljungwall and Tingvall's (2015) meta-analysis of the literature on the effects of R&D spending on economic growth in a large number of economies, however, finds that R&D spending in China has weaker impacts on economic growth than it does in other economies—both Organisation for Economic Co-operation and Development (OECD) and non-OECD countries—covered in the literature. Their finding is supported to some extent by Boeing et al. (2016), who provided micro-level evidence in their finding that a strong increase in patent stock is linked with a falling positive or even vanishing influence on TFP in listed Chinese firms. Boeing et al. (2016) are, however, disputed by Fang et al. (2016), who also used firm-level data. The latter analysis used propensity-score matching methods to demonstrate the link between intra-firm increases in patent stock and TFP growth.

Finally, scholars have also derived estimates of intangible capital in China and examined the related contribution to productivity growth. Intangible capital generally refers to knowledge embedded in intangible products or processes (Li and Wu forthcoming). Examples include software, R&D, designs and advertising. Hulten and Hao (2012) were probably the first to derive these, and they showed that about one-sixth of productivity growth was due to intangibles during 2000–08.

Li and Wu (forthcoming) looked at the role of intangible capital at the provincial level and concluded that TFP growth estimates would be biased if intangibles were not considered. They observed the decline in TFP growth during the GFC; however, Li and Wu also noticed that both human capital deepening and intangible capital deepening played a greater role during the GFC than before it. Fleisher et al. (2015) presented evidence at the micro level that showed that investment in knowledge capital is productivity enhancing among domestically owned and foreign-invested firms.

Growth accounting estimates

To identify new evidence on productivity growth and technological progress using the latest statistics at both the sector and the regional level, we study productivity and economic growth sources using a growth accounting framework. The framework we adopt takes Equations 9.1 and 9.2 and extends them with the inclusion of a time trend in the production function. The coefficient (δ) of the time trend measures the rate of technological progress. The difference between TFP growth rates and δ gives an indication of efficiency changes ($\dot{ec}$). The underlying model is essentially a deterministic one (Aigner and Chu 1968). Given this definition, Equation 9.2 expands as follows (Equation 9.3).

Equation 9.3

$$\dot{y} = \delta + \dot{ec} + (\alpha\dot{k} + \beta\dot{l})$$

To estimate the right-hand side components of Equation 9.3, panel data from 31 Chinese provinces covering the period 1991–2015 are compiled. The raw data are sourced from China's *Statistical Yearbooks* (NBS various issues). Output (y) is measured by value added in three sectors—agriculture, manufacturing and services—at the provincial level. Capital stock (k) estimates are described in Y. Wu (2016), who adopted region-specific and sector-specific rates of capital depreciation. Both output and capital stock are expressed in constant prices. Labour (l) is measured by the year-end employment numbers because information for the actual hours worked is not available.

In the empirical exercises, period-specific dummy variables are included in the production function to capture possible variations in the values of δ, α and β over three subperiods: the 1990s, the 2000s and the period of the GFC. This division is to ensure that the subsamples have approximately equal size. In addition, the three eight-year subperiods coincide with major reform campaigns—starting in 1992 with Deng Xiaoping's 'southern tour', China's accession into the World Trade Organization (WTO) in December 2001 and the period including and following the GFC (since 2008). These major events or policy changes may have led to structural changes in the Chinese economy during the relevant periods. In effect, the inclusion of the dummy variables allows for different production frontiers for the three subperiods. The computation results use the first set of regression outcomes (not reported here due to space limitations) and are summarised in Table 9.1.

From Table 9.1, it is evident that TFP growth has been the dominant driver of economic growth in China since the 1990s. This relates to the fact that the share of TFP growth over output growth ranges from 63 per cent to 93 per cent (column 'TFP/Output' in Table 9.1). The contribution of TFP to economic growth is highest in agriculture, followed, in turn, by services and manufacturing in recent years. This presents a sharp contrast to the findings of H. Wu (2016) and Hoffman and Polk (2014), with the main difference in the latter being their assumption of constant returns to scale by following the conventional growth accounting framework proposed by Solow (1956) and Swan (1956). In fact, the sum of the estimated output elasticity with respect to labour and capital in Table 9.1 is well below one. Since this implies decreasing returns to scale in all three sectors, growth accounting with assumptions of constant returns to scale would in this case inflate the contribution of production inputs and hence underestimate the role of TFP growth.

Table 9.1 Calculated growth rates, shares and returns to scale (per cent, unless otherwise noted)

Period	Output	TFP	TP	EC	TFP/Output	Scale*
Agriculture						
1	5.17	3.90	4.24	–0.33	75.48	0.46
2	4.40	4.05	4.25	–0.19	92.25	0.46
3	4.32	3.90	3.41	0.49	90.30	0.49
Manufacturing						
1	13.45	10.87	9.98	0.89	80.82	0.55
2	14.42	11.31	10.56	0.75	78.43	0.53
3	13.74	8.68	8.09	0.59	63.17	0.56
Services						
1	13.26	10.95	9.92	1.03	82.58	0.26
2	11.89	9.76	9.19	0.57	82.04	0.25
3	10.77	7.73	7.57	0.16	71.77	0.29

* 'Scale' reports the estimated returns to scale and has no unit.

Notes: Period 1 refers to the years 1992–99, period 2 is the second subperiod (2000–07) and period 3 is the third subperiod (2008–15). The values in the columns represent average growth rates of provincial value added (output), TFP, technological progress (TP) and efficiency change (EC). The numbers in the 'TFP/Output' column are shares of TFP growth over output growth. The sum of TP and EC may not be equal to TFP due to rounding.

Source: Authors' own work.

The results in Table 9.1 suggest that technological progress plays a dominant role in productivity growth in all three sectors. The data also suggest that TFP growth in China slowed during the GFC, although growth remains relatively high. Other researchers have also observed this downward trend (e.g. Wang et al. 2013; Yao 2015; Mallick 2017). The implications of this slowdown are worth monitoring as the global economy recovers incrementally. It is also noted in Table 9.1 that the estimated returns to scale in the service sector are much smaller than those in the manufacturing sector. Given that services generated more than 50 per cent of China's total GDP in 2016, Liu and Yang (2015) have argued that China's future growth relies on improvement in the performance of productivity growth in the service sector. Lee (2016) made a similar argument by examining Korea's economic growth and catch-up process. Lee reckons Korean productivity growth was affected by the poor performance in services and China should avoid this by improving productivity in the service sector.

Finally, it is interesting to note that the relatively high rates of TFP growth estimated in this study are consistent with the findings of others (Table 9.2). Examples include Zhu (2012), who reported similar estimates for the Chinese economy, and Gao (2015), who investigated the agricultural sector. Brandt et al. (2012) and Ding et al. (2016) focused on the manufacturing sector.

Table 9.2 Selected estimates of TFP growth and its share in output growth (per cent)

Sources	Years	Growth	TFP/ Output	Sectors
This study	1992–2015	8.9	77.1	Economy wide
	1992–2007	9.4	81.1	Economy wide
	2000–2015	8.7	75.5	Economy wide
	2008–2015	7.9	69.0	Economy wide
Zhu (2012)	1978–2007		78.0	Economy wide
Morrison (2013)	2000–2012	6.0*		Economy wide
Han & Shen (2015)	1990–2009	5.9		Economy wide
Ding et al. (2016)	1998–2007	9.6		Manufacturing
Brandt et al. (2012)	1978–2007	8.0		Manufacturing
Yang (2015)	1998–2009	3.8		Manufacturing
Gao (2015)	1992–2012	3.1	79.2	Agriculture

* This growth rate is estimated by using Figure 3 in Morrison (2013).

Coastal versus non-coastal regions

A major policy focus in China is to reduce regional disparity—in particular, unbalanced development between the coastal and the non-coastal provinces. It is therefore of policy relevance to evaluate and contrast the role of TFP growth in these two broad regions. For this purpose, the above exercises are repeated to allow for regional variations in technology—different values of δ, α and β in Equation 9.3—for the three sectors and the two regions (coastal and non-coastal). This is achieved through the use of both period-specific and regional dummy variables. The estimation results are not listed due to space limitations. Instead, the computational findings are summarised in Table 9.3.

Table 9.3 Computational results: Coastal versus non-coastal regions (per cent)

	Coastal			Non-coastal		
Period	Output	TFP	TFP/Output	Output	TFP	TFP/Output
Agriculture						
1	4.89	3.64	74.53	5.31	4.32	81.40
2	3.69	3.60	97.55	4.73	4.62	97.61
3	2.71	3.08	113.66	5.09	4.81	94.52
Manufacturing						
1	15.84	15.27	96.38	13.40	11.35	84.67
2	14.09	10.64	75.51	14.58	12.24	83.99
3	10.27	4.41	42.96	13.27	8.82	66.51
Services						
1	14.07	12.83	91.19	12.88	9.55	74.14
2	12.32	11.06	89.82	11.69	8.86	75.79
3	10.49	8.48	80.90	10.91	7.38	67.65

Note: See the notes to Table 9.1.

Source: Authors' own work.

Table 9.3 adds weight to our earlier findings that TFP has played an important role in China's growth in recent decades. Both TFP and economic growth have, as also earlier noted, slowed over time. Here we identify, however, that this downward trend is much more serious in the coastal regions than in non-coastal areas. The coastal areas, China's traditional manufacturing heartland, recorded the largest fall in TFP growth. In contrast, the non-coastal regions have maintained strong growth in manufacturing and in turn outperformed the coastal areas in all three sectors during the GFC. This is bad news for the coastal regions but good news for the reduction of regional disparity in the country. For the coastal regions, however, it is interesting to note that the service sector has outperformed the manufacturing sector since the onset of the GFC. Since the service sector dominates coastal economies, relatively fast growth in services may help economic restructuring in these regions and hence contribute to sustainable economic growth.

Conclusion

Understanding the role of productivity and innovation in economic growth in the case of China is controversial. The debate has attracted more attention since the GFC and as China's economy attempts to shift to new sources of growth. From the various methods adopted to analyse related Chinese data at the macro, regional and firm levels, the dominant view in the existing literature appears to support the notion that TFP has made a significant and positive contribution to economic growth in recent decades. Most studies also agree that the rates of both TFP and economic growth have slowed in recent years. Whether this downward trend continues has important implications for China's economic development.

This study has presented some new evidence about TFP and economic growth by examining the latest regional and sectoral statistics from China. Our estimates concur with the existing literature in finding that productivity growth has made a positive contribution to economic growth in China. It is specifically found that productivity growth is the main driver of economic growth in all three sectors: agriculture, manufacturing and services. It is also found that technological progress is primarily responsible for TFP growth.

Though TFP growth tended to fall during the GFC, there are otherwise encouraging developments in the Chinese economy. First, the extensive non-coastal areas have maintained high growth and have outperformed the coastal regions in all three sectors. This is good for the reduction of regional disparity, which has been a major policy focus in China for many years. Second, while manufacturing seems to suffer the most in the coastal areas, growth in the service sector fell only slightly, and, in particular, TFP growth in this sector is still very strong. Since services generate more than 50 per cent of the value added in the coastal areas, strong TFP growth may help these regions sustain economic growth in the future. Finally, the decline in manufacturing and rise in less resource-intensive services may also be a positive development for the environment in the coastal areas of China.

References

Aigner, D. J. and Chu, S.-F. (1968), On estimating the industry production function, *The American Economic Review* 58(4): 826–39.

Aigner, D. J., Lovell, C. A. K. and Schmidt, P. J. (1977), Formulation and estimation of stochastic frontier models, *Journal of Econometrics* 6(1): 21–37. doi.org/10.1016/0304-4076(77)90052-5.

Anand, R., Cheng, K. C., Rehman, S. and Zhang, L. (2014), *Potential growth in emerging Asia*, IMF Working Paper WP/14/2, International Monetary Fund, Washington, DC.

Battese, G. E. and Corra, G. S. (1977), Estimation of a production frontier model: With application to the pastoral zone of eastern Australia, *Australian Journal of Agricultural Economics* 21(3): 169–79. doi.org/10.1111/j.1467-8489.1977.tb00204.x.

Boeing, P., Mueller, E. and Sandner, P. (2016), China's R&D explosion: Analyzing productivity effects across ownership types and over time, *Research Policy* 45(1): 159–76. doi.org/10.1016/j.respol.2015.07.008.

Brandt, L., Biesebroeck, J. V. and Zhang, Y. (2012), Creative accounting or creative destruction? Firm-level productivity growth in Chinese manufacturing, *Journal of Development Economics* 97: 339–51. doi.org/10.1016/j.jdeveco.2011.02.002.

Chen, X. and Funke, M. (2013), The dynamics of catch-up and skill and technology upgrading in China, *Journal of Macroeconomics* 38: 465–80. doi.org/10.1016/j.jmacro.2013.07.002.

Choi, Y., Oh, D.-H. and Zhang, N. (2015), Environmentally sensitive productivity growth and its decompositions in China: A metafrontier Malmquist–Luenberger productivity index approach, *Empirical Economics* 49(3): 1017–43. doi.org/10.1007/s00181-014-0896-5.

Curtis, C. C. (2016), Economic reforms and the evolution of China's total factor productivity, *Review of Economic Dynamics* 21: 225–45. doi.org/10.1016/j.red.2015.02.005.

Ding, S. and Knight, J. (2011), Why has China grown so fast? The role of physical and human capital formation, *Oxford Bulletin of Economics and Statistics* 73(2): 141–74. doi.org/10.1111/j.1468-0084.2010.00625.x.

Ding, S., Guariglia, A. and Harris, R. (2016), The determinants of productivity in Chinese large and medium-sized industrial firms, 1998–2007, *Journal of Productivity Analysis* 45(2): 131–55. doi.org/10.1007/s11123-015-0460-0.

Du, J., Liu, X. and Zhou, Y. (2014), State advances and private retreats? Evidence of aggregate productivity decomposition in China, *China Economic Review* 31: 459–74. doi.org/10.1016/j.chieco.2014.03.002.

Fan, P. (2014), Innovation in China, *Journal of Economic Surveys* 28(4): 725–45. doi.org/10.1111/joes.12083.

Fang, J., He, H. and Li, N. (2016), *China's rising IQ (innovation quotient) and growth: Firm-level evidence*, IMF Working Paper WP/16/249, International Monetary Fund, Washington, DC.

Fleisher, B. M., McGuire, W. H., Smith, A. N. and Zhou, M. (2015), Knowledge capital, innovation and growth in China, *Journal of Asian Economics* 39: 31–42. doi.org/10.1016/j.asieco.2015.05.002.

Gao, F. (2015), Evolution trend and internal mechanism of regional total factor productivity in Chinese agriculture, *Journal of Quantitative and Technical Economics* 32(5): 3–19.

Greene, W. H. (1997), Frontier production functions, in M. H. Pesaran and P. Schmidt (eds), *Handbook of Applied Econometrics II: Microeconomics*, pp. 81–166, Oxford: Blackwell.

Han, J. and Shen, Y. (2015), Financial development and total factor productivity growth: Evidence from China, *Emerging Markets Finance and Trade* 51(Supp. 1): S261–S274. doi.org/10.1080/1540496X.2014.998928.

Hoffman, D. and Polk, A. (2014), *The long soft fall in Chinese growth: Business realities, risks and opportunities*, Conference Board Research Report, US–China Business Council, Washington, DC, and Beijing. Available from: www.uschina.org/china-hub/report-long-soft-fall-chinese-growth.

Hong, E. and Sun, L. (2011), Foreign direct investment and total factor productivity in China: A spatial dynamic panel analysis, *Oxford Bulletin of Economics and Statistics* 73(6): 771–91. doi.org/10.1111/j.1468-0084.2011.00672.x.

Hu, A. G. (2001), Ownership, government R&D, private R&D, and productivity in Chinese industry, *Journal of Comparative Economics* 29(1): 136–57. doi.org/10.1006/jcec.2000.1704.

Hulten, C. R. and Hao, J. X. (2012), *The role of intangible capital in the transformation and growth of the Chinese economy*, NBER Working Paper No. 18405, National Bureau of Economic Research, Cambridge, Mass. doi.org/10.3386/w18405.

Jiang, Y. (2011), Economic environment, technology diffusion, and growth of regional total factor productivity in China, *Journal of Chinese Economic and Business Studies* 9(2): 151–61. doi.org/10.1080/14765284.2011.568684.

Lai, P. (2015), Growth slowdown in China since 2008: Will there be a hard landing in the near future? *China and World Economy* 23(3): 42–58. doi.org/10.1111/cwe.12113.

Lau, K.-T. and Brada, J. C. (1990), Technological progress and technical efficiency in Chinese industrial growth: A frontier production approach, *China Economic Review* 1(2): 113–24. doi.org/10.1016/1043-951X(90)90001-5.

Lee, J.-W. (2016), Korea's economic growth and catch-up: Implications for China, *China and World Economy* 24(5): 71–97. doi.org/10.1111/cwe.12175.

Li, G., You, L. and Feng, Z. (2011), The sources of total factor productivity growth in Chinese agriculture: Technological progress or efficiency gain? *Journal of Chinese Economic and Business Studies* 9(2): 181–203. doi.org/10.1080/14765284.2011.568686.

Li, Q. and Wu, Y. (forthcoming), Intangible capital in Chinese regional economies: Measurement and analysis, *China Economic Review*.

Lin, C.-H., Lee, C.-M. and Yang, C.-H. (2011), Does foreign direct investment really enhance China's regional productivity? *The Journal of International Trade & Economic Development* 20(6): 741–68. doi.org/10.1080/09638190903294866.

Liu, H. and Yang, T. (2015), Explaining the productivity growth gap between China and India: The role of structural transformation, *Developing Economies* 53(2): 100–21. doi.org/10.1111/deve.12071.

Ljungwall, C. and Tingvall, P. G. (2015), Is China different? A meta-analysis of the growth-enhancing effect from R&D spending in China, *China Economic Review* 36: 272–8. doi.org/10.1016/j.chieco.2015.10.001.

Lovell, C. A. K. (1996), Applying efficiency measurement techniques to the measurement of productivity change, *Journal of Productivity Analysis* 7: 329–40. doi.org/10.1007/BF00157047.

Luckstead, J., Choi, S. M., Devadoss, S. and Mittelhammer, R. C. (2014), China's catch-up to the US economy: Decomposing TFP through investment-specific technology and human capital, *Applied Economics* 46(31–3): 3995–4007.

Ma, H., Huang, J. and Oxley, L. (2013), Capital formation and agricultural growth in China, *Asian Economic Papers* 12(1): 166–90. doi.org/10.1162/ASEP_a_00200.

Maliszewski, W. and Zhang, L. (2015), *China's growth: Can Goldilocks outgrow bears?* IMF Working Paper WP/15/113, International Monetary Fund, Washington, DC.

Mallick, J. (2017), *Structural change and productivity growth in India and the People's Republic of China*, ADBI Working Paper No. 656, Asian Development Bank Institute, Tokyo.

Meeusen, W. and van den Broeck, J. (1977), Efficiency estimation from Cobb–Douglas production functions with composed error, *International Economic Review* 18(2): 435–44. doi.org/10.2307/2525757.

Morrison, W. M. (2013), *China's economic rise: History, trends, challenges, and implications for the United States*, CRS Report for Congress 7-5700 RL33534, Congressional Research Service, Washington, DC.

National Bureau of Statistics of China (NBS) (various issues), *China Statistical Yearbook*, Beijing: China Statistics Press.

Nishimizu, M. and Page, J. M. (1982), Total factor productivity growth, technological progress and technical efficiency change, *Economic Journal* 92: 920–36. doi.org/10.2307/2232675.

Solow, R. M. (1956), A contribution to the theory of economic growth, *Quarterly Journal of Economics* 70(1): 65–94. doi.org/10.2307/1884513.

Solow, R. M. (1957), Technical change and the aggregate production function, *Review of Economics and Statistics* 39(3): 312–20. doi.org/10.2307/1926047.

Swan, T. W. (1956), Economic growth and capital accumulation, *Economic Record* 32(2): 334–61. doi.org/10.1111/j.1475-4932.1956.tb00434.x.

Tian, X. and Yu, X. (2012), The enigmas of TFP in China: A meta-analysis, *China Economic Review* 23(2): 396–414. doi.org/10.1016/j.chieco.2012.02.007.

Wang, L. and Szirmai, A. (2013), The unexpected convergence of regional productivity in Chinese industry, 1978–2005, *Oxford Development Studies* 41(1): 29–53. doi.org/10.1080/13600818.2012.756464.

Wang, S. L., Tuan, F., Gale, F., Somwaru, A. and Hansen, J. (2013), China's regional agricultural productivity growth in 1985–2007: A multilateral comparison, *Agricultural Economics* 44(2): 241–51. doi.org/10.1111/agec.12008.

Wang, Y. and Yao, Y. (2003), Sources of China's economic growth 1952–1999: Incorporating human capital accumulation, *China Economic Review* 14: 32–52. doi.org/10.1016/S1043-951X(02)00084-6.

Wei, Z. and Hao, R. (2011), The role of human capital in China's total factor productivity growth: A cross-province analysis, *The Developing Economies* 49(1): 1–35. doi.org/10.1111/j.1746-1049.2010.00120.x.

Wu, H. X. (2016), Sustainability of China's growth model: A productivity perspective, *China & World Economy* 24(5): 42–70. doi.org/10.1111/cwe.12174.

Wu, Y. (1993), Productive efficiency in Chinese industry: A review, *Asian-Pacific Economic Literature* 7(2): 58–66. doi.org/10.1111/j.1467-8411.1993.tb00191.x.

Wu, Y. (1995), Total factor productivity growth, technological progress and technical efficiency change in China: A three sector analysis, *Journal of Comparative Economics* 21(2): 207–29. doi.org/10.1006/jcec.1995.9997.

Wu, Y. (2011), Total factor productivity growth in China: A review, *Journal of Chinese Economic and Business Studies* 9(2): 111–26. doi.org/10.1080/14765284.2011.568682.

Wu, Y. (2012), Trends and prospects in China's research and development sector, *Australian Economic Review* 45(4): 467–74. doi.org/10.1111/j.1467-8462.2012.00707.x.

Wu, Y. (2016), China's capital stock series by region and sector, *Frontiers of Economics in China* 11(1): 156–72.

Yang, R. (2015), Study on the total factor productivity of Chinese manufacturing enterprises, *Economic Research Journal* 50(2): 61–74.

Yao, Z. (2015), Productivity growth and industrial structure adjustment: An analysis of China's provincial panel data, *Chinese Economy* 48(4): 253–68. doi.org/10.1080/10971475.2015.1044848.

You, K. and Sarantis, N. (2013), Structural breaks, rural transformation and total factor productivity growth in China, *Journal of Productivity Analysis* 39(3): 231–42. doi.org/10.1007/s11123-012-0285-z.

Yu, M. (2015), Processing trade, tariff reductions and firm productivity: Evidence from Chinese firms, *Economic Journal* 125(585): 943–88. doi.org/10.1111/ecoj.12127.

Yu, X., Dosi, G., Lei, J. and Nuvolari, A. (2015), Institutional change and productivity growth in China's manufacturing: The microeconomics of knowledge accumulation and 'creative restructuring', *Industrial and Corporate Change* 24(3): 565–602. doi.org/10.1093/icc/dtv011.

Zhang, J., Jiang, C. and Wang, P. (2014), Total factor productivity and China's miraculous growth: An empirical analysis, Unpublished ms. Available from: papers.ssrn.com/sol3/papers.cfm?abstract_id=2456009. doi.org/10.2139ssrn.2456009.

Zhang, Y. (2016), *China's productivity: Past success and future challenges*, MPFD Working Paper No. WP/16/06, Macroeconomics Policy and Financing for Development Division, United Nations Economic and Social Commission for Asia and the Pacific, Bangkok. Available from: www.unescap.org/resources/mpfd-working-paper-chinas-productivity-past-success-and-future-challenges.

Zhu, X. (2012), Understanding China's growth: Past, present and future, *Journal of Economic Perspectives* 26(4): 103–24. doi.org/10.1257/jep.26.4.103.

10. Empirical Study of Regional Innovation Capability and Economic Convergence in China

Chaofeng Yang, Zhiyun Zhao and Zhijuan Zhang

Introduction

Given the correlation of economic activities between regions is becoming stronger, this chapter conducts an empirical study of the convergence of real gross domestic product (GDP) per capita of 31 Chinese provinces and municipalities during the period 2001–15, and explores the impacts of innovation capability on economic convergence, using the inverse centroid distance among different regions as a weight matrix in a spatial econometrics model. The results show that: 1) after considering the spatial effect, China's regional economic development has both conditional convergence and absolute convergence; 2) in recent years, the trend of China's regional economic development convergence is becoming more obvious; and 3) after regional innovation capacity is taken into account, the speed of convergence of China's regional economy will deteriorate.

According to the growth poles theory first proposed by the French economist Perroux (1950), it would be ideal but is impossible in reality for a country to achieve balanced development. Economic growth usually spreads gradually from one or more 'growth centres' to other sectors or regions. Therefore, growth does not appear in all places, but appears first at some growth points or growth poles at different intensities, and these growth points or poles spread out through different channels, generating different final influences on the entire economy.

In the study of modern regional economies, the growth poles theory is used widely as the guiding theory for regional development. It is, however, more realistic in its description of the process of social development, so it is also widely used by many countries, especially developing countries (including China), in strategies for economic planning, productivity and regional economic development. Since the period of reform and opening up, China has achieved rapid economic growth and people's living standards have improved significantly. However, rapid economic growth has not delivered benefits equally to all regions of China, and gaps in regional development have gradually increased. Although in recent years, the government has adopted macroeconomic policy in an attempt to control this situation, and gaps in regional economic development have narrowed slightly, the overall effect is not yet obvious. Moreover, these imbalances in China's economic development have become an increasingly important factor restricting the healthy development of the national economy. Since innovation is now sought as a core source of competitiveness at the national and regional levels, it is timely to ask whether innovation ability has an impact on economic convergence within a country. And, if it does, how should the regional distribution of innovative resources be optimised to narrow the gaps in regional economic development?

It is generally believed that the concept of economic convergence is derived from the neoclassical growth model proposed by Solow (1956). Since the model assumes that the marginal margin of capital diminishes, the underdeveloped areas should grow faster than the developed areas under the circumstance of owning the same technology. The empirical studies of convergence in advanced economies (e.g. Baumol 1986; Barro and Sala-i-Martin 1992) show that the per capita income levels of different states within the United States and those of developed countries have converged. Researchers such as Romer (1994), Baumol (1986) and Barro and Sala-i-Martin (1992) have, however, found that the majority of developing countries fail to narrow their per capita income gap with developed countries. Carrington's (2003) test results show that there is no convergence among European countries in terms of per capita income.

Tests of intra-country regional economic convergence can be divided into two categories. In the first category, the spatial effect is not taken into account. In the case of China, most such tests show that there is no global absolute convergence but there is conditional convergence. Results of tests of the convergence of China's regional economy in the period 1978–95 by We (1997) show that the overall per capita GDP growth in China tends to converge. It has been found from the empirical studies of Cai and Yang (2000) and Shen and Jun (2002) that, since the period of reform and opening-up, there has been no global absolute convergence in China's regional economy, but there is conditional convergence. Studies by Wang and Zhaopan (2002) show that there is club convergence in the country's three main regions: eastern, central and western China. Studies by Lin and Mingxing (2003) show that there was conditional convergence in China's regional economy over the period 1981–99, while research by Ren et al. (2014) shows that the marginal productivity of research and development (R&D) has significant driving effect on regional economic convergence in China.

Tests in the second category of regional economic convergence take spatial correlation into account in the empirical model, with most finding there is global absolute convergence in China's regional economies. Lin et al. (2005) adopted spatial econometric methods and found there was a trend of absolute convergence in China's regional economies between 1978 and 2002. Wu (2006) found that, after taking the spatial effect into account, there was a more significant convergence in the economies of each province and region. Pan (2010) included the spatial effect in the convergence test model and found that, within 30 years of the start of China's reform and opening-up period, there were characteristics of global absolute convergence. All these studies have achieved rich results and provide important implications for follow-up research.

There are, however, two obvious deficiencies in this research in terms of our interests: first, most of the literature uses ordinary least squares (OLS), which neglects the spatial effect, to carry out the model estimation, or, where spatial effects were taken into account, these studies were too simplistic in selecting spatial weights, which often leads to model deviations in actual application, thus resulting in incomplete and unscientific results, lacking due explanatory power (Wu 2007: 149–63). Second, although the existing literature studies the influence on economic convergence of policy and the introduction of new technologies, few regard innovation capacity as the explanatory variable of conditional convergence. In view of this and based on the framework of economic convergence theory, this chapter expands the economic convergence model and uses research methods such as spatial measurement to carry out empirical tests and discuss the influence of innovation on economic convergence to provide theoretical support for the balanced and coordinated development of China's regional economies and the implementation of national innovation-driven development strategies.

Research design

Economic convergence refers to the fact that the growth rate and level of a country's per capita output are negatively correlated, which results in a gradually declining trend for the economic gap between two countries. The concept of economic convergence can also be used in relation to different regions within a country. Economic convergence can be divided into two categories: α convergence and β convergence. α convergence refers to the variance of per capita income in different regions or the fact that the discrete coefficient tends to decrease over time. Macroeconomics focuses on β convergence, and this form is mainly demonstrated by the fact that the economic growth rate of backward areas is higher than that of developed areas, resulting in the per capita income of the former gradually catching up with the latter. If β convergence is conditional on some factors—such as human capital, policy variables and infrastructure—it is called conditional β convergence. Otherwise, it is absolute β convergence. Innovation, which can improve labour and capital productivity, is a major factor in determining long-term economic growth. The impact of innovation capacity on the convergence of regional economic growth is achieved mainly through the diffusion of innovation. The impetus for regional innovation diffusion is the 'potential difference' in innovation ability of each region. Adjacent regions have some coherence and similarities, so innovation can be spread smoothly between them, which gradually reduces the 'potential difference' in innovation ability, some level of convergence of innovation ability can be achieved and, finally, overall regional economic growth tends to converge under certain conditions. Therefore, from this perspective, there is a close relationship between regional innovation capacity and the convergence of economic growth.

Previous empirical studies of economic convergence usually adopt the simplification of convergence analysis framework proposed by Barro and Sala-i-Martin (1992) as the test model. In this chapter, factors controlling innovation capacity are introduced to simplify the model and the test equation of a regional economy's absolute β convergence is shown in Equation 10.1.

Equation 10.1

$$\frac{1}{T}\ln\left(\frac{y_{i,t+T}}{y_{i,t}}\right) = \alpha + \beta\ln(y_{i,t}) + \varepsilon_{i,t}$$

In Equation 10.1, $y_{i,t}$ refers to the per capita GDP of region i in year t; T is the inspection period; $\frac{1}{T}\ln\left(\frac{y_{i,t+T}}{y_{i,t}}\right)$ refers to the annual growth rate of real per capita GDP in region i from t to t + T; $\ln(y_{i,t})$ refers to the natural logarithm of real per capita GDP of region i at period t; α is the constant term; β is the convergence coefficient; and $\varepsilon_{i,t}$ is the random error term. If we add controlling variance (innovation capacity in this chapter) in the absolute β convergence model, it will change to Conditional β convergence, as shown in Equation 10.2.

Equation 10.2

$$\frac{1}{T}\ln\left(\frac{y_{i,t+T}}{y_{i,t}}\right) = \alpha + \beta\ln(y_{i,t}) + \zeta\ln(P_{i,t}) + \varepsilon_{i,t}$$

In Equation 10.2, $P_{i,t}$ is the variance reflecting the innovation capacity of region i in year t. Internationally, cross-country regional innovation capacity depends on the potential of producing a series of innovation products, and among them the most important factor is R&D stock (Furman et al. 2002). Chinese scholars have associated regional innovation capacity with the output of innovation results as well as the ability to carry out innovation activities—the most important factor in which is the number of patent applications. In recent years, patents, especially invention patents, have been playing an increasingly noticeable role in China's regional innovation capacity and economic development and are being taken as an indicator of regional innovation capacity. Provinces and cities with high levels of regional innovation capacity usually have high numbers of invention patents and authorisations. Therefore, in this chapter, the number of invention patent applications is used to measure regional innovation capacity.

We adopt the β convergence test of economic development as noted and measure this using the traditional method in which the spatial effect is not considered. Regions cannot independently develop their own economy; it is instead typically a process closely linked with and affected by the economies of neighbouring regions and those further afield. Spatial effects include spatial dependence and spatial variability: the former refers to the observed value of a sample region being associated with that of other regions; the latter refers to the inhomogeneity of the spatial effect at the regional level due to the heterogeneity of spatial units (Anselin 1988). These two spatial effects correspond to two spatial measurement models: the spatial lag model (SLM) and the spatial error model (SEM). Correspondingly, the SEMs of a regional economy's absolute β convergence and conditional β convergence are shown in Equations 10.3 and 10.4.

Equation 10.3

$$\frac{1}{T}\ln\left(\frac{y_{i,t+T}}{y_{i,t}}\right) = \alpha + \beta\ln(y_{i,t}) + \frac{\rho}{T}W\ln\left(\frac{y_{i,t+T}}{y_{i,t}}\right) + \varepsilon_{i,t}$$

Equation 10.4

$$\frac{1}{T}\ln\left(\frac{y_{i,t+T}}{y_{i,t}}\right) = \alpha + \beta\ln(y_{i,t}) + \zeta\ln(P_{i,t}) + \frac{\rho}{T}W\ln\left(\frac{y_{i,t+T}}{y_{i,t}}\right) + \varepsilon_{i,t}$$

In Equations 10.3 and 10.4, ρ is the spatial lag coefficient that measures the degree of spatial interaction between observed values of the weight matrix and W is the spatial weight coefficient matrix. The spatial weight matrix is the key to the spatial metering model. At present, most research adopts a simple neighbourhood matrix. However, economic linkages between adjacent regions are not identical and, generally, the degree of interregional interaction is weakened by distance. Given spatial distance is generally inversely proportional to the degree of spatial correlation, this chapter takes the reciprocal of the straight-line distance between the centroids of different regions as the value of the elements in W.

Similarly, the formulas for the SEMs of a regional economy's absolute β convergence and conditional β convergence are Equations 10.5 and 10.6.

Equation 10.5

$$\frac{1}{T}\ln\left(\frac{y_{i,t+T}}{y_{i,t}}\right) = \alpha + \beta\ln(y_{i,t}) + (1-\lambda W)^{-1}\mu_{i,t}$$

Equation 10.6

$$\frac{1}{T}\ln\left(\frac{y_{i,t+T}}{y_{i,t}}\right) = \alpha + \beta\ln(y_{i,t}) + \zeta\ln(P_{i,t}) + (1-\lambda W)^{-1}\mu_{i,t}$$

In Equations 10.5 and 10.6, λ is the spatial error coefficient, reflecting the parameters of the spatial correlation between regression residuals, $\mu_{i,t}$~$N(0,\sigma^2 I)$.

In Equation 10.6, if the estimated value of β is significantly negative, the per capita GDP growth rate of a region is negatively correlated with the per capita GDP level at the initial stage. If the per capita GDP growth rate in economically backward regions is higher than that in developed provinces, there is β convergence of the regional economy. The spatial econometric model is no longer suitable for OLS estimation and, generally, the maximum likehood (ML) method is used to estimate the value of the credible parameter. In addition, according to the estimated value of β, the convergence speed, θ, of a region's per capita GDP can be calculated and the semi–life cycle, τ, for convergence can be used to show the time it will take economically backward regions to catch up with economically developed regions (Equations 10.7 and 10.8).

Equation 10.7

$$\theta = -\frac{\ln(1+\beta)}{t}$$

Equation 10.8

$$\tau = \frac{\ln(2)}{\theta}$$

Before using the spatial metering model, it is necessary to first determine whether the spatial correlation exists between regional economies, which is usually verified by Moran's I, first proposed by Moran (1950). The expression is Equation 10.9.

Equation 10.9

$$\text{Mordan's I} = \frac{\sum_{i=1}^{n}\sum_{j=1}^{n}\omega_{ij}(x_i-\bar{x})(x_j-\bar{x})}{S^2\sum_{i=1}^{n}\sum_{j=1}^{n}W_{ij}}$$

In Equation 10.9 $S^2 = \frac{1}{n}\sum_{i=1}^{n}(x_i-\bar{x})^2, \bar{x} = \frac{1}{n}\sum_{i=1}^{n}x_i$, x_i is the observed value of region i; n is the number of regions; and ω_{ij} is the spatial weight value of region i and region j. If the absolute value of Moran's I is close to 1, it indicates that the spatial correlation of regional innovation capacity is stronger. For the selection of spatial lag and SEMs, Anselin et al. (1997) proposed the following criteria: if LMLAG (Lagrange Multiplier Lag) is statistically more significant than LMERR (Lagrange Multiplier Error) in the spatial econometric model, the SLM is selected; if LMERR is more significant than LMLAG statistically, the SEM is chosen.

The scope of this study is 31 provinces in China (excluding Hong Kong, Macau and Taiwan) and the period studied is 2001–15. All data come from the *China Statistics Yearbook* for the corresponding year (NBS various years) and the per capita GDP is the price in 2000.

Estimation results and analysis

Regional per capita GDP spatial correlation test

Moran's I index can be obtained through calculation according to China's provincial per capita GDP in 2001–15 (see Figure 10.1). Moran's I indices for regional per capita GDP in 2001–15 all pass the significance test below the level of 5 per cent. Although there is fluctuation in Moran's I index, all are above 0.3. This indicates that China's regional economic activities are not in a random state, but, rather, demonstrate the phenomenon of clustering in geographical space; and, in our period, this agglomeration demonstrates, first, a rising trend, but, later, a diminishing trend. In other words, China's per capita GDP has a strong spatial correlation and provinces with a relatively higher level of economic development are adjacent to each other while economically backward provinces tend to be adjacent to each other.

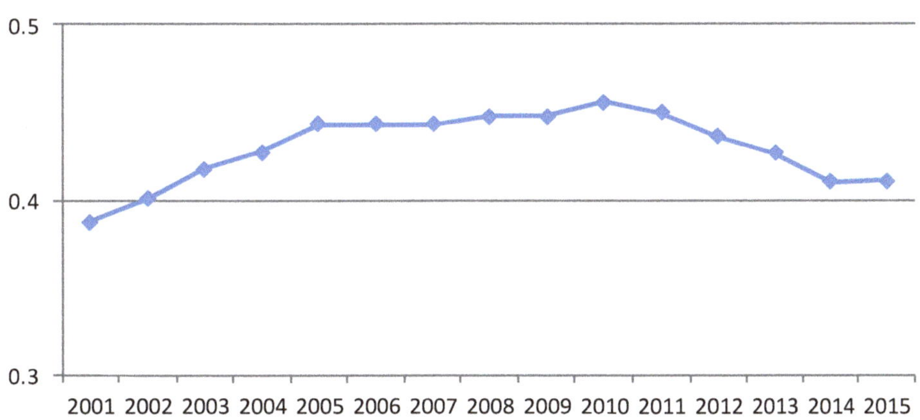

Figure 10.1 Moran's I index of China's regional per capita GDP, 2001–15

Source: National Bureau of Statistics of China (various years).

Model and weight selection

For the sake of comparison, this chapter first adopts OLS estimations without considering the spatial effect in the test equation of a regional economy's absolute β convergence, and the results are shown in Table 10.1.

Table 10.1 Regional economies' absolute β convergence test results (not considering the spatial effect)

Variances	Estimated value	Standard errors
α	4.2753*	0.5316
β	–0.3307*	0.0593
R^2	0.4567	
R^2 after adjustment	0.5011	
Akai information criterion	–18.762	

* significant below 5 per cent

Source: Authors' estimations.

From Table 10.1, we can see that the convergence coefficient is negative, which is consistent with the expectation and is significant at the 1 per cent level. The model's fitting coefficient is relatively low, however, indicating that there are problems with the model setting or estimation model. The spatial correlation results of the model fitting residuals show that there is significant spatial autocorrelation of the residual term, the spatial correction coefficient is 0.0281 and the p value is 0.0274. This further shows that the OLS model ignores the spatial correlation between regions, which leads to the error in results. The way to address these issues with the OLS model is to use a spatial weight matrix.

In the selection of spatial weight, we first use the simple neighbourhood matrix used in most studies to correct the OLS model. The spatial model of regional economies' absolute β convergence is estimated by using the spatial dependence extension package in R language. The results are shown in Table 10.2.

Table 10.2 Regional economies' absolute β convergence test results (adjacent matrix weight)

Variances	Spatial lag model's estimated value	Spatial error model's estimated value
α	3.7585*	0.7463*
β	–0.3028*	0.0637*
ρ/λ	0.0402	0.0189
Log likelihood	12.5247	12.8536
Akai information criterion	–16.891	–16.763

* significant below 5 per cent

Source: Authors' estimations.

It can be seen from Table 10.2 that the spatial lag coefficient, ρ, and the spatial error coefficient, λ, are not significant when the adjacency matrix is used as the weight matrix of the regional economic convergence space measurement model. This indicates that the economic development of neighbouring provinces has no statistical significance for a province's own economic development and the spatial autocorrelation of the error term is not strong, so it has little influence on the model. At the same time, using the Akai information criterion, the SLM and the SEM are –16.891 and –16.763, respectively, which is greater than –18.762 of the OLS model that excludes the spatial effect. If the neighbouring province matrix is used for regional economic convergence, the weight matrix of the model reduces its degree of fit. Adjacent matrices assume that the geographical proximity in the corresponding value in the weight matrix is 1; otherwise, the corresponding value is 0, meaning that the relationship between all adjacent areas is simply regarded as the same without affecting all the non-adjacent regions. In fact, the economic interrelationships between adjacent regions cannot be identical and need to be distinguished; there is still an economic interrelationship in non-adjacent areas.

Absolute convergence test of β regional economy

It can be seen from the above test that, since 2001, the spatial correlation of the economic development level of Chinese provinces is becoming stronger. If spatial correlation between regions is ignored, the reliability of estimated results will be affected. If the neighbourhood matrix is adopted as the weight matrix for the regional economic convergence spatial measurement model, the model cannot be improved. In view of this, in this chapter, the reciprocal of the straight-line distance between different regions is used as the weight of the spatial econometric model.

Since the convergence of regional economic development is often staggered over time (Chen and Guoping 2006), in addition to examining the economic convergence of the entire period, this chapter also divides the period into two (2001–10 and 2011–15) to examine the economic convergence in different periods. To select the appropriate spatial measurement model, this chapter uses the Lagrange multipliers to test the applicability of the SLM and the SEM. The results show that LMLAG is statistically more significant across the entire examination period and also in each of the separate periods, and hence the SLM is selected. The reciprocal matrix of spatial distance is used as the weight to estimate the SLM of absolute b convergence for regional economies, and the results are shown in Table 10.3.

Table 10.3 Results of absolute β convergence of regional economies (reciprocal weight of spatial distance)

Variances	2001–15	2001–10	2011–15
α	5.6449*	3.9415*	1.0277*
β	–0.3706*	–0.2143	–0.0898*
ρ	0.7688**	1.1202**	0.5223**
Log likelihood	12.2190	14.5290	35.6480
Akai information criterion	–16.438	–21.058	–63.296

* significant below 5 per cent

** significant below 1 per cent

Source: Authors' estimations.

The Akai information criterion of the SLM is smaller than that of the OLS model without considering the spatial effect. This shows that if the reciprocal of spatial distance is used as the weight matrix of regional economic convergence, the degree of fit for the weight matrix of the model can be improved. The increase in the logarithmic likelihood also shows that the model is superior to the regional economic convergence spatial model with the adjacent matrix as the weight matrix. The results also show that the spatial lag coefficient, ρ, is 0.7688 and the significance test at the 5 per cent level shows that there is significant positive spatial autocorrelation in interprovincial economic development in China. That is, there is an interprovincial spillover effect on economic development: a region's economic development can promote the economic development of adjacent regions. The convergence coefficient, β, is –0.3706, which is significant at the 1 per cent level. This shows that the speed of economic development in each province is negatively correlated with its initial economic level. In other words, the provinces with relatively high levels of development will slow their growth rate in the beginning, while the provinces with relatively low economic levels will have a higher economic growth rate.

In sum, the results suggest that regional economic development in China shows a general convergence trend from 2001 to 2015. In terms of the results of the economic convergence test for 2001–10, the convergence coefficient, β, is not statistically significant, indicating that there is no convergence phenomenon in China's regional economic development during this period. However, regional economic development is convergent in 2011–15: the convergence coefficient, β, is –0.0898, which is significant at the 1 per cent level.

In fact, in terms of the Gini coefficient, the Tyler index, the variation coefficient, the Herfindahl index and other indices that measure the gap in regional economic development, there is also a declining trend during the period under examination, as shown in Figure 10.2.

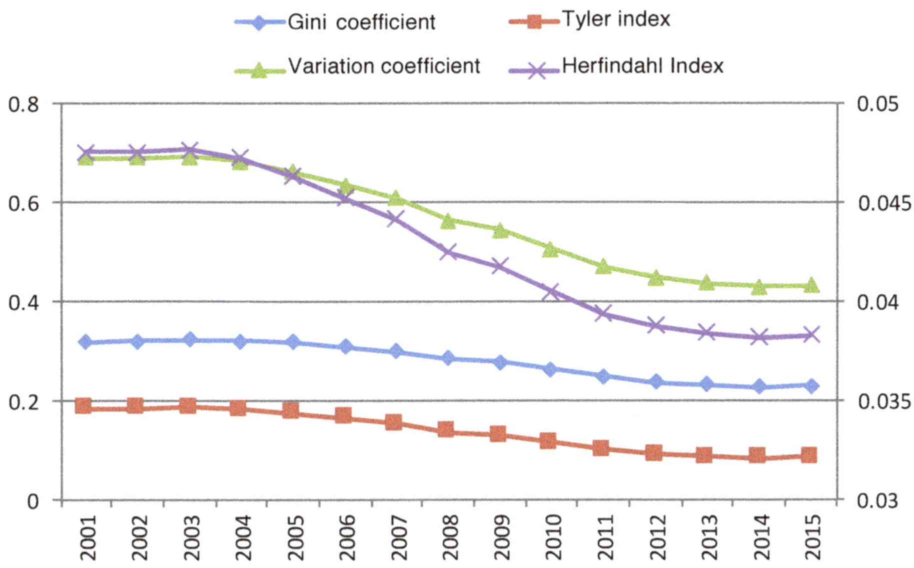

Figure 10.2 Four indicators of the gap in regional economic development

Note: Indicators are calculated using the R language ineq extension package, and the Herfindahl index is on the secondary axis.

Source: National Bureau of Statistics of China (various years).

It can be seen from Figure 10.2 that although the Gini coefficient, the Tyler index, the variation coefficient and the Herfindahl index fell as a whole from 2001 to 2015, they remained relatively stable over the period 2001–06, and thereafter demonstrated a declining trend. This validates the empiriral results of this chapter from one side. In addition, according to the estimated value of β, it is also possible to calculate that the convergence rate of per capita GDP in China from 2001 to 2015 was 3.307 per cent and the half-life cycle of convergence was 20.95 years, which means it will take 20.95 years for economically backward regions to catch up with economically developed regions.

The influence of regional innovation capacity on economic convergence

In addition to absolute convergence analysis, this chapter introduces regional innovation ability to the spatial model and analyses its influence on economic convergence. The estimated results of the SLM of the β convergence test of regional economic conditions are shown in Table 10.4.

Table 10.4 Results of the β convergence test of regional economic conditions

Variances	2001–15	2001–10	2011–15
α	4.4207*	2.7380*	1.4669*
β	–0.3449*	–0.1969	–0.1356*
£	0.0059**	0.0105	0.0401
ρ	1.3102**	0.6321	0.4528
Log likelihood	13.0045	13.7573	36.2550
Akai information criterion	–16.009	–17.515	–62.510

* significant below 5 per cent

** significant below 1 per cent

Source: Authors' estimations.

The results of the β convergence test of regional economic conditions in 2001–15 show that the spatial lag coefficient, ρ, is 1.3102 and passes the significance test at the 5 per cent level. The spatial lag coefficient of the β convergence of regional economic conditions is larger than absolute β convergence, indicating that the spread of China's innovation activities and innovation results helps improve the interaction of provincial economic development. The conditional convergence coefficient, β, was –0.3449 between 2001 and 2015, and significant at the 1 per cent level, suggesting that China's economic development level has conditional β convergence in the whole economic space. The regression coefficient, £, was 0.0059 and significant at the 5 per cent level, indicating that the economic growth rate increase of 5.9 percentage points is associated with a 1 per cent increase in innovation capacity. From 2001 to 2010, the convergence coefficient, β, was statistically insignificant, indicating there was no convergence phenomenon in China's regional economic development, even if the control factor was added, in this period. However, regional economic development in 2011–15 achieved conditional convergence; the convergence coefficient, β, was –0.1356, which was significant at the 1 per cent level. This shows that, in recent years, China's radiation and leading effects of regional innovation have gradually appeared, which have promoted the convergence of regional economic development.

Similarly, according to the estimated value of the conditional convergence coefficient, β, it can be calculated that, after innovation capacity is taken into account, the conditional convergence speed of regional per capita GDP is 3.021 per cent, which is 0.6 per cent slower than the speed of absolute convergence; and, in turn, the half-life cycle of the conditional convergence is 22.94 years. In other words, after the influence of regional innovation capacity is taken into account (and this is slower in economically backward regions), this innovation lag alone will add 3.87 years to the time needed to catch up with economically developed regions, compared with the result when regional innovation capacity is not considered.

Results, conclusion and policy recommendations

In this chapter, the inverse distance between different regions is used as the weight matrix to analyse the actual per capita GDP of 31 provinces and municipal equivalents in China from 2001 to 2015, and the influence of regional innovation ability on economic convergence is discussed. The results show that: 1) after considering the spatial effect, China's regional economic development has both conditional convergence and absolute convergence; 2) in recent years, the trend in China's regional economic development convergence is more obvious than before; and 3) after regional innovation capacity is taken into account, the speed of convergence of China's regional economy deteriorates.

There is absolute convergence in China's regional economic growth, and this conclusion cannot be drawn from the OLS framework. Although from the perspective of economic development, absolute convergence is not obvious in the short term, in the long term, there is a trend of absolute convergence in China, and this trend is becoming increasingly obvious. Therefore, China's regional economic convergence is consistent with the original prediction of the neoclassical growth model, rather than the result achieved after controlling the influence of relevant variables. This also shows that it is not feasible nor would it be effective for China to adopt the growth poles theory to develop its economy. Although geographical conditions, resource endowment and other factors may have a negative impact on the convergence trend, with the gradual establishment and improvement of the market economy, there is still obvious potential for convergence in China's regional economic growth.

China is undergoing economic transformation, so how to control and narrow the regional development gap through effective intervention is not only one of the key objectives of China's current macroeconomic regulation, but also an important problem that needs to be solved urgently. Romer (1990) and many other researchers suggest that the level of human capital is an important factor affecting the rate of economic convergence. The research in this chapter shows that innovation ability also has a significant impact on the speed of economic convergence. If the spatial pattern of the excessive concentration of innovation resources and the serious imbalance in innovation capacity cannot be improved, China's economic development will step into the stage of widening regional disparity caused by innovation. Therefore, in formulating innovation policy, the Chinese Government should pay attention to the spatial interaction mechanism and make full use of the regional innovation resource endowment and differences in innovation ability to reduce the gap in regional economic development.

References

Anselin, L. (1988), *Spatial Econometrics: Methods and models*, Dordrecht: Kluwer Academic Publishers. doi.org/10.1007/978-94-015-7799-1.

Anselin, L., Varga, A. and Acs, Z. (1997), Local geographic spillovers between university research and high technology innovations, *Journal of Urban Economics* (42): 422–48. doi.org/10.1006/juec.1997.2032.

Barro, R. J. and Sala-i-Martin, X. (1992), Convergence, *Journal of Political Economy* 100(2): 223–51. doi.org/10.1086/261816.

Baumol, W. J. (1986), Productivity growth, convergence, and welfare: What the long-run data show, *American Economic Review* 76(5): 1072–85.

Cai, F. and Yang, D. (2000), The convergence and difference of economic growth in China: The Enlightenment to the Western development strategy, *Economic Research* (10): 30–7.

Carrington, A. (2003), A divided Europe? Regional convergence and neighbourhood spillover effects, *Kyklos* 56(3): 381–93. doi.org/10.1046/j.0023-5962.2003.00226.x.

Chen, X. and Guoping, L. (2006), Analysis of spatial panel data model of regional economic convergence in China, *Economic Science* (5): 5–17.

Furman, J. L., Porter, M. E. and Stem, S. (2002), The determinants of national innovative capacity, *Research Policy* 31(6): 899–933. doi.org/10.1016/S0048-7333(01)00152-4.

Lin, G., Zhihe, L. and Mei, W. (2005), An empirical study on the spatial measurement of regional economic convergence in China: 1978–2002, *Economics Quarterly* (B10): 67–82.

Lin, Y. and Lui, M. (2003), China's economic growth convergence and income distribution, *World Economy* (8): 3–14.

Moran, P. A. P. (1950), Notes on continuous stochastic phenomena, *Biometrika* 37(1): 17–23. doi.org/10.1093/biomet/37.1-2.17.

National Bureau of Statistics of China (NBS) (various years), *China Statistics Yearbook*, Beijing: China Statistics Press.

Pan, W. (2010), Regional economic disparity and convergence in China, *Chinese Social Sciences* (1): 72–84.

Perroux, F. (1950), Economic space: Theory and applications, *Quarterly Journal of Economics* 64(1): 89–104.

Ren, L., Xue, J., Liu, Y-g. and Wang, Z. (2014), Research of R&D marginal productivity driving regional economic convergence, *Studies in Science of Science* (11): 1661–7.

Romer, P. M. (1990), Endogenous technological change, *Journal of Political Economy* 98(5): 71–102. doi.org/10.1086/261725.

Romer, P. M. (1994), The origins of endogenous growth, *Journal of Economic Perspectives* (5): 3–22. doi.org/10.1257/jep.8.1.3.

Shen, K. and Jun, M.(2002), A study on the characteristics of 'club convergence' in China's economic growth and its causes, *Economic Research* (1): 33–9.

Solow, R. M. (1956), A contribution to the theory of economic growth, *Quarterly Journal of Economics* 70(1): 65–94. doi.org/10.2307/1884513.

Wang, Z. and Zhaopan, G. (2002), The multiple equilibrium and the precursors of China's regional economic development, *Chinese Social Sciences* (4): 31–9.

Wei, H. (1997), China's regional economic growth and its convergence, *China Industrial Economy* (3): 31–7.

Wu, Y. (2006), Spatial econometric analysis of regional economic growth convergence in China, *Quantitative Economic, Technical and Economic Research* (12): 101–8.

Wu, Y. (2007), *Research on Spatial Econometrics of Regional R&D, Knowledge Spillover and Innovation in China*, Beijing: People's Publishing House.

11. China's Patent Protection and Enterprise R&D Expenditure

Zhifeng Yin and Hao Mao

Based on data from the 2013 National Patent Survey of China, this chapter studies the causal relationship between patent protection and enterprise research and development (R&D) expenditure, and the moderating effect of patent motivation, patent accumulation and patent protection model selection on R&D-promoting effects. The results show: 1) compared with traditional market motives, strong patent protection is not associated with R&D expenditure for enterprises where motivation is administrative driven or strategy driven; 2) the scale effect of patent accumulation has a significant effect on R&D-promoting effects, while the facilitation effect of patent structure (represented by the proportion of invention patents in the total number of patents) on R&D is not significant; and 3) the use of administrative protection has a positive impact on R&D-promoting effects.

Motivation

As an important part of the intellectual property rights system, patent protection regulations are responsible for maintaining a balance between the dynamic efficiency brought about by incentivised innovation and the static inefficiency brought about by market monopolies (Nordhaus 1969; Klemperer 1990). Heated debates have been carried out in academia about the effect of patent protection on the ability of enterprises to increase research and development (R&D) expenditure and promote corporate innovation. Jaffe and Lerner (2006), Boldrin and Levine (2008), Burk and Lemley (2009) and other scholars have highlighted that patent protection does not promote innovation, but in fact may even serve to suppress it to a large degree; overzealous patent protection creates inefficiencies of monopoly in society and also limits knowledge sharing.

From a cross-border perspective, Helpman (1993) found that strict patent protections exacerbate the monopoly rights of property owners, weaken R&D incentives and slow the pace of global technological progress. Shapiro (2001) further shows that overly strong patent protection will increase the cost of learning for developing countries and is not conducive to technological catch-up. Scholars holding the opposite view acknowledge that there are some problems in the patent system, but, on the whole, it is beneficial for encouraging innovation (Gilbert 2011). Yang and

Maskus (2001) point out that, with the help of technology licensing and foreign direct investment (FDI), strengthening the protection of intellectual property rights is conducive to the transfer of production and technological innovation.

Based on these academic arguments, it appears that there is great theoretical value and practical significance in discussing the innovation promotion effects of patent protection. Through the construction of an intellectual property protection index, Ginarte and Park (1997) found that strict protection of intellectual property rights improves innovation and development around the world. Kanwar and Evenson (2009) and Chen and Puttitanun (2005) used cross-border macroeconomic data to investigate the effects of a country's patent protection on its R&D expenditure and innovation output, and found a positive correlation between them. Based on micro data, Mansfield (1986) points out that the impact of patent protection on enterprise R&D varies by industry. Yin et al. (2013) examined mechanisms via which enhanced protection of intellectual property rights serves to promote innovation output in a host country—either through increasing R&D expenditure or through foreign technology spillovers—and found that the mechanism to promote R&D input was significant.

The existing research has important referential value for understanding the effects of patent protection, but there are still many gaps in the literature. Whether through using simultaneous equations or using the lag phase of the level of patent protection (Chen and Puttitanun 2005; Kanwar and Evenson 2009) to analyse the relationship between patent protection and innovation, studies so far have not handled the endogeneity problem well. The degree of patent protection has a self-correlation and, although empirical strategies can reduce the endogeneity problem somewhat, resulting in a two-way causal relationship, the policy effect may be influenced by correlated unobservable factors such that a convincing causal relationship cannot be fully rendered. From a research design and data information perspective, a survey questionnaire offers a better way to avoid two-way causality and, at the same time, isolate the effect of patent protection on enhancing R&D. In the survey, one can ask enterprises questions such as: 'If patent protection is enhanced, will you increase R&D expenditure?' This retrieves first-hand research data. However, because such methods usually have a high implementation cost and time requirement, there have been few attempts in the United States, Europe, Japan, South Korea or other countries to investigate innovation and national patent protection through surveys. We have also not yet found any international literature on the effect of patent protection on innovation that uses survey data as its main subject for analysis.

In this regard, with assistance from the State Intellectual Property Office of China (SIPO), which organised a nationwide large-scale patent survey platform, this chapter uses a unique patent survey dataset from China to study the innovation promotion effects of patent protection. Our goal is to better understand the causal effects of patent protection on innovation and the heterogeneity effects among firms with different motivation, patent structure and protection approaches.

This chapter enriches the existing literature in two ways: first, it identifies the role of patent protection in causally enhancing enterprise R&D expenditure, based on the question proposed in the questionnaire about whether the strength of patent protection impacts on corporate R&D expenditure; and second, based on patent motive, patent structure and protection approaches, it explains the structural differences in the effects of strong patent protection on R&D promotion in enterprises with different characteristics and innovation activities. This research will therefore attempt to provide the scientific basis for strengthening patent protection policies in China. At the same time, it will provide a useful reference for enterprises to give full play to the facilitation effect of strong patent protection on innovation. The rest of this chapter is structured as follows: section two discusses research design, section three illustrates the empirical results and section four presents conclusions and policy suggestions.

Research questions and design

The innovation incentive effect of patent protection is influenced by a country's economic development, technology accumulation and national policy (Maskus 2000; Chen and Puttitanun 2005). For innovation latecomer countries, it might be helpful to use the patent system to stimulate innovation for economic transformation. Based on accumulated theories and market practices from developed economies, strong patent protection is linked with enhanced technology appropriability[1] and increased innovation-derived income, and thereby incentives are offered towards encouraging greater corporate R&D. The related incentive effects of patent protection can, however, fall or shift more categorically as a result of certain factors. Maskus (2000), for example, pointed out that the strength of patent protection and economic development exists in a U-shaped relationship in that only when per capita income reaches the middle-income development level will the facilitation effect of intellectual property protection be notably manifested. Before reaching that income level, the increase in patent protection intensity may have an uncertain effect on economic growth and R&D expenditure. Similarly, Chen and Puttitanun (2005) show that a country's patent protections depend on the level of non-monotonic development first decreasing, then increasing, which is determined by the trade-off between encouraging domestic innovation and imitating foreign technologies. Therefore, we need to study whether patent protection will promote innovation in enterprises; but we also need to examine the heterogeneous effect under different situations.

1 Technology appropriability can be defined as the ability of an innovator to profit from innovation or to internalise the benefits of innovation after solving technical-level issues in technological innovation.

The perspective of strategic connections between the creation, application, protection and management of intellectual property rights of enterprises, and the activities that affect their innovation process, suggests that such moderate factors should at least include the motivation in applying for a patent, the size and quality of the patent and the approach taken to protect patent rights. Accordingly, we arrive at three hypotheses.

Hypothesis 1

Differences in motivations for applying for or maintaining a patent will have different effects on R&D promotion.

Policy-driven and strategic market motivations will, for example, reduce the incentive effect of patent protection. Lin (2003) argued that the Chinese Government is accustomed to allocating resources through administrative authority to enterprises that have been given priority to develop, and to push for reform through administrative orders. When it comes to patents, government policy also has a strong influence on the behaviour of enterprises. When an enterprise submits an application for a patent, but does not intend to commercialise that patent and instead is motivated to acquire some qualification or to meet rigid government requirements, this will inevitably reduce the incentive effect on R&D of strong patent protection. In addition, with the enhancement of patent tools under market competition, the patent system will also become alienated. Research by Harabi (1995), Arundel (1995), Cohen and Goto (2002) and Blind et al. (2006) has shown that, in a competitive market environment, when enterprises apply for and maintain patents, this is not limited to using patents to expand the market, protect innovation, prevent technology from being imitated or other traditional functions. Enterprises driven by strategic 'non-implementation' patent motivations may seek to block competitors, promote and enhance their corporate image or create patent thicket standards,[2] and so on. Compared with traditional patent enforcement motives (such as the industrial use of patents), non-implementation motives place more emphasis on outcomes such as patent advocacy, access to bargaining chips and other strategic tools, and these may serve to inhibit the facilitative effect of patent protection on R&D development.

Hypothesis 2

The number of patents and their structural quality will be positively correlated with the facilitation effect of patent protection on R&D.

2 Patent thicket refers to the scenario in which firms need to acquire access to dozens, hundreds or even thousands of overlapping patents to actually commercialise new technology.

The number of patents is an important indicator of innovation ability. With the growth of patent accumulation, enterprises can obtain more favourable market competition, status, benefits of scale in research costs and prospectively higher operational profits, and thus maintain a virtuous cycle between the scale of patent numbers and sustainable R&D innovation. Patent structure refers to the proportion of invention patents, utility models and designs.[3] Research by Kim et al. (2012) found that the utility model system is an effective learning process during the technological catch-up phase. Through a historical overview, Maskus and McDaniel (1999) also found that during the process of technological catch-up in Japan, the utility model system brought about by technology spillover effects was significant. It is, however, obvious that the utility model is of lower quality than an invention patent and is not conducive to enterprises that are trying to reach the technological innovation frontier. Regarding this point, research by Kim et al. (2012) and Beneito (2006) demonstrated that if an enterprise wants to realise higher technical abilities, it should invest in invention patents and not utility models. Accordingly, we infer that the optimisation of the enterprise's patent structure (that is, a higher proportion of invention patents among all patents) will bring about a greater incentivising effect on R&D.

Hypothesis 3

If enterprises can utilise (administrative and judicial) protection systems to establish and enforce patent protection rights, the positive effect of patents on R&D will be more significant.

China's patent protection system is unique in having a 'double-track' feature via which enterprises can choose either administrative protection or judicial protection to carry out their protection rights. Although there is still some controversy in academic circles about which of the two should be dominant, the patent-related community generally accepts the relative advantages and complementarities of the two. As a private right, patent rights support legal institutional protection, while administrative enforcement influences the cost of enforcing patent infringement and is characterised by being simple, fast and efficient. A sound system of administrative enforcement can substantially shift the cost of patent infringement while significantly reducing the cost of having protection rights. In this regard, we expect that if companies can make full use of both mechanisms of protection then strengthening patent protection will have a greater effect on R&D growth.

3 There are three types of patent in China: invention patents, utility models and designs. Unlike invention patents, utility models and designs require no substantive examination at the patent office for them to be granted.

We test these three hypotheses using the National Patent Survey dataset from the most recent such survey, in 2013.[4] The nationwide survey has been carried out annually since 2008. The survey sample frame for 2013 was based on domestic patents granted in 2012. Sampling proportional to size methodology is used, supplemented by quota sampling. The sample frame for the 2013 survey included 777,308 patents, and the survey covered 65 cities in 26 provinces (including autonomous regions and municipalities). In 2013, there were 11,141 patentees and 9,161 enterprises in the survey; 33,667 patents were selected, of which 22,615 were corporate patents. The final response rate was 87.7 per cent, of which 93.7 per cent were valid questionnaires.

The survey itself examined whether the impact of patent protection is related to R&D expenditure, via the following question from the Enterprise Questionnaire of the 2013 National Patent Survey: 'What is the impact on your R&D expenditure if patent protection is enhanced?' Response options included: 'Increased R&D expenditure due to increased protection', 'Reduced R&D expenditure with enhanced protection', 'No significant impact' and 'Unclear'. The survey also asked a range of questions that would elicit information to help shed light on the variability of policy effects (discussed in detail later), as well as variables that reflect the basic characteristics of the surveyed enterprise, such as location, ownership, size, corporate qualifications (that is, whether it is an intellectual property enterprise recognised by the government at the provincial level or above, whether it is a high-tech enterprise, whether it is a central government–affiliated enterprise), and so on.

We used the multiple regression method to test whether hypotheses 1–3 are valid. Since the explanatory variable is a rank variable that reflects the size of the facilitation effect of patent protection on R&D, we used an ordered probit model for regression analysis (Cameron and Trivedi 2005; Long and Freese 2006). The specific model was designed as follows. Suppose that the R&D facilitation effect produced by patent protection depends on a series of factors captured in vector X. There is a potential policy-promoting effect, y^*, on the basis of each firm's characteristics. Suppose $y^* = X\beta + \varepsilon$, and ε follows the standard normal distribution. There are two critical values, a_1 and a_2, and $a_1 < a_2$. When y^* is less than or equal to a_1, y is equal to 1; when y^* is greater than a_1 and less than a_2, y is equal to 2; when y^* is greater than a_2, y is equal to 3. Specifically, we let Φ be the standard normal distribution function and we then have the following regression equations (Equations 11.1–3).

4 The survey in 2013 contained the key information needed for this study, such as a firm's response to stricter patent protection in terms of R&D expenditure, as well as information used for capturing the firm's patent motive, patent structure and protection approaches.

Equation 11.1

$$p(y = 1|X) = p(y^* \leq a_1|X) = \Phi(a_1 - X\beta)$$

Equation 11.2

$$p(y = 2|X) = p(a_1 < y^* \leq a_2|X) = \Phi(a2{-}X\beta) - \Phi(a_1{-}X\beta)$$

Equation 11.3

$$p(y = 3|X) = p(y^* > a_2|X) = 1 - \Phi(a_2{-}X\beta)$$

Among these, y is the rank variable of the effect of patent protection on promoting R&D, and X includes the following:[5] the variables reflecting hypothesis 1, including the market motivation of the enterprise's patent maintenance behaviour and intensity of strategic patent use; two variables reflecting hypothesis 2, including the enterprise's number of patents and patent structure; and variables reflecting hypothesis 3—namely, the enterprise's choice for patent rights protection and confidence in the enforcement of patents protection. At the same time, combined with the data availability and drawing on the conclusions of previous research, in our regression we also controlled for some of the variables that reflect the qualifications of the enterprise, such as whether it was a government-recognised intellectual property enterprise, a high-tech enterprise, publicly listed or a centrally affiliated enterprise. Variables like the province of the enterprise's location and the industry to which it belonged are also controlled.

Empirical results

Descriptive statistics of the key variables

Table 11.1 shows the descriptive statistics attached to the main variables used in this analysis. Unless otherwise stated, the variables in the table are taken from the corresponding response data from relevant questions of the 2013 National Patent Survey. Variables not directly derived from the questionnaire or that need to be structured through a specific process included market-based patent maintenance motivation, intensity of strategic patent use, number of valid patents, proportion of invention patents, administrative protection of patent rights, judicial protection of patent rights and the level of confidence in patent law enforcement.

5 How these variables are constructed will be discussed in detail in section four.

Table 11.1 Descriptive statistics of the main variables (no. = 4,067)

Variable	Description	Mean	SD	Min. value	Max. value
Rdy	Degree of facilitation of patent protection on R&D (1–3)	2.48	0.61	1	3
dum_mark	Market-based patent maintenance	0.79	0.41	0	1
fss_r	Intensity of strategic patent use	0.56	0.25	0	1
Totpatg	No. of valid patents (1 = above median)	0.60	0.49	0	1
inv_sharg	Percentage of invention patents (1 = above median)	0.55	0.50	0	1
dum_adm_bh	Administrative patent protection	0.83	0.38	0	1
dum_law	Judicial patent protection	0.15	0.36	0	1
Xzbhxx	Confidence in patent law enforcement	0.31	0.46	0	1
Own	Ownership (1–3)	1.32	0.67	1	3
scale1	Size (1 = medium–large)	0.69	0.46	0	1
Zcqy	Intellectual property recognised (1 = yes)	0.34	0.47	0	1
Gxqy	High-tech (1 = yes)	0.70	0.46	0	1
Ssqy	Publicly listed (1 = yes)	0.13	0.33	0	1
Zyqy	Centrally owned (1 = yes)	0.07	0.25	0	1

Note: 1, 2 and 3 in the first variable, 'Rdy', refer, respectively, to: decreased R&D expenditure, no significant or clear impact on R&D expenditure and increased R&D expenditure. 1, 2 and 3 in the variable 'Own' refer, respectively, to domestic-owned enterprises, Hong Kong, Macau and Taiwan–owned enterprises, and foreign-invested enterprises.

We use the two variables capturing market-based motivation and the intensity of strategic patent use to characterise an enterprise's motivation for applying for or maintaining a patent. Among the two, the market-based motivation is defined based on the enterprise patent questionnaire in the National Patent Survey, for which the reasons enterprises could choose for maintaining their patents included 'to increase economic profits and reduce production costs', 'to use the patent as exchange for capital or as a bargaining chip' and 'to protect the enterprise's technology'. If an enterprise chose at least one of these options, they were defined in our study as exhibiting market-based patent maintenance behaviour and were labelled 1; otherwise, they were labelled 0. The intensity of the strategic use of patents in our study was defined according to the survey question about why the enterprise applies for its patent. In response to the information provided by an enterprise when applying for a patent, we count the number of non-traditional patent implementation motives[6] selected, except for those in the questionnaire who chose 'using patents to seize or expand the market' and 'to prevent imitation of enterprise technology

6 Non-traditional patent implementation motives include 'to meet government qualifications', 'to obtain grants and subsidies', 'to complete patent assessments', 'to enhance corporate social influence' and 'to block competitors'.

by others', which were considered the traditional patent implementation motives. We then divide the number of non-traditional motivations by the total number of options the enterprise chose to capture the intensity of strategic patent use.

The number of valid patents and the ratio of invention patents accounted for the two variables used to describe the characteristics of enterprise patents. Based on the name of the enterprise, the number of patents that are 'in force' for the enterprise as of the end of 2012 is calculated from the SIPO patents database; the variable 'Totpatg' is labelled 1 if the number of valid patents is above the sample median; otherwise, it is labelled 0. Similarly, based on the name of the enterprise, we obtained the number of invention patents that are 'in force' as of the end of 2012, calculated the proportion of invention patents in the total number of patents in force and defined enterprises above the median as 1, otherwise 0, thus constructing the 'inv_sharg' variable.

We used administrative patent rights protection, judicial patent rights protection and confidence in patent law enforcement to reflect the features of patent protection behaviour. For administrative patent rights protection, we use the response data for the following question: 'Through which means do you want to protect the patent rights of your enterprise?' Enterprises were limited to two responses from a list of choices.[7] Enterprises choosing 'report to the patent administration authority by calling 12330' or 'hope that the patent management authorities take the initiative to investigate and deal with the claimed violations' were defined as being inclined towards the administrative protection of patents and were labelled 1; otherwise, they were labelled 0. Similarly, the judicial patent rights protection variable was based on how enterprises answered the above question. If one of their two responses was 'go directly to court for litigation', they would be defined as being inclined towards using the judicial system to protect their patents and were labelled 1; otherwise, they were labelled 0. We constructed the confidence variable by including the responses to the question: 'What is the most striking impression of how administrative law enforcement resolves patent disputes in your enterprise?' Responses were limited to three choices and if one of those was 'administrative mediation can resolve disputes', those enterprises were defined as having confidence in administrative enforcement and were labelled 1; otherwise, they were labelled 0. The statistical results in Table 11.1 show that the variables fall within a reasonable range. Furthermore, we calculated the correlation coefficients for the main explanatory variables and found that the pairwise correlation coefficients between the variables were less than 0.3, suggesting that the subsequent regression was less adversely affected by multicollinearity.

7 The choices include 'report to the patent administration authority by calling 12330', 'hope that the patent management authorities take the initiative to investigate and deal with the claimed violations', 'settled through negotiation', 'go directly to court for litigation' and 'other'.

Distribution of the effect of patent protection on R&D expenditure

Table 11.2 shows the statistical distribution of the effect of patent protection on R&D expenditure. The results show that 52.5 per cent of enterprises believe that patent protection will enhance their own R&D expenditure, while 29 per cent believe that enhancing patent protection has no significant impact on their R&D expenditure. This suggests that other incentives—such as trade secrets and government subsidies other than factors of the patent system itself—also play a role (Wright 1983; Teece 1986; Gallini and Scotchmer 2002). The strategic patent application behaviour and the substitution system render the facilitative effect of patent protection on R&D relatively insignificant. At the same time, 11.9 per cent of enterprises believe that the effect of patent protection on R&D expenditure is unclear.[8]

Table 11.2 Distribution of the effect of patent protection intensity on R&D expenditure

Effect of patent protection on promoting R&D	Sample size	Proportion (%)
Patent protection increased R&D expenditure	4,484	52.46
No significant impact	2,478	28.99
Unclear	1,019	11.92
Patent protection decreased R&D expenditure	566	6.62

Source: Authors' calculation.

Structural differences in the effect of patent protection on promoting R&D

Column 1 in Table 11.3 examines the role of market-based motivation and intensity of strategic patent use on R&D promotion. The regression results show that enterprises with market motivation have more favourable evaluations of the effect of patent protection on R&D promotion than their counterparts. This relates to the fact that the patent behaviour of Chinese enterprises has been influenced by public targets and incentives. Enterprises that maintain patents to 'meet government qualifications', 'obtain grants and subsidies' or 'complete patent index assessments' are not as sensitive to patent protection as those that maintain patents to 'increase economic profits and reduce production costs' or 'protect the technology of the enterprise'. Since the enhancement of patent protection can significantly increase the patentability of a technology, the enterprises that follow marketisation principles

8 In our analysis, we classify 'no significant impact' and 'unclear' as one category, and define it as 'no significant impact'. The conclusion is robust even after removing the 'unclear' sample.

can more deeply actualise the important role of increasing patent protection with the goal of increasing the market value of their patents. Therefore, the incentive effect of patent protection on R&D is found to be more significant in such enterprises.

The empirical results also show that the stronger the strategic motivation of enterprises, the lower will be the enterprise's evaluation of the facilitative effect of patent protection on R&D. In other words, benchmark non-strategic motivations can enhance the effects of patent protection more than nascent strategic motivations. For example, enterprises that apply for patents for strategic use will be more likely to apply from a defensive stance, such as being influenced by propaganda, as opposed to those seeking to apply for patents for their industrial use. These patents are driven by a market strategy and do not carry any direct implementation characteristics. Although it helps enterprises secure a certain position in the market, the incentive effect on R&D is still limited.

Column 2 examines the moderate effect of the total number of patents, plus the ratio of invention patents in the total, on R&D promotion. The empirical results show that there is a significant positive correlation between the total number of patents and the facilitative effect of patent protection. The higher the number of patents accumulated by an enterprise, the more patents are applied to the patent portfolio and the greater will be the facilitative effect of patent protection on R&D promotion. At the same time, the proportion of invention patents is positively correlated with the effect of patent protection, but it is not statistically significant. These results show that the utility model still constitutes an important model of technological innovation within China's enterprises, and high-level inventions that incentivise greater R&D are concentrated in special industries and specific samples. They are not yet significantly reflected in the overall sample. For innovation to help upgrade China's industrial structure, there is a need to use multiple and different innovation models, while taking advantage of the roles of inventions, utility models and designs.

Column 3 examines the relationship between the choice of using either the administrative or the judicial system to protect patent rights and the enhancement of R&D. The regression results show that enterprises that choose the administrative protection system are more inclined to believe that intensified patent protection can promote their R&D expenditure than the enterprises that do not adopt the administrative system as their main line of defence. At the same time, compared with enterprises that do not use the judicial system as the main way to protect patent rights, these enterprises show greater incentive to increase R&D. Administrative protection and judicial protection are the two formal systems of patent protection in China that constitute an important institutional basis for enhancing the effect of patent protection on R&D promotion. Both increase the flexibility of choices available to the patent holder in the process of enforcing rights and both promote the development of patent protection, but on different dimensions. At the same time, from the point of view of trusting law enforcement, enterprises that believe in the ability of administrative patent law enforcement to resolve patent disputes are more inclined to think that patent protection has a strong incentivising effect on R&D. The full potential of any facilitative effect of patent protection on R&D rests on the basis of confidence in administrative protection and flexibility on behalf of the patent holder or applicant.

Table 11.3 Analysis of structural differences in the effect of patent protection on promoting R&D

	(1)	(2)	(3)	(4)	(5)
Market-based patent maintenance	0.32***			0.28***	0.28***
	(0.04)			(0.04)	(0.05)
Intensity of strategic patent utilisation	–0.19**			–0.16**	–0.17**
	(0.08)			(0.08)	(0.09)
Total number of patents (1 = above median)		0.13***		0.12***	0.08*
		(0.04)		(0.04)	(0.05)
Invention patents (1 = above median)		0.03		0.02	–0.00
		(0.04)		(0.04)	(0.05)
Administrative protection			0.13***	0.12**	0.12**
			(0.05)	(0.05)	(0.05)
Judicial protection			0.08	0.07	0.12*
			(0.05)	(0.05)	(0.06)
Confidence in patent law enforcement			0.34***	0.30***	0.26***
			(0.05)	(0.05)	(0.05)
Hong Kong, Macau, Taiwan	0.19***	0.20***	0.20***	0.20***	0.23***
	(0.07)	(0.07)	(0.07)	(0.07)	(0.07)
Foreign	0.01	0.01	0.02	0.03	0.03
	(0.06)	(0.06)	(0.06)	(0.06)	(0.06)
Medium–large size	0.11**	0.09**	0.10**	0.07	0.09*
	(0.04)	(0.04)	(0.04)	(0.04)	(0.05)
Intellectual property recognised	0.07	0.08*	0.08*	0.04	0.08
	(0.04)	(0.04)	(0.04)	(0.05)	(0.05)
High-tech	0.08*	0.05	0.10**	0.08*	0.09*
	(0.05)	(0.05)	(0.05)	(0.05)	(0.05)
Publicly listed	–0.04	–0.04	–0.04	–0.07	–0.02
	(0.06)	(0.06)	(0.06)	(0.06)	(0.07)
Centrally affiliated	0.07	–0.02	0.04	0.07	0.08
	(0.07)	(0.08)	(0.08)	(0.08)	(0.08)
cut1_cons	–6.01***	–5.94***	–5.57***	–5.42***	–5.24***
	(0.24)	(0.32)	(0.15)	(0.27)	(0.27)

	(1)	(2)	(3)	(4)	(5)
cut2_cons	–4.56***	–4.50***	–4.12***	–3.95***	–4.01***
	(0.24)	(0.33)	(0.13)	(0.27)	(0.27)
Pseudo r2	0.03	0.02	0.03	0.04	0.04
Log likelihood	–3,520.53	–3,548.13	–3,435.15	–3,404.13	–2,962.72
No.	4,171	4,169	4,071	4,067	3,627

* $p < 0.1$ significance level

** $p < 0.05$ significance level

*** $p < 0.01$ significance level

Notes: An ordered probit model was used. All regressions control for provincial and industrial fixed effects. The base group of enterprise ownership are domestic-owned enterprises; the base group of size are small and micro-enterprises; the base group of intellectual property qualification are enterprises without intellectual property rights acknowledged by the government above the provincial level; the base group of high-tech enterprise qualification are non-high-tech enterprises; the base group of publicly listed enterprises are unlisted enterprises; the base group of centrally affiliated enterprises are non-centrally affiliated enterprises. Robust standard error shown within parentheses.

Source: Authors' estimations.

Column 4 discusses the moderate effect on promoting R&D of patent motives, the number and structure of patents and approaches to protection. Regression results show that these factors are robust in their correlation with the effect of patent protection on R&D. The corresponding economic explanation is the same as that discussed separately, so we will not repeat it here. Finally, given the questionnaire options of 'unclear' and 'no significant impact' were put into one category when constructing the patent protection R&D facilitation effect variable, 'unclear' could contain a lot of noise. Therefore, in column 5, the sample that answered 'unclear' was removed. The empirical results confirm that the basic conclusion is consistent with previous ones, showing that the conclusions for hypotheses 1–3 are robust.

It is worth mentioning that there are significant correlations between some factors in the control variables and effects on R&D promotion. In contrast, Hong Kong, Macau and Taiwan–owned enterprises, large and medium-sized enterprises and high-tech enterprises were more inclined to believe that increased patent protection would significantly enhance their R&D expenditure. Listed companies and centrally affiliated enterprises do not demonstrate stronger belief that patent protection will enhance R&D expenditure compared with non-listed companies and non-centrally affiliated enterprises. The economic explanation is that the competitive advantage of centrally affiliated enterprises is likely to come from trade and resource monopoly, rather than technological innovation, so the evaluation of the incentive effect of patent protection on R&D is limited. Meanwhile, listed enterprises cannot genuinely have technological innovation and corresponding R&D expenditure as prerequisites for the realisation of capital and operational growth, so the incentive effect of patent protection on R&D is also limited there.

Conclusion and policy suggestions

Using data from the 2013 National Patent Survey, this chapter reveals the impact of patent protection on R&D expenditure through the study of the survey question 'How does stricter patent protection affect R&D expenditure in your enterprise', and subsequently analysed the effect of patent protection on R&D facilitation. We then discussed the three main structural differences in how the relationship between patent protection and R&D expenditure is manifested in Chinese enterprises: as patent motives, the number and structure of patents and the selected method of patent rights protection. The main conclusions are as follows.

First, the implementation of national patent protection policies is found to be positively and significantly associated with enterprise expenditure on R&D. The survey data we examined identified some 52.5 per cent of enterprises believed that stricter patent protection would increase their R&D expenditure, whereas 29 per cent of enterprises believed that increased patent protection would have no significant impact on their R&D expenditure.

Second, the facilitative effect of patent protection on R&D differs structurally among the motives behind patent application, the number and structure of patents and the method of patent protection. Compared with traditional market motivations, strong patent protection does not have the effect of increasing R&D expenditure for administrative-driven and strategic-driven models. If the enterprise depends on market forces to apply patents then patent protection is conducive to maintaining strong incentives for R&D expenditure; on the other hand, if the enterprise applies the patent for administrative purposes, the incentive effect will be limited. At the same time, patent applications driven by strategic motives to some extent curb the facilitative effect of patent protection on R&D. This shows that if the purpose of applying for and maintaining a patent is to use the 'patent formation as exchange for capital' and 'to enhance corporate social influence', rather than 'to increase economic profits and reduce production costs', patent protection will greatly reduce any facilitative effects on R&D expenditure. Patent protection also increased the effect of R&D facilitation for enterprises that have accumulated a relatively high number of patents. Patent structure, which is represented by the ratio of invention patents in the total, did not play a significant role in promoting R&D expenditure. Compared with protecting patent rights through non-administrative channels, a decision to use the administrative protection of patent rights resulted in a higher evaluation of the facilitation effect of patent protection on R&D. Moreover, if enterprises have sufficient confidence in the administrative protection of patent rights, their evaluation of a positive effect of patent protection on R&D expenditure will also be higher.

In light of these results, we present the following three policy suggestions.

First, special attention should be given to the motivation behind patent applications. Patents are no longer a straightforward defensive method of protecting innovation, but are now also used as commercial tools. Strong patent protection here is not associated with increased R&D expenditure where the motivations for the patent are administrative and strategic, both of which reduce the innovation incentive effect of the patent system. Second, enterprises should strive to achieve balance between patent quantity and quality and to gradually establish a high-quality growth model. Currently, patent quantity and quality management revolve around the goal of 'quantity first then quality'. In general, R&D expenditure in the majority of Chinese enterprises remains limited, and the most common patent structure is the utility model. Also, there is a lack of will for continuous expenditure on R&D in companies with a favourable (high) invention patent structure. However, international experience suggests that upgrading a country's patent profile must rely on high-end inventions. A reasonable patent structure and the necessary R&D expenditure are the core elements of increasing corporate innovation capacity. Therefore, China needs to utilise multiple innovation models and the role of various types of patents, while establishing a more rational orientation for its national patent policy.

Finally, China's unique 'double-track' judicial and administrative patent rights enforcement and protection mechanism should be strengthened to enhance innovators' level of confidence in enforcement. We found that administrative protection and the ability of enterprises to successfully use administrative enforcement have a positive impact on subsequent R&D expenditure. Administrative enforcement is the consolidation and expansion of the private rights of intellectual property and constitutes a safeguard of these rights. Nonetheless, both judicial protection and administrative enforcement support China's innovation-driven development strategy. Therefore, the government needs to take advantage of the dual aspects of judicial protection and administrative enforcement to strengthen property rights.

References

Arundel, A. (1995), *Innovation strategies of Europe's largest industrial firms: Results of the survey for information sources, public research, protection of innovations and government programmes*, Final Report, MERIT Institute, University of Limburg.

Beneito, P. (2006), The innovative performance of in-house and contracted R&D in terms of patents and utility models, *Research Policy* 35(4): 502–17. doi.org/10.1016/j.respol.2006.01.007.

Blind, K., Edler, J., Frietsch, R. and Schmoch, U. (2006), Motives to patent: Empirical evidence from Germany, *Research Policy* 35(5): 655–72. doi.org/10.1016/j.respol.2006.03.002.

Boldrin, M. and Levine, D. K. (2008), *Against Intellectual Monopoly*, Cambridge: Cambridge University Press.

Burk, D. L. and Lemley, M. A. (2009), *The Patent Crisis and How the Courts Can Solve It*, Chicago: University of Chicago Press. doi.org/10.7208/chicago/9780226080635.001.0001.

Cameron, A. C. and Trivedi, P. K. (2005), *Micro-econometrics: Methods and applications*, New York: Cambridge University Press. doi.org/10.1017/CBO9780511811241.

Chen, Y. and Puttitanun, T. (2005), Intellectual property rights and innovation in developing countries, *Journal of Development Economics* 78(2): 474–93. doi.org/10.1016/j.jdeveco.2004.11.005.

Cohen, W. M. and Goto, A. N. (2002), R&D spillovers, patents and the incentives to innovate in Japan and the United States, *Research Policy* 31(8): 1349–67. doi.org/10.1016/S0048-7333(02)00068-9.

Gallini, N. and Scotchmer, S. (2002), Intellectual property: When is it the best incentive system? *Innovation Policy and the Economy*, 2: 51–77. doi.org/10.1086/653754.

Gilbert, R. (2011), A world without intellectual property? A review of Michele Boldrin and David Levine's 'Against Intellectual Monopoly', *Journal of Economic Literature* 49(2): 421–32. doi.org/10.1257/jel.49.2.421.

Ginarte, J. C. and Park, W. G. (1997), Determinants of patent rights: A cross-national study, *Research Policy* 26(3): 283–301. doi.org/10.1016/S0048-7333(97)00022-X.

Harabi, N. (1995), Appropriability of technical innovations: An empirical analysis, *Research Policy* 24(94): 981–92. doi.org/10.1016/0048-7333(94)00812-4.

Helpman, E. (1993), Innovation, imitation, and intellectual property rights, *Econometrica* 61(6): 1247–80. doi.org/10.2307/2951642.

Jaffe, A. B. and Lerner, J. (2006), *Innovation and its Discontents: How our broken patent system is endangering innovation and progress, and what to do about it*, Princeton, NJ: Princeton University Press.

Kanwar, S. and Evenson, R. (2009), On the strength of intellectual property protection that nations provide, *Journal of Development Economics* 90(90): 50–6. doi.org/10.1016/j.jdeveco.2008.11.006.

Kim, Y. K., Lee, K., Park, W. G. and Choo, K. (2012), Appropriate intellectual property protection and economic growth in countries at different levels of development, *Research Policy* 41(2): 358–75. doi.org/10.1016/j.respol.2011.09.003.

Klemperer, P. (1990), How broad should the scope of patent protection be? *RAND Journal of Economics* 21(1): 113–30. doi.org/10.2307/2555498.

Lin, J. (2003), Backward advantage or backward disadvantage: A discussion with Yang Xiaokai, [in Chinese], *China Economic Quarterly* 2(2): 989–1004.

Long, J. S. and Freese, J. (2006), *Regression Models for Categorical Dependent Variables Using Stata*, 2nd edn, College Station, Tex.: Stata Press.

Mansfield, E. (1986), Patents and innovation: An empirical study, *Management Science* 32(2): 173–81. doi.org/10.1287/mnsc.32.2.173.

Maskus, K. E. (2000), Intellectual property rights and economic development, *Case Western Reserve Journal of International Law* 32(3): 471–506.

Maskus, K. E. and McDaniel, C. (1999), Impacts of the Japanese patent system on productivity growth, *Japan & the World Economy* 11(4): 557–74.

Nordhaus, W. (1969), *Invention, Growth and Welfare: A theoretical treatment of technological change*, Cambridge, Mass.: MIT Press.

Shapiro, B. C. (2001), Navigating the patent thicket: Cross licenses, patent pools, and standard-setting, in A. B. Jaffe, J. Lerner and S. Stern (eds), *Innovation Policy and the Economy: Volume I*, pp. 119–50, Cambridge, Mass.: MIT Press. doi.org/10.2139/ssrn.273550.

Teece, D. (1986), Profiting from technological innovation: Implications for integration, collaboration, licensing and public policy, *Research Policy* 15: 285–94. doi.org/10.1016/0048-7333(86)90027-2.

Wright, B. D. (1983), The economics of invention incentives: Patents, prizes and research contracts, *American Economic Review* 73(4): 691–707.

Yang, G. and Maskus, K. E. (2001), Intellectual property rights, licensing, and innovation in an endogenous product-cycle model, *Journal of International Economics* 53(1): 169–87. doi.org/10.1016/S0022-1996(00)00062-3.

Yin, Z., Ye, J., Huang, Y. and Qin, X. (2013), Intellectual property protection and enterprise innovation: Mechanism and empirical test, [in Chinese], *World Economy* 12: 111–29.

12. Specialist Communities in China's Aerospace Technology and Innovation System: The Cultural Dimension

Alanna Krolikowski

Introduction

Only two decades ago, China was a marginal player in the global aerospace industry. Today, the pace of China's space programs is unparalleled and it has joined the sector's leading ranks. China is the only country after the Soviet Union/Russia and the United States to independently send humans into orbit and a rover to touch down on the Moon. A Chinese station will likely soon be only the only long-term human habitat circling the Earth alongside the International Space Station. Within a decade, China could become only the second country in history to land a person on the Moon's surface. China already has the world's largest radio telescope and is building more large instruments. The country's advances in aeronautics are no less striking. A Chinese firm has disrupted the regional jet market and is poised to enter the large civil aircraft market, challenging the Airbus–Boeing duopoly. Chinese firms already produce advanced military aircraft that fly sensitive missions.

A permissive cause of these developments has been the growing wealth of the Chinese state. Top leaders have declared a political and ideological commitment to science and technology (S&T) modernisation since at least the era of Deng Xiaoping. Yet, as recently as the mid-1990s, advocates of aerospace projects struggled to persuade top leaders that their efforts were worth a share of scarce public funds and fought for the very survival of their programs (Li 2013). Only in the past two decades have the central government's swelling coffers allowed the administrations of Hu Jintao and Xi Jinping to direct substantial resources towards these initiatives (Suttmeier 1980; Liu et al. 2011), as shown in China's accelerated increase in expenditure on research and development (Figure 12.1).

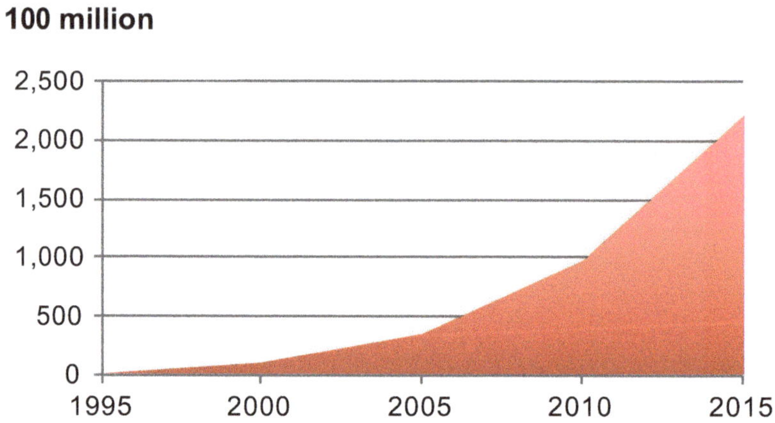

Figure 12.1 China's expenditure on research and development (renminbi)
Source: NBS (2017).

While the central government's material support has made the pursuit of aerospace capabilities possible, it does not explain *how* these capabilities were achieved. A substantial body of scholarship in S&T studies demonstrates that there are multiple pathways to technical achievement and innovation in the aerospace sectors (Zeitlin 1995; Montresor 2001; Keller and Samuels 2003; Pekkanen 2003; Hughes 2004; Pavelec 2004; Hickie 2006; Palmer 2006; Jeon 2010). Diverse configurations of policies, institutions and programs can produce engineering success. And, indeed, China's aerospace sectors illustrate that the country's innovation system accommodates a diversity of approaches to pursuing ambitious technology goals. This chapter examines why and how China's central government has pursued contrasting innovation strategies for developing national capabilities in two adjacent sectors with comparable features: civil commercial aircraft manufacture and civil commercial spacecraft manufacture. The approach to the former sector has stressed drawing in foreign knowledge and systems and embedding Chinese firms in global value chains, while the approach to the latter has prioritised developing indigenous technology to enhance national autonomy.

To grasp how the strategies in the two sectors diverged, it is helpful to keep in view the broader changes that have transformed China's science, technology and innovation system over the past four decades. These changes have allowed distinct communities of specialists to coalesce and influence the design and implementation of major innovation strategies. These communities have become powerful shapers of long-term policy in their respective domains and their policy input helps account for the variation in the strategies adopted for aircraft and spacecraft manufacture.

The first part of this chapter surveys the institutional changes that have transformed China's technology and innovation system and, within it, the aeronautic and space sectors. The second part discusses the culturally distinct specialist communities that have emerged in these two sectors and how they have shaped policymaking to allow for the adoption of distinct sectoral strategies.

The institutional setting

China's pool of scientists and technologists is enormous and growing as a share of the country's workforce (Figure 12.2). Scholars have documented and debated the transformation of this stock of human capital, examining not only the input of newly skilled workers, but also their organisation into new structures (Saich 1989; Dickson 1998; Suttmeier and Cao 1999; Liu and White 2001; Huang et al. 2002; Cao 2003; Sleeboom-Faulkner 2006; Appelbaum et al. 2011). These studies examine how the reform and development of key institutions have structured the conduct of S&T activities, revealing their contributions and limitations.

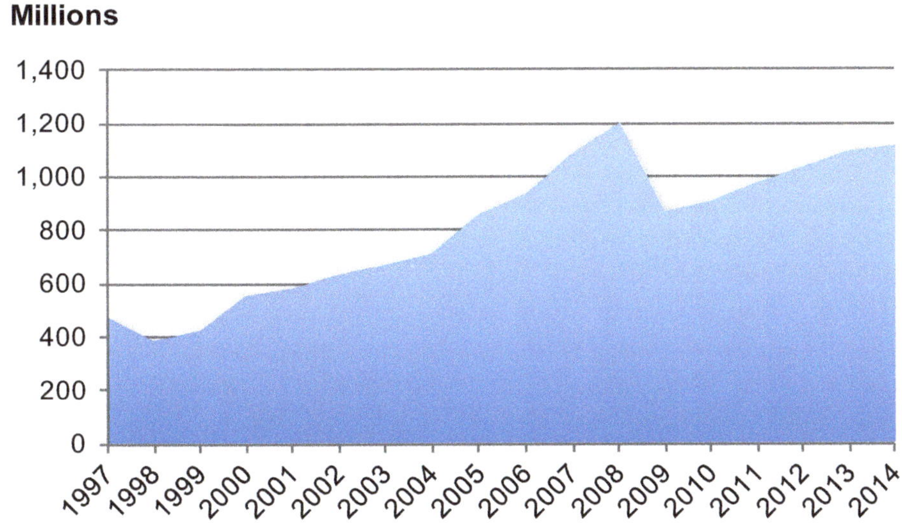

Figure 12.2 Researchers in research and development in China

Source: World Bank (2017).

Often, these institutional changes have created conditions in which the impact on innovation of other inputs has been enhanced. The transformations have allowed China's aerospace S&T establishment to make improved use of resources and more effectively seize opportunities presented by expanded government aerospace procurement and the technological upgrading of the broader economy. These trends—most apparent since the 1990s—include the institutionalisation of S&T

activities, the specialisation of the S&T establishment into distinct functional and sectoral elements and the professionalisation of its workforce. The discussion below delineates the broad contours of these transformations as they have occurred across a range of sectors, including aeronautics and space.

Institutionalisation

'Institutionalisation' here refers to the process of creating and developing stable formal organisational and other processes for the implementation of S&T policies and programs. Since 1978, China's innovation system has transformed from ad hoc, reactive and highly politicised project-driven decision-making and implementation to a system characterised by systematic, stable and coherent institutional mechanisms for developing and implementing major long-term S&T strategies and, within them, medium- and short-term policies and programs (Suttmeier 1980; Simon and Goldman 1988; Saich 1989; Cheung 2011).

This institutionalisation of S&T activities has occurred alongside, and in a mutually supportive fashion with, the institutionalisation of processes across other areas of policymaking within the Chinese state (Liu and White 2001). These include the broad domains of economic reform, public sector governance and defence modernisation.

Several features of this institutionalisation appear to have significantly enhanced the performance of technology-intensive equipment manufacturing industries, such as the manufacture of aircraft and spacecraft. Long-term strategies have provided stability and predictability in policies and programs. Systematic channels for the communication of expert advice to decision-makers have improved the quality of policymaking. The state's supervision of state-owned industrial groups has been refined and harmonised. The interface between equipment manufacturers and end users has improved. These features of the new institutional environment have also intensified interaction between specialists from different work units within the same sector, fostering the emergence of sector-wide specialist communities.

Specialisation

As the innovation system has grown, it has also differentiated internally. Since 2000, new research and development (R&D) initiatives have proliferated, absorbing the swell of personnel and resources. These initiatives take the form of diverse projects, funds, regional development pushes and the building of institutions and facilities across almost every major segment of S&T. The areas affected are diverse, ranging from nuclear engineering and shipbuilding to artificial intelligence.

Today, the national innovation machine is active in almost every major area of S&T that has an impact on economic or defence modernisation. Organisations dedicated to specific technical areas are now established across countless segments of S&T. They have multiplied and expanded in scope (Figure 12.3). Certain large entities have also differentiated internally into subentities that focus on specific production segments or technical areas. In other words, expansion and diversification at the systemic level have co-occurred with specialisation or re-specialisation at the level of sectors, firms and units within them. Like broad institutionalisation, the proliferation of dedicated new entities has fostered the emergence of specialist communities in different sectors and subsectors.

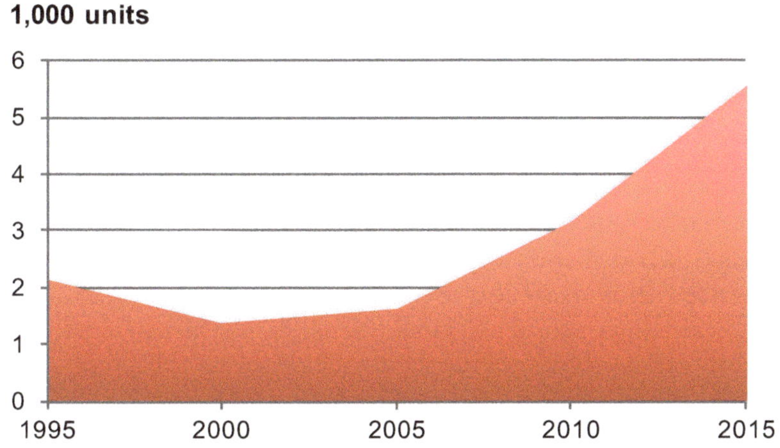

Figure 12.3 Research and development institutions in China
Source: NBS (2017).

Professionalisation

Another factor contributing to the development of high-technology capabilities is the professionalisation of the S&T workforce. In the late 1980s and beyond, major technology programs were led and sometimes created from scratch by elite scientists and engineers. The contributions of these figures, though monumental and enduring in their own right, depended on their personal status and connections to political and military leaders and factions. In general, S&T programs were subject to shifting political winds—encountering adoption, funding and support or fiscal neglect, postponement and termination as they fell in and out of favour with non-technical decision-makers (Schneider 1988; Chang 1996; Feigenbaum 2003; Handberg and Li 2007; Schmalzer 2008; Andreas 2009).

Since the 1980s, however, management at the higher echelons of this workforce has undergone three changes that have mitigated political interference, personalistic authority and erratic management.

The first is depoliticisation. Direct, politically motivated interference by top leaders in specific S&T personnel appointments and activities (Schneider 1988; Handberg and Li 2007; Andreas 2009; Hu 2009; Luk 2015) all but disappeared by the end of the Hu administration. Even under the politicised anticorruption campaign of President Xi Jinping, which has targeted many large state-owned enterprises (SOEs) in high-technology sectors, aircraft and spacecraft manufacturers appear to have eluded significant leadership changes or other disruption. Today, at least within the aerospace sectors, major decisions appear to reflect not struggles over power and privilege within the state, but technical, fiscal or other factors.

The second change is de-personalisation. The fate of an S&T program is far less closely tied with the professional or political fortunes of a single influential figure or group than it was only two decades ago (Lu 2005a; Li 2013). A class of scientific and technical elites has risen (relatively more) meritoriously to program management and other administrative roles (Cao 2004). Within programs, leadership changes are now more standardised. Personal attention from high-level leaders to S&T programs remains a feature of the system (Besha 2010; Cheung 2016), as indicated by President Xi's continuing personal visits to key facilities, but no major aerospace program has recently suffered because of an influential individual's fall from grace.

The third change is routinisation. More robust mechanisms for proposing, adopting and implementing S&T projects developed under former president Hu and persist today. The initiation of a program requires multiple layers of review before it reaches high-level decision-makers.[1] Most programs are proposed at the top of a sectoral or subsectoral hierarchy on the basis of goals identified in the long-term central government plans (Liu et al. 2011). When this involves the acquisition of a large system, as in the case of a large defence aircraft program, leaders of the procuring units must translate goals set out in high-level strategies into concrete program objectives and, in turn, specific system requirements (Puska et al. 2011).

The processes of institutionalisation, specialisation and professionalisation have reshaped the setting for innovation, laying the foundations for more complex and demanding S&T activities. These changes have also fostered the formation of specialist communities in particular sectors, to which we now turn.

1 Interviewee 43-42-18, interview with space expert from Chinese research institution, 2010.

Specialist communities

A specialist is an individual professional in a given technology sector who possesses subject-matter expertise that those outside their sector lack. A specialist community is a collective of professionals active in a given sector who share not only this specialised technical knowledge, but also other basic assumptions about technology and the world around it (Rouse 1993). Experts within a sector often come to share a given world view comprising basic philosophical commitments. These assumptions are so widely accepted that they do not require explicit articulation. Because of their often tacit nature, these assumptions are sometimes called 'background knowledge' (Adler 1992; Adler and Pouliot 2011). These tacit understandings form the bedrock of a specialist community's culture. Members express and reinforce their background knowledge in a wide range of daily professional practices, including habits of speech and writing (Adler and Pouliot 2011). Sectoral experts' shared background knowledge, expressed in common practices, constitutes their community's specialist culture (Rouse 2003). China's S&T establishment comprises countless specialised sectors—from biotechnology to nanotechnology—whose experts form distinct specialist communities.

Elements of the specialist culture shared among members of such a community may transcend national boundaries, language barriers and occupational differences. Scientists, engineers, technicians, investors, lawyers and insurers often belong to a single specialist community. Websites, textbooks, academic journals, trade magazines and conference presentations carry representational practices across continents, diffusing them throughout a transnational specialist community, even while its members remain dispersed. What we observe, then, is not a peculiar 'Chinese' culture of science, technology and innovation, but many specialist cultures that exist within China's S&T establishment and transcend its borders. In aerospace, for example, Chinese specialists' practices and understandings reflect their exposure to Soviet/Russian, US and European counterparts (Krolikowski 2015).

Within every high-technology sector, certain experts do not share the community's dominant stock of background knowledge and practices. In spite of these dissidents, a mainstream specialist culture is usually discernable within a community. When specialists differ on the mere specifics of policies or programs, rather than their basic direction, their disagreement is usually predicated on their common acceptance of more fundamental assumptions about their sector and their work.

Experts draw on this specialist culture when they describe and define their sector and its policy needs to policymakers. When specialists represent their sector in speech or writing, they rely on a set of representational practices—or habits of expression—shared within their community. These discursive acts reflect and convey the underlying philosophical assumptions tacitly shared within the specialist community. Representational practices are important because they 'anchor' other practices, such as programmatic and regulatory practices (Swidler 2001).

Specialist communities shape the S&T system because they discursively constitute distinct sectors as sites requiring particular types of policies. In the process of depicting their sector to policymakers, specialists also impart philosophical assumptions that tacitly lend support to some policy measures over others. Sectoral specialists define their sectors as objects of policy. Their acts of speech and illustration are not merely representational, but also productive of their sectors and technologies (Rouse 1993; MacKenzie 2006).

China's innovation system is home to specialist communities that play these roles. Within the aerospace sectors, at least five conditions help form and maintain tight-knit specialist communities:

1. Barriers to the free circulation of ideas between sectoral experts and outsiders foster an insular specialist culture. Examples include secrecy rules and the program specificity of technical knowledge, both of which characterise work in the defence-industrial conglomerates to which China's aerospace firms belong.[2]
2. Barriers to the entry and exit of individual professionals preserve a specialist community's internal culture. China's aeronautic and space specialists tend to spend their entire careers within their sector, as do their counterparts in many countries, in part because programs have long lifetimes and because attractive opportunities outside a few large industrial groups are scarce.[3]
3. Sectors dominated by large firms and organisations, such as the behemoth aerospace industrial groups, are more likely to have robust internal cultures than sectors fragmented into many smaller entities. Large organisations provide conduits for the maintenance and propagation of such cultures.
4. Hierarchical structures nurture the emergence and consolidation of specialist cultures within organisations. Hierarchies supply role models and reward individuals for the correct performance of a community's cultural practices. Large SOEs feature such structures.
5. Organisations within which professional training and interaction take the form of master–apprentice relationships—for example, supervisor–student, laboratory director–technician, administrative patron–client—are effective at socialising new entrants into their culture (Chang 1996; Qiu 2009; Wang 2011). The aerospace industry features such interactions.[4]

2 Interviewee 25-43-20, interview with space expert from a space-sector operational organisation, 2010.
3 Interviewee 20-36-42, interview with space expert from Chinese research institution, 2010.
4 Interviewee 25-43-20.

Scientists and engineers in policymaking

Specialist communities are worth examining because they are the actors most directly responsible for China's scientific and technological output. They also have an impact on policies and programs, which ultimately shape the long-term prospects for Chinese innovation. Several conditions grant scientists and engineers unique roles in policymaking.

Scientists and engineers form a reservoir of technical expertise for policymakers to consult. Policymakers rarely have any direct experience of the particular sector at stake when devising innovation strategies, so they rely on specialists to interpret these for them. Policymaking bureaucracies tap experts to monitor trends, define problems and policy options and make recommendations. Decision-makers draw on specialist insights when they adopt, evaluate and reform policy for a given technology sector.

Mechanisms exist to channel expert advice to high-level political decision-makers (Halpern 1988). Experts brief leaders, write reports and present at conferences for policymakers who prepare plans and strategies for the sector (Halpern 1988; Zhu 2009).[5]

Since the 1950s, individual elite scientists and engineers have had the ear of senior Chinese leaders, such as Zhou Enlai and Nie Rongzhen (Feigenbaum 2003; Besha 2010; Li 2013). Some have cultivated and used this influence to pursue major S&T projects of their own design and initiative.

Scientific and technical elites derive power and influence from their very status as experts. This is true almost everywhere, but especially so in post-Mao China's technocratic context (Cheng and White 1990; Hua 1995; Greenhalgh 2003). Historically, this status has afforded aerospace experts substantial policy influence, extending even into domains far outside their area of formal training, such as agriculture and family planning (Chang 1996; Greenhalgh 2005).

These factors combine to give China's aeronautic and space experts significant input into and influence over policymaking in their sectors.

5 Interviewee 40-27-18, interview with space expert from Chinese research institution, 2010; Interviewee 24-19-41, interview with export control specialist at a Chinese think tank, 2010.

Aeronautic and space specialists

Aeronautic and space experts have sometimes wielded this influence as individuals or interest groups. However, they have had the most enduring and far-reaching impact as specialist *communities* shaping the landscape within which innovation projects take place. China's aeronautic and space experts belong to distinct specialist communities, each of which is held together by a particular internal culture. As aeronautic and space experts represent their sectors to policymakers, they also implicitly convey distinct policy prescriptions, helping to shape overarching sectoral innovation strategies.

The central government's strategies for developing the nation's aeronautic and space sectors differ markedly. The approach to developing aircraft manufacture has been premised on trade and industrial collaboration with foreign firms since at least the early 1990s. In contrast, the strategy for the spacecraft sector has prioritised autonomously developing critical systems at home and the domestic vertical integration of the national industrial base for several decades, since at least the time of the Sino–Soviet split. To a large degree, these differences reflect the distinct opportunities for trade and foreign collaboration available to Chinese firms and agencies, which have been far more numerous and substantial in aeronautics than in space. However, a close reading of specialist pronouncements reveals that the distinct approaches adopted in each sector long predate Chinese firms' differential access to international technology. This situation suggests that aeronautic and space specialists have understood and depicted the international landscapes before them in fundamentally different ways for several decades.

Aeronautic specialists and policy

Within China, aeronautic specialists are found in a range of organisations spanning SOEs in the defence sector—namely, the Aviation Industry Corporation of China (AVIC) and its arm's-length civil subsidiary, the Commercial Aircraft Corporation of China (Comac)—government agencies, the military and technical universities (Deng et al. 1988; Allen et al. 1995; Goldstein 2006; MIIT 2009; Cliff 2010).

China's aeronautic experts belong to a larger transnational community of aircraft technology specialists, sharing its basic assumptions and discursive practices. Like their counterparts in other countries, China's aeronautic specialists tend to regard aircraft technologies as intrinsically global products (Y. Zhang 2007). Experts define modern aircraft as comprising elements designed and made in different countries. They describe global production networks as the most advanced and self-evident mode of manufacture for this industry. These ideas are rooted in a benign view of the international political economy and world markets. As aeronautic experts explain it, competition between firms and national industries drives innovation and benefits consumers (Chen 2008).

That understanding finds parallels in aeronautic experts' depictions of global aviation activities and the physical environment of flight. Aeronautic engineers tend to envision global airspace as a single transboundary domain. They describe air transportation systems and infrastructure as ideally and naturally forming a seamless global whole that transcends national borders. This view of the aviation environment extends to experts' representations of aircraft operations, regulation and production, all of which require transnational integration in a similar manner (Y. Zhang 2007).

These ideas shape Chinese aeronautic specialists' shared expectations of how their national industry should evolve. Leading experts consistently explain that, like the world's leading airplane manufacturers, Airbus and Boeing, China's national champions should establish global supply chains and facilities to support client airlines all over the world (Zhang 2008; AVIC 2015). These experts also represent offset arrangements with firms in other countries whose airlines will buy their aircraft as a natural part of this evolution.[6]

These views are consistent with other, more fundamental understandings shared by Chinese and international aeronautic specialists. Their perspectives on global trade and transnationally distributed production rest on what could be termed an 'economic' or instrumental philosophy of technology. In this understanding, technical artefacts, such as airliners and aircraft engines, reflect the demands of their social context and the choices of their designers and makers (Y. Zhang 2007; Chen 2008). Aeronautic technology does not evolve according to a logic of its own, but rather develops in response to market pressures, client demands and other human or social factors (Qi and Cheng 2006). Engineers and inventors are the shapers of these devices, which they tailor to meet the needs of their time and place (Yao 1996; Liu 2007).

These understandings reach the high-level policymakers who decide long-term innovation and industrial strategies for the aircraft sector. Aeronautic experts convey their ideas through the analyses and other technical input they supply to policymakers. When experts represent their sector as endowed with specific features, they implicitly prescribe national policies consistent with these characteristics.

When aeronautic experts depict their industry and technologies as inherently global, they represent their sector as one requiring policies that foster trade, transnational industrial integration and intergovernmental civil cooperation (Guo 2000; Lu 2005b). These include measures to facilitate the transboundary sale

6 Interviewee 18-00-18, interview with senior Chinese aircraft industry professional, 2010.

of aircraft articles and investment in aircraft facilities, to harmonise global standards for products and to support partnerships with leading foreign firms (Yu 2009; Mecham and Anselmo 2011). When aircraft items are represented in this way, an insistence on developing and using indigenous technology for the sake of achieving national technological autonomy appears counterproductive and self-limiting. Instead, experts' depictions prioritise easing the inbound and outbound movement of aeronautic articles to China, attracting optimal foreign partners and, ultimately, ensuring the embedding of Chinese firms in global value chains (Frenken 2000; Bowen 2007; Raska and Krolikowski 2013).

These representations in turn support a sectoral strategy with particular features. First, a goal of China's aeronautics strategy has been to integrate Chinese firms into transnational industrial networks at optimal nodes (Grevatt 2012). This approach obviates the total vertical integration of aircraft manufacture within domestic firms (Tyroler-Cooper and Peet 2011). The strategy does not aim at straightforward import substitution, as indicated by the long-term targets of between 10 and 30 per cent indigenous content on the ARJ21 and C919 domestic airliner programs (Lu 2005a).[7] Instead, inserting Chinese firms into transnational networks requires their selective specialisation in high value-added products for both domestic and global markets, alongside the importation and outsourcing of other components and services (Perrett 2009b). The desired end goal is a qualified substitution of high value-added imports with indigenous products in combination with imports and foreign-based industrial collaboration in selected areas (Perrett 2009a; Anselmo et al. 2011). For example, one long-term objective is to develop select national capabilities in commercial aircraft engine manufacture (Central People's Government 2009).

In this vision, AVIC will develop the regionally and globally distributed production processes of today's global top-tier aircraft manufacturers (AVIC 2015). Within this sectoral strategy, the measure of success is twofold: both the technological output and the export success of Chinese firms matter. For these experts, producing viable aircraft domestically is a priority of this approach, but emphasis is also placed on making AVIC entities into profitable, competitive export-oriented businesses.[8] The result is a sectoral strategy with particular features that remains largely uncontested, even while markedly different policies are adopted in the adjacent space sector.

Space specialists and policy

China's space experts belong to their own distinct community and work across a vast range of institutions comparable to those found in the aircraft industry. These include two large state-owned defence-industrial groups, the Chinese Aerospace

7 ibid.

8 ibid.

Science and Technology Corporation (CASC) and the Chinese Aerospace Science and Industry Corporation (CASIC), several government agencies, military entities and technical universities and research institutes (Sun 2007a; Ma 2011).

China's space experts share a specialist culture with space experts in other countries (Miller 2002), but their world view is unlike that of aeronautic specialists. When space experts look beyond their own borders, they see a hierarchical system of competing national industrial bases, each one's position dictated by its mastery of critical technologies.[9] State power and the strength of industry are intertwined in this view, so industrial capabilities remain divided by national boundaries.[10] The natural state of affairs in the space sector is for firms to engage in research, development and production activities within the borders of the country in which they are headquartered and with partners from the same country or, at most, close allies. National industrial bases compete on all fronts.

In these experts' depictions, the prognosis for the global space sector is its inevitable and persistent fragmentation into distinct national industrial bases. Given the sector's strategic role, a rising power must assure its independent access to and utilisation of the space environment by developing an industry of its own (Huang 2006, 2007).

These ideas imply a theory of world politics within which technological factors decide interstate struggles for security and dominance. To space experts, technological breakthroughs are the engines of world history. Advances in space systems are chief among these, bringing revolutionary changes to international politics and other social phenomena (Liu et al. 1996; Chang 2004). For example, in this view, the advent of space weapons has transformed the international system, creating runaway dynamics that governments and militaries cannot control (Zhang 2005; Huang 2006; Dai 2007; Peoples 2008a). Thus, unlike aeronautic experts, space specialists express deterministic and structural assumptions about space technology and its impact on society (Liang 2002; Dai 2007; Ma 2008; Peoples 2008b). While recognising that technological change has many sources, space experts assume that at least one of them is a momentum internal to technology itself (Huang 1999). They often represent technical processes as eluding human control. Technological change proceeds according to its own internal logic, which largely resists management by humans (Xu 2007). Technology advances and the social environment responds (Liu et al. 1996).

This hostile landscape in view, Chinese specialists have interpreted the tightening in 1999 of US restrictions on exports of space items to China as part of a US strategy to suppress China's peaceful rise (Liao 2006; Ning et al. 2006). In this understanding, tight US controls on space exports to China have not only denied

9 Interviewee 19-36-43, interview with space expert from an academic institution, 2010.

10 Interviewee 25-43-20.

it trade opportunities, but also serve a larger US strategy to block China's national rejuvenation: a 'space containment policy' targeting China's core development and security interests (Zhang 2003; Communist Party Member 2008). This 'space embargo' constrains China's economic advance by excluding it from world markets for high-technology goods and, worse, stifles its societal and defence modernisation (Ma 2008). These depictions underpin and rationalise policies to rapidly and autonomously develop capabilities in civil, commercial, military, and intelligence space (Liao 2006; Sun 2006, 2007b; Q. Zhang 2007).

The long-term ideal, then, is national control over critical processes in satellite and launch vehicle manufacture and operation (State Council 2006). This goal demands the near-total vertical integration of manufacture within a national system of firms. The objective of sectoral policy is building a holistic industrial base within China, while selectively pursuing international cooperation projects where they bring significant benefits, but carry few risks (Q. Zhang 2007; Leading Party Group of CASC 2009). Foreign partners' inputs can supplement, but not substitute for or interfere with, homegrown capabilities (Liang 2002; Lan 2007). Success for CASC and CASIC means mission success and its corollary, technological achievement (Guo 2007). Business performance is a distantly secondary objective.[11] Reforms of these conglomerates serve the objective of enhancing their technological output, rather than their profitability or corporate governance for its own sake. Exports are sought and represent industrial achievements, but they are not fundamental goals of the overarching sectoral development strategy.

Table 12.1 Technological development and innovation strategies in China's aerospace sectors

Feature	Aeronautics	Space
Expected structure of global industry	Transnational industrial integration	International industrial fragmentation
Form of industrial structure sought	Import substitution goals qualified, not absolute Vertical integration is not the end goal AVIC to enter global industry at particular nodes	Total in-country vertical integration National control over all critical elements and processes, from R&D through to operations Requires a holistic industrial base within China
Relationship to foreign technology and suppliers	AVIC to produce in global networks Expect offsets, localisation of manufacturing in client states Seek stable supply chains—a means to this are international standards	Foreign inputs supplement, but never substitute for, homegrown inputs
Vision of success for major firms	Exports matter: AVIC's success measured in terms of both technology output and business performance	Success for CASC and CASIC means mission success and technological achievement; business performance is secondary

11 Interviewee 25-43-20.

Through their representations, China's aeronautic and space specialists constitute their sectors as objects requiring specific policies. In the aeronautic sector, these policies foster global trade and cooperation. In the space sector, they constrain trade and cooperation, while prioritising the development of indigenous capabilities (Table 12.1).

Conclusion

China now has perhaps the world's most rapidly advancing space program and is poised to enter the technologically demanding large-carrier segment of the global aircraft industry. Within this evolving innovation system, clusters of experts, sharing specialised knowledge and a particular specialist culture, have coalesced. These communities are significant actors within the S&T system and shapers of innovation policy.

China's specialist communities exert a diffuse and indirect impact on long-term innovation strategies. Experts participate in policymaking as authorities on their subject matter and technical domain. In the process, they perform representational practices that produce their sectors as specific sites for state action. These practices communicate not only experts' technical knowledge, but also their tacit policy recommendations. They reflect the specialist community's culture. Aeronautic and space experts illustrate these processes. Through their representations, these specialists create the enabling conditions for the innovation strategy adopted in each sector. Aeronautic specialists represent their sector as requiring an approach that draws in foreign knowledge and systems and embeds Chinese firms in global value chains. In contrast, space experts depict their sector as demanding a strategy that prioritises developing indigenous technology to enhance national autonomy. These specialists thus define the range of policies and outcomes that policymakers in each sector consider plausible and feasible, in the process setting the parameters on what kind of innovation strategy is possible in their domain. Through their representational practices, specialists produce agreement on the ends and means of policy.

References

Adler, E. (1992), The emergence of cooperation: National epistemic communities and the international evolution of the idea of nuclear arms control, *International Organization* 46: 101–45. doi.org/10.1017/S0020818300001466.

Adler, E. and Pouliot, V. (2011), International practices, *International Theory* 3(1): 1–36. doi.org/10.1017/S175297191000031X.

Allen, K. W., Krumel, G. and Pollack, J. D. (1995), *China's Air Force Enters the 21st Century*, Santa Monica, CA: Rand Corporation.

Andreas, J. (2009), *Rise of the Red Engineers: The Cultural Revolution and the origins of China's new class*, Stanford, CA: Stanford University Press.

Anselmo, J. C., Mecham, M. and Perrett, B. (2011), Made in China: Airbus's Tianjin assembly plant replicates European quality, but at a higher cost, *Aviation Week & Space Technology*, 25 April.

Appelbaum, R. P., Parker, R. and Cao, C. (2011), Developmental state and innovation: Nanotechnology in China, *Global Networks* 11(3): 298–314. doi.org/10.1111/j.1471-0374.2011.00327.x.

Aviation Industry Corporation of China (AVIC) (2015), *AVIC Corporate Strategy*. 7 September. Available from: www.avic.com/en/aboutus/corporatestrategy/index.shtml.

Besha, P. (2010), Policy making in China's space program: A history and analysis of the Chang'e Lunar Orbiter Project, *Space Policy* 26(4): 214–21. doi.org/10.1016/j.spacepol.2010.08.005.

Bowen, J. T., jr, (2007), Global production networks, the developmental state and the articulation of Asia Pacific economies in the commercial aircraft industry, *Asia Pacific Viewpoint* 48(3): 312–29. doi.org/10.1111/j.1467-8373.2007.00350.x.

Cao, C. (2003), Digital dragon: High-technology enterprises in China, *The China Quarterly* (2003): 538–39.

Cao, C. (2004), *China's Scientific Elite*, New York: RoutledgeCurzon.

Central People's Government of the People's Republic of China (Central People's Government) (2009), When will large domestic aircraft have a 'Chinese heart'? [in Chinese], 20 January, Central People's Government of the People's Republic of China, Beijing. Available from: www.gov.cn/fwxx/kp/2009-01/20/content_1209835.htm.

Chang, I. (1996), *Thread of the Silkworm*, New York: Basic Books.

Chang, X. (2004), *Military Astronautics*, [in Chinese], 2nd edn, Beijing: National Defense Industries Press.

Chen, D. (2008), *Discussion of Aviation*, [in Chinese], Beijing: National Defense Industries Press.

Cheng, L. and White, L. (1990), Elite transformation and modern change in Mainland China and Taiwan: Empirical data and the theory of technocracy, *The China Quarterly* 121: 1–35. doi.org/10.1017/S0305741000013497.

Cheung, T. M. (2011), The Chinese defense economy's long march from imitation to innovation, *Journal of Strategic Studies* 34(3): 325–54. doi.org/10.1080/01402390.2011.574976.

Cheung, T. M. (2016), *The rise of the Chinese national security state under Xi Jinping*, CPI Analysis, 15 December, China Policy Institute, Nottingham, UK. Available from: cpianalysis.org/2016/12/15/the-rise-of-the-chinese-national-security-state-under-xi-jinping/.

Cliff, R. (2010), The development of China's air force capabilities, Testimony to the US–China Economic and Security Review Commission, Washington, DC.

Communist Party Member (2008), China says 'no' to space hegemony, [in Chinese], *Communist Party Member* (4): 25.

Dai, X. (2007), Space: War's ultimate high ground, [in Chinese], *Contemporary Military Digest*, Reprinted from *China Defense Daily*, 30 January 2007.

Deng, L., Ma, H. and Wu, H. (eds) (1988), *Contemporary China's Aviation Industry*, [in Chinese], Beijing: China Social Sciences Press.

Dickson, D. (1998), Back on track: The rebirth of human genetics in China, *Nature* 396(6709): 303–6. doi.org/10.1038/24470.

Feigenbaum, E. (2003), *China's Techno-Warriors: National security and strategic competition from the nuclear to the information age*, Stanford, CA: Stanford University Press.

Frenken, K. (2000), A complexity approach to innovation networks: The case of the aircraft industry (1909–1997), *Research Policy* 29(2): 257–72. doi.org/10.1016/S0048-7333(99)00064-5.

Goldstein, A. (2006), The political economy of industrial policy in China: The case of aircraft manufacturing, *Journal of Chinese Economic and Business Studies* 4(3): 259–73. doi.org/10.1080/14765280600991628.

Greenhalgh, S. (2003), Science, modernity, and the making of China's one-child policy, *Population and Development Review* 29(2): 163–96. doi.org/10.1111/j.1728-4457.2003.00163.x.

Greenhalgh, S. (2005), Missile science, population science: The origins of China's one-child policy, *The China Quarterly* (182): 253–76. doi.org/10.1017/S0305741005000184.

Grevatt, J. (2012), AVIC boss eyes M&A activity and teaming to grow 'global industrial chain', *Jane's Defence Weekly*, 19 November.

Guo, B. (2007), Milestones in China's space development: 'China's Space Activities' white paper, [in Chinese], *Aerospace China*, May.

Guo, E. (2000), Development of and responses to aircraft manufacturing technology, [in Chinese], *Aircraft Manufacturing Technology* 6: 16–20.

Halpern, N. M. (1988), Scientific decision making: The organization of expert advice in post-Mao China, in D. F. Simon and M. Goldman (eds), *Science and Technology in Post-Mao China*, pp. 157–74. Cambridge, Mass.: Harvard University Press.

Handberg, R. and Li, Z. (2007), *Chinese Space Policy: A study in domestic and international politics*, London: RoutledgeCurzon.

Hickie, D. (2006), Knowledge and competitiveness in the aerospace industry: The cases of Toulouse, Seattle and north-west England, *European Planning Studies* 14(5): 697–716. doi.org/10.1080/09654310500500254.

Hu, D. (2009), *China and Albert Einstein: The reception of the physicist and his theory in China, 1917–1979*, Cambridge, Mass.: Harvard University Press.

Hua, S. (1995), Science, scientism and humanism, in S. Hua, *Scientism and Humanism: Two cultures in post-Mao China*, pp. 9–32, Albany, NY: State University of New York Press.

Huang, J., Rozelle, S., Pray, C. and Wang, Q. (2002), Plant biotechnology in China, *Science* 295(5555): 674–6. doi.org/10.1126/science.1067226.

Huang, Z. (1999), Reflecting upon space strategy for our country in the early 21st century, [in Chinese], *Journal of Institute of Command and Technology* 10(6): 1–5.

Huang, Z. (2006), Space weaponisation and space deterrence, [in Chinese], *Studies in International Technology and Economy* 9(1): 24–8.

Huang, Z. (2007), *Space Science and Technology and Society: The fourth wave*, [in Chinese], Guangzhou: Guangdong Education Publishing House.

Hughes, T. P. (2004), *Human-Built World: How to think about technology and culture*, Chicago: University of Chicago Press.

Jeon, C. (2010), Technologies of the operator: Engineering the pilot in the US and Japan, 1930–1960, Thesis, Massachusetts Institute of Technology, Cambridge, Mass.

Keller, W. W. and Samuels, R. J. (eds) (2003), *Crisis and Innovation in Asian Technology*, New York: Cambridge University Press.

Krolikowski, A. (2015), *Specialist communities: People and cultures in China's defense science and technology system*, Research Brief, University of California Institute on Global Conflict and Cooperation, La Jolla, CA.

Lan, B. (2007), China's 'Beidou' breaks Western space monopoly, [in Chinese], *Communist Party Member*.

Leading Party Group of Chinese Aerospace Science and Technology Corporation (CASC) (2009), An exploit cast in reform and opening: The achievements, experience and prospects of our country's space development, [in Chinese], *Aerospace China*, January.

Li, C. (2013), The Chinese GNSS: System development and policy analysis, *Space Policy* 29: 9–19. doi.org/10.1016/j.spacepol.2012.11.001.

Liang, S. (2002), *Long March Toward Space*, [in Chinese], Beijing: China Astronautics Publishing House.

Liao, C. (2006), Commentary on the state of the new round of international space competition, [in Chinese], *International Outer Space* (7): 1–6.

Liu, F.-c., Simon, D. F., Sun, Y.-t. and Cao, C. (2011), China's innovation policies: Evolution, institutional structure, and trajectory, *Research Policy* 40(7): 917–31. doi.org/10.1016/j.respol.2011.05.005.

Liu, J., Bai, B.-a. and Liu, J. (eds) (1996), *Space Technology and Modern Society*, [in Chinese], Beijing: China Astronautics Publishing House.

Liu, X. and White, S. (2001), Comparing innovation systems: A framework and application to China's transitional context, *Research Policy* 30(7): 1091–114. doi.org/10.1016/S0048-7333(00)00132-3.

Liu, Y. (ed.) (2007), *China's Aviation History*, [in Chinese], 2nd edn, Changsha, China: Hunan Science and Technology Press.

Lu, F. (2005a), Reflections on our country's large aircraft development strategy, [in Chinese], *China's Soft Sciences*: 10–16.

Lu, F. (2005b), Research report on China's large aircraft development strategy, [in Chinese], *Business Affairs Weekly*, 20 March.

Luk, Y. L. C. (2015), *A History of Biophysics in Contemporary China*, Heidelberg, Germany: Springer. doi.org/10.1007/978-3-319-18093-9.

Ma, X. (2008), Develop space manufacturing, serve the national economy, spur on social progress, [in Chinese], *China Aerospace*, May: 3–7.

Ma, X. (2011), *Space Science and Technology Personnel's Journey to Maturity*, [in Chinese], Beijing: China Astronautics Publishing House and China Aerospace Science and Technology Corporation.

MacKenzie, D. A. (2006), *An Engine, Not a Camera: How financial models shape markets*, Cambridge, Mass.: MIT Press. doi.org/10.7551/mitpress/9780262134606.001.0001.

Mecham, M. and Anselmo, J. C. (2011), Aviation's 'learnaholics': China has the size, money and interest to engage and challenge Western companies, *Aviation Week & Space Technology*, 25 April.

Miller, T. E. (2002), Epistemic communities in the space-policy arena: Evidence of their existence, their evolution, and their influence on policy, PhD thesis, University of Colorado, Denver.

Ministry of Industry and Information Technology of the People's Republic of China (MIIT) (2009), *Overview of China's Civil Aviation Industry Enterprise Units*, [in Chinese], Beijing: Aviation Industry Press.

Montresor, S. (2001), Techno-globalism, techno-nationalism and technological systems: Organizing the evidence, *Technovation* 21(7): 399–412. doi:10.1016/S0166-4972(00)00061-4.

National Bureau of Statistics of China (NBS) (2017), *Annual Data: Statistics database*. Available from: www.stats.gov.cn/english/statisticaldata/AnnualData/.

Ning, L., Wang, C. and Rong, H. (2006), *Confrontation in Space*, [in Chinese], Beijing: Military Affairs Literature Publishing House.

Palmer, S. W. (2006), *Dictatorship of the Air: Aviation culture and the fate of modern Russia*, Cambridge: Cambridge University Press.

Pavelec, S. M. (2004), The development of turbojet aircraft in Germany, Britain, and the United States: A multi-national comparison of aeronautical engineering, 1935–1946, PhD thesis, Ohio State University, Columbus.

Pekkanen, S. (2003), *Picking Winners? From technology catch-up to the space race in Japan*, Stanford, CA: Stanford University Press.

Peoples, C. (2008a), Assuming the inevitable? Overcoming the inevitability of outer space weaponization and conflict, *Contemporary Security Policy* 29(3): 502–20. doi.org/10.1080/13523260802514811.

Peoples, C. (2008b), Sputnik and 'skill thinking' revisited: Technological determinism in American responses to the Soviet missile threat, *Cold War History* 8(1): 55–75. doi.org/10.1080/14682740701791334.

Perrett, B. (2009a), Nosing ahead, *Aviation Week & Space Technology*, 14 September: 26–7.

Perrett, B. (2009b), Cheaper by design, *Aviation Week & Space Technology*, 14 September: 28–9.

Puska, S. M., McReynolds, J. and Geary, D. (2011), *China's military representatives: Striving toward professional contracting and procurement*, SITC Research Brief No. 21, Institute on Global Conflict and Cooperation, University of California. Available from: escholarship.org/uc/item/8kb3g12j.

Qi, X. and Cheng, Z. (eds) (2006), *The Birth and Development of Aircraft*, [in Chinese], Beijing: National Defense Industries Press.

Qiu, J. (2009), Obituary: Qian Xuesen (1911–2009), *Nature* 462(7274): 735. doi.org/10.1038/462735a.

Raska, M. and Krolikowski, A. (2013), *China's military aviation industry: In search of innovation*, SITC Research Brief No. 2013-5, Institute on Global Conflict and Cooperation, University of California. Available from: escholarship.org/uc/item/8t12095f.

Rouse, J. (1993), What are cultural studies of scientific knowledge? *Configurations* 1(1): 1–22. doi.org/10.1353/con.1993.0006.

Rouse, J. (2003), How scientific practices matter: Reclaiming philosophical naturalism, *Isis* 94(4): 791–2.

Saich, T. (1989), *China's Science Policy in the 80s*, Manchester: Manchester University Press.

Schmalzer, S. (2008), *The People's Peking Man: Popular science and human identity in twentieth-century China*, Chicago: University of Chicago Press. doi.org/10.7208/chicago/9780226738611.001.0001.

Schneider, L. (1988), Learning from Russia: Lysenkoism and the fate of genetics in China, 1950–1986, in D. F. Simon and M. Goldman (eds), *Science and Technology in Post-Mao China*, pp. 45–68. Cambridge, Mass.: Harvard University Press.

Simon, D. F. and Goldman, M. (eds) (1988), *Science and Technology in Post-Mao China*, Cambridge, Mass.: Harvard University Press.

Sleeboom-Faulkner, M. (2006), *The Chinese Academy of Social Sciences*, Boston: Brill.

State Council of the People's Republic of China (State Council) (2006), *Government White Papers: China's space activities in 2006*, Beijing: Information Office of the State Council of the People's Republic of China. Available from: www.china.org.cn/english/features/book/183672.htm.

Sun, L. (2006), The brilliant achievements and development strategy of China's space sector, [in Chinese], *Defense Science and Technology Industry*, September: 12–14.

Sun, L. (2007a), The development strategy and key areas of China's space sector, [in Chinese], *Aerospace China*, January: 3–8, 13.

Sun, L. (2007b), Peacefully use military technology, spur on economic and social development, [in Chinese], *Military-Civil Dual-Use Technology and Products* (11): 3–4.

Suttmeier, R. P. (1980), *Science, Technology, and China's Drive for Modernization*, Stanford, CA: Hoover Institution Press.

Suttmeier, R. P. and Cao, C. (1999), China faces the new industrial revolution: Achievement and uncertainty in the search for research and innovation strategies, *Asian Perspective* 23(3): 153–200.

Swidler, A. (2001), What anchors cultural practices, in T. R. Schatzki, K. Knorr-Cetina and E. von Savigny (eds), *The Practice Turn in Contemporary Theory*, pp. 74–92, New York: Routledge.

Tyroler-Cooper, S. and Peet, A. (2011), The Chinese aviation industry: Techno-hybrid patterns of development in the C919 program, *Journal of Strategic Studies* 34(3): 383–404. doi:10.1080/01402390.2011.574981.

Wang, N. (2011), The making of an intellectual hero: Chinese narratives of Qian Xuesen, *The China Quarterly* 206: 352–71. doi.org/10.1017/S0305741011000300.

World Bank (2017), *DataBank: World development indicators*, Washington, DC: The World Bank. Available from: databank.worldbank.org/data/reports.aspx?source=world-development-indicators#.

Xu, N. (2007), Some thoughts on the space security plight, [in Chinese], *Foreign Affairs Review* 96: 59–63.

Yao, J. (ed.) (1996), *China's Aviation History*, [in Chinese], Beijing: Dajia Press.

Yu, D. (2009), First domestic large aircraft engine test flight by 2014, [in Chinese], *Caijing*, 27 August. Available from: www.caijing.com.cn/2009-08-27/110230032.html.

Zeitlin, J. (1995), Flexibility and mass production at war: Aircraft manufacture in Britain, the United States, and Germany, 1939–1945, *Technology and Culture* 36(1): 46–79. doi.org/10.2307/3106341.

Zhang, H. (2005), Action/reaction: US space weaponization and China, *Arms Control Today* 35(10): 6–11.

Zhang, Q. (2003), Exploring diversified international cooperation for China's space industry, [in Chinese], *Aerospace China*, July: 1–4.

Zhang, Q. (2007), Future prospects of China's space development, [in Chinese], *Space Exploration*, September: 22–3.

Zhang, Q. (2008), Resolving to make China's large passenger aircraft soar the blue skies soon, *Seeking Truth*.

Zhang, Y. (ed.) (2007), *Development of Aeronautical Science and Technology*, [in Chinese], Century of Aeronautic Science and Technology Series, Beijing: Aviation Industries Press.

Zhu, X. (2009), The influence of think tanks in the Chinese policy process: Different ways and mechanisms, *Asian Survey* 49(2): 333–57. doi.org/10.1525/as.2009.49.2.333.

Part IV: Technological Change by Sectors

13. Mechanisation Outsourcing and Agricultural Productivity for Small Farms: Implications for Rural Land Reform in China

Yu Sheng, Ligang Song and Qing Yi

Introduction

Agricultural productivity in China has experienced a rapid growth over the past four decades. Between 1978 and 2013, agricultural total factor productivity (TFP) grew at an average rate of 2.86 per cent a year, which is more than three times the global average of 0.95 per cent (Fuglie and Rada 2015). The rapid increase in agricultural productivity has lessened the negative effects of constrained supply of inputs (such as land and water) and adverse seasonal conditions, and contributed to a dramatic expansion of agricultural output. Since the late 1970s, the real gross output value of Chinese agriculture has increased by a multiple of 4.6, from US$129.6 billion in 1978 to US$594.9 billion in 2013 (in the 2004–06 constant price), with total input increasing by just 66.7 per cent over the same period. Increased agricultural productivity has also released rural labour, facilitating rapid urbanisation and industrialisation in China through rural–urban migration. By 2015, about 270 million rural migrants (around 31.7 per cent of the rural population) moved into Chinese cities, providing an abundant labour supply to support urban industrial development.

While this accomplishment is impressive, agricultural productivity growth in China has more recently hit a bottleneck. Previous challenges have intensified and new challenges have emerged. For example, for decades, overuse of fertiliser and crop chemicals has gradually degraded land and slowed the yield growth of major crops (Zhang et al. 2013; Lu et al. 2015). Furthermore, rising wages and rural labour shortages have increased the cost of agricultural production, which continues to rely primarily on the use of labour-intensive technologies (Huang 2013; Han 2015). A more pressing problem is that falling average farm size (in terms of land area operated) has restricted farmers utilising advanced technologies (such as minimum-tillage and no-tillage methods) that are embodied in large plant and machinery (Sheng and Chancellor 2017). Estimates based on annual rural household surveys by the Chinese Ministry of Agriculture show that the average size of farms in China declined from 0.73 hectare in the early 1980s to 0.53 ha in 2003 (NBS 1985–2005; Huang and Ding 2016a). As a consequence, growth in selective crop productivity fell between 2005 and 2014: to 70 per cent for wheat, 73 per cent for maize and 51 per cent for barley of the long-term growth rate since 1961 (FAO 2017).

In recognising the importance of sustainable agricultural productivity growth for the realisation of long-term food security, the Chinese Government has, over the past 13 years, initiated a series of institutional reforms to promote the mechanisation of agricultural production and to encourage the adoption of advanced production technologies (Huang and Yang 2017). Major policy changes include a shift from taxing to subsidising agriculture (Tao and Qin 2007; Liu et al. 2012), an increase in public investment in agricultural research and development (R&D) (Huang and Rozelle 2014; Babu et al. 2016) and gradual market reform and trade liberalisation (Park et al. 2002; Huang and Rozelle 2006; Huang et al. 2009). The most notable change, however, relates to land reforms since 2014 that confirm the 'property right of land contract' for farmers. The purpose of this reform was to resolve the issue of small farm size, with the new institutional arrangement allowing legal transfer of operational rights to land. This was expected to accelerate land consolidation between medium and small farm operators and thus promote agricultural mechanisation in rural China.

It has been argued in the literature that assisting small landholders to either move up or move out of farming can help to improve industry-level mechanisation and agricultural productivity (e.g. FAO 2015; IFPRI 2015). The underlying assumption is that larger farms have greater willingness and capacity to invest in advanced capital equipment compared with their small counterparts, and thus can realise additional productivity gains through increasing returns to scale and access to new technology embodied in plant and machinery (Sheng et al. 2016). Consolidation of farmland via the market, however, remains challenging, even in developed countries with more transparent procedures and relatively lower transportation costs. This is because of the many market, legislative and institutional barriers that smallholders must overcome, as well as the uncertainties and transaction costs caused by cultural factors and the preferences of small landholders. It is noted that the issue of small farm size extends far beyond China: in 2012 more than 50 per cent of farms in the United States were categorised as small, defined as those having sales value and operational land scale below the bottom 20 per cent of the average (Key 2017). Identification of alternative ways to solve small-scale farming efficiency challenges is of broader public interest, especially for China, where more than 50 per cent of farms operate on less than 1 ha of land.

This chapter explores institutional innovation arising from the recent development of capital markets (namely, capital outsourcing) and the related potential for promoting the agricultural mechanisation of small farms in China. We argue that, under certain institutional arrangements, contract mechanisation services (in particular, capital outsourcing) can substitute for farmers' own investment in plant and machinery. This, in turn, can improve the capital–labour ratio of medium and small farms, complementing previous land consolidation reform in China to improve industry-level agricultural productivity. To justify this argument, we analyse the trend of industry-level agricultural productivity in China since 1978 and link this to agricultural capital equipment and average farm size, investigating the interaction between land reform and contract mechanisation services and their impact on farm productivity. Our discussion provides indirect evidence that, under certain conditions, small household farms can significantly increase their capital–labour ratio in production through contracting in mechanisation services. Without incurring the sunk costs related to investment in expensive yet efficient capital equipment, these small farms are now able to explore the productivity benefits from increasing returns to scale and adopting new technology. Moreover, contract mechanisation services can also facilitate land consolidation and change the way in which small farms optimise their production procedures. This provides useful insights for China and other countries attempting to improve agricultural productivity of their small household farms.

The remainder of the chapter is organised as follows. Section two describes the trend of agricultural productivity growth in China over the past three decades and links recent stagnation in productivity growth to the small size of a large share of China's household farms. Section three discusses historical land reforms and their impact on farm size in rural China, and raises the question of whether allowing 'land contract rights' to be legally transferred through markets could facilitate long-term land consolidation and productivity growth for small farms. Section four analyses the development of contract mechanisation services, their potential role in substituting for farmers' own investment in plant and machinery and their impact on levels of industry mechanisation. Section five reviews the literature exploring the impact of contract mechanisation services on farm size and household production in China, and points to its potential role in resolving the issue of small farm size. Section six provides the conclusion.

Agricultural productivity, capital investment and small-farm issues

Agricultural productivity in China grew rapidly after the household responsibility system (HRS) reform in 1978. As an institutional innovation to solve incentive problems inherent in the collective production system under people's communes, the HRS significantly raised agricultural productivity through contracting cultivated land to farm households in each village (Huang and Yang 2017). Compared with the pre-reform period of 1961–78, when agricultural TFP rose by a mere 0.66 per cent a year, the growth rate increased by a multiple of more than 4 per cent per annum, to 3.08 per cent annually, during the early reform years, 1979–84, and by 2.95 per cent a year during the later reform period, 1985–2013 (Figure 13.1). Over the period 1961–2013, the growth of agricultural TFP contributed more than half of China's annual real output growth (4.3 per cent)—a rate that was much higher than those of most developed and developing countries (Figure 13.2).[1]

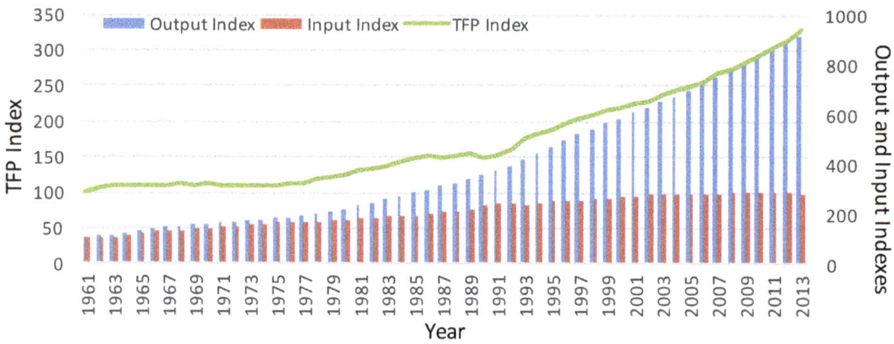

Figure 13.1 Output, input and TFP index in Chinese agriculture, 1961–2013

Source: Authors' estimates based on data from Fuglie and Rada (2015).

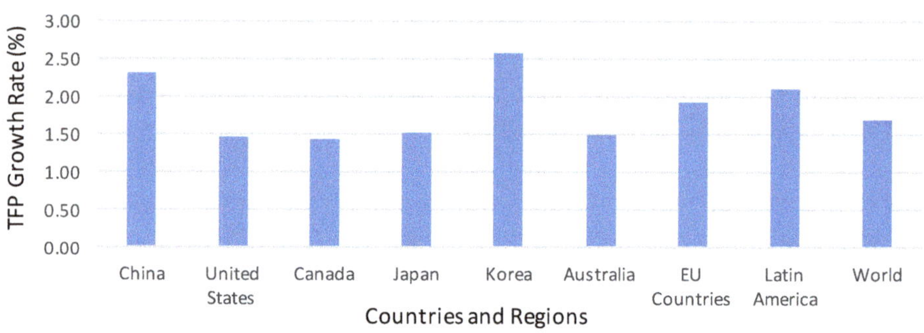

Figure 13.2 Comparison of agricultural TFP growth in China and the rest of the world, 1961–2013

Source: Authors' estimates based on data from Sheng and Song (2017).

Underlying this rapid productivity growth is a dramatic change in the structure of agricultural output and input. Between 1989 and 2014, real total agricultural output in China increased from US$129.6 billion to US$594.9 billion (at the 2004–06 constant price)—an annual growth rate of 4.5 per cent. The proportion of cereals in total agricultural output, however, has declined, from 33.6 per cent to 23.5 per cent. The proportion of vegetables, fruits and nuts, on the other hand, increased, from

1 Note that the comparison of agricultural TFP between countries needs to be approached with some caution because developing countries such as China, Korea and those in Latin America have come from a low base since 1961 compared with the United States, Canada and Australia, which have had access to capital for some time and have operated within very different regulatory and market environments.

8.2 per cent to 19.2 per cent, as did the proportion of livestock and meat products in total agricultural output, from 25.6 per cent to 29.3 per cent. The shift in agricultural production towards higher-value and higher-protein products in particular reflects dramatic improvement in the production efficiency of coarse grains relative to other products, and was partly driven by changing food demand. On the input side, both capital and intermediate inputs increased significantly, substituting for land and labour in production. Between 1978 and 2014, real total inputs into agriculture in China have grown at the rate of 1.58 per cent a year; machinery units (measured by using the number of 40-horsepower tractor equivalents) and fertiliser usage grew at the rate of 6.23 per cent a year and 4.19 per cent a year, respectively. The latter helped to compensate for the decline in labour usage (–0.6 per cent a year) and a mild increase in land usage (0.56 per cent a year) (Figure 13.3).

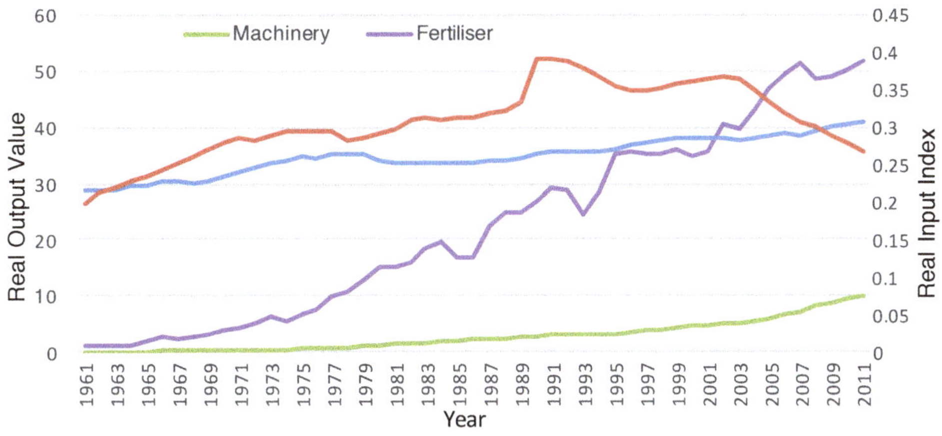

Figure 13.3 Change in input components of agricultural production (US$ million at 2004–06 price)

Source: Authors' estimates based on data from Fuglie and Rada (2015).

At the industry end, it is widely believed that agricultural productivity growth and input–output structural adjustment in China were driven by ongoing technological progress and its diffusion between farms (Huang and Yang 2017). In the technology diffusion process, increasing investment in new plant and machinery is regarded as an essential channel through which farm households improve their level of mechanisation and gain access to the embodied technology. Between 1978 and 2013, the power of plant and machinery per capita in agricultural production increased from 3.5 kilowatts (kW) to 44.7 kW, with an annual growth rate of 6 per cent a year (MOA various issues). Using capital equipment to replace labour has allowed farms not only to increase the efficiency of some primary inputs such as land and labour, but also to expand their TFP and profitability. As such, a strong positive relationship is observed between industry-level agricultural productivity (i.e. yield, labour productivity and TFP) and capital equipment per capita over the past three decades (Figure 13.4).

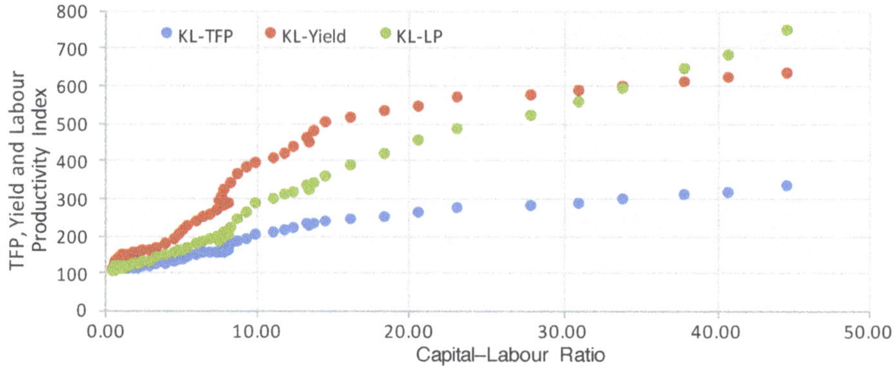

Figure 13.4 Relationship between the capital–labour ratio and agricultural productivity, 1961–2013

Source: Authors' estimates based on data from Fuglie and Rada (2015).

Although the capital–labour ratio in Chinese agriculture has significantly increased over time, it is still much lower than that in developed countries such as the United States, the European Union (EU), Australia and Japan (Figure 13.5). In 2013, China's level of capital equipment per capita in agriculture was only one-twentieth that of Australia, one-forty-seventh of the United States and one-seventy-sixth of that in Japan (Fuglie and Rada 2015). In addition, a majority of the plant and equipment (more than 85 per cent) used in China's agricultural production was smaller and less efficient than that used in developed countries (MOA various years). This relatively low capital–labour ratio and inferior capital equipment prevented Chinese agriculture from further improving its industry-level productivity. A critical issue for policymakers, therefore, is to encourage investment in agricultural capital equipment so as to improve the level of mechanisation in agricultural production.

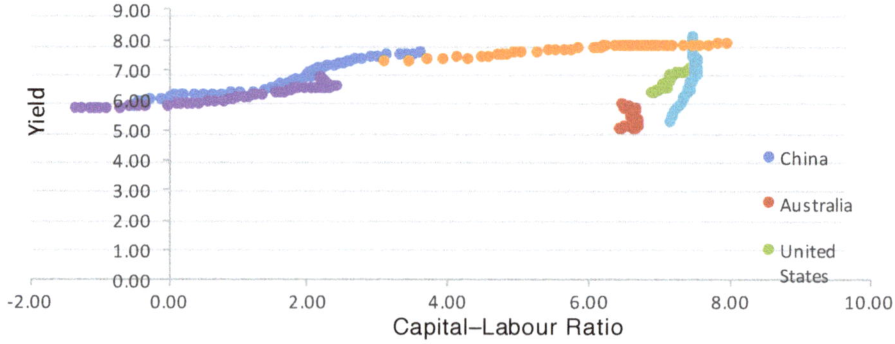

Figure 13.5 Relationship between logarithm of yield and capital–labour ratio between countries, 1961–2013

Source: Authors' estimates based on data from Fuglie and Rada (2015).

Theoretically, large farms have a higher propensity to invest in larger and more advanced equipment than their smaller counterparts. This is not only due to lower budget constraints for capital investment, but also because the average sunk costs of capital investment will decline as output increases. The willingness and ability of small farms to make capital investment are, in contrast, restricted by their lesser financial capacity and limited scope for increasing returns to scale and obtaining gains from adopting new technologies. This logic applies even more so when increased R&D costs result in more expensive and more efficient new capital equipment over time.

In China, agricultural production is based on farming households tending to a small piece of land that is rented from the local rural community. The average size of Chinese household farms is less than 1 ha (just less than 40 per cent of the global average for small farms), and, moreover, until 2004, was in continual decline (Huang and Ding 2016a). While a number of exceptionally small farms are able to achieve high productivity, the majority rely on intensive use of self-employed labour as a substitute for capital. Moreover, much of what capital plant and machinery is used in production is outdated and inefficient. This constrains the industry from improving mechanisation levels and from realising higher levels of productivity growth. To eliminate these obstacles to agricultural mechanisation and productivity growth, it is essential to resolve the investment problem related to small farm size.

Land policy, farm consolidation and transformation

In the agricultural development literature, the effect of farm size (i.e. land size) on agricultural capital investment and productivity has long been debated. Many studies have found an inverse relationship between farm size and productivity in developing countries, including in India, Vietnam and some African countries (i.e. Sen 1962, 1966; Lipton 1993; Dyer 1996; Deininger and Byerlee 2012). There is also evidence that small may not necessarily be beautiful, especially when ongoing technological progress changes methods of agricultural production and management. For example, small farms may face increasing challenges in meeting the structural change of agricultural demand and may also be reluctant to make related capital investments in newly developed production technology (Hazell 2005; Huang et al. 2008). Small farms also lack the capacity to cope with opportunities and risks arising from volatile market and climatic conditions (HLPE 2013). To deal with these issues, a general consensus among economists and policymakers is to transform small farms into large farms (or consolidate agricultural industry) by assisting small farms either to move up or to move out of the farming sector (IFPRI 2015; FAO 2017).

Although the principal need to resolve the challenges of small farms is clear, it is difficult to implement in practice, especially in developing countries where agricultural product and factor markets are usually incomplete. In China, the transformation of small farms is constrained especially by the way in which agricultural land is allocated through leasing and related institutional arrangements. Initiated by the HRS in 1978, cultivated land has been contracted to individual households in each village based on the number of people and/or units of labour in the household (equity). As an institutional innovation to resolve incentive problems inherent in the previous collective production system under people's communes, the HRS succeeded in raising agricultural productivity in the early reform period (1978–84), but it also shifted land-use rights from a collective-based system to a family-based one. Since land-use rights (which are separate from landownership) are not transferable after initial allocation, the average operational scale of farms is constrained by the amount of land initially allocated to each household. An estimate based on rural household surveys showed that the average size of farms in China was 0.73 ha in the early 1980s (NBS 1985–2005), which declined to 0.61 ha until 2013.

Another feature of the land reforms introduced in 1978 that affected the operational scale of farms and farmers' decisions about capital investment relates to the insecure tenure of land contracts. In the early 1980s, land contracts lasted for only three years or less. The short duration of land contracts offered no confidence or incentives for farm operators to make long-term production and investment plans. To improve security of tenure, a new policy was proposed in 1984 to increase the contract duration to 15 years, although it was 'never seriously publicized or implemented' (Zhu and Prosterman 2007). In 1993, the central government issued a further directive, which extended land contracts to a continuous and fixed term of 30 years. However, this new term was not embodied in formal law until 1998, when the government also initiated a massive campaign to publicise the policy (Zhao 2015). These policies generally did little to change farmers' incentives for investment, since village officials (the government) held the privilege (under the regulation) to periodically redistribute land among households in the middle of these fixed terms (Kung and Liu 1997; O'Brien and Li 1999; Pastor and Tan 2000).

Throughout the 1980s and 1990s, a majority of rural land was reallocated by village leaders using administrative methods, although the frequency of land reallocations varied between villages (Brandt et al. 2002; Krusekopf 2002). According to surveys conducted in the 1990s, by 1996, two-thirds of Chinese villages had reallocated land using administrative methods, often in the middle of land contract terms (Brandt et al. 2002). By 2002, 207 of 244 villages in the Ministry of Agriculture's National Fixed-point Survey (NFS) had reallocated land, and the average number of reallocations each village conducted between 1980 and 2002 is two (Zhao 2015). While the exact procedure by which land is redistributed differs between villages

(Figure 13.6), the most common practice is for village leaders to redivide all village land into bundles with equal distribution of land-quality types, and to distribute the bundles to households based on their population and agricultural labour force. Since land redistribution does not necessarily reflect land-use efficiency, but rather seeks to maintain a relatively egalitarian distribution of land, the average operational scale and land size of farms over the period have declined. By 2003, average land areas operated per farm had decreased to 0.53 ha, which was 72.6 per cent of that in 1980 (NBS 1985–2005).

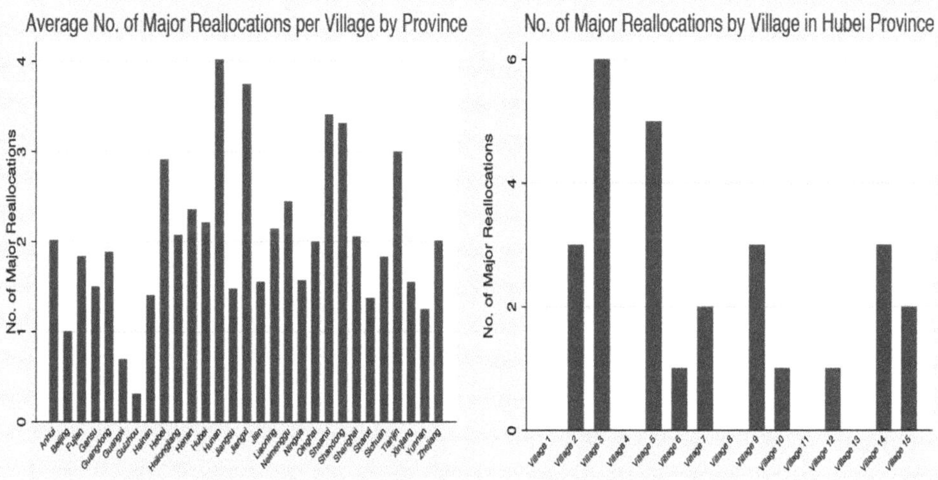

Figure 13.6 Variations in instances of land reallocation

Source: Zhao (2015).

In 2003, the National People's Congress decided to enact the Rural Land Contracting Law (RLCL) with the aim of improving security of tenure. Differing from previous laws, the RLCL was devoted entirely to clarifying the relationship between collective landownership and farmers' use of land, and enforced the contractual arrangements between the two parties (Prosterman et al. 2006). In particular, it explicitly prohibited land reallocation by village officials throughout farmers' 30-year terms of land usage. The frequency of land reallocations has since significantly decreased. On average, only 2 per cent of villages conducted annual reallocations between 2003 and 2006, compared with a yearly average of about 9 per cent before 2003 (Zhao 2015). However, the RLCL still did not allow farm households to exchange land-use contracts via the market. Therefore, the reform helped to improve the security of tenure of land contracts under the HRS, but did not facilitate land transfers between households or land consolidation within China's agricultural industry.

From 2000, China's urbanisation process accelerated, with more and more rural migrants driven to the cities by the prospect of higher wages. By 2010, around 160 million rural migrants had moved into urban regions in China (Meng and Zhang 2010) and the proportion of labour in agriculture decreased from 49.1 per cent in 2003 to 31.4 per cent in 2013 (NBS 1978–2014). The rapid decline in the rural labour supply raised the returns to labour relative to the amount of land in agricultural production, but did not proportionally increase farm size because of the current arrangements for land allocation. Between 2003 and 2013, the relative productivity of labour to land increased by 66.3 per cent, while the average farm size (measured by land area per household) increased by only 15.1 per cent (Figure 13.7). Although land transfers have accelerated since 2000, most of these were between relatives and friends within a village (Huang et al. 2012). By the end of 2013, some 53 million (23 per cent) rural households had rented out their land, accounting for 26 per cent of total agricultural land under the HRS (MOA 2014). However, average farm size remained at 0.61 ha per farm for rural households and 0.78 ha for all agricultural business (Huang and Ding 2016a). This farm size remained too small to benefit from the productivity gains available from the use of larger and more efficient capital equipment.

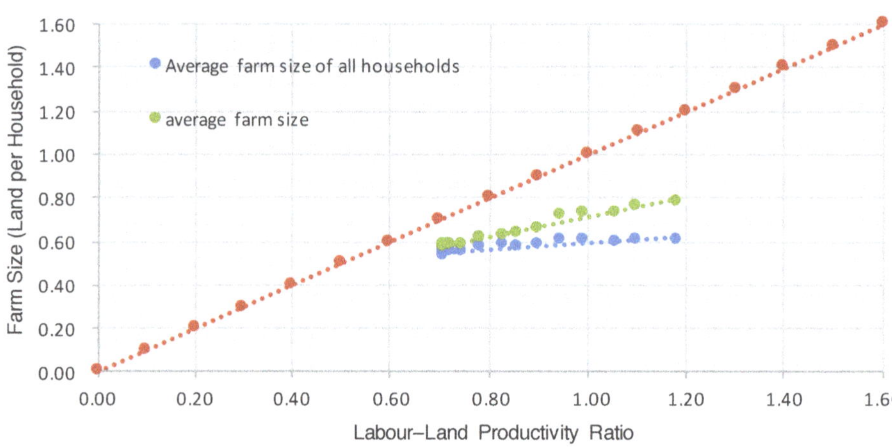

Figure 13.7 Relationship between relative labour–land productivity and farm size, 2000–13

Notes: The share of cultivated land per household is 93 per cent of the total land. The estimates of farm size exclude those households whose members remained in rural areas but were fully engaged in non-farm rural employment.

Source: Authors' estimates based on data from NBS (1978–2014).

Finally, in terms of the distribution of farm size, a majority of farm households operate on a small piece of land, although there appears to be rapid growth in medium and large-scale farms. By the end of 2013, the share of farm households operating on more than 70 ha of land in the total number of farms in north-east and northern China (where average farm size is 1.73 ha, around three times the national average) was still less than 0.02 per cent. Based on estimates using a farm operations survey by the Center for Chinese Agricultural Policy (CCAP) at the Peking University, more than 90 per cent of farm households in north-east and northern China operated on less than 3 ha, among which around two-thirds operated on less than 1 ha (Figure 13.8).

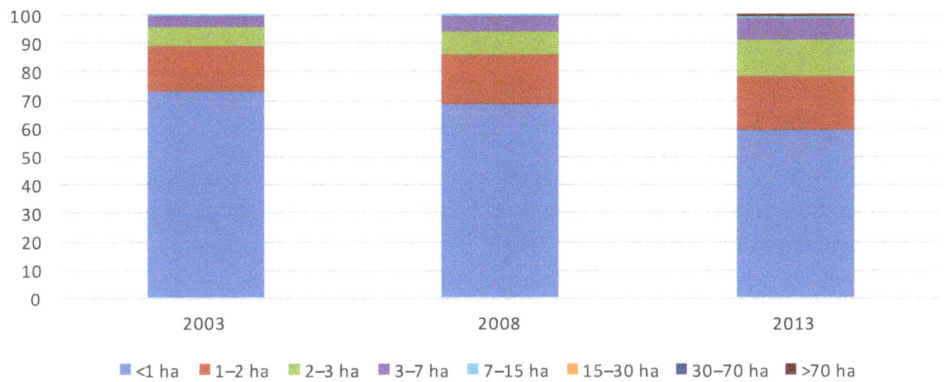

Figure 13.8 Distribution of farm size (by land area) in north-east and northern China: 2003, 2008 and 2013

Source: Authors' estimates based on data from Huang and Ding (2016a).

To encourage land transfers between farm households to improve land consolidation, in 2015 China's State Council amended the national Land Law by formally separating land operation rights from land contract rights. The directive, for the first time, allowed land contract rights to be legally transferred through market mechanisms. Following the directive, a series of institutional innovations—including establishing land transfer service centres to promote land rental and policy support for land consolidation—has been developed to assist small farms to enlarge their operational scale through market transactions (Huang and Ding 2016a). Over time, this kind of institutional arrangement will gradually support land contract consolidation among those farmers who decide to stay in farming and will also improve land distribution and land-use efficiency. This is, however, dependent on whether market failure in the transformation of farm operations (such as high land transaction costs; as in Kimura et al. 2011) can be dealt with appropriately. It is recognised that achieving land consolidation via market transactions that produce larger farming operations, which in turn utilise heavy plant and machinery, is a process that may require more time.

Agricultural mechanisation and contracting capital services

As discussed in section three, land transformation and consolidation can help to improve farm productivity by changing the willingness of household farms to make capital investment. When farms operate on a relatively larger piece of land (or become larger), they are more willing and able to pay the sunk costs for capital investment, and thus can benefit from increasing returns to scale and advanced technology embodied in new plant and machinery. Moreover, the larger the farm size, the higher will be the mechanisation level and productivity. If the literature (i.e. Sheng et al. 2016; Foster and Rosenzweig 2017) proposing this connection is correct, the positive relationship between farm size and productivity can also be interpreted as a consequence of market failure or a mismatch in capital markets due to the non-divisible capital supply, and cannot be accessed by a large number of individual small landholders (or farms).

Although enlarging farm size can moderate this problem, the mismatch between the capital demand of small household farms and capital supply from industrialised production can still exist, and even tends to rise over time as ongoing technological progress makes advanced capital equipment more efficient but also more expensive. To resolve this conflict, institutional innovation in outsourcing capital services may offer a more efficient solution than land consolidation. Specifically, a market-based capital service provider can pool the demand for mechanisation services from individual small farms, and raise funding to purchase the corresponding equipment, matching demand with the capital supplier. Via this process, each party minimises their costs, and farms of different size will gain access to the same capital equipment and embodied technology without incurring the associated large financial outlays that would otherwise be required to individually purchase capital equipment. When market-based contracting of mechanisation services becomes a close substitute for individual farmer's investment in plant and equipment, small farms might be expected to catch up with their larger counterparts in terms of productivity. This implies that using market-based mechanisation services to substitute for individual farm-level investment could be an alternative and more effective way to improve the capital–labour ratio and productivity of small household farms.

For decades after the process of opening up and reform began in 1978, the adoption of advanced production technology (measured using the mechanisation level of agricultural production) in China was positively correlated with levels of per capita capital equipment. Between 1980 and 1990, the mechanisation level of agricultural production stayed at a relatively low level, with the proportions of farmland ploughed, sown and harvested using machinery around 28.8 per cent, 9.4 per cent and 5.4 per cent, respectively (Figure 13.9). This can be attributed to the fact that agricultural production over that period relied on labour-intensive technology. As more and more rural labour moved to urban areas, a rapid increase in agricultural investment raised the capital–labour ratio and improved the mechanisation level of agricultural production in China. Throughout the period 1990–2003, the numbers of tractors, attached equipment and total machinery power per capita increased by two times, four times and 90 per cent, respectively (Figure 13.10). As a consequence, the mechanisation level of agricultural production—measured using the proportion of farmland mechanically ploughed, sown and harvested—more than doubled by 2003. From 2003, the mechanisation level of agricultural production in China increased more quickly, as per capita capital equipment accelerated, with a further increase in capital investment and a decline in rural labour supply. By 2014, more than half of all cultivated land was mechanically sown and harvested and around 80 per cent was mechanically ploughed.

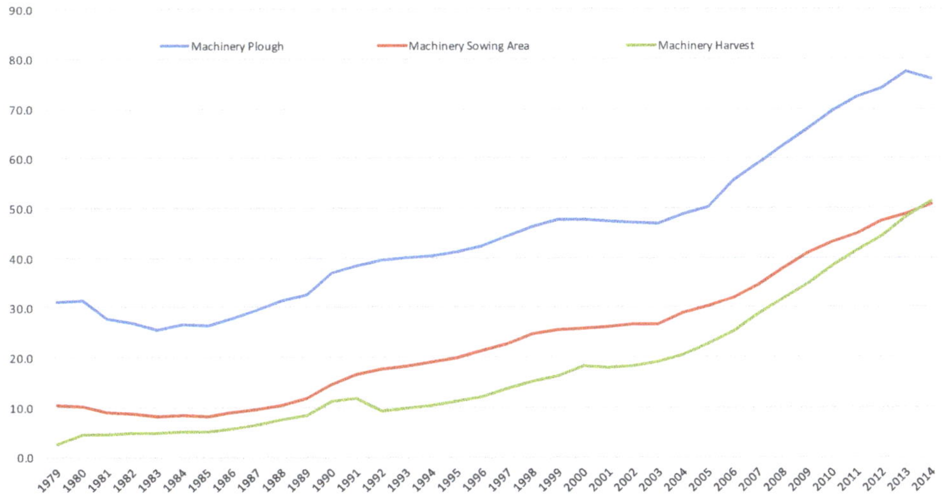

Figure 13.9 Farmland ploughed, sown and harvested using machinery, 1979–2013 (per cent)

Source: Authors' estimates based on data from NBS (1978–2014).

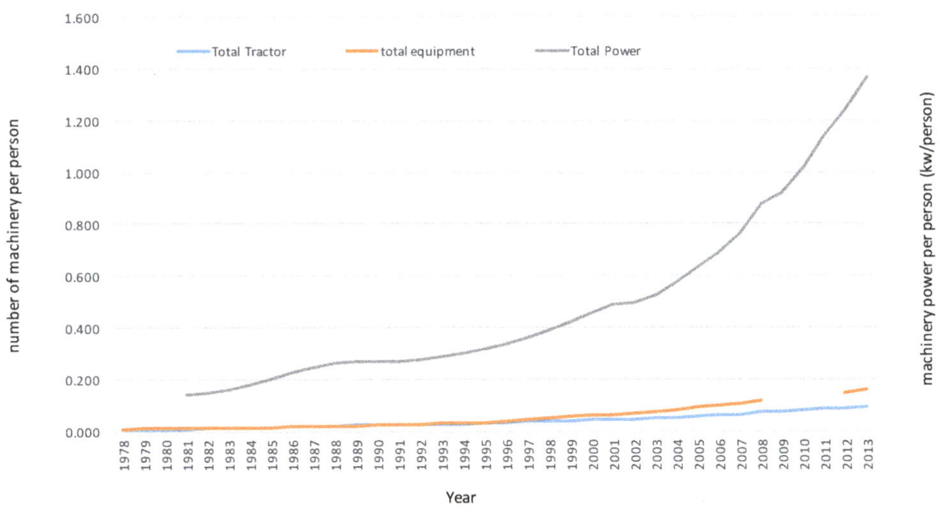

Figure 13.10 Agricultural tractors, attached equipment and total machinery power per capita in China, 1978–2014

Source: Authors' estimates based on data from NBS (1978–2014).

Although the capital–labour ratio in agricultural production has been increasing since the 1980s, the structure of capital equipment (in terms of its per-unit size) has changed over time alongside farm size. Between 1980 and 2003, the share of total engine power of large tractors in total engine power declined from 60 per cent to 20 per cent, while average farm size declined from 0.73 ha to 0.53 ha (Figures 13.11a–b and 13.12). Over this period, the increase in total capital equipment came mainly from increased investment in small tractors and equipment (Figures 13.11a and 13.11b). When average farm size began to increase after 2003, however, the total amount and proportion of large tractors and attached equipment also started to increase. Growth in the use of small tractors and attached equipment, however, began to slow after 2010, implying that the growth in use of large tractors and attached equipment had by then become a driver of growth of total capital equipment. This, in turn, implies that the capital structure of agricultural production in China has, since around 2010, been characterised increasingly by larger plant and equipment as farm size increases, suggesting an increase in capital efficiency (since larger machinery is typically more efficient).

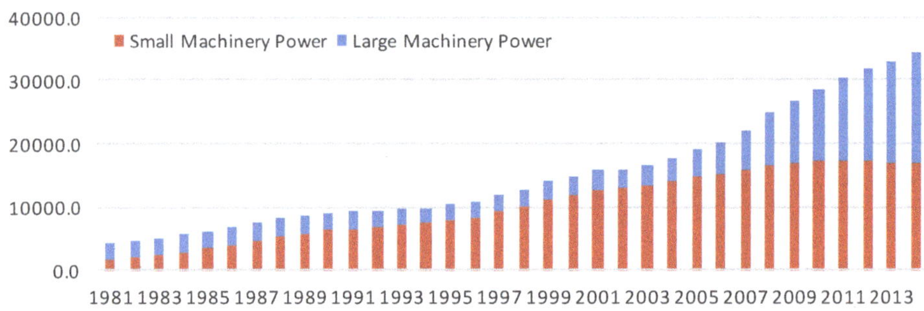

Figure 13.11a Engine power of large tractors and equipment in use, by size: 1978–2014 (billion watts)

Source: Authors' estimates based on data from NBS (1978–2014).

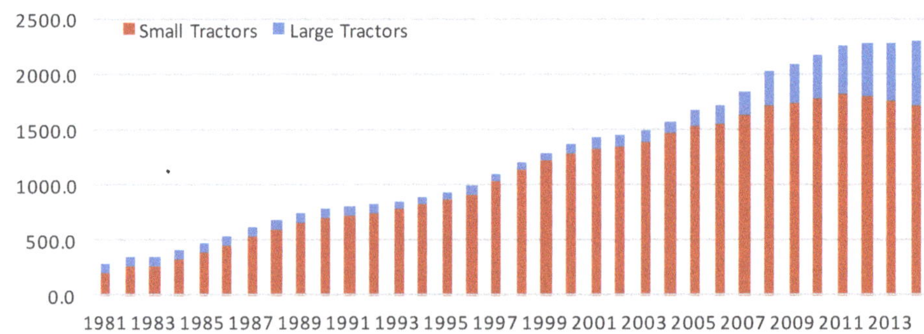

Figure 13.11b Total agricultural machinery in use, by size: 1978–2014 (million)

Source: Authors' estimates based on data from NBS (1978–2014).

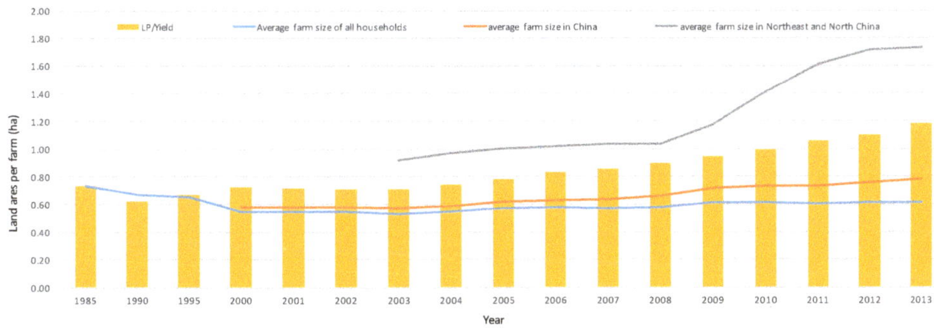

Figure 13.12 Average farm size in China, 1985–2013

Source: Authors' estimates based on data from Huang and Ding (2016b).

In addition to increased farm size, another important factor contributing to the shift in capital structure in China's agricultural production towards large and more efficient plant and equipment after 2003 is rapid development of rural socialisation services (mainly mechanisation services).[2] Between 2008 and 2013, the total number of communities that provided mechanisation services to farm households increased from 8,600 to 42,000—an annual growth rate of 37.2 per cent (Figure 13.13). At the farm level, there were 168,600 professional agencies that provided mechanisation services to farm households in rural China, and more than 12.4 per cent of farm households (5.24 million of 42.4 million) that owned large plant and machinery provided mechanisation services to the market by 2013. This generated total revenue of RMB510.8 billion and total profit of RMB195.6 billion that year. The rapid development of a contract market for capital equipment–related services not only enabled small household farms to access the capital services of large plant and equipment as their large counterparts increased their productivity, but also incentivised capital equipment holders to invest further in large plant and machinery. As a consequence, the relative demand for large and efficient tractors and equipment compared with small and less efficient ones increased rapidly over time.

2 It is also argued that government subsidies for large plant and equipment are another important driver of investment in large plant and machinery (He et al. 2010).

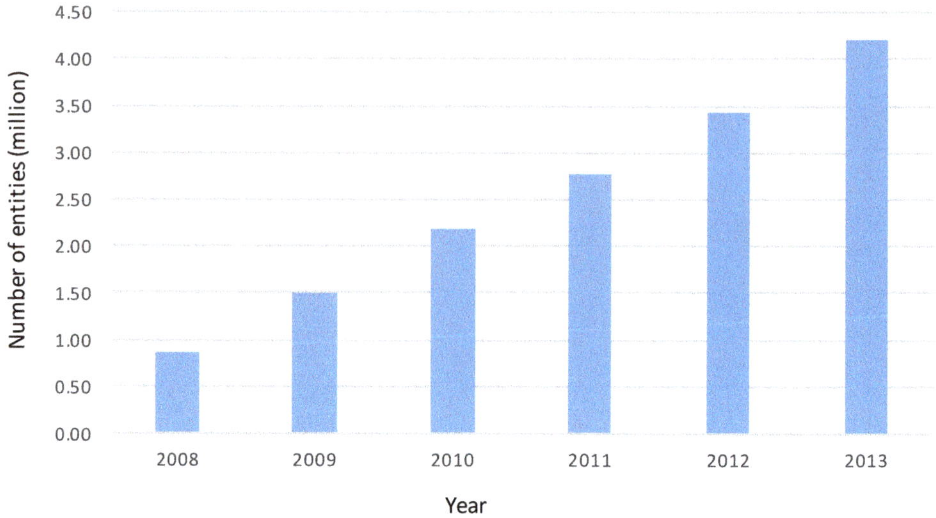

Figure 13.13 The number of communities providing mechanisation services in China, 2008–13

Source: Authors' estimates based on data from NBS (1978–2014).

Although contracted mechanisation services have gradually become an important channel for the promotion of agricultural production mechanisation in China, their impact on total demand for and supply of agricultural capital equipment remains negligible. This is mainly because both land consolidation and average farm size are restricted by high land transaction costs resulting from existing institutional arrangements. In particular, the proportion of market-based contract mechanisation services in total contract mechanisation services is small. By 2013, the total number of market-based contract mechanisation service providers accounted for less than 0.4 per cent of the total number of mechanisation service providers (168,600 out of 425.6 million), among which less than 20 per cent were large machinery holders (with current value of plant and machinery of more than RMB500,000) (Figure 13.14). Increased policy support from the central government since 2014, however, is expected to double the total number of market-based contract mechanisation service providers by 2020 (MOA 2014). Yet, there is still a long way to go before such market-based services can play an important role in substituting for farm-level investment.

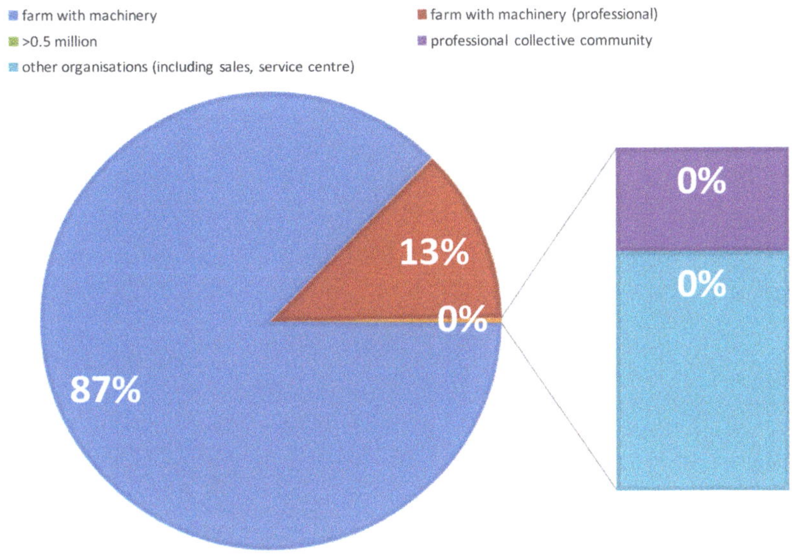

Figure 13.14 Structure of contract mechanisation services, 2013
Source: Authors' estimates based on data from NBS (1978–2014).

Land consolidation and contract mechanisation services: Piece up together

Although land consolidation and contract mechanisation services may help to resolve some of the challenges presented by small-scale farming in China, they are only in a preliminary stage of development, providing different prescriptions for and mechanisms by which to effect on-farm capital equipment use and therefore productivity. Two questions thus arise: 1) Which is more efficient—land consolidation or contract mechanisation services? 2) What is the relationship between land consolidation and contract mechanisation services? To answer these questions, we review three groups of existing studies that analyse the farm size–productivity relationship and its underlying determinants in China, and use findings from these studies to shed light on this issue.

The first body of literature examines the relationship between farm size (in particular, land size) and productivity, which provides useful information to understand the relative contribution of land consolidation to solving small farm–related challenges. Following the literature examining the inverse relationship between farm size and productivity (Assuncao and Ghatak 2003; Deininger and Byerlee 2012), Chen et al. (2010) examine the relationship between farm size and productivity in China using farm-level household survey data between 1995 and 1999. Their study found that total farm output in China declined with cultivated land area, and this could be attributed to local administrative land distribution policies, uneven off-farm work opportunities and heterogeneity in land quality. More recently, Huang and Ding (2016b) re-examined the relationship between farm size and productivity by using farm-level and paddock-level data for the grain industry in north-east and northern China between 2003 and 2013. They provided some evidence of an inverse-U-shaped relationship between farm size and the yield or profitability of the rice, wheat and maize industries in China over the past decade (Figures 13.15 and 13.16), with the optimum land size per farm being 7–15 ha.

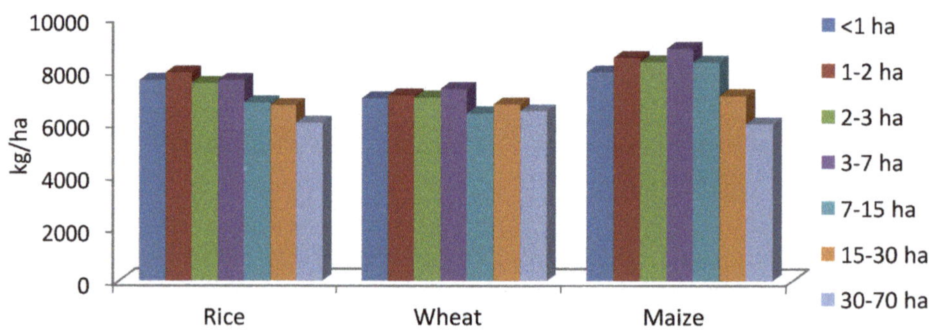

Figure 13.15 Farm size–crop productivity in China, 2013 (hectares)
Source: Huang and Ding (2016b).

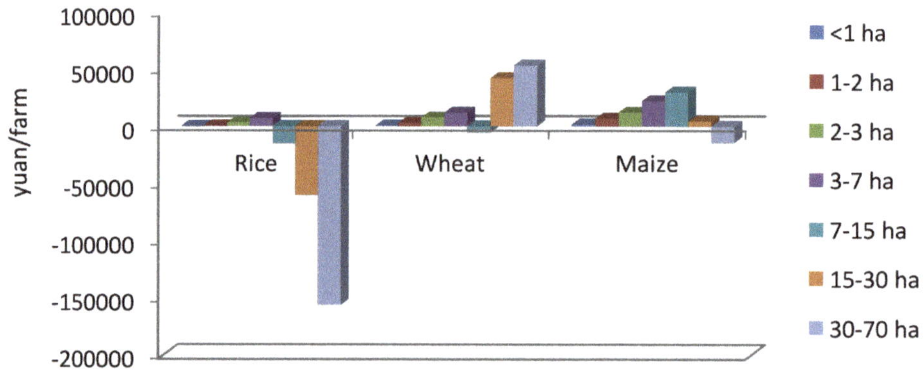

Figure 13.16 Farm size–profitability relationship in China
Source: Huang and Ding (2016b).

Findings from empirical studies examining the farm size–productivity relationship generally suggest that small household farms in China may not benefit from continuing to enlarge their scale of operations. Although this finding about the optimal land size for farm households in China from previous studies is questionable (since the authors did not properly consider the role of increased capital equipment in the farm size–productivity relationship), it highlights the fact that land transactions and consolidation are not sustainable in the long run. It is not known, for example, how quickly land reform could shift the size of most household farms to 7–15 ha (under the current institutional arrangement) and this size, moreover, is probably still too small for farm households to apply new cropping technology (the adoption of minimum-tillage and no-tillage practices requires a minimum of 1,000–2,000 ha of land to apply the traffic control technology) and harvest the increasing returns to scale. In that sense, we can reach a caveat that land reform will facilitate land transfer and consolidation and help to enlarge the operational scale of farms, but it may not necessarily resolve the fundamental issue of small farm size.

Rather than focusing on farm size, a second body of literature (e.g. Yang et al. 2013; Zhang et al. 2017) points out that contract 'mechanised harvesting service clusters' could change the agricultural production of small farms. As the authors argue, a lack of specialisation in labour and capital in particular stages of agricultural production restricted the productivity improvement of small farms in China. To overcome this constraint, small farms could fragment their production process into different stages (as in industrial production and trade) by outsourcing certain stages—for example, those requiring specialised skills such as harvesting and sowing—provided that proper institutional arrangements were in place. The findings of Yang et al. (2013) and Zhang et al. (2017) for the first time draw attention to another option that farms could adopt to compensate for the lack of individually owned labour and capital for production efficiency improvement: cross-regional mechanisation services from related service providers. They tested their argument using a case study of Peixian in Jiangsu province.

Although the mechanism proposed in Yang et al. (2013) and Zhang et al. (2017) does not solve the main problem when agricultural production is broken into stages, and does not seem to be associated only with small farms, it provides an alternative way to think about improving the productivity and profitability of small household farms. In other words, if capital (or labour) services are divisible and separable from their ownership through the market-based contract system to fit the particular size of farms (Figure 13.17), it is no longer necessary to consolidate cultivated land to enlarge farm size (to equip better capital or labour services). In such a process, institutional innovation is essential to erase market failure caused by high transaction costs associated with dividing capital services and allocating them between farms. While outsourced mechanisation services currently account for only a small proportion of total agricultural capital services, a range of farmer cooperatives have begun providing access to capital services across China's provinces in recent years, reflecting the increasing market demand from small farms in Chinese agricultural production (Zhang et al. 2017) and its potential for future development.

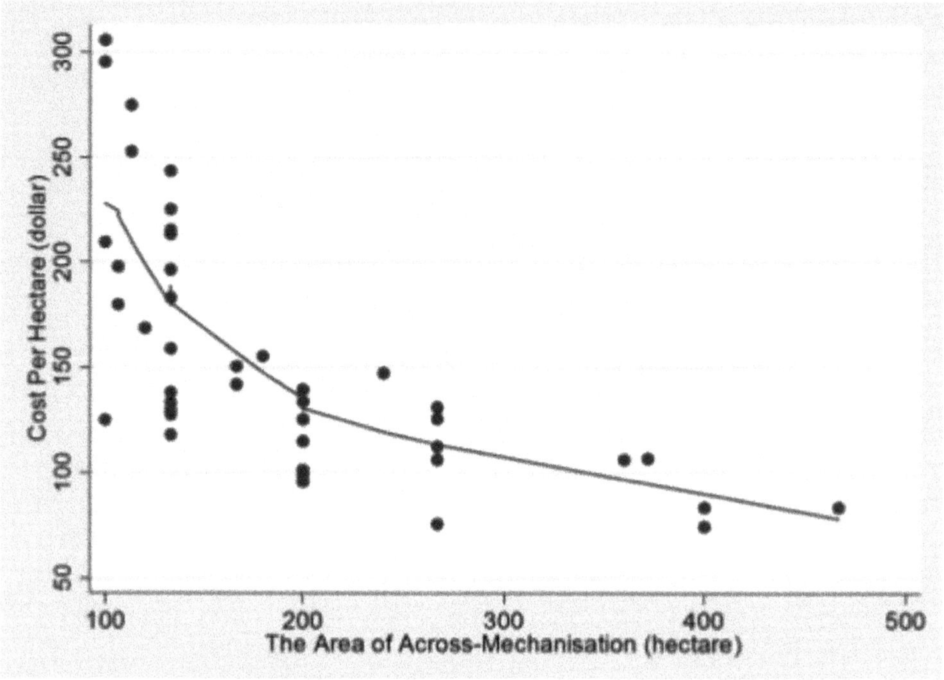

Figure 13.17 Cost per hectare and area harvested of using contracted services from combined service enterprises

Source: Zhang et al. (2017).

Finally, a third body of literature analyses the relationship between land consolidation and contract mechanisation services. While contract mechanisation services allow small farms to catch up with large farms in terms of capital equipment and thus reduce the productivity gap between farms of different size (Sheng and Chancellor 2017), they do not necessarily halt the process of farms becoming larger. In most cases, contract mechanisation services in fact help to facilitate land transfer and consolidation, since farms with superior capital equipment are more likely to efficiently manage larger areas of land. Huang and Ding (2016a) demonstrated that grain farms in China's north-east and north contracting these types of mechanisation services were around 0.12 ha larger than those not using mechanisation services between 2003 and 2013. Moreover, cooperative or company farms were more likely than household farms to preserve this relationship, when other farm and region-specific factors were accounted for. This implies that contract mechanisation services tend to facilitate land consolidation in the Chinese grain industry.

Conclusions

The limited size of household farms in China and in many other developing countries has long been regarded as one of the major constraints on agricultural productivity growth. As an alternative to the conventional recipe in the literature of facilitating land consolidation, this chapter points to the prospect of improving the capital-to-labour ratio of household farms through outsourcing mechanisation services to resolve the issue of small farm size. As a substitute for individual farm investment, market-based capital outsourcing would allow small household farms to access new production technologies embodied in plant and equipment in ways their larger counterparts do and also to capitalise their production process without incurring the corresponding sunk costs. Under certain conditions, the outsourcing of mechanisation services can improve the mechanisation and productivity levels of agricultural production as effectively as land consolidation, but without the huge social and economic costs. In addition, since precision farming technology would improve yields from damaged soil, previous land damage can be overcome with the superior technology available through capital outsourcing.

By outsourcing labour and power-intensive production processes (such as harvesting), some household farms in China have maintained their competitiveness despite their small size and fragmented land (Huang and Ding 2016a; Zhang et al. 2017). Although promising in theory, market-based outsourcing of mechanisation services is constrained by market friction, high transaction costs and various institutional barriers, and therefore is only in its preliminary stages in rural China. By the end of 2013, less than 1 per cent of agricultural capital equipment in Chinese agricultural production came from market-based outsourcing of mechanisation services. Asymmetric information between mechanisation service providers and potential users prevented them from meeting the increasing demand for modernised agricultural production. In turn, institutional innovation is required to reduce market transaction costs to facilitate the use of outsourced mechanisation services, as well as land consolidation reform, to deal with the issue of small farm size in agricultural production.

The Chinese experience provides some useful policy implications for developing new initiatives to improve agricultural productivity in developing countries such as India and Indonesia, where agricultural production is populated with a large share of smallholder farms. Since labour and capital services are divisible, farm size is no longer a limiting factor for scaled production if optimal use of capital equipment can be achieved through the outsourcing of mechanisation.

References

Assuncao, J. and Ghatak, M. (2003), On the inverse relationship between farm size and productivity, *Economics Letters* 80(2): 189–94. doi.org/10.1016/S0165-1765(03)00091-0.

Babu, S. C., Huang, J., Venkatesh, P. and Zhang, Y. (2016), A comparative analysis of agricultural research and extension reforms in China and India, *China Agricultural Economic Review* 7(4): 541–72.

Brandt, L., Huang, J., Li, G. and Rozelle, S. (2002), Land rights in rural China: Facts, fictions and issues, *The China Journal* (47): 67–97. doi.org/10.2307/3182074.

Chen, Z., Huffman, W. E., and Rozelle, S. (2010), Inverse relationship between productivity and farm size: The case of China, *Contemporary Economic Policy* 29(4): 580–92.

Deininger, K. and Byerlee, D. (2012), The rise of large farms in land abundant countries: Do they have a future? *World Development* 40(4): 701–14. doi.org/10.1016/j.worlddev.2011.04.030.

Dyer, G. (1996), Output per acre and size of holding: The logic of peasant agriculture under semi-feudalism, *Journal of Peasant Studies* 24: 103–31. doi.org/10.1080/03066159608438632.

Food and Agriculture Organization of the United Nations (FAO) (2015), *Food and Food Security Data*, October, Rome: FAO.

Food and Agriculture Organization of the United Nations (FAO) (2017), *Statistics*, Rome: FAO. Available from: www.fao.org/statistics/en/.

Foster, A. and Rosenzweig, M. R. (2017), Input transaction costs, mechanization and mis-allocation of land, Conference paper presented to Farm Size and Productivity: A global look, Washington, DC, 2–3 February.

Fuglie, K. and Rada, N. (2015), Methodology for measuring international agricultural total factor productivity (TFP) growth, in *Documentation and Methods*, Washington, DC: United States Department of Agriculture Economic Research Service. Available from: www.ers.usda.gov/data-products/international-agricultural-productivity/documentation-and-methods/.

Han, J. (2015), China: Food security and agricultural going out, in *Strategy Research*, [in Chinese], Beijing: China Development Press.

Hazell, P. B. (2005), Is there a future for small farms? *Agricultural Economics* 32(s1): 93–101. doi.org/10.1111/j.0169-5150.2004.00016.x.

He, W., Zhu, X., Huang, Y., Zhao, X. and Ma, H. (2010), Machinery subsidy policy in China: An empirical analysis, [in Chinese], *Agricultural Mechanisation Study* 4: 195–8.

High Level Panel of Experts on Food Security and Nutrition (HLPE) (2013), *Investing in smallholder agriculture for food security*, Report, Committee on World Food Security, FAO, Rome.

Huang, J. (2013), China's agricultural development in the new era: Opportunities, [in Chinese], *Bulletin of Chinese Academic Science* 3: 295–300.

Huang, J. and Ding, J. (2016a), Institutional innovation and policy support to facilitate small-scale farming transformation in China, *Agricultural Economics* 47: 227–37. doi.org/10.1111/agec.12309.

Huang, J. and Ding, J. (2016b), *An inverse u-shaped relationship between farm size and land productivity or profitability: Evidence from grain production in China*, Working Paper, Center for Chinese Agricultural Policy, Peking University, Beijing.

Huang, J. and Rozelle, S. (2006), The emergence of agricultural commodity markets in China, *China Economic Review* 17: 266–80. doi.org/10.1016/j.chieco.2006.04.008.

Huang, J. and Rozelle, S. (2014), Agricultural R&D and extension, in S. Fan, R. Kanbur, S.-J. Wei and X. Zhang (eds), *The Oxford Companion to the Economics of China*, pp. 315–19, London: Oxford University Press. doi.org/10.1093/acprof:oso/9780199678204.003.0051.

Huang, J. and Yang, G. (2017), Understanding recent challenges and new food policy in China, *Global Food Security* 12(March): 119–26. doi.org/10.1016/j.gfs.2016.10.002.

Huang, J., Gao, L. and Rozelle, S. (2012), The effect of off-farm employment on the decisions of households to rent out and rent in cultivated land in China, *China Agricultural Economic Review* 4: 5–17. doi.org/10.1108/17561371211196748.

Huang, J., Liu, Y., Martin, W. and Rozelle, S. (2009), Changes in trade and domestic distortions affecting China's agriculture, *Food Policy* 34: 407–16. doi.org/10.1016/j.foodpol.2009.04.001.

Huang, J., Wu, Y., Zhi, H. and Rozelle, S. (2008), Small holder incomes, food safety and producing, and marketing China's fruit, *Review of Agricultural Economics* 30: 469–79. doi.org/10.1111/j.1467-9353.2008.00421.x.

International Food Policy Research Institute (IFPRI) (2015), *Global Food Report, 2014–2015*, Washington, DC: IFPRI.

Key, N. (2017), Farm size and productivity growth in the United States corn belt, Conference paper presented to Farm Size and Productivity: A global look, Washington, DC, 2–3 February.

Kimura, S., Otsuka, K. Sonobe, T., Rozelle, S. (2011), Efficiency of land allocation through tenancy markets: evidence from China, *Economic Development Cultural Change* 59: 485–510.

Krusekopf, C. C. (2002), Diversity in land-tenure arrangements under the household responsibility system in China, *China Economic Review* 13(2–3): 297–312. doi.org/10.1016/s1043-951x(02)00071-8.

Kung, J. K.-S. and Liu, S. (1997), Farmers' preferences regarding ownership and land tenure in post-Mao China: Unexpected evidence from eight counties, *The China Journal* (38): 33–63. doi.org/10.2307/2950334.

Lipton, M. (1993), Land reform as commenced business: The evidence against stopping, *World Development* 21(4): 641–57. doi.org/10.1016/0305-750X(93)90116-Q.

Liu, M., Xu, Z., Su, F. and Tao, R. (2012), Rural tax reform and the extractive capacity of local state in China, *China Economic Review* 23: 190–203.

Lu, Y., Jenkins, A., Ferrier, R. C., Bailey, M., Gordon, I. J., Song, S., Huang, J., Jia, S., Zhang, F., Liu, X., Feng, Z. and Zhang, B. (2015), Addressing China's grand challenge of achieving food security while ensuring environmental sustainability, *Science Advances* 1(1): e1400039. doi.org/10.1126/sciadv.1400039.

Meng, X. and Zhang, D. (2010), *Labour market impact of large-scale internal migration on Chinese urban 'native' workers*, IZA Discussion Paper 5288, Institute of Labor Economics, Bonn.

Ministry of Agriculture of China (MOA) (various issues), *China Agriculture Yearbook*, Beijing: China Statistics Press.

Ministry of Agriculture of China (MOA) (2014), The status of transferring rural household responsibility land in 2013, *Rural Business Management* 5: 42.

National Bureau of Statistics of China (NBS) (1978–2014), *China Rural Statistical Yearbook*, Beijing: China Statistics Press.

National Bureau of Statistics of China (NBS) (1985–2005), *China Rural Household Survey Statistical Yearbook*, Beijing: China Statistics Press.

O'Brien, K. and Li, L. (1999), *The Struggle Over Village Elections: The paradox of China's post-Mao reforms*, Cambridge, Mass.: Harvard University Press.

Park, A., Jin, H., Rozelle, S. and Huang, J. (2002), Market emergence and transition: Arbitrage, transition costs, and autarky in China's grain market, *American Journal of Agricultural Economics* 84(1): 67–82. doi.org/10.1111/1467-8276.00243.

Pastor, R. A. and Tan, Q. (2000), The meaning of China's village elections, *The China Quarterly* 162: 490–512. doi.org/10.1017/S0305741000008225.

Prosterman, R., Ping, L. and Zhu, K. (2006), *China's Regulatory Framework on Rural Land: A review and recommendations*, Seattle: Rural Development Institute.

Sen, A. K. (1962), An aspect of Indian agriculture, *Economic Weekly* 14: 243–66.

Sen, A. K. (1966), Peasants and dualism with or without surplus labor, *Journal of Political Economy* 74: 425–50. doi.org/10.1086/259198.

Sheng, Y. and Chancellor, W. (2017), *Exploring the relationship between farm size and productivity: Evidence from the Australian grain industry*, ERS-USDA Working Paper, United States Department of Agriculture Economic Research Service, Washington, DC.

Sheng, Y. and Song, L. (2017), *Agricultural production and food consumption in China: A long-term projection*, CCAP Working Paper Series 2017, Center for Chinese Agricultural Policy, Beijing.

Sheng, Y., Davidson, A., Fuglie, K. and Zhang, D. (2016), Input substitution, productivity performance and farm size, *Australian Journal of Agricultural and Resource Economics* 60(3): 327–47. doi.org/10.1111/1467-8489.12136.

Tao, R. and Qin, P. (2007), How has rural tax reform affected farmers and local governance in China? *China World Economy* 15: 19–32. doi.org/10.1111/j.1749-124X.2007.00066.x.

Yang, J., Huang, Z., Zhang, X. and Reardon, T. (2013), The rapid rise of cross-regional agricultural mechanization services in China, *American Journal of Agricultural Economics* 95(5): 1245–51. doi.org/10.1093/ajae/aat027.

Zhang, F., Chen, X. and Vitousek, P. (2013), Chinese agriculture: An experiment for the world, *Nature* 497: 33–5. doi.org/10.1038/497033a.

Zhang, X., Yang, J. and Reardon, T. (2017), Mechanization outsourcing clusters and division of labor in Chinese agriculture, *China Economic Review* 43(April): 184–95. doi.org/10.1016/j.chieco.2017.01.012.

Zhao, X. (2015), *To Reallocate or Not? Optimal Land Institutions Under Communal Tenure: Evidence from China*, New Haven, Conn.: Campus Press.

Zhu, K. and Prosterman, R. (2007), *Securing land rights for Chinese farmers: A leap forward for stability and growth*, Development Policy Analysis No. 3, Center for Global Liberty and Prosperity, Washington, DC.

14. Technological Progress in Developing Renewable Energies

Kejun Jiang

Recent developments in renewable energy in China

General picture

China is now a leading player in renewable energy development. Annual capacity increases for renewable energy in China account for one-third of the global total. Industry growth has been especially strong since 2011, with annual growth in wind energy of 22 per cent and 110 per cent for solar energy. Since 2015, China has been the world's largest consumer of modern renewable energy. Figure 14.1 illustrates the growth in installed capacity of renewable energy in hydropower, wind power, solar photovoltaic (PV) and biomass in China for the 15 years after 2000.

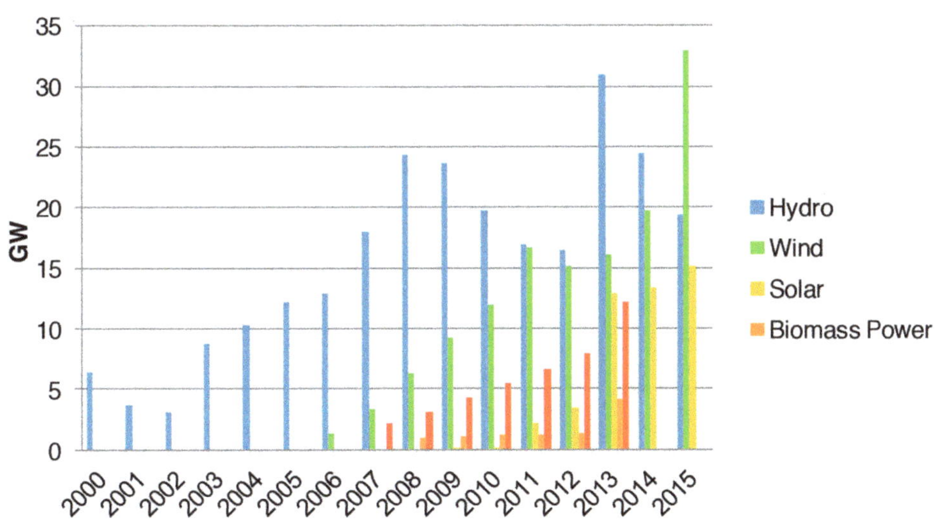

Figure 14.1 Newly installed capacity for selected renewable energy generation in China (gigawatts (GW))

Source: CEC (2017).

Figure 14.1 also draws attention to the importance of policy in promoting the development of renewables in China. After feed-in tariffs (FITs) were announced, wind power and solar power started to expand by largely increasing their annual newly installed capacity.

As an important player in the renewable energy market, China is the leading country, followed by United States, Brazil, Germany and Canada. China has more than one-quarter of the world's total installed renewable power capacity, of some 500 gigawatts (GW). More than half of this, about 296 GW, is hydropower. In terms of non-hydro capacity, the countries with the greatest installed capacity are China, the United States and Germany, followed by Japan, India, Italy and Spain (Figures 14.2 and 14.3).

Global new investment in renewable power and fuels increased to US$285.9 billion in 2015 (not including large hydropower projects that exceed 50 megawatts (MW)), which is 5 per cent higher than in 2014 and exceeds the previous record of US$278.5 billion, set in 2011 (Ren21 2016).

Of the total of US$285.9 billion, China's share of investment was US$102.9 billion—up 17 per cent year-on-year and accounting for 36 per cent of the global total. Most of China's renewables investment was in asset financing, with US$5.5 billion invested in small-scale projects. Wind power led investments in utility-scale projects, of US$47.6 billion, while US$44.3 billion was put into solar power. Offshore wind energy had a breakthrough year in China, with nine projects financed with an around US$5.6 billion. The country also put large investment in large hydropower; 16 GW of new projects started construction during the year, a large portion of which was large hydro.

Overall, this was equivalent to more than one-third of global renewable energy installations in 2015, and generated 3.5 million jobs. In addition, employment in large-scale hydropower in China supported around 440,000 direct jobs, most of which were in construction.

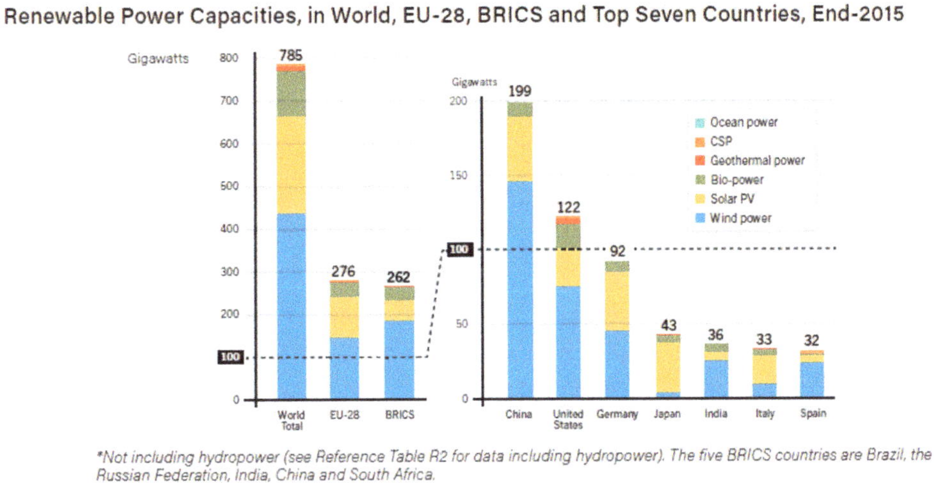

Figure 14.2 Global and selected countries' renewable power capacity
Source: Ren21 (2016).

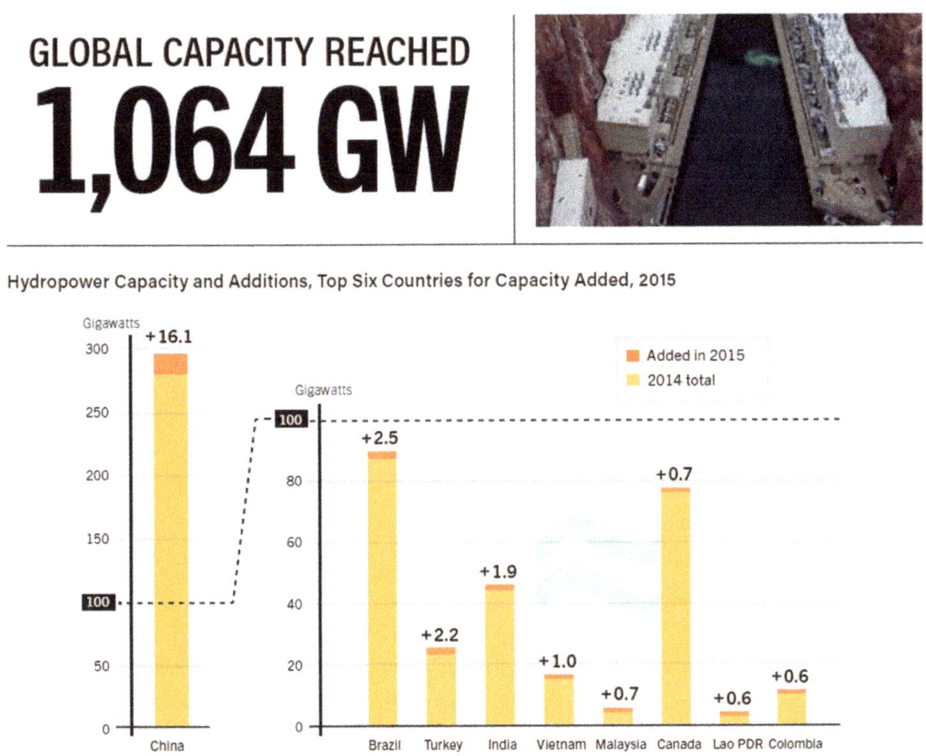

Figure 14.3 Global and selected countries' installed capacity of hydropower
Source: Ren21 (2016).

Progress in 2016

Based on information from the China Electricity Council (CEC), in 2017, China's national electricity demand reached 5919.8 terawatt-hours (TWh)—5 per cent more than in the previous year. Of this, electricity demand from primary industries was 107.5 TWh, the growth rate of which was 5.3 per cent. Electricity consumption of secondary industries was 4,210.8 TWh, up by 11.2 per cent year-on-year. Finally, tertiary industries consumed 796.1 TWh of electricity, up 10.8 per cent on 2015.

In 2016, additional installed national power generation capacity reached 120.6 GW, an increase that was 11.23 GW less than the previous year's increase. In 2016, newly installed capacity for thermal power was 48.36 GW (18.42 GW less than the previous year), 34.59 GW for solar power (20.79 GW more than the previous year), 11.74 GW for hydropower (2.01 GW less than the previous year), 18.73 GW for wind power (12.67 GW less than the previous year) and 7.2 GW for nuclear power (1.08 GW more than the previous year).

By the end of 2016, the total installed capacity of power plants with individual capacity of more than 6 MW reached 1,332.11 GW. The capacity of grid-connected wind power reached 148.64 GW, grid-connected solar power reached 77.42 GW and grid-connected biomass energy reached 12.14 GW. Total national renewable energy capacity reached 570.31 GW, accounting for 34.7 per cent of China's total power capacity.

Non–fossil fuel energy sources accounted for 36.7 per cent of China's total power capacity by 2016. Specifically, national power generation from renewable energy reached 1,552.6 TWh (or 480 million tonnes of coal equivalent (TCE)), accounting for 25.9 per cent of total national power generation. For power plants with individual capacity of more than 6 MW, non–fossil fuel sources generated 1,765.8 TWh (550 million TCE), or 29.5 per cent of the total national power generation from these types of plant.

In 2016, influenced by the benchmark electricity price, solar power capacity increased sharply, with new capacity reaching 34.24 GW—up by 126 per cent year-on-year. In the same year, newly increased capacity for solar PV power stations was 29.98 GW, up by 118 per cent compared with 2015. Newly increased capacity of distributed solar PV power was 4.26 GW, up by 200 per cent compared with 2015; and all together total installed solar PV power capacity was 77.42 GW, up by 79 per cent against 2015, and accounting for 4.7 per cent of the total power capacity.

In 2016, total solar power curtailment[1] reached 74 TWh, up by 53 per cent, the rate of curtailment was 11 per cent, down by 0.3 per cent compared with last year.

1 Curtailment means that renewable energy power plants such as solar PV, wind power and hydropower could not make power generation due to grid dispatch, even though there is solar, wind and water flow available for power generation. This normally happens when there is low electricity demand, some power plants have to reduce their output, grid dispatch will decide which power plant has to shut down or lower its output.

The same year, newly increased capacity for biomass energy was 1.821 GW, for agro-forestry biomass it was 0.746 GW, for waste-to-energy it was 1.057 GW, while for biogas it was 19 MW.

Finally, by the end of 2016, total power capacity for biomass energy reached 12.14 GW, agro-forestry reached 6.05 GW and waste-to-energy generation reached 5.74 GW. In 2016, biomass power generation reached 64.7 TWh, up by 20.1 per cent, while forestry residue and agricultural biomass reached 31.6 TWh.

Technological progress

The rapid development of renewable energy in China has benefited from strong policy support and technological progress (particularly in wind turbines, solar and hydro), which have significantly reduced the costs of these sources.

Wind power

Technological progress for wind power has been concentrated in changes in turbine size, turbine safety and efficiency. China is a leading producer of wind turbines globally, followed by the European Union (EU) and the United States, with manufacturing distributed among relatively few companies. In 2015, by some estimates, China's Goldwind surpassed Vestas of Denmark to become the world's largest supplier of wind turbines—the first time a Chinese company has held this spot. Almost all of Goldwind's recent growth (and that of other Chinese companies) has come from the domestic market, although Chinese companies are increasingly active in new global markets.

One of the major factors in reducing the cost and increasing the efficiency of wind turbines is increasing the generation capacity per unit. In 2009, the global average capacity per wind turbine unit was 1,599 kilowatts (kW); in China it was 1,360 kW, in the United States 1,500 kW and 2–3 MW in Europe. By following the lead of international wind turbine manufacturers, China's producers have increased their unit capacity and are now catching up with their global competitors. In general, the scaling up of wind power plants and price decreases for materials have seen the cost of wind power plants fall significantly over the past decade. In China, in 2015, there was 30.8 GW of new wind power capacity, with total installed capacity more than 145 GW—a level greater than that of the entire European Union (Ren21 2016).

In 2015, new capacity connected into the national grid was 33 GW and started receiving the FIT premium, with approximately 129 GW considered officially grid-connected.

Significant growth was expected in anticipation of reduced FIT levels (as of 1 January 2016), but even amid China's economic slowdown, the market surpassed expectations. The market was also driven by the Chinese Government's push to improve energy security and reduce coal consumption due to growing concerns about climate change and air pollution. Wind energy generated 186.3 TWh of electricity in China during 2015, accounting for 3.3 per cent of total electricity generation in the country (up from 2.8 per cent in 2014) (Ren21 2016).

Across China by province, at the end of 2015, Inner Mongolia had 18.7 per cent of China's total wind power capacity, followed by Xinjiang (12.5 per cent), Gansu (9.7 per cent) and Hebei (7.9 per cent). Since the first three of these areas are far from China's major population centres, difficulties continued in the transmission of this power—a challenge compounded by slow growth in electricity demand (0.6 per cent), which led to significant grid curtailment. Curtailment rose in 2015 to an average 15 per cent, up from 8 per cent in 2014, with 33.9 TWh of potential generation kept from the grid. In addition, many turbines sat unused, awaiting completion of long-distance transmission capacity, which is also the reason some wind power companies have begun building farms in the east and south of the country, where average wind speeds are lower and land is more expensive, but where the turbines are closer to the sources of demand, enabling them to be connected to existing grid infrastructure.

Wind power curtailment in China cost the industry an estimated US$2.77 billion (RMB18 billion) in 2015. To reduce curtailment, the Chinese Government has urged regions in the northwest of the country to attract more energy-intensive industries and to use wind power for heating (with the added benefit that it can displace coal), among other options. Meanwhile, new transmission capacity is under construction and new pumped-hydro storage facilities are being planned. Curtailment challenges could also be seen in other regions—for example, in the United States, curtailment is down dramatically in Texas following the completion of new transmission lines. In 2015, projects were in the planning stage or underway across the globe to strengthen and expand transmission capacity to efficiently move wind-generated electricity to where it is needed.

In 2015 and 2016, newly installed wind power plants were mainly using 1.5–2 MW units. Larger wind turbines were used mainly in offshore wind farms, with the leading manufacturers in Europe and the United States. Siemens, MHI Vestas and Adwen are working to develop wind turbines with a capacity of 8 MW. Chinese companies such as Mingyang are working on units of 6.5–7 MW.

Based on planning in the 'Made in China 2025—Energy Equipment' strategy announced by the National Development and Reform Commission (NDRC), the Ministry of Industry and Information (MII) and the National Energy Administration (NEA) of China, the focus of future research and development (R&D) will be 10 MW offshore wind turbines with a centre height of 100 to 200 m.

One challenge for the wind energy sector is low wind speed. In China, 68 per cent of the total land area experiences low wind speeds, concentrated in central-eastern and southern parts of the country, which are also areas of high population density. Low-speed turbines could run with wind speeds of less than 6.5 metres per second (m/s) or even lower than 5 m/s. With no such kind of technology in other countries, Chinese manufacturers are leading the way in this technology. Since 2015, there has been a greater focus on developing low-speed turbine technologies, both in China and internationally.

By 2014, China had 25.8 GW of low-speed wind power plants installed and grid connected, and the NEA has approved 74.25 GW for development. The first low-speed wind power plant in China was constructed in January 2011 in Lai'an county in Anhui province, with installed capacity of 200 MW and average wind speeds of 5.8 m/s. The plant has 132 wind turbines, each with 1.5 MW of capacity. As with the Lai'an site, most of China's low wind speed areas are hilly or even mountainous and generally complex landscapes, which require more careful site design and higher investment than other areas. At the same time, most low-speed plants are in southeastern China and are therefore close to centres of consumption. Because the utilisation rate for wind turbines is relatively high, there is less problem with curtailment, which is a positive factor for achieving profits from low-speed wind plants. For low-speed plants to be profitable, they need to generate 1,800 to 2,000 equivalent hours per year. While wind turbine blades are becoming longer, it is important to ensure the security and reliability of these power plants.

Plate 14.1 shows the Fenghuangshan wind power plant, developed in 2016, which experiences average wind speeds of less than 6 m/s. In 2016, power generation from Fenghuangshan was 171.6 gigawatt-hours (GWh), the wind turbine utilisation rate was 98.74 per cent and the average wind speed was less than 6m/s. The area is prone to freezing weather and frequent thunderstorms, so the turbine manufacturers had to make technical revisions to respond to these threats.

Plate 14.1 Fenghuangshan wind power plant
Source: www.chinadevelopment.com.cn/news/ny/2017/02/1121750.shtml.

China is also home to offshore wind power generation, with offshore installed capacity reaching 1.627 GW in 2016, an increase from just 900 MW in 2015. In 2016, newly installed offshore wind capacity in China accounted for 26.7 per cent of the global total. Also in 2016, China surpassed Denmark to become the third-largest generator of offshore wind power, after the United Kingdom (5.516 GW) and Germany (3.3 GW).

With more than 18,000 km of coast line, China has potential to generate far greater amounts of offshore wind power than the current 750 GW. Jiangsu, Fujian and Guangdong provinces have the greatest potential for offshore wind power. In 2006, the first offshore wind power plant in China, Rudong, was developed in Zhejiang province.

Development of offshore wind power is growing at a steady pace and is expected to accelerate in the future. China's total installed grid-connected capacity from offshore wind power is forecast to be 30 GW by 2020. Plants in Shanghai, Jiangsu, Zhejiang, Shandong and Fujian provinces are expected to have 25.8 GW of offshore wind power installed by 2020, while in Liaoning, Hebei, Guangdong, Guangxi and Hainan provinces, 9.2 GW of offshore wind energy is planned for 2020. This will mean a total of more than 35 GW of offshore wind power installed by 2020.

The unit capacity of offshore wind turbines has increased, from 2 MW to 4 MW, 5 MW and even larger units. In 2015, among all installed wind turbines, those with a capacity of 2.5 MW accounted for 18.48 per cent, 3 MW 17.74 per cent and 4 MW 34.69 per cent. In 2017, most offshore turbines are 4 to 6 MW units. Offshore turbines must be resistant to corrosion and able to withstand especially high wind speeds—factors that must be incorporated into their design. Engineering modelling and analysis tools are required to lower the costs of offshore facilities and to design the next generation of large-scale turbines optimised for operation in the marine environment.

In May 2014, the total capacity of offshore wind power in China was 565 MW, which increased to about 900 MW in 2015. This is, however, less than one-fifth of the earlier target (Figure 14.4). The development of offshore wind power in China has been slower than expected due mainly to the lack of experience of domestic turbine manufacturers. As a result, local developers must use foreign products, with Siemens the largest supplier of offshore wind turbines in China. Other limiting factors are the huge investment needed and the associated risks of offshore development, which discourage private companies.

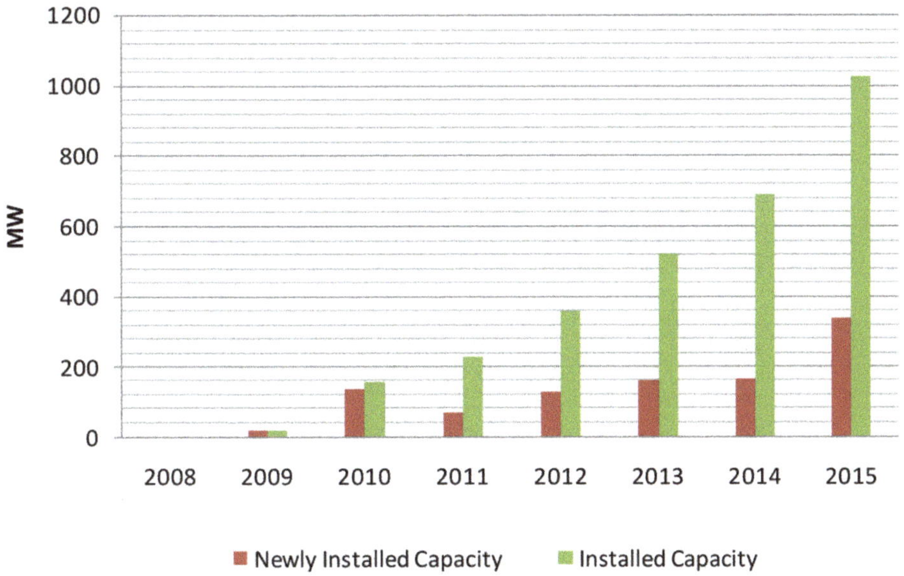

Figure 14.4 Planned and realised installed offshore wind power capacity in China

Source: CEC (2017).

Another key factor in reducing the cost and extending the scale of wind power generation is improving the onsite installation of wind farms. Chinese companies are now leading the world for wind installation, both onshore and offshore.

Wind power costs in general have shifted over time. Since 2008, there has been a cost reduction of about 35 per cent. In 2016, the average cost for onshore wind power was about RMB7,000 per kilowatt-hours (kWh). For example, for low-speed wind power plants in southern China, the cost for turbines is about RMB4,000/kW, with construction costs of RMB4,000–4,500/kW.

By 2016, the investment cost for establishing wind farms in China was the lowest in the world, at US$1,050/kW, compared with US$2,500/kW in Japan and US$1,600/kW in the United States and Europe. In some areas with good wind conditions and relatively high costs for fossil fuel–fired power plants, wind power already competes on cost with new coal-fired thermal power, including in Australia, Chile, Mexico, New Zealand, Turkey and South Africa.

The cost of wind power generation includes the costs of the turbines, base and installation, connection with the grid and ongoing operation costs. For example, for a low-speed wind farm in southern China, the cost of wind turbines is RMB4,000/kW, the installation cost is RMB4,000–4,500/kW, operation costs are RMB120–130/kW, labour costs are RMB30/kW with other material costs of RMB70/kW. Such a wind farm could be RMB0.51 to RMB0.54 per kWh levelised cost of electricity (LCOE) by setting a discount rate of 8 per cent, which is lower than the FIT, making the plant profitable. In northern China, however, construction costs are lower, but, due to curtailment, the equivalent utilisation hours will also be lower. If the investment cost is RMB7,500/kW, the LCOE is RMB 0.57/kWh, which is higher than the local FIT, meaning it will be difficult to make the plant profitable.

Future cost reductions for wind power will be found mainly in lowering the overall cost and increasing power output by, for example: 1) increasing the performance and lowering the cost of turbines; 2) improving turbine module design and lowering the cost of installation; 3) increasing turbine blade diameter, which increases its efficiency; 4) increasing turbine reliability; and 5) lowering the cost of operation and maintenance. There is some potential to reduce the cost of material, which would lower the cost of turbines. Improved wind forecasting would also increase the reliability, and therefore lower the cost of wind power.

Future wind power development will include increasing the unit capacity of turbines, increasing the efficiency of wind capture and conversion, increasing the quality of components and the efficiency of component transportation and increasing the adaptability of turbines to different environments.

Solar

Technological progress

China is the world's leading country for both solar PV and solar thermal energy, with more than 400 solar PV companies alone. Solar water heating is also used extensively, with a total installed capacity of 290 GWh at the end of 2014, accounting for about 70 per cent of the total global installed solar thermal capacity. In 2016, newly installed solar capacity in China reached 34.59 GW, with total solar grid-connected capacity reaching 77.42 GW.

The Chinese Government has continually raised installation targets to increase renewable generation, address the severe pollution problems and promote the domestic manufacturing industry. In 2015, China added an estimated solar PV capacity of 15.2 GW for a total approaching 44 GW, overtaking long-time leader Germany to become the top country for cumulative solar PV capacity, with about 19 per cent of the global total. The provinces of Xinjiang (2.1 GW), Inner Mongolia (1.9 GW) and Jiangsu (1.7 GW) were the top markets for the year, with much of this capacity located far from the country's main population centres. However, six provinces in the eastern and central regions each had more than 1 GW of solar PV capacity at 2015. Large-scale solar PV power plants accounted for 86 per cent of total capacity, with the remainder in distributed rooftop systems and other small-scale installations (Ren21 2016).

In support of the development of the solar sector, various solar PV subsidies have been introduced over the past decade. The 'Golden Sun' program was initiated in 2009, providing capital subsidies for solar PV installations through to 2011 on a project-by-project basis. Off-grid (stand-alone) installations receive 70 per cent capital subsidies while grid-connected installations receive 50 per cent subsidies. Qualifying grid-connected installations, however, must have a peak capacity of 300 kW or larger. There are also program caps, which limit the overall quantity of systems installed; under the terms of the program, installations in any given province are limited to a total of 20 MW.

Almost 300 projects have been proposed under the Golden Sun program, totalling 640 MW and entailing about RMB20 billion (US$2.9 billion) in investment. As a separate part of the program, the Ministries of Finance and Construction are providing subsidies of RMB15 per watt (US$2.20/W) for grid-connected solar PV and RMB20/W (US$2.90/W) for building-integrated PV. Eligible installations must be 50 kW or larger and must utilise solar PV modules achieving minimum efficiency levels (16 per cent for monocrystalline, 14 per cent for polycrystalline and 6 per cent for amorphous). In 2010, the subsidy levels were reduced to RMB13/W (US$1.90/W) for grid-connected modules and RMB17/W ($2.50/W) for building-integrated modules.

With parallels to the early development of the wind power industry, the government initiated a new competitive bidding program for solar PV projects in 2009. This program is creating new benchmark tariffs for solar PV (so-called approved price levels) on the basis of competitive bidding. One example was a bidding process in Dunhuang, in Gansu province, in 2009 for two 10 MW projects. Bid prices ranged from aslo was RMB0.69/kWh (US$0.10/kWh) and resulted in an approved price of RMB1.09/kWh (US$0.16/kWh). Another approved price was RMB1.15/kWh (US$0.17/kWh) in April 2010 for four projects in Ningxia totalling 40 MW.

Finally, at the provincial level, there are also cases of preferential tariffs for solar PV, such as those in Zhejiang and Jiangsu. In Zhejiang in 2009, the tariff was set at a premium of RMB0.70/kWh (US$0.10/kWh), added to the province average coal power generation price, which was RMB0.46/kWh (US$0.07/kWh), thus producing a total tariff of RMB1.16/kWh (US$0.17/kWh). Jiangsu set preferential tariffs significantly higher than Zhejiang, and also established a range of tariffs according to technology type: RMB2.1/kWh (US$0.31/kWh) for ground-based systems, RMB3.7/kWh (US$0.54/kWh) for roof top systems and RMB4.3/kWh (US$0.63/kWh) for building-integrated systems (all prices at 2009 levels). Jiangsu also slated tariffs to decrease progressively, to RMB1.7/kWh for ground-based systems, RMB3/kWh for rooftop systems and RMB3.5/kWh for building-integrated systems in 2010, and to RMB1.4/kWh for ground-based systems, RMB2.4/kWh for rooftop systems and RMB2.9/kWh for building-integrated systems in 2011.

The rapid increase in solar PV capacity in China has, however, caused problems with grid congestion and interconnection delays. Curtailment started to become a serious challenge in 2015, with particularly high rates in the northwestern provinces of Gansu (31 per cent over the year) and Xingjiang Autonomous Region (26 per cent), and a national average of 12 per cent. By year's end, insufficient grid capacity was a significant hurdle for new plants, and investors were growing wary of the sector due to delays in subsidy collection and problems with solar panel quality. To address challenges related to curtailment, the Chinese Government has asked top solar-producing provinces to prioritise transmission of renewable energy, build more transmission capacity and attract more energy-intensive industries to increase local consumption. Against these transmission and curtailment challenges, solar PV generated 2 TWh of electricity in China during 2015—up about 57 per cent from 2014. Chinese companies have also flocked across the border, to Pakistan in particular, where China played an increasingly important role in that country's renewable energy expansion, including in solar PV.

Given the rapid pace of expansion and incentive schemes, many of China's solar product manufacturers experienced low profit margins, excess production capacity and significant debt. For example, Tianwei in 2015 defaulted on an interest payment for a domestic bond and then collapsed, while, in 2017, Yingli required a government bailout and, in 2016, Hanergy came under investigation by Hong Kong's Securities and Futures Commission. In general, power production curtailment and delays in subsidy payments have forced some developers in China to sell off projects and halt further development.

The expansion of renewable energy became one of seven categories of business to receive special attention, including loans and tax incentives, under China's five-year plans, especially the Twelfth Five-Year Plan for industry development. The result was the creation of the world's largest solar manufacturing industry—which has become the price leader in most aspects of the global market, beginning with cheaper solar panels. Another result, however, was that China led the creation of a worldwide glut. There were roughly two panels being made for every one ordered by an overseas customer. Between 2008 and 2013, China's fledgling solar-electric panel industry confronted world prices that had dropped by 80 per cent—a stunning achievement even in a fiercely competitive high-tech market.

China's environment is well suited to an advanced solar industry, with some 70 per cent of the most suitable areas concentrated in the western and northern provinces. The annual solar energy received by China's land surface is estimated to be equivalent to 4.9 trillion tonnes of standard coal. Moreover, China has large areas of desert suitable for hosting concentrating solar power (CSP) stations. It has 2.64 million sq km of arid and desert land, where solar energy resources are abundant. In Xinjiang alone, there are 1.11 million sq km of desert land.

Prominent projects include the first phase of the Qinghai Delingha Solar Thermal Power Generation Project, which will use Bright Source Energy's proven solar tower technology to produce clean, reliable solar electricity for more than 452,000 homes. Located in Qinghai province in northwestern China, the Delingha project will have six 135 MW CSP tower plants, with the first phase including two 135 MW solar plants with up to 3.5 hours of thermal energy storage. It is expected construction will be completed in 2017.

Meanwhile, China is home to the world's largest solar park, which the US National Aeronautics and Space Administration (NASA) has published satellite images of (Plate 14.2). Also in Qinghai province, the plant has a startling scale of some 850 MW. Landsat 8 satellite images taken in January 2017 capture the four million solar panels installed at the site, which cover an area equivalent in size to Macau.

Plate 14.2 Satellite image of Delingha solar PV project in Qinghai province

Source: NASA image. Available from: www.pv-magazine.com/2017/0202/nasa-images-show-stunning-progress-of-chinas-vast-850-mw-longyangxia-solar-park/.

Plate 14.2 comprises two images: the view on the left is from April 2013, while the image on the right shows how the plant looked in February 2017. The Delingha plant became the largest solar power plant in the world, surpassing the 648 MW Kamuthi Solar Power Project in Tamil Nadu, India. China is also currently constructing an even larger installation, in the Ningxia autonomous region, with a capacity of 2 GW.

CSP is still in the early stages of commercial application in China. It is closely related to traditional methods of power generation, which helps to lower the risk of technological development. China has established ambitious goals for CSP deployment and, despite a slow start, it remains a particularly exciting concept with thermal storage applications, especially given the country's strong commitment to diversifying and decarbonising its energy mix.

Solar thermal plants can harness solar energy by using molten salt as a heat-transfer medium, which improves the efficiency of the power generation system by providing higher temperatures and a more stable medium. Old CSP systems used oil or water as the medium, but oil could not reach high temperatures and, while water was easy to turn into steam, it had to be contained at high pressure. China's first molten salt solar thermal power plant has started to send electricity to the grid. The Tianjin Binhai Concentrating Solar Power Investment Co. Ltd said its 50 MW molten salt trough project in Akesai in northwest China's Gansu province demonstrates the maturity of the commercial development of solar thermal technology. The company will carry out large-scale production with the technology in 2018, when it is scheduled to produce facilities with 200 MW of annual solar power output. The Akesai plant was among 20 demonstration solar thermal plants listed for construction by China's NEA in 2016 as the government eyes off the potential of renewable energy.

The Twelfth Five-Year Plan (2011–15) called for the installation of 1 GW by 2015 and 3 GW by 2020 of CSP plants. Plants either being planned or under construction include the following:

1. 1 MW Badaling Pilot Project—a collaboration between the Institute of Electrical Engineering (IEE) and the Chinese Academy of Sciences (CAS).
2. 12 MW (short-term)/300 MW (long-term) collaboration between Xinjiang Qingsong Building Materials and Chemicals (Group) Co. and Guodian Xinjiang Company.
3. 50 MW project in Tibet by Huaneng Tibet Company.
4. 100 MW project in Sichuan's Ngawa Tibetan and Qiang Autonomous Prefecture (Aba) by Tianwei New Energy.
5. 50 MW project (to be determined) by China Huadian Corporation.
6. 100 MW project in Golmud by GD ENERGY.
7. 100 MW project in Ningxia by Beijing Control Technology Co. Ltd.
8. 100 MW project (to be determined) by Avic Xi'an Aero-Engine (Group) Ltd.
9. 100 MW project (to be determined) by Guangdong Kangda.
10. 100 MW project in Gansu by SETC Tianjin.
11. 1,000 MW project in Qinghai by Lion International Investment Ltd.
12. 2,000 MW project in Shaanxi by Shandong PenglaiDianli and eSolar.

CSP is planned to reach 5 GW of electricity generation by 2020, which is more than the total global installed capacity of CSP in 2015. Construction of the 50 MW Qinghai Delingha facility commenced in late 2015. The facility, which will be the country's first commercial CSP plant, is expected to come online in 2017. Additional facilities totalling several hundred megawatts are in various stages of construction, although timelines for completion remain unclear.

Another utilisation of solar energy is for water heating. China dominates the global market for solar water heating, accounting for more than 70 per cent of the world total. China was the largest market by far in 2015, with gross additions of 30.45 GW thermal (GWth) (43.5 million sq m of panel area)—21 times more capacity than was added in second-placed Turkey. At year's end, China's cumulative capacity in operation was an estimated 309.4 GWth, or about 71 per cent of the world's total. China's market contracted for the second consecutive year—falling 17 per cent in 2015 after an 18 per cent drop in 2014—due to the slowdown in the construction industry and the weaker national economy.

Solar water heaters utilise various technologies, such as vacuum tubes, heat pipe solar tubes, flat plate collectors and solar cylinders. Vacuum tubes continued to dominate the Chinese market in 2015, accounting for 87 per cent of added capacity; however, flat plate collectors were still popular, especially for roof and facade integration in urban areas. Heat pipe solar tubes are the most advanced option, but also the most expensive. In China, solar thermal systems for use in multi-family houses and in the tourism and public sectors accounted for 61 per cent of the newly installed collector area in 2015.

Producers and cost changes

China has been the world's largest manufacturer of solar panels since 2008 and, since 2011, has produced the majority of the world's PV systems on an annualised basis. Industry projections estimate that, by the end of 2017, China will have enough manufacturing capacity to produce 51 GW of photovoltaics a year. Domestic demand in China was around 34 GW in 2016—more than twice as much as global production in 2010, of 24 GW.

The industry is dominated by several major manufacturers, including CHINT Group Corporation, JA Solar Holdings, Jinniu Energy, Suntech Power, Yingli, China Sunergy and Hanwha Solar One. Several manufacturers are confronting challenges of large debts.

Within 10 years, the cost of solar PV panels in China dropped significantly, from above RMB50 per watt to RMB4/W, while system costs reduced from RMB60/W to RMB7/W, a decrease rate of more than 85 per cent. With the reduction in investment costs, the cost of solar PV power generation also reduced, by 76 per cent, which increased market competitiveness.

The main driver of such cost reductions is the scaling up of solar PV power via technological innovation. Rapid increases in the market boost manufacturing volumes while lowering production costs. Technological innovation created new products that were more efficient to manufacture and delivered higher efficiency of power generation.

Hydro

Overview

Hydropower in China is still the cheapest source of power generation, and hydro-electricity is the most cost-effective and stable form of renewable energy. This allows developers to install hydro-electric power without the need for considerable FITs. Hydropower also benefits from flexibility, with plants able to adjust their output quickly in response to changing energy demands over certain periods.

From 2010 to the end of 2016, newly installed capacity for hydropower in China reached 103.48 GW, following year-on-year growth of 8.1 per cent. Of this, newly installed large hydropower accounted for 80.76 GW, small hydro for 16.6 GW and pumped storage hydro for 6.12 GW. Total capacity for hydropower reached

319.54 GW, accounting for 27 per cent of the global total. Of that total, large hydro contributed 221.51 GW, small hydro 75 GW and pumped storage hydro 23.03 GW. Hydropower generation in China produces 1,100 TWh, accounting for 19.4 per cent of total national power output and 73.7 per cent of non–fossil fuel power generation. Of the 10 largest hydropower stations in the world, five are in China. Half of all hydropower units with capacity above 700 MW globally are operated by China Three Gorges Corporation.

Moreover, many additional hydro projects are under construction in China (Table 14.1). Newly started construction capacity is 20.9 GW in 2015, which is the highest level in history.

Table 14.1 Hydropower projects under construction in China

Type	River/grid	Power station
Regular hydropower	Jinsha River	Wudongde, Liyuan, Suwalong, Ahai, Ludila, Longkaikou, Guanyinyan
	Yalongjiang River	Lianghekou, Yangfanggou
	Daduhe River	Shuangjiangkou, Houziyan, Huangjinping, Angu, Zhentouba, Shaping second level
	Yellow River	Liujiaxia(extension), Huangfeng
	Other rivers	Mamaya, Fengman(rebuild), Xiaoxuan, Lizhou, Kajiwa, Duobu
Pumped storage hydropower	North China Grid	Fengning, Wendeng, Yimeng
	East China Grid	Jixi, Jinsai, Chuanglongshan
	Middle China Grid	Tianchi, Panlong
	Northeast China Grid	Dunhua, Huanggou
	Southern China Grid	Qiongzhong, Shenzhen, Meizhou, Yangjiang

Source: NDRC (2007).

Although hydropower is an efficient type of renewable energy from a production and FIT perspective, it also presents some challenges, including long development periods, associated social displacement and environmental concerns, as well as the increasing difficulty of accessing potential development sites. These factors suggest that China's investment in hydropower will decline after 2020. The social and environmental consequences of large hydropower installations present another challenge. Almost 1.5 million people were displaced for the construction of the Three Gorges Dam. Migration is becoming a key issue in the development of hydropower and will complicate future development of the sector.

The major international providers of hydropower equipment are GE (United States), Andritz Hydro (Austria) and Voith Hydro (Germany), each with roughly equal market share. Together, they account for about half of the global industry. Other notable manufacturers include Harbin (China), Dongfang (China) and Power Machines (Russian Federation).

A slowdown in the development of hydropower in China and market saturation are inspiring Chinese corporations to increase their involvement in hydropower projects around the world. Their involvement has included both construction and operation, with a particular focus on Africa, South Asia and South America. In early 2016, China Three Gorges Corporation acquired two hydropower plants in Brazil, becoming that country's second-largest private power producer.

Based on the newly published Thirteenth Five-Year Plan for hydropower development in China, the target for installed hydropower capacity is 380 GW, of which 340 GW is normal hydropower and 40 GW is pumped hydro storage. Annual power generation will be 1,250 TWh, accounting for more than 50 per cent of total non–fossil fuel power generation.

Total hydropower resources available for development are 660 GW, with annual power generation of about 3,000 TWh. There is uneven distribution, with 70 per cent of hydropower resources in the south-west of the country.

In terms of technological developments, China is the world leader in developing hydropower, from planning, design and construction to equipment manufacture, operation and maintenance.

In recent years, major technological progress in hydropower has included construction of a 300-m-high arch dam in complex geological conditions, a super high core rockfill dam with gravel soil, a 35-m-wide underground hydropower house and multiple deep-ground water headrace tunnels. The 800 MW Francis-type hydropower turbine and 350 MW pumped hydro power units with 500 m head could be manufactured in China. Constructed in the past few years were the world's highest concrete double-curvature arch dam (Jinping First-Grade Hydropower Station), deep–long tunnel hydropower (Jinping Second-Grade Hydropower Station), the world's third-largest hydropower station (Luoxidu Hydropower Station) and a hydropower station in complex geological conditions (Dagangshan Hydropower Station).

Newly announced hydropower development plans for China focus on development of a grid and transmission system because of the uneven distribution of hydropower resources throughout the country. Based on current planning, more than 100 GW of hydropower will ultimately be transmitted from the west of the country to the east.

There are nonetheless challenges confronting the hydropower sector in China. Environmental issues are receiving increased public attention, making it more difficult to implement new projects. It is becoming more difficult to forcibly relocate populations away from potential hydro project areas. New hydro projects are therefore tending to move towards remote regions and areas of low economic development. In such areas, hydropower is seen as a means of developing the local economy, and low population density also reduces migration costs.

Biomass

Biomass energy refers to energy from agricultural residues and waste, forestry products and waste, bioethanol, biodiesel and biogas from animal husbandry and municipal waste. China has large biomass energy potential. For a long time, the government promoted traditional biomass utilisation including of straw and firewood for energy generation in rural areas. High-efficiency biomass stoves, biomass-heated beds and biomass digesters were supported by rural energy policies for decades. Policies for modern biomass energy utilisation were initiated from 2005. By 2010, the total installed capacity of biomass power generation in China had reached 5.5 GW. The annual utilisation rate of densified biofuels had been as high as 1 million tonnes and that of biogas 19 billion cubic metres; the utilisation rate of ethanol fuel from non-grain raw materials reached 2 million tonnes and that of biodiesel reached 200,000 tonnes (State Council 2011).

Since 1995, China has included biomass energy in its national five-year plans. In the Ninth Five-Year Plan (1996–2000), the development of highly efficient anaerobic technology for treating high-concentration organic wastewater and urban garbage was listed as a key science and technology program. During the Tenth Five-Year Plan (2001–05), development planning for the agricultural biomass energy industry was introduced. Each plan since the Eleventh Five-Year Plan has contained special planning for the biomass energy industry.

A scheme for the comprehensive utilisation of crop straws during the Twelfth Five-Year Plan (2011–15), issued in 2011, points to further development of output generation from this source. It was planned to achieve a straw utilisation rate of more than 80 per cent and straw energy utilisation rate of 13 per cent by 2015. Twelfth Five-Year Plan targets for renewable energy development and biomass energy development, issued in 2012, stipulated that, by 2015, the annual utilisation rate of biomass energy would exceed 50 million TCE. When total installed capacity of biomass power generation reaches 13 GW and related annual power generation is up to about 78 TWh, the annual biomass supply will be up to 22 billion cu m, densified biofuel will be 10 million tonnes and biological liquid fuel 5 million tonnes. Planning for biomass energy in the Thirteenth Five-Year Plan is under way.

On the one hand, the development and utilisation of biomass energy offer potential to replace thermal energy sources and therefore better protect the environment. On the other hand, the costs of development and utilisation are so far unable to compete with those of traditional energy sources. This has led the Chinese

Government to adopt a series of incentive measures for enterprises and users to ease this cost burden and directly subsidise the development and utilisation of biomass energy. The main measures include front-end incentives to encourage development of the biomass energy production chain and market back-end incentives to stimulate sales and use, as well as some indirect incentives to promote the development of the whole industry.

In China, biopower capacity reached 10.3 GW in 2015, an increase of 0.8 GW over the previous year. Generation was up 16 per cent compared with 2014, to around 48.3 TWh. The Twelfth Five-Year Plan set a target of 13 GW by 2015, but actual installed capacity for biomass power generation has not reached that target. Factors that have restricted progress include high prices for feedstock, poor coordination among projects and technical operating difficulties.

China, the world's third-largest ethanol producer, produced an estimated 2.8 billion litres in 2015—a 14 per cent decrease. China increased ethanol imports during that year but added no new production capacity, in part because of a moratorium on maize-based ethanol production. Asia's other major producer, Thailand, saw its ethanol production rise by 10 per cent, from 1.1 billion litres in 2014 to 1.2 billion litres in 2015. China's biodiesel production is estimated to have increased substantially—by an estimated 24 per cent—to 0.35 billion litres in 2015 (Ren21 2016).

Based on the Thirteenth Five-Year Plan's goals for renewable energy, the target for 2020 for total installed capacity of biomass power generation is 30 GW; the annual utilisation rate of densified biofuel will be 50 million tonnes, biogas 44 billion cu m, non-grain raw material fuel ethanol 10 million tonnes and biodiesel 2 million tonnes.

Other renewables

The countries with the largest direct-use geothermal power capacity are China (6.1 GW), Turkey (2.9 GW), Japan (2.1 GW), Iceland (2 GW), India (1 GW), Hungary (0.9 GW), Italy (0.8 GW) and the United States (0.6 GW). In line with installed capacity, China utilised the most direct geothermal heat (20.6 TWh).

China is also developing ocean-energy technologies—both tidal and wave energy. In 2015, there were 10.7 MW of capacity installed, including several projects in development. The Jiangxia tidal power plant was upgraded in 2015, from 3.9 MW to 4.1 MW. Among new development projects is the 100 kW Sharp Eagle wave energy converter, which was deployed in 2015. China's experience to date is that the country's current tidal technologies exhibit significantly lower cost structures than its wave energy projects, but all are limited by immature technology and lack of experience and supporting infrastructure.

Policy development

Development of new and clean sources of renewable energy in China is a key strategic measure for fostering emerging industries of national importance. It is also promoted as part of national action towards protection of the environment, responses to climate change and achievement of sustainable development. China worked to increase the shares of non-fossil fuels in primary energy consumption to 11.4 per cent and installed generation capacity to 20 per cent by the end of 2030.

Against the background of a global energy crisis, local air pollution and climate change, the development of renewable energy utilisation technology has important practical and long-term significance for replacing fossil fuels and realising the sustainable development of humanity. China's energy security has become an increasingly prominent issue, environmental constraints have increased and the situation for energy savings and emission reductions is grim. In this context, the government has prioritised adjustment of China's energy structure and development of alternative, green, clean, low-carbon renewable energy sources. Biomass energy—with plentiful resources and stable supply—can substitute for coal, oil and gas in huge quantities. It can also significantly reduce pollution and achieve near-zero emissions of carbon dioxide. In recent years, therefore, governments at all levels in China have increased their focus on renewable energy and introduced a series of policies and measures for the sector.

The basic framework of China's renewable energy development policies include the Renewable Energy Law, a medium- and long-term development plan for renewable energy and each five-year plan as the short-term plan to attract producers and users to participate in the development and utilisation of renewable energy through the establishment of a series of effective incentive mechanisms.

Legal basis

The Renewable Energy Law of the People's Republic of China was issued in 2005 and formally implemented on 1 January 2006. This is the first energy law in China and indicates the importance the Chinese Government has placed on renewable energy.

The Renewable Energy Law was revised at the end of 2009 and the new edition was implemented on 1 April 2010. The amendment established the Renewable Energy Development Fund to be collected by additional charging from grid on electricity, to support the development of renewable energy.

Target system

The Chinese Government's plan for medium- and long-term renewable energy development aimed to increase renewable energy's share of total energy consumption to 10 per cent in 2010 (from 7.5 per cent in 2005) and to 16 per cent by 2020. The plan treats wind power generation as a key renewable energy source and sets medium and long-term wind power development goals through to 2020 (Table 14.2).

The plan places emphasis on the development of renewable energy, including wind, solar, hydro, biomass, biogas, densified biofuel and biological liquid fuel. Table 14.2 shows the targets set in the plan according to the requirements of China's economic and social development and biomass energy utilisation technology.

Table 14.2 Renewable energy development targets for China

	2005	2010	2020
Renewable energy's share of total energy consumption	7.2%	10%	16%
Annual renewable energy consumption	160 m TCE	270 m TCE	530 m TCE
Renewable energy's share (excluding hydropower) of total power generation	–	1%	3%
Hydropower generation capacity	117 GW	180 GW	300 GW
Wind power generation capacity	1.26 GW	5 GW	30 GW
Biomass power generation capacity	2 GW	5.5 GW	30 GW
Annual methane gas consumption	8b cu m	19b cu m	40b cu m
Photovoltaic power generation capacity	70MW	300MW	1.8GW
Solar water heaters' heat collection area	80b sq m	150b sq m	300m sq m
Annual bioethanol consumption	1.02 m t	2 m t	10 m t

TCE = tonnes of coal equivalent

m = million

b = billion

Source: NDRC (2007).

With the progress of renewable energy technology and strong government policies, renewable energy development in China, especially wind and solar power generation, has always exceeded its targets, meaning these targets undergo constant revision. Table 14.3 presents the revised targets.

Table 14.3 Revised targets for renewable energy in China

Year	Target
2009	80 GW of wind by 2020
2010	150 GW of wind, 20 GW of solar by 2020
2013	Twelfth Five-Year Plan: 20 GW of solar PV, 150 GW of wind by 2015
2013	35 GW of solar PV by 2015
2016	250 GW of wind, 100 GW of solar by 2020

Source: Author.

The 2005 Renewable Energy Law authorised feed-in tariffs for wind power based on 'government guided' prices, which have evolved year-by-year with competitive bidding for wind power capacity, resulting in standardised or 'approved' prices, generally on a province-by-province basis.

According to Article 14 of the Renewable Energy Law, grid enterprises (State Grid) should sign FIT agreements with renewable energy power plant companies that have received permission from the government.

FITs were implemented in China as early as 2003 in support of the deployment of wind power. At first, the tariff amount was determined on a case-by-case basis through bidding or negotiation. However, this arrangement created intense competition among large state-owned renewable power generators, which issued speculative bids that were often insufficient to actually implement the project. This practice was considered harmful to the long-term sustainability of the wind power industry.

In response, the NDRC set baseline prices for wind tariffs in August 2009. The minimum tariff ranged from RMB0.51/kWh to RMB0.61/kWh, depending on the location of the wind farm, with four classes of wind resource ranking.[2] In 2011, the NDRC set the national solar FIT at RMB1/kWh for projects started in 2011 or later. To support the FITs, the NDRC established a renewable electricity surcharge in 2006, of RMB0.001/kWh. The surcharge was increased to RMB0.004/kWh in 2009 and again, to RMB0.008/kWh, in 2011, to support the increasing demand for FITs following rapid growth of renewable energy. Despite the eightfold rate hike, the surcharge remains low by international standards: with an average residential electricity price of RMB0.52/kWh, the surcharge is 1.5 per cent of

2 In order to process benchmark prices for wind power generation, four classes of wind power generation areas were defined based on the wind resource, they are Class I to IV.

the total electricity price. In comparison, Germany's renewable energy surcharge reached €0.053/kWh (RMB0.43/kWh) in 2013, or 20 per cent of the total electricity price. China's low renewable electricity surcharge is important for the sustainable development of renewable energy because it leaves sufficient room for future expansion of FITs.

Finally, there are new provincial-level solar PV preferential tariffs. Zhejiang and Jiangsu have established province-wide preferential tariffs for solar PV. In Zhejiang, the tariff was set as a premium of RMB0.70/kWh (US$0.10/kWh) added to the province-average coal power generation price, which was RMB0.46/kWh in 2009 (US$0.07/kWh), thus producing a total tariff of RMB1.16/kWh (US$0.17/kWh). Jiangsu set preferential tariffs significantly higher than Zhejiang, and also established a range of tariffs depending on technology type: RMB2.1/kWh (US$0.31/kWh) for ground-based systems, RMB3.7/kWh (US$0.54/kWh) for rooftop and RMB4.3/kWh (US$0.63/kWh) for building-integrated systems (all prices at 2009 levels). Jiangsu also slated its tariffs to decrease progressively, to RMB1.7/kWh for ground-based systems, RMB3/kWh for rooftop and RMB3.5/kWh for building-integrated systems in 2010, and to RMB1.4/kWh for ground-based systems, RMB2.4/kWh for rooftop and RMB2.9/kWh for building-integrated systems in 2011. These preferential tariffs were not, however, considered nationally 'approved' prices, which means the money to cover them will have to come from the provincial rather than the national budget.

During 2012–15, it was announced that all new solar projects without state subsidies would be included in Jiangsu's PV subsidy policy, based on the national uniform electricity price. The policy would be implemented for the integrated operation of ground-based, rooftop and building-integrated systems with the electricity price of RMB1.2/kWh in 2014 and RMB1.15/kWh in 2015.

In December 2016, the NDRC released the lower FIT for new projects in 2017. For wind power, the tariffs are 15 per cent, 10 per cent, 9 per cent and 5 per cent lower for the four classes of wind resource rankings, giving rates of RMB0.40/kWh, RMB0.45/kWh, RMB0.49/kWh andRMB0.57/kWh, respectively. For solar power, the FIT reductions are 19 per cent, 15 per cent and 13 per cent for the three solar resource rankings,[3] to rates of RMB0.65/kWh, RMB0.75/kWh and RMB0.85/kWh, respectively. The subsidy for distributed solar power remains at RMB0.42/kWh. The FITs for offshore wind and tidal zone wind power also remain unchanged, at RMB0.85/kWh and RMB0.75/kWh, respectively.

3 Similar to the wind resource ranking, there are also three classes of solar power generation regions based on the resource of solar energy, from Class I to III, to decide the benchmark prices for solar power generation.

Based on a recent announcement by the NEA, power companies will be required to source more than 15 per cent of their power from renewable energy generation, not including large hydro. This is another signal to promote further renewable energy development.

Future development of renewable energy

The goal of keeping the rise in global temperature to 2°C and China's own air quality targets are powerful push factors for the transition of energy systems. Based on the study by the Integrated Policy Assessment Model for China (IPAC) modelling team, energy transition in China alone could support the global climate change target, concurrent with improving air quality. Figure 14.5 presents primary energy demand under the global 2°C target.

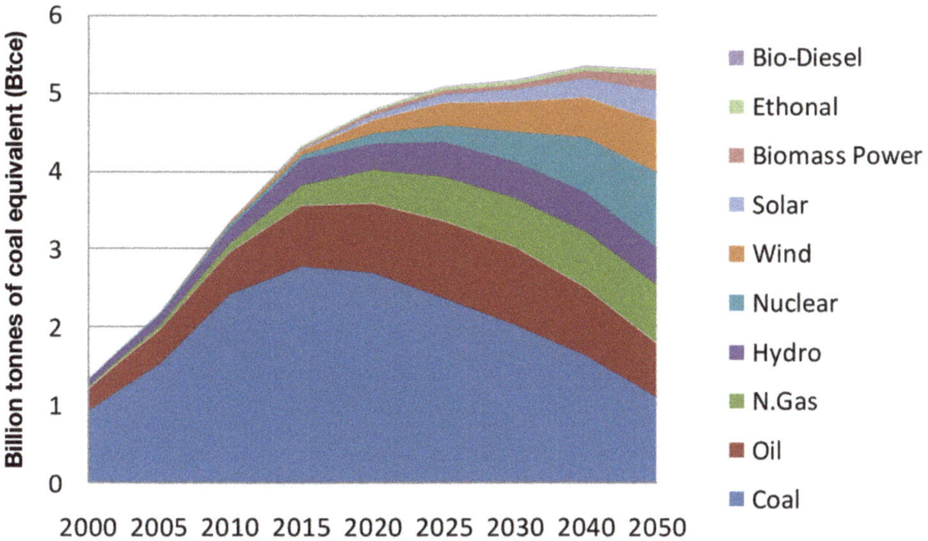

Figure 14.5 Primary energy demand in China under the global 2°C target

Source: Jiang et al. (2013).

By 2050, renewable energy will account for 33.8 per cent of total primary energy demand in China—an increase from 11.4 per cent in 2015. Installed capacity of renewable energy will increase to 289 GW by 2050, while power generation from renewable energy will be 571 TWh by 2050 (Figures 14.6 and 14.7).

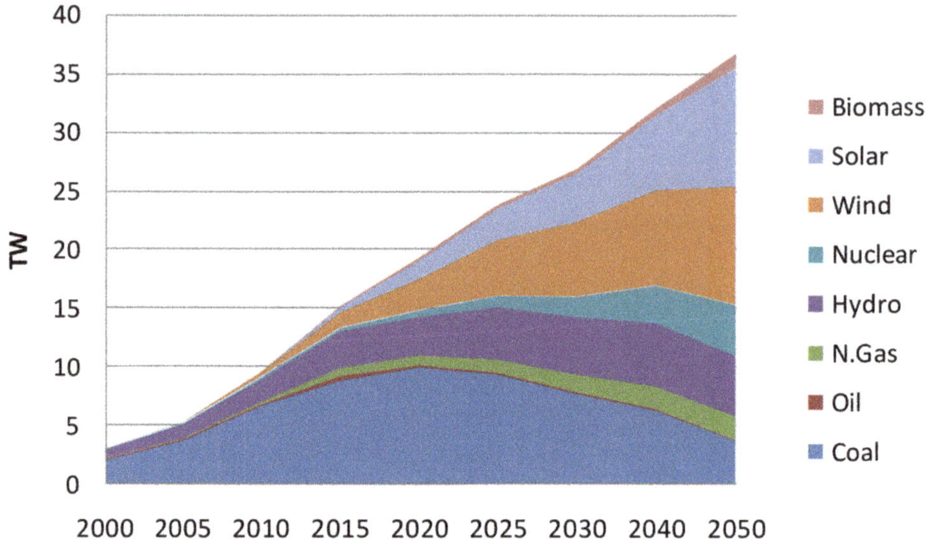

Figure 14.6 Installed capacity in China under the 2°C scenario
Source: Jiang et al. (2013).

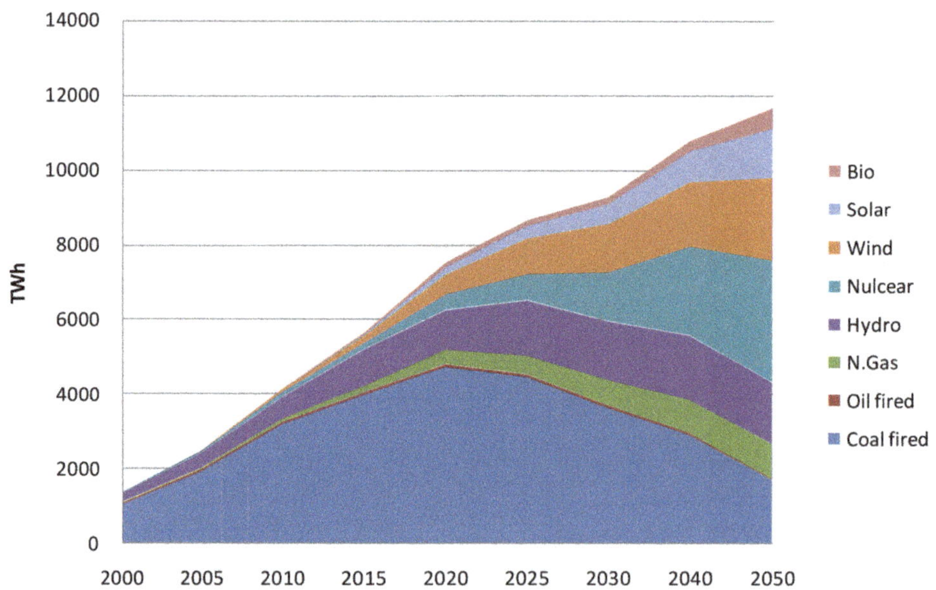

Figure 14.7 Power generation in China under the 2°C scenario
Source: Jiang et al. (2013).

References

China Electricity Council (CEC) (2017), Annual Information on Power Industry in China. Beijing: NEA.

Jiang, K., Zhuang X., Miao, R. and He, C. (2013), China's Role in Attaining the Global 2 Target, *Climate Policy* 13(S01): 55–69. dx.doi.org/10.1080/14693062.2012.746070.

National Bureau of Statistics of China (NBS) (2016), *China Statistics Yearbook 2016*, Beijing: China Statistics Press.

National Bureau of Statistics of China (NBS) Energy Statistics Division (2016), *China Energy Statistics Yearbook 2016*, Beijing: China Statistics Press.

National Development and Reform Commission (NDRC) (2007), *Medium and Long-Term Development Plan for Renewable Energy in China*, Beijing: NDRC.

National Energy Administration (NEA) (2016), *China's 13th Five Year Plan on Energy.* Beijing: NEA.

National Energy Administration (NEA) (2017), *China's 13th Five Year Plan on Renewable Energy.* Beijing: NEA.

National Energy Administration (NEA) (2017), *China's 13th Five Year Plan on Hydro-power.* Beijing: NEA.

Renewable Energy Policy Network for the 21st Century (Ren21) (2016), *Renewables 2016 Global Status Report*, Paris: Ren21 Secretariat. Available from: www.ren21.net/gsr-online/.

The State Council of the People's Republic of China (State Council) (2011), *Twelfth Five-Year Plan 2011–2015*. Available from: english.gov.cn/.

15. The China Interbank Repo Market[1]

Ross Kendall and Jonathan Lees[2]

The market for repurchase agreements ('repo') is an important source of short-term funding for financial institutions operating in China. It is used by the People's Bank of China (PBC) to manage domestic liquidity conditions through its open market operations, and it is likely to become more important over time as a channel for the transmission of monetary policy. This chapter outlines the key features of Chinese repo markets, first focusing on the interbank market, and then discussing recent developments and their impact on the bond market. We highlight that lower and less volatile repo rates over the past couple of years have contributed to greater risk-taking in financial markets and that policy settings in China have been dynamic in shaping and responding to these developments.

Introduction

A repo is an agreement between two parties under which the cash borrower sells or pledges a security (usually a fixed-income security) to the cash lender, with the collateral bought back or released from the pledge at a later date. Repos are therefore economically equivalent to secured loans and are an important part of short-term funding markets in many economies.

In China, a repo can be conducted as an exchange-traded transaction on the Shanghai or Shenzhen stock exchanges or 'over the counter' in the interbank market. The exchange-traded market has grown rapidly in recent years; however, the interbank market—in which a range of bank and non-bank financial institutions are active—is the more significant market, with higher turnover and outstanding lending balances than the exchange-traded repo market (or the unsecured interbank lending market) (Figures 15.1 and 15.2). The People's Bank of China (PBC) also uses the interbank market to adjust domestic liquidity conditions via open market operations. There is around RMB5 trillion (US$720 billion) of lending outstanding in China's interbank repo market, which is around one-third of the size of the US repo market.[3]

1 A version of this article was also published in the June 2017 edition of the Reserve Bank of Australia (RBA) *Bulletin*.

2 The authors are from the International Department of the RBA. The views expressed in this chapter are those of the authors and should not be attributed to the RBA. The content of this chapter was finalised on 21 April 2017.

3 The size of the US repo market is slightly more than US$2 trillion, based on 2016 data on outstanding repurchase agreements from the Federal Reserve Bank of New York Primary Dealer Statistics database.

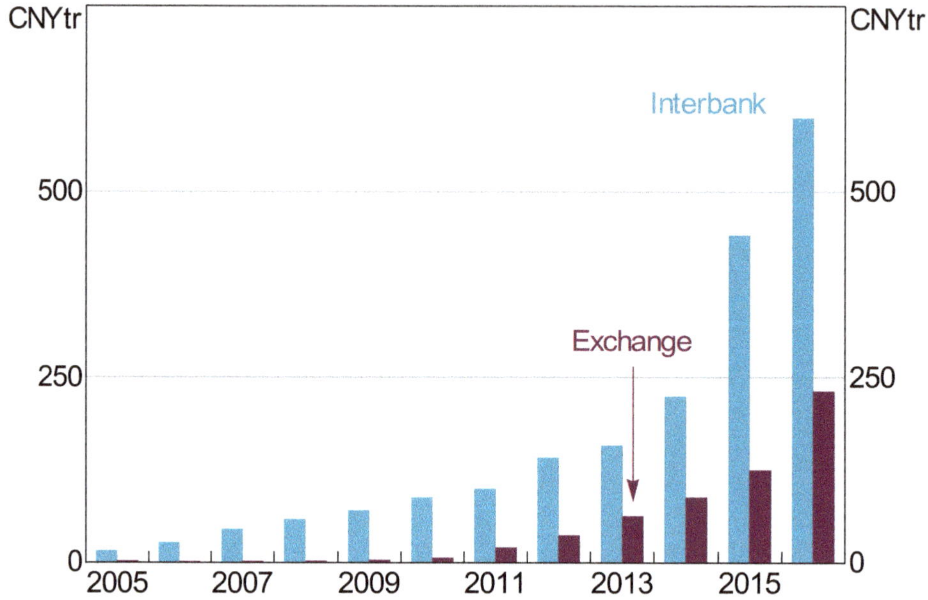

Figure 15.1 Chinese repo turnover (annual, by market)
Sources: Authors' calculations; WIND Information.

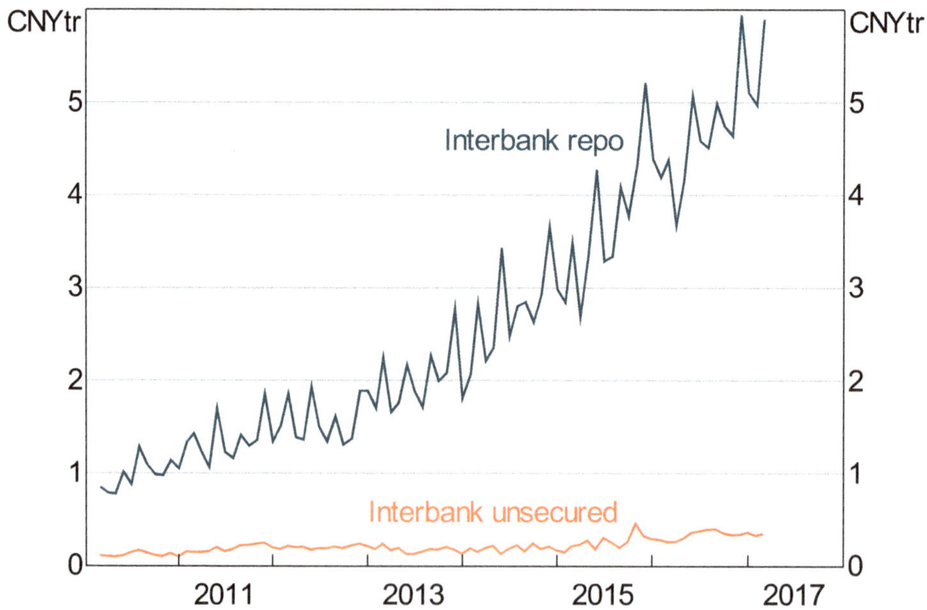

Figure 15.2 Lending balance outstanding (by market)
Sources: CEIC Data; National Interbank Funding Center.

This chapter focuses on the interbank repo market in light of its systemic importance as a major source of short-term funding, the significant role it plays in the PBC's liquidity management and the fact that the PBC views it as an emerging channel for the transmission of monetary policy in China. We outline the key features of the market through the lens of the major cash lenders and borrowers, and go on to discuss recent developments in the repo market, focusing on the build-up of risks and changes to the PBC's liquidity management framework.

Ownership of collateral

As in major repo markets around the world, in China's interbank repo market bonds with low credit risk account for the majority of collateral used. In recent years, Chinese government bonds, together with bonds issued by China's policy banks, have accounted for nearly 90 per cent of repo collateral (Figure 15.3). PBC bills historically accounted for a large share of repo collateral, but their usage has declined as the stock of outstanding PBC bills has fallen.[4] Other instruments (mostly corporate and local government bonds) have accounted for just over 10 per cent of collateral in the interbank repo market in recent years.[5]

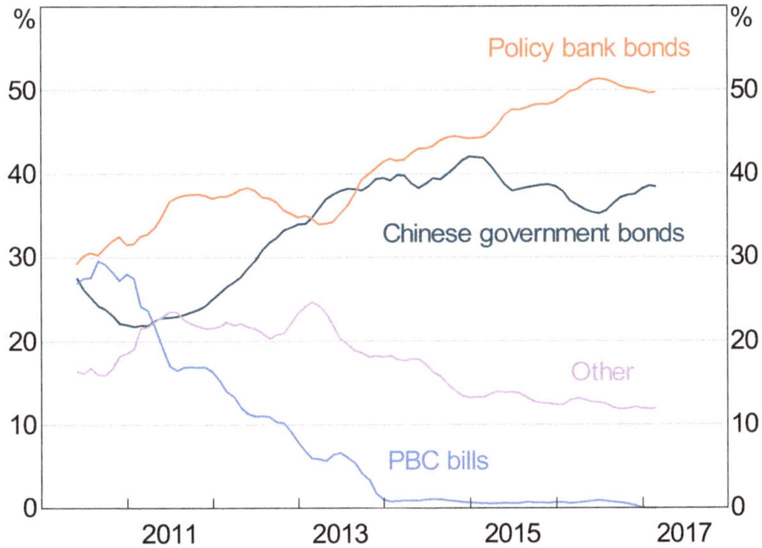

Figure 15.3 Collateral used in repurchase agreements (interbank, pledged collateral, percentage of monthly turnover by value)*

* Six-month rolling average.

Sources: Authors' calculations; CCDC; CEIC Data.

4 There are currently no PBC bills outstanding, with the last remaining bills having matured in 2016.

5 In the pledged interbank market, collateral must meet the requirements specified by the cash lender, but is otherwise generic. That is, cash lenders are not able to request specific or 'special' securities as collateral, as is the case in most major markets.

Repos in the Chinese interbank market are generally conducted on a 'pledged' basis rather than on an 'outright' basis as is common in other major markets (Figure 15.4).[6] Under an outright repo transaction, the ownership of collateral is transferred to the cash lender for the length of the transaction. In contrast, in a pledged repo agreement, ownership of the collateral remains with the borrower but is pledged to the cash lender such that the borrower cannot use it for any other purpose until the cash principal and interest are returned.[7]

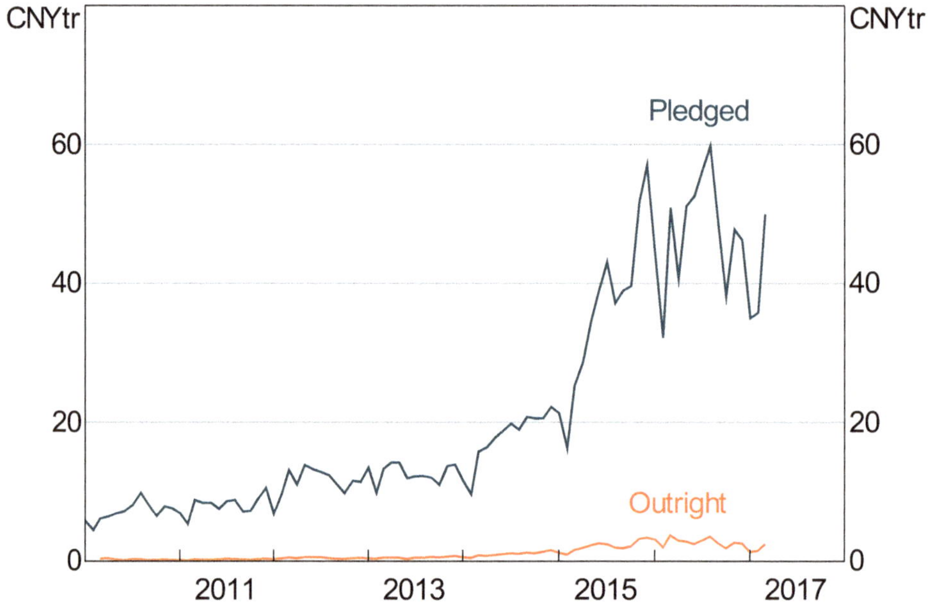

Figure 15.4 Chinese interbank repo market (monthly turnover)

Sources: CEIC Data; National Interbank Funding Center.

As ownership of the collateral is not transferred to the cash lender in a pledged repo transaction, the lender cannot use (or 'rehypothecate') the collateral during the term of the transaction. This has several important implications for the structure of the market in China. First, it precludes the inter-dealer broker model prevalent in other major repo markets. In this model, a dealer acts as an intermediary by lending cash to one counterparty in exchange for collateral, and uses that collateral to borrow cash from another counterparty, taking a spread between the two trades as profit.

6 Pledged agreements accounted for 95 per cent of turnover (by value) in 2016.

7 China Central Depository & Clearing (CCDC), a state-owned entity responsible for the registration, custody and settlement of most fixed-income securities in China, is responsible for ensuring that the pledged securities it holds are not used for any other purpose, including being pledged as collateral to another repo, until the transaction has been unwound.

While market participants may act as an intermediary on an opportunistic basis, the process of on-lending funds in the pledged interbank repo market in China requires substantially more collateral than in repo markets where collateral ownership is transferred outright.

Second, pledged repos are less flexible than outright repos. For example, bond dealers and investors commonly use repo markets to fund bond positions. This involves purchasing a bond outright and using it as collateral in a repo transaction to borrow the cash needed to fund the bond purchase. Net cash flows are thus zero but the investor gains exposure to the bond. In an outright repo market, the investor can unwind their bond position during the term of the repo by borrowing an equivalent bond under a second repo transaction and selling it outright.[8] This creates a short position that offsets the original long position. However, this is not possible in a pledged repo market as the collateral is not available to be sold. Consequently, to retain the ability to exit their positions when desired, bond investors using pledged repo markets to fund their positions are likely to have a preference to borrow cash for shorter terms relative to equivalent investors funding their positions through outright repo markets. Indeed, in the case of China, the use of overnight repos in the pledged repo market increased dramatically during 2015 alongside an increase in the bond–repo carry trade (discussed below).

Finally, the inability to rehypothecate collateral reduces the scope for market participants to profit from interest rate differentials. This may go part of the way to explaining the steep slope of the Chinese repo curve, particularly the spread between overnight and seven-day repo rates, which is persistently large (Figure 15.5). In an outright repo market, participants could take advantage of an interest rate differential such as this by lending cash at the seven-day rate and using the collateral received to borrow at the lower overnight rate. In a pledged repo market, these market participants would need to post their own collateral, increasing the cost of the trade.

8 In most major markets dealers may also exit a bond position by substituting collateral or they may use open-ended repos in which the date of the second leg is not specified at the commencement of the transaction. These approaches are not possible in the pledged interbank market.

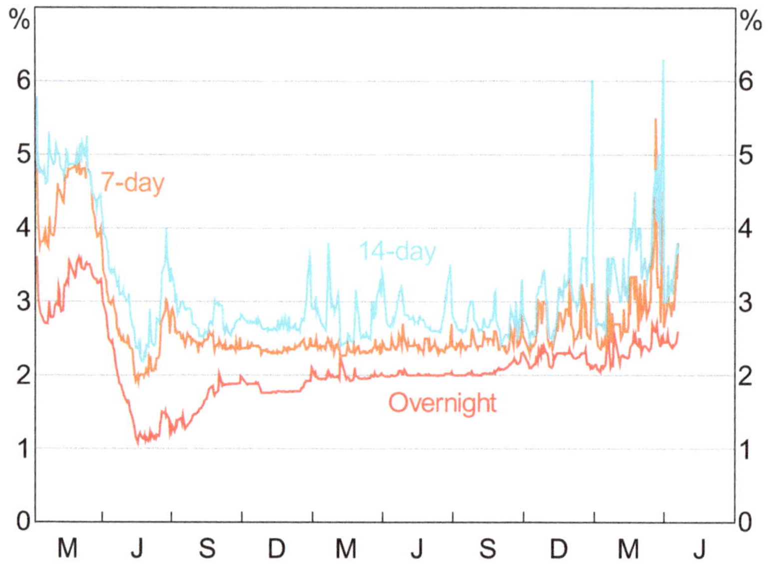

Figure 15.5 Chinese interbank repo rates (by tenor)*

* Fixing repo rates published by the National Interbank Funding Center, calculated as the median rate of trades during the morning of each trading day. M = quarter ending March, J = quarter ending June, S = quarter ending September, D = quarter ending December.

Source: CEIC Data.

Cash lenders

Large Chinese commercial banks have historically been the major suppliers of cash in the interbank pledged repo market (Figure 15.6). In particular, the large state-owned commercial banks account for a substantial share of lending. This reflects their large retail deposit bases and relatively conservative balance sheet management, which have resulted in more funds being available to lend in the repo market.[9]

In contrast with the large national banks, small and medium-sized banks (labelled 'other commercial banks and cooperatives' in Figure 15.6) have been net borrowers in the repo market (discussed below), although they are also responsible for a substantial share of lending. The scale of these institutions' involvement in both the borrowing and the lending sides of the market may be indicative of on-lending activity, whereby institutions take advantage of opportunities to borrow cash at a lower rate than that at which they can lend. However, it is also likely to reflect the diversity of institutions within this group.

9 Data on repo activity by 'national commercial banks' from CCDC cannot be split further between the large state-owned commercial banks and the smaller 'joint-stock banks', but data on the source and use of funds in the domestic banking system from the PBC suggest that the 'four large' state-owned commercial banks account for the majority of repo lending by this category of bank.

Another significant source of funds in the interbank repo market are China's policy banks, whose activity is recorded in the 'special members' category (Cruz et al. 2014). Policy banks play a quasi-fiscal role in channelling government funding to infrastructure and development projects, and also play a significant role in the financial system. Of the three policy banks, the China Development Bank (CDB) appears to be the most active in the repo market, with net lending by 'special members' in the pledged repo market closely aligning with figures on repo lending recorded on the CDB's balance sheet.

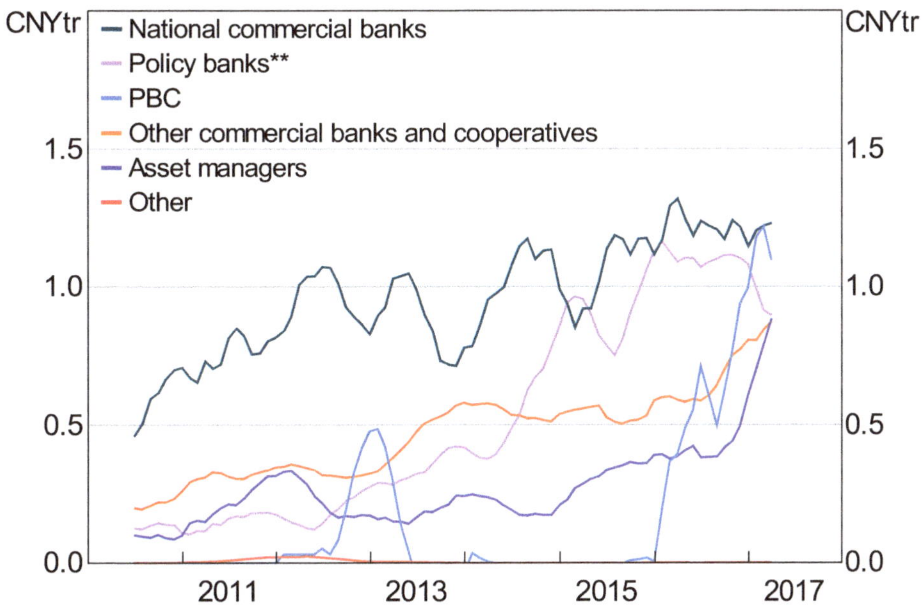

Figure 15.6 Outstanding repo lending balance (interbank, pledged collateral, by type of institution)*

* Six-month rolling average

** Relabelled from 'special members' in source data

Sources: Authors' calculations; CCDC; CEIC Data.

Policy banks' lending in the repo market has increased rapidly since early 2014, tripling in the space of two years and making them systemically important participants in the market. A large increase in policy banks' funding over recent years, via both bond issuance (the traditional funding source for policy banks) and the PBC's Pledged Supplementary Lending Facility (launched in 2014 to provide low-cost funding to policy banks to support development lending), has contributed to an increase in their capacity to lend. It is possible that policy banks' increased repo activity could have been part of a state-led push to reduce volatility in repo rates (see 'Recent developments and their implications' below).

The PBC's lending in the interbank pledged repo market, via its open market operations, has also increased rapidly over the past couple of years.[10] This reflects the PBC's preference to manage liquidity conditions through more active use of open market operations rather than through changes to reserve requirement ratios, as well as the decline in the PBC's foreign currency reserves since 2014, which has required offsetting liquidity injections. Like policy bank activity, this increase in the PBC's activity in the repo market is likely aimed at reducing the volatility of repo rates.

Asset managers use the repo market for liquidity management purposes and have increased their share of lending over recent years as the value of assets under management has grown.[11] However, these institutions individually account for only a small share of outstanding lending, and their cash lending in the interbank repo market is considerably smaller than their borrowing (discussed below).

Cash borrowers

Smaller banks ('other commercial banks and cooperatives' in Figure 15.7) and asset managers account for most of the borrowing in the interbank pledged repo market, with smaller banks accounting for around half of outstanding borrowing. These banks have smaller retail deposit bases than the large state-owned commercial banks and, as a group, have been expanding their balance sheets rapidly over recent years, resulting in an increased reliance on wholesale funding such as repo (RBA 2016).

In recent years, asset managers have increased their borrowing in the interbank pledged repo market and now account for a significant share of outstanding borrowing. This increase has occurred alongside a sharp increase in the value of these funds' assets under management, partly reflecting the generally less restrictive regulation of some types of fund management companies compared with banks' activities. Asset managers are likely to have increased their borrowing in the repo market in recent years to engage in the bond carry trade (discussed below).

10 PBC repo lending and borrowing figures are calculated from PBC open market operations. Lending to or borrowing from the PBC is not captured in the data for other institutions, or in the aggregate turnover or balances data.

11 For the purpose of this chapter, we group together institutions recorded as fund institutions, insurance institutions, securities companies and non-bank financial institutions as asset managers.

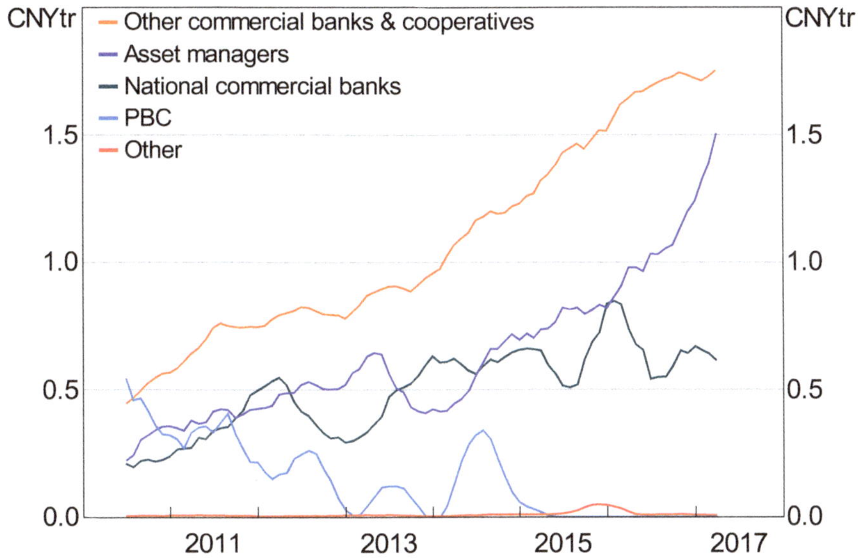

Figure 15.7 Outstanding repo borrowing balance (interbank, pledged collateral, by type of institution)*

* Six-month rolling average

Sources: Authors' calculations; CCDC; CEIC Data.

The borrowing by financial institutions in the 'national commercial banks' category of Figure 15.7 captures borrowing by 'joint-stock' banks (which are smaller than the large state-owned banks that are major suppliers of funds), as well as borrowing by the large state-owned banks for the purpose of on-lending. The interest rates on repo agreements in the interbank market are differentiated based on both the quality of collateral offered and the perceived creditworthiness of the borrower (Shevlin and Chang 2015).[12] Larger state-owned banks are perceived as having the highest credit quality, so borrow at lower rates than smaller banks, while asset managers typically borrow at higher rates than the smaller banks. Higher-rated institutions such as the national commercial banks can take advantage of their creditworthiness by borrowing at relatively low rates and on-lending at higher rates to smaller (less creditworthy) institutions for profit. Figure 15.8 shows net lending in the pledged interbank repo market by type of institution, thereby abstracting from on-lending activities and differences within groups, and hence showing the ultimate suppliers and users of funds. In net terms, the policy banks and the PBC are larger suppliers of funds than the national commercial banks, while smaller banks and asset managers are net borrowers.

12 All else being equal, the credit quality of the borrower should matter more under a pledged repo system, to the extent that it is more difficult for the lender to acquire the collateral that has been pledged in the event of a default. The only reported instance of default in China's interbank repo market that we are aware of involved the failure to repay an overnight repo of less than RMB50 million (US$7 million) in March 2017 (Bloomberg News 2017). This reported default has not been officially confirmed.

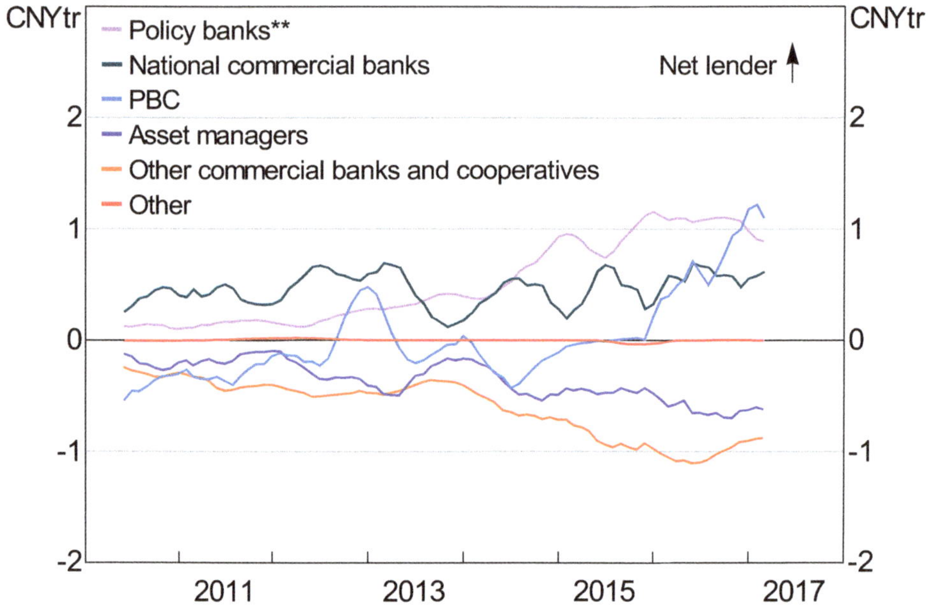

Figure 15.8 Net outstanding repo lending balance (interbank, pledged collateral, by type of institution)*

* Six-month rolling average

** Relabelled from 'special members' in source data.

Sources: Authors' calculations; CCDC; CEIC Data.

Recent developments and their implications

The reduction in the volatility of repo rates

The volatility of Chinese repo rates declined significantly during 2015 and has generally remained low since then, notwithstanding an increase since the second half of 2016 (discussed below; Figure 15.9). One factor contributing to lower volatility was the introduction of reserve averaging for banks in September 2015 (IMF 2016).[13] However, the increased involvement of policy banks and the PBC in the repo market indicates a broader policy objective by the Chinese authorities to dampen volatility. A working paper co-authored by the chief economist of the PBC's research bureau in early 2016 supports this assessment. Specifically, it recommends shifting monetary policy from the current approach (focused on quantitative lending targets, 'window guidance' and central guidance of benchmark lending and deposit rates) towards an interest rate corridor approach and improving the transmission

13 The rule change allows banks to report a required reserve ratio up to 1 per cent lower than the compulsory ratio set by the PBC on any given day, as long as they meet the requirement on average during an assessed period.

from short-term rates (particularly the seven-day repo rate) to other rates in the economy (Ma et al. 2016). In addition, a February 2017 article from PBC Assistant Governor, Zhang Xiaohui, reiterated these goals. It stated that the transmission from short-term rates (especially the seven-day repo rate and the rates on the PBC's Medium-Term Lending Facility) to bond rates and bank loan rates had improved (Zhang 2017).[14]

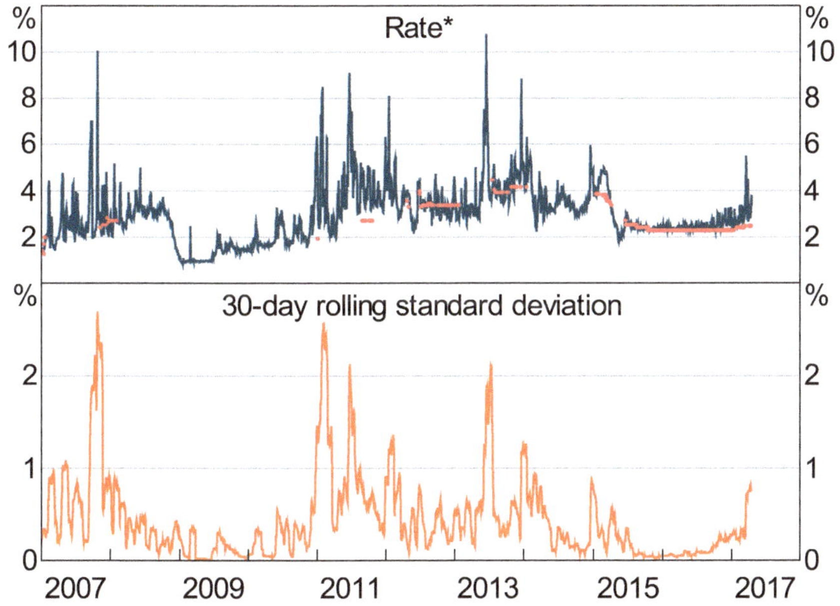

Figure 15.9 Chinese repo rate (seven-day repo fixing rate, daily)

Note: Red dots indicate PBC seven-day open market operation rates on repos (prior to 2012) and reverse repos (since May 2012).

Sources: Authors' calculations; CEIC Data.

Policy banks increased their lending in the interbank pledged repo market from early 2014, with their share of outstanding loans rising from around 20 per cent to almost 40 per cent by early 2015. In early 2016, the share of policy and central bank lending grew further as the PBC increased its activity in the repo market (Figure 15.10). At the same time, the PBC started managing liquidity more actively, increasing the size of injections and withdrawals and moving from bi-weekly open market operations to daily open market operations (Figure 15.11). This enabled the PBC, like other central banks, to more effectively mitigate short-term fluctuations in liquidity conditions—for example, arising from large tax payments or seasonal demand for cash.

14 There have also been numerous reports from market analysts discussing the shift towards an interest rate corridor system, and the International Monetary Fund (IMF 2016) has highlighted this shift and encouraged further progress in its recent communications.

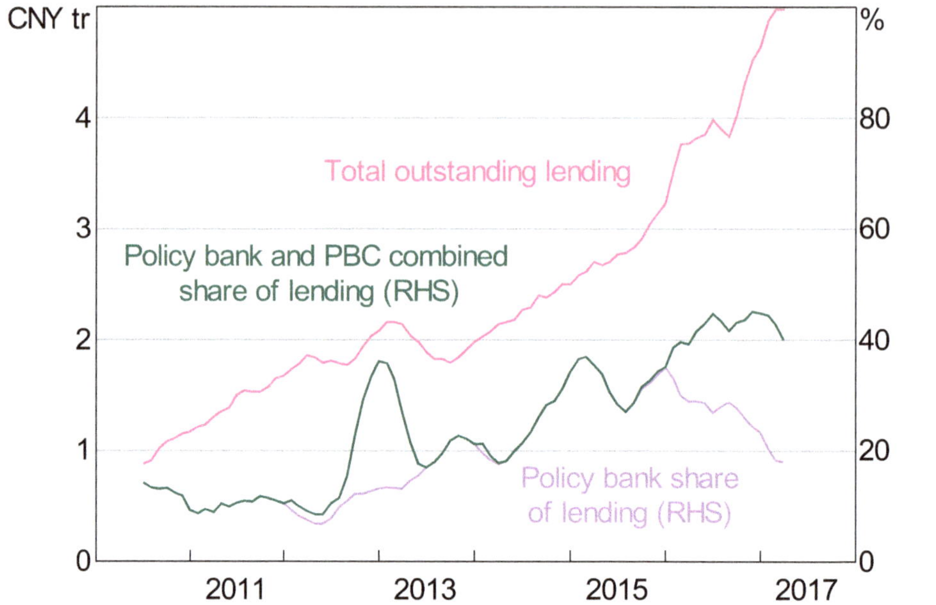

Figure 15.10 Policy bank and PBC repo lending (interbank, pledged collateral)*

* Six-month rolling average.

Sources: Authors' calculations; CCDC; CEIC Data.

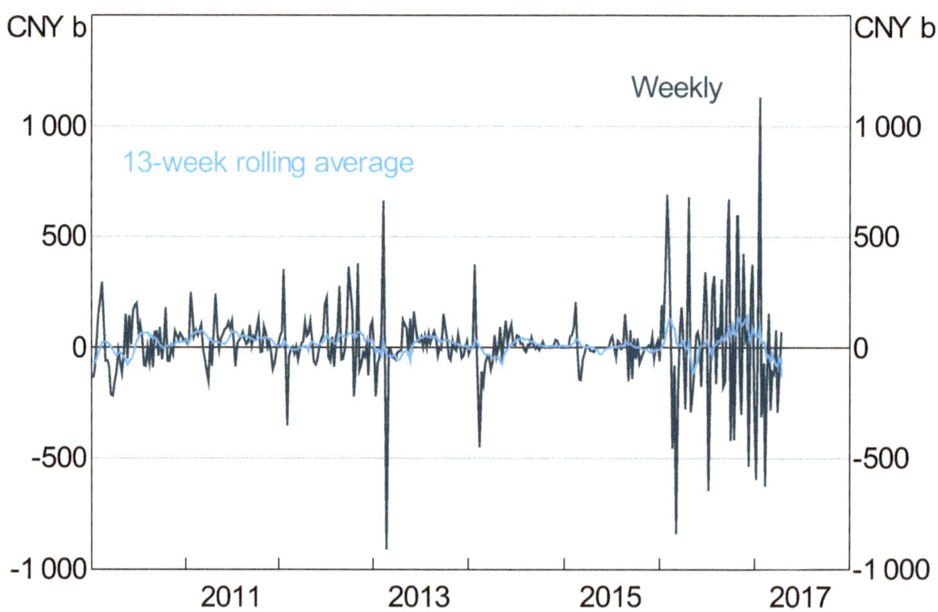

Figure 15.11 PBC liquidity injections and withdrawals (open market operations, net)

Source: Bloomberg.

The bond carry trade

The structural decline in the volatility of repo rates has given rise to a consistent spread between yields on short-term repos and long-term bonds. This spread facilitates the bond 'carry trade'—a leveraged bond investment in which the investor receives the higher long-term interest rate, but pays the lower shorter-term rate (that is, the investor buys a bond and pledges it in exchange for cash through the repo market). Reports suggest that the low level and low volatility of repo rates have indeed led to an increase in leveraged bond investments (see, for example, Bloomberg News 2016; Dongming 2016; Xinhua Finance Agency 2016) and PBC commentary has noted risks to financial institutions related to maturity mismatch (Zhang 2017).

In the case of investments in long-term bonds funded via short-term repo, the trade is subject to refinancing risk whereby the interest differential earned on the trade is eroded or becomes negative if repo rates increase. The carry trade is also subject to the risk of capital losses, as investors would rarely hold a long-term bond funded via repo to maturity. This risk is magnified by the leveraged nature of the investment, with the result that investors funding positions through the repo market are highly sensitive to moves in bond yields.

The widest and most consistent spread has been between overnight repo and long-term bonds (Figure 15.12). This has likely contributed to the sharp increase in overnight repo turnover that occurred from early 2015 alongside growth in repo borrowing by smaller banks and asset managers (Figure 15.13). On the investment side, liquidity as measured by bid–ask spreads improved steadily over the same period, with the carry trade increasing bond trading volumes in an environment of low and stable interest rates. However, to the extent that carry trade supports bond market liquidity, it can be expected to deteriorate quickly when interest rates rise. There was some evidence of this in the December quarter of 2016, when bid–ask spreads widened alongside increases in repo market volatility and bond yields. More generally, the build-up in leveraged bond investments appears to have increased the sensitivity of the bond market to volatility in repo rates. For example, in 2013, large increases in repo rates had little impact on the bond market, while a relatively minor pick-up in the level and volatility of repo rates in late 2016 contributed to a material increase in yields.

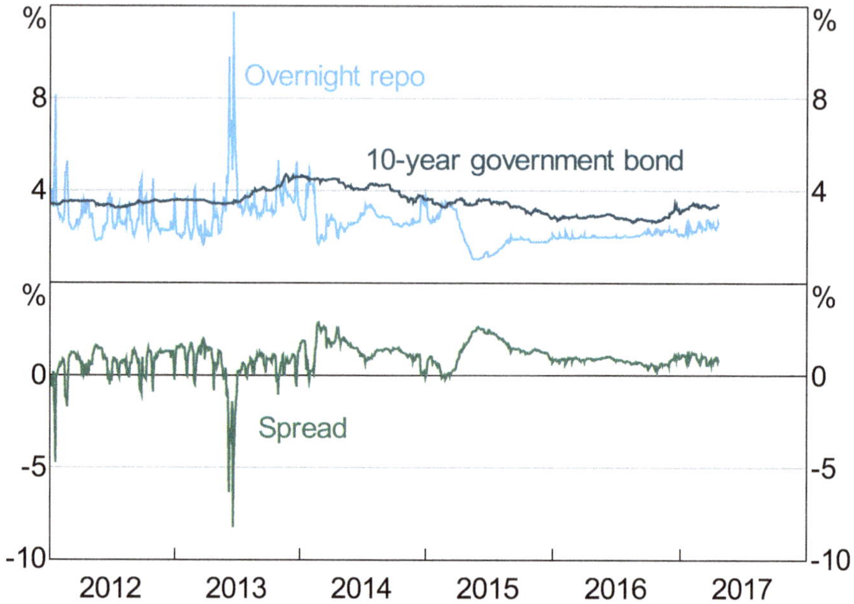

Figure 15.12 Bond and repo rates (daily, on-the-run bond)

Source: Bloomberg.

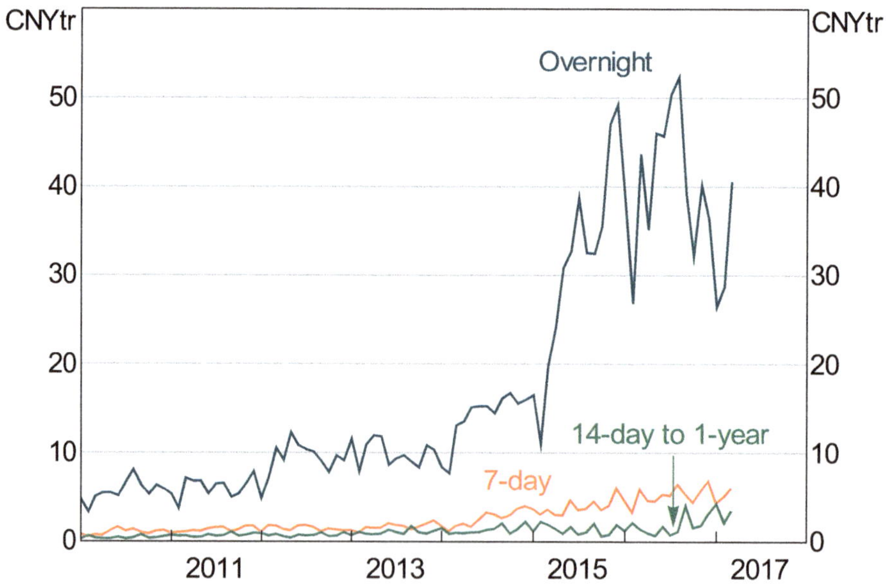

Figure 15.13 Repo turnover (interbank, monthly, pledged collateral, by tenor)

Sources: Authors' calculations; CEIC Data; National Interbank Funding Center.

Part of the pick-up in the level and volatility of repo rates over the second half of 2016 has reflected the increased share of borrowing by asset managers over this period (in addition to changes to the PBC's liquidity operations, discussed below). On average, asset managers likely borrow at a higher rate than banks, contributing to a rise in average repo rates as these institutions' share of turnover increases, and higher volatility to the extent that the rates at which these institutions can borrow are more sensitive to changes in credit risk appetite.[15] In December 2016, repo rates rose substantially as the premium paid by asset managers to borrow relative to banks increased sharply in response to concerns regarding the use of informal repo agreements known as '*dai chi*' by some interbank repo market participants (discussed further below).

The '*dai chi*' market

Dai chi (which translates as 'holding something on someone's behalf') is the practice of selling a bond in exchange for funds and buying the bond back later at a price and time agreed at the start of the trade. *Dai chi* agreements are economically equivalent to a repo agreement, but do not take place via the interbank market trading system and are often informal in nature.[16] Due to this informality, some transactions undertaken in this market may not be legally enforceable—for example, *dai chi* agreements have reportedly been struck using instant messaging services.

There are several reasons that market participants may elect to transact in the *dai chi* market instead of the formal interbank market. *Dai chi* transactions can be used to remove assets from balance sheets for the period of the loan, circumventing regulatory limits on leverage. *Dai chi* also allows collateral rehypothecation, facilitating greater flexibility and leverage than pledged repo.

Though few data are available on this informal market, the practice is reportedly widespread. The president of China Central Depository & Clearing (CCDC) has estimated that the value of outstanding *dai chi* could be as high as RMB12 trillion (US$1.7 trillion), which would make it twice as large as the interbank repo market (Dong 2016; Hong 2017). Without knowing the types of collateral used, the enforceability of contracts or the creditworthiness of the institutions involved, it is difficult to make an assessment of the risks involved with this activity. However, the informality of the *dai chi* market suggests that risks are likely higher than in the

15 Asset managers are likely perceived as having higher credit risk, so are likely to pay a higher rate than banks (Shevlin and Chang 2015). Data from the *Monthly Bulletin on Pledged Repo* retrieved from chinamoney.com.cn/english (the website of the China Foreign Exchange Trade System, which processes interbank repo transactions) show that the average repo rate for 'other' institutions is consistently higher than for any type of Chinese bank (although this does not account for potential differences in the average term of repo funding between different types of institution).

16 The information on the *dai chi* market is based on Dong (2016); Moriyasu (2016); BIS (2017); Hong (2017); Long (2017).

formal repo market. Moreover, there is likely to be some degree of overlap between participants in the formal and informal repo markets, such that risks that manifest in the *dai chi* market could spill over into the interbank and exchange-traded markets.

For example, in mid-December 2016, Sealand Securities announced that two former directors had forged RMB16.5 billion (US$2.4 billion) in *dai chi* contracts in transactions with a number of other financial institutions. Sealand's announcement cast doubt over whether the firm would buy back the bonds being held in relation to the fraudulent transactions, which at the time were carrying mark-to-market losses of around RMB1 billion (US$145 million), or 7 per cent of the firm's shareholder equity.

The announcement resulted in volatility in interest rate markets. In the formal repo market, cash lenders became reluctant to provide funding to non-bank financial institutions, with the spread between interest rates paid by these institutions and those paid by banks increasing sharply.[17] In the bond market, yields rose significantly and bid–ask spreads widened.[18] However, this dislocation was short-lived as the China Securities Regulatory Commission was reported to have stepped in to force a resolution, and large Chinese banks reportedly increased their lending in the repo market via 'X-repo'. X-repo is a repo facility launched by the PBC in 2015 to anonymously match interbank repo lenders and borrowers, with standardised collateral and haircut requirements. Lending through X-repo ensured access to financing for non-bank financial institutions that were unable to borrow via traditional repos due to the spillover of credit concerns from the *dai chi* market into the interbank market.

Extension to the term of the PBC's market operations

The increased use of leveraged bond purchases and informal repo markets has increased the level of risk in China's financial system. In an apparent response to these risks, in August 2016, the PBC started augmenting its standard seven-day open market operations with 14-day and 28-day terms. While there was no official comment on the change in approach at the time, there were widespread reports (see, for example, Reuters 2016) that the PBC was trying to reduce the extent of leveraged bond purchases by encouraging less use of overnight repos and greater use of (more expensive) longer-term repos.

17 The gap between a measure of the seven-day repo rates that includes borrowing by all types of financial institutions and one that includes only borrowing by deposit-taking institutions spiked to around 100 basis points in late December from a normal range of around 10 to 30 basis points.

18 Trading was also suspended in Chinese government bond futures, which reached their daily down limit.

In February, PBC Assistant Governor Zhang noted that the change to the PBC's open market operations had the practical effect of mitigating financial institutions' maturity mismatch and liquidity risks (Zhang 2017). Repo turnover declined following the change, with some investors in the bond carry trade likely to have been deterred by the resulting increase in the level and volatility of repo rates (see Figure 15.12).

Conclusion

Repo markets in China have expanded rapidly in recent years. This is consistent with the broader development of China's financial markets and provides financial market participants the depth and liquidity necessary to effectively manage their short-term assets and liabilities. Moreover, the PBC views the repo market's development as supporting further moves towards a short-term interest rate targeting monetary policy framework in the future. However, as in other financial markets, the expansion of short-term funding markets can give rise to financial stability risks, especially where these markets are informal in nature. It appears these risks have risen with the growth in China's repo markets, and the policy landscape is responding to these risks.

References

Bank for International Settlements (BIS) (2017), *BIS Quarterly Review*, March 2017, Basel: BIS. Available at from: bis.org/publ/qtrpdf/r_qt1703.htm.

Bloomberg News (2016), China's $1 trillion bond leverage unwinds as Pimco senses panic, *Bloomberg.com*, 28 April. Available from: bloomberg.com/news/articles/2016-04-27/china-s-1-trillion-bond-leverage-unwinds-as-pimco-senses-panic.

Bloomberg News (2017), PBOC said to inject funds after missed interbank payments, *Bloomberg.com*, 21 March. Available from: bloomberg.com/news/articles/2017-03-21/pboc-said-to-inject-liquidity-after-interbank-payments-missed-j0jejifd.

Cruz, P. C., Gao, Y. and Song, L. L. (2014), *The People's Republic of China's financial markets: Are they deep and liquid enough for renminbi internationalization?* ADBI Working Paper Series 477, Asian Development Bank Institute, Tokyo.

Dong, J. (2016), 中债登估算代持规模12万亿 建议改进回购交易 [Scale of dai chi market estimated at RMB12 trillion, changes proposed to improve repo market], *Caixin.com*, 27 December. Available from: finance.caixin.com/2016-12-27/101030995.html.

Dongming, T. X. (2016), *The cause of the current bond market turmoil?* OCBC China Insights, 19 December, Overseas-Chinese Banking Corporation, Singapore. Available from: ocbc.com/assets/pdf/regional%20focus/china/china%20insights/2016/china%20insights%2019122016.pdf.

Hong, S. (2017), Behind China's bond selloff, a risky twist on the repo trade, *The Wall Street Journal*, 17 January. Available from: wsj.com/articles/behind-chinas-bond-selloff-a-risky-twist-on-the-repo-trade-1484654059.

International Monetary Fund (IMF) (2016), *The People's Republic of China: Selected issues*, IMF Country Report No. 16/271, International Monetary Fund, Washington, DC.

Long, C. (2017), Dodging a bullet in the interbank market, *Gavekal Dragonomics*, 19 January. Available from: research.gavekal.com/search-result?search=&fr=&to=&au[]=11781&selectItemau[]=11781&sort=date.

Ma, J., Hong, H., Jia, Y., Zhang, S., Yin, L. H. and An, G. (2016), *The role of yield curves in monetary policy transmission*, PBC Working Paper No. 2016/1, People's Bank of China, Beijing.

Moriyasu, K. (2016), China bonds the latest bubble to pop, *Nikkei Asian Review*, 22 December. Available from: asia.nikkei.com/Markets/Capital-Markets/China-bonds-the-latest-bubble-to-pop?page=1.

Reserve Bank of Australia (RBA) (2016), Box A: Recent growth of small and medium-sized Chinese banks, *Financial Stability Review* (October): 14–16. Available from: rba.gov.au/publications/fsr/2016/oct/.

Reuters (2016), China central bank urges banks to spread out tenors of loans: Sources, *Reuters.com*, 25 August. Available from: reuters.com/article/us-china-economy-centralbank-liquidity-idUSKCN110065?il=0.

Shevlin, A. and Chang, A. (2015), China's repo markets, *JP Morgan Liquidity Insights*. Available from: am.jpmorgan.com/au/en/asset-management/gim/liq/liquidity-insights/chinas-repo-markets.

Xinhua Finance Agency (2016), Regulators survey risk of RMB5 trln leverage fund in bond market, *Xinhua Finance*, 21 April. Available from: en.xfafinance.com/html/In_depth/2016/216356.shtml.

Zhang, X. (2017), Review and prospect of monetary policy, *China Finance 2017*, No. 3, 3 February. Available from: business.sohu.com/20170203/n479832292.shtml.

Part V: Technologies with Trade and Investment

16. China's Evolving Role in Global Production Networks: Implications for Trump's Trade War

Prema-chandra Athukorala[1]

Introduction

The early literature on China's rise as an export powerhouse widely interpreted the shift in its export composition away from standard labour-intensive products towards 'high-tech' product lines within global production networks as an indication of China becoming an advanced-technology superpower. It was predicted that the sophistication of China's export basket was rapidly approaching the level of those of most advanced industrial nations (Lall and Albaladejo 2004; Rodrik 2006; Yusuf et al. 2007). China's perceived export prowess, coupled with the rapid increase in intra-regional trade within China-centred production networks, led to the view that East Asia was becoming a self-contained economic entity with potential for maintaining dynamic growth independent of the economic outlook for the traditional developed market economies (Yoshitomi 2007; Park and Shin 2009; Kohli et al. 2011).

Subsequent studies, which analysed trade data by taking into account cross-border linkages within global production networks, challenged this view (Bergsten et al. 2006; Schott 2008; Athukorala 2009; Roach 2014; Yao 2009; Athukorala and Kohpaiboon 2012). These studies demonstrated that the interpretation of China's global economic integration in earlier studies had missed the fact that China was engaged predominantly in the final assembly stages of East Asia–centred global production networks of vertically integrated global high-tech industries. Even though East Asian economies had become the major suppliers of parts and components for assembly operations in China, most destinations for finished products remained markets outside the region. It was, therefore, too early to proclaim that China and East Asia were decoupling from the global economy.

The purpose of this chapter is to revisit this debate by extending the period covered to more recent years. The analysis is motivated by a sizeable recent literature on the deepening of China's engagement in global production sharing. There is evidence coming from firm-level studies that firms engaged in final assembly in China have

1 The author is grateful to Arianto Patunru for valuable comments on an earlier version of this chapter.

begun to procure inputs from domestic sources (Upward et al. 2013; Yang and Hayakawa 2015; Yang and Tsou 2015; Kang and Shen 2016; Kee and Tang 2016; Kong and Kneller 2016). According to these studies, the process of industrial deepening has been underpinned by the relocation of manufacturing facilities to China by foreign component-producing firms to supply the rapidly expanding final assembly activities in China. There is also evidence of a notable decline in the share of foreign-invested enterprises (FIEs) in domestic manufacturing as a result of the rapid expansion of the operations of local firms, a number of which have become significant global players (Lardy 2014). Closely linked with the shift in ownership structure are some signs of Chinese firms moving gradually from a strategy of pure imitation to one of innovation (Wei et al. 2017; Yip and McKern 2016). These structural changes could presumably have led to a greater propensity to procure inputs domestically; however, so far no attempt has been made to examine whether these structural changes in domestic manufacturing have begun to change the patterns of China's engagement in global network trade. Filling this knowledge gap is important for broadening our understanding of China's engagement in the global economy.

A clear understanding of the emerging patterns of China's trade is particularly relevant for the current debate on the possible implications of the 'trade war' declared by US President Donald Trump on Sino–US trade relations and the global economy at large. A recent trade modelling exercise predicts that the implementation of the proposed 45 per cent US tariff would cut Chinese exports to the United States by 73 per cent (Guo et al. 2017). Based on an interview with several China experts, Wu (2017) reports anecdotal evidence of possible export contraction of similar margins. These predictions are based on the conventional notion that trade takes place in goods that are produced from start to finish in a given country (horizontal specialisation).

The validity of these predictions is, however, questionable, given that 'global production sharing'—splitting the production process into discrete activities that are then allocated across countries—has become a prime mover of global trade and China's global economic integration. Modern international trade driven by global production sharing creates interdependence among countries in a way that old-fashioned horizontal approach to trade fails to capture. The goods a country exports are often produced with imported parts and components and the goods it imports often contribute to the expansion of domestic production and indirectly induce its own exports. These intricate complementarities between trade and production have direct implications for both President Trump's ability to implement punitive tariffs and the economic impact if the protectionist threat becomes a reality.

The rest of this chapter is structured as follows. The next section provides an overview of China's emergence as a global export powerhouse. This is followed by an analysis of the emerging patterns of China's engagement in global production sharing, focusing on both its changing commodity composition and the geographic profile of trade. The fourth section examines the implications of the emerging patterns of China's engagement in global production networks for Sino–US trade relations in the context of the current debate about the implications of punitive tariffs proposed by the Trump administration. The final section summarises the key findings and offers some policy suggestions.

China in global production networks

The rise of China as a major trading nation is one of the most momentous developments in the post–World War II era, surpassing even the stunning rise of Germany and Japan. Total merchandise exports from China increased from US$8 billion (around 1 per cent of global exports) in 1978, when the country's liberalisation process began, to US$408 billion (7.7 per cent of global exports) in 2000 and to more than US$2 trillion (14.1 per cent) in 2015.[2] In 2004, China overtook Japan to become the third-largest exporter in the world after the United States and Germany, and, in another three years, it became the second-largest exporter, surpassing the United States. Since 2009, China has been the world's largest exporting nation. China's ratio of exports to gross domestic product (GDP) currently stands at 33 per cent compared with an average level of 10 per cent for other major economies such as the United States, India and Brazil (World Bank various years).

China's phenomenal export expansion has been underpinned by a dramatic shift in the commodity composition of its exports, away from primary products and towards manufactured goods. The share of manufactures in China's total merchandise exports increased from less than 40 per cent in the late 1970s to more than 90 per cent from the late 1990s, compared with a global average of 70 per cent. China accounted for more than half of the increase in total global manufacturing exports between 1990 and 2015. Integration of domestic manufacturing within global production networks has been the prime mover of China's rise as an export powerhouse during this period.

2 The data reported in this chapter are in current US dollars and are taken from the UN Comtrade database (comtrade.un.org/), unless otherwise stated.

In terms of organisational structure, production networks take two major forms: buyer-driven production networks and producer-driven production networks.[3] Until the early 1990s, the expansion of manufacturing exports from China took place predominantly within buyer-driven production networks. China's export composition during this period remained heavily concentrated in traditional labour-intensive manufactures such as apparel, footwear, toys and sporting goods. Hong Kong manufacturing firms, which relocated their plants to the newly established special economic zones (SEZs) in the Chinese mainland, played a pivotal role in linking China to these production networks (Song and Sung 1995; Roach 2014).

Since then, there has been a palpable shift in China's export composition, away from conventional labour-intensive products and towards assembly operations within producer-driven production networks—in particular, those within the broader category of machinery and transport equipment. Within a few years, the increase in the rate of China's market penetration into global machinery trade turned out to be faster than that for traditional labour-intensive manufacturing. Export expansion was underpinned by a notable increase in the entry of multinational enterprises (MNEs) to set up assembly plants in China. The share of MNE subsidiaries in manufacturing exports from China increased from about 10 per cent in the early 1990s to over 60 per cent in 2010 (Lardy 2014).

Successfully linking a developing country to global production networks requires policy reforms to create a business environment conducive to export-oriented production. However, combining economy-wide reforms with public policies specifically designed to attract MNEs to set up production bases is vital, particularly in the case of production sharing within producer-driven networks.

The main drivers of China's emergence as the premier global assembly centre were its ample supply of relatively cheap and trainable labour, trade liberalisation and trade-related infrastructure provision through the establishment of SEZs. In terms of labour supply, China had the specific advantage of the availability of supervisory manpower to complement the vast pool of unskilled workers. Assembly processes within production networks require much greater numbers of middle-level supervisory workers (in addition to the availability of trainable low-cost

3 Buyer-driven networks are common in diffused-technology consumer goods industries (such as clothing, footwear, travel goods and toys). The 'lead firm' in such a network is the international buyer (large retailers such as Walmart, Marks & Spencer, H&M) and production sharing takes place mostly through arm's-length relationships, with global sourcing companies (value chain intermediaries) playing a key role in linking producers and lead firms. Producer-driven networks are common in vertically integrated global industries such as electronics, electrical goods and automobiles. In these networks, the 'lead firm' is a multinational manufacturing enterprise (such as Intel, Motorola, Apple and Samsung) and production sharing takes place through the lead firm's global branch network and/or its close operational links with established contract manufacturers. There is, therefore, a close link between trade and foreign direct investment (FDI) within these networks. On the analytical distinction between these two variants of production networks, see Gereffi (1999).

unskilled labour) than is required in traditional labour-intensive manufacturing.[4] Under global production sharing, developed countries normally shift to developing countries the low-skill-intensive parts of the value chain; however, these low-skill activities can be more skill intensive than even the most skill-intensive activities in the developing country (Feenstra 2010).

If the costs of service linkages associated with production sharing—the costs of connecting and/or coordinating activities into a smooth sequence to produce the final good—had outweighed the gain from the favourable labour market conditions (Jones and Kierzkowski 2004), participation in global production sharing would not have occurred. These extra costs include transportation, communication and related tasks involved in coordinating production activity in a given country with what is being done in other countries within the production network. The SEZ-centred trade and foreign investment policy reforms in China were successful in meeting this requirement.

In addition to these factors, a significant reduction in 'country risk' as a result of the end of the Cold War[5] and China's accession to the World Trade Organization (WTO) in 2001 provided a setting conducive to the smooth functioning of China-centred production networks. Country risk is a key determinant of whether a firm outsources its production processes to another country, either by setting up an affiliated company or by establishing an arm's-length relationship with a local firm. This is because supply disruptions in a given overseas location could disrupt the entire production chain, and it is impossible to fully offset these risks by writing *complete contracts* (Spencer 2005; Helpman 2006).

Trade patterns

To explore the magnitude and patterns of trade arising from cross-border production networks, it is necessary to separate parts and components (henceforth referred to as 'components') from final (assembled) products traded within global production networks in reported standard (customs records–based) trade data. The methodology

4 See Steve Jobs's discussion with former US President Barack Obama on Apple's assembly operations in China in Isaacson (2011: 546): 'At that time, Apple had 700,000 factory workers employed in China, and that was because it needed 30,000 engineers on-site to supervise those workers. If you could educate these engineers, he said, we could move more manufacturing plants here.'

5 Country risk considerations during the Cold War are considered a possible reason US electronics MNEs favoured Singapore (and subsequently Malaysia, Thailand and the Philippines) in which to establish assembly plants in the initial stage of their overseas operations (in the 1960s and 1970s), while bypassing South Korea, Taiwan and Hong Kong (in particular, Hong Kong, a country that followed almost laissez-faire economic policy throughout)—countries that were more familiar to them (Athukorala and Kohpaiboon 2014).

for data compilation is descried in Appendix 16.1. In the following discussion, 'global production network (GPN) products' refers to the sum of components and assembled products.

Exports of GPN products from China increased from US$47 billion in 1992–93 to US$1.5 trillion in 2014–15,[6] when these products accounted for more than 70 per cent of China's total manufacturing exports (Figure 16.1). Within GPN products, assembled products account for a larger share than components throughout the period. This pattern reflects China's dominant role as an assembly centre within global production networks. However, components also account for a sizeable share and that share has increased in recent years, reflecting deepening of the domestic production base.

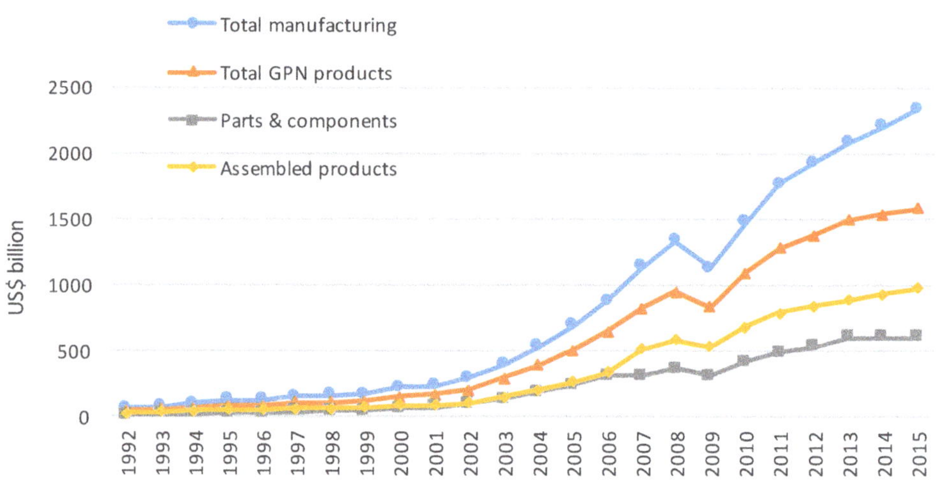

Figure 16.1 China's manufacturing exports, 1992–2015 (US$ billion)

Source: Data compiled from UN Comtrade database (comtrade.un.org/).

From the early 1990s, China's share of global network products remained above its share of total global manufacturing exports (Figure 16.2) and the difference became prominent after about 2005. In 2014–15, China accounted for 27 per cent of total global network product exports in the world compared with an 18 per cent share in total world manufacturing exports. Shares of both final assembly and components were notably higher than the aggregate global export share.

6 To minimise possible random shocks and measurement errors, two-year averages are used in intertemporal comparisons throughout this section.

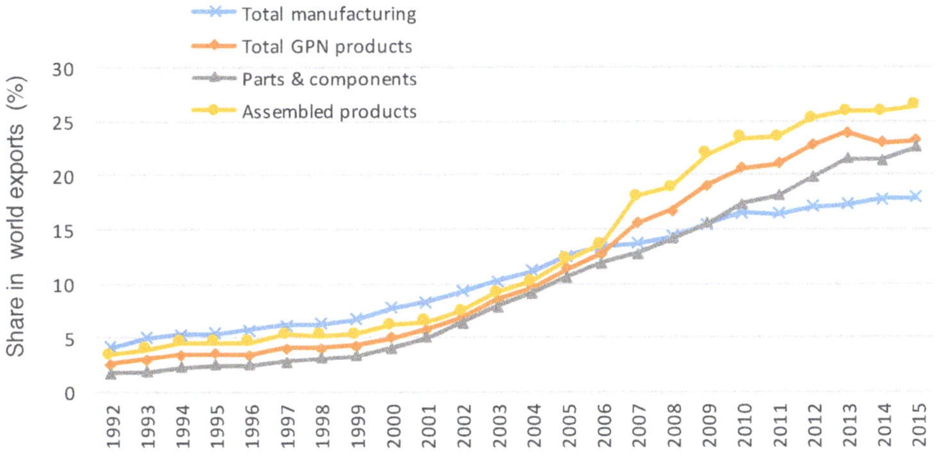

Figure 16.2 China's share in global manufacturing exports, 1992–2015 (per cent)

Source: Data compiled from UN Comtrade database (comtrade.un.org/).

Product composition

China's share of products exported within producer-driven networks in total GPN product exports increased from 52.1 per cent in 2000–01 to 74.2 per cent in 2014–15 (Figure 16.3; Table 16.1). Information technology products (automated data-processing machines, telecommunications and sound recording instruments and electrical machinery) are the prominent export products within this category. These products accounted for over 45 per cent of total global network exports in 2014–15.

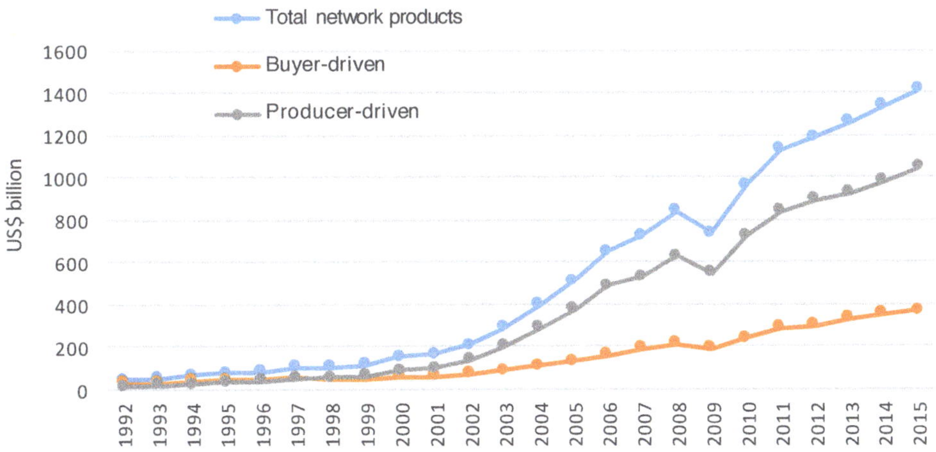

Figure 16.3 Producer-driven, buyer-driven and total global network exports from China, 1992–2015 (US$ billion)

Source: Data compiled from UN Comtrade database (comtrade.un.org/).

Table 16.1 Commodity composition of China's exports within global production networks, 2000–01 and 2014–15 (per cent)[1]

Products[2]	Parts and components		Assembled products		Total GPN products	
	2000–01	2014–15	2000–01	2014–15	2000–01	2014–15
(a) Exports within producer-driven networks	72.0	85.3	34.8	64.5	52.1	74.2
Chemicals (5)	0.3	0.7	-	-	0.1	0.3
Power-generating machines (71)	4.05	5.6	0.25	0.5	1.65	2.7
Specialised industrial machines (72)	1.15	2.0	0.8	3.7	1.6	3.0
Metal-working machines (73)	0.3	0.4	0.6	0.7	0.5	0.6
General industrial machinery (74)	4.35	8.1	1.8	7.2	3.95	7.6
Automated data-processing machines (75)	18.0	14.9	5.7	15.9	12.1	15.7
Telecommunications and sound-recording instruments (76)	18.7	22.3	6.1	8.7	13.9	14.6
Electrical machinery (77)	18.8	22.0	6.75	10.1	11.5	16.2
Road vehicles (78)	2.8	6.1	3.8	4.6	3.45	5.3
Other transport equipment (79)	0.5	0.4	2	4.1	1.4	2.5
Professional and scientific instruments (87)	0.5	1.2	3.4	7.2	2.1	4.6
Photographic apparatus (8)	1.65	0.8	3.3	1.9	2.7	1.4
(b) Exports within buyer-driven networks	27.95	14.7	65.2	35.5	47.9	25.2
Textiles (656–7)	28.15	14.2	0	-	10.1	5.9
Apparel and clothing accessories (84)	0.25	0.5	40.7	24.4	28.1	13.1
Footwear (85)	-	-	10.75	7.3	6.9	4.1
Travel goods (83)	-	-	3.8	3.8	2.4	2.1
Total (a + b)	100	100	100	100	100	100

[1] Two-year averages

[2] Commodity codes of the Standard International Trade Classification (SITC) are in parentheses.

- Zero or negligible

Source: Compiled from UN Comtrade database (comtrade.un.org/).

The shift in product composition towards products within producer-driven networks from those within buyer-driven networks seems to reflect a widening of the domestic production base rather than China losing international competitiveness in products traded within buyer-driven networks. As can be seen in Table 16.2, China's shares of global exports of most products at the two-digit Standard International Trade Classification (SITC) level have increased during this period, notwithstanding the widely perceived decline in China's international competitiveness owing to rising domestic wages. Interestingly, world market shares of buyer-driven exports have recorded notable increases, even though their production is considered relatively more labour intensive. China accounted for a staggering 49.2 per cent of world market share in apparel in 2014–15, up from 30.9 per cent in 2000–01. The world market share of footwear and travel goods increased from 21.9 per cent to 40.5 per cent between the two periods. Within producer-driven exports, automated data-processing machines (SITC 75) and telecommunications and sound-recording instruments (SITC 76) showed the fastest rates of global market penetration: in 2014–15, China accounted for 49.2 per cent and 36.1 per cent, respectively, of total global exports of these products. Interestingly, China's world market share has increased in both components and final assembly within producer-driven production networks, reflecting consolidation of China's role within global production sharing.

Table 16.2 China's share of global network trade, 2000–01 and 2014–15 (per cent)[1]

Products[2]	Parts and components		Final assembly		Total global network products	
	2000–01	2014–15	2000–01	2014–15	2000–01	2014–15
(a) Exports within producer-driven networks	5.85	17.8	13.65	16.2	3.7	11.5
Chemicals (5)	1.8	12.1	-	-	1.8	11.9
Power-generating machines (71)	2.25	9.1	6.0	8.5	1.15	4.8
Specialised industrial machines (72)	2.0	8.4	6.0	9.7	1.6	7.2
Metal-working machines (73)	2.4	9.1	6.15	8.1	1.75	6.5
General industrial machinery (74)	3.8	13.4	10.8	16.3	2.8	9.8
Automated data-processing machines (75)	11.1	29.9	39.8	71.3	7.7	49.28
Telecommunications and sound recording instruments (76)	12.5	46.3	37.3	35.4	8.3	36.1
Electrical machinery (77)	5.0	19.2	18.8	30.6	3.35	12.9
Road vehicles (78)	2.1	8.6	5.35	3.7	1.2	4.0
Other transport equipment (79)	1.2	2.9	3.3	11.1	1.6	7.5
Professional and scientific instruments (87)	2.3	10.5	10.1	16.1	3.9	13.3
Photographic apparatus (88)	9.5	18.5	12.8	13.3	5.5	12
(b) Exports within buyer-driven networks	12.9	32.1	33.8	46.2	19.7	39.6
Textiles (656–7)	13.6	34.5	17.3	-	13.6	34.8
Apparel and clothing accessories (84)	-	-	-	48.1	30.9	49.2
Footwear (85)	8.7	20.6	25.6	42.6	21.9	40.5
Travel goods (83)	0	0	16.5	41.8	23.7	41.6
Total (a + b)	6.5	22.4	16.7	27.6	5.1	17.6

[1] Two-year averages

[2] SITC commodity codes are in parentheses.

- Zero or negligible

Source: Compiled from UN Comtrade database (comtrade.un.org/).

There are at least four possible explanations for this across-the-board increase in global market penetration of manufacturing exports from China. First, even though the average domestic manufacturing wage has significantly increased, China's manufacturing wages are still much lower than those in the United States and other mature industrialised economies (Table 16.3). For instance, in 2014, the annual average wage for manufacturing workers in China was only one-fifth of that in the United States and most other developed countries. Allowing for other factors (discussed below), these 'international' wage differences are presumably a significant determinant of China's attractiveness as a location within production networks.

Second, there is still some slack in the labour markets in China's interior provinces and producers therefore have the option of relocating production within the country in response to labour scarcity and rising wages in the coastal provinces. Large firms located in industrial centres also have the option of using subcontracting arrangements with township and village-owned enterprises (TVEs) as a cushion against increasing wages (Athukorala and Wei 2017). Third, increases in labour costs may have been more than balanced by reductions in service linkage costs resulting from trade and investment policy reforms and, more importantly, improvements in provision of trade-related infrastructure. Finally, as already noted, compared with many countries, China has the advantage of being able to meet labour requirements (unskilled labour and supervisory manpower) for large-scale assembly operations within global production networks.

Deepening of production sharing

As noted at the outset of this chapter, there is some scattered evidence that China's manufacturing base has deepened over the years, with an increase in domestic production of components within global production networks. Has this structural change gained enough significance over time to be reflected in China's trade data?

Two data series compiled to shed light on this issue are plotted in Figure 16.4: the ratio of components exports to imports and the ratio of components imports to exports of assembled products. The former series indicates China's integration into global production networks as a supplier of components; the latter indicates the degree of dependence of final goods assembly in China on imported components.

Table 16.3 Annual average wages for manufacturing workers in selected countries (US$)

Country	2010	2014
Australia	71,420	84,743
Canada	53,454	58,452
France	72,771	74,403
Germany	75,519	78,895
Ireland	-	75,288

Country	2010	2014
Italy	63,757	70,483
Netherlands	73,816	75,216
Sweden	-	78,050
United Kingdom	61,958	70,400
United States	77,055	87,021
Czech Republic	-	24,863
Poland	23,605	24,088
Brazil	32,590	36,735
Mexico	16,021	16,675
China	15,508	16,287
India	14,039	14,708
Indonesia	19,048	18,771
Japan	65,643	66,339
South Korea	46,293	60,039
Malaysia	17,726	21,899
Philippines	10,998	9,526
Singapore	54,997	66,852
Taiwan	29,307	31,845
Vietnam	-	10,652

- Data suppressed to avoid disclosure of data of individual companies.

Notes: Data for the United States relate to US affiliates of foreign MNEs in US manufacturing. For other countries, the data are for foreign affiliates of US MNEs.

Source: US BEA (2014).

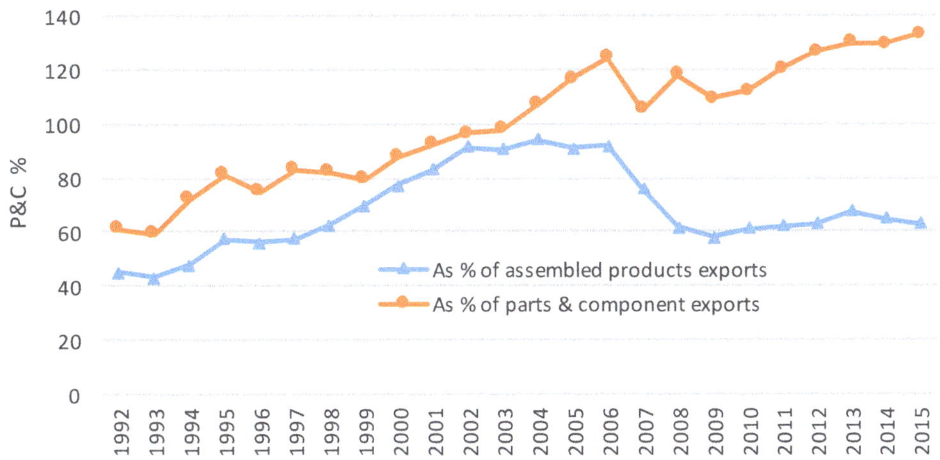

Figure 16.4 China: Imports of parts and components relative to exports of parts and components and assembled products (per cent)

Source: Data compiled from UN Comtrade database (comtrade.un.org/).

China's exports of components amounted to only about 60 per cent of its imports of components in the early 1990s. This share increased continuously during the ensuing years. In 2013–14, components exports exceeded imports by almost 25 per cent. Imports of components as a percentage of assembled goods exports increased from 38 per cent in the mid-1980s to more than 90 per cent by 2005. This was the period of rapid structural transformation from buyer-driven exports to producer-driven exports. This ratio has since come down, reaching 60 per cent by 2014–15. The data clearly indicate, therefore, that China's engagement in global production sharing has deepened over the past two decades.[7]

Geographic profile

Data on the destination-country and source-country composition of China's GPN exports and imports are summarised in Tables 16.4 and 16.5, respectively. A number of interesting developments relating to China's geographic patterns of engagement in global production networks can be observed.

Table 16.4 Destination-country composition of China's global network exports, 2000–01 and 2014–15 (per cent)*

	Parts and components		Assembled products		Total GNP products	
Country/country groups	2000–01	2014–15	2000–01	2014–15	2000–01	2014–15
Japan	19.4	9.4	15.3	7.1	17.8	8.1
South Korea	4.5	7.1	2.8	4.8	3.8	5.7
Taiwan	5.9	2.7	3.9	2.6	5.0	2.6
South-East Asia	11.5	11.5	8.6	12.5	10.1	11.9
South Asia	2.4	5.0	2.6	4.2	2.5	4.6
India	0.4	3.1	0.5	2.4	0.5	2.7
West Asia	1.8	4.3	2.5	5.0	2.1	5.7
Central Asia	0.1	0.6	0.1	0.8	0.1	0.7
Oceania	1.1	1.6	1.7	2.5	1.4	2.1
Australia	1.0	1.5	1.5	2.0	1.2	1.8
NAFTA^	28.8	27.0	31.7	25.3	29.6	24.1
United States	27.1	23.4	29.7	22.2	27.7	22.7
Canada	1.1	1.4	1.3	1.3	1.2	1.4
European Union (EU)	21.1	18.9	21.4	19.9	21.2	19.5
Non-EU Western Europe	0.4	0.3	1.6	0.6	1.0	0.5
Russian Federation	0.1	2.1	0.4	2.3	0.3	2.2
Africa	1.6	3.5	3.2	4.6	2.3	4.1
Latin America and the Caribbean	2.3	6.9	4.4	7.9	3.3	8.5

7 Constantinescu et al. (2014) also report a decline in the ratio of components imports to total manufacturing exports from China, from about 55 per cent in the mid-1990s to about 35 per cent in 2012. However, without looking at what has been happening to component exports, they erroneously interpret these figures as indicative of 'diminishing fragmentation of the production process' (pp. 40–1).

	Parts and components		Assembled products		Total GNP products	
Country/country groups	2000–01	2014–15	2000–01	2014–15	2000–01	2014–15
Total	100	100	100	100	100	100
Memorandum items						
Developed countries#	70.1	52.0	70.3	50.0	69.7	50.2
Developed countries excluding Japan	49.3	42.6	54.9	43.0	51.9	42.8
Developing countries#	29.9	48.0	29.7	50.0	30.3	49.8

* Two-year averages

^ North American Free Trade Agreement

Based on the UN Standard Country Classification.

Source: Compiled from UN Comtrade database (comtrade.un.org/).

Table 16.5 Source-country composition of China's global network imports, 2000–01 and 2014–15 (per cent)*

	Parts and components		Assembled products		Total GNP products	
Country/country groups	2000–01	2014–15	2000–01	2014--5	2000–01	2014–15
Japan	28.5	22.2	28.8	12.8	28.8	15.5
South Korea	8.2	14.1	5.3	19.4	6.7	17.7
Taiwan	16.2	11.4	12.4	19.6	14.3	17.2
South-East Asia	8.7	14.9	3.5	12.9	6.8	13.5
South Asia	0.0	0.4	0.0	0.1	0.0	0.2
India	0.0	0.4	0.0	0.1	0.0	0.2
West Asia	0.1	0.3	0.2	0.3	0.2	0.3
Central Asia	0.0	0.0	0.0	0.0	0.0	0.0
Oceania	0.3	0.2	0.5	0.1	0.3	0.1
Australia	0.2	0.1	0.3	0.1	0.3	0.1
NAFTA^	15.3	10.0	16.4	12.8	15.1	11.4
United States	14.0	9.3	17.4	11.9	15.0	10.6
Canada	1.0	0.4	1.0	0.5	1.0	0.5
European Union (EU)	20.5	24.2	28.5	19.2	24.3	21.1
Non-EU Western Europe	0.8	1.1	1.3	1.3	1.0	1.2
Russian Federation	1.1	0.1	1.2	0.1	1.1	0.1
Africa	0.0	0.1	0.0	0.1	0.0	0.1
Latin America and the Caribbean	0.3	1.2	0.1	1.8	0.2	1.6
Total	100	100	100	100	100	100
Developed countries#	64.5	55.4	77.2	44.4	70.4	47.6
Developed countries excluding Japan	35.6	34.1	48.4	31.6	41.6	32.4
Developing countries#	35.5	44.6	22.8	55.6	29.6	52.2

* Two-year averages

^ North American Free Trade Agreement

Based on the UN Standard Country Classification.

Source: Compiled from UN Comtrade database (comtrade.un.org/).

On the export side, there has been a notable decline in China's share of GPN products destined for developed countries, from 69.7 per cent in 2000–01 to 50.2 per cent in 2014–15. Exports to Japan recorded the sharpest decline, from 17.8 per cent to 8.1 per cent between the two periods. Developed countries other than Japan accounted for 42.8 per cent of China's total GPN product exports, compared with 51.9 per cent in 2000–01. The United States remains the largest market for both components and assembled products, accounting for more than one-fifth of Chinese exports.

While China's market shares in all developing countries/regions, other than Taiwan, have increased across the board, its degree of export penetration in Africa, Latin America and the Caribbean and West Asia (the Middle East) was much sharper, though starting from a low base. The share of Chinese exports destined to the East Asian developing countries (South Korea, Taiwan and the countries of South-East Asia) has increased at a slower rate, from 21.5 per cent in 1992–2003 to 20.5 per cent in 2013–14, compared with the share of exports to other developing countries, which increased from 21.5 per cent to 28.6 per cent.

On the import side, the share accounted for by developed countries in GPN exports has declined at a much faster rate—from 70 per cent in 2000–01 to 47.6 per cent in 2014–15—compared with what we observed for the export side. However, there are notable inter-country differences. The major winners of market share in China are South Korea and Taiwan and the countries in South-East Asia, with South Korea recording the biggest gain. By contrast, Japan's share has declined sharply, from 28.8 per cent in 2000–01 to 15.5 per cent in 2013–15. The data clearly show the heavy concentration of China's components imports from neighbouring East and South-East Asian countries (including Japan). The share accounted for by these countries in total components imports increased from 53 per cent to 62 per cent between 2000–01 and 2014–15.

Production sharing and Sino–US trade relations

China's exports to the United States are dominated by manufactured goods, with other (primary) products accounting for less than 5 per cent of total merchandise exports (Figure 16.5a). GPN products account for the bulk of manufactured goods, with their share increasing from 45 per cent in 2000–01 to over 65 per cent in 2015–16.

The share of manufactured goods in China's imports from the United States (US exports to China) declined from 78 per cent in 2000–01 to 61 per cent in 2015–16. The share of GPN products in total manufacturing exports declined from 73 per cent to 49 per cent between these two periods. In recent years, the annual rate of increase in China's imports has been much slower than the rapid increase in China's exports to the United States (Figure 16.5b).

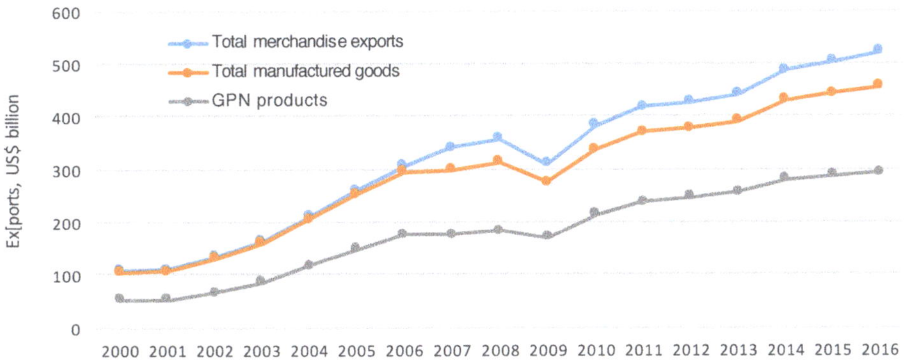

Figure 16.5a China's exports to the United States, 2000–16 (US$ billion)

Source: Data compiled from UN Comtrade database (comtrade.un.org/).

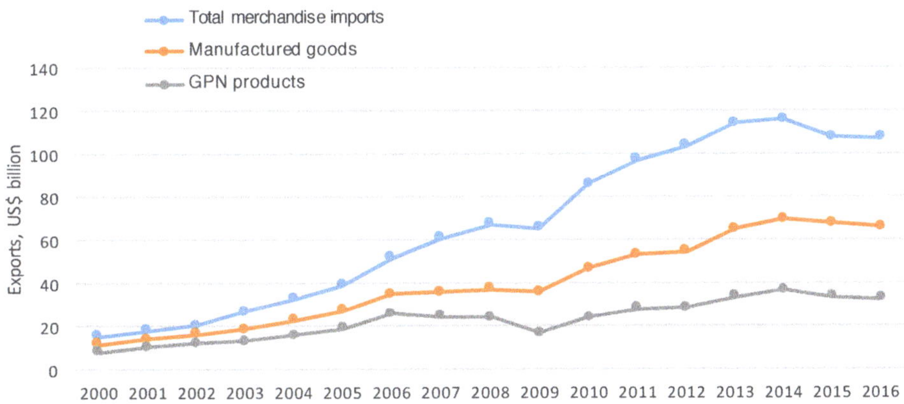

Figure 16.5b China's imports from the United States, 2000–16 (US$ billion)

Source: Data compiled from UN Comtrade database (comtrade.un.org/).

Figure 16.5c China's trade surplus with the United States, 2000–16 (US$ billion)

Source: Data compiled from UN Comtrade database (comtrade.un.org/).

These patterns are consistent with our observation in the previous section of deepening GPN production bases in China. With the rapid expansion of manufacturing production in China—a process in which US MNEs play a significant role—the share of manufacturing in Chinese imports from the United States has declined over time. In particular, given the expansion of components production in China, firms engaged in assembly operations appear to procure inputs from domestic Chinese sources.

The changing export and import patterns of Sino–US trade relations are vividly captured in China's trade surplus with the United States, which is the focal point of that country's China-bashing (Figure 16.5c). Manufacturing trade accounts for almost all of China's trade surplus with the United States. GPN product trade accounted for more than two-thirds of the surplus over the past decade, compared with about 50 per cent during the preceding decade. The actual impact of GPN product trade on the widening trade surplus could be much larger than is depicted in these data: the trade data decomposition procedure used in this study does not cover the entire GPN product trade (see Appendix 16.1).[8]

GPN product imports to the United States increased fivefold (from about US$50 billion to more than US$300 billion between 2000 and 2015). Throughout this period, components, which are mostly inputs to US manufacturing, have accounted for an average of 45 per cent of these imports (Figure 16.6a).

Contrary to popular perceptions based on sensational media stories about massive procurements by Walmart and other US retail stores, standard consumer goods (apparel, footwear, toys and so on) account for a small share of China's total GPN product exports to the United States. Over the past decade, products traded within producer-driven production networks have accounted for more than 85 per cent of GPN product trade between the two countries (Figure 16.6b). This is because most US MNEs in vertically integrated global industries have shifted final assembly processes to China while retaining mostly product design, global marketing and other headquarters functions in the United States.

8 The focus of this chapter is solely on the *record* trade surplus, which is the focus of the current debate on Sino–US trade. The issue of the extent to which this is a reflection of shifting production bases from other countries to China as part of the ongoing process of global production sharing is beyond its scope. On this issue, see Athukorala and Yamashita (2009) and Koopman et al. (2012).

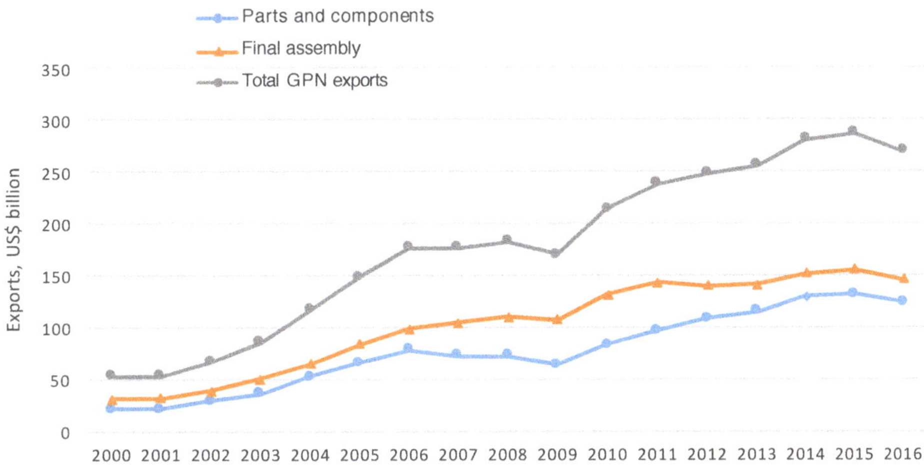

Figure 16.6a Shares of exports of parts and components and final assembly products in total GPN product exports, 2000–16 (US$ billion)

Source: Data compiled from UN Comtrade database (comtrade.un.org/).

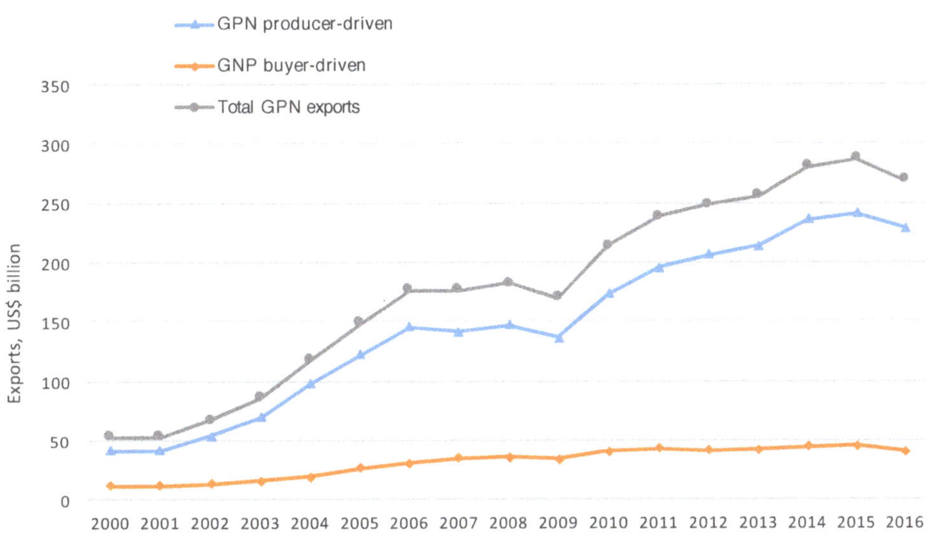

Figure 16.6b Shares of buyer-driven and producer-driven products in GPN product exports, 2000–16 (US$ billion)

Source: Data compiled from UN Comtrade database (comtrade.un.org/).

The debate about the widening Sino–US trade imbalance has mostly, if not entirely, focused on China's exports to the United States. Ignored in the debate is the importance of China for US MNEs as a base for expanding their exports to the rest of the world. In 2013, the latest year for which the relevant data are available, the value of goods exported to the rest of the world by US MNE affiliates in China was US$37.5 billion, which was almost three times the value of their exports to the United States (US$13.6 billion) (Table 16.6).

Table 16.6 Sales values for US multinational enterprises operating in China, 2013 (US$ billion)

	Goods and services	Goods
Total sales	261.8	217.7
Local sales	206.7	166.6
Exports		
To the United States	15.4	13.6
To other countries	39.7	37.5

Source: US BEA (2016).

The discussion in this section supports the view that the widening trade imbalance is essentially a structural phenomenon driven by the process of global production sharing, from which both economies benefit. Protectionist policies would hurt manufacturing production, resulting in job losses in the United States, and hinder the global operations of US MNEs on the back of China's emergence as a manufacturing giant.

Given this intricate interdependence between the two countries, President Trump's attempt to impose punitive tariffs on China is bound to face formidable opposition from major business interests in the United States. So far, his attempt to 'bring factories home' has not materialised beyond the highly publicised cases of Ford Motors and Carrier Corp. abandoning their plans to set up production plants in Mexico. There is anecdotal evidence that US MNEs are already back to their usual practice of 'going global' after a pause in the immediate aftermath of Trump's election victory (Krugman 2017; Black 2017).

Even if punitive tariffs were eventually imposed, the impact on trade flows within global production networks may not be as damaging as commonly thought. There is evidence that global production sharing considerably weakens the link between relative prices and trade performance, particularly when it comes to trade in components (Swenson 2000; Arndt and Huemer 2007; Burstein et al. 2008; Feenstra 2010; Athukorala and Khan 2016). Production units of the value chain located in different countries normally specialise in specific tasks, which are not directly substitutable for tasks undertaken elsewhere. Substitutability of components obtained from various sources is, therefore, rather limited. Also, the establishment of overseas production bases and related service links entails high fixed costs, making relative price/cost changes less important in business decision-making.

Concluding remarks

This chapter has examined the implications of the evolving role of China in East Asia–centred global production networks for regional and global integration of the Chinese economy. Consolidation of its role within Asia-centred global production networks has been the prime mover of China's rapid export growth. The deepening of production bases within global production networks is evident from the notable decline in components imports relative to total processed products exported from China and from its emerging role as a net exporter of components.

China's reliance on its East Asian neighbours for components supply has significantly declined in recent years, reflecting deepening of China's engagement in production networks. China is also emerging as a significant supplier of components within production networks in East Asia and beyond. The shares of components exports to China in total manufacturing exports (to the world) of neighbouring East Asian countries are much smaller than commonly thought. Moreover, in recent years, there has been a notable decline in these shares as the input requirements of final assembly in China are increasingly being met through domestic sourcing.

There has been a notable geographic diversification of final assembly exports from China, but Western countries still account for a sizeable share. The shares of developing countries have generally increased across the board. The degree of China's market penetration in Africa, Latin America and the Caribbean and West Asia (the Middle East) was much sharper, although starting from a low base, than that in East Asia. Therefore, there is no evidence of an East Asia bias in China's evolving export patterns. There is also no evidence that China's rise is reshaping East Asia as a self-contained economic entity with potential for maintaining growth dynamism independent of the developed economies.

The evidence in this chapter supports the view that, in a context in which global production sharing is becoming a symbol of economic globalisation, the real story behind the Sino–US trade gap is much more complicated than what is revealed by standard trade-flow analysis. The widening trade imbalance is basically a structural phenomenon driven by the process of global production sharing and the pivotal role played by China within East Asia–centred global production networks. Initially, China predominantly engaged as the main point of final assembly in Asian production networks, based on its ample supply of labour and moves taken by US firms to supply high-end components from their Asian bases to China. As the production base became more deeply rooted, China's dependence on imported components diminished and China has now become an important supplier of components to the United States and other countries.

The global competitiveness of US MNEs depends on their ability to use China as the production base for supplying the rest of the world. Given this intricate interdependence between the two countries, President Trump's attempt to impose punitive tariffs on China is bound to face formidable opposition from major business interests in the United States. Even if the punitive tariffs were eventually imposed, the impact on trade flows within global production networks may not be as damaging as commonly thought because global production sharing considerably weakens the link between relative prices and trade performance.

References

Arndt, S. W. and Huemer, A. (2007), Trade, production networks and exchange rate, *Journal of Economic Asymmetries* 4(1): 11–39. doi.org/10.1016/j.jeca.2007.01.002.

Athukorala, P. (2009), The rise of China and East Asian export performance: Is the crowding-out fear warranted? *World Economy* 32: 234–65. doi.org/10.1111/j.1467-9701.2008.01151.x.

Athukorala, P. and Khan, F. (2016), Global production sharing and the measurement of price elasticity in international trade, *Economics Letters* 139(1): 27–30.

Athukorala, P. and Kohpaiboon, A. (2012), Intra-regional trade in East Asia: The decoupling fallacy, crisis, and policy challenges, in M. Kawai, M. B. Lamberte and Y. C. Park (eds), *The Global Financial Crisis and Asia: Implications and challenges*, pp. 85–106, New York: Oxford University Press.

Athukorala, P. and Kohpaiboon, A. (2014), Global production sharing, trade patterns and industrialization in Southeast Asia, in I. Coxhead (ed.), *Routledge Handbook of Southeast Asian Economies*, pp. 139–61, London: Routledge.

Athukorala, P. and Wei, Z. (2017), Economic transition and labour market dynamics in China: An interpretative survey of the 'turning point' debate, *Journal of Economic Surveys* [early view]. doi.org/10.1111/joes.12206.

Athukorala, P. and Yamashita, N. (2009), Global production sharing and Sino–US trade relations, *China & World Economy* 17(3): 39–56. doi.org/10.1111/j.1749-124X.2009.01149.x.

Bergsten, C. F., Gill, B., Lardy, N. and Michell, D. (2006), *China: The Balance Sheet*, New York: Public Affairs Publishing.

Black, T. (2017), American jobs are headed to Mexico once again, *Bloomberg Politics*, 31 March, updated 1 April. Available from: www.bloomberg.com/politics/articles/2017-03-31/jobs-departing-u-s-for-mexico-again-as-trump-s-threats-ignored.

Burstein, A., Kurz, C. and Tesar, L. (2008), Trade, production sharing, and international transmission of business cycles, *Journal of Monetary Economics* 55(4): 775–95. doi.org/10.1016/j.jmoneco.2008.03.004.

Constantinescu, C., Mattoo, A. and Rura M. (2015), Slow trade, *Finance & Development* 51(4): 39–41.

Feenstra, R. C. (2010), *Offshoring in the Global Economy*, Cambridge, Mass.: MIT Press.

Gereffi, G. (1999), International trade and industrial upgrading in the apparel commodity chain, *Journal of International Economics* 48(1): 37–70. doi.org/10.1016/S0022-1996(98)00075-0.

Guo, M., Lu, L., Sheng, L. and Yu, M. (2017), *The day after tomorrow: Evaluating the burden of Trump's trade war*, Working Paper E2017003, China Center for Economic Research, Peking University, Beijing. Available from: edirc.repec.org/data/ccpkucn.html.

Helpman, E. (2006), Trade, FDI, and the organization of firms, *Journal of Economic Literature* 44(3): 589–630. doi.org/10.1257/jel.44.3.589.

Hummels, D. (2002), Review of 'Fragmentation: New production pattern in the world economy' by S. W. Arndt and H. Kierzkowskei, *Economic Geography* 2(2): 368–9. doi.org/10.1093/jeg/2.3.368.

Isaacson, W. (2011), *Steve Jobs*, New York: Simon & Schuster.

Johnson, R. C. (2014), Five facts about value-added exports and implications for macroeconomics and trade research, *The Journal of Economic Perspectives* 28: 119–42. doi.org/10.1257/jep.28.2.119.

Jones, R. W. (2000), *Globalization and the Theory of Input Trade*, Cambridge, Mass.: MIT Press.

Jones, R. W. and Kierzkowski, H. (2004), Globalization and the consequences of international fragmentation, in R. Dornbusch, G. Calvo and M. Obstfeld (eds), *Money, Factor Mobility and Trade: Essays in honor of Robert A. Mundell*, pp. 365–81, Cambridge, Mass.: MIT Press.

Kang, H. and Shen, J. (2016), International performance appraisal practices and approaches of South Korean MNEs in China, *The International Journal of Human Resource Management* 27: 291–310. doi.org/10.1080/09585192.2015.1039562.

Kee, H. L. and Tang, H. (2016), Domestic value added in exports: Theory and firm evidence from China, *American Economic Review* 106(6): 1402–36. doi.org/10.1257/aer.20131687.

Kohli, H. S., Sharma, A. and Sood, A. (2011), *Asia 2050: Realizing the Asian century*, New Delhi: Sage.

Kong, Y. F. and Kneller, R. (2016), Measuring the Impact of China's Export Growth on its Asian Neighbours, *World Economy* 39 (2): 195–220.

Koopman, R., Wang, Z. and Wei, S. J. (2012), Estimating domestic content in exports when processing trade is pervasive, *Journal of Development Economics* 99(1): 178–89. doi.org/10.1016/j.jdeveco.2011.12.004.

Krugman, P. (2017), Of tweets and trade, *The New York Times*, 31 March. Available from: krugman.blogs.nytimes.com/.

Lall, S. and Albaladejo, M. (2004), China's competitive performance: A threat to East Asian manufactured exports? *World Development* 32: 1441–66. doi.org/10.1016/j.worlddev.2004.03.006.

Lamy, P. (2013), Foreword, in D. K. Elms and P. Low (eds), *Global Value Chains in a Changing World*, pp. xv–xviii, Geneva: WTO.

Lardy, N. R. (2014), *Markets over Mao: The rise of private business in China*, Washington, DC: Peterson Institute for International Economics.

Nunn, N. (2007), Relationship-specificity, incomplete contracts, and the pattern of trade, *The Quarterly Journal of Economics* 122(2): 569–600. doi.org/10.1162/qjec.122.2.569.

Park, Y. C. and Shin, K. (2009), Economic integration and changes in the business cycles in East Asia: Is the region decoupling from the rest of the world? *Asian Economic Papers* 8(1): 107–40. doi.org/10.1162/asep.2009.8.1.107.

Roach, S. (2014), *Unbalanced: The codependency of America and China*, New Haven, Conn.: Yale University Press.

Rodrik, D. (2006), What's so special about China's exports? *China & World Economy* 14: 1–19. doi.org/10.1111/j.1749-124X.2006.00038.x.

Schott, P. K. (2008), The relative sophistication of Chinese exports, *Economic Policy* 23: 6–49. doi.org/10.1111/j.1468-0327.2007.00195.x.

Song, E. and Sung, Y. W. (1995), *The Fifth Dragon: The emergence of the Pearl River Delta*, New York: Addison-Wesley.

Spencer, B. J. (2005), International outsourcing and incomplete contracts, *Canadian Journal of Economics* 38(4): 1107–35. doi.org/10.1111/j.0008-4085.2005.00317.x.

Swenson, D. L. (2000), Firm outsourcing decisions: Evidence from US foreign trade zones, *Economic Inquiry* 38(2): 175–89. doi.org/10.1111/j.1465-7295.2000.tb00012.x.

United States Bureau of Economic Analysis (US BEA) (2014), *Articles and Publications*, Washington, DC: US BEA. Available from: www.bea.gov/international/ai1.htm#dius.

United States Bureau of Economic Analysis (US BEA) (2016), *Worldwide Activities of US Multinational Enterprises: Revised statistics 2013*, Washington, DC: US BEA. Available from: www.bea.gov/international/usdia2013r.htm.

Upward, R., Wang, Z. and Zheng, J. (2013), Weighing China's export basket: The domestic content and technology intensity of Chinese exports, *Journal of Comparative Economics* 41: 527–43. doi.org/10.1016/j.jce.2012.07.004.

Wei, S.-J., Xie, Z. and Zhang, X. (2017), From "made in China" to "innovated in China": Necessity, prospects and challenges', *Journal of Economic Perspectives*, 31(1): 49–70.

World Bank (various years), *DataBank: World development indicators*, Washington, DC: The World Bank. Available from: databank.worldbank.org/data/reports.aspx?source=world-development-indicators#.

Wu, W. (2017), Just how badly could Trump's threatened 45% tariff hurt China? *South China Morning Post*, 15 January. Available from: www.cnbc.com/2017/01/15/just-how-badly-could-trumps-threatened-45-tariff-hurt-china.html.

Yang, C. H. and Hayakawa, K. (2015), Localization and overseas R&D activity: The case of Taiwanese multinational enterprises in China, *R&D Management* 45: 181–95. doi.org/10.1111/radm.12059.

Yang, C.-H. and Tsou, M.-W. (2015), Multinational exposure, export variety and price: Evidence from Chinese electronics exporters, *Journal of the Japanese and International Economies* 38: 93–110. doi.org/10.1016/j.jjie.2015.05.008.

Yao, S. (2009), Why are Chinese exports not so special? *China & World Economy* 17: 47–65. doi.org/10.1111/j.1749-124X.2009.01130.x.

Yeats, A. (2001), Just how big is global production sharing? In S. Arndt and H. Kierzkowski (eds), *Fragmentation: New production patterns in the world economy*, pp. 108–43, New York: Oxford University Press.

Yip, G. S. and McKern, B. (2016), *China's Next Strategic Advantage: From imitation to innovation*, Cambridge, Mass.: MIT Press.

Yoshitomi, M. (2007), Global imbalances and East Asian monetary cooperation, in D. Chung and B. Eichengreen (eds), *Towards an East Asian Exchange Rate Regime*, pp. 22–48, Washington, DC: Brookings Institution Press.

Yusuf, S., Nabeshima, K. and Perkins, D. (2007), China and India reshape global industrial geography, in A. L. Winters and S. Yusuf (eds), *Dancing with Giants: China, India, and the global economy*, pp. 35–66, Washington, DC: The World Bank.

Appendix 16.1. Trade data compilation

Following the seminal paper by Yeats (2001), it has become common practice to use data on parts and components to measure GPN product trade. However, there has been a remarkable expansion of production sharing, from parts and components to also encompass final assembly. Moreover, the relative importance of these two tasks within production networks varies among countries and over time in a given country, making it problematic to use data on the parts and components trade as general indicators of the trends and patterns of GPN product trade over time and across countries. In this study, we define GPN product trade as incorporating both components and final (assembled) goods exchanged within production networks.

The data used in this study, for all countries except Taiwan, are compiled from the UN Comtrade database. The data for Taiwan (a country not covered in the UN trade data reporting system) come from the database of the Council of Economic Planning and Development, Taipei. The data are compiled at the five-digit level of the SITC, based on SITC Revision 3.

Parts and components are delineated from the reported trade data using a list compiled by mapping parts and components in the intermediate products subcategory of the UN Broad Economic Classification (BEC) with the SITC.[9] It is important to note that parts and components, as defined here, are only a subset of intermediate goods, even though the two terms have been widely used interchangeably in the

9 The lists are available from the author on request.

recent literature on global production sharing. Parts and components—unlike standard intermediate inputs such as iron, steel, industrial chemicals and coal—are 'relationship-specific' intermediate inputs; in most cases, they do not have reference prices are more demanding of the contractual environment (Hummels 2002; Nunn 2007). Most (if not all) parts and components also do not have a 'commercial life' of their own unless they are embodied in a final product.

There is no hard and fast rule for delineating final goods assembled within global production networks from the standard trade data. The only practical way of doing this is to focus on the specific product categories in which GPN product trade is heavily concentrated. Once these product categories are identified, approximate trade in final assembly can be estimated as the difference between parts and components, which are directly identified based on our list, and the total trade of these product categories.

Guided by the available literature on production sharing, we identified 14 product categories: power-generating machinery (SITC 71), specialised industrial machines (SITC 72), metal-working machines (SITC 73), general industrial machinery (SITC 74), office machines and automatic data-processing machines (SITC 75), telecommunications and sound recording equipment (SITC 76), electrical machinery (SITC 77), road vehicles (SITC 78), other transport equipment (SITC 79), travel goods (SITC 83), apparel and clothing accessories (SITC 84), footwear and sport goods (SITC 85), professional and scientific equipment (SITC 87) and photographic apparatus (SITC 88). It is reasonable to assume that these categories contain virtually no products produced from start to finish in a given country. Of these, SITC 83, SITC 84 and SITC 85 can be classified as products predominantly traded within buyer-driven production networks, with the rest belonging to producer-driven production networks. The difference between the value of total exports of these categories and the value of total parts and components falling under these categories was treated as the value of final assembly. Admittedly, however, the estimates based on this list do not provide full coverage of final assembly in global trade. For instance, outsourcing of final assembly does take place in various miscellaneous product categories, such as clothing, furniture, sporting goods and leather products. It is not possible to meaningfully delineate parts and components and assembled goods in reported trade in these product categories because they contain a significant (yet unknown) share of horizontal trade.

A number of recent studies have analysed trade patterns using 'value-added' trade data derived by combining the standard trade data with national input–output tables (Johnson 2014 provides a survey). The underlying rationale is that, in a context of rapidly expanding cross-border trade in components driven by global production sharing, the standard (gross) trade data (trade data based on customs records) tend to give a distorted picture of the bilateral trade imbalances of a given country and the geographic profile of its global trade linkages (Lamy 2013). This approach is, however, not relevant for the present study, which aims to examine patterns and determinants of global production sharing. The pertinent approach is to analyse data on the reported (gross) exports, separated into parts and components and final assembly. Trade and industry policies have the potential to influence only a country's engagement in a given slice of the value chain; domestic value adding evolves over time as the country becomes integrated into the value chain.

17. China's Overseas Direct Investment and Reverse Knowledge Spillovers

Chunlai Chen

Introduction

Since the launch of its 'go global' strategy in 2001, China's outward foreign direct investment (OFDI) has increased dramatically. China's global OFDI stock increased from US$32.69 billion in 2001 (UNCTAD 2003) to US$1.01 trillion in 2005 (UNCTAD 2016). Drivers of outbound investment by Chinese multinational enterprises (MNEs) are diverse. Alongside market-seeking, efficiency-seeking and resource-seeking, one of the main motives of Chinese MNEs is strategic asset–seeking, the aim of which is the acquisition of advanced technology, production knowhow, modern management skills and internationally recognised brands in support of the long-term economic development of China (e.g. Buckley et al. 2007; Liu and Scott-Kennel 2011).

A growing body of literature explores China's OFDI; however, previous studies have focused mainly on either the motivations of Chinese MNEs to conduct OFDI or the location determinants of host countries that make them attractive to Chinese investors (e.g. Liu et al. 2005; Buckley et al. 2007; Cheung and Qian 2009; Tolentino 2010; Wei and Alon 2010; Cheung et al. 2012; Kolstad and Wiig 2012; Amighini et al. 2014; Chen 2015a). Unfortunately, empirical studies of the impact on China's economy of this rising OFDI are limited. Moreover, empirical studies of the impact of reverse knowledge spillovers from OFDI on China's economic growth are rare. It therefore remains unknown whether OFDI flows from China have generated any reverse knowledge spillovers for the Chinese economy, thus contributing via this channel to China's economic growth.

This chapter aims to investigate empirically the impact of reverse knowledge spillovers from OFDI on China's economic growth. It specifically seeks to investigate whether there are reverse knowledge spillovers from OFDI arising from provincial firms and from central government–controlled state-owned enterprises (SOEs) impacting on provincial economic growth.

Analysis of a panel dataset of China's 30 provinces over the years 2004–14 finds that, after controlling for the impact of knowledge spillovers from inward foreign direct investment (IFDI) on provincial economic growth, OFDI from both provincial firms and SOEs is associated with a positive and statistically significant effect on China's provincial economic growth through reverse knowledge spillovers to China's economy. Overall, the study provides strong empirical evidence that OFDI contributes to China's economic growth.

The chapter makes two contributions to the literature. First, this study investigates the impact of both IFDI and OFDI on provincial economic growth in China, adding to the empirical evidence on their impact on economic growth in host and home countries. Second, this study explores how China's OFDI from provincial firms and SOEs affects provincial economic growth. These findings are important for policymakers, especially in developing economies, in designing and implementing policies to facilitate and enhance the diffusion of knowledge spillovers from IFDI and OFDI to host and home economies.

The rest of this chapter is structured as follows: the next section refers to the literature to discuss the theories and channels of reverse knowledge spillovers from OFDI; section three presents the framework for our analysis and empirical model, describes the data and specifies the variables; section four presents the regression results, while section five provides the conclusion and policy implications.

Reverse knowledge spillovers from OFDI: Theory and literature

The term knowledge spillover refers to the flow of knowledge that takes place without any business transactions occurring (Griliches 1992). FDI is one of the most important means by which international knowledge spillovers take place (e.g. Dunning 1993; Dunning and Lundan 2008). Spillovers from IFDI are regarded as an important source of knowledge in developing countries (e.g. Javorcik 2004; Kneller and Pisu 2007; Sheng et al. 2011; Chen et al. 2013).

In the theoretical literature (e.g. Hymer 1976; Dunning 1977, 1980, 1988, 1993, 2000; Caves 1996), through ownership advantages and firm-specific intangible assets, IFDI can bring to host countries a package of capital, advanced technology and knowhow, modern enterprise management and mature marketing skills, well-organised international distribution channels, coordinated relationships with suppliers and clients, good reputation and other intangible assets. IFDI can therefore generate knowledge spillovers to the host country's domestic firms. Knowledge spillovers arising from IFDI can be horizontal—within the same industry and arising through demonstration effects, labour movement and information flows. But IFDI can also impose competition on domestic firms. On the one hand, competition can force local firms to increase their adoption of advanced technology and to be more innovative so as to use existing resources more efficiently, thus increasing efficiency and productivity. On the other hand, it can crowd local firms out of the product market, and also offers completion in local labour and resources markets (e.g. Aitken and Harrison 1999; Hu et al. 2005; Chen 2011, 2015b; Fu 2011; Sheng et al. 2011; Chen et al. 2013). The net effects of horizontal knowledge spillovers from IFDI on domestic firms are inconclusive (Gorg and Greenaway 2004).

Knowledge spillovers arising from IFDI can also be vertical, via forward and backward industrial linkages within the supply chain (e.g. Javorcik 2004; Kneller and Pisu 2007; Sheng et al. 2011; Chen et al. 2013). When IFDI firms supply better intermediate inputs for their customers, or when they transfer knowledge to their suppliers for better quality inputs and on-time delivery, the positive spillovers from IFDI will contribute to domestic firm productivity in downstream and upstream industries.

What about the potential for reverse knowledge spillovers from OFDI back to home-country economies? Theoretically, reverse knowledge spillovers from OFDI can take place in three phases. In the first phase, a subsidiary acquires and absorbs host-country-specific knowledge either directly through cross-border mergers and acquisitions (M&As) or indirectly through reverse knowledge spillovers, such as demonstration effects, labour mobility, vertical industrial linkages and external network linkages with universities, research institutions and business associations in the host country. During the second phase, the acquired knowledge is transferred from the subsidiary to the parent company directly and through intra-firm labour mobility. During the third phase, the acquired foreign knowledge spills over or is transferred to home-country domestic firms or other knowledge recipients and is indirectly absorbed by the home economy.

It is reasonable to assume that the channels for reverse knowledge spillovers and knowledge spillovers from IFDI to host-country domestic firms are similar. The discussion below focuses on the key channels for reverse knowledge spillovers from home-country MNEs to home-country domestic firms, the first two of which are demonstration effects and imitation. If home-country MNEs acquire advanced knowledge abroad, transfer it back to their headquarters and apply the new techniques in their production at home, other domestic firms may also benefit by learning from and imitating that knowledge through demonstration effects. However, if home-country MNEs and other domestic firms are in the same industry, demonstration effects can also create competition between them. This increased competition not only will induce home-country domestic firms to imitate the advanced technology and production techniques of home-country MNEs to ensure their own survival, but will also force the domestic firms to undertake innovation to improve their performance and use existing technology more efficiently (e.g. Blomström and Kokko 1998; Aitken and Harrison 1999; Chen et al. 2013).

A second channel for reverse knowledge spillovers from MNEs to their home economy is labour mobility. Returnees who were employed in subsidiaries abroad and acquired advanced foreign knowledge during those assignments may contribute to the knowledge creation and innovation of their parent MNEs and home economy. Returnees may also bring important external networks that facilitate the continuation of knowledge exchange. Thus, home-country domestic firms profit not only from product or process-related information, but also from the employee's country-specific knowledge, which can be used to open up new export markets. Therefore, the labour mobility of returning employees of home-country MNEs can also add to the aggregate knowledge stock in the home economy. Filatotchev et al. (2011) find that the reverse flows of highly skilled Chinese labour provide an important channel of knowledge transfer to the Chinese economy. Dai and Liu (2009) use a dataset of Chinese small and medium enterprises (SMEs) and find that returnee entrepreneurs are able to develop a competitive advantage by applying the intangible assets they acquired abroad. More importantly, they also find that local entrepreneurs can benefit from returnee entrepreneurs through the establishment of close business linkages.

The third channel for reverse knowledge spillovers from home-country MNEs to the home economy comprises backward (from home-country MNEs to home-country suppliers) and forward (from home-country MNEs to home-country customers) linkages.

Backward linkages of home-country MNEs may benefit the home economy in several ways. First, home-country MNEs may increase the efficiency and product quality of their home-country suppliers by imposing higher requirements for quality and on-time delivery. If home-country MNEs are willing to provide assistance to their home-country suppliers to upgrade production management or technology, the latter may be able to enhance their production and management techniques, and may receive support towards the improvement of product quality or the introduction of innovations (e.g. Lall 1980; Humphrey and Schmitz 2002; Javorcik 2004; Kneller and Pisu 2007). Second, the competition among home-country domestic firms to become suppliers for the home-country MNEs may further increase their efficiency—for example, if they are urged to use their resources more efficiently or to adopt new technologies or production processes (Crespo and Fontoura 2007; Herzer 2009). Third, the business linkages with export-oriented home-country MNEs may provide home-country suppliers with information about foreign market conditions—for example, consumer tastes, design, packaging, product quality requirements and the regulatory environment (Blomström and Kokko 1998). This knowledge in turn may help home-country suppliers to establish their own direct exports to foreign markets. Fourth, by increasing the efficiency and product quality of their home-country suppliers, home-country MNEs may extend the benefits to other home-country downstream producers, who produce end-user consumer goods, as cheaper and more technologically advanced intermediate inputs become available (Kugler 2006; Blalock and Gertler 2008).

Home-country MNEs can also diffuse the acquired foreign knowledge to the home economy through forward linkages if they are suppliers of intermediate goods in their home economy and if they sell their advanced intermediate goods to downstream home-country firms. First, such downstream firms may become more productive as a result of gaining access to new, improved or less costly intermediate inputs produced by home-country MNEs in the upstream sector (Javorcik 2004). Second, the purchase of intermediate goods from home-country MNEs may be accompanied by provision of complementary services that may not be available in connection with imports (Javorcik 2004). Overall, home-country MNE suppliers may increase the home-country pool of knowledge by providing new intermediate goods that were not previously available in their economy.

Therefore, at a theoretical level, OFDI can generate reverse knowledge spillovers on home-country economies, thus increasing productivity and promoting economic growth. However, empirical studies of the impact of reverse knowledge spillovers from OFDI on home-country productivity and economic growth have been limited, especially for developing countries.

Among the existing empirical studies, van Pottelsberghe de la Potterie and Lichtenberg (2001), using country-level data, analyse the impact of OFDI—in particular, technology-sourcing FDI—on the home-country productivity of 13 industrialised economies. They find that total factor productivity (TFP) is increased in cases where OFDI is directed towards research and development (R&D) intensive countries. Herzer (2010), using cross-country data for 50 countries, finds that OFDI positively affects economic growth in the home economies.

Driffield et al. (2009), using industry-level data on OFDI from the United Kingdom to a heterogeneous sample of host locations with varying labour costs and R&D intensity, find that OFDI in high-cost and high R&D-intensive host countries as well as in low-cost and low R&D-intensive locations increases TFP in the United Kingdom. Therefore, they conclude that not only technology-sourcing FDI but also efficiency-seeking FDI positively influences home-country domestic TFP. Similar evidence is also found in Driffield and Chiang (2009), who, using industry-level data, explore the productivity effect of Taiwan's OFDI in Mainland China between 1995 and 2005. They find that Taiwan's labour productivity is positively influenced by OFDI flows to Mainland China and conclude that the productivity gains are due to vertical or efficiency-seeking FDI, which relocates low value-added activities to Mainland China, which has lower labour costs than Taiwan. Therefore, both studies—Driffield et al. (2009) and Driffield and Chiang (2009)—show that productivity gains do not necessarily depend on technology-sourcing FDI.

Given that firms also relocate fewer value-added activities to low-cost locations and retain high value-added activities at home, home-country productivity may also be increased through efficiency-seeking FDI even without reverse knowledge transfers taking place.

A number of studies used firm-level data to investigate the impact of the reverse knowledge spillovers from OFDI on the productivity of home-country domestic firms but reached mixed results. An empirical study based on firm-level data for Irish OFDI, conducted by Copenhagen Economics (2007), finds that OFDI has positive productivity effects for Irish MNEs; however, there is no evidence of productivity spillovers to domestic firms in the Irish economy, regardless of whether these are direct competitors or whether they belong to the MNE's vertical value chain. One of the reasons only the investing MNEs benefit may be the fact that productivity gains stem from cost reduction due to the access to cheaper inputs, which are, however, accessible only to the MNEs and are not transferable back to the home economy (Copenhagen Economics 2007). Vahter and Masso (2007) found a similar result. Based on firm-level data from Estonia, Vahter and Masso find that OFDI has a positive impact on Estonian MNEs' productivity; however, they reveal a lack of general statistical evidence of productivity spillovers via OFDI to other firms in the home economy. In contrast, Castellani and Zanfei (2006), using firm-level data from Italy, find that Italian domestic firms significantly benefit from spillovers from Italian MNEs in the form of increased productivity.

Unfortunately, empirical studies analysing the impact of reverse knowledge spillovers from OFDI on home-country productivity and economic growth from developing countries are very limited. Among the few studies, Herzer (2011), using a sample of 33 developing countries for the period 1980–2005, finds a positive and long-run relationship between OFDI and TFP in the home economy. In the case of China, Zhao and Liu (2008), using national-level data, investigate China's OFDI and reverse R&D spillovers and find that OFDI promotes productivity increases in China by transferring technological spillovers from host countries to the home base. Zhao et al. (2010), using data for Chinese OFDI directed to developed countries for the period 1991–2007, investigate the impact on China's productivity of technology-sourcing OFDI. The findings show that Chinese OFDI in developed economies has a significant effect on China's TFP, and increased efficiency induced by OFDI through demonstration and imitation channels is a greater source of productivity growth than technology change.

The empirical studies mentioned above deliver interesting insights into the dynamics between OFDI activity and home-country economic development. However, there are some shortcomings. For example, previous studies of the impact of OFDI on China's economy do not control for the impact of IFDI in the empirical models when investigating reverse knowledge spillovers from OFDI on home-country productivity and economic growth, which could produce biased estimates. Therefore, studies of reverse knowledge spillovers from OFDI are far from conclusive and more are needed, especially for developing countries, to provide a comprehensive understanding of the impact of OFDI on the economic growth of home countries.

Framework of analysis and empirical model

The basic model

We estimate the impact of OFDI on China's provincial economic growth by specifying an aggregate production function as follows (Equation 17.1).

Equation 17.1

$$Y_{it} = A_{it} LB_{it}^{\beta_1} DK_{it}^{\beta_2} FK_{it}^{\beta_3}$$

In Equation 17.1, Y_{it} is the real gross domestic product (GDP) of province i in year t; A_{it} is the TFP level of province i in year t; LB_{it} is the total labour input of province i in year t; DK_{it} is the domestic capital stock of province i in year t; and FK_{it} is foreign capital stock (IFDI) of province i in year t, which captures the contribution of IFDI as capital input to provincial economic growth.

To investigate the impact of reverse knowledge spillovers from OFDI on provincial economic growth, we need to control for the impact of knowledge spillovers from IFDI. As noted in section two, since IFDI brings to the host country a package of firm-specific intangible assets, it could also generate knowledge spillovers that increase the productivity and efficiency of local firms, thus contributing to the host country's economic growth. Following Chen (2011, 2013), we assume that the higher the share of IFDI stock in a province's total capital stock (*IFDIS/PTK*), the higher will be the spillover effects from IFDI on the economic growth of that province.

OFDI can also increase the home country's economic growth through reverse knowledge spillovers, such as demonstration and imitation effects, labour movement and vertical industrial linkages. Chinese MNEs undertaking OFDI can be categorised into two groups: central government–controlled SOEs and provincial firms. SOEs dominate China's OFDI, accounting for 68.4 per cent of China's total OFDI stock by the end of 2014. However, since 2010, provincial firms have rapidly increased their OFDI flows and, in 2014, surpassed the OFDI flows from SOEs (MOFCOM 2014). Although China's OFDI stock is still dominated by SOEs, the importance of provincial firms in China's OFDI has been increasing. To investigate the impact of OFDI on provincial economic growth, we investigate the impact of

OFDI by provincial firms and by SOEs. We assume that each province has equal opportunity to receive reverse knowledge spillovers from the OFDI of SOEs. We expect also that the higher the share of provincial OFDI stock in provincial total capital stock (*POFDIS/PTK*), and the higher the share of SOEs' OFDI stock in national total capital stock (*SOEOFDIS/NTK*), the higher will be the impact on provincial economic growth of reverse knowledge spillovers from provincial OFDI and SOEs' OFDI.

With the above propositions, A_{it} can be defined as Equation 17.2.

Equation 17.2

$$A_{it} = B_{it}e^{g(IFDIS/PTK_{it-1}, POFDIS/PTK_{it-1}, SOEOFDIS/NTK_{t-1})}$$

In Equation 17.2, A_{it} is the TFP level of province *i* in year *t*; B_{it} is the residual TFP level of province *i* in year *t*; $IFDIS/PTK_{it-1}$ is the share of IFDI stock in provincial total capital stock in province *i* in year *t*–1, which captures the impact on provincial economic growth of knowledge spillovers from IFDI; $POFDIS/PTK_{it-1}$ is the share of provincial OFDI stock in provincial total capital stock of province *i* in year *t*–1, which captures the impact on provincial economic growth of reverse knowledge spillovers from provincial OFDI; $SOEOFDIS/NTK_{t-1}$ is the share of SOEs' OFDI stock in national total capital stock in year *t*–1, which captures the impact on provincial economic growth of reverse knowledge spillovers from SOEs' OFDI.

Incorporating Equation 17.2 into the aggregate production function Equation 17.1—by taking the natural logarithm of the variables of labour (*LB*), domestic capital (*DK*) and foreign capital (*FK*) and rearranging the items on the right-hand side, with the addition of a constant term (β_0) and an error term ($\mathcal{E}_{it}$)—we obtain empirical regression Equation 17.3.

Equation 17.3

$$LnY_{it} = \beta_0 + \beta_1 LnLB_{it} + \beta_2 LnDK_{it} + \beta_3 LnFK_{it} + \beta_4 IFDIS/PTK_{it-1} + \beta_5 POFDIS/PTK_{it-1} + \beta_6 SOEOFDIS/NTK_{t-1} + e_{it}$$

This empirical model allows us to test the impact on provincial economic growth of knowledge spillovers from IFDI as well as the reverse knowledge spillovers from OFDI. First, if the coefficient β_4 is positive and statistically significant, there is evidence that IFDI is correlated with positive impacts from knowledge spillovers on the home country's provincial economic growth. Second, if the coefficient β_5 is positive and statistically significant, there is evidence that provincial OFDI is correlated with impacts from reverse knowledge spillovers on the home country's provincial economic growth. Third, if the coefficient β_6 is positive and statistically significant, there is evidence that SOEs' OFDI is correlated with impacts on the home country's provincial economic growth from reverse knowledge spillovers.

Equation 17.3 is the form of an augmented production function model that we will use to estimate the impact on China's provincial economic growth of knowledge spillovers from IFDI and reverse knowledge spillovers from OFDI.

Data and variable specification

The data for provincial GDP (*Y*) and provincial total capital stock (*PTK*) measured in RMB1 billion at 1978 prices are from Wu (2009).[1] The data for China's national total capital stock are calculated by summing provincial total capital stock measured in RMB1 billion at 1978 prices. Labour (*LB*) is the total number of employed persons in each province measured in one million persons.[2]

Calculating the IFDI stock and the share of IFDI stock in provincial total capital stock

Foreign capital stock (*FK*) is measured as the IFDI stock of each province, which is calculated in several steps. First, the US dollar value of annual FDI inflows[3] is converted into renminbi (RMB) value by using the annual average official exchange rate. Second, the RMB value of annual FDI inflows is deflated into the real value in 1978 prices. Third, a 5 per cent depreciation rate is assumed for IFDI stock. Finally, IFDI stock is accumulated successively at year's end measured in RMB1 billion in 1978 prices.

The domestic capital stock (*DK*) of each province is obtained by deducting the IFDI stock (*FK*) from the provincial total capital stock.

Given the IFDI stock and total provincial capital stock, the share of IFDI stock in provincial total capital stock (*IFDIS/PTK*) for each province is calculated and is used to capture the knowledge spillover effects from IFDI on provincial economic growth. It is reasonable to assume that FDI inflows and knowledge spillover effects from IFDI on the local economy have a time lag, so a one-year lag is applied to *IFDIS/PTK* in the model.

1 Wu uses the conventional perpetual inventory method by employing the recently released national accounts figures to derive a capital stock series for China's 31 provinces and three economic sectors for the period 1977–2009, updated to 2014.

2 Data for labour are collected from NBS (various issues).

3 Data for FDI inflows are from, before and including 2005, NBS (various issues); after 2005, PBS (various issues).

Calculating the OFDI stock and the share of OFDI stock in total capital stock

Methods for calculating the provincial OFDI stock (*POFDIS*) and SOEs' OFDI stock (*SOEOFDIS*) are the same as those for calculating the IFDI stock (*IFDIS*) discussed previously. Data for OFDI flows from provincial firms and from SOEs are taken from the *Statistical Bulletin of China's Outward Foreign Investment* (MOFCOM 2003–14).

Given the provincial OFDI stock (*POFDIS*) and the provincial total capital stock, the share of provincial OFDI stock in provincial total capital stock (*POFDIS/PTK*) is calculated. It is thereafter used to capture the impact on provincial economic growth of reverse knowledge spillovers from provincial OFDI. The share of SOEs' OFDI stock (*SOEOFDIS*) in national total capital stock (*SOEOFDIS/NTK*) is similarly calculated and used to capture the impact on provincial economic growth of reverse knowledge spillovers from SOEs' OFDI. We also assume that OFDI flows and the reverse knowledge spillovers attributed to OFDI experience a time lag, so the value of *POFDIS/PTK* and *SOEOFDIS/NTK* is lagged by one year in the model.

In our estimations, we use the provincial OFDI stock (*POFDIS*) and the SOEs' OFDI stock (*SOEOFDIS*) as alternative measures of OFDI as a robustness check to investigate the impact on China's provincial economic growth of reverse knowledge spillovers from OFDI.

Regression results and explanations

The empirical study in this chapter utilises a province-level panel dataset of China's 30 provinces[4] covering the period from 2004 to 2014.[5] First, we study the impact on provincial economic growth of reverse knowledge spillovers from OFDI using the share of provincial OFDI stock in provincial total capital stock (*POFDIS/PTK*) and the share of SOEs' OFDI stock in national total capital stock (*SOEOFDIS/NTK*) to capture OFDI. For robustness, we also investigate the impact on provincial economic growth of reverse knowledge spillovers from OFDI using provincial OFDI stock (*POFDIS*) and the SOEs' OFDI stock (*OSEOFDIS*) as the variables of OFDI.

Table 17.1 presents the estimation results from Equation 17.3 by using the share of provincial OFDI stock in provincial total capital stock (*POFDIS/PTK*) and the share of SOEs' OFDI stock in national total capital stock (*SOEOFDIS/NTK*) as the independent variables of OFDI. Column 1 reports the random-effects model

4 Tibet is excluded from the dataset because of a lack of data.

5 Data for provincial outward FDI flows are available only after 2003.

estimation and column 2 reports the fixed-effects model estimation. The Hausman test results suggest that a fixed-effects approach is preferred. The estimation results of both models reveal that IFDI and OFDI are associated with positive and statistically significant impacts from knowledge spillovers on provincial economic growth. Because the fixed-effects model has eliminated the province-specific and time-invariant factors that may have impacts on provincial economic growth, our interpretation is based on the results from the fixed-effects model estimation.

Table 17.1 Estimation results of the impact on provincial economic growth of IFDI and OFDI

Independent variables	Random-effects model	Fixed-effects model
Constant	0.1936 (1.36)	1.0751 (6.13)***
LnLB	0.2696 (8.52)***	0.0111 (0.22)
LnDK	0.6181 (23.05)***	0.6051 (23.65)***
LnFK	0.0826 (4.80)***	0.0500 (2.89)***
$IFDIS/PTK_{t-1}$	0.0201 (4.00)***	0.0172 (3.60)***
$POFDIS/PTK_{t-1}$	0.0944 (2.00)**	0.1235 (2.79)***
$SOEOFDIS/NTK_{t-1}$	0.2397 (5.23)***	0.4257 (8.89)***
No. of observations No. of groups R^2 Wald chi^2 F-statistics	322 30 0.98 13,712*** 	322 30 0.93 2,522***

*** $p < 0.01$

** $p < 0.05$

Notes: Numbers in parentheses are t-statistics. The share of OFDI stock in total capital stock is used as the OFDI variable. Hausman test: Chi^2 (6) = 70.35 and Prob > chi^2 = 0.0000, preferring the fixed-effects model.

Source: Author's estimation.

The regression results from the fixed-effects model estimation show that domestic capital input (*DK*) is positive and statistically significant at the 1 per cent level while labour input (*LB*) is positive but not significant. This suggests that domestic capital is important to economic growth relative to labour in China's provinces. The variable of foreign capital (*FK*) is positive and statistically significant at the 1 per cent level, which provides empirical evidence that FDI as a capital input has directly contributed to host-province economic growth.

Turning to the main variables of interest: first, the variable of the share of IFDI stock in provincial total capital stock (*IFDIS/PTK*)—the knowledge spillovers from IFDI—is positive and statistically significant at the 1 per cent level. This finding offers some empirical evidence that IFDI has contributed to China's economic growth through positive knowledge spillovers to the local economy. This finding is consistent with the results of previous empirical studies (e.g. Chen 2011, 2013, 2014).

Second, the variable of *POFDIS/PTK*—the reverse knowledge spillovers from provincial OFDI—is positive and statistically significant at the 1 per cent level. This implies that provincial OFDI is positively associated with knowledge spillovers to the home-province economy, thus promoting provincial economic growth.

Third, the variable of *SOEOFDIS/NTK*—the reverse knowledge spillovers from SOEs' OFDI—is positive and statistically significant at the 1 per cent level, which implies that SOEs' OFDI is associated with positive knowledge spillovers to the home country's economy, thus promoting economic growth across all provinces in China.

For a robustness check, we replace the variables of *POFDIS/PTK* and *SOEOFDIS/NTK* with the variables of *POFDIS* and *SOEOFDIS*, respectively, in Equation 17.3 and rerun the regressions. Table 17.2 reports the estimation results. Column 1 reports the random-effects model estimation and column 2 reports the fixed-effects model estimation. The Hausman test results suggest a fixed-effects model is preferred.

The estimation results of both models suggest that IFDI and OFDI are associated with positive and statistically significant knowledge spillover effects on provincial economic growth. Again, because the fixed-effects model has eliminated the province-specific and time-invariant factors that may have impacts on provincial economic growth, our interpretation will be based on the results from the fixed-effects model estimation.

The regression results from the fixed-effects model estimation show that capital input (*DK*) is positive and statistically significant at the 1 per cent level while labour input (*LB*) is positive but not significant. The variable of foreign capital (*FK*) is positive and statistically significant at the 1 per cent level. These results are consistent with the regression results reported in Table 17.1.

The variable of *IFDIS/PTK* is positive and statistically significant at the 1 per cent level, supporting our earlier finding that IFDI is associated with positive knowledge spillover effects on the local economy, thus promoting host-province economic growth.

Table 17.2 Estimation results of the impact on provincial economic growth of IFDI and OFDI (OFDI stock)

Independent variables	Random-effects model	Fixed-effects model
Constant	0.5169 (3.63)***	1.0683 (6.67)***
LnLB	0.2884 (9.62)***	0.0726 (1.48)
LnDK	0.5730 (22.72)***	0.5852 (23.91)***
LnFK	0.0840 (5.15)***	0.0532 (3.20)***
$IFDIS/PTK_{t-1}$	0.0165 (3.54)***	0.0143 (3.19)***
$LnPOFDIS_{t-1}$	0.0292 (6.19)***	0.0257 (5.75)***
$LnSOEOFDIS_{t-1}$	0.0160 (2.34)**	0.0383 (5.44)***
No. of observations No. of groups R^2 Wald chi^2 F-statistics	322 30 0.98 15,586*** 	322 30 0.95 2,784***

*** $p < 0.01$

** $p < 0.05$

Notes: Numbers in parentheses are t-statistics. The OFDI stock is used as the OFDI variable. Hausman test: Chi^2 (6) = 56.67 and Prob > chi^2 = 0.0000, preferring the fixed-effects model.

Source: Author's estimation.

Now, turning to the variables of main interest, the regression results find that the variables *POFDIS* and *SOEOFDIS* are positive and statistically significant at the 1 per cent level. The results reveal that both OFDI from provincial firms and OFDI from SOEs are correlated with positive reverse knowledge spillover effects on the local economy, thus contributing to provincial economic growth. These results are consistent with the regression results reported in Table 17.1, which suggest that our estimation results are robust.

Referring to the discussion in section two of this chapter, the positive impact of provincial OFDI and SOEs' OFDI on China's provincial economic growth could be the result of reverse knowledge spillovers from home-country MNEs to the home-country economy. These reverse knowledge spillovers may come from demonstration and imitation effects, the movement of labour, vertical industrial linkages, information flows, promotion of local firms' exports and the facilitation of industrial restructuring and technological upgrading of home-country economies, thus increasing the productivity and efficiency of local firms and promoting growth of the home-country economy. This finding provides strong empirical evidence that OFDI has contributed to China's economic growth through positive impacts on the local economy from reverse knowledge spillovers. OFDI could be a new source of economic growth in China in the current environment of deepening globalisation and accelerating industrial restructuring and technological upgrading at home.

Conclusion

The main aim of this study is an empirical investigation of the impacts of reverse knowledge spillovers from OFDI on China's provincial economic growth. The study finds that OFDI from both provincial firms and SOEs has generated positive and statistically significant impacts on provincial economic growth. This positive impact could be the result of reverse knowledge spillovers from OFDI to the home country's provincial economy through demonstration and imitation effects, labour movement, backward and forward industrial linkages, information flows, promotion of local firms' exports and the facilitation of industrial restructuring and technological upgrading in the home-country economies, thus increasing the productivity and efficiency of local firms and promoting growth of the home economy. The study also finds that IFDI has generated positive and significant impacts on the local economy from knowledge spillovers, thus promoting provincial economic growth.

The findings of this study imply that China can gain a lot from OFDI. Given that OFDI brings benefits to the home-country economy through reverse knowledge spillovers, facilitation of exports and acceleration of industrial restructuring and technological upgrading, thus contributing to economic growth, the Chinese Government should consider implementing policies to encourage and facilitate OFDI and to enhance knowledge spillovers from OFDI to China's economy. This includes policies to develop a more open and market-oriented OFDI regime, policies to encourage R&D and technological development to increase the ownership advantages of Chinese domestic firms and policies to encourage interaction between Chinese MNEs and domestic firms to enhance and accelerate the diffusion of positive reverse knowledge spillovers from OFDI to China's economy.

References

Aitken, B. and Harrison, A. (1999), Do domestic firms benefit from direct foreign investment? Evidence from Venezuela, *American Economic Review* 89(3): 605–18. doi.org/10.1257/aer.89.3.605.

Amighini, A., Cozza, C., Rabellotti, R. and Sanfilippo, M. (2014), Investigating Chinese outward foreign direct investments: How can firm-level data help? *China & World Economy* 22(6): 44–63. doi.org/10.1111/cwe.12091.

Blalock, G. and Gertler, P. (2008), Welfare gains from foreign direct investment through technology transfer to local suppliers, *Journal of International Economics* 74(2): 402–21. doi.org/10.1016/j.jinteco.2007.05.011.

Blomström, M. and Kokko, A. (1998), Multinational corporations and spillovers, *Journal of Economic Surveys* 12(3): 247–78. doi.org/10.1111/1467-6419.00056.

Buckley, P., Clegg, J., Cross, A., Liu, X., Voss, H. and Zheng, P. (2007), The determinants of Chinese outward foreign direct investment, *Journal of International Business Studies* 38(4): 499–518. doi.org/10.1057/palgrave.jibs.8400277.

Castellani, D. and Zanfei, A. (2006), *Multinational Firms, Innovation and Productivity*, Cheltenham, UK: Edward Elgar. doi.org/10.4337/9781847201591.

Caves, R. (1996), *Multinational Enterprise and Economic Analysis*, Cambridge: Cambridge University Press.

Chen, C. (2011), *Foreign Direct Investment in China: Location determinants, investor differences and economic impacts*, Cheltenham, UK: Edward Elgar. doi.org/10.4337/9781781001141.

Chen, C. (2013), FDI and economic growth, in Y. Wu (ed.), *Regional Development and Economic Growth in China*, pp. 117–40, Series on Economic Development and Growth No. 7, Singapore: World Scientific.

Chen, C. (2014), The impact of FDI on China's regional economic growth, in L. Song, R. Garnaut and F. Cai (eds), *Deepening Reform for China's Long-Term Growth and Development*, pp. 407–27, Canberra: ANU Press.

Chen, C. (2015a), Determinants and motives of outward foreign direct investment from China's provincial firms, *Transnational Corporations* 23(1): 1–28. doi.org/10.18356/6ba5ab37-en.

Chen, C. (2015b), Do inland provinces benefit from coastal foreign direct investment in China? *China & World Economy* 23(3): 22–41. doi.org/10.1111/cwe.12112.

Chen, C., Sheng, Y. and Findlay, C. (2013), Export spillovers of FDI on China's domestic firms, *Review of International Economics* 21(5): 841–56. doi.org/10.1111/roie.12074.

Cheung, Y. and Qian, X. (2009), The empirics of China's outward direct investment, *Pacific Economic Review* 14(3): 312–41. doi.org/10.1111/j.1468-0106.2009.00451.x.

Cheung, Y., Haan, J., Qian, X. and Yu, S. (2012), China's outward direct investment in Africa, *Review of International Economics* 20(2): 201–20. doi.org/10.1111/j.1467-9396.2012.01017.x.

Copenhagen Economics (2007), *Outward Direct Investment and the Irish Economy*, Dublin: Forfas.

Crespo, N. and Fontoura, M. (2007), Determinant factors of FDI spillovers: What do we really know? *World Development* 35(3): 410–25. doi.org/10.1016/j.worlddev.2006.04.001.

Dai, O. and Liu, X. (2009), Returnee entrepreneurs and firm performance in Chinese high-technology industries, *International Business Review* 18(4): 373–86. doi.org/10.1016/j.ibusrev.2009.03.004.

Driffield, N. and Chiang, P. (2009), The effects of offshoring to China: Reallocation, employment and productivity in Taiwan, *International Journal of the Economics of Business* 16(1): 19–38. doi.org/10.1080/13571510802638916.

Driffield, N., Love, J. and Taylor, K. (2009), Productivity and labour demand effects of inward and outward foreign direct investment on UK industry, *The Manchester School* 77(2): 171–203. doi.org/10.1111/j.1467-9957.2008.02093.x.

Dunning, J. (1977), Trade, location of economic activity and the MNE: A search for an eclectic approach, in B. Ohlin, P. Hesselborn and P. Wijkman (eds), *The International Allocation of Economic Activity*, pp. 395–418, London: Macmillan. doi.org/10.1007/978-1-349-03196-2_38.

Dunning, J. (1980), Toward an eclectic theory of international production: Some empirical tests, *Journal of International Business Studies* 11(1): 9–31. doi.org/10.1057/palgrave.jibs.8490593.

Dunning, J. (1988), The eclectic paradigm of international production: A restatement and some possible extensions, *Journal of International Business Studies* 19(1): 1–31. doi.org/10.1057/palgrave.jibs.8490372.

Dunning, J. (1993), *Multinational Enterprises and the Global Economy*, New York: Addison-Wesley.

Dunning, J. (1995), Reappraising the eclectic paradigm in an age of alliance capitalism, *Journal of International Business Studies* 26(3): 461–91. doi.org/10.1057/palgrave.jibs.8490183.

Dunning, J. (2000), The eclectic paradigm as an envelope for economic and business theories of MNE activity, *International Business Review* 9(2): 163–90. doi.org/10.1016/S0969-5931(99)00035-9.

Dunning, J. and Lundan, S. (2008), *Multinational Enterprises and the Global Economy*, 2nd edn, Cheltenham, UK: Edward Elgar.

Filatotchev, I., Liu, X., Lu, J. and Wright, M. (2011), Knowledge spillovers through human mobility across national borders: Evidence from Zhongguancun Science Park in China, *Research Policy* 40(3): 453–62. doi.org/10.1016/j.respol.2011.01.003.

Fu, X. (2011), Processing trade, FDI and the exports of indigenous firms: Firm-level evidence from technology-intensive industries in China, *Oxford Bulletin of Economics and Statistics* 73(6): 792–817.

Gorg, H. and Greenaway, D. (2004), Much ado about nothing? Do domestic firms really benefit from foreign direct investment? *The World Bank Research Observer* 19(2): 171–97. doi.org/10.1093/wbro/lkh019.

Griliches, Z. (1992), The search for R&D spillovers, *The Scandinavian Journal of Economics* 94(Supplement): S29–S47. doi.org/10.2307/3440244.

Herzer, D. (2009), Outward FDI and domestic output in Japan, *Empirical Economic Letters* 8(12): 1167–76.

Herzer, D. (2010), Outward FDI and economic growth, *Journal of Economic Studies* 37(5): 476–94. doi.org/10.1108/01443581011075424.

Herzer, D. (2011), The long-run relationship between outward FDI and total factor productivity: Evidence for developing countries, *Journal of Development Studies* 47(5): 767–85. doi.org/10.1080/00220388.2010.509790.

Hu, A., Jefferson, G. and Qian, J. (2005), R&D and technology transfer: Firm-level evidence from Chinese industry, *The Review of Economics and Statistics* 87(4): 780–86. doi.org/10.1162/003465305775098143.

Humphrey, J. and Schmitz, H. (2002), How does insertion in global value chains affect upgrading in industrial clusters? *Regional Studies* 36(9): 1017–27. doi.org/10.1080/0034340022000022198.

Hymer, S. (1976), *The International Operations of National Firms: A study of direct foreign investment*, Cambridge, Mass.: MIT.

Javorcik, B. (2004), Does foreign direct investment increase the productivity of domestic firms? In search of spillovers through backward linkages, *The American Economic Review* 94(3): 605–27. doi.org/10.1257/0002828041464605.

Kneller, R. and Pisu, M. (2007), Industrial linkages and export spillovers from FDI, *The World Economy* 30(1): 105–34. doi.org/10.1111/j.1467-9701.2007.00874.x.

Kolstad, I. and Wiig, A. (2012), What determines Chinese outward FDI? *Journal of World Business* 47(1): 26–34. doi.org/10.1016/j.jwb.2010.10.017.

Kugler, M. (2006), Spillovers from foreign direct investment: Within or between industries? *Journal of Development Economics* 80(2): 444–77. doi.org/10.1016/j.jdeveco.2005.03.002.

Lall, S. (1980), Monopolistic advantages and foreign involvement by US manufacturing industry, *Oxford Economic Papers* 32(1): 102–22. doi.org/10.1093/oxfordjournals.oep.a041464.

Liu, J. and Scott-Kennel, J. (2011), Asset-seeking investment by Chinese multinationals: Firm ownership, location, and entry mode, *Asia Pacific and Globalization Review* 1(1): 16–36.

Liu, X., Buck, T. and Shu, C. (2005), Chinese economic development, the next stage: Outward FDI? *International Business Review* 14(1): 97–115. doi.org/10.1016/j.ibusrev.2004.12.003.

Ministry of Commerce of China (MOFCOM) (various issues), *Statistical Bulletin of China's Outward Foreign Investment*, Beijing: MOFCOM.

National Bureau of Statistics of China (NBS) (various issues), *China Statistical Yearbook*, Beijing: China Statistics Press.

Provincial Bureau of Statistics (PBS) (various issues for each province), *Provincial National Economic and Social Development Statistical Bulletin*, China.

Sheng, Y., Chen, C. and Findlay, C. (2011), *Impact of FDI on domestic firms' exports in China*, Research Paper No. 2011015, School of Economics, University of Adelaide, Adelaide.

Tolentino, P. (2010), Home country macroeconomic factors and outward FDI of China and India, *Journal of International Management* 16(1): 102–20. doi.org/10.1016/j.intman.2010.03.002.

United Nations Conference on Trade and Development (UNCTAD) (2003), *World Investment Report 2003: FDI policy for development—National and international perspectives*, New York: United Nations Publications.

United Nations Conference on Trade and Development (UNCTAD) (2016), *World Investment Report 2016: Investor nationality—Policy challenges*, New York: United Nations Publications.

Vahter, P. and Masso, J. (2007), Home versus host country effects of FDI: Searching for new evidence of productivity spillovers, *Applied Economics Quarterly* 53(2): 165–96.

van Pottelsberghe de la Potterie, B. and Lichtenberg, F. (2001), Does foreign direct investment transfer technology across borders? *Review of Economics and Statistics* 83(3): 490–7. doi.org/10.1162/003465301524801 35.

Wei, W. and Alon, I. (2010), Chinese outward direct investment: A study on macroeconomic determinants, *International Journal of Business and Emerging Markets* 2(4): 352–69. doi.org/10.1504/IJBEM.2010.035663.

Wu, Y. (2009), *China's capital stock series by region and sector*, Discussion Paper No. 09.02, Business School, University of Western Australia, Perth.

Zhao, W. and Liu, L. (2008), Outward direct investment and R-D spillovers: China's case, in *Emerging Multinationals: Outward foreign direct investment from emerging and developing economies—Proceedings, International Conference, 9–10 October*, Copenhagen Business School, Copenhagen.

Zhao, W., Liu, L. and Zhao, T. (2010), The contribution of outward direct investment to productivity changes within China, 1991–2007, *Journal of International Management* 16(2): 121–30. doi.org/10.1016/j.intman.2010.03.003.

18. Promoting the Belt and Road Initiative by Strengthening '5 + 1' Cooperation[1]

Biliang Hu, Qingjie Liu and Jiao Yan

Introduction

The concept of '5 + 1' refers to cooperation between the five countries of the Eurasian Economic Union (EEU)—Russia, Belarus, Kazakhstan, Kyrgyzstan and Armenia—and China under the framework of the Belt and Road Initiative (BRI). Commonly abbreviated as '5 + 1', this initiative deepens China's connectivity with the emerging entity of the EEU, which was officially launched on 1 January 2015.

The process of advancing the idea of the EEU began in January 2010, when Russia, Belarus and Kazakhstan formed a customs union. On 29 May 2014, Russia, Belarus and Kazakhstan signed the 'EEU Treaty' in Astana, the capital of Kazakhstan. Finally, on 1 January 2015, the EEU was officially launched, with the medium-term goal of realising the free flow of goods, services, capital and labour between member countries by 2025, and, ultimately, a union similar to the European Union (EU). On 2 January 2015, Armenia also joined the EEU. Kyrgyzstan, which had originally planned to join in May 2015, joined on 12 August that year.

Also in May 2015, China and Russia formally signed an agreement stipulating they would cooperate in the construction of the Silk Road Economic Belt and in building up the EEU to stimulate regional economic growth, strengthen regional economic integration and safeguard regional peace and development.

Proposed by Chinese President Xi Jinping in 2013, the BRI aims to build a prosperous Silk Road Economic Belt and 21st-century Maritime Silk Road together with the countries in the BRI region. This initiative now includes 65 countries (see Appendix Table 18.A1) with a total population of nearly 4.6 billion (62 per cent of the global population), 40 per cent of the global land area and 31 per cent of aggregate gross domestic product (GDP).

1 This research is financially supported by the Fundamental Research Funds for the Central Universities and Beijing Normal University's Interdisciplinary Research Project 'Paths and Implementation of Promoting the Belt and Road Construction through International Cooperation'.

For a number of reasons explained in this chapter, the '5 + 1' initiative is key to the success of the BRI. And there remains substantial scope to enhance infrastructural and trade-related cooperation in particular. In this chapter, we first set out three areas that explain that importance: geography, resources and Sino–Russian relations. Thereafter, we explore the underlying economic trends and issues among '5 + 1' countries, and finally discuss ways to promote cooperation between the two initiatives.

'5 + 1' cooperation and the BRI

Cooperation between China and the EEU is important to the promotion of the BRI because of the unique position of EEU countries geographically, in terms of natural resource endowment advantages and the importance of Sino–Russian relations.

Geographical position

The BRI is one of the most important contemporary initiatives in China. Building an effective '5 + 1' platform is key to the incremental implementation of the BRI. On the one hand, the EEU sits geographically within the hinterland of the Eurasian landmass, which acts as a hub connecting East Asian and European trade and transportation. Thus, construction of the Silk Road Economic Belt requires China to work with Russia and Central and West Asian countries to build links along the Silk Road. The five countries of the EEU are therefore pivotal to extending the Silk Road Economic Belt westward and northward.

The BRI comprises six economic corridors, three of which link directly to EEU member countries: the China–Mongolia–Russia Economic Corridor; the New Eurasian Land Bridge Economic Corridor, which passes through Kazakhstan and Russia, and will eventually reach all the way to the Netherlands; and the China–Central Asia–West Asia Economic Corridor, which stretches from the autonomous region of Xinjiang in China's west through to the five countries of Central Asia, including the EEU's Kazakhstan and Kyrgyzstan. These three economic corridors are fundamental to the promotion and success of the implementation of the BRI. Through '5 + 1' cooperation, moreover, the relationship among the EEU countries may be strengthened via the promotion of infrastructure construction that serves to connect the economic artery of Eurasia with logistics and transport corridors, in the process promoting free trade, capital flows and communication among countries as well as between people of the region.

Resource advantages

The basic geographic, economic and demographic statistics of the '5 + 1' countries define their importance among those of the BRI. According to World Bank data, in 2015, the 64 countries within the BRI (excluding China) comprised 40.5 million square kilometres. The land area of the five EEU countries alone is 19.5 million sq km—48 per cent of the total land area of 64 BRI countries. Their total GDP in 2015 (current US dollars) was roughly US$12 trillion, of which the EEU members contributed US$1.7 trillion, or some 14 per cent of the total. Among the 64 countries (excluding China), however, the EEU members' proportion of total population was only 5.6 per cent. In other words, with less than 6 per cent of the total population, the EEU accounted for nearly 15 per cent of GDP of the BRI countries (excluding China).

The EEU countries are also relatively rich in arable land. Data from the World Bank[2] reveal that the total area of cultivated land in the 64 BRI countries (excluding China) is 575 million hectares, of which the EEU makes up 159 million ha, or 27.63 per cent of the total. Russia's total arable land was 122 million ha, ranking it third in the world (after India and the United States); Kazakhstan had 29.4 million ha, ranking it 12th in the world, but fifth among 64 BRI countries.

Figures 18.1 and 18.2 illustrate per capita arable land and the distribution of water resources in the BRI countries, respectively. In terms of per capita arable land resources, Kazakhstan and Russia, respectively, have 1.7 ha and 0.9 ha per person, ranking them second and sixth in the world, respectively, and top two of the BRI countries. Belarus's per capita arable land area is 0.6 ha, ranking it sixth among the BRI countries. This richness in land resources suggests that Russia, Belarus and Kazakhstan have great potential for agricultural development. In the case of Kazakhstan, its President, Nursultan Nazarbayev, has pointed out his country's agricultural potential directly—and his hopes that China will increase its investment in agriculture there (Zhao 2015). Former Deputy Prime Minister of Kazakhstan Oraz Jandosov put forward a similar view in a BRI lecture on 11 December 2016 at Beijing Normal University's Emerging Markets Institute (Ye 2016).

2 data.worldbank.org/indicator/AG.LND.TOTL.K2.

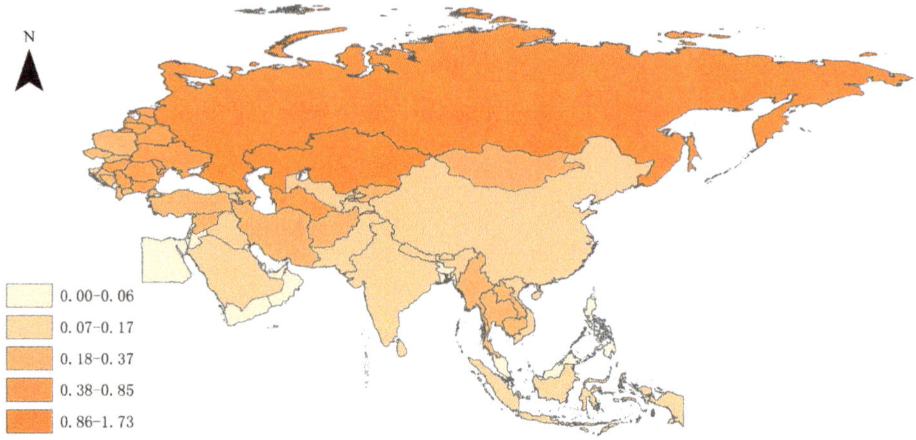

Figure 18.1 Per capita arable land area of BRI countries (hectare per person)
Source: Based on the data from the World Bank: data.worldbank.org/indicator/AG.LND.TOTL.K2.

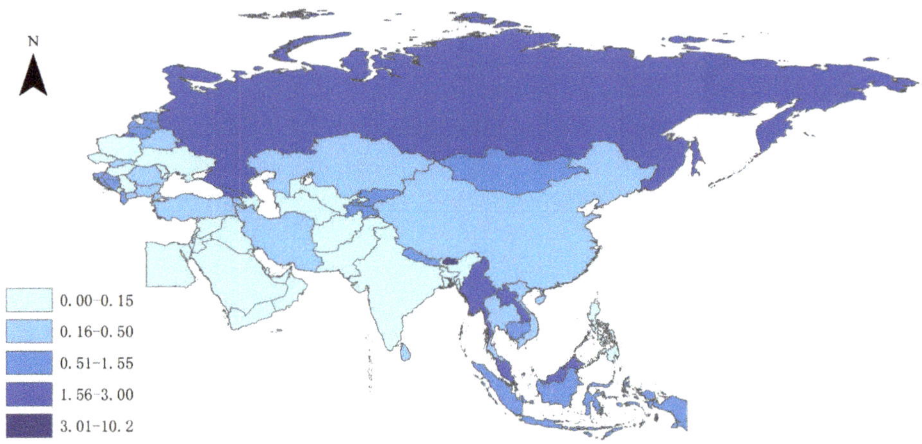

Figure 18.2 Per capita water resources of BRI countries (million cubic metres per person)
Source: Based on the data from the World Bank: data.worldbank.org/indicator/ER.H2O.INTR.K3.

EEU countries are also rich in water resources. Specifically, BRI countries held 12.4 trillion cubic metres of useable water in 2014, of which EEU countries held 4.5 trillion cu m, or 36 per cent of the total.[3] In 2014, Russia's freshwater resources were as high as 4.3 trillion cu m, or 30,000 cu m per capita—a total volume second only to Brazil globally and second among the 64 BRI countries (excluding China), behind Bhutan.

3 data.worldbank.org/indicator/ER.H2O.INTR.K3.

Data from the *World Energy Statistics Yearbook* (BP 2016) suggest that the total energy output from fossil fuels in the 64 BRI countries (excluding China) in 2015 was 4.76 billion tonnes of oil equivalent (toe), of which the production of the five EEU countries was 1.4 billion toe, or 28.93 per cent of the total. Russia's output of 1.2 billion toe was, of course, far ahead of the other countries, and was followed by Kazakhstan's output of 136 million toe.

In 2015, Russia's oil production was 541 million toe, accounting for 12.4 per cent of global output. This placed Russia third in the world in terms of total oil production, after Saudi Arabia (569 million toe) and the United States (567 million toe) (Figure 18.3). Although Africa is also an important oil-producing area, its oil production was only 298 million toe in 2015—less than half that of Russia.

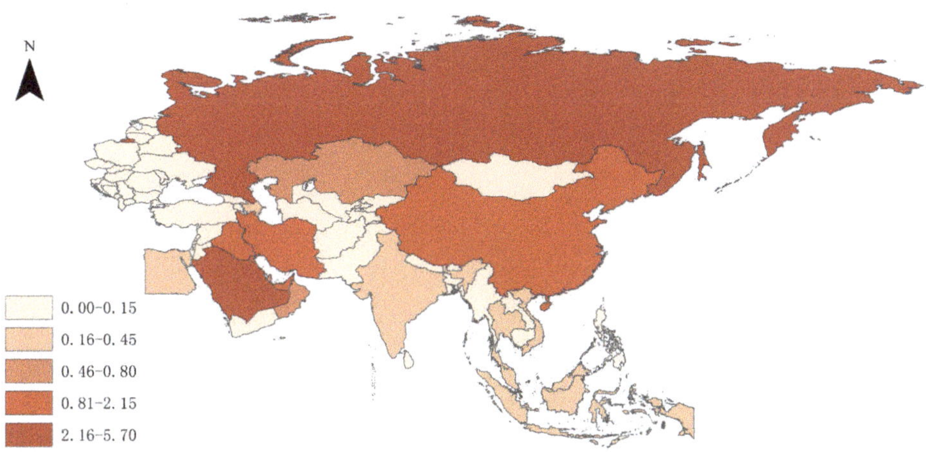

Figure 18.3 Distribution of total oil production of BRI countries (100 million toe)

Source: Based on the data from the *World Energy Statistics Yearbook* (BP 2016): www.bp.com/statisticalreview.

Russia's natural gas production in 2015 was 516 million toe, accounting for 16.1 per cent of total global output—close to the production of the entire Middle East (556 million toe) and second only to the United States (705 million toe), ranking it second in the world (BP 2016). Figure 18.4 provides the distribution of natural gas production of BRI countries (toe).

In sum, EEU countries are richly endowed in agricultural, energy, water and other resources. China is home to a huge domestic market and also capital, and therefore it and the EEU countries have significant potential to cooperate under the BRI framework.

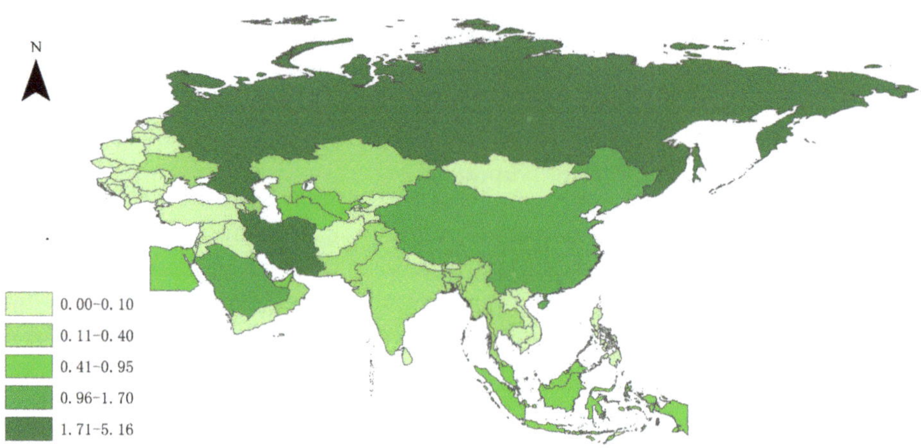

Figure 18.4 Distribution of natural gas production of BRI countries (toe)
Source: Based on the data from the *World Energy Statistics Yearbook* (BP 2016): www.bp.com/statisticalreview.

Sino–Russian relations

It is in the common interests of China and Russia to maintain good bilateral relations, and it is also of great significance to the implementation of the BRI. As an important neighbour of China, Russia shares with it a border of 4,300 kilometres. The BRI runs through the Eurasian landmass, an area in which Russia is a global power. China plans to work with relevant countries to build up the China–Mongolia–Russia Economic Corridor, the New Eurasian Land Bridge Economic Corridor and the China–Central Asia–West Asia Economic Corridor as an important part of strengthening cooperation with these countries, and particularly with Russia.

Under the current complicated international situation, the best choice for both China and Russia is to integrate the construction of the BRI and of the EEU. In the joint statement of the People's Republic of China and the Russian Federation signed on 25 June 2016, the two countries clearly stressed that the signing of the Sino–Russian joint declaration on 8 May 2015 to integrate the construction of the EEU and the Silk Road Economic Belt is of great significance. The comprehensive partnership between China and Russia should be open and transparent, while focusing on the interests of both sides, and should accept the gradual participation of member countries of the EEU, the Association of Southeast Asian Nations (ASEAN) and the Shanghai Cooperation Organisation (SCO) (Global Financial Network 2016).

Trends in '5 + 1' trade and investment relations

The '5 + 1' cooperation also contributes to interregional economic and trade cooperation. In the context of globalisation, countries around the world are, in general, deepening economic ties and social connectivity. Regional economic integration provides effective institutional infrastructure to improve the region's competitiveness. Four of the EEU member countries were states of the former Soviet Union, but gained their independence in 1991: Kazakhstan on 16 December, Armenia on 21 September, Kyrgyzstan on 31 August and Belarus on 25 August. China has worked to establish close relations with all of them, and economic and trade cooperation will be among the most important areas to further these relationships.

Recent relative weakening of trade ties

Trade tightness among the countries is important for future trade development, so we use the trade tightness index to measure the trade dependence of the EEU. In general, the higher the trade density, the closer are the trade ties between the two countries. The basic formula for calculating the degree of trade dependence is as follows (Equation 18.1).

Equation 18.1

$$W_{ij} = \frac{X_{ij}/X_i}{Y_j/Y_w}$$

In Equation 18.1, W_{ij} refers to the trade tightness of country *i* with its trading partner, country *j*; X_{ij} are the exports of country *i* to country *j*; X_i are the total exports of country *i*; Y_j is country *j*'s total imports; and Y_w is total global imports.

Based on this formula, and using trade data from the United Nations Statistical Office,[4] we can establish the trade relations of any one of the five EEU countries with the other four members (here we use the term trade connectivity index, which refers to the level of trade relations between countries; the highest is 100, while the lowest is zero). The results are shown in Appendix Table 18.A2. To more clearly highlight the trends found in our results, we also present the numbers as Figure 18.5, based on Appendix Table 18.A2.

4 comtrade.un.org/data/.

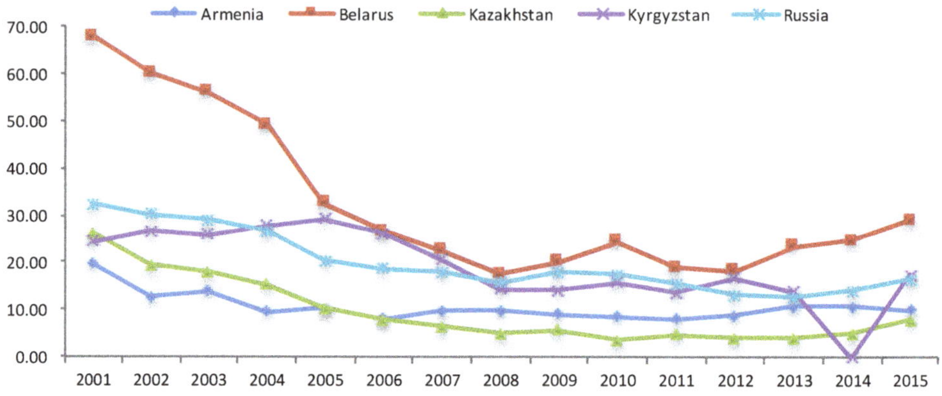

Figure 18.5 Trade tightness between one EEU country and the other four EEU countries

Source: Based on data in Appendix Table 18.A2.

In terms of the trade connectivity index, Figure 18.5 highlights that Belarus trades most tightly with the other four EEU countries. Its index peaked at 67.8 in 2001, and experienced a rapid decline afterwards, but Belarus is still the country with the highest degree of tightness among the EEU countries. Overall, the value of trade of the five EEU countries showed a declining trend, with Kazakhstan falling from 26.1 in 2001 to 7.9 in 2015, a fall of 70 per cent; Belarus fell from 67.8 to 28.97, or 57.3 per cent; Armenia and Russia fell by 49 per cent; and Kyrgyzstan fell by 28 per cent.

In general, and as Figure 18.5 reveals, there have been varying degrees of decline. This is partly explained by the strong convergence in industrial structure among the countries—that is, the trade complementarity between these countries has diminished over time. According to the estimation of Li Jianmin (2014), the degrees of trade complementarity between Russia, Belarus and Kazakhstan are all below 0.5, which is very low, so that the share of trade among these countries (internal trade) is generally lower than the proportions in their total trade (Table 18.1). This simply implies that there is huge potential for these countries to connect to countries outside the EEU, such as China, through improvements in transportation infrastructure and so on; and, therefore, these countries would benefit greatly from the construction of the Silk Road Economic Belt.

According to the data released on the website of the Eurasian Economic Commission,[5] Table 18.1 shows that total internal trade in the EEU in 2015 accounted for only 13.5 per cent of total trade volume, but the trade volume of countries outside the EEU accounted for 86.5 per cent of their total trade volume; external trade was 6.4 times that of internal trade. This indicates that EEU member countries

5 www.eurasiancommission.org.

barely meet the demand for their products and market on average; however, nearly 90 per cent of the goods in the markets of the five countries were satisfied with their trade partners outside the EEU. In terms of the import and export trade volume of the member countries, Russia's trade is the most dependent on countries outside the EEU (91.9 per cent); only 8.1 per cent comes from internal EEU trade. For Kazakhstan, the proportion of external trade was 79.2 per cent. Overall, the five EEU countries have a proportion higher than 50 per cent.

Table 18.1 Comparison of internal trade with external trade of the EEU countries, 2015

	Trade volume inside the EEU to total trade volume (%)			Trade volume outside the EEU to total trade volume (%)		
	Imports and exports	Exports	Imports	Imports and exports	Exports	Imports
Five countries as a whole	13.5	10.8	18.0	86.5	89.2	82.0
Russia	8.1	8.4	7.7	91.9	91.6	92.3
Belarus	49.5	41.2	56.8	50.5	58.8	43.2
Kazakhstan	20.8	10.7	36.1	79.2	89.3	63.9
Kyrgyzstan	44.3	32.2	49.3	55.7	67.8	50.7
Armenia	26.3	15.9	31.1	73.7	84.1	68.9

Source: Eurasian Economic Commission (www.eurasiancommission.org).

Table 18.2 Trade between EEU member countries, 2015

	Percentage of trade volume (US$100 million)				
	Armenia	Belarus	Kazakhstan	Russia	Kyrgyzstan
Armenia	-	0.07%	0.01%	2.82%	0.001%
Belarus	0.333	-	1.26%	57.14%	0.15%
Kazakhstan	0.056	5.724	-	33.45%	1.9%
Russia	12.742	259.282	151.786	-	3.2%
Kyrgyzstan	0.005	0.69	8.636	14.544	-

- not applicable

Source: Eurasian Economic Commission (www.eurasiancommission.org).

From Table 18.2, we find that more than 90 per cent of the total trade volume of US$45.4 billion in 2015 was between Russia, Belarus and Kazakhstan, and, within that, mainly between Russia and Belarus, and Russia and Kazakhstan. The trade volume between Russia and Belarus was US$26 billion, accounting for 57.14 per cent of total trade within the EEU; the trade volume between Russia and Kazakhstan was US$15.2 billion, or 33.45 per cent of total trade within the EEU. In third place, the trade volume between Kyrgyzstan and Russia was US$1.5 billion, or 3.2 per cent, followed by the trade volume between Armenia and

Russia of US$1.3 billion, or 2.82 per cent. In addition to trade with Russia, trade between the other four member countries was less than US$1 billion, especially between Armenia and Kyrgyzstan, which was only US$500,000 in 2015 and only 0.002 per cent of the trade between Russia and Belarus. According to the relevant research, the main reason for this is a relatively high degree of industrial structure homogeneity between the EEU member countries. Exports are essentially resource and energy products, while imports are largely mechanical and electrical products, so the trade demand between each country is weak, and, in terms of competition with the relative high quality of the international market, there is intense competition between each EEU country (Jin 2016).

China is the EEU's most important trade partner

Since the independence of EEU member countries, their trade with China has maintained a positive growth trend. According to trade data released by the United Nations Statistics Office, 12.5 per cent of the EEU's total trade in 2014 was with China, making China the union's largest foreign trade partner (Table 18.3). Due to the decline in commodity and raw material prices in recent years, the volume of foreign trade in the EEU also declined in 2015; however, according to statistics from the Eurasian Economic Commission, China still accounted for 13.61 per cent of the EEU's total foreign trade in 2015, meaning it remained the largest trading partner. As for bilateral trade, China is also Russia's largest trading partner, and the second-largest trade partner of Kazakhstan, Armenia and Kyrgyzstan (Zhang 2016).

Table 18.3 The top-five commodity trading partners of EEU countries

Year	Trading partner	Exports (US$100 million)	Imports (US$100 million)	Share (%)
2014	China	480	606	12.5
	Germany	392	377	8.9
	Italy	528	149	7.8
	Netherlands	784	61	6.1
	Ukraine	229	136	4.2
2015	China	351	438	13.6
	Germany	269	241	8.8
	Netherlands	470	37	8.7
	Italy	306	103	7.1
	Turkey	208	56	4.6

Source: Eurasian Economic Commission (www.eurasiancommission.org).

According to the Eurasian Economic Commission, total trade value among the five EEU members in 2015 was US$45.4 billion, but total imports and exports with countries outside the EEU were as high as US$579.5 billion in the same year

(US$374 billion in exports and US$205.4 billion in imports). Among the top-five trading partners of the EEU, the total trade with China was US$78.9 billion (of which US$43.8 billion was imports from China and US$35.1 billion was exports to China), accounting for 13.61 per cent of total imports and exports between EEU countries and all countries outside the EEU, making China the biggest trading partner, followed by Germany, with a trade value of US$51 billion, accounting for 8.81 per cent. Trade between the Netherlands and the EEU accounted for 8.7 per cent of the total, just less than Germany, and ranking it in third place. In fourth and fifth place were Italy and Turkey, respectively, whose shares were 7.1 per cent and 4.6 per cent, respectively. According to statistics from the Eurasian Economic Commission, until November 2016, China continued to be the EEU's largest trading partner, with 15.4 per cent of the total trading value among all countries outside the union.

If we look over a longer period, the overall commodities trading volume showed an upward trend between China and the five EEU countries from 1992 to 2016: from 1992 to 2005, there was relatively slow growth; from 2006 to 2008, the growth was rapid; and, because of the Global Financial Crisis (GFC), the volume fell after 2009. From 2010 to 2014, high growth continued, increasing 53.43 per cent. In the past two years, the impact of falling commodity prices, such as for crude oil, has seen the trade volume decrease slightly.

China–EEU investment relations

China's direct investment in EEU countries continued to grow over the years, rising from only US$97 million in 2003 to US$22.8 billion in 2015—an increase of 235 times (Figure 18.6). Specifically, China's direct investment in Kazakhstan increased from US$20 million in 2003 to US$5.1 billion in 2015; its foreign direct investment (FDI) in Kyrgyzstan increased from US$16 million to US$1.1 billion, in Russia it increased from US$62 million to US$14 billion and in Belarus and Armenia it rose from almost zero to US$476 million and US$7.5 million, respectively, in 2015. We can see that China's direct investment in Belarus has seen the largest increase, especially since the establishment of the China–Belarus Industrial Park in Minsk, the Belarus capital, which is not only the largest overseas industrial park in which China has invested, but also the largest foreign investment project in Belarus. The China–Belarus Industrial Park is playing an important role in promoting cooperation between China and EEU countries. With the construction of the Moscow–Kazan High-Speed Railway, the China–Belarus Industrial Park, the China–Kazakhstan Border Cooperation Zone and so on, economic and trade relations between China and EEU countries will be further strengthened.

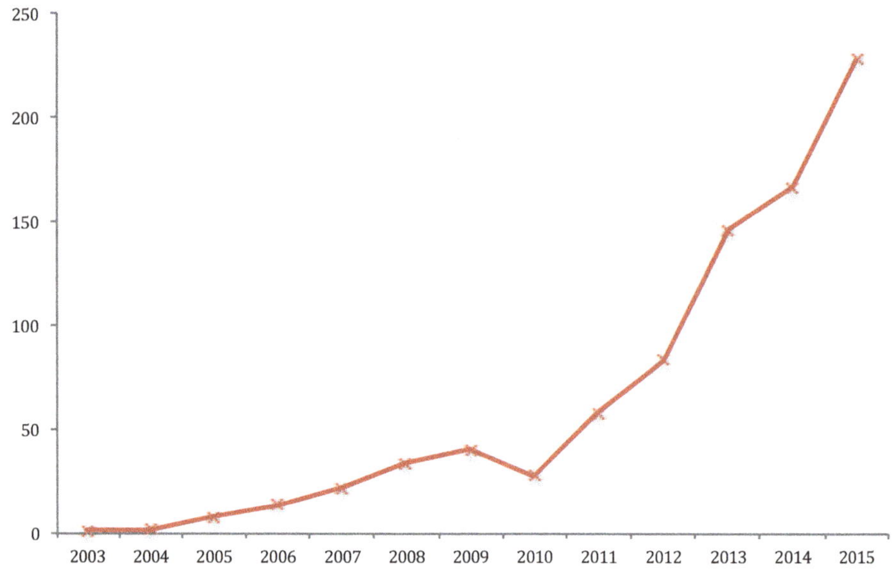

Figure 18.6 China's direct investment in EEU countries, 2003–15 (US$100 million)

Source: MOFCOM et al. (2016).

Infrastructure: The BRI and '5 + 1' cooperation

The EEU area is a key land-based transport hub connecting East Asia and Europe. Achieving infrastructure interoperability and improving the level of infrastructure in the five member countries will create an economic artery connecting the Eurasian landmass.

Transportation infrastructure construction

China is now the biggest commodity trading country in the world, and 90 per cent of Chinese exports and imports are realised through sea transportation.[6] In the case of trade with European countries, about 75 per cent of commodities are transported via ocean shipping.[7] Ocean shipping is normally much slower than rail transport, and, in the case of trade between Europe and China, rail transport takes only 50 per

6 wenku.baidu.com/view/ba13796eff00bed5b8f31d39.html?re=view.

7 www.360doc.com/content/15/0419/12/91243_464334719.shtml.

cent of the time of transportation by sea,[8] with more or less the same transportation costs (Li 2015). It is therefore important for China to use more rail transportation than ocean shipping, which would also benefit European countries.

On 19 March 2011, the Chongqing–Europe International Express Railway was officially opened, which kicks off the operation of China–Europe Express Railways (Figure 18.7). The Chongqing–Europe Railway runs from Chongqing City in China, via Xi'an and Lanzhou, to Alashankou (Alataw Pass) within China. Beyond the Alataw Pass, the railway crosses Kazakhstan, Russia, Belarus and Poland, before arriving in Duisburg in Germany. This line is the southern channel of the Eurasian Land Bridge, which stretches for 11,179 km. The construction of the Chongqing–Europe Railway route is being undertaken jointly by six countries along the line—China, Kazakhstan, Russia, Belarus, Poland and Germany—and it will become one of the main routes of the China–Europe Express Railways system.

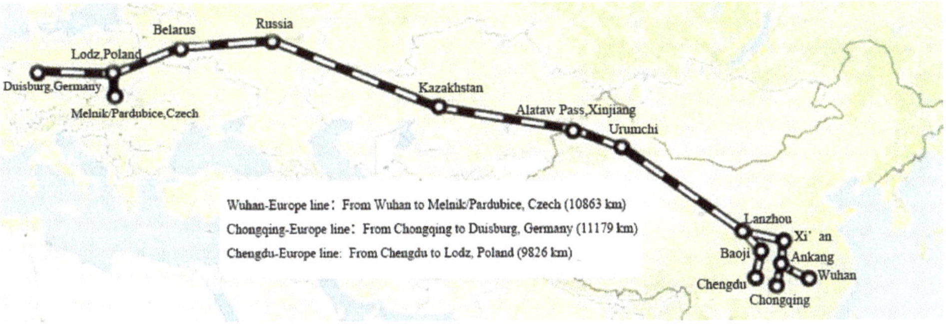

Figure 18.7 China–Europe Express Railways: Chongqing–Europe line, Wuhan–Europe line and Chengdu–Europe line

Source: finance.sina.com.cn/roll/2016-10-18/doc-ifxwvpqh7761641.shtml.

China–Europe Express Railways passes through three EEU countries—Russia, Belarus and Kazakhstan—with trains running from Chinese cities such as Zhengzhou, Wuhan, Chongqing and Chengdu to various European cities. Figure 18.7 shows three of these important lines. According to statistics from the China Railway Corporation, from the successful opening of China–Europe Express Railways in March 2011 until June 2016, 1,881 trains passed through the EEU countries, realising a total of US$17 billion in import and export value during this time (Sina Online 2016). China–Europe Express Railways directly supports the promotion of trade between China and Europe, and it has become an important part of the construction of the Silk Road Economic Belt.

8 www.china.com.cn/news/2017-04/19/content_40649951.htm.

As the main countries of the EEU, Russia, Kazakhstan and Belarus will also be important in building up the Silk Road Economic Belt. The EEU countries have also put forward ideas for building Eurasian transport corridors, including the Far East region development strategy proposed by Russia, the 'Bright Road' infrastructure development strategy proposed by Kazakhstan, Kyrgyzstan's railway construction strategy, along with the BRI, which focuses very much on infrastructure interconnection; all of these therefore have strong complementarity.

Energy infrastructure

At present, although Russia and Central Asian countries are among the big oil and natural gas producers in the world and China is a big oil and natural gas importer, they do not have much of a voice in the energy arena. Western developed countries have placed economic sanctions on Russia over the Ukraine crisis, and China's oil imports have long been from the 'turbulent arc' of the Middle East, which constantly threatens China's oil security (Figure 18.8). To address this situation, promoting '5 + 1' cooperation through the framework of the Silk Road Economic Belt to facilitate the establishment of an energy community is a viable option, and energy infrastructure construction has become the primary task.

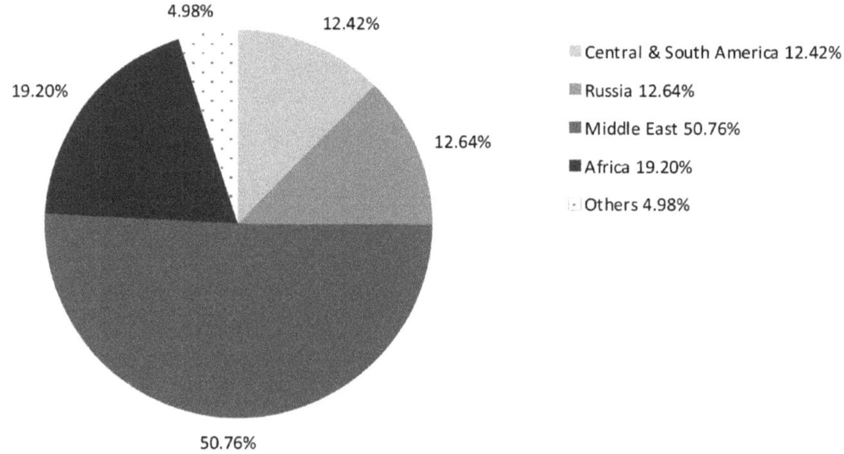

Figure 18.8 Sources of China's oil imports
Source: BP (2016).

The China–Central Asia gas pipeline starts on the border of Turkmenistan and Uzbekistan, on the right bank of the Amu Darya (Amu River), crosses Central Uzbekistan and southern Kazakhstan and enters China east of Horgos, thus forming the 'West–East natural gas transmission' corridor. The natural gas pipeline is about 10,000 km long, with 8,000 km of that inside China, 188 km inside Turkmenistan, 530 km in Uzbekistan and 1,300 km in Kazakhstan. As of December 2016, all three sections of the line—China–Central Asia gas pipeline A, B and C—operated successfully. The D line is being laid, and will be completed in 2020, with a total length of 1,000 km and capacity to deliver 30 billion cu m of gas annually (Table 18.4). Assuming that China consumed 400–420 billion cu m of natural gas in 2010, completion of the D line will meet more than 20 per cent of the country's domestic demand for natural gas (Ma and Wei 2017). The four China–Central Asia gas pipeline sections will form an artery of gas transport from Central Asia to China.

Table 18.4 China–Central Asia natural gas pipeline construction

Line	Source country	Pipe length (km)	Gas delivery per year (billion cu m)	Start of operations
Line A	Turkmenistan	1,830	30	December 2009
Line B	Uzbekistan	1,830	30	October 2010
Line C	Uzbekistan	1,830	25	May 2014
Line D	Turkmenistan	1,000	30	2020

Source: news.cnpc.com.cn/system/2014/09/15/001507242.shtml.

A total of 2,018 km of pipeline lies outside China, 64.42 per cent of which passes through Kazakhstan (an important EEU member), representing almost two-thirds of the total length of China's overseas pipelines; Turkmenistan and Uzbekistan account for 9.32 per cent and 26.26 per cent of the total, respectively. It is clear that promotion of '5 + 1' energy infrastructure cooperation between China and the EEU is essential to smooth construction of the China–Central Asia natural gas pipeline.

China and Kazakhstan have already worked closely together on energy infrastructure construction. The China–Kazakhstan crude oil pipeline is the first such transnational pipeline and is of strategic significance for both countries, transporting crude oil directly from Kazakhstan to the Chinese consumer market without crossing a third country. The China–Kazakhstan crude oil pipeline begins in Kazakhstan's western Atyrau District and crosses into China via the Alataw Pass. The first phase of the project was completed in May 2006 and the second phase was put into operation in 2009, and was included in the Twelfth Five-Year Plan's focus on energy transport construction (State Council of China 2013). In 2015, the pipeline transported 10.8 million tonnes of crude oil to China, the volume having exceeded 10 million tonnes for five consecutive years—for a total of 56.8 million tonnes from 2011 to 2015. From July 2006 to the end of 2015, the pipeline transported 87.2 million tonnes of crude oil to China from Kazakhstan, playing an important role in China's quest for energy security (China Petroleum News Center 2016).

Promoting policy coordination through '5 + 1' cooperation

We have discussed how to promote the construction of the BRI through '5 + 1' cooperation in terms of trade, investment and infrastructure construction. Establishing an effective cooperation mechanism to coordinate all aspects of the BRI is essential. In light of one of the author's recent field surveys in Kazakhstan and Kyrgyzstan—two EEU countries—combined with our discussion above, we propose the following important policy coordination to strengthen '5 + 1' cooperation and further promote the BRI.

The first area is funding. We suggest the following actions:

1. Encourage Chinese financial institutions to provide finance to the five EEU countries—in particular, to support qualified Chinese private companies to open financial businesses in those countries.
2. Establish a number of special funds through policy coordination. China has already set up the Silk Road Fund to support the BRI, but relying solely on state funding will not be enough. At present, China and the EEU countries have large volumes of private capital looking for investment opportunities, so the establishment of special funds would help attract private sector funding.
3. Issue special bonds to support important infrastructure projects.
4. Consider a special BRI international board on the Chinese stock exchange to raise funds for companies investing in countries along the BRI, particularly the EEU members.
5. In recent years, there has been widespread exchange rate instability among the EEU countries. Since the renminbi has been defined as a special drawing rights (SDR) basket currency, meaning it can be used for international settlement and exchange, it is possible to build a financial stability zone based on the renminbi in the BRI and especially in the Silk Road Economic Belt, therefore helping maintain regional financial stability.

A second avenue for deepening cooperation is through investment policy coordination. Through field surveys, we found that the EEU countries have interests in establishing closer investment partnerships with China; Kazakhstan's demands are particularly apparent. In fact, the Kazakh Government and the Chinese Government have had some good communication relating to investment policy coordination—with, for example, the two countries signing an agreement on investment cooperation for 2016–22. However, some Chinese businesspeople told the authors that it was sometimes difficult to obtain a visa for Kazakhstan even for investment purposes, thus policy coordination in this area will be good for both sides in terms of increasing Chinese investment in Kazakhstan.

A third vehicle via which EEU relations can be deepened is enhanced trade policy coordination. Since China and Russia have signed an agreement to promote '5 + 1' cooperation at the highest levels of leadership, we propose the formation of a '5 + 1' free-trade agreement (FTA) as soon as possible. This would be good not only for promoting the BRI, but also to drive trade prosperity and economic growth for the five EEU countries.

Finally, the '5 + 1' countries could also increase industrial policy coordination. The five EEU countries have industrial advantages in agriculture, energy and minerals, but the manufacturing industry is underdeveloped and industrialisation is lagging behind. Further coordination of industrial policy would directly contribute to the promotion of complementary development between China and these countries in relevant industries, to promote regional economic prosperity.

References

BP (2016), *Statistical Review of World Energy*, London: BP. Available from: www.bp.com/statisticalreview.

China Petroleum News Center (2016), More than 10 million tons of oil per year transported by China—Kazakhstan pipeline during the past five years Available from: news.cnpc.com.cn/system/2016/01/12/001575462.shtml.

Global Financial Network (2016), *Sino–Russian joint statement: The establishment of Eurasian comprehensive partnership*, *Global Financial Network*, 27 June. Available from: www.qqjr.com/quanqiu/zc/2016-06-27/3537.html.

Jin, R. (2016), Speed up to integrate the Belt and Road strategy and the Eurasian Economic Union, *Macroeconomic Management* 3: 41–3.

Li, G. (2015), Railway cost is the same as ocean shipping: Chongqing–Europe Express Railways becomes the new channel of China–Europe trading, *21st Century Economic Report*, 15 May.

Li, J. (2014), Silk Road Economic Belt, Eurasian Economic Union and Sino Russian cooperation, *Academic Journal of Russian Studies* 5:7-18.

Ma, X. and Wei, M. (2017), Development status and construction progress of the six economic corridors along the Belt and Road, the First Financial Research Institute of China. Available from: mt.sohu.com/20170201/n479757185.shtml.

Ming, H., Zhang, Q. and Xin, Q. (2009), Kazakhstan oil industry overview, *International Petroleum Economy* 2: 41.

Ministry of Commerce of China (MOFCOM), National Bureau of Statistics of China (NBS) and State Administration of Foreign Exchange of China (2016), *China's Outward Foreign Direct Investment Statistics Bulletin*, Beijing: China Statistics Press.

Sina Online (2016), The Belt and Road construction accelerates: China-Europe express railway trains will be about 5000 a year by 2020, , *Sina Online*, 18 October. Available from: finance.sina.com.cn/roll/2016-10-18/doc-ifxwvpqh7761641.shtml.

State Council of China (2013), *State Council on printing and distributing the 'Twelfth Five-Year Plan' for Energy Development*, No. 2 [2013], State Council of China. Available from: www.gov.cn/zwgk/2013-01/23/content_2318554.htm.

Wang, W., Zhu, M. and Wu, W. (2011), Study on the trade structure and effect of the Russian–Belarus–Kazakhstan Customs Union, *Russia, Central Asia and Eastern European Market* 12: 29–35.

Wu, J. (2013), *Choosing the Growth Model in China*, Shanghai: Shanghai Far East Publishing House.

Ye, X. (2016), Chinese and foreign well-known people on the Belt and Road Initiative, *People's Daily Overseas Edition*, 19 December: 2. Available from: paper.people.com.cn/rmrbhwb/html/2016-12/19/content_1736845.htm.

Zhang, G. (2016), On the foundation, problems and countermeasures of a free trade zone between China and Eurasian Economic Union, *Chinese University Social Sciences* 4: 96–107.

Zhao, Y. (2015), Nazarbayev says Kazakhstan's agricultural development potential is huge, *International Online*, 5 June. Available from: gb.cri.cn/42071/2015/06/05/8011s4987823.htm.

Zhou, M. (2015), Huge potential for cooperation between the Belt and Road and Eurasian Economic Union, *China Economic Weekly* 18: 22–4.

Appendix 18.1

Table 18.A1 Basic information about 65 BRI countries, 2015

Country code	Country	GDP (US$ billion)	Population (million)	Land area (million sq km)
1	China	11,007.70	1,371.220	9.3882
2	Russian Federation	1,331.21	144.097	16.3769
3	Mongolia	11.74	2.959	1.5536
4	Singapore	292.74	5.535	0.0007
5	Brunei Darussalam	12.93	0.423	0.0053
6	Thailand	395.17	67.959	0.5109
7	Malaysia	296.28	30.331	0.3286
8	Indonesia	861.93	257.564	1.8116
9	Vietnam	193.60	91.704	0.3101
10	Philippines	292.45	100.699	0.2982
11	Myanmar	62.60	53.897	0.6531
12	Cambodia	18.05	15.578	0.1765
13	Laos	12.37	6.802	0.2308
14	Timor-Leste	1.44	1.245	0.0149
15	Afghanistan	19.33	32.527	0.6529
16	Nepal	21.19	28.514	0.1434
17	Maldives	3.44	0.409	0.0003
18	India	2,095.40	1,311.051	2.9732
19	Pakistan	271.05	188.925	0.7709
20	Bangladesh	195.08	160.996	0.1302
21	Sri Lanka	82.32	20.966	0.0627
22	Bhutan	2.06	0.775	0.0381
23	Saudi Arabia	646.00	31.540	2.1497
24	United Arab Emirates	370.30	9.157	0.0836
25	Oman	69.83	4.491	0.3095
26	Israel	299.42	8.380	0.0216
27	Kuwait	114.04	3.892	0.0178
28	Qatar	164.64	2.235	0.0116
29	Bahrain	31.13	1.377	0.0008
30	Iran	425.33	79.109	1.6286
31	Turkey	717.88	78.666	0.7696
32	Iraq	180.07	36.423	0.4343
33	Jordan	37.52	7.595	0.0888
34	Lebanon	47.08	5.851	0.0102
35	Egypt	330.78	91.508	0.9955

Country code	Country	GDP (US$ billion)	Population (million)	Land area (million sq km)
36	Yemen	37.73	26.832	0.5280
37	Syria	n.a.	18.502	0.1836
38	Palestine	12.68	4.422	0.0060
39	Belarus	54.61	9.513	0.2029
40	Georgia	13.97	3.679	0.0695
41	Azerbaijan	53.05	9.651	0.0827
42	Ukraine	90.62	45.198	0.5793
43	Armenia	10.53	3.018	0.0285
44	Moldova	6.57	3.554	0.0329
45	Poland	477.07	37.999	0.3062
46	Czech Republic	185.16	10.551	0.0772
47	Slovakia	87.26	5.424	0.0481
48	Hungary	121.72	9.845	0.0905
49	Latvia	27.00	1.978	0.0622
50	Lithuania	41.17	2.910	0.0627
51	Slovenia	42.77	2.064	0.0201
52	Estonia	22.46	1.312	0.0424
53	Croatia	48.73	4.224	0.0560
54	Romania	177.95	19.832	0.2300
55	Bulgaria	50.20	7.178	0.1086
56	Albania	11.40	2.889	0.0274
57	Serbia	37.16	7.098	0.0875
58	Macedonia	10.09	2.078	0.0252
59	Bosnia and Herzegovina	16.19	3.810	0.0512
60	Montenegro	3.99	0.622	0.0135
61	Kazakhstan	184.39	17.544	2.6997
62	Turkmenistan	35.85	5.374	0.4699
63	Uzbekistan	66.73	31.300	0.4254
64	Kyrgyzstan	6.57	5.957	0.1918
65	Tajikistan	7.85	8.482	0.1400

Source: World Bank statistical database (data.worldbank.org).

Table 18.A2 Trade connectivity index between EEU member countries, 2001–15

Year	Armenia	Belarus	Kazakhstan	Kyrgyzstan	Russia
2001	19.66	67.80	26.10	24.44	32.26
2002	12.64	60.07	19.24	26.43	30.19
2003	13.70	56.00	17.79	25.89	28.99
2004	9.60	49.10	15.14	27.73	26.49
2005	10.08	32.62	10.24	29.18	20.26
2006	8.09	26.53	7.88	26.02	18.53
2007	9.82	22.39	6.42	20.50	17.79
2008	9.64	17.33	4.92	14.28	15.71
2009	8.95	20.15	5.57	14.02	17.80
2010	8.62	24.30	3.40	15.64	17.44
2011	8.02	18.90	4.61	13.45	15.40
2012	8.84	18.13	3.97	16.58	13.12
2013	10.61	23.47	3.90	13.85	12.53
2014	10.76	24.68	5.00	0.00	14.06
2015	10.07	28.97	7.90	17.51	16.35

Note: The trade connectivity index between countries can be as high as 100 and as low as zero, which means there is no trade relationship.

Source: Authors' calculations based on the trade database of the United Nations Statistical Office (comtrade.un.org/data/).

19. China's 'Innovative and Pragmatic' Foreign Aid: Shaped by and now Shaping Globalisation

Lauren Johnston and Marina Rudyak[1]

Introduction

In his address to the 2017 annual meeting of the World Economic Forum in Davos, Switzerland, Chinese President Xi Jinping said:

> [W]hen the global economy is under downward pressure, it is hard to make the cake of the global economy bigger. It may even shrink, which will strain the relations between growth and distribution, between capital and labour, and between efficiency and equity. Both developed and developing countries have felt the punch. (Xi 2017)

But this, he added, does not mean the world should write off economic globalisation completely. He said it was a natural outcome of human progress and therefore 'we should adapt to and guide economic globalization, cushion its negative impact, and deliver its benefits to all countries and all nations' (Xi 2017).

As the plenary speech on the first visit to Davos by a Chinese president, the speech itself is significant, but it offers little in the way of predictions of any material results on economic policy—a result both of the dynamic complexities of globalisation and of policymaking in China. Nonetheless, Xi's call for greater adaptation to and better guidance of globalisation implies that any change will itself be dynamic. A stated goal of China's increasing leadership in globalisation is delivery of mutually positive benefits to developing countries. In his Davos address, Xi therefore drew particular attention to China's foreign aid and its contribution to global growth.

One estimate says China's net Organisation for Economic Co-operation and Development (OECD) equivalent foreign aid disbursement (minus aid received by China) over the period 2009–13 increased annually by some 11 per cent (Kitano 2016). It was estimated that by 2013, China's net aid had reached US$5.4 billion, most of which was being disbursed bilaterally, as both grants and loans (Figure 19.1) (Kitano 2016). Estimated net foreign aid fell between 2013 and 2014,

1 The authors thank the organisers, ANU College of Asia and the Pacific and participants of the 'China: Wealth and Power' conference held in Canberra, 7–8 April 2016, for helpful feedback and the opportunity for this collaboration.

to US$4.9 billion, however, this did not affect China's ranking among international aid donors, of ninth place. This puts China immediately behind Norway, Sweden and the Netherlands as a provider of foreign aid (Kitano 2016), allowing room for expansion of China's 'adaptive' approach to globalisation and economic governance while also fostering global growth.

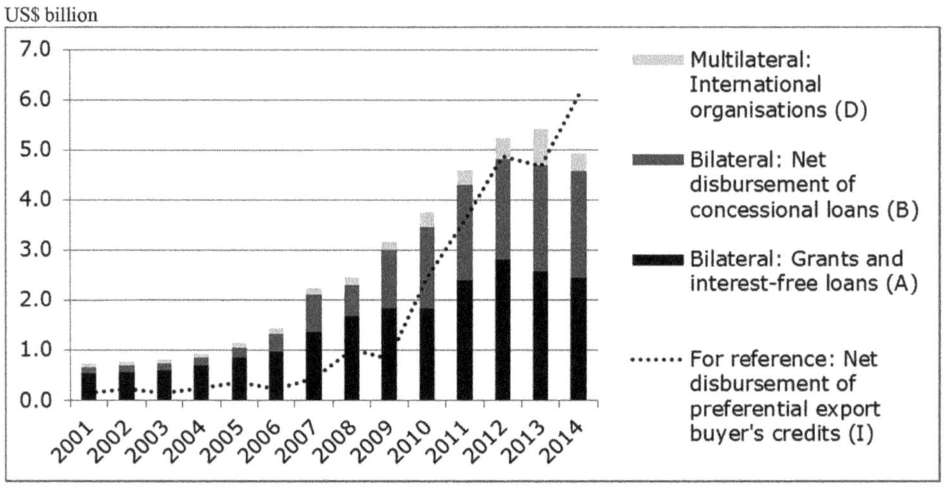

Figure 19.1 China's net foreign aid (estimates)
Source: Kitano (2016).

African countries receive around half of China's total foreign aid (SCIO 2011a, 2014). Africa is also important to China's foreign aid because of its mutually beneficial economic potential (e.g. Johnston 2015a), the significance of which has been noted by China's current leadership on recent visits to the continent. During Xi's inaugural visit to Africa as president, in February 2013, he noted that China–Africa relations had already entered a 'fast track of comprehensive development' (Xi 2013). Adding direction to that track in April 2014, while speaking at the Ethiopian headquarters of the African Union, Chinese Premier Li Keqiang laid out four principles for deepening China–Africa cooperation: sincerity and equality; solidarity and mutual trust; jointly pursuing inclusive development; and innovative pragmatic cooperation (Li 2014). The notion of 'innovative pragmatic cooperation' itself marked a turning point, added for the first time to the traditional static notions of 'equality' and 'solidarity' (Johnston 2014).

The meaning of Li's reference to innovation in the 2014 speech was quickly revealed, with China establishing several new financing institutions to promote international development in various areas: the Asian Infrastructure Investment Bank (AIIB), the Silk Road Fund and a South–South climate fund. It has also made new and substantial investments in a range of existing development finance institutions, including the African Development Bank (AfDB) and the European Investment Bank (EIB), and in several industrial cooperation funds, such as the China–Africa Industrial Capacity Cooperation Fund (CAICCF) (Kamal and Gallagher 2016).

The 'adaptive' approach to increasing China's leadership in globalisation may have its roots in the concept of 'Chinese characteristics'. In this chapter, however, we suggest that the story of China's new globally ambitious and potentially transformative foreign aid policy is itself the product of a bigger global development story. First, the 'trinity' of aid, trade and investment at the core of the Chinese foreign aid model was shaped by a 'chain of knowledge creation' (Shimomura and Wang 2015: 9–16) with its origins in Soviet and Japanese aid to China, China's own development experience and the country's half-century role in South–South cooperation. Second, China—the world's largest economy in purchasing power parity terms—has experienced a growing scarcity of labour and therefore higher labour costs since about 2005. This drop in the availability of cheap labour coincides with the increase in the working-age and primary school–educated population in Africa, offering the prospect of a 'demographic dividend' (Johnston 2015a, 2015b, forthcoming; Chen and Nord 2017).

We argue that greater elaboration of China's development experience as an aid recipient, and the related links to its own outbound foreign aid, can shed light on China's otherwise difficult to decipher foreign aid policy. This in turn may offer insight into the role aid might play in a China-led process of adaptive globalisation. This chapter therefore summarises the evolution of China's inbound and outbound foreign aid policy. By highlighting seminal domestic and international political and economic influences and drivers, we set out a series of internal and external points of inflection in Chinese foreign aid policy over some six decades. We discuss the significance of China's foreign aid for recipient countries, with particular reference to Africa, and turning points that may elucidate how China could influence global development and the globalisation agenda from now on.

The evolution of Chinese foreign aid

Although often misleadingly referred to as an 'emerging' or 'new' foreign aid donor (e.g. Manning 2006; Hernandez 2016), China has a history of outbound aid comparable in length with its inbound aid history, dating back to the early 1950s. In fact, it has been providing aid longer than many of the so-called traditional donors.[2] China's aid model has been uniquely shaped by its experience as an aid recipient, particularly its exposure to concessional loans from the Soviet Union

2 In the contemporary literature, a 'traditional donor' typically refers to donors that are members of the OECD's Development Assistance Committee.

from the 1950s until the Sino–Soviet split in the early 1960s, and also loans from Japan from the late 1970s, followed by aid from Western donors from the 1980s. Our survey here is divided around selected turning points.

Pre-reform and opening-up (before 1978): The ideal of economic self-reliance

In the early years of the People's Republic of China (PRC), the influence of the Soviet Union shaped the country's own planned economy. It also exposed China to tied concessional lending, which is the mode China uses for its outbound aid today. This laid the foundation for two core principles of Chinese aid: China should not impose any political conditions on its aid[3]—which has been criticised by some Western observers as 'no strings attached aid'—and Chinese aid should promote the independent economic development capabilities of its recipients.

In February 1950, in lockstep with the Sino–Soviet friendship treaty, China signed its first concessional loan, worth US$300 million, with annual interest charges of 1 per cent and a disbursement period of five years (Watanabe 2013). The loan was 'tied' to China's purchase of commodities and military materials from the Soviet Union. China agreed to repay the sum through the supply of commodities or foreign currency within 10 years of 1953. A number of other concessional loan agreements followed, mostly packaged with provision of Soviet technical experts who would be responsible for carrying out the aid projects. In the process, Chinese leaders grasped a sense of ownership over the assistance through clear formulation of how such projects fitted within their strategy for building a new country (Watanabe 2013: 88–9). The view that development assistance should primarily serve a country's self-determined development strategy is evident today in the statements of China's aid experts. Speaking about global aid to Africa, Peking University African studies scholar Li Anshan said, 'we cannot set up a plan for Africa. We can rather join them in their efforts and not impose a plan for them' (Adu-Gyamerah 2014).

While receiving Soviet aid, China also instigated its own aid program, starting with support for the reconstruction of postwar North Korea in 1953 and aid to recently decolonised South-East Asian countries. The circle of recipients was expanded following the first Asian–African Conference, held in Bandung, Indonesia, in 1955, when China gradually began to provide aid to African countries. Hereby, China clearly linked its early foreign aid to the Soviet aid model, which was formally based on the notion of 'mutual benefit and mutual respect for national sovereignty'. It also linked economic independence (which foreign aid could help to achieve) to political independence:

3 One notable exception is, however, the strong adherence to the 'One China Policy' and non-recognition of Taiwan.

> It is on this principle [of mutual benefit and mutual respect for national sovereignty] that Socialist countries have established a new type of economic relations amongst each other. The friendly aid in economy and technology given by the Soviet Union to China is a great example of this type of relationship … China is a country that just recently has been liberated. Our economy is still very backward; we still haven't achieved full economic independence … But we have understood that economic independence is of major significance for consolidating political independence. Therefore, while we advance the building up of our own economy, we wish, within the bounds of our possibilities, to contribute our meagre forces to help the economic development of other countries. (Zhou 1956; translated from Chinese)

These links constitute a core principle of Chinese foreign aid today and are almost identical to those in its foreign aid White Papers (SCIO 2011a, 2014) and other government aid documents (Rudyak 2014).

The Sino–Soviet split that occurred in the aftermath of Joseph Stalin's death in the early 1960s was the second profound influence on early Chinese aid. When, under president Nikita Khrushchev, Soviet aid to China came to an abrupt halt, China was forced to continue alone on projects started with Soviet assistance while still repaying the loans. This led to an even stronger insistence on the Chinese side that aid should be used only as a means to achieving economic self-reliance. The aid model of the PRC's early years then manifested in the announcement by Premier Zhou Enlai on a visit to Africa in 1964 of the 'Eight Principles of Economic and Technical Aid'. Along with mutual benefit and the development of self-reliance, these principles include strict respect for the sovereignty of recipient countries and political non-conditionality, and constitute the fundamental guidelines for China's foreign aid that remain in place today (Chen 2010, Chen 2011). From the outset, therefore, China's foreign aid and foreign policy were linked. This, however, does not differentiate China from other major donor countries. For example, the United States instigated the Marshall Plan to both rebuild European countries after World War II and limit the spread of Soviet communism.

Early reform and opening-up (1978 to mid-1990s): Nascent mutual benefit for common (economic) development

From the late 1970s, the beginning of the period of 'reform and opening up' under Deng Xiaoping and the new primacy given to economic modernisation cemented a gradual shift from primarily political to economic drivers of aid. The concurrent transformation of various ministerial structures into state-owned enterprises (SOEs) laid the groundwork for the way in which Chinese aid is implemented today—mostly through turnkey projects executed by SOEs.

With reform and opening up, China was again open to inbound aid. In 1979, it signed concessional loan agreements with Japan. Development aid from Western countries followed and, in April 1980, China joined the World Bank. In Chinese policy circles, there was, however, debate as to whether China should remain a parallel foreign aid provider when limited available resources were needed for national development. In response, the Central Committee of the Chinese Communist Party and the State Council decided that aid would remain central to foreign policy because China needed a stable international environment in which to develop (Shi 1989). Foreign aid spending was nonetheless reduced and greater emphasis placed on projects that were of more direct benefit to China's modernisation and reform agenda (Shi 1989). That shift was cemented during Premier Zhao Ziyang's visit to Tanzania in 1983 (People's Daily 1983), where he announced the 'Four Principles of Sino–African Economic and Technical Cooperation'. Alongside continued emphasis on mutual benefit, as articulated in the earlier years, the 'four principles' reflected Deng Xiaoping's renunciation of Mao Zedong's ideal of self-reliance and his belief that it was not suited to China's opening up. Deng introduced the notion of 'common development'—thus emphasising the economic aspect of China's mutually beneficial aid. In the early 1980s, in other words, foreign aid started to develop into an economic tool for China.

Concurrent change in domestic policy was also influencing China's approach to foreign aid. In the 1980s, China's extensive ministries were selectively transformed into SOEs or their functions were outsourced to new SOEs under the supervision of the parent ministry. The Ministry of State Farms and Land Reclamation, for example, established the China State Farms Agriculture Industry and Commerce Joint Venture Corporation under its own authority in 1980, delegating to it the implementation of agricultural aid projects (Tang et al. 2014).[4] In 1994, this was transformed into the China State Farms Agribusiness Group Corporation (CSFAGC), which is now a leading SOE in China's international agribusiness investments. The China National Complete Plant Import Export Corporation (Complant) offers another example. Established in 1959, Complant's purpose was to undertake turnkey projects (such as the Tanzania–Zambia railway) and to provide technical assistance under the Ministry of Foreign Trade and Economic Cooperation (MOFTEC), which later became the Ministry of Commerce (MOFCOM) (Tang et al. 2014). It was reorganised in 1993 as a comprehensive conglomerate with subsidiaries in many African countries that engage in aid, trade and investment. Similarly, at the provincial level, foreign aid construction departments were also transformed into international economic and technical cooperation corporations (Tang et al. 2014). In general, aid became subject to more competitive forces, but the companies implementing aid projects continued to retain the mentality of a state bureaucracy and the stovepipe channels to their former host ministries.[5]

4 In 1994 it was again transformed, to the China State Farms Agribusiness Group Corporation (CSFAGC).

5 Interview with Zha Daojiong, Beijing, March 2016.

Mid-1990s to 2010: Going out with the trinity of aid, trade and investment

From the mid-1990s, China's foreign aid became increasingly important to its global trade strategy (Wang 2013), and was thus incrementally converted into a channel for promoting foreign trade and investment. Resonant with how early Soviet aid to the PRC had influenced China's foreign aid, in this new period, Japan's development assistance became influential. Yet, China's appropriation of certain features of Japan's cooperation trinity—the integration of aid, trade and investment—from the 1980s was facilitated by two major macroeconomic shifts: one in China and one in Africa.

In China, reform and opening up were producing what would later be called a 'growth miracle' (Lin et al. 2003). By the mid-1990s, China had passed an industrialisation milestone: exports of machinery and electronics had exceeded those of textiles and clothing (Lin and Wang 2014: 4). In turn, China became a net oil importer in 1993, when 7.5 per cent of oil for domestic consumption had to be imported (Leung 2011). China's timber-consuming industries had also grown rapidly: by 2000, China had emerged as the main processing hub for the world's forestry industry (Buckingham 2016). This gave rise to an expansive search for greater and diversified access to oil, minerals and timber, which also served to identify new markets for Chinese goods and services (Pannell 2013).

There was also timely political change on a continent with an abundance of such resources—Africa. The end of apartheid in South Africa in 1994, for example, allowed Africa's then largest economy to integrate into its region and place a greater overall focus on regional economic development. From the mid-1990s, most countries in sub-Saharan Africa experienced increased macroeconomic stability (Arbache and Page 2007). Then Ethiopian prime minister Meles Zenawi, whose Ethiopian People's Revolutionary Democratic Front party had grasped power in 1991, made an important visit to China in 1995. A series of important agreements on trade and economic and technical cooperation followed (Shinn 2014; Venkatamaran and Gofie 2015), helping to set the foundations for today's rapidly intensifying economic ties between the two countries (see Adem 2012).

With its explicit aim to promote export-oriented industrialisation, Japan's aid had made a positive contribution to China's economic growth. The approach adopted to achieve this had three main characteristics: 1) coordination of all three types of developmental financial flows;[6] 2) a strong link between Japan's official aid and foreign direct investment in and trade flows with recipient countries; and 3) close collaboration between the public and private sectors (Shimomura and Wang 2012). Aid projects were thus commissioned by request, amid distinct efforts to develop

6 Official development assistance, other official flows and private finance.

recipient-country self-reliance and with Japan itself steering away from domestic policy issues and extensive conditionality (Shimomura and Wang 2012).[7] Chinese officials were reportedly impressed. First, by the fact that Japan's investment in China's infrastructure and heavy industry made an important concurrent contribution to the latter's economic development and poverty reduction, at the same time as helping Japanese industry internationalise (Nissanke and Schimomura 2013: 25). Second, the substantial number of Chinese aid policy officials of this period who received training in Japan also showed the Japanese approach to aid was pragmatic and effective for both sides (Nissanke and Schimomura 2013).

In December 1994, then trade minister Wu Yi introduced the 'Grand Strategy of Economy and Trade', which in essence embodied the Japanese approach of the interlinking of aid, investment and trade (Ma 1994). Moreover, the grand strategy introduced the concept of government-subsidised concessional loans and joint-venture projects. Following in the footsteps of equivalent institutions in Japan and South Korea, the Export–Import Bank of China (Exim Bank) was set up under the State Council to operationalise this new concessional lending agenda.

The new aid strategy was immediately reflected in China's policies towards Africa. Following a visit to seven African countries in 1995, then prime minister Zhu Rongji stressed that Africa's economic and social development had entered a new period and China's economic assistance to Africa subsequently needed reform—namely, 'encouraging outstanding Chinese enterprises to engage in economic cooperation with Africa' (Zhu 1995). The shift was cemented in 1996, when then president Jiang Zemin proposed a new concept of 'comprehensive cooperation' while visiting the headquarters of the Organisation of African Unity—core components of which were mutually beneficial and seeking common development through joint ventures with strong Chinese enterprises in Africa (Jiang 1996). The number of companies using preferential loans to carry out joint ventures and international cooperation projects increased from eight in 1995 to 70 by 1998 (Liu 2001, cited in Wang 2013).

This also laid the foundation for the launch in 1999 of China's 'Going Out' strategy. 'Going Out' was a package of incentives for Chinese outbound investors that sought to support not only the acquisition of natural resources, but also Chinese companies with the potential to build global brands. The timing coincided with advanced preparations for China to join the World Trade Organization (WTO). Negotiations had begun in 1986 and were concluded in 2001, with China's WTO accession taking place on 11 December of that year.

7 During the 1980s and 1990s, Japanese aid faced the same critique China has been facing since the mid-2000s—namely, being too commercial, weak on development-oriented interests and too focused on infrastructure (Lancaster 2007: 110–42).

Again following equivalent forums in Korea and Japan, China's WTO membership and with its greater role in world trade at last in sight, China in 2000 initiated the Forum On China–Africa Cooperation (FOCAC). This aimed to create 'a platform [for] China and friendly African countries for collective consultation and dialogue and a cooperation mechanism between the developing countries, which falls into the category of South–South cooperation' (PRC Foreign Ministry 2017). A triennial summit has since rotated between China and an African country. The 2006 summit drew particular international attention when China promised to double its aid to African countries by 2009 in the framework of the Beijing Action Plan, and also to establish a US$5 billion China–Africa Development Fund (FOCAC 2009).

The mid-1990s is often noted as a turning point in China–Africa ties, with a shift from politics to economics as the driving force (Alden 2007; Jiang 2012; Johnston 2016). China's experience as a recipient and observer of Japanese aid would now enable it to similarly reshape its relations with, and to become a major economic player in, Africa.

2010 to the present: Timely reform and opening-up of Chinese aid

In the introduction, we indicated that Chinese aid was from the outset part of a global development story. In the previous three subsections, we have, moreover, shown how it evolved through contact points with other donors and how this evolution was enabled by macroeconomic shifts. Yet, if we could say that Chinese aid was *shaped by globalisation*, from 2011 it began to transition to *shaping globalisation*. Three important factors that likely helped trigger this change were: 1) the growing debate about Chinese aid outside China; 2) changes to the global economy following the 2008 Global Financial Crisis; and 3) demographic change in China and Africa.

On the first point, since the mid-2000s, as analysed comprehensively by Mawdsley (2012), there has been an increasingly controversial debate about the implications of China's aid replacing 'traditional' development aid. OECD aid practitioners and development researchers as well as developing-country political, civil society and academic voices were especially concerned by the intertwining of trade and investment in the context of the Chinese Government's pledge to provide aid free from political and measureable transparency conditions. In the second half of 2010, when China officially celebrated 60 years of delivering aid, the Chinese Government appeared to respond to this debate. In a speech to the National Aid Work Conference in August, then premier Wen Jiabao emphasised the need for reforms in the aid system, including raising standards for companies implementing foreign aid projects abroad (Rudyak 2014).

In an article in the Central Committee of the Communist Party's periodical *Qiushi* in 2010, then Minister of Commerce Chen Deming highlighted: 1) the reputational risks of foreign aid–supported investment not being seen to deliver optimal benefits to recipient countries; and 2) the role of foreign aid in making China a responsible stakeholder:

> Foreign investment should be closely integrated with efforts to help recipient countries cultivate personnel and transfer applicable technology while abiding by local laws and regulations, respecting local customs and habits, maintaining good relations with the local people, actively participating in public welfare undertakings and working to protect the ecological environment. (Chen 2010; translated from Chinese)[8]

In 'response to Western criticism' (SCIO 2011b), in April 2011, China issued its first White Paper on foreign aid (SCIO 2011a). This was the first comprehensive English-language document published on Chinese aid activities and included an overview of China's foreign aid policy, financial resources and forms and distribution and management of foreign aid. It also outlined the Chinese state's perspective on international cooperation in foreign aid. That it did not, however, provide data on bilateral aid disappointed some critics (e.g. Provost 2011). The data provided instead extended only to a breakdown of aid by region (Figure 19.2), which confirmed that Africa received more than half of the Chinese aid pie.

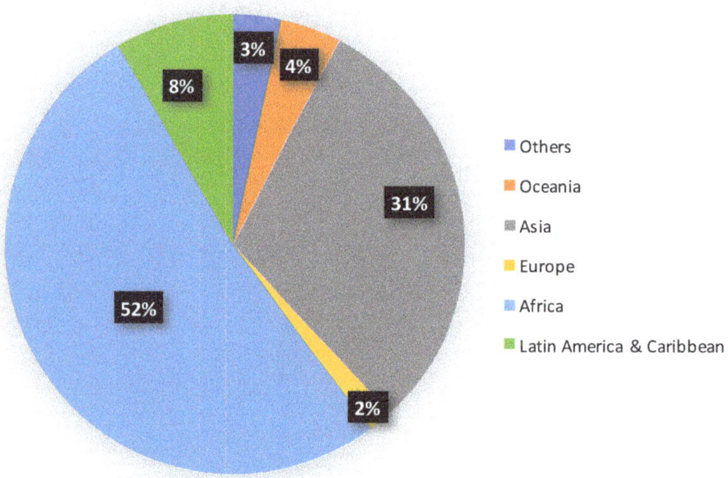

Figure 19.2 China's foreign aid by recipient region

Source: SCIO (2014).

8 An English version of Chen's articles appeared half a year later in the English edition of *Seeking Truth*, in April 2011, just before the release of the first White Paper on foreign aid, and was obviously intended to show the international community that China was working on improving its system (Chen 2011).

Concurrent with that institutional story, economic conditions in China had tightened. Between the mid-1980s and 2011, China's growth was underpinned by uninhibited investment and growth led by exports of low-cost manufactured goods (Garnaut et al. 2014: 2). Changes within China's economy and also in the global economy following the collapse of Lehmann Brothers in 2008 meant that from around 2011 an era of tighter growth conditions and shifting economic priorities began (Garnaut et al. 2014). One result was that new sources of growth were more actively sought, which in turn meant a heightened growth imperative was attached to innovation, services and foreign investment—and their optimal delivery (see Song et al. 2015).

An important factor underlying those tightening conditions was demographics. Restrictive family planning policies of the late 1970s mean that, since about 2005, China has experienced growing labour scarcity and also higher labour costs (Garnaut et al. 2014). In contrast, many of the countries with which China has an aid program are demographically young. In the case of Africa, not only are sub-Saharan Africa's low-income countries youth-filled, but also, thanks to the United Nations Millennium Development Goals, which recently prioritised investment in primary education, the proportion of children finishing primary education in sub-Saharan Africa has increased to some 70 per cent (see Johnston 2015b).

The 28th summit of the African Union convened in January 2017 under the theme 'Harnessing the demographic dividend through investments in youth'. A demographic dividend can arise after a decline in the mortality and fertility rates induces change in the population age structure. This is typically characterised as an increase over several decades in the working-age population share, which produces accelerated growth—and therefore a demographic dividend. When this coincides with economic development, as in China's recent case, the returns can be substantial. Given the current political prioritisation and the underlying economic potential—alongside China's own ageing population—China's foreign aid to Africa is increasing, targeting labour-intensive investments by Chinese firms and infrastructure to sustain their competitiveness (see Lin and Wang 2014; Johnston 2015a, 2015b).

The links between China's foreign investment and its aid program in Africa have, however, added political pressure—such as that noted in the periodical *Qiushi*—for the aid system to become more efficient in meeting Chinese and recipient-country expectations. Resonant again with the earlier approach of Japan, Vice-President of China's Exim Bank Zhu Hongjie spoke of a strengthened merging of the 'going out' plan and China's foreign aid:

> Considering the present situation, we need to expand foreign aid and help developing countries increase their development capacity. This will promote South–South trade cooperation and resolve the difficulties brought to developing countries by the drop of exports. We need to further strengthen the scientific quality and coherence of foreign aid planning, and adopt innovative methods to increase the efficiency of aid spending. At the same time, we need to further broaden the scope of concessionary loans, and actively encourage and support strong Chinese enterprises with good reputations to participate in concessionary loan programs. While serving the country's political and economic diplomacy strategy, we need to make the best use of concessionary loans to promote Chinese exports. (China Economic Net 2012; translated from Chinese)

As well as fostering opportunities for established domestic players in low-cost manufacturing and infrastructure, this new emphasis coincides with China's more nascent push into services and innovation. China has a long history of promoting agricultural innovation and development in Africa, which it sees as having an important link to food security and poverty reduction (Xu et al. 2016). Recent documents, especially the 2015 FOCAC Johannesburg Action Plan (for the period 2016–18), reiterated a commitment that both sides would continue to implement the 'China–Africa Science and Technology Partnership Plan' and build joint laboratories and science and innovation parks. One such example is the Sino-Africa Joint Research Centre at Kenya's Jomo Kenyatta University of Agriculture and Technology, which was opened in September 2016. The centre focuses on biodiversity protection, remote sensing of resources, microbiology and the promotion of modern agriculture, and has a partner relationship with the Chinese Academy of Sciences (CAS). Another example is the April 2017 launch of the China–South Africa Science Cooperation Park. With a focus on mining and minerals technology, the park is expected to play a leading role in the promotion of bilateral research collaboration and the development of joint research institutes.

In general, these aid-based investments by China are part of its efforts to ensure its foreign aid can meet the previously noted international expectations that it will act 'responsibly' as a donor. The importance of this was directly acknowledged by Xi Jinping in his AIIB inauguration ceremony speech in January 2016:

> China has taken an active part in, contributed a constructive part and benefited from the international development system. The initiative to establish the AIIB is a constructive move. It will enable China to undertake more international obligations, promote improvement of the current international economic system and provide more international public goods. (Xi 2016)

Scholars have agreed that the AIIB is a seminal test of expectations of China's international development assistance agenda (e.g. Callaghan and Hubbard 2016). The AIIB's founding also marks a major step in the direction of development financing noted by former World Bank chief economist Justin Lin in 2014, when he wrote of a shift away from official development assistance (ODA) towards other official flows (OOFs), 'OOF-like loans, and OOF-like investments from development banks, and sovereign wealth funds' (SWFs) (Lin and Wang 2014: 18). Brautigam (2011) elaborates the complex links between these diverse financial instruments and funding pots in the context of whether China's aid could be governed according to OECD foreign aid benchmarks. For China meantime, these shifts may also serve to support the incremental internationalisation of China's currency, the renminbi. In April 2017, for example, the renminbi was used for the first time as a currency of bond issuance in Africa by the Bank of China in Johannesburg (Dai 2017).

Discussion

Slower growth in China since about 2011 has increased the importance of foreign aid to its own economic ambitions. Demographic change in other countries, especially in sub-Saharan Africa, makes this change timely. Given China's contemporary economic weight, this situation presents an implicit challenge to leading sovereign and multinational firms, most of which are attached to the OECD, as drivers of globalisation.

Lesser understood internationally, however, is that with China's increasing global economic weight, pressures on its aid domestically and in recipient countries are also increasing. The range and number of tasks China's aid is expected to deliver are growing rapidly: supporting the success of China's 'Going Out' firms; supporting the implementation of China's emerging Belt and Road Initiative (BRI); promoting China's image as a responsible international stakeholder; and, last but not least, helping China promote its own global governance reform agenda to shape globalisation. Such external pressures, moreover, sit against a backdrop of an ever more vocal Chinese public asking why the government is generously spending rising sums of money abroad while large parts of the Chinese countryside remain entrenched in poverty. Outbound Chinese firms are not making the job easier. A 2015 report by the United Nations Development Programme in China (UNDP in China 2015) attests that the government and Chinese companies have, at best, only limited awareness of sustainability issues. At the recipient end, there are equivalent concerns. In January 2015, for example, Cambodian Prime Minister Hun Sen suspended construction of the Stung Cheay Areng hydropower plant involving China's state-owned hydropower giant Sinohydro, following massive environmental protests by the local population (Parameswaran 2015). Similar tensions have emerged around the quality of Chinese-funded projects in Africa, most prominently in the case of a power plant in Botswana. The complex organisation of China's aid institutions and hierarchy, and the non-comparability of China's aid figures, likely do not help the reputation of its aid program within recipient countries, nor efforts at donor coordination (Johnston and Rudyak 2016).

Exogenous factors are meanwhile converging to ensure greater efficiency in the use of China's aid funds. By the end of January 2017, China's foreign exchange reserves unexpectedly fell below the US$3 trillion level, the lowest point in six years. It is not surprising, therefore, that the Chinese Communist Party's Central Leading Group for Comprehensively Deepening Reforms, set up by Xi Jinping in late 2013 to ensure that reforms are implemented, for the first time took on the issue of foreign aid, in February 2017 (Rudyak 2017, People's Daily Online 2017). Following that meeting, Xi Jinping was himself quoted in the *South China Morning Post*, saying that 'China must act more wisely when giving money to foreign countries by "optimising the strategic layout" of foreign aid' (Huang 2017). So, it may be realistic to expect that China's aid institutions and delivery mechanisms will become not only more 'innovative and pragmatic' in coming years, but also more efficient and streamlined. The internationalised learning opportunity presented by the creation of the AIIB—which, like a majority of leading Chinese aid and aid-related institutions, has its headquarters in Beijing—may, following the evolution outlined in this chapter, henceforth also serve as a useful learning mechanism for that process.

Conclusion

Outlining his vision for economic globalisation in Davos in January 2017, President Xi argued for:

> growing an open global economy to share opportunities and interests through opening-up and achieving win–win outcomes. One should not just retreat to the harbour when encountering a storm, for this will never get us to the other shore of the ocean. (Xi 2017)

Consistent with Xi's use of Chinese-language analogies in this speech, this notion could be thought of as an outbound equivalent of Deng Xiaoping's famous 1978 description of China's domestic reform process as an experimental journey of 'crossing the river by feeling the stones'. We see it also as something of a globalisation of Premier Li's call in April 2014 for China's aid to Africa to adhere to principles of pragmatism and innovation (Johnston 2014).

In this chapter, we have specifically outlined China's transition from aid recipient to aid provider. We understand that China's aid from the outset has been shaped by its own political and economic agenda, alongside critical shifts in the global political economy. Our chronology offers a lens through which to understand and project how and why China may now develop its own economic interests and those of other developing countries to more actively and directly shape globalisation.

In so doing, we have added to the literature on foreign aid, and specifically to the far more limited literature on China's foreign aid. Our political economy chronology of China's mutually beneficial approach to foreign aid highlights the external origins of many of China's basic institutions and approaches, especially the trinity approach and the importance of inducing self-reliance. It also highlights the importance of China's own progress in its push to help other countries. Consistent with broader criticisms of China's foreign aid as raised herein, our analysis is constrained by the limited data on China's foreign aid and the scale of fragmentation of China's aid architecture.

In the longer term, whether China's relative economic scale and changing economic growth imperative are among the catalysts of a new, innovative, pragmatic and widespread era of development in Africa and other developing regions remains to be seen. Moreover, African countries and other Chinese aid recipients will ultimately—like contemporary China before them—carve out their own narrative and demands. In turn, a successful China-led globalisation may help instigate a more literal globalisation. To that end, much of the world is now effectively 'crossing the river by feeling the stones', but the globalisation equivalent of that process is really just beginning.

References

Adem, S. (2012), China in Ethiopia: Diplomacy and economics of Sino-optimism, *African Studies Review* 55(1): 143–60. doi.org/10.1353/arw.2012.0008.

Adu-Gyamerah, E. (2014), Africa needs fair trade, not aids: Prof Li Anshan, *Graphic Online*, 2 April. Available from: www.graphic.com.gh/international/international-news/africa-needs-fair-trade-not-aids-prof-li-anshan.html.

Alden, C. (2007), *China in Africa*, London: Zed Books.

Arbache, J. and Page, J. (2007), *Patterns of long term growth in sub-Saharan Africa*, Policy Research Working Paper 4398, Office of the Chief Economist for the Africa Region, The World Bank, Washington, DC. Available from: www-wds.worldbank.org/external/default/WDSContentServer/WDSP/IB/2007/11/14/000158349_20071114124045/Rendered/PDF/wps4398.pdf.

Brautigam, D. (2011), Aid 'With Chinese Characteristics': Chinese Foreign Aid and Development Finance Meet the OECD-DAC Aid Regime, J. Int. Dev., 23: 752-764. doi.org/10.1002/jid.1798.

Buckingham, K. (2016), Beyond trees: Restoration lessons from China's Loess Plateau, in L. Song, R. Garnaut, C. Fang and L. Johnston (eds), *China's New Sources of Economic Growth. Vol. 1: Reform, resources, and climate change*, pp. 379–95, Canberra and Beijing: ANU Press.

Callaghan, M. and Hubbard, P. (2016), The Asian Infrastructure Investment Bank: Multilateralism on the Silk Road, *China Economic Journal* 9(2): 116–39. doi.org/10.1080/17538963.2016.1162970.

Chen, D. (2010), Strive to initiate new progress in foreign aid work: Thoroughly carry out the spirit of the National Working Conference on Foreign Aid, [in Chinese], *Qiushi* [*Seeking Truth*) (19): 42–4.

Chen, D. (2011), China's foreign aid work, *Qiushi* [English edn] 3(2). Available from: english.qstheory.cn/international/201109/t20110924_112578.htm.

Chen, W. and Nord, R. (2017), *A rebalancing act for China and Africa: The effects of rebalancing on sub-Saharan Africa's trade and growth*, IMF Working Paper, International Monetary Fund, Washington, DC.

China Economic Net (2012), Zhu Hongjie: Expand foreign aid, grasp the new opportunities of overseas investment, [in Chinese], *Sina Online*, 23 February. Available from: finance.sina.com.cn/roll/20120323/100411662171.shtml.

Dai, T. (2017), First renminbi-denominated bond well received in Africa, *China Daily*, 20 April. Available from: www.chinadaily.com.cn/business/2017-04/20/content_29010547.htm.

Forum On China–Africa Cooperation (FOCAC) (2016), *Beijing Action Plan (2007–2009)*, 16 November, Ministry of Foreign Affairs, the People's Republic of China, Beijing. Available from: www.fmprc.gov.cn/zflt/eng/zyzl/hywj/t280369.htm.

Garnaut, R., Cai, F. and Song, L. (eds) (2014), *Deepening Reform for China's Long-Term Growth and Development*, Canberra: ANU Press.

Hernandez, D. (2016), *Are 'new' donors challenging World Bank conditionality?* AidData Working Paper No. 19, January, AidData, College of William & Mary, Williamsburg, Va. Available from: aiddata.org/sites/default/files/wps19_are_new_donors_challenging_world_bank_conditionality.pdf.

Huang, K. (2017), China must act more wisely in giving out foreign aid, says Xi Jinping, *South China Morning Post*, 9 February. Available from: www.scmp.com/news/article/2069414/chinas-president-xi-wants-wiser-approach-foreign-aid-donation?utm_source=&utm_medium=&.

Jiang, S. (2012), Historical evolution and future prospects of China–Africa trade cooperative development, [in Chinese], *Practice in Foreign Economic Relations and Trade* 10: 9–13.

Jiang, Z. (1996), Building a new historical pillar for Chinese–African friendship: Speech at the Organisation of African Unity, [in Chinese], *People's Daily*, 14 May: 6.

Johnston, L. (2014), Premier Li calls for 'innovative and pragmatic' cooperation in Africa, *East Asia Forum*, 11 June. Available from: www.eastasiaforum.org/2014/06/11/premier-li-calls-for-innovative-and-pragmatic-cooperation-in-africa/.

Johnston, L. (2015a), Boom to cusp: Prospecting the 'new normal' in China and Africa, in R. Garnaut, L. Song, F. Cai and L. Johnston (eds), *China's Domestic Transformation in a Global Context*, pp. 383–408, Canberra and Beijing: ANU Press.

Johnston, L. A. (2015b), China–Africa economic integration: Striving for common development, *Australian Outlook*, 14 December, Canberra: Australian Institute of International Affairs. Available from: www.internationalaffairs.org.au/australian_outlook/china-africa-cooperation-striving-for-common-development/.

Johnston, L. (2015c), China, Australia and the African frontier, *Pursuit* [*Inside Business*] [University of Melbourne], 14 October. Available from: pursuit.unimelb.edu.au/articles/china-australia-and-the-african-frontier.

Johnston, L. A. (2016), China–Africa economic transitions survey: Charting the return of a fleeting old normal, in M. Kelly (ed.), *21st Century Tensions and Transformation in Africa: The 2015 AFSAAP Annual Conference Proceedings*, Melbourne: Deakin University. Available from: afsaap.org.au/assets/Lauren_Johnston_AFSAAP2015.pdf.

Johnston, L. (forthcoming), China's Africa return: Economic trends and prospects, in J. Binns, K. Lynch and E. Nel (eds), *Handbook on African Development*, London: Routledge.

Johnston, L. A. and Rudyak, M. (2016), Red aid: A fair grasp of China's plan for growth at home and abroad, Paper presented to China: Wealth and Power Conference, The Australian National University, Canberra, April.

Kamal, R. and Gallagher, K. P. (2016), *China goes global with development banks*, 5 April, Bretton Woods Project, London. Available from: www.brettonwoodsproject.org/2016/04/20508/.

Kitano, N. (2016), *Estimating China's foreign aid II: 2014 update*, JICA-RI Working Paper No. 131, June, JICA Research Institute, Tokyo. Available from: www.jica.go.jp/jica-ri/publication/workingpaper/wp_131.html.

Lancaster, C. (2007), *Foreign Aid: Diplomacy, Development, Domestic Politics*, Chicago: University of Chicago Press.

Leung, G. C. K. (2011), China's energy security: Perception and reality, *Energy Policy* 39(3): 1330–7. doi.org/10.1016/j.enpol.2010.12.005.

Li, K. (2014), Li Keqiang delivers a speech at African Union Conference Centre, [in Chinese], 6 May, Ministry of Foreign Affairs of the People's Republic of China, Beijing. Available from: www.mfa.gov.cn/chn//gxh/zlb/ldzyjh/t1152894.htm.

Lin, J. and Wang, Y. (2014), *China–Africa co-operation in structural transformation*, WIDER Working Paper No. 2014/046, February, United Nations University World Institute for Development Economics Research, Helsinki.

Lin, J. Y., Cai, F. and Zhou, L. (2003), *The China Miracle: Development strategy and economic reform*, Hong Kong: Chinese University Press.

Ma, J. (1994), Wu Yi introduces the concept of 'grand strategies of economy and trade', [in Chinese], *China Market* (7): 9.

Manning, R. (2006), Will 'emerging donors' change the face of international co-operation? *Development Policy Review* 24(4): 371–85. doi.org/10.1111/j.1467-7679.2006.00330.x.

Mawdsley, E. (2012), *From Recipients to Donors: Emerging Powers and the Changing Development Landscape*, London; New York: Zed Books.

Nissanke, M. and Shimomura, Y. (2013), Institutional evolution through development cooperation: An overview, in M. Nissanke (ed.), *Aid as Handmaiden for the Development of Institutions: A new comparative perspective*, pp. 1–47, Basingstoke, UK: Palgrave Macmillan. doi.org/10.1057/9781137023483_1.

Pannell, C. (2013), China's economic and political penetration in Africa, *Eurasian Geography and Economics* (49): 706–13.

Parameswaran, P. (2015), Cambodia suspends China dam project to silence opposition, *The Diplomat*, 25 February. Available from: thediplomat.com/2015/02/cambodia-suspends-china-dam-project-to-silence-opposition/.

Provost, C. (2011), China publishes first report on foreign aid policy, *The Guardian*, 28 April. Available from: www.theguardian.com/global-development/2011/apr/28/china-foreign-aid-policy-report.

People's Daily (1983), Premier Zhao spoke at a press conference in Dar es Salaam: Said that the visit to 10 African countries achieved the expected results, [in Chinese], *People's Daily*, 15 January: 1.

People's Daily Online (2017), First session of the year 2017 of the Central Leading Group for Comprehensively Deepening Reforms: Nine major areas will undergo reform, [in Chinese], *CPC News*, 7 February. Available from: cpc.people.com.cn/n1/2017/0207/c164113-29064057.html.

People's Republic of China, Ministry of Foreign Affairs (2017). Characteristics of FOCAC. Available from: www.fmprc.gov.cn/zflt/eng/gylt/ltjj/t157576.htm.

Rudyak, M. (2014), The hidden reform debate: China's foreign aid system reacts to Western critique, Paper delivered to the South–South Development Cooperation: Chances and Challenges for the International Development Architecture Workshop, Heidelberg University, Germany, September.

Rudyak, M. (2017), Too Complex and Too Fragmented. China Must Urgently Reform its Development Aid Structures, [in German], *International Politics*, May/June 2017, pp. 102–106. Available from: zeitschrift-ip.dgap.org/de/ip-die-zeitschrift/archiv/jahrgang-2017/mai-juni/zu-komplex-und-fragmentiert.

Shi, L. (1989), *China's Economic Cooperation with Foreign Countries Today*, [in Chinese], Beijing: Social Sciences Academic Press.

Shimomura, Y. and Wang, P. (2012), *The Evolution of "Aid, Investment, Trade Synthesis" in China and Japan*, in J. Sato & Y. Shimomura (eds), *The Rise of Asian Donors: Japan's Impact on the Evolution of Emerging Donors*, Ebington: Routledge, pp. 114–132.

Shimomura, Y. and Wang, P. (2015), *Chains of knowledge creation and emerging donors*, JICA-RI Working Paper No. 88, March, JICA Research Institute, Tokyo. Available from: www.jica.go.jp/jica-ri/publication/workingpaper/chains_of_knowledge_creation_and_emerging_donors.html.

Shinn, D. (2014), Ethiopia and China: How two former empires connected, *International Policy Digest*, 11 June.

Song, L., Garnaut, R., Cai, F. and Johnston, L. (eds) (2015), *China's Domestic Transformation in a Global Context*, Canberra and Beijing: ANU Press.

State Council Information Office of the People's Republic of China (SCIO) (2011a), *China's foreign aid*, [in Chinese], White Paper, State Council of the People's Republic of China, Beijing. Available from: www.scio.gov.cn/zxbd/wz/201104/t896900.htm.

State Council Information Office of the People's Republic of China (SCIO) (2011b), Foreign media follow closely China's white paper on foreign aid: Praise that aid does not impose political conditions, [in Chinese], 25 April, State Council of the People's Republic of China, Beijing. Available from: www.scio.gov.cn/xwfbh/xwbfbh/yg/2/Document/898670/898670.htm.

State Council Information Office of the People's Republic of China (SCIO) (2014), Chinese foreign aid (2014) white paper, [in Chinese], *PLA Daily*, 11 July: 3.

Strange, A. M., Dreher, A., Fuchs, A., Parks, B. and Tierney, M. J. (2015), Tracking underreported financial flows: China's development finance and the aid–conflict nexus revisited, *Journal of Conflict Resolution*, 20 September.

Tang, L., Li, X. and Qi, G. (2014), Evolution and results of China's agricultural aid management model in Africa, [in Chinese], *International Studies* (6). Available from: www.ciis.org.cn/gyzz/2014-11/20/content_7385069.htm.

United Nations Development Programme (UNDP) in China (2015), *2015 Report on the Sustainable Development of Chinese Enterprises Overseas*, Beijing: UNDP in China. Available from: www.cn.undp.org/content/china/en/home/library/south-south-cooperation/2015-report-on-the-sustainable-development-of-chinese-enterprise/.

Venkataraman, M. and Gofie, S. M. (2015), The dynamics of China–Ethiopia trade relations: Economic capacity, balance of trade and trade regimes, *Bandung: Journal of the Global South* 2(1): 8. doi.org/10.1186/s40728-014-0007-1.

Wang, P. (2013), The Chinese view: Reflection of the long-term experience of aid receiving and giving, in Y. Shimomura and H. Ōhashi (eds), *A Study of China's Foreign Aid: An Asian perspective*, pp. 125–44, Basingstoke, UK: Palgrave Macmillan.

Watanabe, S. (2013), How have major donors affected China's economic development and foreign aid policy? In J. Sato and Y. Shimomura (eds), *The Rise of Asian Donors: Japan's impact on the evolution of emerging donors*, pp. 87–113, Basingstoke, UK: Routledge.

Xi, J. (2013), Xi Jinping's speech in Tanzania's Nyerere International Conference Centre: Full text, [in Chinese], 25 March, Ministry of Foreign Affairs of China, Beijing. Available from: www.mfa.gov.cn/chn//pds/ziliao/zyjh/t1024949.htm.

Xi, J. (2016), Full text of Chinese President Xi Jinping's address at AIIB inauguration ceremony, [in Chinese], *Xinhuanet*, 16 January. Available from: news.xinhuanet.com/english/china/2016-01/16/c_135015661.htm.

Xi, J. (2017), Jointly shoulder responsibility of our time, promote global growth, Keynote speech to opening session of World Economic Forum Annual Meeting, 17 January, Davos, Switzerland. Available from: america.cgtn.com/2017/01/17/full-text-of-xi-jinping-keynote-at-the-world-economic-forum.

Xu, X., Li, X., Qi, G., Tang, L. and Mukwereza, L. (2016), Science, technology, and the politics of knowledge: The case of China's agricultural technology demonstration centers in Africa, *World Development* 81(2016): 82–91. doi.org/10.1016/j.worlddev.2016.01.003.

Zhou, E. (1956), On our foreign policy and the question of Taiwan's liberation, [in Chinese], *People's Daily*, 29 June: 1. Available from: cpc.people.com.cn/GB/64184/64186/66662/4493079.html.

Zhu, R. (1995), Zhu Ronji talks about the visit to seven African countries, [in Chinese], *People's Daily*, 6 August: 1.

Index

www.ingramcontent.com/pod-product-compliance
Lightning Source LLC
LaVergne TN
LVHW070031011026
849160LV00020B/1701